W9-AFM-097

MIKHAIL BAKHTIN

Stanford University Press
Stanford, California
1990

MIKHAIL
BAKHTIN

Creation
of a
Prosaics

Gary Saul Morson & Caryl Emerson

Stanford University Press
Stanford, California
© 1990 by the Board of Trustees of the
Leland Stanford Junior University
Printed in the United States of America

CIP data appear at the end of the book

Published with the assistance of the
National Endowment for the Humanities

Title-page photo by Robert Louis Jackson

For Jane and Ivan,
our superaddressees

Acknowledgments

Helena Goscilo patiently searched every page of this manuscript for solecisms, awkward sentences, and unclear formulations. We are indebted to her, to William Mills Todd III, whose comments guided our revisions, and to Sara Burson, who helped track down obscure facts and bibliographical references. Jane Morson keyed on countless adjustments to the text under considerable time pressure and with grace and humor. Unflaggingly conscientious, Annette Pein verified all citations. In the course of writing this book, we have benefited from discussions with too many people to enumerate here, but special appreciation is due to Carol Avins, Michael André Bernstein, Wayne C. Booth, Victor Erlich, Robert Fagles, Gerald Graff, Robert Louis Jackson, Aron Katsenelinboigen, Lawrence Lipking, Sidney Monas, Nina Perlina, Alfred Rieber, Frank Silbajoris, Anna Tavis, Stephen Toulmin, Charles Townsend, and Alexander Zholkovsky. Patient and wise in her advice, Helen Tartar was, as always, a model editor.

G.S.M.
C.E.

Contents

Prosaics, 15. Prosaics and everyday language, 21. Prosaics as a philosophy of the ordinary, 23. Prosaics and ethics, 25. Prosaics and systems, 27. The unnoticed and the ordinary, 32. Unfinalizability, 36. Unfinalizability as immanent, 38. Bakhtin versus Bakunin, 40. Unfinalizability and historicity, 43. Dialogue, 49. Toward dialogue, 52. Dialogue and other cultures, 54. Monologization, 56. Truth as dialogic, 59.

Four periods, 64. 1919–24: The early writings, 68. Responsibility and architectonics, 71. Others: Real and "unspecified" potential, 74. "The Problem of Content, Material, and Form": Confronting the Formalists over content, 77. 1924–29: The potential of the word, 83. The 1930's to the early 1950's: Historicizing and idealizing the word, 86. Carnival: The apotheosis of unfinalizability, 89. The early 1950's to 1975: Spokesman for the profession, 96.

The dispute, 102. Proving actions by alleging motives, 109. Are the Marxist books Marxist?, 111. The debate does not abate, 112. What is at stake, 116.

Utterance versus sentence, 125. Active understanding: The joint creation of the word, 127. Dialogue, 130.

nival, 452. The historical fate of folklore laughter, 454. Carnival and the two editions of the Dostoevsky book, 456. The carnivalization of literature and the seriocomic genres, 460. Reduced laughter, 463. Polyphony and menippean satire, 465. Genre conditions, 466. Problems with the carnival approach to Dostoevsky, 467. The carnivalesque among Bakhtin's global concepts, 469.

Charts

Biographical Sketch

Mikhail Mikhailovich Bakhtin was born on November 16, 1895, in Orel (south of Moscow), the second of five children in a cultured family of liberal views. His father worked as manager of a bank. Bakhtin grew up in two cosmopolitan border towns of the Russian Empire, Vilnius and later Odessa, and then earned a degree in classics and philology at the University of Petrograd (1913–18). His education in the classics is evident in his choice of topics and examples in his work.

After graduation, to avoid the terrible privations in the capital during the Civil War, Bakhtin moved to the small town of Nevel in western Russia. There he worked as a schoolteacher and participated in lecture series and study circles devoted to the relationship between philosophy, religion, and politics. In 1920, Bakhtin resettled in Vitebsk (the hometown of Marc Chagall and a center for the artistic avant-garde), where his study circle, including among others Valentin Voloshinov and Pavel Medvedev, continued to meet. During the early 1920's, Bakhtin defined himself against the neo-Kantianism of his own mentors and worked on a massive treatise concerning the nature of moral responsibility and aesthetics. In 1924, with the country more stabilized economically and politically, Bakhtin and his wife—who quickly became indispensable to her impractical, often ailing, and yet remarkably productive husband—moved back to Leningrad.

Most of Bakhtin's associates in his circle were able to find official and stable employment during the 1920's, because of either their Marxism or their versatility; Bakhtin was not. This was due in part to his illness, a bone disease that left him frequently bedridden and resulted in the amputation of his right leg in 1938. In part it was due to Bakhtin's lack of political credentials under the new regime.

In 1929, Bakhtin was arrested. In the mass raids on intellectuals in the early Stalinist years, almost any political eccentricity could serve as pretext; the particular charge against Bakhtin concerned his alleged activity in the underground Russian Orthodox Church. It is not clear to what extent the young Bakhtin actually involved himself in the various above- and underground Christian study groups during this time. He was sentenced to ten years on the So-lovetsky Islands, a death camp in the Soviet Far North. Thanks to the intervention of influential friends and to his own precarious health, Bakhtin's sentence was commuted to six years internal exile in Kazakhstan. During the 1930's, while working as a bookkeeper on a collective farm and at other odd jobs in exile, Bakhtin wrote his most famous essays on the theory of the novel.

He also researched a major work on Rabelais, which he was to submit as his doctoral dissertation in 1941 to the Gorky Institute of World Literature in Moscow. The Rabelais project—with its irreverence, celebration of carnival and sexuality, and utopian, philosophical anarchism—became something of a scandal. A degree (although not the *doktorat*) was eventually granted to Bakhtin, but the book was not published until 1965.

In 1936, Bakhtin took up a professorship at the fledgling and remote Mordovia State Teachers College in the town of Saransk, east of Moscow. There he taught courses in Russian and world literature until the rumors (and soon the reality) of new political purges—always a danger to former exiles—prompted him to resign and retire to a still less visible town. At the end of the Second World War, he returned to work at the Teachers College. His relative obscurity and low profile in print during this time of mass repression most likely saved his life.

Bakhtin's final years are the story of rediscovery and rising fame. In the 1950's, on the other side of the Stalinist night, a group of Moscow graduate students who had read Bakhtin's 1929 Dostoevsky book learned, to their astonishment, that its author was still alive, teaching at what had by then been upgraded to the University of Saransk. "Pilgrimages" to Saransk, to a survivor from a past believed lost, took on the character of a temporal crossing. Bakhtin was persuaded to rework the Dostoevsky book for a second edition. Once this book was reapproved for print (1963), other long-delayed Bakhtin manuscripts were published. Bakhtin became a bellwether for a post-Stalinist rethinking of literary studies, his advice sought by both the structuralist semioticians of the Tartu School and the more conservative Marxist-Leninist humanists of the Soviet establishment.

By the time of his death on March 7, 1975, Bakhtin was already the object of a cult in the Soviet Union. The cult spread through Paris to the United States in the 1980's. This phase has somewhat receded in Russia and in the West, but to date Western scholars of

Bakhtin's thought have been more active than their Soviet counter-parts in the difficult task of assessing the legacy. If hopes are real-ized, this situation will change, as it becomes more possible in the Soviet Union to analyze the writings of Bakhtin and his associates dispassionately. A Soviet Academy Edition of the works of the Bakhtin circle now is projected for the mid-1990's.

Abbreviations

All works below are by Bakhtin unless otherwise identified.

Anthologies

The 1986 Russian collection   M. M. Bakhtin, *Literaturno-kriti-cheskie stat'i*. Ed. S. G. Bocharov and V. V. Kozhinov. Moscow: Khudozhestvennaia literatura, 1986.

The 1979 Russian collection   M. M. Bakhtin, *Estetika slovesnogo tvorchestva*. Ed. S. G. Bocharov. Moscow: Iskusstvo, 1979.

The 1975 Russian collection   M. Bakhtin, *Voprosy literatury i estetiki: Issledovaniia raznykh let*. Moscow: Khudozhestvennaia literatura, 1975.

DI   *The Dialogic Imagination: Four Essays by M. M. Bakhtin*. Ed. Michael Holquist. Tr. Caryl Emerson and Michael Holquist. Austin: Univ. of Texas Press, 1981.

RB   *Rethinking Bakhtin: Extensions and Challenges*. Ed. Gary Saul Morson and Caryl Emerson. Evanston, Ill.: Northwestern Univ. Press, 1989.

SG&   M. M. Bakhtin, *Speech Genres and Other Late Essays*. Ed. Caryl Emerson and Michael Holquist. Tr. Vern W. McGee. Austin: Univ. of Texas Press, 1986.

Individual Works

AiG   "Avtor i geroi v esteticheskoi deiatel'nosti" [Author and hero in aesthetic activity]. In the 1979 Russian collection, pp. 7–180. Translations ours.

BiK   "M. M. Bakhtin i M. I. Kagan (po materialam semeinogo arkhiva)." Publikatsiia K. Nevel'skoi. [Correspondence of Mikhail Bakhtin and Matvei Kagan from the 1920's, from the Kagan family archive.] In *Pamyat'*, no. 4 (Moscow samizdat, 1979; Paris: YMCA Press, 1981), pp. 249–81. Portions of this material have since appeared in the USSR in "Sovetskaia Mordoviia" and reviewed in *Voprosy literatury*, no. 7 (1989) ("Sredi zhurnalov i gazet": "Novoe o M. M. Bakhtine").

BSHR   "The *Bildungsroman* and Its Significance in the History of Realism (Toward a Historical Typology of the Novel)." In SG&, pp. 10–59. Russian text in the 1979 Russian collection, pp. 188–236.

DiN   "Discourse in the Novel." In DI, pp. 259–422. Russian text in the 1975 Russian collection, pp. 72–233.

EaN   "Epic and Novel." In DI, pp. 3–40. Russian text in the 1975 collection, pp. 447–83.

FTC   "Forms of Time and of the Chronotope in the Novel: Notes Toward a Historical Poetics." In DI, pp. 84–258. Russian text in the 1975 Russian collection, pp. 234–407.

IiO   "Iskusstvo i otvetstvennost'" [Art and responsibility]. In the 1979 Russian collection, pp. 5–6. Translations ours.

KFP   "K filosofii postupka" [Toward a philosophy of the act]. In the 1984–85 issue of *Filosofiia i sotsiologiia nauki i tekhniki*, a yearbook of the Soviet Academy of Sciences. Moscow: Nauka, 1986, pp. 80–160. Translations ours.

M:FM   *The Formal Method in Literary Scholarship: A Critical Introduction to Sociological Poetics.* By P. N. Medvedev. Tr. Albert J. Wehrle. Cambridge, Mass.: Harvard Univ. Press, 1985. Published under the names M. M. Bakhtin / P. N. Medvedev. This translation was first published under the names P. N. Medvedev / M. M. Bakhtin (Baltimore, Md.: Johns Hopkins Univ. Press, 1978). For the Russian text, see Mikhail Bakhtin [sic], *Formal'nyi metod v literaturovedenii*. New York: Serebrianyi vek, 1982. Originally published as P. N. Medvedev, *Formal'nyi metod v literaturovedenii (Kriticheskoe vvedenie v sotsiologicheskuiu poetiku).* Leningrad: Priboi, 1928.

MHS   "Toward a Methodology for the Human Sciences." In SG&, pp. 159–72. Russian text in the 1979 Russian collection, pp. 361–73.

M:VLP *V laboratorii pisatelia* [In the writer's laboratory]. By P. N. Medvedev. Leningrad: Sovetskii pisatel', 1971. Originally published in Leningrad by Izdatel'stvo pisatelei v Leningrade, in 1933.

N70–71 "From Notes Made in 1970–71." In SG&, pp. 132–58. Russian text in the 1979 Russian collection, pp. 336–60.

PDP   *Problems of Dostoevsky's Poetics* [the 1963 edition of the Dostoevsky book]. Ed. and tr. Caryl Emerson. Minneapolis: Univ. of Minnesota Press, 1984. For the Russian text, see

Problemy poetiki Dostoevskogo. 3rd ed. Moscow: Khudo-zhestvennaia literatura, 1972.

PND   "From the Prehistory of Novelistic Discourse." In DI, pp. 41–83. Russian text in the 1975 Russian collection, pp. 408–46.

PS   "Problema soderzhaniia, materiala, i formy v slovesnom khu-dozhestvennom tvorchestve" [The problem of content, material, and form in verbal creative art]. In the 1975 Russian collection, pp. 6–71. Translations ours.

PT   "The Problem of the Text in Linguistics, Philology, and the Human Sciences: An Experiment in Philosophical Analysis." In SG&, pp. 103–31. Russian text in the 1979 Russian collection, pp. 281–307.

PTD   *Problemy tvorchestva Dostoevskogo* [Problems of Dostoevsky's creative art; the 1929 edition of the Dostoevsky book]. Leningrad: Priboi, 1929. Translations ours.

RAHW   *Rabelais and His World.* Tr. Hélène Iswolsky. Cambridge, Mass.: MIT Press, 1968. For the Russian text, see *Tvorchestvo Fransua Rable i narodnaia kul'tura srednevekov'ia i renessansa.* Moscow: Khudozhestvennaia literatura, 1965.

RQ   "Response to a Question from the *Novyi Mir* Editorial Staff." In SG&, pp. 1–9. Russian text in the 1979 Russian collection, pp. 328–35.

SG   "The Problem of Speech Genres." In SG&, pp. 60–102. Russian text in the 1979 Russian collection, pp. 237–80.

TF1929   "Three Fragments from the 1929 Dostoevsky Book." Appendix 1 in PDP, pp. 275–82. Russian text in PTD, pp. 3–4, 100–102, 238–41.

TP1   Preface to vol. 11 (dramas) of Tolstoy's works. In RB, pp. 227–36. Russian text in the 1986 Russian collection, pp. 90–99.

TP2   Preface to vol. 13 (*Resurrection*) of Tolstoy's works. In RB, pp. 237–57. Russian text in the 1986 Russian collection, pp. 100–120.

TRDB   "Toward a Reworking of the Dostoevsky Book." Appendix 2 in PDP, pp. 283–302. Russian text in the 1979 Russian collection, pp. 308–27.

V:DiL   "Discourse in Life and Discourse in Poetry (Concerning Sociological Poetics)." By V. N. Voloshinov. In V:F, pp. 93–116. Originally published as "Slovo v zhizni i slovo v poezii." *Zvezda* 6 (1926).

V:F   *Freudianism: A Critical Sketch.* By V. N. Voloshinov. Ed. I. R. Titunik and Neil R. Bruss. Tr. I. R. Titunik. Bloomington: Indiana Univ. Press, 1987. Earlier edition published as *Freudianism: A Marxist Critique.* New York: Harcourt Brace, 1976. For the Russian text, see M. M. Bakhtin / V. N. Voloshinov, *Freidizm: Kriticheskii ocherk.* New York: Chalidze, 1983. Originally published as V. N. Voloshinov, *Freidizm: Kriticheskii ocherk.* Moscow–Leningrad: Gosudarstvennoe izdatel'stvo, 1927.

V:MPL   *Marxism and the Philosophy of Language.* By V. N. Voloshinov. Tr. Ladislav Matejka and I. R. Titunik. New York: Seminar, 1973. For the Russian text, see *Marksizm i filosofiia iazyka: Osnovnye problemy sotsiologicheskogo metoda v nauke o iazyke.* 2nd ed. Leningrad: Priboi, 1930.

Zam   "Zametki." In the 1986 Russian collection, pp. 509–31.

MIKHAIL BAKHTIN

Glory be to God for dappled things—
For skies of couple-colour as a brindled cow;
    . . .
And all trades, their gear and tackle and trim.
All things counter, original, spare, strange.
                —Gerard Manley Hopkins,
                    "Pied Beauty"

Introduction

The unity of the Einsteinian world is more complex and profound than that of the Newtonian world, it is a unity of a higher order (a qualitatively different unity).　　　—TRDB, p. 298

Unity not as an innate one-and-only, but as a dialogic *concordance* of unmerged twos or multiples.　　　—TRDB, p. 289

Dostoevsky's plans contain by their very nature an open-endedness which in effect refutes them as plans.　　　—PDP, p. 39

Books about thinkers require a kind of unity that their thought may not possess. This cautionary statement is especially applicable to Mikhail Bakhtin, whose intellectual development displays a diversity of insights that cannot be easily integrated or accurately described in terms of a single overriding concern. Indeed, in a career spanning some sixty years, he experienced both dramatic and gradual changes in his thinking, returned to abandoned insights that he then developed in unexpected ways, and worked through new ideas only loosely related to his earlier concerns.

Small wonder, then, that Bakhtin should have speculated on the relations among received notions of biography, unity, innovation, and the creative process. Unity—with respect not only to individuals but also to art, culture, and the world generally—is usually understood as conformity to an underlying structure or an overarching scheme. Bakhtin believed that this idea of unity contradicts the possibility of true creativity. For if everything conforms to a preexisting pattern, then genuine development is reduced to mere discovery, to a mere uncovering of something that, in a strong sense, is already there. And yet Bakhtin accepted that some concept of unity was essential. Without it, the world ceases to make sense and creativity again disappears, this time replaced by the purely aleatory. There would again be no possibility of anything meaningfully new. The grim truth of these two extremes was expressed well by Borges: an inescapable labyrinth could consist of an infinite number of turns or of no turns at all.

Bakhtin attempted to rethink the concept of unity in order to allow for the possibility of genuine creativity. The goal, in his words, was a "nonmonologic unity," in which real change (or "surprisingness") is an essential component of the creative process. As it happens, such change was characteristic of Bakhtin's own thought, which seems to have developed by continually diverging from his initial intentions. Although it would not necessarily follow that the development of Bakhtin's thought corresponded to his ideas about unity and creativity, we believe that in this case his ideas on nonmonologic unity are useful in understanding his own thought—as well as that of other thinkers whose careers are comparably varied and productive.

In one partially finished essay that remains for the most part an assemblage of notes and jottings from his last years, Bakhtin both discusses and dramatizes his favorite themes of unity and the creative process. He differentiates between "two aspects that define the text as utterance: its plan (intention) and the realization of this plan. Their divergence can reveal a great deal" (PT, p. 104). There follows a cryptic but crucial comment: "Change of plan in the process of its realization."

At best, Bakhtin's work exhibits this unstable kind of unity. We say "at best" because—as Bakhtin himself realized—some of his changing ideas cannot be subsumed even by an open, nonmonologic, plan. Not only does Bakhtin appear to alter his ideas in the course of working them out, but, it must be admitted, at times he simply contradicts himself. At other times, he goes off on tangents; at still others, he pursues weak ideas to a rapid dead end.

In a rare meditation on his own work near the end of his life, Bakhtin attributed some misunderstanding of his ideas to his nonmonologic habits of thought and writing: "My love for variations and for a diversity of terms for a single phenomenon. The multiplicity of focuses. Bringing distant things closer without indicating the intermediate links" (N70–71, p. 155). But in that same note, Bakhtin also admits to a less exalted form of inconsistency, the failure to think an idea through or to express himself clearly. One kind of open-endedness is both intrinsic to his thought and desirable, but the other is a shortcoming: "The unity of the emerging (developing) idea. Hence a certain *internal* open-endedness to many of my ideas. But I do not want to turn shortcomings into virtues: in these works there is much external open-endedness. . . . Sometimes it is difficult to separate one open-endedness from another" (ibid.). To appreciate Bakhtin's strengths without apologizing for his weaknesses, we must try to distinguish between these two kinds of ambiguity and openness.

Lives are not works of fiction. Meetings full of promise do not always ripen into friendship, and ideas rich in potential sometimes lead nowhere. Important people and concerns enter our lives and thought early and late, for various lengths of time, and then depart, never to return. Although in retrospect we may trace causal lines between events and see direct linkages between thoughts, in doing so, we may misrepresent the connections between them. The work we do to make events cohere in a sequence is easily underestimated. Overlooking the role of contingent factors that need not have happened, we imagine only the outcome realized to the exclusion of others equally possible. Ideas that seem to anticipate others might in fact have led in another direction, and apparent resemblances across time may testify to little more than characteristic habits of thought. Memory and biographies tend to be obsessive in excluding accident and insisting on patterns, but lives and intellectual careers, as Bakhtin maintained, are not. Rather, they are wasteful, producing not only diverse achievements, but also unrealized or only partially realized potential.

Bakhtin did not make it easy for anyone to reconstruct the "labyrinth of linkages" among his own ideas. Documentary evidence about his life is relatively scanty. He was reticent about the "personal trace": he did not often illustrate theory with his own experiences. According to those who knew him, he rarely inquired about the personal lives of his students or associates, and wrote few letters to others about his own. Least of all did he discuss the relation of his works to each other. It has been claimed (in our view, mistakenly) that he authored texts published under the names of others, but the very lack of information has contributed to the rumors that he did so, and to other legends about him. Dating his work is difficult, because decades often elapsed between composition and publication; it is often hard to say when a work was begun, and still harder to know how it evolved in the interim.

The rediscovery of Bakhtin in the Soviet Union and the West in the 1960's and 1970's has complicated matters still more. His influence in a given culture has been in part dependent upon the sequence in which his works have been translated and published, which in turn casts its hermeneutic shadow over each new text and translation that appears. In the United States, for example, the fact that *Rabelais and His World* was the first study to be translated (1968) has led to misreadings of his other works, which derive from different and more characteristic lines of his thought. In various cultures, translators and reviewers have imposed radically different grids upon him. He has been described as structuralist and poststructuralist, Marxist and post-Marxist, speech act theorist, sociolinguist, liberal, pluralist, mystic, vitalist, Christian, and materialist. To take just one example, Julia Kristeva—an early and influential conduit for Bakhtin's thought in the West—first appropriated Bakhtin for high structuralism ("Word, Dialogue, and Novel," 1967) and then for intertextuality ("The Ruin of a Poetics," 1970). Both appropriations offer a French "Bachtine" alien in spirit to many versions in Germany, the United States, and Russia.

Those who have tried to "put Bakhtin's legacy in order" have therefore faced no small challenge. Perhaps understandably, some have looked for rhetorically effective shortcuts—for example, recruiting Bakhtin's own heroes and values as aids for the ordering of his intellectual biography. Because Bakhtin loved jesters, fools, and the quintessentially novelistic hero, perhaps—so this argument goes—he modeled his life on them. This hypothesis is as tempting as it is dubious. Readers of the current literature on Bakhtin often encounter a special genre of Russian hagiography: not the suffering martyred writer that Russia so often offers us, but a lesser-known yet also common persona, the clowning fool-in-Christ. But as data, these descriptions lie on the boundary between a life and the cult or myth of a life. That is, they are based not on what a person said or did, but on what others now say or remember about him, at best refracted through the memory of what a man wrote, and at worst shaped by the need for cultural heroes of a given type.

A closely related approach is to invoke Bakhtin's distrust of closed systems as a justification for incoherent judgments of his thought. The New Critics used to call this "the imitative fallacy," which, in the case of some of Bakhtin's critics, has led to rejections of clarity, precision, and careful reasoning as qualities somehow inappropriate to Bakhtin himself.

As Bakhtin wrote in his early manuscripts, it is only after our death that another can begin to "aestheticize" our personality (AiG, p. 115). Are there ways of doing so that cause minimal distortion? What possible models are there? Bakhtin's critics have used a number of interesting ones.[1]

One common model for organizing an author's oeuvre is the structuralist one, first developed by Roman Jakobson, and later used by a number of critics of similar persuasion. A writer's life is described as a set of variations on a theme, of surface transformations of an unchanging "deep structure." In this model, the passage of time, and the work of the biographer, may illuminate one or another aspect of that structure, but the whole is essentially timeless. Evolution, if it exists at all, is itself given in the underlying structure. Tzvetan Todorov's primer on Bakhtin (*Mikhail Bakhtin: The Dialogical Principle*) adopts this approach. In his introduction, Todorov promises to present Bakhtin's thought as a coherent, orderly, "general system" (Todorov, *Dialogical Principle*, p. xii), a synchronic guide to the sixty-year career. Todorov's strengths and weaknesses derive from the forthrightness of his project, in which biography is almost irrelevant, change immaterial, and development essentially nonexistent. Todorov observes:

Properly speaking, there is no *development* in Bakhtin's work. Bakhtin does change his focus; sometimes he alters his formulations, but, from his first to his last text, from 1922 to 1974, his thinking remains fundamentally the same; one can even find identical sentences written fifty years apart. Instead of development, there is *repetition* . . . each one [of Bakhtin's writings] contains, in a way, the whole of his thought. [Todorov, *Dialogical Principle*, p. 12]

Todorov is certainly correct that there is a great deal of repetition in Bakhtin's work, and his study admirably demonstrates that one can construct an interesting and useful *system* (in the strong sense of that word) out of Bakhtin's work.[2] And yet to do so is to "monologize" Bakhtin's texts and thought, to dampen their resonance, and so—to use one of Bakhtin's metaphors—to "transpose a symphonic (orchestrated) theme on to the piano keyboard" (DiN, p. 263).

In our view, Todorov's approach also leads to some significant miscasting of Bakhtin's ideas. Because Todorov insists on an underlying structure in Bakhtin's thought, he is disappointed when he fails to find it. When Bakhtin does not fit his model, Bakhtin is to blame. "The not very coherent and ultimately irrational character of Bakhtin's description of the genre of the novel," he writes, "is indication that this category does not occupy its own place in the system" (Todorov, *Dialogical Principle*, p. 90). Considering how central the novel was to Bakhtin's thought, this judgment is on the face of it very curious.[3] We would reply that Bakhtin was not interested in a "system" in Todorov's sense. Because Todorov identifies system with rationality, he does not appreciate that Bakhtin's approach to the novel is not "irrational" at all. Rather, it is a highly rational attempt to imagine the world as incommensurate with systems.

Todorov's assimilation of Bakhtin's concept of genre to a "modeling" system (ibid., p. 83) and his reduction of dialogue to "intertextuality" (ibid., ch. 5) reveal the same impulse at work. Both concepts belong to the heritage of structuralism and its attendant terms: the opposition of signifier to signified, language and the self as systems; and texts as whole entities that are not dialogized from the start but enter into dialogue only subsequently. Todorov translates Bakhtin's concepts into a framework to which Bakhtin was explicitly opposed. What appears to matter to Todorov ultimately is the impersonal slot and the autotelic text, rather than the developing person and the dialogic voice, which were Bakhtin's main concerns.

One possible alternative to the structuralist approach is what we call the "embryonic" model, because it describes the author's work as variants not of a deep structure but of an initial idea or problem.[4] That idea is largely present at the outset of the author's career, and is restated throughout his life—a life that simply "unfolds" rather than genuinely develops. Katerina Clark and Michael Holquist's pioneering biography *Mikhail Bakhtin* (1984) would seem to adopt such a model. In their reading of him, Bakhtin had one central idea, which appears in a protomanuscript of the early 1920's provisionally entitled by Clark and Holquist "The Architectonics of Answerability." According to these two biographers, Bakhtin sought to restate this idea in various idioms and languages, and to apply it to different topics, in all his writings—whether early or late, finished or unfinished, signed by Bakhtin or by one of his associates. Taken together, his collected works constitute many "different attempts to write the same book" (Clark and Holquist, *Bakhtin*, p. 63). This thesis constitutes, in effect, a biographical version of Todorov's, and entails many of the same consequences as its structuralist rival. The role played by a hypothetical deep structure in Todorov's account is here played by an originating and partly hypothetical Ur-text. What remains the same is that throughout Bakhtin's life things remain pretty much the same.

Clark and Holquist base their conclusions on a reading of Bakhtin's early manuscripts, one of which ("Author and Hero") had not been translated, and another of which ("Toward a Philosophy of the Act") had not yet appeared in any language. "Toward a Philosophy of the Act" was at last published in Russian in 1986.[5] In our reading, these texts suggest not a smooth continuity, but something closer to a decisive break—a watershed—between them and the works for which Bakhtin is currently best known. Though important for understanding his development and thought, the early manuscripts are very much the product of influences Bakhtin soon outgrew (Bergson and neo-Kantianism) and are in large part the expression of formulations he abandoned. If all that Bakhtin had done was to restate and apply the ideas in these manuscripts, he would not have become the original and profound thinker that he later became. Bakhtin's later works can be read back into the early manuscripts only at the expense of blunting their most interesting and radical points, or by anachronistically reading into the early texts ideas that Bakhtin had not yet developed.

The Clark-Holquist and Todorov studies are undoubtedly the most extensive and well researched, but they are by no means the only attempts to reduce Bakhtin's thought to a systematic unity. Other critics have tended to endorse a teleological inversion of the embryonic approach. Rather than locating the crucial point at the beginning, these critics choose the end, and describe Bakhtin's work not as deriving from an initial idea but as tending to a final outcome. In such an approach, everything is seen as flowing toward a predetermined ideology or resting point, which is authoritative for understanding everything that came before it.[6]

Valuable insights into Bakhtin's intellectual development are made available by these three approaches. Each has developed latent potentials in Bakhtin's thought, as each fills in the gaps so as to make each part fit the whole. But, in our view, such an *application* of Bakhtin's ideas should be distinguished from an exposition of them.

For all their profound differences, the structuralist, embryonic, and teleological approaches discussed above are alike in their division of Bakhtin's life into active foreground and passive background. The context of his life belongs to the background, because otherwise something outside the structure, origin, or end could decisively shape his intellectual development—instead of merely providing the necessary material for the preexisting idea. Historical and contingent events are consequently allowed to intensify or diminish the rate and local contours of an unfolding idea, but not to change it in fundamental ways. As Bakhtin would say of such scenarios, "time forges nothing new." Everything is "given," nothing is a "task" or problem.

In this study we attempt a different approach. We have sought above all to communicate our sense of Bakhtin the thinker, in all the rich strangeness and surprising fruitfulness of his intellectual career. Yet we did not want to write an intellectual biography, which would treat his works in chronological order. Rather, our aim is to introduce readers to his key ideas—with their reformulations and inconsistencies intact. We began by asking ourselves how best to understand a thinker's career, how to understand, without exaggerating, its unity, and what constitutes the open development of an idea. Without turning "shortcomings into virtues," how should we describe the "unity of the emerging (developing) idea"—and ideas—in Bakhtin's life?

As it happens, Bakhtin himself devoted a considerable part of his work to exploring these very questions. We understand that there is no special virtue in representing a thinker's life according to his own models of biography. It could well be the case that Freud's life is best described in non-Freudian terms, Marx's thought in non-Marxist ones, and Aristotle's oeuvre in terms Aristotle never dreamed of. Nevertheless, we are persuaded that Bakhtin's theories of development are remarkably sophisticated, and, for that reason, we have allowed them, we hope with due caution, to inform our own account. For there does seem to be a correlation between Bakhtin's account of his favorite writers (Dostoevsky, Goethe, and Rabelais) and his own way of "living through" his thoughts. Bakhtin's account of the various genres that might be used to represent a life, from ancient romance and biography to the nineteenth-century novel, does offer a powerful alternative to the three models we have discussed.

Bakhtin himself examines these three models, although he calls them by different names. In a section of his essay on the "chronotope" ("Ancient Biography and Autobiography"), he describes what he calls the "Platonic" type of biography. This end-determined model, the story of "the life course of one seeking true knowledge" (FTC, p. 130), has myth, metamorphosis, and a final conversion at its base. It corresponds to what we have called the teleological model. The other two models correspond to Aristotelian categories developed, according to Bakhtin, in the Hellenistic and Roman worlds. Answering to the embryonic model is what Bakhtin calls an approach in terms of "energia," the unfolding of an essence through time. As Bakhtin describes them, biographies of this sort represent "not at all the time of a person's 'becoming' or growth" (FTC, p. 141), but a time in which the source is all. By contrast, the *analytic* (our structuralist) biography invokes a finished whole to which time is irrelevant. The first strokes establish the contours of a life that all events merely serve to repeat or fill in.

Bakhtin rejects each of these models as inadequate to a real sense of time as he understands it. He prefers the kind of insights characteristic of novels, which take real "becoming" into consideration. The novel, as he describes it, allows ideas to grow, change, and struggle against a background that is active in shaping a life. The novelistic background is no mere backdrop. One of Bakhtin's favorite examples of this mode of understanding the life of people or ideas was the Dostoevskian novel, which he describes in *Problems of Dostoevsky's Creative Art* (1929).

According to Bakhtin, Dostoevsky changed the novel by creating a character governed neither by plot (as in the epic) nor by an impersonal authorial idea (as in monologic works). This new type of hero carries his own idea, which develops "at a distance" from the author. In such a plan, the hero cannot be conceived without his developing idea, which is essential to his identity; and the idea, in turn, has no existence apart from the hero's developing personality. As a result, Bakhtin wrote, "Dostoevsky's form-shaping ideology lacks those two basic elements upon which any ideology is built: *the separate thought*, and a unified world of objects giving rise to a *system* of thoughts" (PDP, p. 93). Thoughts are not separate, because they live by dialogic interaction with other thoughts of the hero, with the ideas of those around him, and with the vagaries of the environment; instead of "gravitating" to a "system," thoughts exist as "live events."

According to Bakhtin, Dostoevsky, the biographer of his heroes, did not rely on plot in the usual sense because his heroes do not fit "into the procrustean bed of the plot, which, in any case, is conceived of as only one of many possible plots and is consequently in the final analysis merely accidental for a given hero" (PDP, p. 84). Rather than focus on where an idea had to lead, Dostoevsky stresses that it might have led elsewhere and could still lead elsewhere. Part of any idea or any person is "its *potentialities*, and precisely this potential is of the utmost importance for the artistic image" (PDP, p. 91)—or, for that matter, for the image of any thinker's life, properly understood. Nothing in an idea *necessarily* leads anywhere. To describe such a life, one must avoid the procrustean plot so convenient for creating a readable book but so destructive of the sense of contingency, "other plots," and potentiality.

In the present study, we have tried to avoid those dangers without reducing our own account to incoherence. We proceeded topic by topic, so that we could project our sense of how Bakhtin's thoughts might speak to us. We have tried to draw what Bakhtin called "dotted lines" from his ideas to our own concerns, all the while trying to distinguish his explicit arguments from their potential (as we understand it), and to trace connections without imposing a system.

Much of Bakhtin's fame today rests on a few neologisms and new uses of existing words that have rapidly been reduced to cliché. Polyphony, the double-voiced word, carnival and carnivalization, the chronotope, heteroglossia, metalinguistics, the surplus, the loophole, and a host of others now circulate in sometimes creative, sometimes merely curious, and at other times flatly mechanical paraphrases and applications. Where Bakhtin is not forced into a "system," he is taken as the author of "separate thoughts," a tendency that distorts those thoughts by robbing them of their spirit and, at times, simply by misstating their specified meaning. One of our purposes, then, is to offer an interpretation of Bakhtin's key terms, their relation to each other, his evolving and at times inconsistent use of them, and, especially, the questions they were formulated to answer.

Although Bakhtin's thought underwent real development and surprising change, one can discover certain problems that recur with varying but impressive intensity throughout his life. An awareness of these problems can help us to understand what Bakhtin wanted to accomplish when he turned to diverse fields. Two of the most important were the dynamics of the creative process and the nature of ethics. Closely related to both was a third, the value of work, the moment-to-moment effort that constitutes the project of living.

Bakhtin developed a number of global concepts over the years, which he brought to bear on specific fields rich in implications for understanding his recurrent problems. In our first chapter, we present three such concepts that we deem most important for grasping his style of thought.

These three global concepts are *prosaics* (our term), *unfinalizability*, and *dialogue*. They appear separately and together, explicitly and implicitly, in various combinations and emphases in Bakhtin's work. We do not suppose that Bakhtin mechanically combined these several concepts to produce specific new ones, nor do we imagine that they constitute elements that underwent chemical combination to produce new ideational compounds. Prosaics multiplied by unfinalizability does not yield chronotope. But we do suppose that when Bakhtin hit upon the idea of the chronotope, it

reflected and enriched his understanding of unfinalizability and prosaics. In short, we suggest that when, by whatever means, Bakhtin
arrived at an idea, he judged it by how well it contributed to solving
his recurrent questions and by how well it fit with or helped to enrich his global concepts—which were themselves always evolving.
These three concepts do not cover everything. But we think they
are broad enough to serve as a good starting point and will facilitate
an understanding of Bakhtin's particular theories, methods of exposition, and style of framing questions.

The present study is divided into three parts. The first is a broad
overview of key issues pertaining to Bakhtin's thought taken as a
whole. After reviewing his global concepts in Chapter One, we
offer a chronological account of his development in Chapter Two.
Here we try to indicate both continuities and discontinuities, and to
show side roads and dead ends as well as what proved to be main
lines of development. In Chapter Three, we offer our reasons for
believing that Bakhtin did *not* write the "disputed texts"—works
published by his associates, Valentin Voloshinov and Pavel Medvedev, which some have taken to have been written by Bakhtin himself. We also indicate why the issue is of central importance to
understanding each of these three thinkers, especially the relation of
each to Marxism and semiotics. We believe that Bakhtin not only
influenced Voloshinov and Medvedev, but that their ideas had an
important effect on his own development.

Part Two considers three broad, and closely related, topics pertaining to the nature of authorship in Bakhtin's thought. Chapter
Four discusses his many theories of language, Chapter Five his diverse theories of the self, and Chapter Six the difficult but key concept of polyphony. In Part Three, we consider Bakhtin's theories of
genre and of the novel. His general theories of literary genres are
outlined in Chapter Seven. We devote Chapters Eight through Ten
to Bakhtin's three major theories of the novel. Those theories are
arguably his most durable contribution to literary study.

Thus, the volume is organized by topics and problems, rather
than by works. In presenting Bakhtin's theories, we alternate between two approaches, which might be called analytic and chronological. When considering Bakhtin's theories of language, for instance, we prefer to pose general problems and present his specific
solutions, always keeping in mind the differences suggested by his
other concerns in a given period of his life. By contrast, his theories of the self, which differ from each other in fundamental ways,

are presented chronologically. In part, then, these two methods of presentation answer to the material itself. In part, it must also be .dmitted, they answer to the fact that the two authors of the present volume have different intellectual styles. Both of us believe that neither approach enjoys any special privilege over the other, and we hope that the double focus will serve to enrich our readers' understanding of Bakhtin as a thinker whose thought genuinely "became."[7]

PART I

Key Concepts and Periods

I

Global Concepts: Prosaics, Unfinalizability, Dialogue

Prosaics

Bakhtin used the terms *unfinalizability* and *dialogue* constantly; *prosaics*, however, is our own neologism.[1] We have coined the term to cover a concept that permeates Bakhtin's work. As we discuss in Chapter Eight, Bakhtin uses a number of phrases roughly synonymous with prosaics: "prosaic wisdom" or "prosaic intelligence" as the "form-shaping ideology" of the novel.

Prosaics encompasses two related, but distinct, concepts. First, as opposed to "poetics," prosaics designates a theory of literature that privileges prose in general and the novel in particular over the poetic genres. Prosaics in the second sense is far broader than theory of literature: it is a form of thinking that presumes the importance of the everyday, the ordinary, the "prosaic."

In developing prosaics in the second sense, Bakhtin follows a number of other thinkers, both Russian and Western, the most significant of whom was probably Leo Tolstoy. A number of other modern thinkers, including Ludwig Wittgenstein, Gregory Bateson, and Fernand Braudel, developed similar ideas, and so we will briefly situate Bakhtin's prosaics in this wider context. Prosaics in the first sense—a serious, comprehensive theory of literature that privileges prose and the novel—is, so far as we know, Bakhtin's unique and original creation.

Critics have become so accustomed to using the term *poetics* as a virtual synonym for "theory of literature" that they often overlook or underestimate the implications of the word *poetics* for an understanding of prose. For if literature is defined primarily with verse genres (or dramas) in mind, then prose necessarily emerges as something less than fully literary, as literary only by association, or, perhaps, as not really literary at all. At best, poetics tends to describe prose as poetry with some poetic features missing and some unpoetic features added; which is something like defining mammals as reptiles who do not lay eggs and who have warm blood.

In offering a prosaics, we will argue here, Bakhtin sought not to *supplement* traditional poetics with a "poetics of prose" but to change our approach to all literary genres, both poetic and prosaic. Once one understands the nature of the novel, he argued, one must regard all literary forms differently, and undertake "a radical revision of the fundamental philosophical conception of poetic discourse" (DiN, p. 267). As a result, the entire tradition of poetics, from Aristotle to the Russian Formalists, must be thoroughly reconceived.

For Bakhtin, the Formalists embodied the philosophical conception of poetics in its most extreme form, and could therefore serve as a convenient stand-in for the tradition as a whole. Leading Formalists, it will be recalled, founded a "Society for the Study of Poetic Language" (OPOIAZ) and, having identified what they took to be the specific nature of poetic language, defined all literature in terms of it. This step is characteristic of poetics in its essence. Perhaps mistakenly and certainly polemically, Bakhtin's associate Pavel Medvedev insists that the idea of poetic language, as developed by Shklovsky and Jakobson, was the basis for all later Formalist work—work that, Medvedev argued, would make no sense without it (M:FM, pp. 61–63). Indeed, both Medvedev and Bakhtin argued that poetic language does not even characterize verse forms accurately, and fails completely when applied to prose.[2]

What, then, do the Formalists do when they must consider the language and style of prose? According to Bakhtin, they adopt one of two approaches, both of which lead to a misunderstanding and an undervaluing of novels. At times, they apply to prose the tradition of stylistics, as developed for poetry, and then discuss the tropes of the author, narrator, or characters. Quite consistently they arrive at conclusions as untenable as they are provocative: that Gogol's "Overcoat" is only a play on discrepant styles, that Don Quixote's personality is an irrelevant by-product of innovative plot techniques, and that the philosophical essays in *War and Peace* have no thematic significance but serve only as a stylistic device. In a different tone, American criticism has also produced studies of a particular author's "prose style" from the standpoint of traditional poetics, for example William Wimsatt's *The Prose Style of Samuel Johnson*.

In studies of this sort, Bakhtin argues, style is understood as the author's individual instantiation of the system of language. Consequently, the sense that novels as a group may have specific stylistic features—that a generic tradition may intervene between language as a whole and the author—escapes analysis, at least in any fundamental sense. The style *of* the novel is reduced to the sum of styles *in* the novel. But the genre of the novel, Bakhtin insists, cannot be understood except as a style of styles, an orchestration of the diverse languages of everyday life into a heterogeneous sort of whole. One can easily analyze the parts without having any sense of the whole. Accordingly, to Bakhtin, the resources of poetics and traditional stylistics are entirely inadequate to an understanding of this higher order of style.

The second method characteristically adopted by practitioners of poetics is to approach the novel as a nonliterary form. "There is a highly characteristic and widespread point of view that sees novelistic discourse as an extra-artistic medium. . . . After failure to find in novelistic discourse a purely poetic formulation ('poetic' in the narrow sense) . . . prose discourse is denied any artistic value at all; it is the same as practical speech for everyday life, or speech for scientific purposes, an artistically neutral means of communication" (DiN, p. 260). Bakhtin cites as exemplary of this approach the Formalist fellow traveler Victor Zhirmunsky, who argued quite consistently from his premises against regarding novels as works of verbal art. According to Zhirmunsky,

Whereas lyrical poetry appears to be authentically a work of *verbal art* . . . Tolstoy's novel, by contrast, which is free in its verbal composition, does not use words as an artistically significant element of interaction but as a neutral medium or as a system of significations subordinated (as happens in practical speech) to the communicative function. . . . We cannot call such a *literary work* a work of *verbal art* or, in any case, not in the sense that the term is used for lyrical poetry. [Zhirmunsky, "On the Problem of the Formal Method" ("K voprosu o 'formal'nom metode'"), as cited in DiN, pp. 260–261, n. 1]

If artistic discourse is necessarily poetic discourse, and if artistic discourse defines verbal art, then *Anna Karenina* is not a work of "verbal art."

The evident problem with this conclusion led a number of Formalists and quasi-Formalists to modify their argument. Some sought to practice two kinds of stylistic analyses: poetry would be studied in terms of traditional stylistic categories, whereas prose would be handled by a revival of rhetoric. Similar projects have, of course, been common in American literary theory. According to Bakhtin, "the re-establishment of rhetoric, with all its rights, greatly strengthens the Formalist position" (DiN, p. 267, n. 3) because at the very least it provides critics with a way to analyze rather than merely dismiss the language of novels.

However, this solution still retains intact the equation of art with the poetic, and analyzes novels according to methods that were derived from nonartistic uses of language. Novels, to be sure, make use of rhetorical forms (much as their narrators may cite poems), and so both rhetoric and poetics may contribute to our understanding of novels. But rhetorical analysis cannot substitute for an approach to novels that starts from a recognition of their status as verbal art, distinct from poetry on the one hand and rhetoric on the other.

To apply nothing but rhetorical analysis to prose is to deny its literariness. Bakhtin cites one practitioner of this approach, Gustav Shpet, who, no less than Zhirmunsky, argued consistently from his poetic premises:

Here is what Shpet says about the novel: "The recognition that contemporary forms of moral propaganda—i.e., the *novel*—do not spring from *poetic creativity* but are purely rhetorical compositions, is an admission, and a conception, that apparently cannot arise without immediately confronting a formidable obstacle in the form of the universal recognition, despite everything, that the novel *does* have a certain aesthetic value."

Shpet utterly denies the novel any aesthetic significance. The novel is an extra-artistic rhetorical genre, "the contemporary form of moral propaganda"; artistic discourse is exclusively poetic discourse (in the sense we have indicated above). [DiN, p. 268]

One cannot improve on Shpet's position, Bakhtin argues, by treating the novel as "a hybrid formation" (as Viktor Vinogradov does), because the root problem—equating artistry or literariness with the poetic—remains.

Bakhtin was no less dismissive of yet another approach to the novel, which regards the literariness of the genre as a function of features other than language. The Formalists suggested that prose could properly be treated in terms of features it shares with the epic, namely, plot, motif, and theme. Strictly speaking, this approach is inconsistent with Formalist premises, which, according to Medvedev, define "literariness" in terms of poetic language. Although the Formalists tried to specify "The Link Between Devices of Plot Composition and General Stylistic Devices" (the title of an article by Victor Shklovsky), this argument by analogy could not really resolve the fundamental inconsistency of the Formalist approach. Bakhtin and Medvedev concede that Formalist theory did yield a valuable, though limited, set of techniques for analyzing prose works. What it could not offer was a way of treating prose as something other than fallen poetry or promoted rhetoric.

In advancing these objections, Bakhtin and Medvedev had in mind the great tradition of Formalist plot studies as developed by Shklovsky, Boris Tomashevsky, Boris Eichenbaum, and Vladimir Propp. In our day, that tradition has inspired, among others, the "narratology" of Seymour Chatman, Gerard Genette, and Tzvetan Todorov. The many Formalist studies in this tradition describe how narratives are "made" by "deforming" everyday narrative much as poetry is "made" by deforming everyday language. They developed an arsenal of techniques and concepts that are by now familiar: *fabula*, *siuzhet*, repetition, retardation, parallelism, morphology, substitution, motivation, and baring the device.

But as numerous theorists of our own tradition have pointed out, although these techniques seem more or less adequate for analyzing folk tales, detective stories, and utopias, they appear wanting when applied to short stories and novels. As Thomas Greene has observed, they are powerless to explain what makes *The Decameron* stories different from hundreds of others with similar plots. The interest and life of Boccaccio's stories derive not only from their plots, but from something harder to specify, the manner of their telling. Formalism and narratology, Greene concludes, give us "nouns and verbs," but we need "adverbs." [3] In Bakhtin's view, Formalist plot analyses were even more inadequate when applied to great novels—not only because there is much more to a novel than plot, but also because plot itself cannot be properly understood as a collection of narrative techniques.

Novels have a special way of conceiving events and of understanding the interrelations of space, time, social milieu, character, and action, according to Bakhtin. Plot in a novel is as special as language. Much as Bakhtin's essay "Discourse in the Novel" was devoted to exploring the special qualities of novelistic language, his essay "Forms of Time and of the Chronotope in the Novel" distinguishes novelistic plots from those of other genres. The fundamental problem with Formalist and narratological approaches to the novel, in sum, is that they develop *The Poetics of Prose* (the title of a book by Todorov). What is needed, however, is "the prosaics of prose."

In short, all the methods by which prose is analyzed are derived from poetry, and so they cannot reveal the "prosiness" of prose and the "novelness" of novels. Prose must necessarily appear as incomplete poetry and as a mere concession to nonliterary purposes.

Bakhtin contends that once we examine prose in its own terms, we will come to see all verbal art, poetry included, in a different way. In the light of prosaics, poetics itself appears inadequate even for its own object, poetry. "Novelistic discourse" is for Bakhtin "the acid test for this whole way of conceiving style, exposing the narrowness of this type of thinking and its inadequacy in all areas of discourse's artistic life" (DiN, p. 261). Theory confronts a dilemma: "either to acknowledge the novel (and consequently all artistic prose tending in that direction) an unartistic or quasi-artistic genre, or to reconsider radically that conception of poetic discourse in which traditional stylistics is grounded and which determines all its categories" (DiN, p. 267). To be sure, Bakhtin continues, "this dilemma . . . is by no means universally recognized. Most scholars are not inclined to undertake a radical revision of the fundamental philosophical conception of poetic discourse" (ibid.). But it is just such a radical revision that is required.

Of course, one might object that Bakhtin's suggestions could lead to a simple inversion of poetics, that is, to a sort of novelistic imperialism, rather than a comprehensive literary theory privileging neither prose nor poetry. As we suggest in Chapter Two, Bakhtin was not immune to this imperializing move on behalf of the novel.

Bakhtin's theories of language and the novel constitute just such a radical rethinking of literary categories. We stress this point, because his admirers often take his work too narrowly. They integrate one or another of his concepts—dialogue, polyphony, chronotope—into analyses whose basic presuppositions remain unchanged, and thus these Bakhtinian categories are misunderstood or misapplied. Bakhtin means to offer not just a set of detachable terms, nor even a new set of techniques, but a fundamentally different approach to both language and literary discourse in their entirety.

Although his linguistic and literary studies do make amply clear just what this prosaic approach entails for nonliterary discourse, for the novel, and for numerous genres of narrative poetry, Bakhtin never did fully work out its implications for lyric poetry. He indicates that once we start thinking in these terms, we will discern features of lyric poems previously overlooked, and that even those features that have been analyzed will be understood quite differently. The development of his ideas in this direction remains to be done.

Prosaics and Everyday Language

We have mentioned that, for Bakhtin, poetics—especially in the extreme form represented by Russian Formalism—leads to a misunderstanding of nonliterary as well as literary discourse. Indeed, poetics in large part *derives* from the errors of general philology and linguistics. According to Bakhtin, poetics, philology, traditional linguistics, and Russian Formalism all make fundamentally the same mistake. Medvedev cites as exemplary the following passages from the principal Formalists:

Thus we arrive at the definition of poetry as speech that is braked, distorted. Poetic speech is a speech construction. And prose is usual speech: economical, easy, correct (*dea prosae* is the goddess of normal, easy births, of the nondistorted position of the infant). [Shklovsky, "Art as Device," as cited in M:FM, p. 89]

Poetry is indifferent to the object of expression. [Roman Jakobson, *Noveishaia russkaia poeziia*, as cited in M:FM, p. 87]

In order to put into practice and strengthen this specifying principle without recourse to speculative esthetics, it was necessary to contrast the literary fact to another series of facts. . . . The contrast of "poetic language" to "practical language" was such a methodological device. It was worked out in the first collections of OPOIAZ . . . and served as a point of departure for the formalists' work on the basic problems of poetics. [Boris Eichenbaum, "The Theory of the Formal Method," as cited in M:FM, p. 88]

The rhythm of prose is, on the one hand, the rhythm of the work song, the "dubinushka," and replaces the order to "heave-ho"; but, on the other hand, it makes work easier, automatizes it. . . . Thus prosaic rhythm is important as an automatizing factor. But the rhythm of poetry is different. . . . Artistic rhythm is prosaic rhythm disrupted. [Shklovsky, "Art as Device," as cited in M:FM, p. 90]

These and similar passages, which Medvedev calls "typical [of Formalism] to the highest degree" (ibid.), exhibit simultaneously several key errors of poetics. They equate the "artistic" with the "poetic"; they consequently equate prose with nonliterary discourse; nonliterary discourse, in turn, is characterized as "practical" or (in other cases) habitual; and practical or everyday (*bytovaia*) speech is described as something homogeneous, uncreative, and "automatized." These characterizations not only distort the nature of poetry and prose, they also profoundly misconceive the nature of nonliterary discourse.

To begin with, Medvedev points out, the Formalists' "apophatic method" (definition by negation) leads them to consider the entire realm of nonliterary language as one undifferentiated mass. Even if we grant that poetic language does have some special features, it does not follow that other realms of discourse cannot also have their own special features. "We know that there exists no construction true to life as it is lived, and that the utterances of life, the reality that underlies the nature of language's communicative functions, are formed in various ways, depending on the different spheres and goals of real-life interaction. The formal differences between individual communicative constructions in real life can be even more profound and important than those between a scientific and a poetic work" (M:FM, p. 93).

Following the Formalists' logic, one might just as well identify the characteristic features of legal, or journalistic, or any other kind of language, and proclaim all the rest—including poetry—an undifferentiated mass. In fact, the sort of language the Formalists called "practical" characterizes only extremely limited areas of commercial life. "The Formalists saw none of the difficulties of the concept of practical language. They immediately took it as self-evident" (ibid.). The Bakhtin circle remedied this error. Much of Bakhtin's and Voloshinov's work dealt with the heterogeneous and subtle forms of nonliterary discourse, to which Bakhtin returned much later when he wrote "The Problem of Speech Genres."

According to the Bakhtin circle, the Formalist framework leads to a denigration of the everyday realm. If everyday speech is by definition automatized, then it cannot be the locus of vitality or of social and individual creativity:

In reality, real-life intercourse is constantly generating, although slowly and in a narrow sphere. The interrelationships between speakers are always changing, even if the degree is hardly noticeable. In the process of this generation, the content being generated also generates. Practical interchange is full of event-potential, and the most insignificant philological exchange participates in this incessant generation of the event. The word lives its most intense life in this generation, although one different from its life in artistic creation. [M:FM, p. 95]

For the Formalists and their Futurist allies, the everyday world (*byt*) was dead, automatized, essentially unconscious, and certainly uncreative. The Formalists and Futurists were attracted to bohemian romanticism—to slaps in the face of public taste, dramatic beginnings and endings, crises, the storming of barricades, to unrequited love and "braked" emotion, to apocalyptic time and historical leaps. What they did not like was *byt*: "Love's boat has smashed against the daily grind [*byt*]," wrote Vladimir Mayakovsky in his suicide poem. By contrast, Bakhtin set out to explore "the problem of the author of the most ordinary, standard, everyday utterance" (SG, p. 109). For Bakhtin, Voloshinov, and Medvedev, the everyday is a sphere of constant activity, the source of all social change and individual creativity. The prosaic is the truly interesting and the ordinary is what is truly noteworthy.

To be sure, prosaic creativity generally proceeds slowly, begins in narrow spheres, and is hardly noticeable. For that reason we do not see it, and think that innovation must come from somewhere else. But innovation is in fact the product of innumerable small changes taking place "incessantly." The difficulty we have in perceiving and understanding it results from its very familiarity.

Prosaics as a Philosophy of the Ordinary

> He had learned to see the great, the eternal, the infinite in everything, and therefore, in order to enjoy his comprehension of it, he naturally discarded the telescope through which he had been gazing over the heads of men, and joyfully surveyed the everchanging, eternally great, unfathomable, and infinite life around him.   —Tolstoy, *War and Peace*, p. 1320

Bakhtin was the first to formulate a comprehensive prosaics in what we have called its first sense (prosaics as opposed to poetics), but he was only one of the most important "prosaic" thinkers in the second sense. In his meditations on the everyday and the ordinary, Bakhtin follows a tradition of Russian anti-ideological thinkers that includes Alexander Herzen, Leo Tolstoy, and Anton Chekhov. In *Uncle Vanya*, Elena Andreevna pleads against the dominant and antithetical tradition of Russian thought: "Ivan Petrovich, you are an educated, intelligent man, and I should think you would understand that the world is being destroyed not by crime and fire, but by . . . all these petty squabbles" (Chekhov, *Vanya*, Act II, p. 191).[4]

In his essay "Why Do Men Stupefy Themselves?," Tolstoy develops the idea that real ethical decisions are made, and one's true life is lived, at everyday moments we rarely if ever notice. Anything that darkens our judgment at any moment is potentially very harmful, even if the changes are only trifling. To assume that only big effects at crucial moments are important is "like assuming that it may harm a watch to be struck against a stone, but that a little dirt introduced into it cannot be harmful" (Tolstoy, "Stupefy," p. 196).

In this essay, Tolstoy retells the story of the painter Bryullov, who was correcting a student's work. You only changed it a tiny bit, the amazed student remarked, but it is quite a different thing. Bryullov replied: "Art begins where the tiny bit begins." Tolstoy draws momentous conclusions:

> That saying is strikingly true not only of art but of all of life. One may say that true life begins where the tiny bit begins—where what seem to us minute and infinitely small alterations take place. True life is not lived where great external changes take place—where people move about, clash, fight, and slay one another—it is lived only where these tiny, tiny infinitesimally small changes occur. [Tolstoy, "Stupefy," p. 197]

Tolstoy chooses an example from *Crime and Punishment*, which he then proceeds to read as if he had written it. According to Tolstoy, "Raskolnikov did not live his true life when he murdered the old woman or her sister," nor did he decide to commit murder at any single, "decisive" moment. He made his choice, and lived his true life, neither when he entered the old woman's lodgings with a concealed axe, nor when he made plans for the perfect crime, nor when he worried about whether murder is morally permitted. No, the choice was made when he was just lying on his couch, thinking about the most everyday questions—whether he should take money from his mother or not, whether he should live in his present apartment, and other questions not at all related to the old woman. "That question was decided . . . when he was doing nothing and only his consciousness was active; and in that consciousness, tiny, tiny, alterations were taking place. . . . Tiny, tiny alterations—but on them depend the most important and terrible consequences" (Tolstoy, "Stupefy," pp. 197–98).

In *Anna Karenina*, Tolstoy applies this argument to love, work, and daily ethics. His characters learn the value of routine family life, of daily tasks that meet an immediate need, and of unsystematic judgment reflecting a life lived rightly moment to moment. Levin escapes his suicidal skepticism when he comes to a renewed appreciation of the rich ordinariness of daily life. "And I watched for miracles, complained that I did not see a miracle that would convince me. . . . And here is a miracle, the sole miracle possible, continually existing, surrounding me on all sides, and I never noticed it!" (Tolstoy, *Anna Karenina*, pt. 8, ch. 12, p. 829). He finds the solution to the philosophical problems disturbing him when he realizes they cannot have a philosophical solution. Or as Tolstoy's admirer Wittgenstein observed: "The solution to the problem of life is seen in the vanishing of the problem. (Is this not the reason why those who have found after a long period of doubt that the sense of life became clear to them have been unable to say what constituted that sense?)" (Wittgenstein, *Tractatus*, 6.521).

Prosaics and Ethics

Tolstoyan prosaics has immediate implications for ethics. Bakhtin approached ethical problems in much the same spirit in his earliest writings, especially in "Toward a Philosophy of the Act" and in "Art and Responsibility." Taken together, the two thinkers offer a special perspective on ethical problems.

Levin in *Anna Karenina* and Pierre in *War and Peace* have both been troubled by the impossibility of grounding an ethical theory, and therefore of knowing for sure what is right and wrong. On the one hand, absolutist approaches not only proved inadequate to particular situations but also contradicted each other. On the other hand, relativism absurdly denied the meaningfulness of the question and led to a paralyzing indifference. After oscillating between absolutes and absences, they eventually recognize that their mistake lay in presuming that morality is a matter of applying rules and that ethics is a field of systematic knowledge. Both discover that they can make correct moral decisions without a general philosophy. Instead of a system, they come to rely on a moral wisdom derived from living rightly moment to moment and attending carefully to the irreducible particularities of each case.

Bakhtin makes a similar point in his early manuscripts when he argues against Kant, whom he takes as representative of all abstract, philosophical approaches to ethics dominant in the West since Descartes and Pascal. According to Bakhtin, such approaches typically regard ethics as a matter of general norms or principles, and the individual act as a mere instantiation (or failure to instantiate) a norm. Making an ethical decision therefore comes to resemble adjudicating a court case. Like that brilliant jurist, Tolstoy's Ivan Ilich, one sorts through the particular facts, excludes all that are irrelevant, and applies the norm to arrive at the correct decision. According to Bakhtin, this approach overlooks everything essential to genuine ethical thinking.

In Bakhtin's view, all approaches to ethics in terms of rules not only ignore essential particulars that fail to fit a rule, but also function in a fundamentally mechanical way.[5] Today, we might say: if morality were a matter of applying norms, we might hope for a computer that could do it better than we could. Bakhtin insists that ethics in this sense is at best retrospective: it cannot be a guide to any particular decision, but is at best "the principle of possible generalizations from already completed acts in their theoretical transcription" (KFP, p. 102). Like translations of poetry, such transcriptions tend to lose what is most important about the event, "the sense of its eventness, precisely that which it knows responsibly and toward which the act is oriented" (KFP, p. 105). Obligation, the "oughtness" of responsibility, arises in and responds to each particular situation in a way that cannot be adequately generalized without depriving it of its very essence.

Like Tolstoy, Bakhtin cautions over and over again that this rejection of absolutes does not imply an acceptance of relativism or subjectivism. For relativism and subjectivism are themselves wholly located in the realm of abstract theory, and are as far from the "oughtness" and "eventness" of the event as is any theory of general norms. As he so often did throughout his life, Bakhtin insisted in these early writings that relativism (or subjectivism) and absolutism (or dogmatism) are two sides of the same coin.

In ethics, absolutism destroys the oughtness of an event by replacing it with rules; relativists agree that ethics is a matter of rules, but deny that nonarbitrary rules can exist. Neither position is compatible with ethical action as either Bakhtin or Tolstoy understood it.

If ethics is not generalizable, not a matter of rules, that in no sense makes it any less of a burden. On the contrary, if ethics were a matter of rules, and we could know those rules, all the *work* of an ethical action would disappear, because we could simply and thoughtlessly apply them. Conversely, if "anything goes," there is also no work. But if ethics is real, and is located fundamentally in particular situations, then real work is *always* required. That work of judging necessarily involves a risk, a special attention to the particulars of the situation and a special involvement with unique other people at a given moment of their lives. It is precisely in such a nexus that morality, like love, lives.

Bakhtin wants to link the ethical with every ordinary moment of our lives. Why, one might ask, need the ordinary be linked with the moral? Might not catastrophe—or, for that matter, extraordinary good luck—also generate ethical accomplishment? In general, the extraordinary puts the ethical at risk. Catastrophes undo the network of small, reasoned obligations built up around a person or an event—which is why, of course, their horror is also "liberating." Crisis tends to dissolve personal responsibility in the same way norms and principles do: the focus is no longer on the small, prosaic decisions taken by me after much inner debate, but on the large, impersonal mandate, which is either already in place before I came on the scene or imposed on me by an outer source.

Bakhtin does not mean to reject entirely the value of philosophical approaches to ethics. In considering particular situations, Bakhtin believed, we may come to understand their ramifications better by identifying just where norms fall short; and this exercise may educate our responsiveness to future situations. Of course, the very abstractness of such discussions, which tend to rely on case studies stripped of the wealth of detail characterizing all real situations, severely limits their usefulness. Philosophers' examples tend to be too schematic and spare of detail to be of much use from a prosaic standpoint. Indeed, even situations in real life can be deficient, because we usually have no way of knowing numerous particulars, such as the state of mind of each person just before the encounter. Far superior would be case studies extending over hundreds of pages and locating the moments to be considered in the network of all concerned persons, together with their histories and perceptions, and describing all these events within their multivalent social milieu. Far superior, in short, would be the rich and "thick" accounts found in great novels.

For both Tolstoy and Bakhtin, novels, the most prosaic of prosaic forms, occupy a special place in ethical education. For good or ill, they are powerful tools for enriching our moral sense of particular situations. They locate obligation in eventness—still incompletely of course, but much more fully than other available forms of representation. It should be clear why the very length of Tolstoy's novels, with so many details irrelevant to the overall plot, is itself essential to their purpose; and why novels in general and the long Russian novel in particular became central to Bakhtin's understanding of "art and responsibility." If ethics were an object of knowledge, then philosophy would be the best moral education. But ethics is a matter not of knowledge, but of wisdom. And wisdom, Bakhtin believed, is not systematizable.

Prosaics and Systems

It would be helpful to clarify the basic characteristics of prosaic thought, and to specify how it conceives of the "ordinary" and the "everyday."

Prosaics is suspicious of systems in the strong sense, in the sense used by structuralists, semioticians, and general systems theorists: an organization in which every element has a place in a rigorous

hierarchy, "a set of interrelated entities, of which no subset is unrelated to any other subset" (Kramer and Smit, *Systems Thinking*,
p. 14).[6] If one thinks prosaically, one doubts that any aspect of culture, from the self to a language, from daily life to all of history,
could be organized tightly enough to exhibit an all-encompassing
pattern.

As we have seen, Tolstoy, an ideologist of prosaics, explicitly rejected the possibility of any laws of history or of any underlying
order that could explain away the disorder of everyday life. He explicitly denied the existence of a "law of progress" governing history, and insisted that neither that nor any other law could exist.
Tolstoy meant to question the very axioms of all the great system
builders, "from Hegel to Buckle." Bakhtin's frequent targets were
Saussure, the Formalists, and (apparently) Freud; he also attacked
the entire tradition of "dialectics," including both Hegel and Marx.

Bakhtin used a variety of terms for the mistaken attachment to
systems. His earliest term for this error was *theoretism*; later, he
tended to call it *monologism*. Our own covering term for this tendency is *semiotic totalitarianism*, the assumption that everything has a
meaning relating to the seamless whole, a meaning one could discover if one only had the code.[7] This kind of thinking is totalitarian
in its assumption that it can, in principle, explain the totality of
things; it is semiotic (or cryptographic) in its approach to all apparent accidents as signs of an underlying order to which the given system has the key. Freud offers a convenient example.

Bakhtin (and, in his own studies, Voloshinov) had many reasons
for disliking Freudianism's particular doctrines, but what most distinguishes Bakhtin from Freud is Freud's very style of thought.
That style rules out the very possibility of mental events being accidental, meaningless, or unrelated. "I believe that an unintentional
manifestation of my own mental activity *does* . . . disclose something hidden. . . . I believe in external (real) chance, it is true, but
not in internal (psychical) accidental events," Freud insists (Freud,
Psychopathology, p. 257).

From this assumption Freud derives his insight that errors are
necessarily purposeful, and that forgetting results from "an intention to forget" (ibid., p. 4). Characteristically, Freud will not allow
the unobjectionable position that only some forgetting is meaningful whereas other lapses result from the inefficiency of the mind.

Since we overcame the error of supposing that the forgetting we are familiar with signified a destruction of the memory-trace—that is, an annihila-
tion—we have been inclined to take the opposite view, that in mental life

nothing which has once been formed can perish—that everything is some-how preserved and that in suitable circumstances (when, for instance, re-gression goes back far enough) it can once more be brought to light. [Freud, *Civilization*, p. 17]

It is, of course, just this approach that gives Freudianism its ex-planatory power, and it is just this power that Bakhtin suspects.

In some versions of modern semiotics and other literary or cul-tural theories, the same impulse leads to the interpretation of di-verse aspects of life and behavior—from dreams to gestures to whole periods of social history—as entirely meaningful, if one only had the key, which the theory purportedly provides. In literary criticism, we recognize the same form of thinking in the common assumption that everything in a text can be justified in terms of structure, meaning, or thematic integrity.

By contrast, Gregory Bateson defended an alternative view in one of his splendid conversations with his daughter. Bateson called these dialogues "metalogues," because their shapes recapitulate their themes; and in "Why Do Things Get in a Muddle?," father and daughter muddle and meander their way to a series of prosaic insights. "People spend a lot of time tidying things," the daughter observes, "but they never seem to spend time muddling them. Things just seem to get in a muddle by themselves. And then people have to tidy them again" (Bateson, "Muddle," p. 3). If one does not work at it, tidy things get messy, but messy things never get tidy. Why?

Bateson's answer is disarmingly simple. There are an indefinitely large number of ways in which things can be messy, but very few one would call tidy. His daughter expresses dissatisfaction with this answer, because she thinks that disorder must be explained by some active force for disorder (something, perhaps, like Freud's death instinct):

D[aughter]: Daddy, you didn't finish. Why do things get the way I say isn't tidy?
F[ather]: But I *have* finished—it's just because there are more ways which you call "untidy" than there are ways which you call "tidy."
D: But that isn't a reason why—
F: But, yes, it is. And it is the real and only and very important reason.
D: Oh, Daddy! Stop it.
F: No, I'm not fooling. That is the reason, *and all of science is hooked up with that reason.* [Bateson, "Muddle," p. 5]

Whether or not all of science is hooked up with that reason, all of prosaics is. Order needs justification, disorder does not. The natural state of things is *mess*.

Freud, and semiotic totalitarianism generally, makes the opposite assumption. By contrast, Tolstoy insists that although some things happen for a reason, others happen simply "for some reason" (a favorite phrase of Tolstoy's); that is, they happen for a reason that does not "fit." Bakhtin also presumed that, at least in culture, mess was the normal, and at times even the healthy, state.

The cultural world, Bakhtin argued, consists of both "centripetal" (or "official") and "centrifugal" (or "unofficial") forces. The former seek to impose order on an essentially heterogeneous and messy world; the latter either purposefully or *for no particular reason* continually disrupt that order. We stress "for no particular reason" because it is quite common among Bakhtin's admirers, especially Marxists, to misinterpret centrifugal forces as a unified opposition. Bakhtin's point, however, is that although forces of organized opposition sometimes *do* coalesce, centrifugal forces are generally speaking messy and disorganized.

Even calling them by a single name can be misleading. Rather than a unity, centrifugal forces are a panoply of the most heterogeneous elements. They may have no relation to each other except their divergence from the "official." Because this divergence from the official (which is itself never as unified as it pretends to be) can differ in degree as well as in kind, it may in principle be impossible to draw a sharp line between the centripetal and the centrifugal. These categories are themselves subject to the centrifuge.

Centrifugal forces register and respond to the most diverse events of daily life, to the prosaic facts that never quite fit any official or unofficial definition. They are an essential part of our moment-to-moment lives, and our responses to them record their effect on all our cultural institutions, on language, and on ourselves. *Heteroglossia*—Bakhtin's term for linguistic centrifugal forces and their products—continually translates the minute alterations and re-evaluations of everyday life into new meanings and tones, which, in sum and over time, always threaten the wholeness of any language. Language and all of culture are made by tiny and unsystematic alterations. Indeed, the wholeness of any cultural artifact is never "something given, but is always in essence posited—and at every moment . . . is opposed to the realities of heteroglossia" or other centrifugal forces (DiN, p. 270).

As a result, wholeness is always a matter of work; it is not a gift, but a project. When Bakhtin writes that unity is always "posited," the word he chooses is *zadan*; he seems to be playing on closely related words, *zadacha*, a problem, and *zadanie*, a task. Thus wholeness is never a given, it is always a task. Disorder, by contrast, is often (though not always) a given.

Semiotic totalitarians typically presume that it is disorder that requires an explanation. Prosaics begins by placing the burden of proof the other way. One cannot assume that disorder has any specific cause, it may happen just "for some reason"; however, order must have been a task, a problem that has been more or less successfully solved.

In the self, in culture, and in language, it is not (as Freud would have us believe) disorder or fragmentation that requires explanation: it is integrity. The creation of an integral self is the work of a lifetime, and although that work can never be completed, it is nonetheless an ethical responsibility. Here, we perceive the connection between Bakhtin's prosaics and his ethics, which demands that we create integrity so as to *take* responsibility. Dishonesty may result not from a motive, but, quite often, from the failure to undertake the project of responsibility.

These ethical concerns appear explicitly in Bakhtin's early writings and reappear, in more or less concealed forms, throughout his life. In "Toward a Philosophy of the Act," he argues that each self is unique because each aggregate of the related and the unrelated is different. There can be no formula for integrity, no substitute for each person's own project of selfhood, no escape from the ethical obligations of every situation at every moment. Or, as Bakhtin often sums up the point: "There is no alibi for being" (e.g., KFP, pp. 112, 119).

To assume otherwise is to become what Bakhtin calls a "pretender," by which he means not someone who feigns someone else's identity, but someone who avoids the project of selfhood and so tries to live without an identity of his own. The pretender tries to live as the theorists of ethical "norms" say we all should live, by simply performing or failing to perform abstract demands. The pretender lives "representatively" and "ritualistically" (KFP, p. 121). Such a life is one "washed from all sides by the waves of an endless, empty potentiality" (KFP, p. 120).

In his earliest published essay, "Art and Responsibility," Bakhtin contends that ideally "personality must become responsible through and through. All its aspects must not only arrange themselves alongside the temporal flow of its life, but must also intersect one another in the unity of blame and responsibility" (IiO, pp. 5–6). This demand entails an endless and necessary obligation. Applying these ideas to authors and readers, Bakhtin concludes that "art and life are not one, but they must become united in me, in the unity of my responsibility" (IiO, p. 6).

Specifying the sort of unity one might seek in a world of centrifugal forces was to become one of Bakhtin's recurrent problems. What remains constant throughout his diverse formulations—from the "knitting together" of genres to the unity of polyphony—is Bakhtin's insistence that this unity is never complete, and that it is a "unity of another order," distinct from "mechanical" or "systemic" unity.

The Unnoticed and the Ordinary

Prosaics requires both a suspicion of system and an emphasis on ordinary events as the most important. Though closely related, these criteria must be carefully distinguished, because it is quite common for a thinker to satisfy one but not the other. For example, in calling his book *The Psychopathology of Everyday Life*, Freud signals his interest in the ordinary; but he seeks to look through the chaos of daily events to discern an underlying system. Some Marxist examinations of everyday events are guided by a similar procedure. Conversely, it is quite possible to insist that great events shape history, but that those events do not conform to any discernable laws. All forms of catastrophism follow this approach; and we may perhaps discern its traces in Victor Hugo's argument that an unforeseen rainstorm during Napoleon's campaign changed the course of history.[8] Somewhat inconsistently, Hugo also embraces the fourth possibility, that great events shaping history happen according to discernible laws: "Bonaparte, victor at Waterloo, did not harmonize with the law of the nineteenth century. Another series of facts was preparing, in which Napoleon no longer had a place. . . . It was time for this man to fall" (Hugo, *Misérables*, vol. 2, bk. 1, ch. 8, p. 29).

We may summarize these four possibilities as follows:

Prosaics and Its Rivals

	Presumption of System	Suspicion of System
Efficacy of extraordinary and dramatic	Religious apocalypticism Bolshevism	Catastrophism Romantic inspiration
Efficacy of ordinary and prosaic	Freud in *The Psychopathology of Everyday Life*	Prosaics

It is of course necessary to allow for transitional states and for disagreements over the nature of any particular style of thought.[9]

Prosaics focuses on quotidian events that in principle elude reduction to "underlying" laws or systems. The impulse to such reduction probably derives from some of the hard sciences, but according to Bakhtin, it is precisely the nature and challenge of the human sciences to find a responsible way to study a very different order of facts. In "The Problem of the Text," he raises the question "as to whether science can deal with such absolutely unrepeatable individualities as utterances, or whether they extend beyond the bounds of generalizing scientific cognition. And the answer is, of course, it *can*. . . . Science, and above all philosophy, can and should study the specific form and function of individuality" (PT, p. 108).

We are so used to thinking of "science" as a matter of timeless laws, which are by definition general, that a science of the individual seems paradoxical. Bakhtin's point is that this sense of paradox itself reflects habits of thought inadequate to an understanding of culture. Indeed, Bakhtin even suggested that the natural sciences were coming to understand the physical world as he understood the humanities.

To appreciate what Bakhtin had in mind, one might consider the new "science of chaos" that has arisen, both in Russia and the United States, in the past quarter century. The founding insight of this science apparently belongs to Edward Lorenz, who demonstrated that long-term weather forecasting was in principle impossible. The reason is that weather exhibits "sensitive dependence on initial conditions," which means that infinitesimal differences rapidly multiply to produce major differences in result. Whereas a scientist who is a few feet off in measuring the position of Halley's comet will only be a few feet off in estimating its position years later, a meteorologist who overlooks the flapping of "a butterfly's wing" in Peking may be unable to predict the weather a month later in New York. Hence the more popular term for this phenomenon: *the butterfly effect*. It appears that nature, as well as culture, may work by Tolstoyan "tiny alterations"—by prosaics.

The butterfly effect and a host of similar qualities characterize phenomena as diverse as heartbeat, coastlines, and turbulence in liquids. Indeed, these effects seem essential to an understanding of all those things that make life on earth the rough, unpredictable thing that it is. Then why did it take scientists so long to notice it? Because, as James Gleick explains, the whole burden of scientific training lay in looking for more conventional and linear regularities:

When people stumbled across such things—and people did—all their training argued for dismissing them as aberrations. Only a few were able to remember that the solvable, orderly, linear systems were the aberrations. Only a few, that is, understood how nonlinear nature is in its soul. Enrico Fermi once explained, "It does not say in the Bible that all laws of nature are expressible linearly!" The mathematician Stanislaw Ulam remarked that to call the study of chaos "nonlinear science" was like calling zoology "the study of nonelephant animals." [Gleick, *Chaos*, p. 68] [10]

Ordinary, unsystematizable events are hard to study. Indeed, they are very difficult even to notice. "The aspect of things that are most important for us are hidden because of their simplicity and familiarity. (One is unable to notice something—because it is always before one's eyes)," observed Wittgenstein. "And this means: we fail to be struck by what, when seen, is most striking and most powerful" (Wittgenstein, *Philosophical Investigations*, para. 129).

Bakhtin's various theories of language, the novel, the self, and society reflect his concern with prosaic events in this sense. When he speaks of authorship, he is concerned not only to understand great writers but also to appreciate the most everyday ways we have of imagining other people. A model of language, he feels, is nothing unless it can help us appreciate the overlooked richness, complexity, and power of the most intimate and most ordinary exchanges.

Bakhtin often remarks on the irony that anthropologists study remote languages and cultures, linguists construct complex structural models, and literary scholars employ abstruse methods to decipher great works, and yet so few should have thought to learn from the richly varied dialogues they hear every day. "In real life," he digresses in the Dostoevsky book,

we very keenly and subtly hear all those nuances in the speech of people surrounding us, and we ourselves work very skillfully with all these colors on the verbal palette. We very sensitively catch the smallest shift in intonation, the slightest interruption of voices in anything of importance to us in another person's practical everyday discourse. All those verbal sideward glances, reservations, loopholes, hints, thrusts do not slip past our ear, are not foreign to our lips. All the more astonishing, then, that up to now all this has found no precise theoretical cognizance, nor the assessment it deserves! [PDP, p. 201]

According to Bakhtin, literary scholars have circumvented this sort of study with other forms of contextual analysis. At the worst, they examine literature the way crude Marxists do, by correlating it "with socioeconomic factors, as it were, behind culture's back"

(RQ, p. 2). Alternatively, they imagine that they have understood a work's context when they have situated it among the literary polemics and schools of its time. An especially impoverishing form of analysis, such scholarship turns literature itself into "a trivial instead of a serious pursuit" (RQ, p. 3). Of course, Formalist and neo-Formalist approaches that see nothing at all outside the text are the most trivializing of all, according to Bakhtin.

What each of these methods fails to see is the rich texture of prosaic life that conditions everything about the work, from its language, to its "devices," to its complex layers of meaning. Literary works draw not only on their literary and philosophical forebears, but also on "the powerful deep currents of culture (especially the lower, popular ones), which actually determine the creativity of writers" (RQ, p. 3). The very words a novelist uses carry the intonations and evaluations accumulated in daily life, in diverse contexts and heterogeneous speech genres whose existence has not been recognized. Bakhtin writes characteristically:

At the time when major divisions of the poetic genres were developing under the influence of the unifying, centralizing, centripetal forces of verbal-ideological life, the novel—and those artistic-prose genres that gravitate toward it—was being historically shaped by the current of decentralizing, centrifugal forces. . . . on the lower levels, on the stages of local fairs and at buffoon spectacles, the heteroglossia of the clown sounded forth. . . . there developed the literature of the *fabliaux* and *Schwänke* of street songs, folk-sayings, anecdotes, where there was no language-center at all, where there was to be found a lively play with the "languages" of poets, scholars, monks, knights and others. [DiN, pp. 272–73]

Bakhtin stresses the importance of heterogeneous everyday genres and meanings not only in the author's epoch, but over centuries of a culture's development. Words and speech genres gradually accumulate meaning over centuries of diverse experience that layer evaluation upon evaluation, place intonation over intonation. Attentiveness to the ordinary requires the perspective of centuries, of what Bakhtin calls "great time" (RQ, p. 5).[11]

Bakhtin's concept of great time recalls Fernand Braudel's idea of the *longue durée*, perhaps because both thinkers begin with similar prosaic assumptions (as well as some important differences; we focus here on the similarities). Like Bakhtin and Tolstoy, Braudel objects, first of all, to the attempt to reduce history to a system: "So we can no longer believe in the explanation of history in terms of this or that dominant factor. There is no unilateral history. No one thing is dominant" (Braudel, "Situation," p. 10). "There is never any problem, ever, which can be confined within a single framework" (ibid., p. 15). He also insists that history is not a matter of crises or dramatic events, which are themselves the product of an indefinitely large number of daily actions, habits, and rhythms. "To the narrative historians, the life of men is dominated by dramatic accidents. . . . And when they speak of 'general history,' what they are really thinking of is the intercrossing of such exceptional destinies" (ibid., p. 11).

For Braudel, narrative history necessarily tends to the dramatic, to what makes a good story. It therefore usually overlooks those ordinary elements of life that do not change, or change only imperceptibly. When historians look at such social realities, they treat them as mere "backdrop" instead of studying them "*in themselves and for themselves*" (ibid.). Because ordinary events may have no discernible effect for long stretches of time, they do not lend themselves to narrative description, and scholars must be prepared for "a history slower than the history of civilizations" (ibid., p. 12)—the *longue durée*. We will see that there are other important similarities between Bakhtin and Braudel.

It is, of course, quite possible to overstate prosaic insights, even to make a system out of renouncing system. Tolstoy in particular seems to succumb to this temptation rather often, and Bakhtin sometimes makes a fetish of the clowns, fools, and other centrifugal figures that people his social history. The danger lies in making prosaics into a dogma rather than a style of inquiry.

At their best, prosaic thinkers do not deny that great events can be important. Rather, they are inclined to ask whether other, much more important events have been overlooked simply because they are not striking. Prosaics assuredly does not deny that order may exist, only that it may be presumed to exist behind every apparently messy event. Prosaics requires evidence of order, which must overcome the indefinitely numerous and heterogeneous centrifugal forces of everyday life.

Unfinalizability

Bakhtin advances the term *unfinalizability* (*nezavershennost'*) as an all-purpose carrier of his conviction that the world is not only a messy place, but is also an open place. The term appears frequently in his works and in many different contexts. It designates a complex of values central to his thinking: innovation, "surprisingness," the genuinely new, openness, potentiality, freedom, and creativity—terms that he also uses frequently. His paraphrase of one of Dostoevsky's ideas also expresses his own: "*Nothing conclusive has yet taken place in the world, the ultimate word of the world and about the world has not yet been spoken, the world is open and free, everything is still in the future and will always be in the future*" (PDP, p. 166).

In his concern for openness, Bakhtin was knowingly wrestling with some of the most difficult problems in philosophy and with the "accursed questions" asked so often in Russian literature. Like Berdyaev's, Shestov's, and Vyacheslav Ivanov's studies of Dostoevsky, Bakhtin's *Problems of Dostoesvky's Poetics* is not only an analysis of that writer but also an attempt to answer his central questions. As so often happens in Russia, criticism and theory become the practice of philosophy by other means.

How is it possible for the world to be open and free? For events to make sense, it has been argued, they must be governed by laws, which, if known, must reduce freedom and responsibility to illusions and actors to mere puppets. As Tolstoy observed, "if we concede that human life can be governed by reason, the possibility of life is destroyed" (Tolstoy, *War and Peace*, p. 1354).

From Lermontov's "The Fatalist" to Zamyatin's *We,* this problem has been an obsession of Russian writers. For Bakhtin, the most important work concerned with it was probably Dostoevsky's *Notes from Underground.* To understand Bakhtin's formulations, it would be helpful to paraphrase Dostoevsky's themes as Bakhtin chose to interpret them.

The underground man, who desperately wants to believe in freedom, taunts himself with an extreme version of determinism. Some day, he supposes, we shall know all the laws of history and be able to calculate human actions with the same precision now used to pinpoint the location of a planet. A "table of logarithms" indicating all the details of our lives will be drawn up, and "a real mathematical formula" will specify all our desires (Dostoevsky, *Underground*, pp. 22, 24):

Then, after all, man would most likely at once stop to feel desire, indeed he will be certain to. For who would want to choose by rule? . . . After all if they calculate and prove to me that I stuck my tongue out at someone because I could not help sticking my tongue out at him and that I had to do it in that particular way, what sort of *freedom* is left me, especially if I am a learned man and have taken my degree somewhere? [Dostoevsky, *Underground*, pp. 24, 25]

Surprising action would then be as inconceivable as an unexpected answer when multiplying two by two. It may take time to perform an act, just as it takes time to solve a mathematical problem, but time is basically irrelevant to both. In Bakhtin's terms, this would be a world in which "time forges nothing new," a world without "surprisingness." Indeed, this conclusion follows even if the laws are not yet known; the mere fact that they can be known is sufficient to eliminate the possibility of freedom, choice, and the genuinely new. Creation becomes mere discovery, and life is reduced to "extracting square roots."

What life needs above all is something unexpected. In perhaps his most celebrated outburst, the underground man hisses that "two times two makes four is, after all, to me simply a piece of insolence. . . . I admit that two times two makes four is an excellent thing, but if we are going to give everything its due, two times two makes five is sometimes also a very charming little thing" (Dostoevsky, *Underground*, p. 30; trans. emended).

Bakhtin was not willing to select commonly available solutions to this problem. Unlike so many thinkers, he was unsatisfied with proclaiming the irreducibility of both objective laws and our subjective sense of freedom. Such a solution still would leave the "table of logarithms" intact. Freedom, openness, real innovation, and creativity had to be possible in the phenomenal world.

Bakhtin's several theories of language, literature, culture, and the self offer visions of the world in which freedom and unfinalizability are real. Polyphony, the novelistic chronotope, certain types of dialogue, the "open unity" of culture, and many other key concepts serve as ways of understanding how the world could be sufficiently orderly for genuine scientific knowledge and yet sufficiently open for true creativity. Indeed, some of Bakhtin's models demonstrate that freedom is, paradoxically, inevitable: "We live in freedom by necessity," as W. H. Auden wrote.

If freedom is possible, then ethical problems, always of central importance to Bakhtin, are also possible. If freedom is necessary, then responsibility is unavoidable. "There is no alibi for being."

Unfinalizability as Immanent

Although *unfinalizability* is etymologically a negative term, Bakhtin wanted to define it positively and to specify its nature and function in our lives. In each of his formulations, he did so by describing it as immanent in and essential to quotidian existence.

Only if freedom was immanent and essential, he believed, could it be real.

Bakhtin argued that certain common ways of formulating philosophical questions preclude the possibility of unfinalizability from the outset. In particular, Bakhtin repeatedly rejects models of any cultural process that investigate that process in terms of laws or systems while treating actual events as mere instantiations of preexisting laws. The original cultural process disappears under such scrutiny. With laws distilled, the residue becomes a mere assembly of accidental, incomprehensible, unclassifiable phenomena. Ferdinand de Saussure was Bakhtin's favorite, though by no means only, example of this approach. In Bakhtin's view, when Saussure abstracted *langue* from *langage*, the remainder, *parole*, could only be an accessory phenomenon, a formless realm outside scientific inquiry. Laws and residues are twin consequences of an untenable style of thought.

According to Bakhtin, the main problem with such an approach is *not* that the actual concrete event—*parole* or its analogue in other areas—remains unstudied. In that case, one could always simply supplement a study of *langue* with a theory of *parole*. Bakhtin is often misunderstood as simply calling for such a supplement. Rather, Bakhtin believed that all such approaches, in the very act of abstraction, lose something essential about language or any other cultural entity: their "eventness," which means they also lose their unfinalizability.[12] For it is clear that unfinalizability, real creativity, cannot be located in a system of laws. If systems are treated synchronically, then, of course, there is no principle of change at all; and if they are treated diachronically, as in some forms of structuralism or in dialectical materialism, change becomes mere exfoliation of alternatives that are essentially already given. Moreover, the laws of systemic change are necessarily beyond human agency and therefore at crucial points beyond human creativity.

It is equally clear, on the other hand, that creativity cannot exist in a realm of passive, chance phenomena. For creativity is equally absent whether those phenomena merely follow the given laws or randomly disobey them. Neither possibility allows for meaningful creative acts or for responsible ethical ones.

Russian Formalism, which owed so much to Saussurean linguistics, was guilty of just this sort of error, and the result was that real creativity became inexplicable. "The creation of the really new is at a dead end here," wrote Medvedev. "There is no place for it in any of the Formalists' conceptions" (M:FM, p. 97). Such systems can only recombine old elements and turn from one already existing alternative to another. Thus, the Formalists at times explained literary change as the "canonization of the younger line." But the younger line is, as Medvedev observed, "already assumed present. Nowhere is it shown how something initially new appears" (ibid.).[13]

The Formalists saw only one alternative to such models, namely, the attribution of creativity to pure randomness, an alternative they correctly rejected as incompatible with any meaningful approach to literary history. Reasoning correctly from their Saussurean framework, they had to choose between two positions equally incapable of explaining the origin of the new. According to Bakhtin, and later Medvedev, the Formalists' problem lay in their initial assumptions. Bakhtin also recognized that this sort of problem is not unique to Saussure and the Formalists but is characteristic of all models that separate the particular from the general, the individual from the social, or the law from the act, regardless of which side of the duality is privileged.

Bakhtin always tries to find a way to approach cultural entities without this illegitimate division. The only way for creativity to be real is for it to be *immanent* in constant, ongoing processes. We might say that Bakhtin attempts here to rethink the tradition of vitalism in a responsible way.

To understand language as creative, the self as unfinalizable, and history as fundamentally open, each had to be described so that creativity was inherent in it. Without creativity, they would each be something quite different. Creativity is always and everywhere. We can now appreciate the connection between unfinalizability and prosaics: the way to construct models of openness is to locate unfinalizability in ordinary processes, as Bakhtin puts it, in the very "prose of everyday life" (IiO, p. 5). Those processes are open to the future because they are and have been the product of accumulated tiny alterations constituting the daily "event of being."

Bakhtin Versus Bakunin

Bakhtin's use of unfinalizability must be carefully distinguished from a number of other familiar defenses of freedom and openness. To Bakhtin, Medvedev, and Voloshinov, those earlier formulations were inadequate, not only because their arguments were weak, but also because the kind of freedom they described was not truly meaningful according to Bakhtin's criteria. For Bakhtin, freedom had to be immanent in daily life, and had to be inseparable from the ongoing demands of ethical responsibility.

For these reasons, the Bakhtin group rejected Romantic conceptions of freedom and creativity, which tended to view the creative act as a sudden irruption from outside the causal chain. This sort of freedom is by definition catastrophic rather than prosaic. Creativity becomes something exceptional, mysterious, and, most important, beyond human agency. "A man cannot say, 'I will compose poetry,'" Shelley maintains in "A Defense of Poetry." "The greatest poet cannot even say it; for the mind in creation is as a fading coal, which some invisible influence, like an inconstant wind, awakens to transitory brightness. . . . I appeal to the greatest poets of the present day, whether it is not an error to assert that the finest passages of poetry are produced by labor and study" (Shelley, "Defense," p. 511).

Medvedev's book *In the Writer's Laboratory* reads like one long polemic against such ideas. In chapters on "intuition," "inspiration," and "freedom of creativity," he objects that the Romantic view severs the creative moment from both its subsequent working out and from its everyday context, thus leaving creativity completely unintelligible.

Bakhtin found the Romantic view of creativity unacceptable for another reason as well, one closely connected with his ethical concerns. For Bakhtin, creativity and responsibility were inseparable, both part of the "task" and work of daily life. Romantic separation of creativity from "labor and study" was therefore objectionable on ethical grounds. In his early manuscript *Author and Hero,* Bakhtin characterizes the Romantic poet as an artist defined by "a striving to act and create immediately in the common event of being as its sole participant; [by] an inability to resign himself to laboring, to defining his place in the event through others or to place himself along side of them" (AiG, p. 176).

So understood, the Romantic view of creativity is, of course, a "poetic" rather than a "prosaic" one. Creativity is left homeless on earth, which is understood as dead and law governed; it cannot be found in the daily work of real people, whose lives are necessarily formulaic except for unaccountable irruptions of creative energy. These irruptions are always passively experienced, as Shelley emphasized; they are not truly worked for, not truly created by human effort.

No more acceptable to Bakhtin was a solution offered by some heroes in Dostoevsky's novels: freedom and innovation are entirely random acts, like spite or causeless self-annihilation. We may recall that in *The Possessed,* Kirillov decides to kill himself and so prove his freedom. As the first person to do so, he will become the "man-god." "But you won't be the only one to kill yourself; there are lots of suicides," Stavrogin objects. "[Those were all] with good cause," Kirillov answers. "But to do so without any cause at all, simply for my own self-will, I am the only one" (Dostoevsky, *Possessed*, p. 628). The underground man, for similar reasons but with considerably less confidence, offers senseless acts of spite as quintessentially free acts. Insofar as existentialists, such as Camus, embrace similar ideas, they also defend a position Bakhtin rejects.

When we see Kirillov shoot himself, not out of a metaphysical quest for freedom but tracked down like an animal by a fellow revolutionary who stands to profit by his death, and then read of his brains splattered on the floor, we may reflect on the inexorability of the laws he hoped to transcend and the meaninglessness of freedom so conceived. And when we become familiar with the underground man's spite, it is all too easy to anticipate his actions, as he himself well knows. Spite, too, may have its iron, if perverse, laws.[14] And even if these acts *could* be momentarily free, they would lead nowhere and would still exclude the possibility of creativity in everyday, lived life.

The underground man's other and more interesting attempt to prove his freedom is no better, in Bakhtin's view. Reasoning that all actions limit and "finalize" him, the underground man strives to do nothing at all and so to have no finalizing definition. In Bakhtin's phrase, he endeavors to be a man of "pure function." But pure function creates nothing, according to Bakhtin; it is mere "empty potentiality," which to be real must at times be realized and answered for.

Bakhtin is so often treated merely as a kind of philosophic anarchist, as the Bakunin of our times, that we stress his suspicion of such "solutions." For Bakhtin, the absence of any finalization destroys freedom and creativity as surely as complete finalization. Absolute lack of commitment precludes genuine responsibility no less than a mechanical application of universal norms. According to Bakhtin, the ethical individual must make commitments that are real, if provisional. As Voloshinov writes, one needs not only irony and the loophole, but also "the word that really means and takes responsibility for what it says" (V: MPL, p. 159).

According to Bakunin's famous aphorism, "the passion to destroy is a creative passion." According to Bakhtin, creativity cannot proceed entirely by destruction if it is to be genuinely creative: mere negation, he suggests, can never produce a meaningful word.

The initial critical reception of Bakhtin in the West focused primarily on those passages in Bakhtin that do sound a great deal like
Bakunin. His admirers described libertarian Bakhtin, an apostle of
pure freedom and carnival license, who rejoices in the undoing of
rules, in centrifugal energy for its own sake, in clowning, and the
rejection of all authority and "official culture." It must be admitted
that there are indeed elements of antinomianism, theoretical anarchism, and holy foolishness in his thought about carnival. But on
the whole Bakhtin insulates himself against that sort of thinking
better than it might at first appear. Judged by the entirety of his
work, Bakhtin is, if anything, an apostle of constraints. For without constraints of the right sort, he believed, neither freedom nor
creativity, neither unfinalizability nor responsibility, can be real.

Unfinalizability and prosaics, taken together, also help to explain Bakhtin's oft-noted equanimity, even benevolence. At several
points in the early manuscripts, Bakhtin makes his implicit case
against the everyday temptations of envy, passivity, and despair in
the following terms: because of the multiple factors particularizing
me, *no one else* is ever in a position to do what I, at this moment, can
do (KFP, pp. 112–13).

Unfinalizability and Historicity

Unfinalizability and prosaics shaped Bakhtin's understanding of
historicity. Bakhtin (and Medvedev) dismissed with impatience
many narrative models and philosophical conceptions that were ostensibly but only superficially historical. For example, the Russian
Formalists advanced models of change, but, according to Medvedev, those models were themselves "profoundly nonhistorical."
"The qualitative development of existence . . . is completely inaccessible to Formalism" (M:FM, p. 97). For Bakhtin and Medvedev,
history is much more than mere change.

But what is historicity? For Bakhtin, this question was simultaneously a philosophical and a historical one. Time and again, he examines it not only by exposition of the concept but also by nar-
rating his own history of historical awareness. He considers both
explicit theories of history and implicit ones shaping various forms
of narrative. For example, he describes the history of the novel as
the gradual (and truly historical) development of what he calls "real
historical time" (BSHR, p. 19). (We consider Bakhtin's thoughts on
this aspect of the problem in Chapter Nine of the present study.)

For Bakhtin, an awareness of real historical time entails much more than an awareness of flux. Historicity cannot be equated, as modern literary theorists so often do, with the sort of thinking that is content to indicate variability and conclude that all things are relative. Such a conclusion, which can always be drawn equally well under all circumstances, is itself profoundly nonhistorical. In fact, it is antihistorical, because the end of each investigation is always known in advance, and so the examination of any particular historical event is superfluous.

The great historical models, including Marxism, also fail to be more than superficially historical according to Bakhtin's criteria. For as those models are usually employed, they more or less guarantee in advance the significance of anything one might find. In his Soviet context, Bakhtin would have ample reason to fault this kind of thinking. But Western Marxism would also usually fall short.

Jean-Paul Sartre observed that "lazy Marxism," based on "apriorism," endlessly discovers what it already knows (Sartre, *Search*, pp. 53, 42). As a result, Marxism tends to "dissolve" real, historical people "in a bath of sulphuric acid" (ibid., pp. 43–44). The "dialectic" becomes "a celestial law . . . a metaphysical force which by itself engenders the historical process" and we lose all sense of the value of particular action, of "human creativity" (ibid., p. 99). Bakhtin would doubtless have agreed with this critique. History is not history unless particular experience is meaningful, actions are responsible, results are partially unexpected, and the lives of people, both individually and in groups, are surprising. In short, historicity requires unfinalizability.

Historicity also cannot be equated with mere diachrony, as Formalists, structuralists, and semioticians use the word. For diachrony can be, and often is, nothing but a series of synchronic slices, with no intelligible historical links. Or at times, it is a sort of synchrony sliced sideways, a system that unfolds over time in a systemic and systematic way. Unfinalizability and prosaics are missing from such models, which make change the result of causes outside human agency, uniform in nature, and, at least in principle, knowable in advance.

Bakhtin may be regarded as a major contributor to a distinctively modern sense of historicity, quite at odds with nineteenth-century historicist and more recent structuralist models. His work on this concept was complex and extensive. We shall explore his ideas in greater depth later in this book, but it would be useful to describe at the outset a few recurrent patterns of his thought and to identify in general terms his minimum requirements for a profound sense of real historical time.

According to Bakhtin, history must be understood so that it is neither random nor completely ordered, neither of which would allow for genuine "becoming." Because social and psychological entities cannot be completely ordered, they cannot be described in terms of "structures" in the structuralist sense. Because they are *partially* ordered, they do exhibit structure in the looser sense apparently employed by Braudel in *The Structures of Everyday Life*. General systems theorists distinguish a system (defined, it will be recalled, as "a set of interrelated entities, of which no subset is unrelated to any other subset") from a looser form they call an aggregate, "a set of entities which may perhaps be partly interrelated, but in which at least one entity or subset of entities is unrelated to the complementary set of entities" (Kramer and Smit, *Systems Thinking*, p. 14). In Bakhtin's view, social entities tend to resemble aggregates more than systems.

For Bakhtin, the world clusters and unclusters. Particular elements interact with existing aggregates, which are in turn modified by interactions with other aggregates; particular elements are also continually detached from aggregates, cluster anew, and form the basis for yet more unforeseen interactions. Unfinalizability characterizes the whole as well as the particular parts.

All cultural entities, whether psychological or social, behave in this way. Social formations are never perfectly designed; rather, they make do with the resources they have at hand. Whatever forms they develop come complete with unforeseen by-products, which have in turn the potential to affect future developments in unexpected ways.

Bakhtin was quite interested in biological science, and an analogy from evolutionary biology might be useful. Stephen Jay Gould has repeatedly reminded us that according to Darwin, the best proof of evolution is *imperfect* design, compromise structures that work more or less well, but not as efficiently as other conceivable structures. No cosmic designer would have built them in that compromise way; therefore, they must have come about by making do with the resources of changing environments and natural history. In other words, messiness and tinkering, not perfect adaptation, are the true marks of historicity.[15]

Gould further argues that a common misunderstanding of Darwin, "hyperselectionism," in fact misconstrues the very point of

Darwin's proof of evolutionary history. Hyperselectionists such as Alfred Russel Wallace viewed "each bit of morphology, each function of an organ, each behavior as an adaptation, a product of selection leading to a 'better' organism. They held a deep belief in nature's 'rightness,' in the exquisite fit of all creatures to their environments" (Gould, *Panda's Thumb,* p. 50). If an organic or behavioral feature should exhibit no apparent function, that lack only shows the incompleteness of our knowledge, according to the hyperselectionist view. We may recognize in this view a style of thought analogous to semiotic totalitarianism.

As Gould stresses, this caricature of Darwin almost returns, in a curious way, to the creationist view of perfect design. It thinks away history, what Gould calls the "messier universe" that Darwin saw (ibid.). Darwin realized that natural selection was not the only force at work, and that not everything fits. For one thing, "adaptive change in one part [of an organism] can lead to nonadaptive modifications of other features." Moreover, "an organ built under the influence of selection for a specific role may be able, as a consequence of its structure, to perform many other, unselected features as well" (ibid.). And once in place, unselected features provide the material for future changes. In short, biological structures, like social entities, are at once designed, undesigned, and ill-designed— they change in an imperfect way, and they give rise to by-products. For all these reasons, they exhibit the potential for the unforeseen.

If that is true of natural processes, it is still more likely to be true of social ones, where human agency and a multiplicity of heterogeneous purposes always operate. In this context, grand historical systems, with all their closedness, appear to describe history in terms too simple and inflexible even for inanimate or nonhuman natural forces.

Bakhtin's concept of historicity as a matter of multiple potentials led him to meditate on the nature of time. He consistently opposed all ways of thinking that reduced the present moment—each present moment—to a simple derivative of what went before. As he emphasized the "eventness" of the event and the necessity of responsibility here and now, he also insisted on the *presentness* of each moment. Time is open and each moment has multiple possibilities.

In understanding the historical past, or earlier stages of a person's life, it is instructive to note how frequently we interpret the past anachronistically. We tend to see in it only those possibilities that were in fact realized. In so doing, we misrepresent the past, because every past moment exhibited "presentness" when it occurred; it had the potential to lead in many directions. Each participant in the moment experienced that distinct sense of time.

When Bakhtin discusses narrative genres, he stresses the way in which each one represents the sense of the present. Does a given genre describe the present as open or closed, conclusive or inconclusive? How near is the position of the author to the throb of events in his own time, and in his character's time? As we will see, for Bakhtin only the novel could come close to representing the "open present" and real historicity. "[Represented] reality as we have it in the novel is only one of many possible realities; it is not inevitable, not arbitrary, it bears within itself other possibilities" (EaN, p. 37). This sense of time becomes intrinsic to the way novels describe moments in history and in the lives of characters: "The world as an event (and not as existence in ready-made form)" (MHS, p. 162).

If and only if history is a matter of unique and unrepeatable events, each of which has unrevealed potential, then time is, as Bakhtin writes, "irreversible." By "irreversibility" Bakhtin means more than the mere fact that it flows in only one direction. He means that retrodiction, no less than prediction, is in principle impossible, and that classical deterministic notions of time, which reduce it to an emptiness that events merely fill, are mistaken.

Bakhtin was interested in the physical as well as the biological sciences. It is difficult to tell how thoroughly he understood them, but he appears to have especially appreciated their reconceptualization of temporality.[16]

As Ilya Prigogine (*Being to Becoming*) has eloquently explained, Newtonian mechanics and classical determinism view time as a mere "parameter" and physical processes as essentially "reversible." That is, events could just as easily happen in the opposite direction; and one can retrodict the position of physical objects as easily as one can predict them. But from the development of thermodynamics to the debates on quantum mechanics, physics and chemistry began to understand time as irreversible, directionality as essential, and retrodiction as often impossible. It may well be impossible in principle to predict the future state of a system from the state that immediately precedes it. Prior states constrain, but do not necessarily determine, outcomes. Prigogine dwells at length on the implications for both science and the humanities of an understanding of irreversibility. He believes that our conceptions must move *From Being to Becoming*.[17]

It may seem paradoxical that freedom should be associated with the *ir*reversibility of time, but upon reflection it becomes clear that only such a view can grant real importance to a unique event at a particular moment. And if unique events do not have such importance, if they are wholly predictable from prior or future states of the system, then freedom is an illusion and genuine historicity disappears.

Time is not a mere parameter, but an operator. It fills events as much as events fill it.[18] And if that is true of physical, geological, and biological events, it is of course even truer of social and cultural events. Bakhtin explored the development of the concept of temporal incommensurability since the Renaissance in several works, including his studies of Rabelais and Dostoevsky, and especially in his study of Goethe and his essay on the chronotope.

Bakhtin argues that European prose, which began with a static hero placed in a static world, learned to represent genuine development first in individuals, and then in individuals and society together. More accurate narrative prose often preceded more accurate philosophical discussions, according to Bakhtin.

Beginning with the fiction written during the Enlightenment, it was understood that a person "emerges *along with the world* and he reflects the historical emergence of the world itself" (BSHR, p. 23). The result was a profound conception of unfinalizability. "Understandably, in such a novel of emergence, problems of reality and man's potential, problems of freedom and necessity, and the problem of creative initiative rise to their full height. The image of the emerging man begins to surmount its private nature . . . and enters into a completely new, *spatial* sphere of historical existence" (BSHR, p. 24).

Bakhtin's metaphor of spatiality alludes to another criterion of historicity. Historicity includes not only *anachronism* but also what we might call *anatopism*. From place to place, nook to nook, and room to room, time and the sense of time show qualitative differences and shape events in dissimilar ways. According to Bakhtin, Goethe had the perspicacity to perceive different kinds of time at work simultaneously. "Behind each [apparently] static multiformity he saw heterochrony" (BSHR, p. 28). *Heterochrony* (also translated as "multitemporality") is a key element, usually overlooked, in Bakhtin's own sense of history.

Interestingly enough, Braudel also faults traditional narrative historians for overlooking the "plurality of social time . . . the multiplicity of time" (Braudel, "History," pp. 26–27). The rhythms of history range from extremely slow ones, perceptible, if at all, only over centuries, to those that are almost instantaneous; according to Braudel, at any given time diverse rhythms operate in different spheres. "Science, technology, political institutions, conceptual changes, civilizations . . . all have their own rhythms of life and growth, and the new history of conjunctures will be complete only when it has made up a whole orchestra of them all" (ibid., p. 30). What is required, Bakhtin would say, is "a polyphonic unity" of heterogeneous chronotopes.

Dialogue

A reified model of the world is now being replaced by a dialogic model.   —TRDB, p. 293

Dialogic relationships are a much broader phenomenon than mere rejoinders in a dialogue laid out compositionally in the text; they are an almost universal phenomenon, permeating all human speech and all relationships and manifestations of human life—in general, everything that has meaning and significance.

—PDP, p. 40

Bakhtin's third recurrent concern, in addition to prosaics and unfinalizability, is that complex of ideas he calls "dialogue." He uses the term in so many contexts and in such diverse senses that it often seems devoid of clear definition. In subsequent chapters, we will explore its significance in Bakhtin's theories of language (Chapter Four), the self (Chapter Five), and literature (Chapters Six through Ten). At present, we would like to discuss it in its broadest sense, as "a model of the world."

Dialogue for Bakhtin is a special sort of interaction. Unfortunately, it has often been taken as a synonym for interaction, or verbal interaction in general, and is thereby trivialized. As Bakhtin used the term, dialogue cannot be equated with argument, nor is it equivalent to "compositionally expressed dialogue," that is, the sequential representation of transcribed voices in a novel or a play. Bakhtin also cautions us against confusing dialogue with logical contradiction. It is different from Buber's I-Thou relation. Least of all does it resemble Hegelian or Marxist dialectics.

When we imagine dialogue, we tend to think of two monads that come to interact in a given way: for example, opposites contradict, producing a synthesis. This common conception is a necessary consequence of the kind of thought that Bakhtin calls "theoretism," and which he regards as dominant in modern Western history. As

Bakhtin uses the term, theoretism always understands events in terms of a set of rules to which they conform or a structure that they exhibit. In semiotics, for instance, particular people are reduced to counters, and their intimate and ethical relations to their actions are lost. The same is true of Marxist dialectics. As Bakhtin puts it in his early writings, theoretism thinks away the "eventness" of events, which becomes secondary rather than primary.

That which makes real dialogue a live process transcends received models, none of which allow for unfinalizability. The problem with theoretism is that it begins analysis from the wrong place. According to Bakhtin, "we cannot break out into the world of events from *within* the theoretical world. One must start with the act itself, and not with its theoretical transcription" (KFP, p. 91). This kind of "transcription" reduces time to a mere parameter and loses the real historicity of an event. In theoretism, Bakhtin observes, "the temporality of the actual historicity of existence is only a moment of abstractly cognized history" (KFP, p. 89).

In fact, all social and psychological entities are processual in nature, according to Bakhtin. Their unfinalizable activity is essential to their identity. And for people, the most important activity is dialogue. Thus, for any individual or social entity, we cannot properly separate existence from the ongoing process of communication. "*To be* means *to communicate*" (TRDB, p. 287). It is therefore inaccurate to speak of entering into dialogue, as if the components that do so could exist in any other way. To be sure, particular dialogues may break off (they never truly end), but dialogue itself is always going on. In his linguistic work, Bakhtin endeavors to describe language so that dialogue is not a subsequent act of combination but is itself the starting point.

The second problem with the image of interacting monads is that, as we have seen, for Bakhtin neither individuals nor social entities ever constitute a monad. They are much looser, "messier," and more open than that. The most interesting and most unfinalizable aspects of any interaction arise from the relative disorder of the participants.

Moreover, we usually think of monads as wholes with clear boundaries. Bakhtin warns us, however, that neither individuals nor any other social entities are locked within their boundaries. They are extraterritorial, partially "located outside" themselves. Thus, Bakhtin refers to the "nonself-sufficiency" of the self (TRDB, p. 287). "To be means to be for another, and through the other for oneself. A person has no sovereign internal territory, he is wholly and always on the boundary; looking inside himself, he looks *into the eyes of another* or *with the eyes of another*" (ibid.).

Indeed, the very metaphor of "territory" and "boundary" is faulty, according to Bakhtin. If one insists on using it, one necessarily winds up with paradoxical formulations. Bakhtin insists that cultural entities are, in effect, *all* boundary:

> One must not, however, imagine the realm of culture as some sort of spatial whole, having boundaries but also having internal territory. The realm of culture has no internal territory: it is entirely distributed along the boundaries, boundaries pass everywhere, through its every aspect. . . . Every cultural act lives essentially on the boundaries: in this is its seriousness and significance; abstracted from boundaries it loses its soil, it becomes empty, arrogant, it degenerates and dies. [PS, p. 25][19]

Perhaps we are inclined to metaphors of territory and boundary because we think of individual selves occupying a specific place at a specific time. But although that is true of and necessary for physical bodies, it is untrue of psyches or of any other cultural entities. It would clearly be best to avoid such metaphors altogether. Bakhtin either avoids them or reminds us of their problems by paradoxically defining his favorite heroes as always liminal, always on a boundary.

Bakhtin will come to favor a host of other metaphors to replace the usual ones of monads, territories, and bodies. Each of these three, he felt, is essentially "Newtonian" or "Ptolemaic"; they imagine physical entities as bodies in collision or planets traveling in fixed orbits around a given center. But if one must look to the sciences, more recent work offers better ground. Cultural entities more closely resemble oscillating "fields," a play of force lines rather than an assembly of objects. At other times, he speaks of "obscuring mists," "elastic environments," and "live media." Consider the sequence of metaphors in one characteristic description of "the word":

> But no living word relates to its object in a *singular* way: between the word and its object, between the word and the speaking subject, there exists an elastic environment of other, alien words about the same object. . . . It is precisely in the process of living interaction with this specific environment that the word may be individualized and given stylistic shape.
>
> Indeed, any concrete discourse (utterance) finds the object at which it was directed already as it were overlain with qualifications, open to dispute, charged with value, already enveloped in an obscuring mist—or, on

the contrary, by the "light" of alien words that have already been spoken about it. It is entangled, shot through with shared thoughts, points of view, alien value judgments and accents. The word, directed toward its object, enters a dialogically agitated and tension-filled environment of alien words, value judgments, and accents, weaves in and out of complex inter-relationships, merges with some, recoils from others, intersects with yet a third group. [DiN, p. 276]

Here Bakhtin's own prose becomes a "tension-filled environment," an "obscuring mist" of mixed metaphors upon mixed metaphors, as he tries to escape the fixedness that any single metaphor— however fluid, active, incomplete, and open to interpenetration— might imply. As this passage continues, the metaphors multiply: the word is a ray that produces "a play of light and shadow," a thick "atmosphere," and "spectral dispersion" (DiN, p. 277). Here we see Bakhtin trying to take advantage of light's quality of pure energy while trying to escape its tendency to travel in a straight line. What he says here of the word, he suggests is true of everything in culture.

These cultural "fields" consist not only of diverse elements and forces, but are also "shot through" with multiple temporalities and diverse rhythms. The interaction of such fields, therefore, does not resemble the collision of billiard balls, nor can it be categorized in terms of "contradictions." The complexity of such dialogic inter-actions is immense, and might itself be the primary topic for a general theory of culture.

It is clear that dialogue so conceived involves the constant redefinition of its participants, develops and creates numerous potentials "in" each of them "separately" and between them "interactively" and "dialogically." It is also clear that no single interaction could exhaust the potential value of future exchanges. Both dialogue and the potentials of dialogue are endless. No word can be taken back, but the final word has not yet been spoken and never will be spoken.

Toward Dialogue

In his early writings, Bakhtin was still struggling toward his later sense of dialogue. Viewing his own development at a later point in his life, he may have seen this period as testing the limits of a model of interaction of "self" and "other" by so complicating each term that the model pretty much collapsed under its own qualifications. To develop one of his favorite analogies, his early work tinkers with a "Ptolemaic" model by adding more and more epicycles until, at last, he abandons it altogether in his own "Copernican" revolution. So long as he still thought of self and other (or society) as a primary opposition, he was still in his Ptolemaic phase; his Copernican revolution was to make dialogue central and primary, and the old opposition of self and society a secondary abstraction. It is therefore mistaken to view Bakhtin's mature work as a meditation on alterity in the usual sense.

When Bakhtin did arrive at his mature understanding of dialogue, he was able to reinterpret and partially rehabilitate some of the concepts he developed in his early period. Many of his favorite early terms and concepts reappear in his later work, now with new significance in a different and richer view of the world. It would be helpful to consider some of these earliest concepts.

According to the young Bakhtin, every action of every person is conditioned by the singularity of each in time and place. When "theoretists" of ethics or action consider the world, they generalize to patterns, norms, and rules, in which these singularities are lost. Their descriptions are "reversible" in that they allow either person to be in the other's place. Analysis can reverse participants as surely as people can alternate the first person pronoun. But the essence of real actions is that they are irreversible and particular. This is another way in which Bakhtin arrives at his concept of the "nonalibi."

When one person faces another, his experience is conditioned by his "outsideness." Even in the physical sense, one always sees something in the other that one does not see in oneself. I can see the world behind your back; when I see another person suffering, I, but not he, can "see the clear blue sky against whose background his suffering external image takes on meaning for me" (AiG, p. 25). And I am aware that each other has the same "surplus" of vision with respect to me. Different forms of aesthetic, ethical, political, or religious activity (Bakhtin proposes to write on all these topics) make different use of this "surplus."

How shall I respond to another person's suffering? What is most productive? We sometimes recommend empathy—merging as much as possible with the other's position, attempting to "see the world from his point of view," and renouncing one's own outsideness and surplus of vision. But to the extent that such empathy is possible, it is also sterile. "What would I have to gain," Bakhtin asks, "if another were to fuse with me? He would see and know only what I already see and know, he would only repeat in himself the inescapable closed circle of my own life; let him rather remain outside me" (AiG, p. 78).

Rather than empathy, we need what Bakhtin calls "live entering" or "living into" another [*vzhivanie*]. In this process one simultaneously renounces and exploits one's surplus; one brings into interaction both perspectives simultaneously and creates an "architectonics" of vision reducible to neither. This architectonics produces new understanding. "I *actively* enter as a living being [*vzhivaius'*] into an individuality, and consequently do not, for a single moment, lose myself completely or lose my singular place outside that individuality. It's not the subject who unexpectedly takes possession of a passive me, but *I* who actively enter into him; *vzhivanie* is *my* act, and only in it can there be productiveness and innovation" (KFP, p. 93).

When he discovered dialogue, Bakhtin largely abandoned this model. His early term for the complex of action was *architectonics* (KFP, p. 139), but this must have seemed too static a metaphor, and it was replaced by *fields* and *live media*. Above all, the abstractness of the formulation, its sense of self and other as irreducibly counterposed starting points, gave way to a richer sense of dialogue as the starting point. He arrived at more profound and integrated conceptions of self and society—two categories that were derivative, reified, and partially misleading when opposed to each other.

Dialogue and Other Cultures

We can see the dialogic enrichment of Bakhtin's thought over a lifetime in his "Response to a Question from the *Novyi mir* Editorial Staff" (1970). Asked to state his opinion of contemporary Russian literary and cultural studies, Bakhtin complains of "a certain fear of investigatory risk, a fear of hypotheses" (RQ, p. 1). "There is no bold statement of general problems" (ibid.), he writes. "And without this we cannot rise to the heights or descend to the depths" (RQ, p. 7). He gives several examples of timidity and recommends various types of boldness.

In investigating foreign cultures, he argues, one should be content neither with the gathering of new factual material nor even with the reconstruction of a foreign point of view. Both these kinds of anthropology are merely preliminary to the more important task of revealing "new *semantic* depths" (RQ, p. 6) in other cultures— and in our own.

One must proceed dialogically. "There exists a very strong, but

one-sided and thus untrustworthy, idea that in order better to understand a foreign culture, one must enter into it, forgetting one's own,
and view the world [entirely] through the eyes of this foreign culture" (RQ, pp. 6–7), Bakhtin begins. This step is necessary, but if
it is viewed as a goal, then research becomes mere "duplication and
would not entail anything new or enriching" for either side (RQ,
p. 7). This step is the equivalent of mere "empathy" in his early
writings; what is needed is *vzhivanie*. Or, as he puts it in 1970, our
goal should be the dialogic one of "creative understanding":

Creative understanding does not renounce itself, its own place in time, its
own culture; and it forgets nothing. In order to understand, it is immensely
important for the person who understands to be *located outside* the object of
his or her creative understanding—in time, in space, in culture. For one
cannot even really see one's own exterior and comprehend it as a whole,
and no mirrors or photographs can help; our real exterior can be seen and
understood only by other people, because they are located outside us in
space and because they are *others*. [RQ, p. 7]

Outsideness creates the possibility of dialogue, and dialogue helps
us understand a culture in a profound way. For any culture contains
meanings that it itself does not know, that it itself has not realized;
they are there, but as a *potential*. As we will see, the concept of a
potential is immensely important for Bakhtin's thought on many
topics. (We will consider it in more detail in our chapter on genres.)

Only dialogue reveals potentials. It does so by addressing them,
by provoking a specific answer that actualizes the potential, albeit in
a particular and incomplete way. At the same time, the questioner
necessarily undergoes the same process, which helps him comprehend unsuspected potentials in his own culture. The process, then,
is multiply enriching: it educates each side about itself and about the
other, and it not only discovers but activates potentials. Indeed, the
process of dialogue may itself create new potentials, realizable only
through future activity and dialogue.

This process cannot take place if one renounces or attempts to
insulate one's point of view. It also cannot take place if one adopts a
position of total relativism, assuming (as some modern theorists
teach) that one can only learn what one knows in advance and that
one necessarily turns everything into a mirror of one's self. No less
than dogmatism, relativism precludes dialogue, as Bakhtin frequently points out. Nor should we expect some "synthesis" or
"merging" of points of view: dialogue is not a self-consuming artifact, nor is it "dialectic," for dialectic (in the Hegelian or Marxist

sense) can be contained within a single consciousness and over-comes contradictions in a single, monologic view. By contrast, in "a dialogic encounter of two cultures . . . each retains its own unity and *open* totality, but they are mutually enriched" (RQ, p. 7).

In literary studies, Bakhtin insists, outsideness is equally valuable. To understand an author in the richest way, one must neither reduce him to an image of oneself, nor make oneself a version of him. Both methods exemplify "the false tendency toward reducing everything to a single consciousness, dissolving in it the other's consciousness" (N70–71, p. 141). Each participant must retain outsideness. "One cannot understand understanding as emotional empathy, as the placement of the self in the other's position (loss of one's own position). This is required only for peripheral aspects of understanding. One [also] cannot understand understanding as a translation from the other's language into one's own" (ibid.).

Rather than merely understand a text "as the author himself understood it," we should seek something "better" (ibid.). True understanding both recognizes the integrity of the text and seeks to "supplement" it. Such understanding "is active and creative by nature. Creative understanding continues creativity, and multiplies the artistic wealth of humanity." We must therefore value "the co-creativity of those who understand" (N70–71, p. 142). And this is true whatever the basis of our outsideness: personal, spatial, temporal, national, or any other.[20]

Monologization

> *Question* and *answer* are not logical relations (categories); they cannot be placed in one consciousness (unified and closed in itself); any response gives rise to a new question. Question and answer presuppose mutual outsideness. If an answer does not give rise to a new question from itself, it falls out of the dialogue.
>
> —MHS, p. 168

Because of mental habits, intellectual traditions, and centripetal cultural forces, we often lose a sense of the dialogic quality of an event. The live medium becomes dead: activity is represented by stasis, heterochrony is reduced to singularity, irreversibility is perceived as reversibility, openness is reduced to a closed systematicity, and potentials are completely overlooked. Bakhtin uses a variety of terms for this deadening process. In his earliest writings, he calls it "transcription"; later, he speaks of "finalization" and "monologization," depending on which kind of loss concerns him.

"Monologization" appears most frequently. Like dialogue, monologue has many different meanings for Bakhtin. At present, we are concerned with it in its broadest sense, as a form of thinking that turns dialogue into an empty form and a lifeless interaction.

According to Bakhtin, dialectics is one such monologization. "Dialogue and dialectics," he writes boldly. "Take a dialogue and remove the voices (the partitioning of voices), remove the intonations (emotional and individualizing ones), carve out abstract concepts and judgments from living words and responses, cram everything into one abstract consciousness—and that's how you get dialectics" (N70–71, p. 147). Bakhtin's contempt for dialectics was a constant, and appears in writings of the 1920's as well as of the 1970's.

Dialectics abstracts the dialogic from dialogue. It finalizes and systematizes dialogue. Individual agency, particular evaluations, the rootedness in the world that creates real potential for the unforeseen are reified and die. "Reified (materializing, objectified) images are profoundly inadequate for life and discourse," Bakhtin insists. "A reified model of the world is now being replaced by a dialogic model. Every thought and every life merges in the open-ended dialogue. Also impermissible is any materialization of the word: its nature is dialogic. Dialectics is the abstract product of dialogue" (TRDB, p. 293). Dialectics is a typical product of the old, Newtonian, monologic view of the world.

From the point of view of dialogics, "the world is a [live] event," whereas in dialectics it is "a mechanical contact of 'oppositions,'" a contact of "things," rather than people. "If we transform dialogue into one continuous text, that is, erase the divisions between voices (changes of speaking subjects), which is possible at the extreme (Hegel's monological dialectic), then the deep-seated (infinite) contextual meaning disappears (we hit the bottom, reach a standstill). [In dialectics, we have] a thought that, like a fish in an aquarium, knocks against the bottom and the sides and cannot swim farther or deeper. Dogmatic thoughts" (MHS, p. 162).

No less than dialectics, Bakhtin suggests, semiotics "materializes" and reifies the word: it takes the life out of language and culture. In part, such reification derives from a misunderstanding of history. The misunderstanding lies in mistaking habits or clusters for rules or laws.

According to Bakhtin, culture and individuals accumulate habits and procedures, which are the "sclerotic deposits" (DiN, p. 292) of earlier activity; forms are "congealed" events and situations (MHS,

p. 165). Habits and inherited forms produce some regularity in present behavior; they also serve as the ground for new kinds of future activity. Characteristically, the centripetal forces of culture often codify these habits by turning them into a fixed set of rules. This codification serves in part to restrain change. Such disciplines as semiotics, philology, and linguistics, which are themselves products of centripetal cultural forces, tend to mistake the codification for reality and so misunderstand both present potential and past activity.

Forgetting that activity and discourse are always evaluatively charged and context specific, semiotics typically generalizes away the particularities of context. "Semiotics deals primarily with the transmission of ready-made communication using a ready-made code. But in live speech, strictly speaking, communication is first created in the process of transmission, and there is, in essence, no code" (N70–71, p. 147). For Bakhtin, there is a crucial difference between "context" and "code." "A context is potentially unfinalized; a code must be finalized. A code is only a technical means of transmitting information; it does not have cognitive, creative significance. A code is a deliberately established, killed context" (ibid.).[21] Bakhtin often pairs criticism of semiotics with criticism of dialectics, because both approaches embody the same context-killing impulse.

Bakhtin would doubtless have advanced similar objections to speech act theory, insofar as it tries to describe a grammar of situation and to codify context itself.[22] Both speech act theory and semiotics still employ a model of monads acting according to rules. Bakhtin would find in them insufficient recognition of the way "discourse lives, as it were, beyond itself, in a living impulse toward the object; if we detach ourselves completely from this impulse all we have left is the naked corpse of the word. . . . *To study the word as such, ignoring the impulse that reaches out beyond it, is just as senseless as to study psychological experience outside the context of that real life toward which it was directed and by which it is determined*" (DiN, p. 292; in quoted text, italics are in the original unless otherwise noted). Opposition to the monologization of the psyche is a central theme of Bakhtin's theories of the self, which we will discuss in Chapter Five.

In his earliest writings, before the concept of dialogue became central, Bakhtin faults theoretism for an error analogous to monologization. Those who understand ethics in terms of rules make a mistake similar to the understanding of language in terms of codes.

They assume that it is possible to "transcribe" an event so as not to lose its essential features, but in so doing, the event loses all the singularity from which responsibility derives. "Of course it is possible to transcribe all this in theoretical terms and express it as a constant law of the act; the ambiguity of language permits us to do this, but we will end up with an empty formula" (KFP, p. 111).

Such transcriptions and monologizations are certainly not useless. Taken as a starting point, they can facilitate an understanding of an event or dialogue, much as codes can help us to understand a language, and rules may be a useful first step in ethical thought. At times, Bakhtin himself resorts to monologization, although he cautions us not to mistake it for the real thing. For example, he writes: "The catharsis that finalizes Dostoevsky's novels might be—*of course inadequately and somewhat rationalistically*—expressed in this way: nothing conclusive has yet taken place in the world" (PDP, p. 166; italics ours). In his notes "Toward a Reworking of the Dostoevsky Book," he explicitly reminds himself to include such cautionary words: "I translate into the language of an abstract worldview that which was the object of concrete and living artistic visualization and which then became a principle of form. Such a translation is always inadequate" (TRDB, p. 288). Falsification arises when one, forgetting that such statements are provisional, reifies them.

Bakhtin, we have observed, is often misunderstood as a relativist. But in his view, relativism is itself a form of monologization. Assuming that all descriptions are equally arbitrary, relativists simply leave us with an infinity of monologizations. We consequently lose the dialogic quality of events even more surely than ever, for at least single monologizations—that is dogmatic statements—take a stand, and therefore may be transcended. Pure relativism leaves us in a world where even this transcendence is impossible, and where responsibility in any meaningful sense is absent.

Truth as Dialogic

Sciences of the spirit; their real field of inquiry is not one but two 'spirits.'. . . The real object of study is the interrelation and interaction of 'spirits.'   —N70–71, p. 144

Bakhtin envisaged all of life as an ongoing, unfinalizable dialogue, which takes place at every moment of daily existence:

The dialogic nature of consciousness. The dialogic nature of human life itself. The single adequate form for *verbally expressing* authentic human life is the *open-ended dialogue*. Life by its very nature is dialogic. To live means to participate in dialogue: to ask questions, to heed, to respond, to agree, and so forth. In this dialogue a person participates wholly and throughout his whole life: with his eyes, lips, hands, soul, spirit, with his whole body and deeds. He invests his entire self in discourse, and this discourse enters into the dialogic fabric of human life, into the world symposium. [TRDB, p. 293]

According to Bakhtin, existing forms of knowledge inevitably monologize the world by turning an open-ended dialogue into a monologic statement "summarizing" its contents but misrepresenting its unfinalizable spirit. The dialogue of life requires a dialogic method and a dialogic conception of truth to represent it. But in Bakhtin's view, such a concept of truth is missing from modern Western thought, at least insofar as that thought is represented in the tradition of philosophy. So far, only literary works have approached this more adequate representation. The best novelists are far ahead of the philosophers.

Bakhtin's reference to the "world symposium" suggests his approach to Socratic dialogues. In a rudimentary way, this genre goes some distance toward representing the world dialogically. "At the base of the genre lies the Socratic notion of . . . the dialogic nature of human thinking about truth," he writes in the Dostoevsky book (PDP, p. 110). As opposed to "official monologism" with its "ready-made truth" (ibid.), this genre embodies the opposite idea: "Truth is not born nor is it to be found inside the head of an individual person, it is born *between people* collectively searching for truth, in the process of their dialogic interaction" (ibid.). According to Bakhtin, Plato later monologized the dialogue, turning it into an empty vehicle of exposition, a mere "catechism." [23] But in the earliest dialogues Socrates avoids ever stating a ready-made truth, for his truth was one of activity itself.

Or at least, that is the tendency, the hidden but barely exploited potential of this genre, according to Bakhtin. In it, dialogic notions of truth determine "its *form,* but they did not by any means always find expression in the actual content of the individual dialogues. The content often assumed a monologic character that contradicted the form-shaping idea of the genre" (ibid.). [24]

Some later dialogic forms of literature also share this core idea and also realize it in a rudimentary way. For example, the "threshold dialogues" of Lucian and later writers trace "dotted lines" from existing thinkers until they intersect. Typically, they describe the resulting dialogue as a conversation at the gates of the other world (e.g., Lucian's "Dialogues of the Dead," Gulliver's conversations with the dead in book three of *Gulliver's Travels,* or innumerable stories about interviews at the gates of heaven or hell). At their best, these dialogues reveal and create new potentials from each thinker's ideas and from their interaction. But they still do not fully represent the dialogic nature of the world.

For Bakhtin, Dostoevsky came closest to succeeding at this task. We will discuss Bakhtin's understanding of Dostoevsky's "polyphonic novel" in Chapter Six. Here we would stress that this understanding of Dostoevsky goes far beyond a mere critical analysis of that writer, far beyond even a general literary theory. Bakhtin finds in Dostoevsky support for his own radical revision of knowledge. Bakhtin tries to indicate in his own monologic form of exposition the essential features of a dialogic view of the world; it is as if he thought of his work as gesturing toward Dostoevsky's novels, so we could see in them all that escapes any monologic paraphrase, including Bakhtin's. Only then can we appreciate and extend the implications of Dostoevsky's work. "Dostoevsky's influence has still far from reached its culmination," Bakhtin wrote in 1961. "We are even today still being drawn into his dialogue on transient themes, but the dialogism he revealed to us, the dialogism of artistic thinking and of an artistic picture of the world, his new model of the internally dialogized world, has not yet been thoroughly examined" (TRDB, p. 291). Nevertheless, it is already evident that, by comparison with Dostoevsky, the Socratic dialogue is "mere dialogue, little more than an external form of dialogism" (ibid.). Real dialogism will incarnate a world whose unity is essentially one of multiple voices, whose conversations never reach finality and cannot be transcribed in monologic form. The unity of the world will then appear as it really is: polyphonic.

At such moments, Bakhtin's prophetic tone verges on the theological. In his earliest writings, he envisages Christ as the One who performed a live entering into the world without ever losing his divine outsideness. Bakhtin's theology, to the extent he had one, is not of resurrection but of incarnation. It recommends not "faith (in the sense of a specific faith in orthodoxy, in progress, in man, in revolution, etc.)" (TRDB, p. 294), for this kind of faith would be a monologic doctrine. Rather, Bakhtin recommends something quite different, "a *sense of faith,* that is, an integral attitude . . . toward a higher and ultimate value" (ibid.), the sort of faith that Father Zosima has in *The Brothers Karamazov* or, we might add, that Levin reaches precariously at the end of *Anna Karenina*. This faith must be continually reasserted, and is always the product (and process) of hard work. Its "effect must be that it becomes an altogether different world. It must, so to speak, wax and wane as a whole," as Wittgenstein writes (Wittgenstein, *Tractatus,* 6.43).[25] Knowledge, too, must become "not theory (transient content), but 'a sense of theory'" (TRDB, p. 294).

Bakhtin's ultimate image of such dialogic faith is, characteristically, a *conversation* with Christ. "The word as something personal. Christ as Truth. I put the question to him" (N70–71, p. 148; trans. emended). What would Bakhtin's conversation with Christ, the ultimate threshold dialogue, be like? One may imagine it would resemble the vision of Pontius Pilate in Mikhail Bulgakov's novel, *The Master and Margarita.* Pilate dreams of a walk with his dog along a moonbeam, as he and Christ, the "vagrant philosopher," converse: "He was walking with Banga and the vagrant philosopher beside him. They were arguing about a weighty and complex problem, over which neither could gain the upper hand. They disagreed entirely, which made their argument all the more absorbing and interminable" (Bulgakov, *Master,* ch. 26, p. 310).

2

The Shape of a Career

In the previous chapter we approached globally three of
Bakhtin's major ideas: prosaics, unfinalizability, and dialogue. Since
global concepts are not designed to reflect chronology, our discussion of them may seem to flatten Bakhtin's development as a
thinker. We will now attempt a dynamic and chronological survey
of Bakhtin's career. For it is an important premise of this book that
the development of Bakhtin's lifework, not only the content of his
philosophy, was genuinely dialogic and unfinalized—that is, it had
clusters of ideas, some very productive and others less so; it had unexpected encounters, watersheds, both creative and fallow periods,
and some contradictory dead ends. There are also several points
where Bakhtin's general ideas, developed in different directions by
his associates, might in turn have spurred Bakhtin himself on to
new formulations. This premise, that Bakhtin sometimes surprised
himself, implies that his ideas genuinely *grew*, and that not all
of them were equally fruitful. It also underscores the need to explain the kind of coherence that his work did possess.

The hypothesis we offer in this chapter is not the result of any
new oral evidence or documentation from unpublished sources.
The periodization in many respects is not original,[1] but we differ
from much current biobibliographical opinion in that we *exclude*
the so-called disputed texts from the Bakhtin canon. Our reasons
for doing so are developed at length in Chapter Three. The primary
"new" influence shaping our hypothesis was the publication, in
1986, of a second installment of Bakhtin's early writings previously
available only to those with access to the archive. (A first installment had already been published in Russian in 1979.)[2] These materials were never prepared for publication by Bakhtin himself. Like
all rough drafts, they must be used with care; their publication in
the Soviet Union was itself a politicized event, made possible by literary executors who had their own reasons for creating a particular
posthumous image of Bakhtin. Even in their unfinished state, however, these early writings are significant. They impart a certain spi-
raled symmetry to the life, for Bakhtin returned to their concerns

half a century later in ways that provide an interesting frame for his well-known works on carnivalization and the history of the novel.

In our chronological survey we devote the most attention to the period before 1929, because those years contain the two most significant watersheds of Bakhtin's career and because the writings of that period are still relatively unknown. In our reading of the works of this period, Bakhtin was seeking—and for a decade not finding—his own critical voice. It is not our purpose in this chapter to reconstruct the various traditions of continental philosophy that contributed to this search; that work has been undertaken by others.[3] Rather, we will focus on Bakhtin himself: on the frameworks he developed during these years, their relation to the challenge of Russian Formalism, and their shortcomings—which, in our view, provoked him to the conceptual breakthrough of *Problems of Dostoevsky's Creative Art* in 1929. The masterwork on Dostoevsky is not only Bakhtin's first major theoretical statement, but is also the first sustained evidence that Bakhtin had found his own "internally persuasive" voice.

The major books and essays after 1929—on the history and theory of the novel, on the Bildungsroman and on Rabelais, and the revised Dostoevsky book—constitute the "canonical Bakhtin" best known and most influential in the West. Our treatment of these texts and concepts in this present chapter will be brief; they are allotted their own chapters in Parts Two and Three.

Four Periods

We see four periods and hence three watersheds in Bakhtin's thought (see our chart, "The Shape of a Career"). The first period, 1919 to 1924, began with Bakhtin's earliest published article, a six-paragraph programmatic statement entitled "Art and Responsibility," and ended with the submission (although unfortunately not the publication) of his major 1924 essay, "The Problem of Content, Material, and Form in Verbal Art." During this period, Bakhtin, true to his Kantian or neo-Kantian beginnings, was concerned to link the realms of the ethical and the cognitive—and he found such a link in the aesthetic.

At this time, however, the *word* as such was not yet central for Bakhtin; what he investigated were ethical and aesthetic *acts*. When the Formalists advanced "literariness" as their own special marker of aesthetic value, Bakhtin countered in his 1924 essay with a five-point critique of their "material aesthetics" and decried their lack of a unified theory of art. By "material aesthetics" Bakhtin meant the Formalist tendency to reduce a work to the "material"—the language and its "devices"—from which the work is made, but without considering what the work, as an act in its own right, accomplishes.

At this point Bakhtin's critique was still largely negative. He called for an aesthetics of *content*, but was hard put to devise a specific methodology; aware of the twin dangers of subjectivism and abstraction, he foundered on a positive agenda. At the watershed he was apparently asking: can there be a "nonmaterial aesthetics" that possesses the rigor and objectivity promised by Formalism?

The second period, 1924 to 1930, started with this question and ended with its provisional solution: the typology of the prose word that Bakhtin offers in *Problems of Dostoevsky's Creative Art*. The major event of this period was the discovery of language as a crucial topic. This discovery led to a redefinition of language—not as structural linguists, Formalists, or Russian Futurists understood it, but as uttered (spoken or written) dialogic discourse. In the Dostoevsky book, the act of speaking becomes the most privileged human act, and Bakhtin begins to suggest that prose is the most privileged category of literature. In his typology of double-voiced words (discussed by us in Chapter Four), Bakhtin finally achieved the degree of "nonpoetic" rigor that he sought in the 1924 essay. He had devised a "prosaics" to match Formalist poetics, and had based his theory, even more soundly than his opponents had, on a unified philosophy of language.

The discovery of the word, and particularly of the novelistic word, made possible a third period, 1930 through the early 1950's. Two related but distinct lines of thought can be said to issue from the Dostoevsky book. In the first line, Bakhtin expanded his focus from Dostoevsky, sole creator of the polyphonic novel, to "novelness" in general, with Dostoevsky as only one main exemplar. Some of the features that make Dostoevsky great—the double-voiced word and dialogized language—were generalized into desirable "qualities of consciousness" to be assimilated by all truly novelistic prose. (Polyphony, however, was *not* reinterpreted as a characteristic of all novels.) From here Bakhtin went on to speculate provocatively on the history of "novelistic consciousness" in terms of time and space (the chronotope), on the difference between novels and other literary forms, and on the way language works in novels as opposed to other genres. These insights, we feel, are among Bakhtin's strongest and most productive.

The Shape of a Career:
Four Periods and Their Interrelationships

	Works	Style	Topics	New Concepts	Global Concepts
Period I	"Art and Responsibility" "Philosophy of the Act" "Author and Hero" "Problem of Content" (transitional)	Heavily philosophical Influenced by Kantian tradition	Ethics General aesthetics	Theoretism Outsideness Surplus Live entering	Prosaics Finalization *over* unfinalizability (No dialogue yet)
Period II	*Problems of Dostoevsky's Creative Art* (1929)	Discovery of the word, and Bakhtin finds his own voice	Language Selfhood Ethics	Polyphony Dialogue (types 1 and 2) Double-voiced word	Prosaics Shift toward unfinalizability Dialogue (type 3)
Period IIIa	"Discourse in Novel" "Forms of Time and Chronotope" "Prehistory of Novelistic Word" "Bildungsroman"	Discursive, analytic	Genre The novel "Historical poetics"	Novelness Chronotope Heteroglossia	Balanced blend of all 3 global concepts
Period IIIb	*Rabelais and his World* "Epic and Novel"	Poetic, even ecstatic Hyperbolic	Folk rituals Laughter Antigenres	Carnival Joyful relativity Novelization (novel imperialism)	Unfinalizability to extreme, virtually excluding prosaics and dialogue
Period IV	"Speech Genres" "Methodology for Human Sciences" "Problem of Text" "Toward a Reworking of Dostoevsky Book" "Notes 1970–71"	Professional, meditative, metaphilosophical	Nature of humanities Texts Cultural studies Literary history	Great time Creative understanding Genre memory Genre potential	Blend of all 3 global concepts

But Bakhtin then succumbed to exaggerating and idealizing "novelization" in a second line of thought that reached its peak during the 1930's and 1940's, the line concerned with carnival and carnivalization. In our view, this concept, for all its current vogue, is one of Bakhtin's weaker formulations. Reinforced by some misplaced emphases on the part of Bakhtin's early interpreters, including ourselves, the "carnival texts" (which include the book on Rabelais and portions of the essay "Epic and Novel") have given rise to a dominant critical image of an anarchistic Bakhtin. He is described as an antinomian rejoicing, Bakunin-like, in joyful destruction, carnival clowning, and novels-as-loopholes. He is said to have engaged in sly denials of authorship because, after all, in this topsy-turvy world we author each other's texts all the time—only some of us roguishly refuse to sign. Bakhtin, who never gave up his commitment to ethical responsibility, is presented as playfully and anarchically irresponsible.

This carnival mode is the canonic base for a number of very peculiar appropriations of Bakhtin, from Marxist to deconstructionist, and, in our view, it has tended to obscure the larger and more consistent shape of his thought. Generally speaking, Bakhtin was much less concerned with millenarian fantasies and holy foolishness than with the constraints and responsibilities of everyday living. Carnival, while offering a provocative insight into much of Rabelais and some of Dostoevsky, ultimately proved a dead end. In his last period, laughter but not the idealization of carnival anarchy remained—and the functions of laughter were more closely specified.

Bakhtin's fourth and final period, stretching from the early 1950's until his death in 1975, was a time of recapitulation, of return to the earlier ethical themes of the 1920's, and—for want of a better word—of "professionalization." When Bakhtin was rediscovered by a group of Moscow graduate students in the late 1950's, he had been teaching intermittently since 1936 at the obscure Mordovia State Teachers College, later the University of Saransk. He had submitted his dissertation (on Rabelais) to the Gorky Institute of World Literature in 1941, and, after a decade of controversy and delay, had been granted a doctorate in 1952. Beginning in 1963, the fame that accrued to Bakhtin's newly published and republished writings no longer belonged to an eccentric political exile but to an established academic. By the early 1970's, Bakhtin was already something of a cult figure in the post-Stalinist Soviet Union. In that capacity he was interviewed by a leading literary journal on the question of the future of literary studies; the last essay he wrote concerned the place of the humanities in contemporary culture. From marginalized intellectual Bakhtin had moved to spokesman for a profession. It is worth noting that the ideas he outlined during these final years owe at least as much to his earliest manuscripts as to his well-known essays on the novel from his third period.

There is, of course, a fifth and "posthumous" stage in Bakhtin's career: the migration of his texts and reputation to France in the 1960's and then to the United States in the 1970's, accompanied by a renewed debate in the Soviet Union over Bakhtin's legacy. Is he a structuralist, a semiotician, a Marxist-Leninist humanist, or an opponent of all these things?

1919–24: The Early Writings

Bakhtin's early writings have been published in three segments: a single-page essay entitled "Art and Responsibility" that appeared in a provincial journal in 1919; a 150-page unfinished essay entitled by its editors "Author and Hero in Aesthetic Activity" (not published until 1975); and a somewhat shorter piece, "Toward a Philosophy of the Act," which did not appear until 1986. "Act" is cast in categories that grow out of Kant's Third Critique, and is argued in the language and terms of theoretical philosophy. "Author and Hero," which appears to have been written subsequently, reworks the same categories on the aesthetic plane.

Both "Act" and "Author and Hero" deal broadly with the same three central concerns, all widely debated at the beginning of the century. First, Bakhtin weighs the relative merits of the personally ethical act as opposed to the abstract and philosophical proposition. Where, he asks, can personal morality be grounded in the absence of a Supreme Being or even of a categorical imperative? Second, Bakhtin recasts this contrast as one between the "radically singular event" and the systematically applied rule. And last, through a detailed reading of a lyric by Pushkin, he asks how the ethical becomes the aesthetic. This third concern also motivates "Problem of Content" (1924), but by that time his argument was in dialogue not with neo-Kantianism but with Russian Formalism.

Near the beginning of "Act," Bakhtin provides a plan for a future project (KFP, p. 122). It was to consist of four parts. First there would be a discussion of the "architectonics" of the real world (the world not as schematized but as individually experienced), followed by a section on aesthetic activity perceived as action or *act* (that is, not as a product viewed externally but as a process lived through from the point of view of a responsible participant). The third part was to deal with the ethics of politics, and the fourth with the ethics of religion.

Half of this agenda—the politics and the religion—presumably became unrealizable by the end of the 1920's, as the Stalinization of Soviet culture got underway. But the initial outline is still instructive, in part for what it omits. We note, for example, that the verbal arts were originally quite peripheral to the project. The crucial concept was the *act*, which Bakhtin divided into acts of thought, of feeling, and of external deed. What defines an act is not primarily its content or its mode of realization, but rather the degree and kind of personal responsibility one assumes for it—that is, the *concreteness* of the identification between a given act and a given personality. Bakhtin begins his critique of Kant's reliance on imperatives and moral norms from this very point: a sense of obligation or "oughtness" (*dolzhestvovanie*) must be grounded in the concrete instance, not in the general rule or the abstractly hypothetical situation. Bakhtin even insists at one point that there are "no moral norms signifying in themselves," but only the "moral subject with his specific structuring . . . upon which one must rely" (KFP, p. 85).

The major philosophical challenge of our time, Bakhtin writes, is not to appreciate the abstract value of time, space, or morality, but to resist the temptations of the theoretical and the abstract. One must rescue the "I" from the realm of infinite and purely abstract meaning—what Bakhtin calls the world of cognition—and so free it for genuine responsibility (*otvetstvennost'*). What is most important about a given act, then, is the fact that *I* "sign" it. Bakhtin insists that this concept, if properly understood, is neither solipsistic nor selfish; Nietzsche's big mistake, in fact, was to assume that living *from* oneself meant living *for* oneself (KFP, p. 119). Signing an act does not mean accepting all blame or assuming absolute control over it. Rather, signing is that indispensable enabling gesture that makes it possible for morality to coalesce around a human being, in what Bakhtin calls the "architectonics" of a life. The abstract and "projective" side of things, which theorists identify with life, will always remain a sort of "rough draft of possible accomplishment," "a document without a signature, obligating no one and obliged to nothing" (KFP, p. 115). Only the singular act can release us "from endless rough-draft variants" and permit us "to write out our own life in fair copy, once and for all" (ibid.).

Signing, then, is the first step toward the truth of any situation. Only what is personalized can become available for clarification, wholeness, and interaction. Thus, the most important thing about any act is: did I do it and do I accept responsibility for it, or do I behave as if someone else, or nobody in particular, did it?

Viewed in retrospect, this "ethics of the act" seems to be in actual, and very curious, opposition to several of Bakhtin's later and more celebrated concepts. To get at this apparent discrepancy we must open up another key term in the early manuscripts, *architectonics*. Bakhtin defines architectonics (in one of his more paradoxical formulations) as "a focused and indispensable non-arbitrary distribution and linkage of concrete, singular parts and aspects into a finished whole, [something that is] possible only around a given human being as hero" (KFP, p. 139). The paradox here is that an architectonics strives to articulate the general aspects of particular acts so that their particularity is nevertheless not compromised.

Bakhtin intends the concept as an alternative to the idea of system. For the problem with systems, Bakhtin implies, is not only their inaccuracy, artificiality, and predictability (*non*system can exhibit those traits too); the problem with system is that it does not necessarily contain any human beings. Without concrete individual instances there is no obligation, because only the particular can obligate us.

If we compare the idea of the architectonic act with the later (and more familiar) "dialogic word," two differences immediately come into view. First, what is remarkable about the act is its high degree of closure. "The act gathers together, correlates, resolves in an . . . already finalized context," Bakhtin writes (KFP, p. 103). In marked contrast to the novelistic *word*, which Bakhtin will come to define as open, unfinalized, inhabited by many voices and therefore shot through with sideward glances or loopholes, the *act* is valuable as a concrete closed event around which I can wrap my responsibility.

A corollary quickly follows. In the early manuscripts, authorship is a relatively unproblematic idea. What is important about the act is the fact that I sign it, and how my signature got to be mine is not targeted as a special problem. The architectonic whole of the world is distributed around *me*, Bakhtin argues, in an image that suggests a very "Ptolemaic" universe (KFP, p. 124). In contrast, we might recall the Bakhtin of 1929, who celebrates precisely the opposite position in his discussion of the Dostoevskian word. In the first edition of the Dostoevsky book, Bakhtin praises that author for initiating a "Copernican Revolution" in his novels, displacing the authoring "I" from the center of things and thereby giving weight or gravitational pull to the created other (PTD, p. 56). By the time of that book's writing, legitimation of the personality had shifted outward. For Bakhtin, the word had become a vehicle for *others'* creation of me, or for my creation of myself out of others. What is important about the dialogic word, therefore, is the impossibility of my ever *completely* signing it, because the very concept of "my" is multiple. The word, it seems, has loopholes; the act has obligations. The word also has obligations, to be sure, but only by virtue of being an act.

Once one understands the nature of acts, Bakhtin intimates, one can comprehend "aesthetic acts." Near the end of "Toward a Philosophy of the Act," Bakhtin introduces the concept of "aesthetic acts" in lyric, epic, and drama. He was later to dismiss these genres as "monologic" when he discovered the novelistic word, but at this point he is reasonably tolerant of them. We might consider his one detailed reading, of a lyric poem, along with his sole published article prior to the Dostoevsky book, the one-page "Art and Responsibility" (1919). Both these pieces attempt to answer—one in theory, the other in practice—the most difficult questions raised by the writings of this first period: how do I gain the right to author? What do I owe an authored object? And is there a way for the *aesthetic event* to be released from real life and yet at the same time require me to be responsible for it?

Responsibility and Architectonics

"Art and Responsibility" can be read, in part, as a response to Victor Shklovsky's early Formalist essay "Art as Device" (1917). In that essay, Shklovsky elaborates the now-famous concept of "defamiliarization," the device of "making strange," by which a literary artist marks his art off from everyday life and thereby molds it into an aesthetic whole. In their discussions of artistic creativity, the Formalists distinguished between "material"—the raw material of life—and "form," the shape imposed by the artist. What this dichotomy eliminated was content, for that was seen as too subjective and thus not appropriate for literary science. Indeed, the early Formalists posited this alienation between art and topic, or art and "life," as the ideal for both art and criticism; for Bakhtin, such alienation was precisely what had to be overcome.

Mechanical depersonalization in the interests of artistic unity is in fact rather easy to achieve, Bakhtin argued in his 1919 essay. The whole fraught question of the art-life boundary has in fact worked nefariously to the mutual convenience of *both* sides. "Both life and art desire to lighten their respective burdens, to remove responsibility," he writes, "for it is, after all, easier to create without answering to life, and easier to live not reckoning with art" (IiO, p. 6). Keeping art and life separate, therefore, cannot be the primary task of an aesthetics. That happens all too easily as it is. If the artist leaves life behind and enters the world of pure inspiration, then "art becomes too brazenly self-confident, too emotional" (IiO, p. 5), and life loses interest in art. In one of his characteristic personifications, Bakhtin whimsically speaks for life: " 'So where's our place in all this?' life says; 'that is art, and all we have is the prose of everyday life' " (ibid.). We see here the germ of prosaics.

To relate art to the "prose of life" in a meaningful yet rigorous way would become Bakhtin's project for the 1920's. Mechanical play with devices was too dehumanized; it could achieve no more than a "mechanical whole." Inspiration and isolation from life, on the other hand, was too transcendental: "Inspiration which ignores life . . . is simply an obsession" (IiO, p. 6). Bakhtin ends this little essay with the statement: "Art and life are not one, but they must become united in me, in the unity of my responsibility" (ibid.).

In some way as yet only dimly hinted at, responsibility in art must involve an interaction between the aesthetic and the ethical spheres. Bakhtin was to offer many scenarios for this interaction throughout his life. In his earliest writings, in contradistinction to the Formalists, Bakhtin reinstates the integral position of the author. But this position does not grant a creator sole control, nor license the creator's every whim. Constraints are immediately operative. Bakhtin insists that the aesthetic project always begins with the creation of a whole human being, a *second consciousness* in addition to the author's (AiG, pp. 170–75). Here Bakhtin has in mind not the reader of the work, but its character or "hero." What makes any work aesthetic is the degree to which this second consciousness has a logic and a dynamics of its own, with which the author interacts. In this project, form belongs primarily to the author, content primarily to the hero. Bakhtin stresses that authors must act in good faith: they are obliged to surmount content with "loving form," which in turn has the capacity to redeem. Since form and content are equally powerful generators of meaning, the interaction between author and hero is a genuine one.

Bakhtin provides a good example of this "aesthetic struggle" in his reading of Pushkin's short lyric, "Parting" (*Razluka*) (KFP, pp. 131–38; pp. 141–54).[4] The poem, one of the most famous of Russian lyrics, is addressed to the poet's mistress, who had left Russia for her native Italy; from that distant land the poet hears of her death. Bakhtin analyzes the overlapping, interacting value centers in the poem (what is being spoken from whose point of view) and then suggests categories for interrelating these voices. He posits two "poles," one "realistic" and the other "formal." The poem's heroes react "realistically" to events from within the poem: they do not know that they are fictions, and so their acts—of loving, remembering, reconciling—are open-ended, and have for them real ethical significance. The author creating the heroes reacts "formally"; his primary role is to create a finalized aesthetic whole. The aesthetic act is thus "a reaction to a reaction": the reaction of the author to his heroes' reaction to an event. Should an author fail to separate himself from the hero in this way, the work would become a mere confession, and be responsible in a different way.

Bakhtin's analysis is remarkable for what it leaves out. In contrast to the Russian tradition of prosodic analysis, Bakhtin does not deal at all with the quantifiable or statistical aspects of verse analysis, nor does he introduce a historical and generic dimension by discussing prototypes or tropes. The closest he gets to an analysis of structural components is the interesting—but ultimately rather mechanical—distinction between "realistic" and "formal" intonations and rhythms: realistic intonation is the realm of the hero, formal rhythm the realm of the author. Voice complexity does not stop there, of course: if the hero "recites," plays the poet, or stylizes his own discourse, then his intonation will take on formal rhythms. Since all these variables must necessarily be expressed on the same verbal plane, conflicts or subtle ambiguities are inevitable. The more nuanced and well crafted this struggle, Bakhtin intimates, the more successful the aesthetic work.

This early reading is important, if only because it shows us a Bakhtin much more sympathetic to the complexities of lyrical form than the Bakhtin we see in the later, novel-centered third period. As an analysis of a poem, however, it not only omits a great deal but is also rather shortsighted in the way it opposes ethics to aesthetics. For as Bakhtin argues here and elsewhere, even in real life people are to some degree aestheticized (KFP, p. 153). Moreover, the very act of aestheticization has moral significance. A more subtle discussion of the responsibility of the aesthetic to the ethical realms, which for Bakhtin meant the relationship of a creating to a created consciousness, was to come in "Author and Hero" and "The Problem of Content." Appropriately, the insights in these essays were developed into an alternative poetics only when Bakhtin himself moved from a general problem to a particular instantiation of it, in his book on Dostoevsky.

Others: Real and "Unspecified" Potential

> But the Princess never saw the lovely expression of her own eyes, the look they had when she was not thinking of herself. As with everyone, her face assumed an unnaturally strained, ugly expression, as soon as she looked in a glass.
>
> —Tolstoy, *War and Peace*, p. 128

"Author and Hero in Aesthetic Activity" begins with a typology of human events in terms of the number of participating consciousnesses and their interrelationships (AiG, p. 22). Bakhtin discerns four basic categories. An *aesthetic* event must involve two non-coincident consciousnesses. In an *ethical* event, hero and author coincide; I stand for my act. In a *cognitive* event, which deals with abstract truths, the hero is altogether absent. And finally, in a *religious* event, there are two consciousnesses, but they are not even potentially equal; the other is supreme and all-embracing. Bakhtin does not investigate the religious event as such in his early writings, at least not in those that have been released for publication in the Soviet Union. But the other three categories are central to his reworking of the architectonics of the act.

We should note, first, that "Author and Hero" is more than an extension and "aestheticization" of issues discussed in "Toward a Philosophy of the Act." It is also a shift in methodology, that is, a change in the plane on which the problem is cast. It is as if Bakhtin realized that his doubts about system could only be expressed in a new approach to the very gathering of data. This new approach was—to invoke a global concept from our opening chapter—"prosaic." If in his earlier work he tended to cite (and to polemicize with) Kant and Bergson, evoking their general schema even as he argued on behalf of the concrete, in the later text he more often begins with local needs and goals, with everyday observations rather than generalizations. He asks prosaically: what happens when we look in the mirror, and why are self-portraits always untrue to the way others see us? Why will certain acts—say, a high jump—fail if we think them through step by step from within ourselves rather than concentrate on a projected goal in space? When investigating the possibility of empathy toward a person in pain, Bakhtin meditates on an (his own?) ailing leg.

"Author and Hero" is divided into five basic parts. Three are devoted to the hero: his spatial form, temporal wholeness, and the possibility of a wholeness of meaning around his person. We will mention here only those features of Bakhtin's wide-ranging discussion that appear to signal a realignment in his own concerns, and thus serve as markers in his intellectual evolution.

Bakhtin discusses the hero's spatial form in terms of the hero's external appearance, external boundaries, and acts. Although these categories suggest "externality," Bakhtin's emphasis here is on the language of internal *self*-sensation: how we imagine ourselves as the heroes of our own fantasies and dreams; how we experience from within the externalization of our own image; the difference between trying unsuccessfully to visualize our own face and failing to recall someone else's forgotten face. In each of these single-consciousness situations, the same result obtains: we can never create ourselves as others see us. The "unspecific potential other" that we try to be for ourselves renders us unfocused, transparent, empty, alone. Only a genuine *other* consciousness can draw convincing boundaries for us, complete us, and fill us in. From this follows the terrible difficulty of autobiography as a form, and also—on another, less literary plane—the frustrating inability ever to consummate a fantasy.

It might be instructive at this point to contrast Bakhtin's discussion of a hero's acts in this essay (AiG, pp. 40–47) with the scenario in "Toward a Philosophy of the Act." In the earlier discussion, we recall, the act is something around which I wrap my responsibility: the focus is singular and radically personal. Tone, intonation, and unrepeatability combine to create the "ultimate singular unity (*edinstvo*)" of each of my acts (KFP, p. 109). Here the word *unity* indicates not a fusing of boundaries or a fitting together of disparate things but rather a wholeness, a "unit-y." It refers to the way in which everything in me forms a unit—so that nothing in a given complex is dispensable or replaceable. Unity, in this sense, means singularity and moral responsibility.

In "Author and Hero," Bakhtin, now examining the ground for aesthetic rather than ethical acts, shifts his focus. Although his examples are still drawn from real-life prosaic situations, what he stresses is the *im*possibility of self-actualization and self-realization without the other as a necessary witness to what *I* do. In the context of this more complex relationship between self and other—with primacy being given to the other—radically singular responsibility begins to be transformed. Eventually it will be redefined as *addressivity* [*obrashchennost'*]. The absolute need for response begins to compete with the moral requirement of responsibility.[5]

Since the Russian word *otvetstvennost'* contains, as does its English equivalent, both "answer" and "response," a translator's decision to render the term as *responsibility* or as *answerability* has some effect on one's perception of Bakhtin's intellectual evolution and on the validity of the watersheds posited for him. Responsibility, which has a manifestly ethical resonance, is what is most likely intended in the 1919 piece, "Art and Responsibility." By the mid-1920's, however, a case could be made for either translation, ethical responsibility or addressive answerability (that is, the presence of response). There is an ethical component in answerability as well, of course, but it is more abstract and less tied to a specific act. One's obligation in answerability is to rescue the other from pure potential; reaching out to another consciousness makes the other coalesce, and turns the other's "mere potential" into space that is open to the living event (AiG, p. 39).

In his chapters on spatial form in "Author and Hero," Bakhtin discusses at length the role of the body in history. He also treats the aestheticization of both body and personality that is made possible by death. Not until Bakhtin addresses the "meaningful whole" of the hero does he return to aesthetic questions in the traditional sense of the term (literary genres and study of character).

In these areas, too, we see a shift from responsibility toward answerability. Bakhtin treats the genres of personal confession, biography, autobiography, lyric, and saint's life (and classical and romantic character types) in terms of their attempts to exile, incorporate, or engage various forms of the other (AiG, pp. 121–61). This other can be neighbor, God, or the everyday "choral support" required before we can make our own voice manifest. In line with the prosaic orientation of his earlier comments, Bakhtin shows a predictable fondness here for what he calls the "social-everyday" type of biography. In this type, history is presented not as fundamentally organized but as fundamentally diverse, that is, as a social cross section. Its small, present events have value for a "humanity of living people, not of dead heroes or future descendants" (AiG, p. 140).

The final section in "Author and Hero" deals with the problem of the author. Bakhtin repeats here in an aesthetic context the ethical conclusions of his ruminations on the hero: only the other can be a value-endowing center and wholeness must be bestowed from without. As author I am always "not yet," and thus my task *as* author is "to find a fundamental approach to life from without" (AiG, p. 166).

As legitimation for acts moves successively *outward* in these writings—that is, as the role of being "other to a self" assumes increasing importance—Bakhtin approaches his first watershed. Here a contrast with other members of his circle is helpful. It is often remarked that the polemics of the circle thrived on polarizations: in the 1920's its members debated the most controversial topics of the day (Saussurean linguistics, Freudianism, Formalism, Marxism) by identifying opposing trends, showing the inadequacy of each extreme, and then mapping out a proper middle course. Voloshinov follows just this pattern in his two books, *Freudianism: A Critical Sketch* and *Marxism and the Philosophy of Language*.[6] Bakhtin, however, appears less willing than his associates to deal in dichotomies. Where they were prepared to absorb the individual into the social (and into the historical), he was working on ways to dissolve the very distinction.

Bakhtin had already shown that self and other are indispensable to each other. He then began to suspect that the very distinction itself might be misdrawn. Until his discovery of language as a governing metaphor for consciousness, however, Bakhtin was unable to find a fully satisfactory way beyond the self-other opposition. When he did find his new formulation, he saw the need to separate the word from system—both from the system of grammatical structures and from any systematically preprogrammed inner (or psychic) space. In Chapter Five we offer some hypotheses about Bakhtin's psychology of the self, which developed in tandem with, but still separately from, the psychological theories offered by other members of his circle.

"The Problem of Content, Material, and Form": Confronting the Formalists over Content

Bakhtin is known to have written and prepared for publication only one essay in the mid-to-late 1920's: "The Problem of Content, Material, and Form in Verbal Creative Art." In style and approach it is quite different from the works on psychology and linguistics written by other members of his circle, and quite different as well from his own magnum opus at the end of the 1920's, *Problems of Dostoevsky's Creative Art.*

"The Problem of Content" reads as if chunks of the early manuscripts collided with the Formalists. It is a difficult essay—in part because its agenda is largely negative, and in part because Bakhtin is still straining, somewhat awkwardly, toward a style of his own. He is at home neither in the Kantian categories he is trying to outgrow nor in the Formalist terminology he is trying to resist. In this essay Bakhtin does not, or cannot, do what his associate Pavel Medvedev will accomplish so successfully in 1928 in *The Formal Method*: provide an efficient, straightforward, and pragmatic critique of Formalist readings based on the provocative inconsistencies contained in early Shklovskian manifestos. Bakhtin is still very far from that sort of criticism; he is still too intent upon devising mediating structures to bridge the mind (cognition) and the act (ethics). We have seen that in his early writings Bakhtin proposed the category of the aesthetic as primary mediator between the two. It is no surprise, then, that "The Problem of Content" opens with the comment that Formalism, whatever its local successes might be, cannot ultimately be productive because it lacks a unified aesthetics. It has operating procedures but no "task," devices but no larger positive purpose.

Bakhtin's response to Formalism in this essay complements, on another plane, the final chapter of "Author and Hero," which deals with the proper tasks of an author and the ways in which literary devices can be made legitimate (AiG, pp. 162–80). Heroes cannot be "made" out of pure form, Bakhtin insists; the Formalists notwithstanding, characters are not bundles of devices that work between author and reader. To recognize a work as aesthetic is to "feel" another consciousness inside it, as one feels the presence of another human being.

The author's task, therefore, is to organize a concrete world with three attributes: a spatial world with a living body as its value-generating center, a temporal world with a soul as its center, and a world endowed with meaning as the unity of the two (AiG, p. 165). In the 1930's, Bakhtin would develop these three prerequisites for an aesthetic world into a new concept, the *chronotope*. In 1924, he is more concerned to argue against the exiling of these worlds from the aesthetic project altogether.

The key task of "The Problem of Content," as well as its collision with the Formalist project, can be found at the point where it echoes the 1919 essay "Art and Responsibility" on the question of art's duty to life and life's duty to art. These two duties are connected "in the unity of my responsibility," Bakhtin had written in his earliest published essay. But to what "sphere of culture" does this unity belong? In 1924, Bakhtin provides an answer: to the aesthetic sphere.

Where the aesthetic fits into other human activity is a question that has not been properly investigated, Bakhtin claims. To this end, he reiterates the three possible relations that human beings can have with reality, as he discussed them in his early manuscripts: cognitive action, ethical action, and aesthetic action (PS, p. 30). Cognition is unified; it is "knowledge in general," and knows no separate acts or works. Ethics, on the other hand, is conflict; it knows only individual particularized value. What links them is aesthetics, which creates a "concrete intuitive unity" of the two worlds and permits them to communicate. The position of the author-artist can only be understood in relation to these two flanking realms. "The usual opposition of reality to art, or life to art, and the striving to find some essential link between them, are absolutely justified," Bakhtin writes, "but they are in need of a more precise scientific formulation" (PS, p. 26). This is "literary science" in a very different sense from the one intended by the Formalists. We will readily see where it intersects with the architectonics of the act.

In their pursuit of precision the Formalists err in two directions, Bakhtin indicates. First, real-life material cannot be so easily excised from art even if such a move were desirable, because "real life" is *already* aestheticized; life becomes real for us in "aesthetic intuition," and there is no "neutral reality" that can be opposed to art (PS, pp. 24–26). In addition, the Formal (or morphological) Method errs in its assumption that "science" results from *isolating* things. But in fact, if somewhat paradoxically, the autonomy of art is guaranteed not by its isolation from life but by its precise participation in it—by the "unique, necessary, and irreplaceable place" it occupies *within* life (PS, p. 9). Not surprisingly, Bakhtin demands of art the same qualities that he demands of a person living a real ethical life: particularization, commitment, and "no alibi for being." In both instances Bakhtin is concerned to identify "the right sort of specificity." Such specificity is obtained not by abstracting a phenomenon or linking it up within a system, but by making it answer for its unique effects in the real world.

Bakhtin organizes his case against the Formal Method around a number of faults he finds with "materialist aesthetics," that is, with "literariness" achieved through applying devices to inert material (PS, pp. 14–24).[7] First, "defamiliarization" and similar devices can offer at best a "physiological hedonism" because they can neither constitute a ground for artistic form nor generate real values. Second, material aesthetics cannot draw the distinction—crucial for understanding works of art—between the aesthetic object (which is an *activity* directed toward the work, something individualized, architectonic, linked with the acting consciousness), and the external work of art (the technical realization). In a third and related criticism, the materialist approach is said to blur the distinction between "architectonic" and "compositional" forms. The latter are structural, teleological, implemental, and necessary to realize limited goals; in this realm, Bakhtin asserts, Formalism has made genuinely valuable contributions. Architectonic forms, however, are beyond the Formalist reach. They belong to the realm of content, and "contemporary poetics" has rejected content—dismissing it as either a mere aspect of form or as a mere aspect of material (PS, pp. 33–34). This procedure gets things backward, Bakhtin insists. First one must understand content (a very complex notion) and how content transforms material; only then is it possible to understand the "value-bearing functions of form" (PS, p. 24).

Architectonic and compositional forms must not be confused. As Bakhtin argues, it is possible to have texts that do not deal with the world but with the word *world*, and in such texts, form is genuinely indifferent to content. Those works can indeed be mere exercises in "defamiliarization" (PS, p. 35). But most literary works intend worlds, not just the word *world*; indeed, Bakhtin remarks, this is one of the reasons that material has become so problematic in the modern period, because *too much is expected of the word*. The poet must overcome the word as the sculptor overcomes marble—that is, as all artists subdue their raw material. Precisely because linguists and formalists deal so exclusively with the material word, they cannot transcend its matter-ness (PS, pp. 50–53).

We see that Bakhtin in this essay is still far from the *logos*-centric universe of his later writings. Just as his early manuscripts concentrated on acts (of which the word was only one type), so this 1924 essay on early Formalist poetics backs only gingerly, as it were, into the word itself, reluctant to investigate its properly verbal resources. Although Bakhtin does grant the word its material elements (sound, intonation, and so forth), its most important feature is "the feeling that meaning is being actively generated." This meaning is not itself necessarily verbal, Bakhtin hastens to add; "the act of the word is related to the unity of an ethical event" (PS, pp. 62–63). Only in the special case of poetry is the feeling of verbal activity—the generation of meaning by the word alone—the governing factor. The fact that Bakhtin evidently regards poetry as a special case perhaps shows how far he had already come toward privileging prose.

Form, then, is realized on material and conditioned by the nature of the material, but its primary action is on content. What does aesthetic form do to content? Bakhtin asks (PS, pp. 59–60). It serves to *isolate* and to *renounce*. It liberates content from its real-world contexts—not, to be sure, from identification and ethical evaluation—in order to fix content so that it can become tranquil, complete, and open to contemplation. The purpose of form is to "free content of responsibility before a [particular] future event. . . . The word, the utterance, ceases to wait and to desire something of the real beyond its borders" (PS, pp. 61–62). The aesthetic "freezes" life in place, and gives the author the power to motivate and interpret—but it does not make that life less available for moral judgment. That judgment is not negated but resituated.

One might object at this point that the Formalist device of *ostranenie*, or "defamiliarization," also isolates. But Bakhtin reminds us that Formalist devices isolate raw *material*, not meaningful *content*. And material can never mediate between the cognitive and the ethical spheres, so it can never play an essential role in aesthetic experience. Bakhtin suggests that the Formalists feared content because they misunderstood it. They appeared to believe that content was a question of propositional paraphrase or extractable theme, and thus could be safely exiled as an impoverishment of the artwork. Art can indeed be free from such cognition and from narrow reference, Bakhtin grants, but it *cannot* be free from content. He offers the example of music: "Music is denied referential specificity and cognitive differentiation, but is profound in content: its form leads us beyond the boundaries of acoustical sound production, but does not lead us into an axiological void—content here is, at base, ethical" (PS, p. 16).

This 1924 essay contains very few footnotes, but Bakhtin does make one reference in passing to a "splendid article" by A. A. Smirnov, "The Paths and Tasks of the Study of Literature" (1923) (PS, p. 10). Although Bakhtin does not discuss the article, Smirnov's comments on the ethical in art might serve as eloquent summary of Bakhtin's position: "All those judgments about the 'amorality' of poetry are the purest misunderstanding. Poetry can be called amoral only in the sense that it casts up a challenge to every concrete system of morals, but poetry not only does not reject the principle of ethical self-definition, but in its very essence awakens it" (Smirnov, "Puti," p. 97).[8]

Let us summarize briefly Bakhtin's assessment of the Formalists, the positive aspects that he saw as well as the dangers. Unlike Medvedev in *The Formal Method*, Bakhtin offers a truly balanced critique. In his view, it was good, first, that the Formalists undermined the mimesis argument for art and preferred to speak of refraction rather than reflection. But what the Formalists saw as "refracted" in art was material reshaped by device; what Bakhtin would see as refracted was the personality (as form) working on content. Second, it was good that the Formalists stressed not mystical genius or intuition but craftsmanship and analysis in both the genesis and the reception of art—qualities realized through real, responsible work. But for the Formalists, "work" was the device applied to the material; for Bakhtin, work was the personal responsibility of creating a second consciousness in the artwork.

Further, the Formalists believed (correctly, in Bakhtin's view) that the author should be located "outside" the work of art; the subjective attributes of the author's psychology and biography should not be indiscriminately mingled with artistic features. But for the Formalists, outsideness was technical, amoral, and mechanical; for Bakhtin, outsideness was the moral position necessary to co-experience a work of art, to finalize it, and then take responsibility for its content. Last, both Bakhtin and the Formalists agreed that literariness depended not on the intrinsic qualities in an artwork but on their function. For the Formalists, however, function was to become function within a system, potentially author-free. For Bakhtin, the aesthetic effect was precisely *function without a system*, that is, the radical singularity of the artist who transferred ethical responsibility from the content onto his own person by means of an active application of form.

As we conclude this section, it is worth noting how the 1924 essay appears to mark a true watershed in Bakhtin's development. "The Problem of Content" is Bakhtin's first extended discussion of the aesthetic function in literature, but he is still no exclusive devotee of the word. If anything, it is music to which he repeatedly returns to illustrate the interaction between form, content, and material. With the Symbolists apparently in mind, he even remarks that too much of culture at the present time has been reduced to the word and to the metaphysics of the word; "it would be easy to conclude that, except for the word, there is nothing else in culture at all, that all of culture is nothing more than a phenomenon of language, that the scholar and the poet in equal measure have only to do with the [mere] word" (PS, p. 43). A unified theory of literary aesthetics cannot deal only with words, it must also deal with ethics and with cognition. Words are just material, and poets must overcome words; "the aesthetic object arises on the boundaries of words" (PS, p. 49).

Thirty-five years later, in the late 1950's, Bakhtin was to write: "Language and the word are almost everything in human life" (PT, p. 118). The fact that language could eventually occupy such a central position for Bakhtin is due, in part, to a breakthrough in his own thought between the writing of "The Problem of Content" and *Problems of Dostoevsky's Creative Art*. In the 1924 essay, Bakhtin is trying to understand how words can transmit ethical judgments (what he calls "content") in aesthetic form. But he is aware that any such understanding of content does not easily translate into a "scientific" methodology; although lamenting the Formalists' lack of a unified aesthetics, he does acknowledge that their operating procedures can yield objectively concrete, if limited, results.

Bakhtin is understandably nervous at the task of setting up a "methodology based on content." Analysis of content is very difficult, he concedes; only "scholarly tact" can keep us within the proper limits (PS, p. 43). This task is taken no further in 1924. It is only when Bakhtin develops his model of the dialogic word at the end of the decade that he can devise a precise methodology for analyzing content, one that is not subjective but at the same time is not impersonal.

1924–29: The Potential of the Word

The development of a typology for the dialogic word also enabled Bakhtin to shift his distinction between "architectonics" and "composition" onto new ground. As expressed in "The Problem of Content," the opposition was basically that between relationships-around-a-single-center (architectonics) and technique or teleology (composition). In that essay, these two components of creative literary production appear quite polarized. It is as if the *living* and the *structuring* aspects of art could not meet at a single point without compromise. Once Bakhtin comes to understand the word not merely as one among many types of material but as, first and foremost, the feeling that meaning is being actively generated, then he can recast the idea of composition out of its vaguely Formalist framework and into a dialogic one. The word can be reinvested with "technique" and restored to a typology with no fear of "mechanization," because the typology now concerns not devices but voices. Voices already have "tone" and "content." Once Bakhtin recuperates verbal composition for non-Formalist (i.e., dialogic) literary scholarship, he can then develop the idea of architectonics along other lines during the 1930's. Specifically, he rethinks the issues that led him to architectonics as a problem of genre and of chronotope—which, as we will see, can be thought of as a sort of repeatable and historically sensitive architectonics.

With *Problems of Dostoevsky's Creative Art*, Bakhtin first entered upon his positive agenda. In Chapter Four of the present study we provide an account of the theory of language first explicated in that book, and in Chapter Six a discussion of polyphony and its implications. Our purpose in this chapter is to stress the connecting tissue, as it were, that binds the Dostoevsky book to Bakhtin's writings that preceded and followed it, and also to comment on the shape and proportions of the first edition.[9] The original version has not been translated into Western languages, and its structure has been obscured by the popularity and canonic status of the revised and greatly expanded 1963 edition.

The following table of contents and number of pages per chapter might be helpful in assessing the original Dostoevsky book:

Contents of the 1929 Dostoevsky Book

First and most important, we note that the book in its original form gives proportionately a much larger emphasis to prose discourse typology than does the 1963 edition. Not only is the word *poetics* absent from the title and table of contents, but the word *prosaic* is present; part two, the greater half of the book, is called "The Word in Dostoevsky," and its first chapter is entitled "Types of the Prosaic Word." Less space is devoted to a survey of Dostoevsky criticism (understandably, for in his 1963 edition Bakhtin updates that discussion with thirty years of Soviet scholarship); accordingly, Bakhtin's *rebuttal* of one critic (Boris Engelhardt), who reads Dostoevsky's works dialectically, occupies a much more prominent place in the "critique of the criticism" (part one, chapter one). And what in the revised version becomes the massive 80-page chapter four ("Genre and Plot Composition," tracing Dostoevsky's roots back to the ancient world) was originally a modest 9-page discussion of the functions of the adventure plot in Dostoevsky (part one, chapter four). In the 1963 chapter, that adventure-plot discussion serves as mere introduction to a major and new excursus on menippean satire, folklore, and genre memory—clearly the fruit of Bakhtin's several decades of work in carnivalization and history of the novel.

Compared with the later redaction, then, the 1929 volume is a leaner study, more oriented toward the prosaic word. There is little on literary history and there are relatively few readings. The precise relationship of this first book to the early writings is difficult to trace.[10] But it is clear that the tract on Dostoevsky served Bakhtin as their continuation in several ways at once. It was, first, a (veiled) statement against Marxism: despite some general asides on culture and capitalism, the first chapter is largely a polemic against applying the dialectic as a key to the development of literary figures or their authors.[11] The book also disputed the Formalist rejection of content and personality, while at the same time taking on Dostoevsky—the most ideological, content-encrusted novelist of the nineteenth century—and insisting that his works be analyzed with *formal questions* in mind. Bakhtin asks rigorous analytical questions, but his analysis focuses not on device or system but rather on content, in the sense that he had used the word in 1924 (PS, p. 37). His concern was content conceived not as theoretical unity, not as thought or idea, but as aesthetic activity directed toward an object, as something cognized that is then linked with an acting consciousness.

The 1929 book also betrays little sympathy for purely psychological structures in Dostoevsky's novels, whether immanent to

Dostoevsky's own thinking or supplied by his readers. For Bakhtin, psychology was at best a pedagogic and at worst a monologic science. Its explanations required the wrong sort of outsideness, the sort that finalizes rather than enables. Indeed, Bakhtin resisted seeing psychology in Dostoevsky even where it was manifestly present. In a 1929 passage later excised from the revised edition, Bakhtin remarked that Dostoevsky does not "transform [Romanticism] into psychology" because he "never has anything up his sleeve, never attacks from behind" (TF1929, p. 278). Bakhtin's benevolent interpretation of Dostoevsky (and Dostoevsky's narrators), his reluctance to see in them anything unalterably cruel and pathological, is in large part a result of this rejection of psychology. (A more complete discussion of Bakhtin's case against the psychologies of his time, and some of the blind spots that thus result in his readings, can be found in Chapter Five of the present study.) As Bakhtin was to jot down many years later in his notes for revising the Dostoevsky book, "Consciousness is much more terrifying than any unconscious complexes" (TRDB, p. 288).

The major positive achievements of this period are the concepts of polyphony and double-voicedness. Bakhtin at last devises a *prose* typology that can match the rigor of prosody studies, and can counter the general assumption—fostered by the Formalists but not exclusive to them—that "literariness" was primarily the language of poetry.[12]

The discovery of double-voicedness, so immensely productive in Bakhtin's third period, was not without its cost. That cost was registered largely in a shift in Bakhtin's focus from responsibility to addressivity. Bakhtin remained concerned with ethics throughout his life, but the topic receded from the foreground of his works and was transformed, as it were, into a hidden or presumed agenda. In the Dostoevsky book, and later in the writings on the theory of the novel, this new emphasis on addressivity marking the watershed from Bakhtin's second to third period produces powerful, curiously provocative, yet often misconstrued readings.

The 1930's to the Early 1950's: Historicizing and Idealizing the Word

It is important to keep in mind that *Problems of Dostoevsky's Creative Art* was not only a book about Dostoevsky, nor only a book about Dostoevskian polyphony. It was also—and this is perhaps its richest vein, connecting it with the work of the early 1920's—about the creative process. According to Bakhtin, what polyphonic authors accomplish is a sort of creation both unknown to, and undesired by, authors following classical and Romantic models of creativity. Polyphonic writing relies neither on formulaic plotting nor on pure inspiration (both of which might be called "already over" before the act of composition begins), but on the identification and provocation of voices whose own potentials for surprising dialogue create the shape of the work. This association of Dostoevskian polyphony with the potential for unexpected self-realization opened up several new topics in the 1930's: historical, metalinguistic, and folkloristic.

We divide Bakhtin's accomplishments in this period into two basic lines leading out, as it were, from his typology of the prose word. The first line was prompted by a new interest in *genre*. Here belong Bakhtin's major essays on heteroglossia, language use in the novel, and historical poetics: "Discourse in the Novel," "From the Prehistory of Novelistic Discourse," "Forms of Time and of the Chronotope," and "The *Bildungsroman* and its Significance." The second line was an idealization of parody that culminated, in the early 1940's, in Bakhtin's doctoral dissertation on carnival laughter in Rabelais. In a sense, the genre-marking chronotope (a tool in historical poetics) and carnivalization (an ahistorical concept) can be seen as two extremes of the same continuum. Chronotopes measure norms and celebrate the prosaic regularities that make any given world, day after day, recognizable for the consciousnesses that live in it; carnival, on the other hand, is almost an antichronotope, mocking all possible norms and suspending definitions. Chronotope and carnival will be further developed in chapters of their own (Nine and Ten). In the present chapter we will comment only on the general direction of the two lines and how they contribute to the shape of Bakhtin's career.

Apart from several pages in the 1929 Dostoevsky book on the "adventure plot," Bakhtin had not engaged questions of genre in the 1920's. But his associate in the circle, Pavel Medvedev, had devoted a chapter of his 1928 critique of Formalism to the problem of genre (M:FM, pp. 129–37). Elsewhere in this study we suggest that Bakhtin might have been spurred to articulate a social, but *non-*Marxist, theory of discourse after confronting the Marxification of his ideas in Voloshinov's book. Here we suggest a parallel move, that Bakhtin might have been stimulated to investigate questions of genre after considering Medvedev's thoughtful treatment of the problem in the *Formal Method in Literary Scholarship*.

Medvedev's argument, in brief, is as follows. The Formalists approached genre mechanically, from the bottom up, as an accumulation of devices organized by a specific dominant. But genre must be approached from the top down, Medvedev counters; it is the "typical totality of the artistic utterance," "a finished and resolved whole"; "the problem of finalization [*zavershenie*] is one of the most important problems of genre history" (M:FM, p. 129). Medvedev goes on to argue that of all spheres of ideological creativity, only art knows finalization in the strict sense of the word. "Every genre represents a special way of constructing and finalizing a whole, finalizing it essentially and thematically (we repeat), and not just conditionally or compositionally" (M:FM, p. 130).

Now, Bakhtin was not hostile to finalization in all situations; nor was he hostile to the notion of a whole, so long as wholeness was not the product of a system. He understood aesthetic finalization, however, in a way quite different from Medvedev. In the opening pages of "Author and Hero," Bakhtin defined the general relationship of author to created character as the relationship of any "I" to any "other." But one important difference obtains between real-life and aesthetic authoring.

In life, Bakhtin argued, we author fragments under pressure of daily events and we have neither the time nor the attention span to interact in any other way; "we are not interested in the whole of a person but only in his separate acts" (AiG, pp. 7–8). In art, however, the author must assume "a unified reaction to the *whole* of a hero" (AiG, p. 8). Getting the whole of a hero right is an arduous task, Bakhtin admits; how many "grimaces, random masks, false gestures" (ibid.) can result from the whims of the author's own subjectivity and caprice. But the task is necessary, for only then can a hero be released to develop freely within the logic of his *own* reality. The author's most responsible act is to grant integral wholeness to another consciousness, which is a way of granting to that consciousness not only "given traits" but also unexpected potential.

This perspective on created characters within a work suggests a model for genres within literary history. The "wholeness" that Medvedev sees as definitive for genre ("finalizing it essentially and thematically . . . not just conditionally or compositionally") would appear to Bakhtin in the period after *Problems of Dostoevsky's Creative Art* as too Aristotelian, too dependent upon models of plot closure, to satisfy the genuine potential of novels. Finalizing a whole, for Bakhtin, is more a question of the author's approach to the task of creative activity. Proper wholes are achieved by visualizing radical singularities and the worlds that they potentially generate. Orchestrate many such worlds in a verbal work of art, make them sensitive to one another and reflect that sensitivity in the languages of the work, and one may arrive at dialogized heteroglossia. Extend these worlds in literary history, and one has a sequence of chronotopes.

What genres of speech and literature do, in other words, is provide specific complexes of values, definitions of situation, *potentials* (not merely structures) for kinds of action. They are complexes, clusters, "congealed events," as opposed to closed wholes or systems. Genres are themselves neither systematic nor parts of larger systems, as the Formalists tried to argue; nor need they be structurally finalized or thematically unified, in spite of Medvedev's argument in his critique of the Formalists. The complexes Bakhtin has in mind provide a *relative* stability, but they do not exhaustively define the members of any given genre. We need genres to understand specific acts, Bakhtin argued, but in understanding genre we have not understood everything that is important about those acts or literary works. Genre provides the "given," but the work or act provides the "created," something new. As he would eventually elaborate, each act of speech and each literary work uses the resources of the genre in a specific way in response to a specific individual situation. The genre—similar to the uttered word—is thus changed slightly by each usage; it "remembers" its usage and acquires what Bakhtin will call, anthropomorphically, "genre memory" (see Chapter Seven).

Bakhtin's understanding of genre was one of his several attempts to overcome the paradox of architectonics, the paradox of radical singularity that nevertheless communicates and accumulates a history. Needless to say, such an open concept of genre fits poorly into a fixed hierarchy of literary forms, and leads to a privileging of the novel as a maximally open genre. Once Bakhtin began to integrate his ideas on "aesthetic wholes" into his earlier commitments to radical singularity and creative potential, the concepts of genre, chronotope, and dialogized heteroglossia appeared as so many solutions-in-progress.

Carnival: The Apotheosis of Unfinalizability

In "Discourse in the Novel" (1934–35), Bakhtin succeeded in combining the best of his old ideas in a theory that broke new ground. Written in a relatively clear and confident discursive style, the work constitutes a mature development of Bakhtinian premises. With good reason, many critics have read it as his most characteristic, and perhaps also most profound, theoretical study.[13]

In writing it, Bakhtin apparently set himself the task of fusing his three global concepts. The suggestion in the Dostoevsky book that prose language is radically different from poetic language is now defended explicitly, as Bakhtin constructs a prosaics to oppose all traditional poetics. The work also argues for prosaics in the second sense, as it stresses the value of everyday experience as the source of all responsibility and creativity. In Bakhtin's other major study of the 1930's ("Forms of Time and of the Chronotope: Notes Toward a Historical Poetics"), he went still further, and intimated that the nineteenth-century novel's prosaic sense of time, social space, and character made it the first genre to convey a truly historical sense of the world. In both these essays, he argued that the prosaic historical sense required a dialogic conception of truth and language. He argued as well that only an appreciation of genuine dialogue and of truly prosaic experience permits a vision of humanity and culture as they really are: responsible to the core, creative at every moment, and, above all, unfinalizable in their very essence.

This successful fusion of his favorite concepts was only one way in which Bakhtin's thought developed during this period. A second line of thought chronologically overlaps the first. In "Epic and Novel" (1941) and in the manuscript eventually published as *Rabelais and His World*, Bakhtin appears to have experimented by taking one of his global concepts to an extreme, even to the point where it excluded or contradicted the other two. The concept he chose was "unfinalizability," and the tone he adopted was poetic, optimistic, and breathlessly exaggerated. Bakhtin's choice of Rabelais as a topic seems appropriate to his newfound delight in free play and radical experimentation.

One might contrast the style of the Rabelais book (written in the late 1930's and early 1940's, although not published until 1965) with that of Bakhtin's early manuscripts. "Toward a Philosophy of the Act" is turgidly polemical; *Rabelais and His World* strives after an effervescent critical apostrophe. In *Rabelais*, we witness Bakhtin working against his discursive habits and his earlier labored style to reach an inspirational mode of presentation:

The ritual of the feast tended to project the play of time itself, which kills and gives birth at the same time, recasting the old into the new, allowing nothing to perpetuate itself. Time plays and laughs! It is the playing boy of Heraclitus who possesses supreme power in the universe ("dominion belongs to the child"). The accent is placed on the future; utopian traits are always present. [RAHW, p. 82]

As a result, *Rabelais* presents a peculiar mix of the repetitive or plodding (the work was originally a dissertation) with Rabelaisian excess and the ecstatic.

In terms of content as well, the works of this carnival group contrast markedly with Bakhtin's other writings. Throughout his career, Bakhtin explored the proper ratio of unfinalizability to finalization. In his earliest works, he stressed the value of finalization, so long as it is not carried to excess and so long as a person does not assume he can finalize himself. After all, Bakhtin argued, without a finalizing other, "I" cannot achieve an image of myself, just as I cannot be aware of how my mind works when I am unselfconscious, and cannot know how I really appear to the world by looking in a mirror. An integral self, a tentative self-definition, requires an *other*. To know oneself, to know one's image in the world, one needs another's finalizing outsideness.

Bakhtin also argued that the creation of all art requires a similar outsideness. Fantasies and dreams never congeal into a whole, because in dreams the author is himself the hero and therefore cannot stand *outside* the hero (AiG, pp. 67–68). Works of art, however, offer an aesthetic whole because an act of finalization is undertaken by an author who is located outside the hero and able to offer an integral image of him. Finally, ethics requires finalization and outsideness, because ethical action by its very nature consists of a free gift to another from a different integral position. The ethical person seeks not full identity with a sufferer, but "live entering," a special relation that adds something new and valuable from an outside and temporarily finalizing perspective. In short, these manuscripts contend that without finalization, there would be no art, no self, and no responsibility.

In the 1929 Dostoevsky book, the ratio of unfinalizability to finalization shifts in favor of the former. Though necessary and valuable when properly used, finalization is also seen as profoundly dangerous when abused—as it often is. The act of finalizing, defining, or accounting for another "causally and genetically" and "secondhand" is described as a fundamental threat to the essence of selfhood, which lies in the ability to render untrue all finalizing definitions. So long as a person is alive, Bakhtin writes, he retains the power to make conditional all external definitions of himself and is therefore "noncoincident" with himself. The sin of "theoretism"— or as he now calls it, the "monologic" conception of truth prevalent in Western thought of the past few centuries—is to reduce people to the circumstances that produced them, without seeing their genuine freedom to remake themselves and take responsibility for their action. Now Bakhtin argues that without *un*finalizability, there is neither selfhood nor ethical responsibility. He was evidently much concerned with the threat of the great -isms, especially psychologism (or Freudianism) and Marxism. Dostoevsky's novels became his weapon and Dostoevsky's characters his distilled essence of unfinalizability.

In the Dostoevsky book, Bakhtin also implicitly challenges his earlier theory that art necessarily finalizes. Now he argues that only monologic art functions by finalization. Dostoevsky's great discovery was to invent a way within art to represent people as genuinely unfinalizable, and to do so he developed a creative method that was itself unfinalizable. The polyphonic novel renounces the author's "outside essential surplus" with respect to the characters in order to represent people as truly open.

In *Rabelais*, Bakhtin goes still further and presents unfinalizability as the only supreme value. The proper ratio of unfinalizability to finalization is now infinite, because the value of finalization has been reduced to zero. Everything completed, fixed, or defined is declared to be dogmatic and repressive; only the destruction of all extant or conceivable norms has value. It is as if Bakhtin had taken for his mottos the anticommand of the Abbey of Thélème—"Do as you like!"—as well as Bakunin's famous invocation of rebellion for its own sake: "The will to destroy is a creative will!"

If aesthetic experience requires outsideness and finalization, so much the worse for it, Bakhtin seems to say. In carnival no one is outside, and nothing ever reaches a whole image, which could only be restrictive. Carnival "is by no means a purely artistic form nor a spectacle and does not, generally speaking, belong to the sphere of art. . . . In fact, carnival does not know footlights, in the sense that it does not acknowledge any distinction between actors and spectators. Footlights would destroy a carnival, as the absence of footlights would destroy a theatrical performance" (RAHW, p. 7).

In carnival, Bakhtin thought he had discovered a social ritual of pure antinomianism, and in carnival laughter he detected an eternally "unofficial," "second truth about the world"—a truth that rejects the existence of all Truth. Laughter becomes a "universal philosophical form" (RAHW, p. 67)—and its philosophy temporarily became Bakhtin's own.

"The principle of laughter," declares *Rabelais*, "destroys . . . all pretense of an extratemporal meaning and unconditional value of necessity. It frees human consciousness, thought, and imagination for new potentialities" (RAHW, p. 49). In his early writings, Bakhtin derided views like this as a cultivation of "mere empty potential," which is a delusion because potential without any concrete realization necessarily turns into a mere shadow of itself. But in *Rabelais*, pure potential is pure freedom, and pure freedom is almost the only true value.

The claims Bakhtin offers for carnival laughter are themselves extravagant and "Rabelaisian." Carnival laughter, he argues, not only overcomes all oppressive social norms, it also banishes death and the fear of death. Taking sheer delight in the Heraclitian flux, carnival understands the human body not as the mortal husk of an individual bound to suffering and articled to end, but as the collective great body of the people, given to Rabelaisian orgiastic excess and destined to continue through all change, all history. "In Rabelais's novel the image of death is devoid of all tragic or terrifying overtones. Death is the necessary link in the process of the people's growth and renewal. It is [nothing more than] the 'other side' of birth" (RAHW, p. 407). Thus, Rabelais's book "is the most fearless book in world literature" (RAHW, p. 39).

In "Epic and Novel," Bakhtin describes the novel in much the same spirit as he was soon to describe carnival. Personifying his favorite genre, he treats literary history as an ongoing battle between the spirit of "finalized" or "completed" genres, with their "ready-made" truths and established canons, and the eternally itinerant novel, the scion of carnival and the prophet of pure becoming. "The novel is not merely one genre among other genres. . . . Compared with them, the novel appears to be a creature from an alien species. . . . It fights for its own hegemony in literature; wherever it triumphs, the other older genres go into decline" (EaN, p. 4). Like carnival, the novel is pure parody and pure antinomianism: "The novel parodies other genres (precisely in their role as [fixed and canonical] genres); it exposes the conventionality of their forms and language" (EaN, p. 5). Consequently, the novel is the only genre to lack a canon; the novel never fixes itself because "it is plasticity itself" (EaN, p. 39). Needless to say, this view is in marked contrast with the one expressed in "Discourse in the Novel," which confidently describes novelistic discourse as the language of Dickens,

Fielding, and Turgenev—authors who not only wrote traditional novels, but who in fact even serve as Bakhtin's canonical examples of distinct "lines" in the development of the genre.

When one recalls that *Rabelais and His World* and "Epic and Novel" were written in Stalinist Russia, with its great purges and its Terror, one is tempted to read the two works as maximalist reactions to a totalitarian state.[14] One may be especially struck by Bakhtin's extensive description of the pure "freedom of speech" characteristic of carnival. In our view, it would be a mistake to reduce the book to this allegorical dimension alone; the work clearly grows out of Bakhtin's lifelong concern with unfinalizability and his more recent interest in parody and the novel. Nevertheless, the political allegory does appear to be present, and it helps to explain one peculiar dimension of the Rabelais book.

We have in mind the work's professed utopianism, which is so much at odds with the anti-utopianism of Bakhtin's other writings. Bakhtin's lifelong dislike of systems, his distrust of final answers, and his preference for the messy facts of everyday life made him deeply suspicious of all utopian visions. In the chronotope essay, which contains a substantial discussion of Rabelais and carnival, Bakhtin has some harsh words for "historical inversion"—which, in projecting myths of a past Golden Age onto a utopian vision, empties out and impoverishes the real and immediate future (FTC, pp. 147–48). We do not mean to argue that this inconsistency should lead us to characterize the utopian passages of the Rabelais book as mere window dressing. So much of that book is inconsistent with Bakhtin's other writings that there is no reason to single out its utopianism as insincere. What we do mean is that the utopianism of this book is decidedly odd and radically different from the utopian tradition generally. Perhaps intended as a fig leaf for Bakhtin's unorthodox views, the term *utopian* may be misleading. In context, it appears to designate something close to its opposite: an idealization of unremitting skepticism and unending change without a goal. What Bakhtin offers us is the utopia of an anti-utopian thinker.

Carnival and laughter are described as utopian in the sense that they challenge all social norms that have ever been or *ever will be*; they incorporate a spirit of joyful negation of everything completed or to be completed. Because there are always some norms in force, this negation can never ultimately succeed—nor does it strive to succeed—in replacing the world as we know it with another world. Political utopianism could only replace one set of norms with another, but in Rabelais and in carnival laughter "we discover the joyful relativity of [political] events as well as of the entire political problem" (RAHW, p. 448) in Rabelais's time, or at any other time. Carnival and Bakhtin offer us the paradox of a radically *apoliti-cal* utopianism. The Rabelais book is political only in the sense that apoliticism—especially in the Stalinist context, which defined everything as political—is in itself a kind of politics.

This "second line" of Bakhtin's third period, then, may be seen in two ways. It is in part a response to the times and in part a development understandable within the context of Bakhtin's intellectual life. Specifically, it is an extreme extension of one of Bakhtin's three global concepts, a continuation of the trajectory that led from "Toward a Philosophy of the Act" to *Problems of Dostoevsky's Creative Art*.

Nevertheless, the exclusive and extreme focus on unfinalizability led Bakhtin to some conclusions that appear aberrant within the context of his career. In contrast to his earlier and later work, the Rabelais book evinces a contempt for the prosaic activities of minute-to-minute ordinary living. Carnival liberates by freeing us from "all that is humdrum" (RAHW, p. 34) in daily life. Language in Rabelais is described not as a dialogue that generates new and valuable truths, but as the joyful destruction of all truths. And individual responsibility entirely disappears from view when the individual is merged into the great body of the feasting people. There is no longer a self, there is only the carnival mask; other people can accomplish what "I" can if they adopt my festive clothes. Carnival as a whole appears to offer a perfect "alibi for being."

In Bakhtin's last period, he returned to the theme of laughter and carnival, but in a different spirit. When Bakhtin decided to revise and republish his book on Dostoevsky, he added a lengthy section (constituting most of the fourth chapter) on carnivalization and laughter. Although this chapter reflects the research Bakhtin did in writing the Rabelais book, it differs markedly from that book in tone. Carnival is now described not as a pure force of antinomian destruction, but as a clearing away of dogma *so that* new creation can take place. It allows potential to be realized. Laughter, too, is recharacterized in more positive and creative terms. It becomes part of a skeptical, but not antinomian, enterprise of experimentation, "familiarization," and exploration—the role it had played in some of Bakhtin's more sober discussions of parody from the 1930's, such as that in "Toward a Prehistory of Novelistic Discourse" (PND, pp. 51–56). In *Rabelais*, laughter takes place against the background of mass violence, but in his "Notes of 1970–71" Bakhtin writes:

Violence does not know laughter. Analysis of a serious face (fear or threat).
Analysis of a laughing face. . . . The sense of anonymous threat in the tone
of an announcer who is transmitting important communications. Seriousness burdens us with hopeless situations, but laughter lifts us above them
and delivers us from them. Laughter does not encumber man, it liberates
him. . . . Everything that is truly great must include an element of laughter. Otherwise it becomes threatening, terrible, or pompous; in any case,
it is limited. Laughter lifts the barrier and clears the path. [N70–71,
pp. 134–35]

In the Rabelais book, carnival speech is described as an explosion
of obscene epithets and a torrent of playful vituperation, shouted in
various "genres of billingsgate." It is farthest of all from true open
dialogue (in the second sense). But in his late writings, laughter
"clears the path" of violence and threat so as to make room for dialogue. In fact, laughter ceases to require carnival or other extreme
situations; on the contrary, it takes place (or should take place)
in the most prosaic situations. "Laughter can be combined with
profoundly intimate emotionality (Sterne, Jean Paul, and others)"
(N70–71, p. 135). Laughter belongs not to the culture of Satur-
nalian excess, but to "the culture of the weekday" (ibid.).

The Early 1950's to 1975:
Spokesman for the Profession

The "rediscovery" of Bakhtin in the early 1960's and his subsequent rise to national and international acclaim created a strange
tunneling, almost a collapse, of all periods of his biography into
one. The last book Bakhtin saw through press, containing work
written between 1924 and 1973, seems to capture in its subtitle
("Research from Various Years") this conflation. That book was
followed by a posthumous volume of even more widely disparate
essays, ranging from 1919 to Bakhtin's final, incomplete projects.
All the periods of Bakhtin's life were becoming known to Russians
at once. Revisions of earlier work, genuinely new insights, and
lapsed, outmoded concepts were assimilated and translated in any
order, imparting a sort of synchronic patina to his legacy.

It has been our thesis in this chapter that Bakhtin's ideas genuinely changed over time, as he produced new insights that grew
from, but were not contained in, earlier work. In his final period,
Bakhtin seems to have set himself the task of culling the best ideas
from his career and forging a synthesis that would lead to still richer

questions. He had undertaken a similar project in the mid-1930's when writing "Discourse in the Novel," but now he had much more to integrate.

In his new writings of the final period, Bakhtin returns to many of the concerns of the early 1920's. Perhaps as part of his effort to integrate the writings of a long and disjointed career, he again places in the foreground many of the moral issues central to his early work: outsideness, ethical responsibility, creativity (and what he now calls "creative understanding"). In subject matter and style, he retreats from the novel imperialism, carnival maximalism, and utopian constructs of the Stalinist years. In fact, his most interesting essays from this period (in particular "The Problem of Speech Genres," a transitional piece) demonstrate a renewed appreciation of the value of finalization and a renewed interest in constraints.

But these familiar ethical issues are now discussed with a difference. In the early manuscripts, we recall, Bakhtin refuted Kant and other systematizers in "philosopher's discourse." Soon after, he sensed that his own language was inadequate to his message, and so developed a style more dependent upon local detail and prosaic observation. In his final period, this prosaicism is retained, but the language has become less erratic. It is now meditative and metaphilosophical. The titles of his later essays or working drafts for essays are indicative of their broad scope: for example, "The Problem of the Text in Linguistics, Philology, and the Human Sciences: An Experiment in Philosophical Analysis" (1959–61), and "Toward a Methodology for the Human Sciences" (begun in the 1930's or early 1940's; reworked in 1974).[15] This breadth is combined with a return—calculated or no—to the short form: many of Bakhtin's most lapidary formulations are in the form of unfinished sentences, notebook entries for future projects or unrealized revisions of past projects, and isolated juxtapositions for some later rethinking.

Newly present in this final period was what we might call a "professionalism" in Bakhtin's tone and topics. As his work became recognized and his advice was sought by the academic establishment, Bakhtin turned his attention to the future of literary studies. The first period's dichotomy between systems and singularity reemerged as the distinction between the natural (or exact) and the human sciences. On the boundary between the two are the Formalists and structuralists, whom he therefore characterized as both valuable and flawed.[16]

In his comments on these two powerful alternatives to his own thought, Bakhtin sketched the groundwork for a moral prosaics in the humanities. As he wrote in "Toward a Methodology of the Human Sciences":

> My attitude toward Formalism: a different understanding of specification; ignoring content leads to "material aesthetics" (criticism of this in my article of 1924); not "making" but creativity. . . .
>
> My attitude toward structuralism: I am against enclosure in a text. Mechanical categories: "opposition," "change of codes" . . . sequential formalization and depersonalization: all relations are logical (in the broad sense of the word). But I hear *voices* in everything and dialogic relations among them. . . . The problem of "precision" and "depth." [MHS, p. 169]

"Precision" is the goal for the natural sciences, "depth" for the humanities. In this formulation Bakhtin is recasting on another plane a distinction that had pursued him all his life: that between *znachenie* (the objective, generalizable, dictionary meaning of something) and *smysl* (its sense or particular meaning in a given, unrepeatable context).

The exact sciences, Bakhtin claims, are characterized by *znachenie,* specifically, formal definition and verifiability through repetition. Natural science knows only one genuine subject, the researcher, and that subject studies "voiceless things." The techniques of the natural sciences have only a preparatory significance to the humanities, properly understood. On Bakhtin's map of the world, we must recall, things (as opposed to personalities) can have surroundings, but they cannot have genuine contexts. True context requires at least two consciousnesses. It is impossible where mere "objective knowledge" is the only goal—because context, Bakhtin maintains, is always personalized from two ends, an interrupted dialogue.

Such a "contextual" state of affairs obtains only in the humanities, which always must deal with two or more subjects. These subjects can, of course, *choose* to treat one another like things. Varying degrees of "thing-ness" can be beneficial for certain tasks, Bakhtin readily admits, especially those in which a usable extract rather than an "essence" is needed. Bakhtin has in mind the sort of point he liked to make about linguistics, which he considered a useful discipline, but still one that does not touch the metalinguistic essence of speech and writing.

All knowledge in the humanities begins as an interaction between two points of view. This kind of interaction, which is what Bakhtin means by an "event," inevitably entails an evaluation that must in turn anticipate a counterevaluation. Unlike scientific propositions, such knowledge cannot be confirmed or reproduced by further experiments, because "[human] thought knows only conditional points; thought erodes all previously established points" (MHS, p. 162).

This profoundly non-Platonic conviction about human thought is Bakhtin's starting point for his concept of *creative understanding* (RQ, p. 7; MHS, p. 159). Revising the Kantian triad of his earliest period, Bakhtin now claims that understanding is in fact a four-tiered process: first, the physical perception, then its recognition, then a grasping of its significance in context, and finally— and this is the crucial step—"active-dialogic understanding." This fourth step is *more* than an acknowledgment of existing context; it is implicitly creative, and presumes ever-new, and surprisingly new, contexts. Most contemporary analysis, Bakhtin writes, "fusses about in the narrow space of small time. . . . There is no understanding of evaluative nonpredetermination, unexpectedness, as it were 'surprisingness,' absolute innovation, miracle" (MHS, p. 167).

Such an understanding of understanding—which stresses outsideness, live entering, nonfusion, and active dialogue—took Bakhtin into other disciplines, especially cultural anthropology. Asked to comment on the future of literary studies in the Soviet Union, Bakhtin responded with a call for more diversity, more boldness, and for a methodology that viewed culture as an "open unity." He had in mind "unity" in the same fraught sense that we discussed earlier in this chapter; a singular unit-y that was irreplaceable and in essence multiple, always requiring for its self-realization and creative development an outside and other perspective (RQ, pp. 5–7). No cultural text could be understood merely "on its own terms": "*Creative understanding* does not renounce itself, its own place in time, its own culture; and it forgets nothing. In order to understand, it is immensely important for the person who understands to be *located outside* the object of his or her creative understanding—in time, in space, in culture" (RQ, p. 7).

How, then, does one deal creatively and responsibly with otherness? One cannot become a mere duplicate of the other through total empathy or "fusing" of horizons; that could add nothing truly new. Nor should one "modernize and distort" the other by turning the other into a version of oneself. Both these alternatives, which are often seen as the only possible ones, reduce two voices and two perspectives to one. But true responsibility and creative understanding are dialogic, and dialogue gives rise to *unexpected* questions. "If an answer does not give rise to a new question from itself, it falls out of dialogue and enters systemic cognition, which is essentially impersonal" (MHS, p. 168).

To the four periods outlined here, we might add a postscript on the fifth, posthumous period. In contrast to Bakhtin's initial reception in his homeland—where "dialogism" and "carnivalization" were often applied to literary texts rather mechanically—recent Soviet symposia on Bakhtin's work have tended to emphasize the early writings and their strong moral message.

In a brief essay on the "ethical dominant" in Bakhtin's philosophy, for example, one scholar recommends Bakhtin's "participatory or act-oriented thinking," his resistance to "fatal theoretism" in philosophy, and his idea of the primacy of the ethical in a work of art (Brandt, p. 24). The essay concludes on a hopeful and personal note: "It seems to me that today, when we are trying to determine maxims for 'new thinking,' alongside affirmations of the priority of generally-human considerations over 'class' ones and affirmations of the human being as 'the measure of all things,' an honored place should be occupied by Bakhtin's position on the responsibility of each person for his or her own singularity" (ibid.).

As Bakhtin's early writings are gradually integrated into the final notes that so richly echo them, his legacy is beginning to be seen *whole*. In order to see Bakhtin as a whole, however, one must look more closely at what he did and did not write. That debate is the subject of the next chapter.

3

The Disputed Texts

Hostility to all forms of theoretism was one constant in Bakhtin's long career. His many attacks on dialectics, his criticisms of the Saussurean view of language, and his attempts to outline a theory of psychology inimical to both Freud's and Pavlov's all derive from his concern for the eventness of the event. They reflect as well his belief in the unsystematicity of culture, the unfinalizability of people, and the centrality of genuine responsibility to human experience.

Bakhtin imagined himself as offering an alternative to the view that knowledge in the humanities must be modeled on the hard sciences and that culture, language, and the mind could ultimately be described as systems. According to Bakhtin, this view constitutes pseudoscientific reductionism, which was bound to lead to terrible moral consequences and to provoke a sterile relativism in response. To explain what sort of knowledge is possible without theoretism, Bakhtin developed numerous conceptual alternatives: "live entering," "dialogue," "novelness," and "creative understanding."

In his "Notes of 1970–71," for instance, we find him rejecting Marxism (and dialectics) along with semiotics and structuralism (with their concept of "code") as twin errors:

Semiotics deals primarily with the transmission of ready-made communication using a ready-made code. But in live speech, strictly speaking, communication is first created in the process of transmission, and there is, in essence, no code. . . .

Dialogue and dialectics. Take a dialogue and remove the voices (the partitioning of voices), remove the intonations (emotional and individualizing ones), carve out abstract concepts and judgments from living words and responses, cram everything into one abstract consciousness—and that's how you get dialectics.

Context and code. A context is potentially unfinalized; a code must be finalized. A code is only a technical means of transmitting information; it does not have cognitive, creative significance. A code is a deliberately established, killed context. [N70–71, p. 147]

Readers of passages like these may wonder at the by-now-widespread ascription to Bakhtin of three other books—Valentin

Voloshinov's *Marxism and the Philosohy of Language* and *Freudianism: A Critical Sketch* and Pavel Medvedev's *The Formal Method in Literary Scholarship* (as well as a number of articles by Voloshinov and Medvedev). Each of these books is avowedly and consistently Marxist, and Voloshinov's book on language is also a work of semiotics. On what basis, then, has Bakhtin been credited with works fundamentally at odds with his most cherished convictions?

The Dispute

What would I have to gain if another were to fuse with me?

—AiG, p. 78

It is now commonplace for critics to cite Voloshinov's and Medvedev's works as Bakhtin's, often without offering any qualification, but in fact the authorship of these texts is far from a settled question. In the United States, the influence of Katerina Clark and Michael Holquist's pioneering biography, which takes a strong stand for Bakhtin's authorship of these books, has led to a widespread assumption by nonspecialists that an open question is in fact closed.[1]

For a number of years, we followed and contributed to this practice of attributing Voloshinov's and Medvedev's works to Bakhtin.[2] The case finally offered in the Clark-Holquist biography, plus our own reading of the newly published manuscripts, led us to reconsider our previous assumption. In 1986, *Slavic and East European Journal* published a forum on Bakhtin in which the question was addressed by three contributors. I. R. Titunik, a translator of Voloshinov and an advocate of Voloshinov's authorship, raised serious objections to Clark and Holquist's position.[3] Elsewhere, other scholars, including Nina Perlina and Edward J. Brown, have also objected on grounds of methodology and internal consistency to the double assumption that the works of the Bakhtin group can be treated as the product of a single author and that the author is Bakhtin.[4]

We have since come to the conclusion that, barring the presentation of new evidence, there is no convincing reason to credit Bakhtin with the authorship of the disputed texts.

In arguments of this sort, a good deal of skepticism is in order. Politics and academic politics color the issues, as do the economics of publishing and the "economics" of scholarly reputation in the professional marketplace. In the Bakhtin case, both Soviet and American politics have played a conspicuous role.

In the Soviet Union, the rediscovery of Bakhtin in the early 1960's coincided with a lengthy debate over the emergence of semiotics, structuralism, and related methods of literary, linguistic, and cultural analysis. "Physicists" and "lyricists," semioticians and traditionalists, took varying and complex positions over such questions as the "mathematization" of literary studies, the use of cybernetics in the humanities, the place of linguistics in literary scholarship, the value of the Formalist heritage, the formalizability of "intuition" and "creativity," and the role of neurophysiology in aesthetics. Intense debates, covered by Peter Seyffert in *Soviet Literary Structuralism*, involved accusations of "reductionism," "scientism," "vitalism," and "vulgar sociologism."[5] Undercurrents of Russian nationalism and the revival of Russian Orthodoxy further confused the matter. Understandably in the Soviet context, opposing camps cited Marx and Lenin; equally understandably, opposing polemicists used Bakhtin, whose prestige was at its height, as a cudgel. Bakhtin was too significant for any side to abandon him to the opposition.

In this context, the attribution of Voloshinov's and Medvedev's works to Bakhtin offered various kinds of ammunition. If Bakhtin were allowed to be the author of works in semiotics, the semioticians stood to gain; if one stressed Medvedev's attack on Formalism, their opponents might profit. A more generous reading of events is also possible: that Bakhtin, now approved and even celebrated in his homeland, was being used as a conduit through which to reintroduce texts by his associates long banned or out of print.[6] The result was a kind of biographical imperialism, that is, the expansion of the Bakhtin canon to include powerful works by the other two scholars.

In the West, other interests have come into play. To state only the most obvious: Jakobsonians have endeavored to claim Bakhtin for structuralism and semiotics (despite Bakhtin's frequent attacks on both). Marxists have also claimed Bakhtin, and the attribution to him of the avowedly Marxist disputed texts has aided them in doing so. Scholars whose careers are linked to Bakhtin's stature have an understandable sympathy for arguments that magnify his legacy. The economics of effort has also played a role: in assembling a coherent account of the three theorists' ideas, critics often find it convenient to treat them as the product of one author, and to take advantage of claims tending to free their text from awkward qualifications. And, of course, publishers are clearly likely to sell more books with Bakhtin's name on the cover.[7]

To clarify the arguments on both sides, it would be useful to state what is *not* in dispute. There really were a Voloshinov and a Medvedev; nobody believes those names are pseudonyms in the sense that "Mark Twain" is a pseudonym. It is clear that Medvedev and Voloshinov were close friends of Bakhtin, who exchanged ideas with him and with each other frequently. It is also clear to all that Bakhtin's ideas exercised a profound influence on his friends' books. Voloshinov and Medvedev appear to have been sincere Marxists. They were both dead by 1938. From the time of the publication of the works in question (approximately the late 1920's) until 1970, no one publicly disputed that Voloshinov and Medvedev wrote the books published under their names.

Because no one contests the influence of Bakhtin's ideas on his friends, the presence of important similarities between works signed by Bakhtin and works signed by Voloshinov and Medvedev is not germane to the argument. Because Voloshinov's and Medvedev's works are avowedly Marxist, the significance of the broader framework of their studies *is* relevant. Is the Marxism window dressing for the censor, as Clark and Holquist maintain, and is it in fact compatible with Bakhtin's beliefs?

Vyacheslav Ivanov, the Soviet semiotician who claimed Bakhtin for his discipline, was the first to take a public stand for Bakhtin's authorship. In a lecture delivered in 1970 and published in an expanded version in 1973, Ivanov made the following statement, which we quote in its entirety:

The basic texts of works 1–5 and 7 [of the article's bibliography] are by M. M. Bakhtin. His students V. N. Voloshinov and P. N. Medvedev, under whose names they were published, made only small insertions and changes in particular parts (and in some cases, such as #5, in the titles) of these articles and books. That all the works belong to the same author, which is confirmed by the testimony of witnesses, is evident from their very texts, as one may easily convince oneself by the quotations presented. [Ivanov, "Significance," p. 366, n. 101; item 5 is V:MPL. Items 1–4 and 7 are: V:DiL; V:F; M:FM; Voloshinov, "Latest Trends in Linguistic Thought in the West" (1928); and Voloshinov, "The Construction of the Utterance" (1939)][8]

As Voloshinov's defenders have noted, Ivanov offered no evidence to substantiate the assertion. The "witnesses" were not named. Similarity of ideas, as we have noted, would be entirely compatible with the assumption that Voloshinov's and Medvedev's books were influenced, but not necessarily written, by Bakhtin.

In their biography of Bakhtin, Clark and Holquist present the extant evidence for Bakhtin's authorship. According to them, Bakhtin wrote the works either entirely or almost entirely: "The disputed works were written by Bakhtin to the extent that he should be listed as the sole author, Medvedev and Voloshinov having played a largely editorial role in each instance" (Clark and Holquist, *Bakhtin*, p. 147).[9]

Immediately after this assertion, Clark and Holquist advance a methodological argument that goes to the heart of the issue: "For one thing, nothing has established that Bakhtin could *not* have written the disputed texts and published them under friends' names." That is, the burden of proof is assumed to lie with the skeptics rather than with them. This argument is crucial, because in fact very little of Clark and Holquist's chapter on "The Disputed Texts" presents evidence that Bakhtin *did* write the works in question. The preponderance of the chapter either attempts to discredit arguments against Bakhtin's authorship or else offers motives why Bakhtin would have wanted to publish under others' names if indeed he did so.

It seems to us, however, that the burden of proof must lie with those who claim that Bakhtin wrote works signed by others. After all, Voloshinov's and Medvedev's names appear on the title pages, and their authorship was not disputed for some four decades. To our knowledge, no one has shown conclusively that the Earl of Oxford or Francis Bacon could *not* have written Shakespeare's works, but the burden of proof still lies with those who claim they did.[10]

Refuting counterarguments is therefore largely beside the point unless convincing evidence for Bakhtin's authorship is first presented. What evidence has been offered?

Clark and Holquist cite four kinds of evidence. The first and most important kind on which they rely is anecdotal, the reported testimony of "eyewitnesses" of Bakhtin and his wife "on private occasions." Most of this anecdotal evidence is presented in footnote 3 of the chapter, where we learn that "Bakhtin claimed authorship in a conversation with the American Slavist Thomas Winner in 1973" and that he made the same claim to his literary executor, Sergei Bocharov. Moreover, "in Ivanov's presence Bakhtin's wife once reminded Bakhtin that he had dictated the Freud book to her," according to an interview of Clark and Holquist with Ivanov. "The American Slavist Albert J. Wehrle observed that when a copy of the 'Medvedev' book was produced in front of Bakhtin and his wife, Bakhtin said nothing, but his wife exclaimed, 'Oh, how many times I copied that!'" We are also told that the Formalist Victor Shklovsky "knew as early as the 1920's that Bakhtin was the sole

author of the Medvedev book about his own group, the Formalists," according to Clark and Holquist's interview with Shklovsky
in 1978 (ibid., p. 375, n. 3).

In addition to the oral character of this evidence, which under
any circumstances would be difficult to substantiate, Clark and
Holquist indicate that there are other problems with it. In another
footnote, they concede that "as a former Formalist, Shklovsky had
reason for putting a negative construction on the affair" (ibid.,
p. 376, n. 9). Moreover, when other people questioned Bakhtin
about the disputed texts, Bakhtin did not confirm his authorship:
"Indeed, during the 1960's and 1970's most people found that if
they asked Bakhtin directly about whether he authored the disputed texts, he either avoided the question or was silent" (ibid.,
p. 148; no references are cited). "At first he [Bakhtin] did not even
admit authorship to his literary executors, and when he later did
admit it, he did not like to talk on the subject" (ibid.). Like Ivanov,
the executors were deeply involved in polemics over the significance of Bakhtin's legacy. Finally, Clark and Holquist report that
when the Soviet copyright agency (VAAP) asked Bakhtin to sign a
prepared document stating that he wrote the three disputed books
and one of the disputed articles, "he refused to sign it" (ibid., p. 147).
The Soviet Union became part of international copyright agree-
ments shortly before this document was prepared, and stood to
profit from anything tending to raise Bakhtin's prestige in the West.
In short, the anecdotal evidence is not only oral and mostly unverifiable but also far from unambiguous.

Another problem with this sort of evidence is that it is not always clear how precise the question was, or just what answer
Bakhtin actually gave on the few occasions when he allegedly did
speak about the matter. Was the question framed clearly enough to
distinguish between Bakhtin's actual composition of the disputed
texts and his influence on them? Did the question clearly differentiate between mere mechanical changes in Bakhtin's text (on the one
hand) and (on the other) composition by Voloshinov and Medvedev after extensive discussions with Bakhtin? Since these are the
only issues in dispute, the precision of the question is crucial. Many
students and colleagues are profoundly influenced by a talented
friend's ideas, but still digest those ideas, deploy them in a framework of their own, and creatively transform the overall significance
of those ideas in the process.

In our reading, Albert Wehrle's account of the anecdotal evidence would seem to indicate that information often taken to prove Bakhtin's authorship could be taken just as well to indicate his influence. Reporting a conversation he had with V. N. Turbin, Wehrle writes:

The few pieces of the puzzle we have now are hard to put together. Ivanov reports that Voloshinov and Medvedev "made only small insertions and changes in particular parts" of the books and articles in question and changed some titles. V. N. Turbin seems to support Ivanov when he quotes Bakhtin as saying, with regard to *The Formal Method:* "Pavel Nikolaevich [Medvedev] added to it, and not always for the better." According to Turbin, this was as much as Bakhtin ever said about the book. At other times he would confine himself to the remark that he "helped" with it. Knowing Bakhtin's reticence about the book, Turbin decided to conduct an experiment. In 1965, on a visit to Bakhtin, Turbin laid a copy of *The Formal Method* on the table without a word. Bakhtin said nothing, but his wife exclaimed: "Oh, how many times I copied that!" On the other hand, the latest published information, provided by Vadim V. Kozhinov, is that the problematic books and articles were written "on the basis of conversations with Mikhail Mikhailovich [Bakhtin]." [Wehrle, Introduction to M:FM, p. xvi]

Let us imagine that Medvedev wrote his own book "on the basis of conversations with" Bakhtin, but that, having thought profoundly about the issues, he transformed Bakhtin's ideas into a Marxist framework. Then Bakhtin might well have felt that he "helped" Medvedev but that Medvedev's additions "were not always for the better." Given the close relations of the Bakhtins with Medvedev, and given their considerable dependence on the largesse and protection afforded by Medvedev's influential position in the academic and publishing worlds, Bakhtin's wife might well have copied the manuscript even if her husband had not written it (Bakhtin was unemployed at the time). Moreover, if Bakhtin was himself influenced by Medvedev's book, as we suspect, his wife may have copied extensive parts of it as notes. In short, it is easy to imagine that people who had only recently learned that there was any connection among Bakhtin, Medvedev, and Voloshinov, may have asked imprecise questions and leaped to conclusions, especially in the charged atmosphere of the time and given the importance of Bakhtin's newfound prestige to all groups.

Clark and Holquist's second type of evidence is also inconclusive. Because Voloshinov and Medvedev died more than three decades before the controversy began, American scholars, unable to consult them, interviewed their families. According to one scholar, Voloshinov's first wife attributed her husband's books to Bakhtin;

according to another, Medvedev's son and daughter insisted that their father wrote *The Formal Method* and only "consulted with" Bakhtin (Clark and Holquist, *Bakhtin*, pp. 148, 376, n. 4).

The third type of evidence cited is dubious for several reasons, although it evokes our sympathy. In 1929, Bakhtin was arrested and faced imprisonment in a camp on the Solovetsky Islands in the Soviet Far North; because of his ill health, he appealed on the grounds that the sentence would kill him. According to Clark and Holquist, investigators called on Bakhtin to inquire about his possible authorship of the Medvedev and Voloshinov texts, since they knew he was familiar with "Marxist methods." The implication here, presumably, is that Marxist books written by Bakhtin could help the investigators contribute to a stronger defense of Bakhtin and so lighten his sentence. In these circumstances, it is said, Bakhtin admitted authorship (ibid., pp. 143–44). No oral or written documentation is offered for this story; and, in any case, the circumstances would hardly allow for Bakhtin *not* to have admitted authorship. (Bakhtin's sentence was eventually changed to six years' internal exile and his life saved.)

Finally, Clark and Holquist argue that examination of the texts themselves confirms Bakhtin's authorship. Their argument here depends on judgments of quality. According to Clark and Holquist, Medvedev's undisputed texts—that is, the ones they believe he really wrote, such as *In the Writer's Laboratory*—are of a much lower quality than *The Formal Method*. They also state that the texts that are genuinely Voloshinov's are, though better than Medvedev's undisputed texts, still not as good as the disputed Voloshinov texts. They conclude that Voloshinov and especially Medvedev were not intelligent enough to have written on their own the texts they signed, except, perhaps, for their poorest (and most Marxist) passages. So Shakespeare scholars used to argue that only the best passages of his plays were written by Shakespeare and that worse ones must have been written by someone else.

This argument assumes that a great writer must be consistently great, and a less great one consistently less great—an assumption it would be difficult to justify. Are Bakhtin's prefaces to Tolstoy as good as his study of Dostoevsky, published in the same year?[11] Besides, if the argument were accepted, it could just as easily demonstrate that Voloshinov, rather than Bakhtin, wrote *The Formal Method*, because Voloshinov is also said to be intellectually superior to Medvedev. Above all, it must be noted that judgments about the quality of a work are profoundly disputable. We are persuaded by

Wlad Godzich's observation in his foreword to the reprint of *The Formal Method*:

One must be wary of a phenomenon that seems to have grown quite strong in the Soviet Union in recent years: a veritable (though "unofficial") cult of Bakhtin, who thus becomes the recipient of all praise while the more questionable aspects of the works attributed to him are alleged to be the products of collaborators and name-lenders, especially when it comes to Marxist views. The rewriting of history is not the monopoly of state ideology in the Soviet Union today. [Godzich, Foreword to M:FM, p. ix]

Proving Actions by Alleging Motives

In presenting their case, Clark and Holquist devote much of their attention to describing Bakhtin's motives for publishing under others' names. To us, this argument seems to put the cart before the horse. Of course, if it were shown that Bakhtin did write the works in question, one would want to know why he might have done so. But the fact that one can suggest possible motives for someone's having done something does not prove that he or she did it.

In the Soviet context, it is especially easy to discover possible motives, hidden meanings, and Byzantine strategies, because censorship, restrictions on publishing, and the fear of punishment are always factors. As a certain kind of American critic can handle any passage that offers counterevidence to his interpretation by discovering "irony," so Slavists learn very early in their training to resort to the censor. And since original thinkers in Russia always do worry about the censor, this argument is always possible. But for that very reason, the argument is not sufficient, because it can in principle justify any interpretation of any text. Surely even in Russia people sometimes mean what they say.

In order to describe Bakhtin's motives, Clark and Holquist first need to answer a number of obvious objections to their account, some of which had already been raised and others of which were bound to occur. In 1929, *Marxism and the Philosophy of Language* appeared under Voloshinov's name; in the very same year, *Problems of Dostoevsky's Creative Art* was published under Bakhtin's name. How then can one argue that Bakhtin published under his friends' names because that was the only way he could get into print? Why would Bakhtin, who was a non-Marxist and a religious man (according to Clark and Holquist), labor to defend Marxism against its most powerful enemies?

To begin with, Clark and Holquist contend, Bakhtin was fond

of "recherché jokes": "Bakhtin was himself a great lover of rascals and would have taken delight in pulling off so large-scale a hoax" (Clark and Holquist, *Bakhtin*, p. 151). In effect, Bakhtin was illustrating his own theory of carnivalization. Paraphrasing a conversation with Vadim Kozhinov, one of Bakhtin's Soviet executors, Albert Wehrle endorses this explanation: "Vadim Kozhinov has observed that Bakhtin was associated with other people of the 'carnival' type. Perhaps the exchange of identities within the Bakhtin circle owed something to this carnival atmosphere, or at least was stimulated by Bakhtin's attraction to ambivalence, disguises, the 'unofficial,' and nonwritten popular tradition" (Wehrle, Introduction to M:FM, p. xxi).

Bakhtin's behavior, in short, is described as performing his theories. Elsewhere, Holquist has argued that pseudonymy was a way of dramatizing Bakhtin's lifelong concern with polyphony, dialogue, and the complexities of authorship.[12] Alternatively, Holquist argues that publishing Christian views in Marxist language was Bakhtin's way of dramatizing the Incarnation.[13]

Of course, it is possible that such motives would have occurred to Bakhtin, if he did indeed publish under others' names. But as Titunik has observed, why then should the exchange of identities have been only in one direction?[14] If carnivalization was so characteristic of the Bakhtin group, then it is equally possible that *Problems of Dostoevsky's Creative Art* was written in whole or in part by Voloshinov. In any case, as Titunik mentions, the concept of carnival had not yet appeared in any of Bakhtin's works at this time (Titunik, "Baxtin Problem," p. 93).[15]

Titunik also questions the ethical implications of this account for Voloshinov's doctoral dissertation, which, according to Clark and Holquist, "was probably 'the problem of how to present reported speech'" (Clark and Holquist, *Bakhtin*, p. 110), that is, the very problem to which one third of *Marxism and the Philosophy of Language* was devoted. If Voloshinov wrote his own dissertation, then surely he could have written the passages in *Marxism*. If Bakhtin wrote the dissertation, "then Baxtin and Vološinov perpetrated no mere 'hoax' but out-and-out fraud—again no laughing matter" (Titunik, "Baxtin Problem," pp. 93–94).[16]

As for the thesis that Bakhtin dramatized his concern with dialogue and incarnation by ascribing his works to others, Titunik objects that there is no necessary reason why someone would have to make scholarly works instances of their own theories (ibid., p. 94). The thesis, which seems to project current American critical practice onto Bakhtin, is suspiciously anachronistic. Moreover, this sort of false ascription of his work to others would not illustrate, but contradict, Bakhtin's key belief (in "Toward a Philosophy of the Act") that action must be "responsible." It will be recalled that for Bakhtin "signature" was a fundamental ethical act. And one might add that attributing books worked out in group discussion to a single person is a rather odd way to dramatize dialogue.

Are the Marxist Books Marxist?

One of the reasons that the authorship question matters is that it bears directly on the status of three books that have often been considered exemplars of sophisticated, nonreductive Marxist criticism. If Bakhtin was not a Marxist, and if Bakhtin wrote *Marxism and the Philosophy of Language*, *The Formal Method*, and *Freudianism*, then the Marxism of those books turns out to be mere "window dressing," as Clark and Holquist assert (Clark and Holquist, *Bakhtin*, p. 168). On the other hand, if Voloshinov and Medvedev were the real authors, albeit authors strongly influenced by Bakhtin, then the Marxism of the books may be taken seriously. The books become attempts to construct a sophisticated Marxist theory of culture. Rather than theology in code, they constitute alternatives to the rather unsophisticated Marxism prevalent in the Soviet Union at the time.[17]

In part, this argument depends on how one reads the disputed texts. "The Marxist aspects of *Freudianism*, which have been cited to prove that it was not written by Bakhtin, have been exaggerated," Clark and Holquist contend (ibid., p. 164). Regarding *Marxism and the Philosophy of Language*, Clark and Holquist assert that "the farther one reads in the book, the more the Marxist terminology fades from view" (ibid., p. 166). It does not fade from our view; we invite our readers to test theirs.

Clark and Holquist are committed to two views of Bakhtin's works that we believe are open to question. First, they argue that all of Bakhtin's key ideas were already present in his earliest writings (before 1924), after which he simply sought different ways to express or apply them; as Holquist puts it, Bakhtin's first work "*contains, in embryonic form, every major idea Bakhtin was to have for the rest of his long life*" (Holquist, "Politics," p. 171). Second, they contend that Bakhtin's fundamental concerns were religious and that his works are a disguised theology. Because they characterize Bakhtin's early work as explicitly theological, the two contentions are closely linked. Their argument concerning the Marxism of the disputed texts is grounded in these premises.

To them, the question is why a "religious man," as they believe him to have been, would have allowed his ideas to be presented as a kind of Marxism, especially at a time when persecution of religion was at its height in Russia. In addition to the argument about incarnation, they suggest that Bakhtin's version of religion was not inimical to Marxism, because his early Kantian meditations on the relation of self to other were already "social" in character. But in this loose sense almost all cultural theories could be described as social.

Clark and Holquist thus simultaneously maintain two premises: that the Marxism of the "pseudonymous" texts is mere window dressing, but that Bakhtin was nevertheless not hostile to Marxism. For example, they claim that the argument of the Dostoevsky book (or certain parts of it) "is in a general sense Marxist" (Clark and Holquist, *Bakhtin*, p. 154). As evidence, they cite a passage in which Bakhtin states that the polyphonic novel "could have been realized only in the capitalist epoch" because capitalism brought diverse and previously iolated social groups together and, of course, created an acute sense of individuality.[18] But one hardly has to be a Marxist even in a "general sense" to see a connection between the genre of the novel, the rise of the middle class, and concern for individual identity. In the West, the theme is a cliché of non-Marxist novel criticism, and in Russia it was a commonplace in non-Marxist Dostoevsky criticism. Clark and Holquist do not mention passages in the Dostoevsky book that are overtly critical of dialectics.[19]

Clark and Holquist do mention the two texts of Bakhtin's that are overtly Marxist, two prefaces that Bakhtin provided for a 1929 edition of Tolstoy's literary works (see TP1 and TP2). Wisely, they do not press the point. To just about all concerned, the Marxism of these essays does indeed seem like "window dressing" of some sort. It is as far from the sophisticated, flexible Marxism of the disputed texts as it is from the discursive openness of Bakhtin's other works. Clark and Holquist cite with approval an early version of Ann Shukman's article "Bakhtin's Tolstoy Prefaces," in which Shukman suggests that the Tolstoy prefaces may in fact be parodic (Clark and Holquist, *Bakhtin*, p. 377).

The Debate Does Not Abate

In their 1986 reply to Titunik and Morson, Clark and Holquist not only went over some familiar ground but also made some new arguments, some of which Titunik seemed to have already anticipated.

First, Clark and Holquist concede that the "hearsay evidence" is provided by "witnesses with varying claims to direct knowledge and differing degrees of disinterestedness," and that it cannot stand on its own, although they also assert that it cannot "be dismissed out of hand" (Clark and Holquist, "Continuing," p. 96). They concede as well that the evidence of "the texts themselves" does not prove their case. They therefore present a new piece of evidence.

In their book, they claim that in addition to authoring works signed by Medvedev and Voloshinov, Bakhtin wrote an article published under the name of a third friend, I. I. Kanaev. Their book offers no evidence to support this assertion, and Titunik bypassed discussion of it: "One article by I. I. Kanaev is also attributed to Baxtin, but it is not a disputed text for the simple reason that only Clark and Holquist seem to know about it" (Titunik, "Baxtin Problem," p. 93). The article in question is Kanaev's "Contemporary Vitalism" (1926).

In brief, Clark and Holquist argue (1) that they have proof, which they cannot reveal, of Bakhtin's authorship of the Kanaev article, and (2) that if Bakhtin wrote the Kanaev piece, he might well have written the Medvedev and Voloshinov works as well. In our view, the second statement does not follow from the first. In the Soviet context, as we noted, the censorship and the state control of publishing frequently produce complex scenarios. What is in question, however, is whether Bakhtin wrote Voloshinov's and Medvedev's works, not whether he ever shared in the Soviet practice of labyrinthine publishing maneuvers.

To support the contention that Bakhtin wrote the vitalism essay, Clark and Holquist state that Kanaev himself "confirmed" Bakhtin's authorship of the article, although not to them personally (Clark and Holquist, "Continuing," p. 96).[20] To explain why they cannot reveal to whom Kanaev credited Bakhtin's authorship, and why they cannot reveal certain other evidence about the authorship question, Clark and Holquist then mention the sensitivity of the issues involved, including Bakhtin's "Marxism" and "Christianity," and state that many people supplied them with information but asked not to be identified. In the Soviet context, such a situation is, of course, quite common.

One answer to this argument is already implicit in the Titunik essay to which Clark and Holquist reply. Titunik's central point is the responsibility of scholars to be skeptical, especially when information is impossible to verify and sources of information may not be disinterested. He also suggests that Clark and Holquist's evident enthusiasm for Bakhtin may have led them astray. Like a number of other commentators, Titunik discovers a strong element of hagiography in the Clark-Holquist biography. Its authors may have been convinced by their sources, but, again, how are we to judge how skeptically those sources were evaluated or how precise were the questions asked?[21]

Titunik places special emphasis on the Clark-Holquist attempt to read Bakhtin's works as a kind of theology in code.[22] Whether or not Bakhtin was religious, it is quite possible to be religious without making all of one's writing a concealed theology. In particular, Titunik objects to the biography's characterization of Bakhtin's early works (which Clark and Holquist believe to be part of one large work to which they give the name "The Architectonics of Answerability"). The text on which Clark and Holquist concentrate, "Author and Hero," would appear from their characterization to be largely theological, but in fact "the 'Christological' passage of the fraction dealt with [in their account]—the key passage for the authors—is approximately a page and a half [out of 175]" (Titunik, "Baxtin Problem," p. 92). Moreover, the authors often do not distinguish their paraphrases of Bakhtin's ideas from their own "excursuses and digressions" and so "it takes special acquaintance with the original text to discern what is and what is not paraphrase" (ibid.). Our own examination of the more recently published early manuscript "Toward a Philosophy of the Act" confirms Titunik's objections to the characterization of Bakhtin's early writing as primarily theological. (See our introduction to *Rethinking Bakhtin*.)

We also concur with one other point Titunik makes about these paraphrases. Titunik charges Clark and Holquist with a kind of biographical anachronism, that is, with paraphrasing the early manuscripts in terms of language and concepts not present in them but present in Bakhtin's later works—without indicating to the reader that later concepts are being invoked (Titunik, "Baxtin Problem," p. 93). The reader of the Clark-Holquist chapter on "The Architectonics" might well come away with the idea that "Author and Hero," "Toward a Philosophy of the Act," and "Art and Answerability [sic]" have lengthy discussions of dialogue similar to those in the Dostoevsky book and in "Discourse in the Novel." But that is not the case. We may recall that the very use of the word *answerabil-*

ity to translate *otvetstvennost'* (the Russian word for "responsibility") is itself a kind of anachronism, because it suggests that language and dialogue were central to Bakhtin's work at the time—but the available texts do not support that view.[23] The issue of anachronism is not crucial, of course, if one accepts Clark and Holquist's thesis that all of Bakhtin's later ideas are already present in the early texts; but that is itself one of the issues in dispute.

At the time Clark and Holquist made this "embryonic" assertion, they alone among Western scholars had access to "Toward a Philosophy of the Act." (As the present volume goes to press, none of these three earliest texts are available in English.) Titunik's central point is the possibility of interpreting texts in different ways, the consequent need for skepticism about unverifiable evidence, and the need to reassess conclusions when previously unavailable texts do at last appear.

Nina Perlina raises a quite different objection to Clark and Holquist's attribution of the Kanaev article "Contemporary Vitalism" to Bakhtin.[24] It appears that the philosopher Nicholas Lossky (1870–1965), who was expelled from the Soviet Union in 1922, had published a brochure entitled *Contemporary Vitalism* shortly before his expulsion. Bakhtin was apparently familiar with Lossky's work, to which he refers very positively in "Toward a Philosophy of the Act" (KFP, p. 92). "Including Losskii's brochure on vitalism into a discussion of Bakhtin's vexing texts is like sowing the wind and reaping a whirlwind," Perlina observes (Perlina, "Funny Things," p. 18). For the Kanaev (or Bakhtin) article "Contemporary Vitalism" repeats large sections of the Lossky brochure, which it would have been imprudent to mention (as the work of an exile) by 1926. Inverting Lossky's conclusions, Kanaev (or Bakhtin) managed "to drag several chunks of Losskii's writings, which had already stopped circulating in the country, through the machinery of Soviet censorship" (ibid., p. 20). Perlina comments: "Without denying the validity of Kanaev's statement that Bakhtin had published at least one text under his name, we still are not sure whether Bakhtin *actually wrote the article*" (ibid.). If Bakhtin "copied several parts of Lossky's brochure on vitalism for his friend Kanaev," she asks, does that make Bakhtin the author? What precisely did Kanaev say when he admitted Bakhtin's authorship, and how reliable was his admission? The questions here are complex indeed, and, it would seem, derive from a situation quite different from the circumstances surrounding the Medvedev and Voloshinov books. In any case, evidence about the Kanaev incident cannot go very far toward proving Bakhtin's authorship of *The Formal Method* and *Marxism and the Philosophy of Language*.

It will be recalled that Clark and Holquist concede that neither the anecdotal evidence nor the evidence of the texts themselves can demonstrate their claims. They then appear to claim that the Kanaev incident does demonstrate it. Since the Kanaev incident does not even concern the Voloshinov and Medvedev texts, it would seem that this new claim cannot rectify the deficiencies of the old ones. It is therefore hard to understand what basis there is for continuing to attribute the disputed texts to Bakhtin.

But why should the question matter?

What Is at Stake

> The critics often invent authors: they select two dissimilar works—the *Tao Te Ching* and the *1001 Nights*, say—and attribute them to the same writer and then determine most scrupulously the psychology of this interesting *homme de lettres*.
>
> —Borges, "Tlön, Uqbar," p. 13

Any thinker with original and challenging views is subject to degrees of misunderstanding, superficial readings, and careless appropriations of terminology. In Bakhtin's case, understanding has been impeded by delayed and inconsistent translations, by a lack of familiarity with the tradition of Russian critical and linguistic thought, and by the fact that comparatively few Americans can read his texts in the original. Add to these factors the charged Russian atmosphere from which the texts emerged and the charged American debates into which they were rapidly recruited, and it ceases to surprise us that his work has so often been read in disappointing ways. The debate over the disputed texts has added an extra and particularly obscuring layer to the already complex problem of interpreting his ideas.

As imperialist countries are often weakened, rather than strengthened, by territorial expansion, so imperialist biographers and interpreters, in our view, can harm the cause of understanding Bakhtin. More is not always better or stronger. The attribution to Bakhtin of works that Voloshinov and Medvedev signed seems to have obscured the meanings both of those studies and of Bakhtin's own works. Early attempts to present Bakhtin as a Marxist or a semiotician still affect large numbers of readers, who come to his texts with presuppositions that the texts themselves do not justify and often contradict. Alternatively, attempts to present the Marxism of Voloshinov's and Medvedev's works as "window dressing" lead to Byzantine reading strategies at the expense of real consideration of the import of those books. Confusion and diminution result, and the distinctive ideas of all three thinkers are lost in the attempt to treat them as one.

Voloshinov's and Medvedev's works are sincerely Marxist. In our view, they represent a particularly complex and rewarding form of Marxism, and are among the strongest works on language and literature of our century; that is especially true of *Marxism and the Philosophy of Language*. No disrespect is intended or should be inferred by the idea that Bakhtin did not write, but merely influenced, the books and articles of Voloshinov and Medvedev. The time has passed when the very mention of Bakhtin's name should evoke a talismanic aura.

Bakhtin was neither a Marxist nor a semiotician. Neither was he a Freudian or a Formalist. In his view—as the early manuscripts illustrate—all these approaches share the errors of theoretism in especially destructive ways. As we have seen, a fundamental tenet of Bakhtin's thought is that knowledge, to be genuine and valuable, does not have to be a system; neither does it have to describe its object as a system. On the contrary, the most important aspects of language, literature, ethics, the psyche, history, and culture are lost if one assumes that either there is a system or there is nothing. Bakhtin dedicated his intellectual life to finding a way around this faulty assumption. The description of him as a Marxist, a semiotician, a structuralist, or an adherent of any other -ism is therefore bound to result in a trivialization of his ideas.

In "Toward a Philosophy of the Act," Bakhtin accuses theoretism of "transcribing" events in such a way that they lose their "eventness." Later in his life, the concept of monologization replaced that of transcription. To be sure, Bakhtin concedes that monologization and transcription have their legitimate uses. In the hard sciences, for instance, a researcher's interest may lie precisely in what is repeatable and stateable as monologic propositions. Those who decipher dead, or even living, languages may be interested in what can be codified into a systematic grammar. But in most areas of the humanities, monologization destroys the essence of the object under investigation.

Evidently, Voloshinov and Medvedev did not share this hostility to systems of whatever sort. They appear to have taken some of Bakhtin's specific concepts and shown that they could be integrated into systems. Voloshinov described language as dialogic, but he incorporated this description into a Marxist, dialectical system. The fact that he effected this change so well indicates that Bakhtin's specific concepts are not necessarily dependent on the overall framework they were designed to serve. Voloshinov and Medvedev produced remarkable books about literature and language using Bakhtin's ideas. But the books as wholes, we suggest, are fundamentally alien to Bakhtin in their informing vision and in their very spirit. They are excellent books, but they are not Bakhtin's. They are highly sophisticated *monologizations* of Bakhtin's thought.

Oddly enough, defenders of the great proponent of dialogue have themselves monologized a deeply dialogic relationship. As Bakhtin often observed, real dialogue is destroyed by the attempt to make a synthesis (dialectical or otherwise) that conflates distinct voices. We believe that the relations among Bakhtin, Voloshinov, and Medvedev were genuinely dialogic.[25] Their readers can only be the poorer for losing the chance to choose among them.

It is hard to tell just how the attribution of the disputed texts to Bakhtin has obscured readers' sense of Bakhtin's own intellectual development. But it is clear that the resulting distortions are bound to be considerable. The attempt to create an image of a thinker who in the course of the 1920's wrote such disparate works as "Toward a Philosophy of the Act," "Author and Hero," *Problems of Dostoevsky's Creative Art, Marxism and the Philosophy of Language, Freudianism*, and *The Formal Method* could only make the outlines of Bakhtin's own concerns more imprecise and opaque. If it came to be believed that Chekhov had written Gorky's works, would our sense of Chekhov (or for that matter of Gorky) be more precise? In place of understanding, we have been given a Borgesian parable.

Once one begins to think in terms of dialogue and influence, rather than identity and pseudonymy, other possibilities come into view. If Bakhtin influenced Voloshinov and Medvedev, why could they not have influenced him? In our view, that is very likely what happened. Bakhtin's early writings were emphatically *not* sociological, except in the trivial sense in which every meditation on selves and others is sociological. But his writings of the 1930's and 1940's (for example, "Discourse in the Novel" and the book on Rabelais) were deeply sociological. Is it not possible that the encounter with strong Marxist renditions of his own ideas provoked the change? Faced with the challenge of a sophisticated sociological poetics, based to a considerable extent on Bakhtin's own ideas,

Bakhtin appears to have responded with theories of language and literature that were sociological without being Marxist; he answered the challenge of his friends with his sociology without theoretism. He seems to have believed that Marxism, for all its help in prodding thinkers to consider sociological questions, falls short in answering them.

PART II

Problems of Authorship

4

Metalinguistics: The Dialogue of Authorship

> The unique nature of dialogic relations. The problem of inner dialogism. The seams of the boundaries between utterances. The problem of the double-voiced word. Understanding as dialogue. Here we are approaching the frontier of the philosophy of language and of thinking in the human sciences in general, virgin land. A new statement of the problem of authorship (the creating individual).   —PT, p. 119

The dialogic conception of language was central to Bakhtin's thought from 1924 on. It forms the basis for his account of the psyche and of culture, and it led him to his remarkable discourse theory of the novel. Postponing these topics for later chapters, we would like to outline here the core ideas that led Bakhtin to lay aside a great triumvirate of traditional disciplines concerned with language: stylistics, poetics, and, of course, linguistics.

In arguing against these disciplines, Bakhtin stressed that he did not want simply to "add" a dialogic dimension to their descriptions of language. Rather, he considered their inability to appreciate the nature and importance of dialogue as reason to rethink them in the most radical way. Though useful for certain local and limited purposes, the insights of these disciplines were flawed and misleading in their very approach to the object of study. So (to use one of his analogies) Ptolemaic astronomy, though not without its contributions, nevertheless offered a fundamentally misleading picture of the universe, which, if uncorrected, would condemn future work to more and more trivial and faulty results.

By traditional linguistics, Bakhtin meant not only the great heritage of preceding centuries, but also, and especially, the work of Saussure and those influenced by him: the Formalists, structuralists, and, later, the semioticians. Indeed, he felt that the quintessential errors of traditional linguistics were particularly evident in Saussurean work, which he questioned, synecdochically, as a kind of distilled essence of traditional linguistic thought. In criticizing stylistics, he was, again, not taking a stand among competing schools, but rejecting the very basis of the enterprise. Like linguistics, stylistics would have to be fundamentally reconceived. We postpone his radical critique of poetics to a later chapter, but we may note here that Bakhtin regarded poetics as grounded in the same concept of language that has informed linguistics and stylistics. All these disciplines are ideologies of language, and, according to Bakhtin, their ideologies, if totalized, are inadequate to their presumed object.

Bakhtin outlines his theory of language somewhat differently in different studies, depending on the problem immediately before him. In the Dostoevsky book (1929, 1963), he proceeds from the concept of voicing and the relation of speakers to their listeners and topics. The structure of this argument accommodates the book's broader concern with the relation of author to hero in the "monologic" and "polyphonic" novel. "Discourse in the Novel" (1934–35) discusses the orchestration of diverse ways of speaking in novels and therefore approaches language from a new starting point, "heteroglossia." As its title suggests, Bakhtin's late essay, "Speech Genres" (1952–53), primarily concerns the genres of daily speech and their relation to the genres of literary discourse. In "The Problem of the Text," another essay from Bakhtin's last period, language is approached with broader problems of cultural analysis in mind. Each of these discussions recasts a few concepts central to all of them: the nature of the utterance (as opposed to the sentence); the asystematicity of language; and the problem of "dialogization" or "double-voicing" (the terminology varies). If one imagines double-voicing as a center, one can picture Bakhtin's studies of language as different radii leading from that center.

Voloshinov's work on language, most notably his book *Marxism and the Philosophy of Language*, explicates a similar theory of discourse, and it, too, converges on a center that can be regarded as yet another variant of double-voiced discourse: the forms of reported speech. With due caution, Voloshinov's explication can be used to supplement Bakhtin's, so long as we keep in mind two key differences between Bakhtin and his associate.

First, whereas Bakhtin celebrates intense dialogization and double-voicing, Voloshinov, writing as a Marxist, describes such phenomena disapprovingly (e.g., V:MPL, pp. 158–59). The forms so central to Bakhtin's ideas of unfinalizability and so characteristic of his prosaic approach to the cultural world are regarded by

Voloshinov as symptoms of decadent "relativistic individualism" (V:MPL, p. 122). Voloshinov expects and calls for the decay, if not the abolition, of these forms of speech, and he believes that the triumph of the working class is the death knell for these forms.

Second, Voloshinov changes Bakhtin's theories by accepting his specific descriptions of language but then accounting for language so described in historical-materialist terms. Bakhtin describe language as not systematic; Voloshinov agrees, but argues that this asystematicity only leads us to look for an external system to explain it. That system is Marxism as Voloshinov understood it. Indeed, the reformulation of Marxism was central to Voloshinov's whole enterprise, as it was not for the non-Marxist Bakhtin.

Utterance Versus Sentence

One of Bakhtin's many objections to the Saussurean division of language into *langue* (the system) and *parole* (the individual speech act) is that this model leads to a fundamental misconception of the utterance. In particular, it endorses a traditional view that the utterance is an *instantiation* of the linguistic system, which in turn implies that utterances are mechanical accumulations composed of units of language (words, sentences, etc.). Bakhtin objects that although utterances do typically contain words and sentences, those sorts of entities do not exhaust the utterance's defining features. An utterance is also constituted by elements that are, from the point of view of traditional and Saussurean linguistics, extralinguistic.

Utterances are not the same sort of thing as sentences; there is no possible combination of words, sentences, or other linguistic units that can compose an utterance. We are dealing with entities that are different in kind. To offer a rough analogy, linguistics is in the position of someone trying to explain clothing in terms of fibers and shapes, but who has not based his or her analysis on the fact that clothes are designed to be worn, and worn for specific reasons (warmth, fashion, self-expression). Although the chemistry of fibers is certainly not irrelevant to a study of clothing, a study of clothing that either relied on fibers alone or treated clothing as an instantiation of fibrous resources would provide a decidedly odd picture of the product. Something crucial and definitive of clothing as a social object would have been omitted.

The sentence is a unit of language (in the traditional sense); the utterance is a unit of "speech communication" (*rechevoe obshchenie*). Utterances may be as short as a grunt and as long as *War and Peace*, and the distinction between them and sentences is not one of length. Even when an utterance is one sentence long, something must be added to the sentence's linguistic composition to make it an utterance. Someone must *say* it to someone, must respond to something and anticipate a response, must be accomplishing something by the saying of it. One can *respond* to an utterance, but one cannot respond to a sentence. A sentence that is assertive in form asserts nothing unless it is framed as an utterance; and, according to Bakhtin, it is the nature of this framing that is crucial.

The point is often overlooked because linguists sometimes choose sentences as examples and then, without taking account of their assumptions, imagine particular simple situations in which those sentences are utterances. Thus, they "smuggle into" the sentence characteristics of an utterance (PT, p. 123). "A great many linguists and linguistic schools (in the area of syntax) are held captive by this confusion, and what they study as a sentence is in essence a kind of *hybrid* of the sentence (unit of language) and the utterance (unit of speech communication)" (SG, p. 75). This confusion not only leads linguists to mischaracterize both sentences and utterances, but also blinds them to the real complexities of utterances and how they work. "One does not exchange sentences any more than one exchanges words (in the strict linguistic sense) or phrases. One exchanges utterances that are [partially] constructed from language units" (ibid.).

Sentences are repeatable. Sentences are repeatable. They may coincide like congruent geometric forms. They or other linguistic elements may be quoted, or simply appear an indefinitely large number of times in diverse situations—as simple questions, for instance, often do ("What time is it?"). But each utterance is by its very nature unrepeatable. Its context and reason for being differ from those of every other utterance, including those that are verbally identical to it. Two verbally identical utterances never *mean* the same thing, if only because the reader or listener confronts them twice and reacts differently the second time. Context is never the same. Speaker and listener, writer and reader, also change. People never respond nor are asked to respond in exactly the same way. No matter how many features they may share, two utterances can never share everything. Each is unique, and each therefore means and is understood to mean something different, even when they are verbally the same.

The reasons we speak, the very reasons texts are made, lie in what is *un*repeatable about them. The unrepeatable aspects of an utterance reflect our daily purposes, which are always changing, if ever so slightly. Or, in other utterances, "this is the aspect that pertains to honesty, truth, goodness, beauty, history. With respect to this aspect, everything repeatable and reproducible proves to be material, a means to an end," which is "the purpose for which it [the utterance] was created" (PT, p. 105). And purposes are never reducible to linguistic categories.

It is therefore necessary to draw a distinction between two kinds of meaning. In Russian, Bakhtin distinguishes between *znachenie* (which he employs to mean "abstract [or dictionary] meaning") and *smysl*, which he uses to indicate "contextual meaning"—or the sense of a situation. The former enables but does not exhaust the latter. Linguists tend to recognize only abstract meaning, and so collapse contextual (or real) meaning into abstract meaning.

According to Bakhtin, abstract meaning is "pure potential" to mean—but only when that potential is exploited for a particular purpose on a particular occasion is there real meaning. Voloshinov draws essentially the same distinction in different words. He retains the same word for the meaning of a sentence (*znachenie*, translated literally in the English version of *Marxism and the Philosophy of Language* as "meaning") but calls the real meaning of an utterance its "theme" (*tema*, an unfortunate choice because his book also uses *tema* in the more usual sense as well, e.g., the theme of a novel). "In essence, only theme means something definite," writes Voloshinov. "Meaning, in essence, means nothing; it only possesses potentiality—the possibility of having a meaning within a concrete theme" (V:MPL, p. 101). Or as Bakhtin puts it, one can "curl up comfortably and die" with the abstract meaning of a sentence (MHS, p. 160), but not with its contextual meaning.

Active Understanding: The Joint Creation of the Word

Corresponding to these two kinds of meaning are two kinds of understanding. "Passive understanding" (Voloshinov's term is "recognition") is what one uses to grasp the meaning of a sentence and is all that traditional linguists posit. But just as no concrete utterance can be exhausted by analyzing the properties of a sentence, so no concrete act of understanding can be exhausted by the concept of "recognizing" or "decoding" the sentence's meaning. Each act of real, "active understanding" is much more complicated than that. The listener must not only decode the utterance, but also grasp why it is being said, relate it to his own complex of interests and assumptions, imagine how the utterance responds to future utterances and what sort of response it invites, evaluate it, and intuit how potential third parties would understand it. Above all, the listener must go through a complex process of *preparing a response* to the utterance. These various elements are in fact separable only for purposes of analysis, but in essence are inseparable elements of any act of real understanding. That is, we do not first passively decode and then decide how to respond; rather, we engage in an act of active understanding, for which passive understanding is necessary.

Bakhtin criticizes the misleading aspects of traditional diagrams of communication, the best known of which is the complex "telegraphic" model formulated by Saussure and refined by Jakobson:

$$
\begin{array}{c}
\text{Context} \\
\text{Addresser} \text{------} \text{Message} \longrightarrow \text{Addressee} \\
\text{Contact} \\
\text{Code}
\end{array}
$$

From Bakhtin's perspective, there are many things wrong with this model. One immediate problem is that it represents a "message" as something formulated by the speaker, encoded, and then decoded by the listener. As we have seen, understanding is not merely a matter of decoding. Moreover, utterances are not really "sent" from a speaker to a listener, except perhaps in a purely physical or physiological sense.

Utterances do not just happen to be understood. In the Jakobson model, strictly speaking, nothing about the message would change if the addressee were asleep or entirely absent. But with actual utterances, that is not so. The process of active understanding is anticipated by the speaker; he counts on it at every point, and could not continue to formulate his utterance without counting on it. Indeed, his own utterance is itself the result of such a process inasmuch as it responds to previous utterances. Much as a painter may step back from his canvas and imagine how it may be seen, "the speaker strives to get a reading on his own word, and on his own conceptual horizon, that determines this word, within the alien horizon of the understanding receiver; he enters into dialogical relationships with certain aspects of this horizon. The speaker breaks through the alien horizon of the listener, constructs his utterance on alien territory, against his, the listener's, apperceptive background" (DiN, p. 282).

This process of constructing an utterance shapes everything about it, from its choice of words and syntax to its content and intonation. In other words, the listener (real or imagined) shapes the utterance from the outset. In contrast to reader reception theory, which is usually concerned with how readers interpret texts *after* they are made, Bakhtin's dialogic model represents readers as shaping the utterance *as* it is being made. That is why utterances can belong to their speakers (or writers) only in the least interesting, purely physiological sense; but as meaningful communication, they always belong to (at least) two people, the speaker and his or her listener.

To put the point differently: In Bakhtin's view, linguists misunderstand the question of "ownership" of the utterance, which they assign to the speaker. But the words and linguistic units themselves belong to "no one" so long as they are viewed as just linguistic units. And as soon as we consider the utterance, we encounter something

interindividual. Everything that is said, expressed, is located outside the "soul" of the speaker and does not belong only to him. The word cannot be assigned to a single speaker. The author (speaker) has his own inalienable right to the word, but the listener also has his rights, and those whose voices are heard in the word before the author comes upon it have their rights (after all, there are no words that belong to no one). The word . . . is performed outside the author, and it cannot be introjected into the author. [PT, pp. 121–22]

For similar reasons, Voloshinov compares utterances ("the word") to a "bridge," which depends on both sides. "In point of fact, *the word is a two-sided act*. It is determined equally by *whose* word it is and *for whom* it is meant. As word, it is precisely *the product of the reciprocal relationship between speaker and listener, addresser and addressee*. . . . I give myself verbal shape from another's point of view" (V : MPL, p. 86).

Applying this analysis to stylistics, we see that this discipline also fundamentally misconceives its object. In determining a writer's style, the stylistician typically envisages the situation as one of instantiation: how does the writer use the resources of the language? In later chapters, we will see that this model overlooks some key categories, such as genre, and leads to disaster when applied to novels. Here we may note that the model leaves no place for an active listener. In fact, an author's style is developed over the course of a lifetime, on the basis of constant interactions with others, which become part of the way he or she speaks and thinks. Each of these interactions is two- (or multi-) sided, as are all utterances. As Voloshinov observes: "'Style is the man,' they say; but we might say: Style is at least two persons or, more accurately, one person plus his social group in the form of its authoritative representative, the listener—the constant participant in a person's inner and outward speech" (V:DiL, p. 114). Bakhtin uses a political metaphor to make the point:

Style organically contains within itself indices that reach outside itself, a correspondence of its own elements and the elements of an alien context. The internal politics of style (how the elements are put together) is determined by its external politics (its relationship to someone else's words). The word [discourse] lives, as it were, on the boundary between its own context and another, alien context. [DiN, p. 284]

One might be tempted to answer that to resolve these problems one need only supplement linguistics with some contextually based approach, such as rhetoric, pragmatics, or speech act theory. Bakhtin's implicit reply, again, is that one must not just supplement but rather reconceive the whole question. That is because many key problems traditionally treated by linguistics change their character when one appreciates the dialogic nature of language. For example, the syntax of utterances, their "internal politics," are shaped by their "external politics," their dialogicality. Indeed, Bakhtin and Voloshinov argue, syntactic forms arise in response to changing dialogic situations.

Bakhtin was also suspicious of all attempts to supplement grammars of language with grammars of context, as speech act theorists typically do. Instead of realizing the important effect of extralinguistic factors on language, these theorists simply annex the extralinguistic and treat it, grammatically, as another kind of language. Rhetoric has indeed made contributions to the study of language as dialogic, but its failure to reconceive the very nature of language has blinded it to some central dialogic phenomena. To understand these phenomena, we must first explore what Bakhtin means by dialogue.

Dialogue

Language lives only in the dialogic interaction of those who make use of it.   —PDP, p. 183

Bakhtin used the term *dialogue* in at least three distinct senses, and considerable misunderstanding has resulted from their confusion. In Chapter One, we discussed dialogue as a global concept, as a view of truth and the world; we think of this as the third sense of dialogue. At present we are concerned with what we call the first sense of dialogue, according to which *every* utterance is by definition dialogic. Later in the present chapter, we will consider the second sense of dialogue, which allows some utterances to be dialogic and some to be nondialogic (or monologic).

To understand dialogue (in the first sense), it is necessary to recognize that dialogue is possible only among people, not among abstract elements of language. There can be no dialogue between sentences. An utterance requires both a speaker and a listener (or a writer and a reader), who, as we have seen, have joint proprietorship of it. In other words, a constituent, necessary feature of every utterance is its "addressivity" (*obrashchennost'*), its "quality of turning to someone . . . without it [addressivity] the utterance does not and cannot exist" (SG, p. 99). Purely linguistic elements lack addressivity.

Dialogue cannot be found, then, by looking at language (in the traditional sense). It is an extralinguistic feature of utterances, and so falls outside the domain of linguistics (PDP, p. 183). The whole complex "life of the word" that is Bakhtin's main concern therefore requires a new discipline, which will make use of the resources of "pure linguistics" but which will also fundamentally reconceive it, transcend it, and reflect upon its procedures. Bakhtin's name for this projected new discipline is "metalinguistics" (*metalingvistika*; the term has also been translated as "translinguistics").

Metalinguistic relations are no more reducible to logical relations than they are to linguistic ones. Like linguistic relations, logical relations are necessary but not sufficient for dialogicality, which uses them as "material." As linguists often improperly smuggle dialogical relations into sentences, so philosophers often smuggle them into logical propositions. But logical relationships (such as contradiction) do not become dialogue unless someone says something to someone else. Logical propositions may contradict each other, but only people can disagree.

Bakhtin asks us to consider two sentences: "Life is good" and "Life is not good." A specific logical relation exists between these two sentences, namely, negation. "But between them there are not and cannot be any dialogic relationships; they do not argue with one another in any way (although they can provide the referential material and logical basis for argument). Both these judgments must be embodied, if a dialogical relationship is to arise between them and toward them" (PDP, p. 183).

By contrast, let us imagine two specific people speaking the following two utterances, the second person replying to the first: "Life is good," says the first person; "Life is good," answers the other. From the point of view of linguistics, we have a repetition of the same sentence. From the point of view of logic, we have a specific logical relation, namely, identity. But from the metalinguistic point of view we have something quite different, the dialogic relation of *agreement*. The second person, from his own experience, confirms the judgment of the first, who has arrived at it by a different experience. One might imagine, for instance, that the second person means something like: "Even from the perspective of my life, which, as you know, has been filled with illness and tragedy, it appears to me that life is good, though perhaps not for the reasons you might give." What we have here are concrete relations between two people, for whom the resources of language and logic provide the material to enter into a relationship that is not to be found in the material itself, no matter how hard or systematically one looks.

Bakhtin cautions that it is a crude understanding of dialogue to picture it as "disagreement," and this crudity is only one short step from the outright mistake of reducing dialogue to the logical relation of contradiction. Agreement is as dialogic as disagreement. Agreement has countless varieties, infinite shadings and gradations, and enormously complex interactions. In *War and Peace*, Pierre Bezukhov delivers a speech to his fellow Freemasons and is dissatisfied not only with the disagreement but still more with the agreement he provokes:

At this meeting Pierre for the first time was struck by the endless variety of men's minds, which prevents a truth from ever appearing the same to any two persons. Even those members who seemed to be on his side understood him in their own way, with stipulations and modifications he could not agree to, since what he chiefly desired was to convey his thought to others exactly as he himself understood it. [Tolstoy, *War and Peace*, p. 528]

The idea that agreement can be full identity is utopian, which is why Pierre, at this stage in his spiritual development, falls into despair at the anti-utopian implications of his discovery. For Bakhtin, this anti-utopian insight is central to his "prosaic" sense of the world, and marks the connection between his dialogic theory of language and his prosaic sense of the world's unfinalizability.

Bakhtin cautions that dialectical relations, although often mistaken for dialogic ones, are fundamentally different. They are still essentially logical, not dialogical. If one considers two antithetical propositions, thesis and antithesis, yielding a synthesis, this entire process is still not necessarily embodied by anyone; and if it were embodied, it could easily be embodied as a single speaker's utterance. All this could be "united in a single utterance of a single subject, expressing his unified dialectical position. . . . In such a case no dialogic relationships arise" (PDP, p. 183).

Authors: Voice and Intonation

"Yes," said Mr. Casaubon, with that peculiar pitch of voice which makes the word half a negative.

—Eliot, *Middlemarch*, p. 194

In speaking of "embodiment," Bakhtin stresses that utterances must have "authors" just as they must have listeners. One can relate dialogically only to a person; there must be "a creator of the utterance whose position it expresses" (PDP, p. 184). Or to put the point differently, when we respond to an utterance, when we treat it *as* an utterance, we are necessarily positing an author, even if there really is no author. We may know that a given work was produced by a collective, by the effort of successive generations, but to respond to it we endow it with a "voice," imagine someone possessing the experience of those generations, speaking to us out of its wisdom (or folly). If we respond to a proverb (by denying its wisdom or preferring the insight of a contrary proverb), we imagine someone who might have said it, and may imply that the experience that led to it was partial: we treat it as a German or Russian proverb, say, and imagine the sort of "typical" German or Russian from whom it might have emanated. One can respond dialogically even to distinct styles of speaking if we imagine a "typical" speaker who would unself-consciously use that style. We may even respond to inanimate, naturally produced objects if we imagine them as signs that express someone's personality or voice.

The idea of "voice" is important because it immediately suggests "tone," another key concept of Bakhtin's. Even before Bakhtin turned his attention to language, tone was a central category of his thought. In his earliest writings, where the central category is the "act" (*postupok*) rather than the "word" (*slovo*), Bakhtin maintains that a constitutive feature of every act is its tone. In every act I impart something new to it, something particular to me. Tone bears witness to the singularity of the act and its singular relation to its performer: "Emotional-volitional tone opens up the locked-in, self-sufficient potential content of a thought, attaches it to a unified and singular being-event. Every generally signifying value becomes truly signifying only in an individual context" (KFP, pp. 108–9). Approaching the utterance in the same way, Bakhtin will later say that tone, in the form of intonation, is witness to the singularity of the dialogic situation and the particular addressivity and responsibility of the participants.

That "something new" which an actor imparts to his actions or which interlocutors impart to an utterance must always include an evaluative stance, which is carried by the "emotional-volitional tone" of the act or utterance. Since the past experience of each particular person is unique, tone carries an "imprint of individuality" (or, rather, individualities). The shadings of tone are infinitely complex and varied. No grammar of tone is possible; that would be a typical delusion of theoretism.[1] In his early manuscripts, Bakhtin writes: "Of course, it is possible to transcribe all this [individuality] in theoretical terms and express it as a constant law of the act; the ambiguity of language permits us to do this, but we will end up with an empty formula" (KFP, p. 111).

Thus, whatever else an utterance may do—refer, perform, question, command—it always evaluates. Voloshinov insists that "no utterance can be put together without value judgment. Every utterance is above all an *evaluative orientation*" (V:MPL, p. 105). It follows that any "disjuncture between referential meaning and evaluation is totally inadmissible" (ibid.). Bakhtin agrees, and takes one further step: evaluation always has ethical import.

Often tone is *all* an utterance conveys. A meaningless word or a mere interjection may be uttered simply to carry tone. Indeed, Voloshinov observes, "in living speech, intonation often does have a meaning quite independent of the semantic composition of speech. Intonational material pent up inside us often does find outlet in linguistic constructions completely inappropriate to the particular kind of intonation involved" (V:MPL, p. 104). And Bakhtin, in his last years, echoed the point: "To a certain degree, one can speak by means of intonations alone, making the verbally expressed part of speech relative and replaceable" (MHS, p. 166). Both Voloshinov and Bakhtin observed that people frequently have their favorite words (*eh, well-well*), typically lengthened or doubled so as to serve as a better carrier of intonation, which they habitually use to convey an emotional-volitional tone. Often, gestures serve a similar function, carrying a silent intonation (or they may be accompanied by an intoned word). Indeed, tone itself is a sort of gesture, and the two are typically fused. Such "meaningless" words and gestures may be complete, and highly expressive, utterances.

The Superaddressee

If one pays close attention to tone, another constitutive feature of the utterance comes into view. We have seen that all utterances presuppose and require a listener, a "second person" (however many of them there may be; the term is not to be taken in "an arithmetical sense"; PT, p. 126). The utterance counts on and is shaped by the second person's responsive understanding. But in addition to this second person, there is also a third person for every utterance, whom Bakhtin calls the "superaddressee" (*nadadresat*).

No author (or speaker) can ever count on perfect understanding by his listener, and so he cannot "turn over his whole self and his speech work to the complete and *final* will of addressees who are on hand or nearby" (ibid.). Thus, with a greater or lesser degree of awareness, every utterance is also constituted by another kind of listener, a supreme one "whose absolutely just responsive understanding is presumed, either in some metaphysical distance or in distant historical time" (ibid.). This superaddressee would actively and sympathetically respond to the utterance and understand it in "just the right way." "Each dialogue takes place against the background of the responsive understanding of an invisibly present third party who stands above all the participants in the dialogue" (ibid.). (We might view the superaddressee as a necessary corrective to a model of communication that—unlike the model of Jürgen Habermas, to take a close competitor—*refuses* to deal in ideal situations of "undistorted and uncoerced communication.")

Bakhtin gives no examples illustrating the superaddressee, but it is not hard to think of some. In everyday speech between two people, one might turn to an invisible third person and say about the person actually present: "Would you just listen to him!" Or one of the two may gesture: roll up his eyes or put his body into a questioning position, as if asking some invisible person for guidance in understanding the recalcitrant other. At times, we speak to someone as if our real concern is with a possible listener not present, one whose judgment would *really* count or whose advice would really help us. Stated more positively, the superaddressee embodies a principle of hope. It is present, more or less consciously, in *every* utterance. The superaddressee "is a constitutive aspect of the whole utterance, who, under deeper analysis, can be revealed in it" (PT, pp. 126–27).

Bakhtin adds that the superaddressee can be and has been personified in "various ideological expressions (God, absolute truth, the court of dispassionate human conscience, the people, the court of history, science, and so forth)" (PT, p. 126). But although these ideological expressions are projected, they must not be confused with the superaddressee itself, which is, strictly speaking, not an ideological but a metalinguistic fact constitutive of all utterances. Cultures, subcultures, and individuals may change their image of the ideally responsive listener, or they may have no concrete and generally shared image, but their utterances still presume this "third party." God may be dead, but in some form the superaddressee is always with us.

The necessary "invisible presence" of the superaddressee follows from the very nature of discourse, "which always wants to be *heard*, always seeks responsive understanding, and does not stop at *immediate* understanding but presses further and further on (indefinitely)" (PT, p. 127). It follows that there would be special terror in a situation where one knew that the quest for deeper and growing understanding was groundless and that the very thing we appeal to in a superaddressee is a fiction—as O'Brien convinces Winston Smith in *1984*. Discourse, aborted in its very shaping, would turn into an absurdity and a nightmare. In an allusion to Thomas Mann's *Dr. Faustus*, Bakhtin adds: "Cf. the understanding of the Fascist torture chamber or hell in Thomas Mann as absolute *lack of being heard*, as the absolute absence of a *third party*" (PT, p. 126).

In one of his few openly theological notes, Bakhtin comments on the need to be heard in relation to the need for God. If one thinks of God in terms of the superaddressee, God takes on a very special character: he listens, but he does not necessarily answer. He is willing to understand, but he does not require understanding in return. As Bakhtin comments cryptically: "God can get along without man, but man cannot get along without Him" (TRDB, p. 285).

Speaking About the "Already-Spoken-About"

Bakhtin's use of the term *third person* (or *party*) for the superaddressee is potentially confusing, because in his earlier study, "Discourse in the Novel," he used the term to name yet another constitutive aspect of every utterance: its "hero" or topic (corresponding

to the third person pronoun). What we talk about also complicates
the utterance and constitutes it dialogically.

We have seen that utterances are shaped by the anticipation of a
response—by the "not-yet-spoken" (*esche ne skazannoe*). They are
also shaped by previous utterances about the topic—the "already-
spoken." Of course, the topic of our discourse does not literally
speak to us, but as we speak, it affects us as if it did. The topic is in
effect a third *person*, and Bakhtin's rhetoric treats it as animate. We
detect here Bakhtin's conviction that embodiment is necessary for
genuine expression. In every utterance we enter into dialogic relations with our topic, with its hero, and the hero's "words" contribute to the tone, shape, and meaning of what we say.

No speaker is ever the first to talk about the topic of his discourse. The speaker, after all, is not "the biblical Adam" (SG, p. 93)
who names, characterizes, and evaluates the world for the first
time. Each of us encounters a world that is "already-spoken-about"
(*ogovorennyi, uzhe skazannyi*), already "articulated, disputed, eluci-
dated and evaluated in various ways" (ibid.). In the Jakobson model,
nothing essential would change if the speaker were the first to break
the eternal silence of the universe, but, from Bakhtin's perspective,
that is yet another crucial mistake of all models of that kind. Like
the active listener, the already-spoken-about topic is a category that
finds no significant place in the view of utterances as *parole*, as mere
instantiations of the resources of abstract language.

Every time we speak, we respond to something spoken before
and we take a stand in relation to earlier utterances about the topic.
The way we sense those earlier utterances—as hostile or sympathetic, authoritative or feeble, socially and temporally close or distant—shapes the content and style of what we say. We sense these
alien utterances in the object itself. It is as if the object were coated
with a sort of glue preserving earlier characterizations of it.

In using words and speaking about topics, we find them "already
populated" (*naselen*), indeed "overpopulated" (*perenaselen*) with
other people's utterances about them. Consequently, our speech becomes extremely complex. "No living word relates to its object in a
singular [and direct] way: between the word and its object, between
the word and the speaking subject, there exists an elastic environment of other, alien words about the same object, the same theme,
and this is an environment that it is often difficult to penetrate"; the
environment is "tension-filled" (DiN, p. 276). In this "agitated"
realm of alien words and value judgments, the speaker's word
"merges with some, recoils from others, intersects with yet a third

group; and all this may crucially shape discourse, may leave a trace in all its semantic layers, may complicate its expression and influence its entire stylistic profile" (ibid.).

It follows that words must "conceptualize" their object in ways that are anything but simple and direct. As we have seen, Bakhtin compares this act of conceptualization (*kontsipirovanie*) to a ray of light entering an "atmosphere" laden with value judgments, judgments that have been shaped by social and historical events and by the experiences of the speaker and listener as specific people:

If we imagine the *intention* of such a word, that is, its *directionality toward the object,* in the form of a ray of light, then the living and unrepeatable play of colors and light on the facets of the image that it constructs can be explained as the spectral dispersion of the ray-word . . . in an atmosphere filled with the alien words, value judgments and accents through which the ray passes on its way toward the object; the social atmosphere of the word, the atmosphere that surrounds the object and makes the facets of the image sparkle. [DiN, p. 277]

We may better understand the utterance if we recognize that crucial aspects of reported speech—the fact that direct and indirect discourse are utterances about other utterances—are present in every utterance. In a sense, all speech is reported speech. That is because any utterance, when analyzed in depth in its social context, "reveals to us many half-concealed or completely concealed words of others with varying degree of foreignness. Therefore, the utterance appears to be furrowed with distant and barely audible echoes of changes of speech subjects and dialogic overtones, greatly weakened utterance boundaries that are completely permeable to the author's expression" (SG, p. 93).

This account suggests some reasons why Bakhtin considered it conceptually disastrous to think of dialogue after the model of a script, "compositionally expressed dialogue," where one speech simply follows another. The complexities created by the already-spoken-about quality of the word, and by the listener's active understanding, create an *internal dialogism* of the word. Every utterance is dialogized *from within* by these (and some other) factors. Indeed, even a specific word can be dialogized in ways different from those dialogizing the rest of the utterance to which it belongs. In such cases, we sense that the word is somehow cited from another speaker whose tone is felt in it. In this case, not only is there the internal dialogism of the whole utterance but also a "microdialogue" in that word.

Words "remember" earlier contexts, and so achieve a "stylistic aura," often misconceived as the word's "connotations" around a semantic center. This aura is, in fact, the effect of manifold voices that do not reduce to unity or yield a center. In using a word, speakers may intone the word so as to question the values present in its aura and the presuppositions of its earlier usage. In other words, the word may be "reaccented" (as *sentimental* was in the nineteenth century). As they accumulate and come to be shared, reaccentuations add to and alter the already-spoken-about quality of the word. This process is an essential factor in shaping a word's evolution.

A word's memory and aura also contain the style and ways of speaking in which the word has figured. To understand Bakhtin's point about ways of speaking and their import, we must turn to another key concept, which he developed in the 1930's: "hetero-glossia" (*raznorechie*, literally "varied-speechedness").

Heteroglossia

We have considered so far Bakhtin's objections to the concept of *parole* and to the view of the utterance as a mere instantiation of the system of language. Both Bakhtin and Voloshinov also object stren-uously to the view of language as *langue*, as a *system* of abstract norms, and they indicate some of the crucial aspects of discourse to which this view blinds scholars. In "Discourse in the Novel," Bakh-tin attacks linguistics, poetics, and stylistics for misconstruing or insufficiently appreciating the fact that different people and groups speak differently. The problem is typically reduced to purely per-sonal idiosyncrasy, to conscious or unconscious error, or to dialec-tology. None of these approaches, alone or in combination, is ade-quate to an appreciation of heteroglossia's rich significance.

According to Bakhtin, language is *never* a unitary system of norms. On the contrary, in language, as in the psyche and every-where else in culture, order is never complete and always requires work. It is a *task*, a *project*, always ongoing and ever unfinished; and it is always opposed to the essential messiness of the world. In lan-guage, messiness is the result of the complexities of daily living, with all its unforeseen, small, prosaic purposes and shifts in mood and evaluation, which are not reducible to a system.

These "centrifugal" forces, which continually upset order, are not themselves in any way unified *as* forces of opposition. Those whose encounters with Bakhtin have been shaped by the idea of carnivalization or been mediated by a Marxist framework often misunderstand him on this crucial point. Centrifugal forces are essentially disparate and disunified; relative order may be produced among some of them, but the production of such order is itself a project. As we have noted, even the choice of a single word for these forces (*centrifugal*) may itself be misleading, suggesting as it does lines of force radiating from a center in an organized way.

Nevertheless, cultures strive for unity and order. That striving is reflected in the European regularization of national languages—in the writing of grammars and dictionaries, and in the defining of standard and nonstandard usage. Bakhtin does not mean to say that there is anything wrong with this effort. But he does mean to say that we must understand it for what it is—an attempt to create order by positing it. "A unitary language is not something given [*dan*] but is always in essence posited [*zadan*]" (DiN, p. 270). The essential mistake of philology, linguistics, stylistics, and poetics is to take as something real what is in essence an ideal, something merely posited in a social struggle for unity. The constructed system is reified—Voloshinov says "hypostasized"—and then mistaken for what language really is and for an account of how it really functions.

The legacy of theoretism encourages this error. We may see it, for instance, in all attempts, from Leibniz on, to construct abstract universal grammars and in all essentially Cartesian ways of approaching language. Philology's heritage of examining dead languages, where the traces of living dialogue are especially difficult to discern or are largely lost, makes it particularly prone to this sort of thinking. And philology, Bakhtin and Voloshinov agree, has had a profound influence on Western linguistic thought. Although they may not be aware of it, linguists reflect and tend to contribute to the "centripetal" forces of language and so misidentify as a scientific or descriptive activity what is essentially a polemical or political one.

Language, Bakhtin reiterates, is always language*s*. Not only are there always "linguistic dialects in the strict sense of the word (according to formal linguistic markers, especially phonetic)" (DiN, pp. 271–72), but, much more important, there are always many different ways of speaking, many "languages," reflecting the diversity of social experience, conceptualizations, and values. In practice, we are all extremely sensitive to this diversity, the importance of which linguists have not appreciated or have not devised adequate ways of registering.

Different professions each have their own way of speaking, as do different generations, different classes, areas, ethnic groups, and any number of other possible divisions. The important thing to understand is that for Bakhtin these different "languages" are not just a matter of, let us say, a professional jargon. In that case, the specialized vocabulary of the profession could simply be recorded in a dictionary, and the idea of a unified language would not be threatened. No, what constitutes these different languages is something that is itself extralinguistic: a specific way of conceptualizing, understanding, and evaluating the world. A complex of experiences, shared (more or less) evaluations, ideas, and attitudes "knit together" to produce a way of speaking. The term *srastat'sia*, meaning to knit together—to inosculate, or to grow together in the way bones grow together—suggests an organic process of blending separate entities. It is evidently chosen to avoid suggesting that these languages are systems or subsystems of the whole. Insofar as there is a whole, it is a growing together of numerous elements, which have themselves been formed by inosculation, that is, by a daily process of adjustment and growth.

We might also say: Each language reflects in its particular unsystematic clustering and clumping the contingent historical and social forces that have made it.

Attitudes and views of the world identify languages. Whatever linguistic features there may be are not themselves definitive (as a dialectologist might assume). They are the consequences, or as Bakhtin variously puts it, the "traces," "crystallizations," or "sclerotic deposits" of these attitudes—and beyond that, of the whole activity of living in particular ways. These activities are deeply creative, always reponding to the quotidian pressures and opportunities of life. And so, "discourse lives, as it were, beyond itself, in a living impulse [*napravlennost'*] toward the object; if we wholly detach ourselves from this impulse all we have left is the naked corpse of the word, from which we can learn nothing at all about the social situation or the fate of a given word in life" (DiN, p. 292).

The various languages of heteroglossia have their own ways of "accenting" and "intoning" given words, and there may be a tonality to the whole "language." But in using the inherited resource of linguistic experience (which is to say, other languages of heteroglossia), each way of speaking employs "a completely different principle for marking differences and for establishing units (for some this principle is functional, in others it is the principle of theme and content, in yet others, it is, properly speaking, a socio-dialectological principle)" (DiN, p. 291). It should be obvious, then, that a common linguistic methodology, a search for a particular kind of linguistic sign, would be inadequate for discovering even the "traces" of heteroglossia. For what these languages have in common—the only thing they all have in common—is that they are each "specific points of view on the world, forms for conceptualizing the world in words, specific world views, each characterized by its own objects, meanings and values" (DiN, pp. 291–92).

If we examine particular languages, we will see there is an astonishing variety of them, and, moreover, that there are languages within languages, languages overlapping other languages, languages of small social groups as well as large, languages with staying power and languages that quickly pass, leaving their values and resources to be reaccented by other languages in the making. Each academic institution, each class in a school, may have its own language, and not only each age but also each year, each "day." Language dates, and we can intimately sense its datedness. All these diverse groupings are more or less "capable of attracting its [language's] words and forms into their orbit by means of their own characteristic intentions and accents, and in so doing to a certain extent alienating these words and forms from other tendencies, parties, artistic works and persons" (DiN, p. 290).

If we consider particular words, we will see that there are no "neutral words," no "no one's words." Words characteristically function in different ways of speaking and are intoned and evaluated differently in each of them. Again we see how this process is impoverished by the idea that words (or their "naked corpse," as embalmed in dictionaries) first have a central denotative meaning and then peripheral connotative ones—or even by the idea that words are "polysemic."

Dialogized Heteroglossia

> It was one of Caleb's quaintnesses, that in his difficulty of finding speech for his thought, he caught, as it were, snatches of diction which he associated with various points of view or states of mind; and whenever he had a feeling of awe, he was haunted by a sense of Biblical phraseology, though he could hardly have given a strict quotation.   —Eliot, *Middlemarch*, bk. IV, ch. 40, p. 395

Because the principles constituting ways of speaking are so various, each of us participates at all times in several languages and their attendant sets of views and evaluations. We are all a specific age, belong to a given class, come from a given region, may work in a specific profession, and have developed private languages with unique sets of intimates; and so we speak differently on different occasions. For the given speaker, what is the relation of the distinct languages he or she uses to each other? Bakhtin's answer is that in real life heteroglossia is itself "dialogized" in various ways and to different degrees.

The concept of "dialogized heteroglossia" is often confused with the concept of heteroglossia, so it would be helpful to explore just what Bakhtin means when he says that languages may be dialogized. He clarifies his point by asking us to consider a hypothetical person, who probably could not exist: an illiterate peasant, for whom languages are *not* dialogized (see DiN, pp. 295–96). We may imagine that this peasant uses several languages—prays to God in one, sings songs in another, speaks to his family in a third, and, when he needs to dictate petitions to the authorities, employs a scribe to write in a "paper" language. Our hypothetical peasant employs each language at the appropriate time; his various languages are, as it were, automatically activated by these different contexts, and he does not dispute the adequacy of each language to its topic and task.

By contrast, we may also imagine that another peasant is capable of regarding "one language (and the verbal world corresponding to it) through the eyes of another language" (DiN, p. 296). He may try to approach the language of everyday life through the language of prayer and song, or the reverse. When this happens, the value systems and worldviews in these languages come to interact; they "interanimate" each other as they enter into dialogue. To the extent that this happens, it becomes more difficult to take for granted the value system of a given language. Those values may still be felt to be right and the language may still seem adequate to its topic, but not indisputably so, because they have been, however cautiously, disputed.

In fact, this dialogizing of languages is always going on, and so when words attract tones and meanings from the languages of heteroglossia, they are often attracting already dialogized meanings. Having participated in more than one value system, these words become dialogized, disputed, and reaccented in yet another way as they encounter yet another. This potentially endless process pertains not only to particular words but also to other elements of language—to given styles, syntactic forms, even grammatical norms. Complex interactions of this sort serve as a driving force in the history of any language.

We may contrast this account of the history of a language with the structuralist notion of systemic imbalances, continually correcting themselves and in the process creating new systemic imbalances, thus creating further change. "The history of a system is in turn a system," wrote Tynyanov and Jakobson in 1929; "every system necessarily exists as an evolution, whereas, on the other hand, evolution is inescapably of a systemic nature" (Tynyanov and Jakobson, "Problems," pp. 79–80). This insight, which was to prove central for Prague structuralism, led to descriptions of linguistic history as guided by laws of immanent evolution. Language preserves its integrity and systemic character over time by continually adjusting to changes and imbalances by means of new changes that restore balance, readjust the system, and may produce still more imbalances, which in turn serve as engines of future change. Saussure had argued that linguistic history was random, like a fortuitous change of rules in a game of chess; Tynyanov and Jakobson countered that such changes themselves produce adjustments in a systemic way. The concepts of laws, equilibrium, and dynamic system were central to the Russian and Czech models of language history.[2]

For Bakhtin, on the other hand, linguistic change is not systemic, but messy, produced by the unforeseeable events of everyday activity. Moreover, it is not the result of purely abstract forces (systemic imbalances), but of real people's actions in response to their daily lives. Least of all is it governed by overarching laws. For Tynyanov and Jakobson, outside disruptions themselves result from changes in other cultural "series," and so events that might at first glance seem random are really the result of systemic dynamics elsewhere in culture. According to these two theorists, apparent randomness really testifies to the fact that culture as a whole is a "system of systems." For Bakhtin, the attempt to explain away messiness by postulating still more systems and the higher order of a system of systems is at best like adding epicycles to a Ptolemaic astronomy and at worst a wholly unjustified leap of theoretist faith.

Voloshinov also rebuts a softer version of "abstract objectivism" (his term for the systemic view of language). He distinguishes between the "hypostasizing sort" of abstract objectivism, which insists on the objective reality of the system, and another kind, which does not. Instead, nonhypostasizing abstract objectivism maintains that even if language is not objectively a system, it still functions as one for each individual speaker. The position is an improvement, Voloshinov concedes, but it is still wrong (V:MPL, p. 67). We will see in the next chapter that both Bakhtin and Voloshinov deny that the psyche is a system in any meaningful sense. Consciousness, too, is a "tension-filled environment" of centripetal and centrifugal forces. It would be surprising if they allowed language, which for them is constitutive of all or almost all thought, to be systemic even for particular speakers.

According to Voloshinov, we can recognize why language cannot be a system for each speaker when we recall that we do not learn our native language (and we are always learning it) from dictionaries and grammars, but from specific exchanges in which we participate. As a result, the language we assimilate comes to us already dialogized, already spoken about, already evaluated; it is encountered and learned as something used and patched, as an aggregate rather than a system. As we master new words and syntactic forms, we do not strip them of accents and addressivity in order to systematize them. After all, when we ourselves speak we will make use of those accents. Words and forms exist in us as they exist in the social world, not as "naked corpses" but as "living impulses," with a memory and an activity.

Native speakers do not apply rules, they enter the stream of communication. To be sure, native speakers do internalize norms and they do become aware of some grammatical regularities, but they do not strictly speaking apply rules, even unconsciously. They talk or write, they use the resources of language to accomplish something. Rather than decode, they understand and respond. When linguists encounter an exception to a rule, and foreign language teachers present a paradigm with its exceptions, they may assume (and transmit to the students) that the exceptions are somehow not genuine and that there must be a higher rule to explain both paradigm and ostensible violations. And the linguists may indeed be right in many cases. But unless the exceptions are very numerous, it will often be economically wasteful of effort for the mind to make a rule for every exception. Only if one begins with the faith that behind all apparent unsystematicity there must be a system, is there any good reason to presume that a system of higher rules necessarily exists.

Moreover, the entire approach of abstract objectivism depends on speech being entirely a matter of language in the narrow sense. But language as it is actually used is not just affected but actually constituted by "extralinguistic" forces. To repeat, speech is always dialogic, and dialogue cannot be reduced to any conceivable linguistic categories; it is metalinguistic.

Dialogue in the Second Sense

We have seen that for Bakhtin all utterances are by definition dialogic in the first sense. Bakhtin also uses the term *dialogue* in a second sense that allows some utterances to be dialogic and others more or less nondialogic (or monologic). It is important to grasp these two senses of the term and to identify which one he has in mind on a given occasion.

To understand the second sense of dialogue, it is necessary to introduce yet another concept, which Bakhtin variously and anthropomorphically calls the "tasks," "aim," or "project" of the utterance. Roughly speaking, an utterance's tasks are the complex of purposes it is designed to serve.

Let us consider two different cases. We have seen that with the right sort of analysis, the words of all utterances can be shown to be cited or reported from other contexts. But we can also appreciate that when we speak it is often not part of our purpose for our listener to consider the sources of our words. We may want him or her simply to consider what we are trying to say, to regard the discourse as our direct, unmediated, uncited word—spoken without "quotation marks"—about our topic. We may contrast this case with a second one, in which the very same words may be spoken but we want the listener to hear them *with* quotation marks. For example, a speaker may be alluding ironically to what someone else, known to both speaker and listener, might say on the topic. The speaker may incorporate into his utterance characteristic expressions or intonations of this common acquaintance in order to distinguish these from what "we"—the speaker and his listener—would say. In the first case, the voices of others and the quotation marks are not part of the tasks of the utterance, or may in fact be directly contrary to it. In the second case, they *are* part of the utterance's tasks. Both utterances are dialogic in the first sense. But only the second is dialogic in the second sense.

Bakhtin argues that the tradition of stylistics and poetics derives from analyses of the first, simpler type of utterance (without quotation marks) and so is reasonably well adapted to everyday, rhetorical, and literary forms of that type. Utterances, of course, are very rarely pure, and so this form of analysis has shortcomings in dealing with texts that may be composed of both types of expression. Those shortcomings turn into complete failures in dealing with texts composed entirely or primarily of utterances that are dialogic in the second sense. In fact, we frequently use such utterances in everyday life, and the novel as Bakhtin conceives the genre relies almost exclusively on language dialogized in the second sense. In such cases, we may recognize why we need not a "poetics" but a "prosaics."

In Chapter Eight, we will consider in some detail how this line of thinking appears to have led to Bakhtin's discourse theory of the novel. Here, we would like to give some examples of the sort of discourse Bakhtin has in mind and some reasons why poetics, linguistics, and stylistics are less satisfactory than metalinguistics and prosaics for understanding the real life of language.

To paraphrase what we have stated so far, we may say that there are two basic types of discourse: single-voiced (without quotation marks) and double-voiced (with quotation marks). In the final chapter of the Dostoevsky book, Bakhtin refers to double-voiced discourse as the true "hero" of his discussion (PDP, p. 185).

Bakhtin's analysis in that chapter is complex and too long to summarize in detail.[3] For current purposes, we would like to indicate the basic logic of Bakhtin's discussion, which he often leaves unclear. To do so, it would be helpful to adapt his chart of "words" (or "types of discourse"—the Russian *slovo*, literally "word," is frequently used in the sense of "discourse"). We say "adapt," rather than "reproduce" or "gloss," because Bakhtin offers his chart (PDP, p. 199) as a summary of a lengthy discussion, and much detail included there may obscure his basic framework. Also, Bakhtin neglects to include in his chart some key distinctions present in his discussion and important for understanding the logic of his analysis. The following version of the chart will guide our presentation of Bakhtin's ideas:

Discourse Types

I. Single-Voiced Words
   A. "Words of the first type": Direct, unmediated discourse
   B. "Words of the second type": Objectified discourse (of a represented person)
II. Double-Voiced Words: "Words of the third type"
   A. Passive double-voiced words
      1. Unidirectional passive double-voiced words (such as stylization)
      2. Varidirectional passive double-voiced words (such as parody)
   B. Active double-voiced words

Bakhtin is primarily interested in the final category, active double-voiced words, because such discourse displays the most complex kinds of "internal dialogization" (in the second sense) and therefore most clearly indicates the limitations of traditional poetics and stylistics.

Let us proceed from the simplest to the most complex kinds of discourse and begin with words of the first type. In analyzing this discourse type, traditional approaches overlook its internal dialogism in the first sense, but do not overlook internal dialogism in the second sense—because there is no such dialogism to overlook. Discourse of the first type is monologic.

Specifically, discourse of the first type is "direct," "unmediated," and "referentially oriented" in that it "recognizes only itself and its object, to which it strives to be maximally adequate" (PDP, pp. 186–87). The speaker says what he wants to say as if there were no question that his way of saying it will accomplish his purpose, and that there could be no other equally adequate way. For example, members of a given profession discussing a professional problem may simply assume that the problem must be discussed in their profession's "language." They do not worry whether some other form of speaking might be better. If words fail them, it is because they need to learn some other terms within the profession's language, or because language—all of it, not just their particular language—must ultimately fail when applied to that topic. The possibility that another language of heteroglossia may be more adequate is not taken into account.

Speakers of "direct, unmediated discourse" also do not take into account the already-spoken-about quality of the object or, at least, not in a way that implicitly challenges the authority of their own speech. They speak as if there were no "spectral dispersion" of the word; they simply name their referent. Of course, under metalinguistic analysis their discourse would reveal the effect of other people's words about their topic and expose the cited elements in their own discourse; but these effects and elements "do not enter into the project that discourse has set itself" (PDP, p. 187). What we detect by analysis resembles "scaffolding, which is not incorporated into the architectural whole even though it is indispensable and taken into account by the builder" (ibid.). If the scaffolding were included in the architectural design—if the speaker wanted his use of other people's words to be detected—then we would have a word of the third type, a "double-voiced word."

Direct, unmediated discourse is the only form that "directly" expresses the author's "ultimate semantic authority." Of course, that authority is (indirectly) present in other types of utterances, but there may be no single compositional expression of it. In drama, for example, the author's ultimate semantic authority is to be found in the whole work, but may not be expressed by any character.

Bakhtin now turns to words of the second type, what he calls "represented" or "objectified" discourse. What he basically intends to include in this category is a narrator's representation of a character's words in a way felt to be somehow characteristic or typical of the character as an individual or a member of a social group. From the perspective of the character himself, his words belong to the first type. He is directly saying what he wants to say—referring to an object, giving a command, accomplishing a purpose. But in fact there is another "speech center" here, invisibly present but detectable by the reader, that represents the character's way of speaking and makes it an object for an audience, as it is not for the character himself. We may detect here a trace of Bakhtin's earliest author and hero scenarios, in which the created character lives his ethical life "unself-consciously," whereas the author imposes "from outside" aesthetic finalization on that life.

Since there are two speech centers in words of the second type, it may be hard to understand why Bakhtin nevertheless calls this kind of discourse single-voiced. He explains that no dialogic relations exist between the author and his character; they do not lie on the same plane and so they can neither dispute nor agree with each other. Of course, if the "monologic context" should weaken, if the voices should approach equality, then dialogic relations could arise, and we might have a different kind of discourse—either two utterances of the first type in dialogue with each other or an utterance of the third type.

The crucial fact about words of the second type is that the character's speech is not shaped by his or her *awareness* of a second speech center. The hero is alive and speaking in his or her own world. "Discourse that has become an object is, as it were, itself unaware of the fact, like the person who goes about his business unaware that he is being watched; objectified discourse [consequently] sounds as if it were direct single-voiced discourse" (PDP, p. 189). It should be remembered that a work composed entirely of this second type of discourse would have no direct expression of the author's ultimate authority to make meaning (although that authority would still be there).

Passive Double-Voiced Words: Stylization

In the third type of word, the double-voiced word, the sounding of a second voice *is* a part of the project of the utterance. In one way or another, for one reason or another, the author makes use "of someone else's discourse for his own purposes by inserting a new semantic intention into a discourse which already has, and which retains, an intention of its own" (PDP, p. 189). If we reflect on how much of our daily discourse alludes to or incorporates the words of others and on the extent to which the full panoply of dialogic relations seeks expression, we will immediately appreciate why the forms of double-voiced discourse are so numerous and varied. Changing social attitudes (toward authority, toward other people, and toward received truths, for example) are always generating new varieties of double-voiced discourse, which are consequently an excellent document of that change.

Double-voiced discourse can be either passive or active. In the passive variety, the author or speaker is in control. He uses the other's discourse for his own purposes, and if he allows it to be heard and sensed, that is because his purposes require it to be. In short, the "passivity" giving this class of double-voiced words its name belongs to the "word of the other," which remains a passive tool in the author's (or speaker's) hands. By contrast, in active double-voiced words, the word of the other does not submit so easily. It actively resists the author's purposes and disputes his intentions, thereby reshaping the meaning and stylistic profile of the utterance. The active type of double-voiced words is the more interesting.

Passive double-voiced discourse is in turn classified as either "unidirectional" or "varidirectional." The distinction pertains to the relationship between the speaker's purposes and the purposes of the other. Whereas in unidirectional discourse, the "tasks" of the two are essentially the same, in varidirectional, they are more or less different and opposed: as Bakhtin puts it, the author and the other want to go in different "directions." Obviously, this distinction simply names two poles of a continuum, and there are bound to be an indefinitely large number of gradations in between.

The exemplary case of unidirectional passive double-voiced discourse is what Bakhtin calls "stylization." The stylizer adopts the discourse of an earlier speaker or writer whose way of speaking or writing is regarded as essentially correct and in accord with the task to be accomplished. A critic revives a style inherited from a previous generation he admires, or a writer adopts a style marked as belonging to a particular earlier school because he has concluded that he agrees with that school. One might ask why this discourse need be considered double-voiced and dialogic in the second sense, if the two speakers want to do essentially the same thing. The answer is that, as we have seen, agreement, no less than disagreement, is a dialogic relation. There is a radical and qualitative difference between, on the one hand, one speaker being consistent with himself, and on the other, two speakers who happen to agree, each from his own perspective. Analogously, there is a difference between direct unmediated discourse and stylization.

The crucial point is that the stylizer constructs his utterance so that the voice of the other will be heard to sound within his own. If he did not, if he wanted his source to be undetected and constructed his utterance accordingly, the voice of the other would become scaffolding and we would have an utterance of the first type. But if he wants the voice of the other to be heard, and himself to be heard as agreeing with and perhaps even reinforcing that voice, the utterance becomes double-voiced.

In this case, the status of the other's voice changes. To appreciate the nature of the change, one must understand that the very act of agreeing with someone implies the possibility of disagreement. The speaker agrees with his predecessor, but is aware that not everyone will concur. The speaker has considered *whether* to agree with the other and has then decided, as he might not have, that the other's discourse is "right." In other words, the discourse of the other has been *tested*. It has passed the test, but the very fact that it was necessary to test it changes the nature of its authority. As Bakhtin explains, "a slight shadow of objectification" (PDP, p. 189) has been cast over the predecessor's style. What was once "unconditional"— which is to say, direct, unmediated, referentially oriented discourse —is now "conditional" (accepted because of specific conditions). In the course of being tested, it has been treated like the discourse of a character and could have remained as such if it had failed the test; that is why, even after being tested, the "shadow of objectification" remains on it. In short, stylization incorporates a dialogue.

Of course, over time, the dialogue may be muted and ultimately erased. The stylizer's "enthusiasm for his model [may] destroy the distance and weaken the deliberate sense of a reproduced style as *someone else's* style" (PDP, p. 190). When that happens, the two voices "merge," and only one is meant to be sensed. Instead of stylization, we then have mere "imitation" (in the narrow sense). Imitation in this sense is single-voiced. Conversely, imitation may over time develop into stylization. One may identify many intermediate stages from period to period; distance may grow or diminish and authority wax and wane. Metalinguistic and socially grounded literary history would pay close attention to this sort of change, which might otherwise be invisible.

Another topic for a new historical stylistics would be the relative dominance of direct discourse over stylization in a given period. Sometimes skepticism may be so central to a group's sense of the world that direct unmediated discourse, in which language is presumed to be fully adequate to its object, may seem impossibly naive. To avoid naivete, authors may cultivate various styles with "quotation marks," and use various forms of stylization in preference to direct unmediated discourse. For intellectuals, the present may be such a period, and historically there have been others. "Direct authorial discourse is not possible in every epoch, nor can every epoch command a style—for style [in this sense] presupposes the presence of authoritative points of view and authoritative, stabilized ideological value judgments" (PDP, p. 192).

Voloshinov, but not Bakhtin, regards epochs as decadent when stylization predominates over direct style. He maintains that pre-revolutionary Russia was decadent in this way, but expresses confidence that the triumphant proletariat will restore the direct, "categorical," "declaratory" word to all its ancient rights (V:MPL, pp. 158–59). Here we see a primary difference between Voloshinov and Bakhtin. For Voloshinov the central opposition is usually between the eternally true and the harmfully false. Bakhtin tends to favor the dialogic and to value the rhetoric of plurality and messiness. For him, the important opposition is between what is untested (or unquestioned) and what has been tested (or passed through "the crucible of doubt").

Passive Double-Voiced Words: Parody and *Skaz*

In contrast to unidirectional passive double-voiced words, varidirectional passive double-voiced words treat the discourse of the other in a critical or hostile fashion. The discourse of the other has been tested, and found not only wanting, but necessary to dispute. Parody is Bakhtin's exemplary case of this phenomenon.

As a double-voiced word, parody, like stylization, allows us to sense the discourse of the other. Unlike stylization, parody subjects the other's words to harsh treatment. Specifically, it "introduces into that discourse a semantic intention that is directly opposed to the original one" (PDP, p. 193). Parodistic discourse consequently becomes "an arena of battle between two voices" (ibid.).

Now, it is possible to disagree with something for many reasons, and so the parodist will indicate the grounds of his disagreement by making the objectionable aspect of the target's discourse deliberately "palpable" (ibid.). If he does not, the point of the parody is likely to be missed. For instance, the parodist may exaggerate stylistic features of the target that betray a set of attitudes the parodist finds objectionable. In other words, the stylistic outline of the other voice is likely to be felt more sharply (but not necessarily more accurately) in parody than in stylization, and the author's intentions with respect to the original are likely to be more "individualized" (ibid.). For this reason, and because disagreement may generally seem more interesting than agreement, more critical attention has been paid to parody than to stylization.[4]

In the course of his discussion, Bakhtin digresses to consider a vexed problem raised by the Russian Formalists, the nature of *skaz*. *Skaz* was the subject of a great deal of important Formalist work, and it has been frequently analyzed and redefined ever since. Roughly speaking, the term refers to the form of discourse present in such works as Gogol's "The Overcoat" (the exemplary case) or, to choose American examples, Mark Twain's "The Celebrated Jumping Frog of Calaveras County" and his "Story of the Old Ram," or Ring Lardner's "Haircut." The Formalists stressed two features present in this sort of narrative. The first, which links *skaz* to their beloved *Tristram Shandy*, is the scripted sense that the narrator is not in control and that the work is being created "in process" and without revisions. Thus, "The Overcoat" begins: "In the department of . . . but I had better not say which department. There is nothing in the world more touchy than a department, a regiment, a government office, and, in fact any sort of official body" (Gogol, "Overcoat," p. 562)—and so on, for another page, until the narrator starts all over again, without, however, canceling what he has written. Or, rather, not *written*, but *said*, because the second and truly important feature of *skaz* is that the narrative is oral. It is oriented toward the idiosyncrasies of oral speech, preferably in dialect. In *skaz*, according to the Formalists, the more idiosyncratic and markedly oral, the better.

Bakhtin objects that the Formalist treatment of *skaz* relies on essentially formal categories, most notably, orality. According to Bakhtin, many oral narratives do not sound anything like "The Overcoat." For example, Turgenev's stories often use oral discourse in a quite different way. In his stories, there "is an orientation toward oral speech but not toward another person's [distinctive] discourse" (PDP, p. 192), as there is in Gogol's fiction. In a third variant, Leskov's stories—cited by the Formalists as exemplary of *skaz*—use dialect only secondarily for its orality but primarily "for the sake of a socially foreign discourse and a socially foreign worldview" (ibid.).

In such cases, *skaz* is not "double-voiced" as it is in "The Overcoat." Leskov's oral narration is really composed of words of the second type—represented, objectified discourse—whereas the more interesting instances of *skaz* are double-voiced. In particular, they are examples of varidirectional passive double-voiced words. "To ignore in *skaz* its orientation toward someone else's discourse and, consequently, its double-voicedness, is to be denied any understanding of those complex interrelationships into which voices, once they have become varidirectional, may enter within the limits of *skaz* discourse" (PDP, p. 194).

Because the Formalists focused on linguistic rather than on metalinguistic categories, they ended by grouping together phenomena that are in fact quite different. Bakhtin proposes to distinguish "simple" *skaz* (using words of the second type) from "parodistic" *skaz* (using double-voiced words). From a metalinguistic perspective, parodistic *skaz* is much closer to double-voiced narratives representing written discourse than it is to single-voiced narratives representing oral discourse. "The Overcoat" resembles Dostoevsky's epistolary novella *Poor Folk* more than it resembles Leskov's stories or the speech and thought of Adam Bede.

Active Double-Voiced Words

Let us tinker with the notion of parody. Consider a case of parody, in which the author ironically cites and exaggerates the utterance of another. Let us gradually reduce the "objectification" of the target voice and allow it to *resist* what the parodist is doing to it. Allow the target to assert its rights, to aspire to and ultimately reach equality with the parodist. Let us imagine, moreover, that this gradual achievement of dialogic equality does not bifurcate the utterance, but takes place within the original single utterance. The utterance is still an "arena of battle," as it was before, but now the parodist is no longer in control. We keenly sense two voices and detect two accents competing for hegemony. "In such discourse, the author's thought no longer oppressively dominates the other's thought, discourse loses its composure and confidence, becomes agitated, internally undecided and two-faced" (PDP, p. 198). Par-

ody—a passive type of double-voiced word—has been transformed
into an active double-voiced word.

In fact, one can find many gradations between passive and active
double-voiced words. This distinction is one of several in which
Bakhtin defines opposite tendencies not in order to postulate an un-
bridgeable opposition, but in order to gesture toward the complexity of the space between.

Active double-voiced words are internally dialogized (in the second sense) to a great degree. If this internal dialogization is intense
and complex enough, as it often is in Dostoevsky, then there may
be too many competing and contrary intonations to be retained
when the text is read aloud. But silently we may still "hear" the
intonational play. Directors of plays adapted from novels may well
experience their greatest challenge in overcoming this difficulty.
Bakhtin is sympathetic to the problem of realizing multiply-
accented discourse in performance: "It is [sometimes] difficult to
speak it aloud," he writes, "for loud and living intonation excessively monologizes discourse and cannot do justice to the other person's voice present in it" (PDP, p. 198).

Bakhtin's first example of active double-voiced discourse, the
"hidden polemic," may clarify the basic features of this category. In
hidden polemic, the author's discourse is partially directed at its referential object, like discourse of the first type. But at the same time,
it seems to cringe in the presence of a listener's word, to take a
"sideward glance" at a possible hostile answer. It responds to this
anticipated answer by striking "a polemical blow . . . at the other's
discourse on the same theme" (PDP, p. 195), and so we sense that
the word has a double orientation. This double orientation is reflected in its style, intonation, and syntax. It will not be understood
if one treats it as discourse of the first type and focuses exclusively
on its referential meaning or ostensible direction.

In its basic features, this sort of discourse is extremely common
in everyday life. We see it in all those cases where a speaker uses
"barbed" words, words that "make digs at others," and "self-
deprecating overblown speech that repudiates itself in advance,
speech with a thousand reservations, concessions, loopholes, and
the like" (PDP, p. 196). Prosaic practices could be a guide to a metalinguistic perspective. All the more surprising, then, and all the
more indicative of the wrong-headedness of traditional stylistics,
that scholars have not appreciated the complexities of this phenomenon—as, indeed, they could not, so long as they thought of speech
and writing as an individual's instantiation of a system's resources.

If we consider literary speech, we will see that a certain element of hidden polemic must always be present in every style, if for no other reason than its sense of differing from some preceding style. But in direct unmediated discourse, that element of hidden polemic is not part of the utterance's tasks. The author does not mean for us to perceive what close analysis might reveal. But in active double-voiced words, the task of the utterance does include a sense of resistance by another and a sense of the speaker's preemptive response to that resistance.

If we consider rejoinders in compositionally expressed dialogues, we may sometimes find active double-voicing with a sideward glance. Indeed, to some degree, this phenomenon will always be present, though often only minimally. In most cases, the internal dialogism of the word is almost entirely dialogism in the *first* sense. Sometimes, however, the rejoinder in a dialogue may, like a hidden polemic, "cringe" in anticipation of a response and take a sideward glance at an expected answer. When this happens, the rejoinder becomes a type of active double-voiced word that Bakhtin calls "intensely dialogic discourse" (PDP, p. 197).

Or we may examine the phenomenon of "hidden dialogicality," which is related to but still quite different from the hidden polemic and from "intensely dialogic discourse." If we imagine a conversation between two persons in which the statements of one have been omitted in such a way that the conversation's overall sense is preserved, then the omitted speaker's words may have left deep traces on the speech we do hear. Its style may be shaped by the invisible other. In fact, a great deal of discourse sounds as if this process has taken place, even if it has not. In speech of this sort, "we sense that this is a conversation, although only one person is speaking, and it is a conversation of the most intense kind, for each present, uttered word responds and reacts with its every fiber to the invisible speaker, points to something outside itself, beyond its own limits, to the unspoken words of another person" (PDP, p. 197).

Having discussed the most general features of active double-voiced dicourse, Bakhtin offers a number of progressively more complex examples drawn from Dostoevsky's fiction. Each of these examples suggests further refinements, distinctions, and categories, too numerous to discuss here. But a few highlights are in order.

The simplest case is drawn from Dostoevsky's *Poor Folk*, an epistolary novel. In principle, of course, epistolary fiction does not demand a particular type of discourse, but the correspondents' sensed presence of each other makes the form well suited to active double-voiced words. When the young Dostoevsky took advantage of this generic appropriateness to dramatize the psychology of insult and humiliation, he arrived at a remarkable display of double-voiced words. In *Poor Folk*, the other's anticipated answer continually "wedges its way" into the letters of the impoverished and self-conscious hero, Makar Devushkin, and shapes their stylistic profile.

When Devushkin writes to his young and sentimental lady correspondent, he never ceases to consider how his discourse will sound. To an almost pathological degree, he continually anticipates replies to his statements before he has quite finished making them, phrases them so as to preempt responses he fears, and consequently betrays his fear—which he also cautions us to disregard. Bakhtin cites the following example: "So don't you imagine, my darling, there is anything else about it, any mysterious significance in it; 'here he is living in the *kitchen!*' Well, if you like, I really am living in the kitchen, behind the partition, but that is nothing." (Dostoevsky, *Poor Folk*, as cited in PDP, p. 208). Here the word *kitchen* bursts into Devushkin's discourse as the dreaded word of another, with its objectionable accent and overtones polemically exaggerated to discredit them in advance. We sense that Devushkin resents this word but also acknowledges its power, and his speech is shaped by all sorts of attempts to evade it and to prevent it from being uttered. If it *must* be uttered, then Devushkin wants to be its carrier and thus gain some authority by confronting the truth manfully: but the otherness of the word ever threatens an integrated style. "From this other discourse embedded in him, circles fan out, as it were, across the smooth surface of his [Devushkin's] speech, furrowing it" (PDP, p. 208). If one were simply to class this passage as "direct discourse" one would miss what is really going on.

Throughout *Poor Folk*, Devushkin chooses his words simultaneously from two distinct viewpoints: "as he himself understands them and wants others to understand them and as another might actually understand them" (ibid.). The second viewpoint leads to a third: how he would respond to the way in which another might actually understand his words.

When this process of multiple accentuation and double-voicing is intensified, it may produce phenomena even more complex and lead to constant shifts among "microdialogues." Virtually every phase of the text can become "interruption prone." Interruptions of this sort penetrate into "the subtlest structural elements of speech" and consciousness (PDP, p. 209); two voices interrupt each other "intra-atomically" (PDP, p. 211).

Dostoevsky develops this technique further in his next novella, *The Double*. By comparison with Yakov Petrovich Golyadkin, the schizophrenic hero of this new work, Devushkin is a model of sanity. Golyadkin's sense of identity is always threatened, and he talks to himself so as to simulate total indifference to others' opinions, which in fact trouble him very much. Thus, his inner "monologue" becomes long-winded and endlessly repetitive as he calms himself with reassuring phrases. Golyadkin continually caresses and comforts himself with a "substitute second voice" belonging to an imagined, charitable other. Indeed, this second voice often drowns out what real others are saying to the point where he does not understand them and replies in weird, inappropriate ways.

But created consolations cannot ever attain full authority; one's own fears and awareness of artifice will leak through. Golyadkin's substitute second voice often turns hostile and switches from caresses to taunts. Alert as only an insider could be to Golyadkin's sore spots, and probing them all, this voice mocks Golyadkin's feigned indifference to others and makes fun of his reassuring phrases. Golyadkin then responds by trying to hide from this hostile voice, attempting to bury himself in the crowd and insisting he is just like everyone else. In a single passage describing Golyadkin's thought, all these voices may answer each other with dizzying rapidity, thus producing an ascending spiral of interruptions, caresses, taunts, and evasions.

As if this complexity were not enough, Dostoevsky uses a special narrative voice to tell the story. According to Bakhtin, *The Double* is narrated with one of Golyadkin's own voices, specifically the substitute second voice that taunts the hero. It is as if the story were addressed not to us but, dialogically, to Golyadkin himself. The narrative we read seems to ring in Golyadkin's ears, driving him mad. Nowhere is Dostoevsky's "cruel talent" more cruel than in this taunting narrative describing Golyadkin's uninvited presence at his superior's ball:

Let us rather turn to Mr. Golyadkin, the real and sole hero of our true-to-life story.

The fact is that he is now in a position that is, to say the least, rather strange. He is here too, ladies and gentlemen, that to say, not at the ball but almost at the ball; he is all right, ladies and gentlemen; he may be on his own, yet at this moment he stands upon a path that is not altogether straight; he stands now—it is strange even to say it—he stands now in the passage from the back entrance of Olsufy Ivanovich's flat. But that he is standing there means nothing; he is all right. He is standing, though, ladies and gentlemen, in a corner, lurking in a much darker, if no warmer place, half concealed by an enormous cupboard and an old screen, among every kind of dusty rubbish, trash, and lumber, hiding until the proper time and meanwhile only watching the progress of the general business in the capacity of a casual looker-on. He is only watching now, ladies and gentlemen; but, you know, he may also go in, ladies and gentlemen . . . why not? He has only to take a step, and he is in, and very neatly. [Dostoevsky, *Double*, as cited in PDP, p. 218; ellipses Dostoevsky's]

In contrast to the example from *Poor Folk*, here the voice of the other predominates, telling the story its own way, swallowing up all other discourse. This other voice makes sure to include Golyadkin's own "self-assuring" words—he's all right, he's on his own—exposing them to ridicule, pronouncing them in a deeply mocking tone, teasing and provoking Golyadkin. This provocation is bound to be especially painful to the hero, because as Golyadkin well knows, he talks to himself in just this way and justifies himself before "ladies and gentlemen" without believing in his own justifications.

Thus, it is very easy for this narration to slide into Golyadkin's direct words to himself. "The question 'Why not?' belongs to Golyadkin himself, but is given in the teasing, aggressive tone of the narrator" (PDP, p. 218). Although quotation marks are omitted in the passage just cited, they could be supplied at many points. Indeed, the rhythms of the narrator's speech are so close to those of Golyadkin's taunting second voice that the author could in principle insert quotation marks almost anywhere. At times Dostoevsky does slide into and out of direct discourse, but in such a way that we feel the quotation, in effect, really began somewhere earlier. The *sense*—rather than the actual typographical presence—of quotation marks and their capricious or subtle distribution throughout a text was later to become one of Bakhtin's generic markers for the novel.

The Word with a Loophole

The famous, contorted speech of *Notes from Underground* is tailor-made for Bakhtin's analysis. All of the underground man's speech is actively double-voiced in an astonishing variety of ways. The underground man is always trying to elude the power of the other to define him and always trying to prevent any "finalized" image of himself from fixing. He therefore continually polemicizes with the impressions his words might make, and seems to mock and retract what he has said before he has finished saying it. He even retracts his own tendency to retractions, and ridicules in advance even his tendency to use preemptive double-voiced discourse. It is as if he understood all possible analyses of himself, including Bakhtin's, and was trying to disarm them, to stun the analysts before the words were out of their mouths.

Of course, as the underground man also knows, the very fact that he denies the other any power over him proves he acknowledges and fears that power. As a result, he does in his speech what he does with his old schoolmates: he purposefully tries to *show* them that he is *ignoring* them. Bakhtin analyzes the complex interaction of accents, counteraccents, and countercounteraccents in these passages. In fact, the underground man even seems to be addressing his entire dialogue with his imagined audience to yet another audience, the readers who "overhear" both sides of the dialogue. It should be no surprise that the underground man engages in hidden polemics with this audience as well; his discourse, as Bakhtin observes, is not just double-directed but triple-directed.

In his discussion of *Notes from Underground*, Bakhtin also introduces one of his most intriguing discourse types, the "word with a loophole" (*slovo s lazeikoi*). The idea of "loophole" goes back to Bakhtin's earliest writings, before the act gave way to the word. "I always have an exit along the line of my inner experience of myself in the act," Bakhtin writes of the "I-for-myself." "There is, as it were, a loophole through which I can save myself from nature's utter givenness" (AiG, p. 38).

The word with a loophole is thus not only a metalinguistic form, it is a whole ideology and view of the world. This ideology is also reflected in the underground man's "loophole consciousness" and loophole image of his body. Most basically,

a loophole is the retention for oneself of the possibility of altering the ultimate, final meaning of one's words. If a word retains such a loophole, this must inevitably be reflected in its structure. This potential other meaning, that is, the loophole left open, accompanies the word like a shadow. Judged by its meaning alone, the word with a loophole should be an ultimate word and does present itself as such, but in fact it is only the penultimate word and places after itself only a conditional, not a final period. [PDP, p. 233]

In *Notes from Underground*, loophole discourse is the desire for unfinalizability made pathological. The underground man may, for instance, repent or condemn himself, but he does so in order to provoke a denial from the other. But just in case the other does not dispute his self-definition, he leaves himself a loophole, so that if necessary he can say (as he often does): so you believed me! "Can you imagine that I am ashamed of it all, and that it was stupider than anything in your life, gentlemen?" (Dostoevsky, *Underground*, p. 51). The presence of the loophole can be felt in the tone of the initial statement, which has an element of exaggerated as well as authentic self-mockery. Contrary tones switch places without specifying which has the higher authority, and in such a way that the statement can be recharacterized in contradictory ways as circumstances warrant.

In discussing these examples from Dostoevsky, of which the preceding is only a small sample, Bakhtin occasionally cites Formalist work on Dostoevsky's style. He treats Formalist analyses as the best work possible within the tradition of conventional stylistics and poetics. As such, these analyses can sensitively describe syntactic roughness and distortions, but they do not deal with what is truly at stake. The Formalists cannot appreciate the nature of those distortions because their methods are not adequate for understanding the double-voiced discourse producing them. Without metalinguistic categories, the Formalists were bound not only to simplify the examples they cite, but also to miss all play of tone that lacks a specific formal and stylistic marker.

Voloshinov on Reported Speech

The Formalists were Bakhtin's most constant opponents in the 1920's, and they had an important effect on his thought. But there were equally important "friendly others" to whom Bakhtin was also indebted, specifically, the members of his own circle. Working with the same network of ideas that concerned Bakhtin, Valentin Voloshinov developed them in a Marxist direction. We will explicate Voloshinov's conclusions in some detail because it appears that the influence was mutual and that Bakhtin's works of the 1930's were shaped in part by Voloshinov's earlier contributions. In formulating his discourse theory of the novel, Bakhtin seems to have borrowed equally from Voloshinov and from his own earlier study of Dostoevsky. Bakhtin stripped Voloshinov's models of their Marxist framework, but retained many of the insights Voloshinov produced while generating that framework. Moreover, Voloshinov's discussion of reported speech (in Russian, *chuzhaia rech'*, "another's speech") is immensely interesting in its own right and worth discussing in some detail as a major contribution of the Bakhtin group.[5]

Voloshinov's *Marxism and the Philosophy of Language* was published in the same year as the first edition of Bakhtin's Dostoevsky book (1929). The third and final section of *Marxism* traverses some of the same ground covered in the Dostoevsky book, but from another angle and with a different, larger agenda in mind. Voloshinov's ultimate purpose is to link a dialogic approach to language to a dialectical view of history, a purpose completely at odds with Bakhtin's.[6]

We have seen that Voloshinov's evaluation of the metalinguistic phenomena he discusses differs from Bakhtin's. Voloshinov also outlines a rather crude periodization of European "ideology" since the Middle Ages. His four periods—"authoritarian dogmatism," "rationalistic dogmatism," "realistic and critical individualism," and "relativistic individualism" (V:MPL, p. 123)—are linked to historical materialist categories, and therefore suggest a fifth, unnamed period, initiated by the Russian Revolution (V:MPL, pp. 154, 159). Bakhtin would doubtless have objected to this scheme for many reasons, not the least of which is its homogenization of periods and languages. But whatever the crudeness of Voloshinov's periodization, his argument for a sociological approach to linguistic form and history is anything but crude. Although his account is not, in our opinion, as sophisticated as Bakhtin's, it offers numerous important insights.

To speak in the most general terms, Voloshinov contends that at any given time the resources of language—its patterns—exist only insofar as they are implemented by particular speakers. Crucially, speakers never just instantiate a pattern, they modify it (more accurately, they modify their socially shaped sense of it) in response to the pressures of ongoing social activity. As pressures change, so do the modifications; the more widespread and lasting the pressures, the more generally shared the modifications will be. Modifications repeatedly used become "crystallized" into distinct styles; and styles may in turn become accepted as grammatical norms. Grammar is nothing but style of very hard crystallization.

A continuum extends from the most idiosyncratic ways of speaking to the most incontestable grammatical norms. Movement along the continuum is shaped by the pressures of low-level social behavior and may serve as an index to social trends. Processes of grammaticization and "degrammaticization" are always going on in any language.

It follows that the difference between stylistic and grammatical norms is one of degree and not one of kind. It is therefore to be expected that debates will often arise about the status of particular norms and forms: are they grammatical or merely stylistic? According to Voloshinov, such debates are completely unresolvable in principle because they presuppose a hard and fast boundary between grammar and style, between the system and some uses of it. In fact, "the borderline [between grammar and style] is fluid because of the very mode of existence of language, in which, simultaneously, some forms are undergoing grammaticization while others are undergoing degrammaticization. . . . This is precisely where the developmental tendencies of a language may be discerned" (V:MPL, p. 126). The real significance of these debates is their symptomaticity: they call attention to borderline forms in motion and thereby serve as valuable documents of a language's history.

Voloshinov chooses to illustrate his social and historical approach to language with a discussion of syntax, and in particular, of reported speech. In choosing this topic, Voloshinov can immediately stress the dialogic aspect of language, because, after all, "reported speech is speech within speech, utterance within utterance, and at the same time also *speech about speech, utterance about utterance*" (V:MPL, p. 115).

Moreover, an analysis of reported speech could in principle be useful for understanding understanding itself. As we discuss in the next chapter, Bakhtin and Voloshinov describe thought as internalized dialogues, as "inner [dialogic] speech." Thought adapts the forms of social dialogue, which we subsequently learn to perform silently in our heads. Therefore, with certain important modifications, what we learn about dialogue will be important for psychology. The special importance of reported speech, according to Voloshinov, is that any act of understanding necessarily does something resembling reported speech. When we understand, we must somehow "take in" an utterance and prepare a reply to it, and so understanding must involve something like a citation and commentary—that is, an analogue to reported speech set in a reporting, evaluating context. Something akin to indirect discourse is also going on within us.

Voloshinov cautions that this analogy cannot be pushed too far because, after all, active understanding does not sequentially "recognize" and then "reply." The two actions are organically fused, can be separated only analytically, and must not be reified as distinct processes. Moreover, outer reported speech, as a whole utterance in which two speakers can be heard, must necessarily have its own audience, a third person to whom the report is directed and who therefore actively shapes it as it is being made. That may not be so in each act of inner understanding. Moreover, as the Russian psychologist Lev Vygotsky was to demonstrate, inner speech typically abbreviates utterances to a far greater extent than we can ever do in dialogues with real other people.[7] In spite of these differences between outer reported speech and inner understanding, the similarities are important enough for the former to serve as an important clue to the latter.

Authority and the Discourse of the Other

In part three of *Marxism and the Philosophy of Language*, Voloshinov deliberately avoids beginning his discussion of reported speech with a classification of its syntactical forms (direct, indirect, quasi-direct). Rather, he first discusses the attitudes and social values that have shaped these forms, and which may cut across them. His most general point is that different kinds of reported speech crystallize different sets of values and purposes with respect to the discourse of others.

For example, if an utterance is felt to be highly authoritative (Scripture, for instance), it will probably be cited in a type of reported speech allowing for little opportunity to express agreement, disagreement, or other personal opinions. There may also be a tendency to "depersonalize" and "disembody" the authoritative figure's speech, so that it is not perceived as merely one person's opinion. Voloshinov offers a number of examples, which illustrate that concepts of authority, attitudes toward personality, and ideas about social typicality may all shape the forms of reported speech that are used, modified, or created.

Voloshinov begins the second chapter of part three with a preliminary and rough classification of possibilities within reported speech (V : MPL, pp. 120–22). For the sake of clarity, it will be useful to represent this classification in a simple outline:

Styles of Reported Speech

I. The Linear Style (boundaries strong, personalization minimized).
II. Its opposite, the Pictorial Style (boundaries weak, personalization maximized).
   A. The pictorial style (report*ing* speech resolves report*ed* context). The extreme form of IIA is its "decorative" trend.

B. An unnamed subclass: the report*ed* speech resolves the report*ing* context.

It will be seen immediately why Voloshinov's discussion may be difficult to follow. The term *pictorial style* is used both for a class and one of its subclasses, the other of which is unnamed. Some terms are freely adapted from other scholars (*linear style* from Wölfflin). It should also be kept in mind that Voloshinov is defining trends, or poles of a continuum, not categories with hard and fast boundaries; and that many other continua describing important sets of attitudes are needed to supplement this one.

To explicate the outline: if a group approaches a class of utterances as authoritative and not to be tampered with, it will tend toward the linear style. The linear style constructs clear-cut outlines between reported speech and reporting context so that there will be minimal interaction between them. Also, the linear style minimizes the stylistic individuality of the reported speech in order to prevent audiences from regarding it as simply the product of a specific, therefore partial, set of experiences. Thus, the linear style tends to display "stylistic homogeneity" to the point where "the author and his characters all speak exactly the same language" (V : MPL, p. 120). Different periods may develop different kinds and degrees of linear style, which reflect the attitudes that have shaped its use.

The opposite tendency is the "pictorial style," which strives to break down or obliterate the boundaries between reported and reporting speech, the better to allow maximal dialogic interaction. The stylistic profile of speech will be emphasized so as to call attention to what style betrays about individual or social attitudes. Stylistic homogeneity will thereby be minimized.

There are two possible ways in which this pictorial process may take place. Control may belong either to the reporting or to the reported speech. In the first case, which is the easier to understand, "the impetus for weakening the peripheries of the utterance" belongs to the reporting author, whose "own intonation—humor, love or hate, enthusiasm or scorn" pervades the reported speech (V : MPL, p. 121). At its extreme, this impulse leads to a complete neglect of what the reported speech was trying to say as the reporting author concentrates entirely on its stylistic features. For example, characters in Gogol often utter entirely meaningless phrases except insofar as their style and choice of meaningless words betray something about them. Voloshinov calls this extreme trend "decorative."

The opposite kind of pictorial speech reverses control, so that somehow the reported speech "begins to resolve, as it were, the reporting context, instead of the other way around" (ibid.). The reporting author begins to perceive his own speech as "subjective," as typical of something, much as he might perceive the speech of another. In fiction, we see this phenomenon in various unstable narrators. Like Bakhtin, Voloshinov cites Dostoevsky as an example, and it is clear that he has in mind the sort of phenomenon that Bakhtin almost simultaneously describes more richly and more carefully as "active double-voiced words."

It would be worth noting a characteristic difference in emphasis between Bakhtin's and Voloshinov's formulations. Voloshinov, with his special interest in shared horizons and synthesizing dialectical processes, stresses how the elimination or overcoming of boundaries between speech acts facilitates complex communication. By contrast, Bakhtin tends to stress the importance of boundaries and of unmerged horizons, which provide the outsideness that ultimately makes all dialogue and all creativity possible.

Indirect, Direct, and Quasi-Direct Discourse

With these considerations in mind, Voloshinov turns to the broad categories of direct, indirect, and quasi-direct speech. Obviously, there is a relation between the use of these forms and the classification of reported speech trends just presented. For example, quasi-direct discourse (or "free indirect discourse") offers rich possibilities for weakening the boundaries between reporting and reported speech. It is therefore especially well adapted to the pictorial style, particularly its second variety in which the reported speech has the upper hand. Indeed, quasi-direct discourse may even have arisen in response to this very need. Nevertheless, no one-to-one correspondence can be made between formal and attitudinal categories. One can identify forms of direct and indirect discourse adapted to all attitudes. If we concentrate on the forms alone, we will miss the complexities and potentialities of their use.

It is also necessary to keep in mind that different languages have different resources available for transmitting speech, and that what grammar books often represent as equivalent forms in two languages may in fact do different things. According to Voloshinov, Russian displays "the unqualified primacy of direct discourse" (V:MPL, p. 127); other languages may have more richly developed forms of indirect discourse. Voloshinov claims as well that Russian is especially well suited for the pictorial style of reported speech, "though, granted, of a somewhat vague and flaccid kind, that is, without that sense of boundaries being forced and resistance being overcome (as in other languages). An extraordinary ease of interaction and interpenetration . . . is the rule" (ibid.). Voloshinov repeatedly cautions us against the tendency to treat forms of reported speech mechanically, as mere *forms*. We must think, rather, in terms of verbal interaction, of utterances responding to utterances dialogically, and of interlocutors orienting themselves, with greater or lesser ease, among the possibilities a given language offers for their adaptive use.

Different forms and styles of reporting speech might usefully be regarded as different ways of "hearing" another's words. When we use indirect discourse, we do not just apply a grammatical rule, we must necessarily *analyze* and respond to the reported utterance and show our dialogic relation to it. We may be concerned with different aspects of a reported utterance. Some forms of indirect discourse focus on the "content" of the original, a tendency that Voloshinov refers to as the "content-analyzing modification" (*predmetno-analiticheskii*, translated in V:MPL as "referent-analyzing"). These forms are well suited to discursive or rhetorical contexts where one is concerned primarily with explaining or comparing opinions. When they are used, anything not relevant to the topic— stylistic idiosyncrasy, pauses, disconnectedness—is not "heard"; or if the topic itself requires that such features be heard, they are turned into content and placed in the reporting context ("He said angrily that . . ."). Obviously, the content-analyzing modification accords well with the linear style.

A second kind of indirect discourse, which Voloshinov calls the "word-analyzing modification" (*slovesno-analiticheskii*, rendered in V:MPL as "texture-analyzing modification"), focuses on the "subjective and stylistic physiognomy" of the reported utterance, that is, on its emotive, socially typical, or personally characteristic features. A third tendency, the "impressionistic modification," is rather free with the reported utterance: "It abbreviates it, often only highlighting its themes . . . [so that] authorial intonation easily and freely ripples over its fluid structure" (V:MPL, p. 133). What one senses most in the impressionistic modification is the author's irony, his deft hand in abbreviating and reorganizing the material. Voloshinov offers these tendencies, described with examples, as illustrative, not exhaustive of indirect discourse.

One might at first imagine that direct discourse offers little possibility for dialogue and verbal interaction inasmuch as it quotes, rather than paraphrases, the reported speech. There are indeed many examples of such "inert" reporting (ibid.), which Voloshinov calls the "monumental style," but they far from exhaust the rich resources of direct discourse, which has numerous ways of creating dialogue. Russian and other languages possess "modifications which display a mutual exchange of intonations, a sort of reciprocal infectiousness between the reporting context and the reported speech" in both directions (ibid.).

Voloshinov relegates to a footnote some illustrative phenomena he finds too obvious to discuss in detail: the use of "sic!," italics that change the tone of what is reported, or interpolations (where the citation is interrupted with a framing comment, such as "he admitted") (V:MPL, p. 134, n. 5). He turns to more interesting examples, which recall Bakhtin's discussion of double-voiced words.

For example, in "prepared-for direct discourse" (*podgotovlennyi*, translated in V:MPL as "preset direct discourse"), the citation emerges out of indirect or quasi-direct discourse, which already colors it with the author's intonations. In *The Idiot*, for example, the description of Myshkin's thoughts on the verge of an epileptic fit is cast in quasi-direct discourse, which shades into and out of direct discourse. We move from complex and deeply dialogic paraphrases of Myshkin's conversations with others and with himself to direct quotations not clearly distinct from their surrounding context. (We have already seen a similar phenomenon in Bakhtin's discussion of *The Double*.)

Voloshinov compares another modification, "materially realized [*oveshchestvlennyi*] direct discourse," to a comic act in which a comedian's makeup, costume, gestures, and bearing make us ready to laugh at his words before he says them. According to Voloshinov, Gogol and the early Dostoevsky were masters of this technique.

His most interesting and complex example, "anticipated and dispersed reported speech," involves the report*ed* speech infiltrating the report*ing* context with its accents, typical words, and tones. In this case, the reporter's own speech begins to sound as if it were somehow reported. For example, a story's narrator may so admire a character that his speech becomes saturated with the character's way of speaking. Voloshinov chooses an example from the beginning of Dostoevsky's "A Nasty Story":

Once in winter, on a cold and frosty evening—very late, rather, it being already the twelfth hour—three *extremely distinguished* gentlemen were sitting in a *comfortable*, even sumptuously appointed, room inside a *handsome* two-storey house on Petersburg Island and were occupied in *weighty* and *superlative* talk on an *extremely remarkable* topic. All three gentlemen were officials of the rank of general. They were seated around a small table, each in a *handsome* upholstered chair, and during pauses in the conversation they *comfortably* sipped champagne. [Dostoevsky, "Nasty Story," as cited in V:MPL, p. 135; italics Voloshinov's]

Unless one understands what is happening here, Voloshinov observes, the passage will seem extraordinarily banal, with its constant repetition of overblown and uninformative words. But as the story progresses, it becomes clear retrospectively that this and similar examples of the narrator's speech are infected with a pompous character's speech. We detect in the narrator's speech "anticipated and dispersed [*predvoskhishchennyi i rasseiannyi*] direct discourse." One could easily put the words Voloshinov italicizes in quotation marks because they are the sort of words a character uses. If Dostoevsky does not use quotation marks, that is because these are also the narrator's words; the narrator speaks naturally in just this way, incorporating the words and worldviews of those upon whom he fawns. To be sure, the narrator is a bad imitator, overdoes it, and so exposes both himself and his model to an irony he does not sense.

In each of these examples, given words and phrases come to serve "two masters, participating simultaneously in two speech acts" (V:MPL, p. 137). Voloshinov names this phenomenon "speech interference"; it is clearly a version of what Bakhtin calls "double-voiced discourse."

After offering several other varieties of direct discourse that are anything but "inert," Voloshinov turns to quasi-direct discourse. He chooses this designation, his rendition of the German *uneigentliche direkte Rede*, over *style indirect libre* or "free indirect discourse," because it seems to bring along with it the least amount of objectionable theory. The theory Voloshinov wants to avoid is mechanical and based on abstract grammatical forms.

Quasi-direct discourse has often been described as "a mixture of direct and indirect discourse." Alternatively, it is identified as reported speech in which grammatically it is the author who speaks whereas according to sense and general orientation it is the character who speaks. Voloshinov considers the first of these two descriptions objectionable because it implies a thoroughly mechanical origin—two received forms "mixed" or pasted together. The second might serve as a good mnemonic device, but misses what is really going on here, namely, the creation of new ways to dialogize utterances. Quasi-direct discourse offers especially interesting ways of allowing reported and reporting contexts to interpenetrate.

Voloshinov devotes most of his discussion to refuting "mechanical approaches" and, finally, to expressing discomfort with the "relativistic individualism" such forms convey. Therefore, he is rather short on examples and illustrative varieties. Some may be found in the course of Bakhtin's discussion of double-voicing in the Dostoevsky book. In "Discourse in the Novel," Bakhtin discusses reported speech in much greater detail, as we will see in Chapter Eight.

Given and Created

Both Bakhtin and Voloshinov contest the equation of utterance with instantiation, maintain that language is fundamentally dialogic, and attack the notion that language is somehow a system, whether closed or open, static or dynamic. For them, language is not an autonomous or semiautonomous whole that *comes to interact* with extralinguistic forces. Rather, extralinguistic forces are *constitutive* of language and of its history. Thus, language must be understood from a "metalinguistic" (Voloshinov says "sociological") perspective.[8]

In contrast to Voloshinov, Bakhtin does not try to explain this asystematicity in terms of some other system, whether historical materialism or any other. From the standpoint of prosaics, the messiness of the world is fundamental.

In his theories of language, culture, and the psyche, Bakhtin opposes the impulse of theoretism to reduce human actions to a set of causal rules that produced them. Rules exist, of course, but their domain is limited, and they must not be understood as potentially explaining everything. If they did, there would be no room for human agency, for people to create themselves and their world. To stress this point, Bakhtin draws a distinction between the "given" [*dan*] and the "created" [*sozdan*], a distinction not to be confused with that between the "given" and the "posited" discussed above.

The given, which is all the theoretists see, is the "material," the resources, with which we speak and act. It includes our language, cultural norms, personal history—in short, everything already finalized for us. But an utterance or an action is never just the "product" of what is given. "It always creates something that never existed before, something absolutely new and unrepeatable. . . . What is given is completely transformed in what is created" (PT, pp. 119–20).

Of course, it is easier to study what is given than what is created, to reduce a work to the things that made it possible. But to stop at the given is to live in a world where everything is prefabricated, "ready-made," but in which no one genuinely does or creates anything:

An object is ready-made, the linguistic means for its depiction are ready-made, the artist himself is ready-made, and his world view is ready-made. And here with ready-made means, in light of a ready-made world view, the ready-made poet reflects a ready-made object. But in fact the object is created in the process of creativity, as are the poet himself, his world view, and his means of expression. [PT, p. 120]

We are always creating ourselves and our world. Prosaically, moment to moment, our actions matter and have moral value. We may detect a deep, organic connection between Bakhtin's approach to ethics and his theories of language. Just as utterances are unrepeatable, so actions can be performed once and only once by a given person (KFP, p. 112). Neither speech nor ethical action can ever be merely an instantiation of rules.

5

Psychology: Authoring a Self

> The problem of the soul . . . cannot be a problem in psychology, a science that is non-evaluative and causal, because the soul—although it develops and comes to be in time—is a whole that is individual, evaluative, and free.　　　　—AiG, p. 89

In the preceding chapter we examined Bakhtin's and Voloshinov's theories of language. We now turn to a closely connected topic, their theories of the self. Long before he turned his attention to language, Bakhtin was concerned with the nature of selfhood and, in his early manuscripts, he developed a number of concepts he was to rethink and reaccentuate throughout his life. When during his second and third periods language became central to his thought, he formulated a metalinguistic model of selfhood in terms of inner speech and in so doing integrated his earlier ideas into a new framework.

Presenting a picture of Bakhtin's views of the self entails special difficulties, because so many earlier accounts—including our own—have been based on the belief that Voloshinov's book on Freud and his comments on psychology in *Marxism and the Philosophy of Language* belong to Bakhtin. The assumption that Bakhtin is the real author of Voloshinov's two books has worked not only to refashion Bakhtin into a Marxist, but has also obscured Bakhtin's own subtler polemic against Freudian-style thought. It has also worked to veil the weaknesses and strengths of Voloshinov's contribution. Perhaps the most difficult part of writing the present book was the task of rethinking the discrete contributions of Bakhtin, Medvedev, and Voloshinov without conflating them into one, as we had on earlier occasions.

To suggest the logic and genesis of Bakhtin's ideas on selfhood, we will proceed chronologically. Because Bakhtin's earliest manuscripts are still almost unknown and because their central concerns were continually modified, we devote considerable attention to

Bakhtin's starting point, especially his essay "Author and Hero." In our consideration of Bakhtin's second period, we also discuss Voloshinov's rather disappointing tract against Freud and his much more successful comments on inner speech in his book on language. Comparisons are drawn with the work of the developmental psychologist Lev Vygotsky, especially with his provocative contributions to a theory of psychic life as inner speech.

In what we have called the first phase of Bakhtin's third period, he developed his own and Voloshinov's ideas on inner speech into some remarkable models for exploring the ways people use the resources of language to shape selves. We call this approach to the self "novelistic" because it is intimately related to Bakhtin's discourse theory of the novel, it makes the novel the richest form yet devised for understanding selves, and it in fact appears as a lengthy digression in "Discourse in the Novel."

In the second phase of his third period, Bakhtin developed views whose origins can indeed be traced to earlier ideas, but which nevertheless differ from them radically in tone, content, and spirit. In this phase, Bakhtin attempted to imagine unfinalizability independent of his other two global ideas and, in the process, he proposed a model of the "carnivalistic" self. As in his first period, he paid particular attention to the body as a determinant of selfhood, but his conclusions were almost unrecognizably different. In his final period, Bakhtin returned to the precarnivalistic perspective, and at the time of his death appeared to be reintegrating ideas from all stages of his thought. It is worth noting that many of Bakhtin's most challenging ideas on selfhood were developed in the course of his studies of polyphony, chronotope, and other topics related to the general theory of the novel and its depiction of "the image of a person," which we describe elsewhere in this volume.

The Context of the 1920's

Like so many other areas of intellectual life, the study of psychology in the Soviet Union was much more diverse in the 1920's than it was soon to become.[1] There were vigorous public debates over "idealist" and "behaviorist" approaches, the value and dangers of reductionism, and the relation of Marxism to particular schools of psychology and to psychology as a discipline. The Moscow Psychological Society, in existence from 1885 to 1922, counted among its active members not only psychiatrists and psychologists but also speculative philosophers. Although Pavlov's international fame earned him a special place in the Russian context, he was far from unchallenged.

In light of later events, it is important to stress that Freud had not yet been decisively rejected by the Party and that lively debate centered on his views. To be sure, *Civilization and Its Discontents*, with its explicit criticism of Bolshevism and the view of human nature on which it rests, had still not been written. Other writings of Freud, however, had been widely known in intellectual circles in Odessa and Moscow since the turn of the century, and his major works were rapidly translated into Russian. The Russian Psychoanalytic Society, founded in 1910, remained active until Leon Trotsky (who had offered a qualified defense of Freud) was expelled from the Soviet Union in 1927.

Freud was not yet perceived as necessarily inimical to Marxism. Some considered his ideas compatible with dialectical materialism. Regarding his system as a victory for "determinism," they viewed his displacement of the ego as a strike at bourgeois individualism. More recent Western attempts to construct a combined Freudian-Marxist discourse at times seem to reenact these earlier Russian discussions. In his early book *Psychology and Marxism* (1925), for example, Alexander Luria stressed the compatibility of the two systems: both were monist, materialist, antibehavioralist, hospitable to clinical experiment, and reassuringly "scientific" rather than speculative or mystical (or so it seemed to Luria). The very possibility of such discussions, of course, points to the relative flexibility of Soviet Marxism and the relative openness of debates about its more general applicability. Marxists of this kind tended to emphasize process, change, and interaction between organism and environment. This state of affairs would soon contrast painfully with the extreme rigidity and dogmatism of the Stalinist period. In the 1920's, Voloshinov might reasonably have hoped that his flexible and sophisticated Marxism could prove persuasive in official circles; such hopes would have been entirely chimerical in the decades to follow.

Bakhtin's concerns intersect with controversial questions of his time, but in the 1920's he did not engage in direct debate with psychologists, as did Voloshinov. For Bakhtin, the problem of the self was not strictly a psychological problem but more broadly and loosely a philosophical one. In his Dostoevsky book, he cites with approval Dostoevsky's assertion that, in spite of all the psychological insight of his novels, he was *not* a psychologist—a line Bakhtin interprets as an attack on those who would account for human thought and action causally. Bakhtin cites as exemplary Lise's observation in *The Brothers Karamazov* that Alyosha's analysis of Snegir-yov is, however subtle and well founded, fundamentally wrong in spirit because Alyosha is so *certain* about Snegiryov's motives and actions. Such certainty denies a person's freedom of response. For Bakhtin, as for Dostoevsky in Bakhtin's reading of him, a rich understanding of selves must begin with a sense of people as free and morally responsible agents who are truly unfinalizable.

Bakhtin differs from Freud, then, not only on particular doc-trines about the mind but in the very spirit of their enterprise. The "determinist" approach to the mind that made some Russians adum-brate a synthesis of Freudianism and Marxism marked Bakhtin's dislike of both. The fact that both unabashedly presented them-selves as systems—forms of theoretism—undoubtedly also made Bakhtin suspicious of them, as he was of Formalism and, later, of structuralism.

Beyond these differences in spirit and tone, we may note one other crucial difference between Bakhtin's and Freud's many ap-proaches to the mind. Bakhtin's theories studiously avoid invoking an unconscious as Freud understood it. To be sure, Bakhtin, like Voloshinov and Vygotsky, did not believe—and who ever has?—that we are fully aware of the implications of our actions and that everything we do or think emerges from the center of our atten-tion. But rather than invoking an unconscious, these Russian think-ers were more likely to turn to the dynamics of memory and habit (as psychologists from the associationists to the cognitivists have done). Most important, they resisted the notion of a separate and inaccessible structure out of which our impulses, fears, and sur-prises come, and argued instead for a richer, more varied, and more diverse picture of *consciousness*.

Where Freud describes a conflict between the conscious and the unconscious, Voloshinov (in the 1920's) and Bakhtin (in the 1920's and 1930's) describe a complex dialogue among the numerous, di-verse, socially heteroglot voices present in inner speech. Basically, their contention is that thinkers turn to an unconscious when they have an extraordinarily impoverished idea of consciousness. As Bakhtin was to write in the early 1960's in his notes for reworking the Dostoevsky book, "consciousness is much more terrifying than any unconscious complexes" (TRDB, p. 288).

Curiously enough, both Bakhtin and Freud invoke Dostoevsky as an illustration of their very different theories of the mind. It was almost as if an explanation of Dostoevsky's characters was a nec-essary test for any psychological theory to pass. This is under-

standable: Dostoevsky's novels contain sufficient support for a
Freudian theory of the unconscious as well as for a description of
the mind in terms of inner speech. But in invoking Dostoevsky,
each thinker tends to overlook crucial aspects of Dostoevsky's
works, Freud reacting with bemused dismay to Dostoevsky's invo-
cations of a theologically based human freedom, and Bakhtin offering a rather benign account of all those perversities that we now call
"Dostoevskian."[2]

Act and Self

Bakhtin's earliest extant writings, as we have seen, are concerned
largely with ethical questions. Two such questions are of special
relevance to an understanding of his theories of the self: How is the
self constituted as an entity that performs responsible acts in the
world? How does my "I" and the acts it performs fit into culture
understood as a whole? According to Bakhtin in his early period,
the crisis facing the philosophy of his day was in essence a crisis in
understanding the nature of the act (KFP, pp. 95–97).

Bakhtin sees the roots of this crisis in a tendency to split the act
in two, into its meaning or content (perceived as objective and
transhistorical) and into the subjective process of carrying it out.
Later in his career, he would raise a similar objection to the Saussurean division of language into its abstract system of rules and
their individual instantiation. Such binary divisions, Bakhtin contends, may be useful for certain analytic purposes, but are fundamentally misleading as a description of language or action as a
whole. Thinkers in this tradition tend to regard language or action
as combinations of the analytic categories that they have themselves
created by an act of abstraction; they then lose their way in endless
discussions about how these hypostasized entities, which they have
mistaken as primary and as existing, may interact. In the late 1920's
and the 1930's, Bakhtin was to argue that this division of language
transcribes away its real life. In the same way, Bakhtin argues in the
early 1920's that reigning philosophies of action transcribe away the
essence of the act and the eventness of events by similar kinds of
analytic division that "absolutize the derivative" and misrepresent
the original phenomenon.[3]

For Bakhtin, as we recall, such errors are the natural consequence of theoretism and its tendency to think away particulars.[4] It
is a sad "legacy of rationalism [and theoretism], that truth can only
be the sort of truth that is put together out of general moments,

that the truth of a proposition is precisely what is repeatable and constant in it" (KFP, p. 110). When opposite derivatives (*langue* and *parole*, or social and individual) are absolutized, the temptation is to ignore or resolve away one or the other category. Some thinkers will resolve the individual entirely into the social, some the reverse. In Bakhtin's early manuscripts, Kant's ethics serves as an example of emphasis on the general; for Bakhtin, morality must be a matter of "the historical concreteness of the individual fact, and not . . . the theoretical truth of a proposition" (KFP, p. 84).

Moreover, all of us, as constant participants in the "event of being," are always aware of the inevitable concreteness of decisions for which no set or sets of timeless rules are adequate. Understanding the self as a person who acts and who faces ethical choices involves understanding the self at particular moments and in unrepeatable circumstances.

This summary might suggest that Bakhtin would have been sympathetic to Henri Bergson, whose basic ideas he knew: Bergson as the celebrator of open-ended flow, champion of intuition against the disembodied workings of "spatialized" intellect, and proponent of the creative capacities of time. Bakhtin seems to take this overall compatibility for granted, in much the same way that he does not bother to comment on the ways in which his approach does resemble Kant's. He focuses instead on his differences from Bergson, whom he appears to view as someone who repeats the errors of theoretism by inverting them—that is, as someone who accepts the hypostasizing division of acts into abstractions and instantiations even if he privileges the instantiation.

According to Bakhtin, Bergson is "methodologically inconsistent" in opposing intuition to rational cognition (KFP, pp. 91–92). For in the process, the concept of intuition—which fuses the theoretical and the aesthetic—remains abstract, and so does not permit the self access to the real "event of being" (KFP, p. 95). In Bakhtin's view, both components of intuition are impoverished. A theoretical transcription of an act merely relates it to preexisting moral norms, an aesthetic expression of an act releases it from real responsibility to the future, and no combination of the two can commit the self to risk-laden moral work.

In the course of his dicussion, Bakhtin cites Nicholas Lossky's book *The Intuitive Philosophy of Bergson* (Losskii, *Intuitivnaia*), which appears to have influenced Bakhtin's interpretation of the French philosopher. In mentioning the book here, we do not presume to assess it; we aim rather to read Bakhtin's reading of Bergson through

Lossky's reading of Bergson. Lossky's book, which went into its third edition the year in which its author was exiled from the Soviet Union (1922), is largely a summary of Bergson's thought for the nonspecialist. But it does contain one chapter devoted to a critique, and in that chapter we can see where the interests of Lossky's "intuitivist idealism" and Bakhtin's prosaics overlap. Specifically, we see Bakhtin's skepticism of exuberant irrationalism, that is, Bakhtin in an intellectual mood quite different from the one in which he was to write the book on Rabelais. The moment has some significance, for it could be seen as an early instance of a braking move, a "corrective to unfinalizability" in Bakhtin's own thought.

Lossky objects initially to the rigid separation of intuition and reason: "There is no abyss [between them] . . . since reason is itself intuitive" (Losskii, *Intuitivnaia*, p. 40). He also resists descriptions of human reasoning that are in fact caricatures of reason—a move that may have appealed to Bakhtin, who felt that "psychologisms" of all sorts offered an impoverished account of the complexities of conscious thought. Lossky argues that to allow reason only two faculties, analysis and generalization, and then to assume that these faculties will be exercised on wholly inert, passive material, is to reduce reason to a shadow of itself (ibid., pp. 98–99). Reason is much more than "calculation." According to Lossky, Bergson also errs in his understanding of the sort of knowledge at which reason can arrive, as well as in his reluctance to credit the multiple ways in which reason can deal and interact with the particulars of the world. In effect, both critics and celebrators of purely abstract reason unjustifiably narrow its range, even if their evaluations of that range differ. "The error of the mechanistic worldview consists not in the fact that it grants existence to the abstract sides of reality, but that it invests those abstractions with an autonomous existence and tries to understand the whole merely by *externally attaching these abstractions to one another*. This is an error not of reason but of people making use of reason in an inadequate way" (ibid., p. 102).

It follows for Lossky that Bergson has chosen the wrong target and so arrived at a mistaken conclusion. "After all, there are no fewer distortions when one affirms that no extra-temporal principles exist in the world, *as if the world were only a flow of changes*" (ibid.).

Ultimately, Bakhtin could be sympathetic neither to Lossky's intuitivist idealism nor to his belief that the world somehow constitutes an organic, systematic whole. But Bakhtin could strongly endorse Lossky's defense of the complexities of reason, which must not be understood as mere analysis enacted on material; and he could certainly accept Lossky's suspicion of rigid dualistic boundaries between functions of the mind. Most important, Bakhtin could accept Lossky's criticism of a concept of personality defined largely as an endless flow of inner changes. In Bakhtin's terms, Bergson was correct in focusing on process more than on product, but he was nevertheless too indifferent to the *act*. Since Bakhtin understood the act as something that the self must pin down and "acknowledge" rationally, consciously, and responsibly, his difficulties with the Bergsonian view apparently begin here. Bergson makes it hard to understand how actions could be ethically "signed" or socially shared in a meaningful way. If, to Bakhtin, Kantianism became a symbol for the systemic, impersonal, and fundamentally static, Bergsonism came to represent pure inner change and flow, the pure Heraclitian flux of self, the river one cannot step into twice. If the self is only such a flow, *who* is it that can be held morally responsible?

For ethical action to be real, Bakhtin believed, a new conception of the responsible self is needed. "Toward a Philosophy of the Act" looks to a model of the self as both *non*systemic and *inter*personal. What unites selves who act? What is it that joins them in the ethical "event of being," which is also the "co-being of being," as Bakhtin seems to pun on the Russian phrase (*sobytie bytiia*)? To understand these things, Bakhtin writes, I must "know the truth that unites us, and the event in which we are participants and in which my act flows" (KFP, pp. 94–95).

In a similar spirit, Bakhtin writes that the proper way to affirm selfhood at any moment is as "an unmerged, indivisible affirmation of myself in existence" (KFP, p. 112). Neither the flow of the moment nor the eternal norms are responsible, but *I* am responsible. To understand responsibility, one must recognize a unique self acting at a unique time and place. Ethical action is born of a sense that each act is unrepeatable and responsibility is nontransferable. "What can be accomplished by me cannot be accomplished by anyone else, ever" (ibid.).

Pretendership and Alibis for Being

In the second part of his early manuscripts, the portion eventually published under the title "Author and Hero in Aesthetic Activity," Bakhtin extends his ethical concepts into the realm of the aesthetic. Now his primary concern is not so much with individual responsibility and the ways in which we answer for ourselves in an act as with the ways in which we come to create images of others, and images of ourselves *for* others. For Bakhtin, the creation of such finalized images is the essence of aesthetic activity. He intends not only to describe aesthetic activity, but also to consider its possible and proper relations to ethical activity and to the total project of selfhood.

Throughout the essay, Bakhtin examines the process of self-formation in both art and life. He deals with the self in three related categories. First there is the I-for-myself (how my self looks and feels to my own consciousness), and then two categories of outsideness and otherness, I-for-others (how my self appears to those outside it) and the reverse, the-other-for-me (how outsiders appear to my self). Working with this triad, Bakhtin poses a number of questions about selfhood; his answers define the parameters of his early approach to psychology.

Bakhtin asks first how a self establishes a relationship to the world. He begins by rejecting some traditional subject-object oppositions as fundamentally flawed because there exists neither a stable self nor a stable "given" world to which it might be opposed. Rather, the outside world *becomes* determinate and concrete for us only through our willed relationship to it; in this sense, "our relationship determines an object and its structure, and not the other way around" (AiG, p. 8).

Our environment seems most arbitrary and alien to us not when we create or perceive the wrong relationship with the world, but when we attempt to refuse to have any relationship with the world at all—when we live, that is, as if we had an "alibi for being." But the fundamental fact of human existence is that there can be no alibis for being. Nevertheless, people have devised ways to simulate them.

In his early writings, Bakhtin calls those who try to live by such alibis "pretenders." The use of the word *pretender* (*samozvanets*, literally "self-caller") is curious, because normally in Russian (as in English) the term means someone who tries to take another's place, such as a pretender to the throne. In Bakhtin's idiosyncratic usage, however, a pretender is not someone who usurps another's place but someone who tries to live in no particular place at all, or from a purely generalized abstract place. (Dostoevsky created just such a pretender in Stavrogin, the hero of *The Possessed*.) People who live this way "pass meaning by" or "irresponsibly sneak meaning past existence" (KFP, p. 115). Each of their acts is merely a sort of "rough draft for a possible accomplishment, a document without signature, obligating no one and obliged to nothing" (ibid.).

Those who live as pretenders frequently do so by living, in effect, as if they were characters in a novel. An early Dostoevsky character observes that one should live so as to make a work of art of oneself, and the peculiar pathology of many Dostoevsky characters derives from that sort of attempt. *Notes from Underground*, with its hero who thinks and speaks to himself and about himself "like a book," may serve as an especially cruel example.

There are several real-life ways to accomplish self-abdication, and one that Bakhtin dwells on at length concerns one's image in the mirror (AiG, pp. 28–31). Pretenders in effect identify with such images and overlook their peculiar falsity. When I look in the mirror, I never see what others see when they see me, because any authentic outer self requires the finalizing efforts of a *second* consciousness. The falsity therefore lies in confusing an I-for-others with an I-for-myself; an I-for-others requires that second, outside other, who in fact supplies that image of self. Looking at myself, I can only impersonate such an other; and even if such impersonation could be successful, I would still only have a sense of myself-for-others, which is still a very different thing from the I-for-myself. My own body, my own voice cannot be the same for me as it is for someone else.

For myself, my body can at best be a sort of semidetached "bas-relief" image; "what strikes us in our external image is its own peculiar emptiness, ghostliness, its vaguely oppressive loneliness" (AiG, pp. 28–29). Responding to my own face in a mirror—by talking, smiling, pretending to be a second consciousness—I can only play the role of an "indeterminate potential other" (AiG, p. 31). I cannot be a real other at all, but only a fraudulent "soul-slave without a place of its own, without a name and without a role" (AiG, p. 30). This "soul-slave," part self and part other, registers the "expression of a potential other's evaluation," but since a real other is absent, the expression on my reflected face is always "somewhat false," moving in various directions at once, a mix of satisfaction and dissatisfaction (AiG, p. 31). Life offers many kinds of mirrors, Bakhtin intimates, and many invitations to soul-slavery. We become pretenders whenever we live in a world we irresponsibly aestheticize, which happens whenever we turn subjects into mere "pretender-doubles" (KFP, p. 95).

People can also become pretenders by living lives that are "ritualized" or "represented" (KFP, p. 121). In using these terms, Bakhtin most likely has in mind political or religious officials who so identify with their role that they lose any responsible orientation to it. In a possible allusion to the revolutionary politicization of his own country, Bakhtin criticizes the "pride" of those who become pure "representatives of some large whole" (ibid.). This forfeiture of singular "participation" in the name of "representation" is a constant temptation of political activity, and has the potential for catastrophe.

Bakhtin seems to regard political ideologies as incorporating all the dangers of Kantian ethics, and adding a few of their own. All systematic ethics, and all attempts to dissolve personal responsibility into a general political system, deny the value of one's own particular moral obligation. "There is no person in general, there is me, there is a definite concrete other: my close friend, my contemporary (social humanity), the past and future of real people (of real historical humanity)" (KFP, p. 117). From the perspective of the categorical imperative or of political ideology, all deaths are alike. "Loving flesh becomes signifying only as an aspect of infinite matter, indifferent to us, or as an exemplar of *homo sapiens*" (KFP, p. 120). "But no one lives in a world where all people are mortal in an axiologically equal way" (KFP, p. 118).

In one remarkable passage—which potentially throws into ambiguous relief some of our most time-honored juridical principles—Bakhtin asks us to consider "the destruction and fully justified shaming of a person beloved by me" (KFP, p. 128). From the point of view of norms, rules, and abstract "content," one might recognize the justice of the punishment. Nevertheless, the agony I experience suggests that this situation would and should be different from a similar situation in which the person is a stranger. Indeed, one would be behaving irresponsibly and immorally if one reacted the same way in both instances. "The highest value is a human being, and the subordinated value is 'the good,' and not the other way around" (KFP, p. 129). If one views ethics in terms of abstract norms, or if one lives ritualistically, such distinctions become invisible. Bakhtin does not address the problems his position implies for those who would responsibly fill public roles, a weakness not atypical of Russian thinkers.

In "Author and Hero" and in his first published essay "Art and Responsibility," Bakhtin is most concerned with aesthetic escapes from responsibility. Properly understood, aesthetics can play an important role in ethical daily life. It can do so only if it enriches our sense of that life and does *not* serve to distance ourselves from it or, still worse, to replace our presence in daily life with an aestheticized double. Bakhtin is clearly unsympathetic to all forms of "aestheticism," largely because he takes the moral person and what he calls "the prose of everyday life" (IiO, p. 5) as the basis for his entire prosaic project.

The unity of art and life is not a given, Bakhtin argues, it is a project. Unity may be entirely absent, or it may be purely "mechanical." The only thing that can truly unify art and life, that can "guarantee the internal connections among these elements of a personality" is

the unity of responsibility. Whatever I have experienced and understood in art I must answer for with my life, so that everything experienced and understood should not remain ineffective in that life. . . . The poet must remember that his poetry is guilty before the vulgar prose of life, and the human being of life should know that his modest and simple tastes and the frivolity of his everyday questions are to blame for the barrenness of art. Personality must become responsible through and through; all its aspects must not only arrange themselves alongside the temporal flow of its life, but must also intersect one another in the unity of blame and responsibility. [IiO, pp. 5–6]

Art and life must be responsible to each other, but only I can take that responsibility. "Art and life are not one, but they must become united in me, in the unity of my responsibility" (IiO, p. 6).

What precisely can aesthetics contribute to the prose of life? We shall see that it offers the special benefits of finalization performable only by another specific consciousness. It follows for Bakhtin that all those "impoverishing aesthetic theories" (AiG, p. 78) based on collapsing many consciousnesses into a single abstract generalizable consciousness miss the whole point of aesthetic activity. (To take a more recent example, Bakhtin would have been entirely unsympathetic to constructs of an abstract "ideal reader.") For Bakhtin, whatever serves to "fuse" serves to impoverish because it destroys outsideness and otherness; it replaces interactive processes with consummated products, and thus sacrifices the eventness of events for a mere theoretical "transcription."

Impoverishing theories ground cultural creativity in the rejection of one's own place, in a refusal to juxtapose oneself to others, in *attachment to unitary consciousness*, in solidarity and even in merging. . . . The theory of knowledge has become the model for theories of all other realms of culture. Ethics, or a theory of the act, is replaced by a theory of knowledge of actions already performed; aesthetics, or a theory of aesthetic activity, is replaced by a theory of the knowledge of already completed aesthetic activity. [AiG, p. 79]

Ethics, responsible action, and aesthetic activity require multiple consciousnesses and a recognition that particular actions, people, times, and places cannot be generalized away.

"Author and Hero": Seeing Other Bodies and Being Seen

> What would I have to gain if another were to fuse with me? . . . let
> him rather remain outside me.   —AiG, p. 78

The crucial values for real selves are *non*fusion and *inter*action. These categories differ radically depending on one's point of view. To begin with the category of I-for-myself (that is, looking from the inside out): my "I" strives to see how others see me, an activity that is of necessity never completed. Although I am forever on the "lookout" for reflections of myself in others—reflections both of parts and of the projected whole of my life—these reflections cannot and do not coalesce into a unitary image. Every image of myself constructed by another is necessarily partial for several reasons—not the least of which is that the very act of finalization required by all images is false to the project of my unfinalizable life, because my life is always (as Bakhtin was later to say) noncoincident with itself. I seek the consummating power of each finalizing image for certain limited purposes, but these images "do not disrupt the unity of my life as lived, which is always directed toward a yet-to-come event" (AiG, p. 17). "Wholes"—all of them—are always transcended by our inner selves, and a recognition of such endlessly forward momentum is, in fact, constitutive of a healthy inner perspective. If "alien reflections" ever do "take on flesh" within us, they become "dead spots of accomplishment, a brake" on our lives (ibid.).

When Bakhtin turns to the categories of the-other-for-me and I-for-another (how I see others and how others see me), he introduces his crucial idea of "surplus." We have discussed this idea in Chapter One and shall have more to say about its importance in Bakhtin's theory of polyphony (Chapter Six). Here it is worth stressing that the idea of surplus is essential for Bakhtin's early understanding of the self because it is a way of locating and describing what makes each self radically singular and ir-replace-able. In using these spatial words, we imitate Bakhtin, who took the simple fact that each of us occupies a singular place at a given time as a figure for (and a consequence of) our radical singularity in many other respects. Physical and temporal specificity is a sort of synecdoche of our larger irreplaceability.

To begin with the physical facts: each of us sees the world in a particular way that is a specific "field of vision" (*krugozor*), a parameter not to be confused with one's "surroundings" (*okruzheniia*), which is our environment viewed as if from nowhere (AiG, p. 87). My surroundings, but not my field of vision, include the back of my head. When we meet, we share surroundings but cannot share fields of vision; for one thing, each of us appears in the other's field of vision but not in our own. Even if I look at my own body, my act of looking cannot appear in my own field of vision, as it can in yours. Each of us knows these facts about ourselves, and much of the drama and value of daily life develop from them. What I can see about you that you cannot see about yourself constitutes my surplus with respect to you (each surplus is always relative and contingent, even if there absolutely must always be some surplus).

The surplus allows me to finalize and complete an image of you, to create a finalizing environment in which you are located for me. Whereas my own totality is open and "my position must change every moment and I cannot linger or relax" (ibid.), I can relate to you as an author relates to a hero, for I provide form and create an image of you. This analogy is the central one informing Bakhtin's essay "Author and Hero."

The essentially aesthetic act of creating such an image of another is most valuable when we seek not to merge with or duplicate each other, but rather to supplement each other, to take full advantage of our special fields of vision. In daily creativity—the real prosaic creativity on which more noticeable creative acts depend—you and I formally enrich each other and the world. Properly performed, the aesthetic act in daily life involves a reassumption and a reconfirmation of one's own place after the other is encountered. Rather than fuse, we produce something new and valuable. As Bakhtin concludes, "I experience [another's suffering] precisely as *his* suffering, in the category of the *other*, and my reaction to him is not a cry of pain but a word of consolation and a gesture of assistance" (AiG, pp. 25–26).

Aesthetic activity begins for the self only after it returns to itself and takes advantage of its own surplus and outsideness. It follows that the task of providing artistic form requires two distinct centers of consciousness. Or as Bakhtin puts the point later in the essay, "form is a boundary that has been aesthetically reworked. . . . A boundary of the body as well as of the spirit and soul" (AiG, p. 81).

This characterization of aesthetic form nicely illustrates one noteworthy aspect of "Author and Hero": the great attention Bakhtin devotes to enfleshment, to the physicality of bodies in space, and to the interaction of *bounded entities*. The essay contains whole chapters devoted to the body as a spatial form. Bakhtin begins with the complexities of "external appearance" (how we experience our own exterior and why such experience is always somewhat artificial and false). He then takes up the outer boundaries of the body (and the emotional fallacy of trying to embrace or caress oneself) and considers various modes of experiencing our external actions (why the successful completion of physical acts—his example is the high jump—requires that we *not* concentrate on our outer sensations but rather on our inner impulse toward a goal). Bakhtin also includes a lengthy excursus on the evaluation of the human body in history and traces a gradual shift in emphasis, from ancient times to the Enlightenment, from the category of "my-body-for-others" to the category of "my-body-for-me."

One might ask why Bakhtin concentrates so much attention in these early writings on the body as a carrier or "marker" of the self. The answer might be related to the more general roles of "embodiment" and "play" in creative art. One way to approach these questions is to contrast Bakhtin's psychology of the creative act with Freud's more familiar psychoanalytic model.

Psychoanalysis, Fantasy, and the Creation of Art

In the 1920's, it was common for many critics of "psychologism" and Freud to mention Freud by name. Among those close to Bakhtin, Voloshinov wrote an entire book on the subject (*Freudianism: A Critical Sketch*) and Lev Vygotsky, not an associate but close to Bakhtin in spirit, explicitly criticized Freudian explanations of artistic creativity.[5] Bakhtin, however, usually avoids an explicit attack, perhaps because he saw Freud as an example of a more common error, the attempt to account for people in ways that deprived them of openness, continual responsibility, and creativity. Nevertheless, Freud appears implicitly as a significant other throughout Bakhtin's early work and, indeed, in later periods as well.

Bakhtin's model of the responsible and creative self offers a fundamental challenge to the Freudian model. It will be recalled that

Freud distinguishes real, lived experience from three other activities that he groups together in one category: play, daydreams or fantasy, and art. "The opposite of play is not what is serious, but what is real," Freud observes. "The creative writer does the same as the child at play. He creates a world of fantasy which he takes very seriously—that is, which he invests with large amounts of emotion—while separating it sharply from reality" (Freud, "Creative Writers," p. 749). The creative impulse in art, Freud surmises, results from a repression of fantasy, and the pleasure we feel in creating or viewing art can serve as compensation for unrealized desire. Art offers a "liberation of tensions in our minds" (ibid., p. 753). Art, play, and fantasy all arise from a *lack*: "We may lay it down that a happy person never fantasizes, only an unsatisfied one. The motive forces of fantasies are unsatisfied wishes, and every single fantasy is the fulfillment of a wish, a correction of unsatisfying reality" (ibid., p. 750).

To be sure, Bakhtin might reply, art and play, like fantasy, may indeed result from a lack or from unsatisfied wishes. But from a Bakhtinian perspective one may note Freud's "semiotic totalizing" tendency to use words like *never* and *always*, much as he argues elsewhere that every one of our experiences without exception is preserved in memory. Bakhtin would argue that there are other sources of creativity beyond wish fulfillment, unsatisfied desire, or lack.

For Bakhtin, creativity is built into prosaic experience, into all the ways in which we continually turn what is given into what is created. To live is to create, and the larger, more noticeable acts we honor with the name *creative* are extensions and developments of the sorts of activity we perform all the time. Freud, in short, partakes of the romantic tendency to regard creativity and inspiration as exceptional. To see creativity only as a kind of redirected unhappiness or a healthful use of a potential pathology, Bakhtin intimates, is to misunderstand the very nature of human experience and daily activity.

Of course, some creativity may indeed be "Freudian." But according to Bakhtin, creativity is as a rule positive, conscious, and the result of work undertaken by the whole personality. Furthermore, since personalities develop by interaction with others, creativity is a special kind of social act, as is the formation of an individual, unrepeatable self.

Bakhtin's description of fantasy also differs markedly from Freud's. For Bakhtin, fantasy—though a somewhat aestheticized activity—is not only a perfectly normal, everyday experience, but also an activity requiring no repression and generating no necessary guilt. In his own model of the life-art, or ethical-aesthetic, relationship, Bakhtin does *not* oppose real experience to the triumvirate of dreams, fantasy, and art. Although that categorization has its uses, Bakhtin prefers to classify real experience, dreams, and fantasy together and to distinguish all three, as a group, from art (AiG, pp. 67–68). The distinctions he draws derive from the concepts we have already explored: the triad I-for-myself, I-for-another, and the other-for-me; outsideness and the surplus; finalization and unfinalizability.

What characterizes the first group (life *and* fantasy) is "inner self-sensation," the absence of an "outward expressed quality" to the self (AiG, p. 67) and thus the inability to consummate or finalize the primary actor, the I-for-myself. I can see another, Bakhtin reasons, but myself I can only sense as acting (AiG, p. 28). In a dream, too, I can only sense myself acting. Only when I retell a dream or a fantasy can it become finalized or (in Bakhtin's sense) artistic. In that case, however, I become not the author but a "hero" of the fantasy (I am now the author of the act of retelling). In retelling a dream, I must cast myself on the same pictorial plane as the other heroes; it follows that "the first act of the artist [or reteller] is to invest the leading hero with a body" (ibid.), a body with "surroundings." Fundamentally, creative art is produced not as a response to unconscious bodily frustration but as an act of conscious embodiment. Once something has a body, the artist can be "outside" it and the aesthetic act is born.

Whether its genesis is pathological or prosaic, Bakhtin insists, fantasy alone cannot give rise to art. Fantasy must remain an "inner imitation"; it lacks the kind of outsideness necessary for art (AiG, p. 67). Fantasy can "imagine" but it cannot "impart an image" to anything, because fantasy allows for no genuine other (ibid.). Bakhtin does not illustrate this point, but he seems to have in mind the sort of dilemma Dostoevsky explores in his portrait of the "dreamer" (*mechtatel'*) in several of his shorter narratives. Dostoevsky's early novella *White Nights: A Sentimental Tale* is a case in point. It offers a superb illustration of the paradoxes, dangers, and dynamics of fantasy without consummation (in Bakhtin's sense). Read in this way, what sometimes seems like either an overly mawkish plot, or a rather dated parody of that plot, becomes instead a polemical exploration of a much more powerful idea: what Bakhtin might have called "psychological otherlessness," or the refusal to risk genuine encounters with the other's finalizing power. By the very logic of life as fantasy, such dreamers always wake up alone. The hero of Dostoevsky's story "The Landlady" also fails to make the transition from dreamer to artist, as he wishes to do, because he can never consummate and finalize.[6] The underground man may be viewed as a culmination of this type.

Bakhtin then discusses the relationship between play and art in a healthy (rather than a pathological) social and prosaic context, namely, children's games (AiG, pp. 67–68). While children are in the midst of a game, it is real experience for them, something innerly experienced, imagined but not given as an image. But play may approach art when an "actively contemplating" outside spectator begins to admire it. As long as such a spectator watches, we have the kernel of a dramatic aesthetic event. When the spectator leaves, or when he becomes so interested that he joins the game, what Bakhtin in later years would call "footlights" disappears from the scenario and the aesthetic event returns to the status of play. What is indispensable for art, it seems, is a second self who perceives the creation *as* art, that is, as a finalized image viewed from the outside. Art requires someone exercising a surplus with respect to the event.

Artistic creators and their audiences are alike in that they must remain outside the heroes' event in both space and time, or, more accurately, in a kind of space and time. So important to Bakhtin is this shared status of outsideness that he often combines the functions of author and reader into one composite term, *author-contemplator (avtor-sozertsatel')*. In retrospect, such a term looks forward to Bakhtin's later treatment of speaker and listener as co-authors of an utterance, and it recalls his frequently expressed belief that creativity combines activities usually distinguished as authorship and interpretation. In the early manuscripts, Bakhtin avoids drawing a boundary between the creator and the contemplator of a work of art. An author is always like a contemplator because in the act of creation he "always encompasses the whole temporally, he is always *later*, not only in time but *in meaning* as well" (AiG, p. 104).

Integrity, Creativity, and Form

Bakhtin next describes requirements for a set of desirable relationships among various created and creating selves. Because the problem of author and hero is also the problem of each self's relation to others, Bakhtin's larger ethical concerns are always present.

The first requirement is a recognition of outsideness and a willingness to make proper use of it: "One must come to feel at home in the world of other people" (AiG, p. 98). The second requirement is that all participants (created as well as creating) must be treated as potentially able to create something new. In Bakhtin's thinking at this stage, this requirement is rather opaquely expressed and, in the terms he sets, apparently impossible to fulfill, because it is hard to see how a created character could have the same ability as his creator to initiate the unexpected. The theory of polyphony (discussed in Chapter Six of this study) emerged as his eventual solution to how such initiatory equality *is* possible.

These requirements are as much spiritual—in Bakhtin's incarnated, body-centered sense of that word—as they are aesthetic, and to link the two realms is clearly part of Bakhtin's master quest. The temporal whole of the hero, Bakhtin writes, is "the problem of the inner man, the soul" and "the problem of the soul is methodologically a problem of aesthetics" (AiG, p. 89).

For art, the proper relation of author to hero demands, first of all, what Bakhtin calls integrity or wholeness (*tsel'nost'*). From what vantage point does one self determine the wholeness or integrity of another self? And is there a way to achieve compositional wholeness in art that does not undermine or compromise the hero's openness and growth? In short, how does an author describe a hero as a whole without sacrificing the hero's capacity to develop in surprising ways? Here again the problematics of these manuscripts suggest why Bakhtin found it necessary to develop his theory of polyphony and its attendant concept of a "wholeness of a higher order" (TRDB, p. 298).

Earlier we saw that for Bakhtin *events* may have wholeness or "unit-y" (*edinstvo*). He now extends this idea of unity to the *personality*, and specifically to personality viewed from an aesthetic perspective. In this context, the counterpart to "unity" is "integrity," *tsel'nost'*: "The human being in art is an integral [*tsel'nyi*] human being" (AiG, p. 88). Integrity in this sense is not primarily a matter of consistency, measured by coherence of plot or in the fate of heroes. Rather, and at first glance a bit strangely, it is a matter of the heroes' *potential*, their capacity to exceed expectations in a meaningful way, and to disappoint predictions. Integrity or wholeness of this sort cannot be "mechanical," and the hero who possesses it can be neither fully completed (in which case surprise would be impossible) nor entirely random (which rules out both real surprise and true meaningfulness). Only if heroes are visualized by their authors as "integral" wholes can their personalities be robust enough to be released by their authors as genuine creators in their own worlds. The test of integrity is creativity.

Precisely here, when discussing potential, Bakhtin provides his strongest statements against what he calls (albeit somewhat obscurely) the "psychological approach" in ethics and aesthetics. Such an approach includes but would not be limited to Freud. Because integrity involves genuine creativity, "the problem of the soul cannot be a problem in psychology, *a science that is non-evaluative and causal*, because the soul—although it develops and comes to be in time—is a whole that is individual, evaluative, and free" (AiG, p. 89; italics ours). Psychology cannot think creativity without thinking a good deal of it away.

For Bakhtin, selves are creative in response to images of themselves given by others. The other bestows form, an aesthetic act, and, as part of my inner life, I react to that form. I-for-myself is never identical with but always learning from the image of I-for-others, transcending that image, and so giving rise to yet other aesthetic acts that bestow on me new kinds of form. One task of form is to permit its own transcendence and to create a field of open potential. "The soul [conceived] as an empirical reality neutral to these forms is nothing more than an abstract product of the thinking [characteristic] of psychology" (AiG, p. 92). These ideas on form look forward to Bakhtin's later concept of "form-shaping ideology" (or "form-shaping force"), which describes how forms may be bestowed in ways that allow for meaningful finalization without sacrificing the potential for the new.

Because my sense of self is so intricately involved with images provided by others, Bakhtin contends, the concept of what is truly "mine" becomes especially complicated. If I do not understand the role of others in shaping what is mine, I can cause myself profound confusion. In daily life, a conviction that something is genuinely mine merely because it appears to be internally generated is necessarily the result of "illegitimate subjectivity"—and so may give rise to feelings of guilt or penance. Such reactions need not occur if the other bestows the gift of mine upon me and if I accept that gift and the responsibility it entails. Psychology usually errs in how it studies the concept of mine:

A sense of *mine* in the experiencing of an object is something studied by psychology, but in complete abstraction from the value-generating weight of *I* and *other*, and from that which makes them singularly unique; psychology knows only a "hypothetical individuality." . . . [In psychology,] inner givenness is not contemplated but rather studied [improperly] in a value-free context, in the posited unity of rule-governed psychological regularities. [AiG, p. 101]

For Bakhtin, "rule-governed psychological regularities" (and a psychological discipline of abstract, value-neutral descriptions and systems of rules or laws) are the predictable consequence of theoretism's cast of mind.

Spirit Versus Soul, Loophole Versus Rhythm

Ethical freedom (the so-called freedom of the will) is not only freedom from cognitive (causal) necessity, but also freedom from aesthetic necessity.   —AiG, p. 105

For Bakhtin, the self is not divided into a conscious and an unconscious, nor is it shaped by the "socialization" of an originary individuality. The idea of socialization, of an initial self forced to accommodate its fantasies and desires to the realities of social pressure, was for Bakhtin a typical product of Western psychological thought, Freudian and other. Bakhtin favored models in which the fundamental units of psychology precede (or entirely dissolve) the distinction between individual and social—two categories that may be seen as reifications produced by mistaking analytic categories for actual, existent entities. Something exists prior to this analytic division, and Bakhtin was to name and rename these "prior entities" throughout his life. His most sophisticated account was to focus on the idea of psychic life as dialogized, heteroglot inner speech. That account, of course, was not available to Bakhtin before his appreciation of language as a central locus for personality. In "Author and Hero," his prior categories are registered in the distinction between "spirit" (*dukh*) and "soul" (*dusha*).

Spirit describes I-for-myself, my experience of myself from within, and it possesses no firm points of consummation. Consummation belongs to soul, a consequence of I-for-others. Others must partake in the process of engendering soul out of me for themselves, which means that soul is inevitably partial and purposeful. Depending on particular instances of outsideness and specific acts of finalization performed by others, my soul always responds to someone else's concrete need. As we saw in Chapter Four, Bakhtin was later to make a similar argument regarding "the word."

The phrase *my soul* must therefore be seen as a sort of paradox or oxymoron, because soul results from a complex process in which others finalize me and I incorporate their finalization of me. That is why my soul is simultaneously "social" and "individual." My soul is a moment of my inner, open-ended, task-oriented self (my spirit) that some other consciousness has temporarily stabilized, embodied, enclosed in boundaries, and returned to me "as a gift [*dar*]" (AiG, pp. 89, 90). "The soul is a gift of my spirit to the other" (AiG, p. 116).

Bakhtin explains this scenario in richly paradoxical formulations: "In spirit I can and must lose my soul; my soul can be preserved, but not through my own powers" (AiG, p. 90); by myself I cannot create a soul within myself because self-reflection can only produce a "false and disjointed subjectivity" (ibid.). Another's existence for me has "the weight of an event," but my own life as I live it has no "aesthetic plot" or "story line weight" (AiG, p. 94). I am a "condition for potential" in my own life, but not its hero, inasmuch as the concept of hero presupposes another's perspective (ibid.).

Spirit cannot be the function or carrier of a story line because stories have a beginning, middle, and end—an end that is in a sense already present and simply waiting to unfold. Spirits are unfinalized, noncoincident with themselves, and always yet-to-be. Or as Bakhtin also puts the point in "Author and Hero," spirits always have a "loophole": spirit and inner perspective provide us with an "intuitively experienced loophole out of time, out of everything given, everything already present and on hand" (AiG, p. 97). The term loophole was later extended in the Dostoevsky book to describe words, utterances, addresses, and entire worldviews.

Story line creates its own weight, its own finalization and meaning, by uniting the moment with its past and future (with birth and death), by discovering the "rhythm" of the whole process, and by representing the present moment in terms of that rhythm (AiG, pp. 103–16). By "rhythm" Bakhtin means not just metric pulse, which is in fact a consequence of what he has in mind: projected expectation or patterning. Rhythm in Bakhtin's sense is the opposite of loophole; rhythm expresses closure in the present moment, as the loophole expresses openness. Successful imposition of rhythm overcomes the open and risk-laden future and makes that future in effect already past and consummated. It thus implies "a certain hopelessness with regard to meaning" (*smyslovaia beznadezhnost'*; AiG, p. 103).

Bakhtin's use of the word *hopelessness* here is instructive. The curious assumption that rhythm, once definitively established, must inevitably be "hopeless" goes to the heart of Bakhtin's very definition of "meaning": to be real, meaning must always include the possibility of *new* meaning. Every self has rhythmicized patches, of course, because soul is continually bestowed upon us. But these patches are themselves always changing. Thus, an attitude of "hope" in this sense need not imply a faith in improvement; it merely implies the assurance of some sort of significant change.

Rhythm, like an aestheticized life, works against responsibility. "By rhythm I can only be possessed," Bakhtin writes; "in rhythm, as if in a trance, I am not aware of myself. . . . In this sense, ethical freedom (the so-called freedom of the will) is not only freedom from cognitive (causal) necessity, but also freedom from aesthetic necessity. . . . Everywhere I am present I am free, and I cannot free myself from 'oughtness'" (AiG, p. 105).

Rhythm therefore has dangers as well as advantages. It properly serves as a part of the other's created image of me, as a part of the "soul" the other offers me but which I can and should transcend. In this sense, "rhythm is possible as a form for relating to the other, but not to my own self" (AiG, p. 106). I can be enriched by the other's "rhythmicizing" of me because I know that a particular image of me does not define me completely. But I can only be impoverished if I try to live as if another could rhythmicize me completely; such an attempt would be another path to pretendership. If I become alienated from myself, if I no longer live so as to generate value from myself, and if I try to live completely in and for patterns set by others, then I will readily assimilate myself to their rhythm. In that case, I will live as if I had no creativity, no loophole. If, in Bakhtin's example, I live as a mere part of a social order or movement, a nation, or even all of humanity, and if I passively join myself to these larger entities, then I submit too unreservedly to rhythm and speak merely as part of a "chorus" of others (ibid.). In this way, I lose (or rather live as if I had lost) my uniquely responsible voice (ibid.).

In one of the reasonably rare places in his early writings when Bakhtin discusses language as such, he does so to offer an analogy with the pretendership of rhythmicized and "story line" lives. Near the end of "Author and Hero," Bakhtin remarks on the "daring and obstinance" of any embodiment: "Everything that *already is*, is so unjustifiably; it has, as it were, dared to already define itself and to linger (stubbornly) in all its definitiveness in a world that is yet all-to-come in its meaning, in its justification" (AiG, pp. 116–17). Such an embodiment must "resemble a word that would like to be fully defined within a sentence that had not yet been spoken or thought through to the end" (AiG, p. 117). In a sense, Bakhtin concludes, every spoken word is ashamed of the "unitary light of meaning" in which it had to be pronounced; "as long as the word remained unspoken, there had remained the possibility to believe and hope—after all, there had been such a nagging fullness of meaning—now it's spoken, now it's completely here in all its stubborn real-life concreteness—it's all here, there's nothing more!" (ibid.). In this passage we glimpse Bakhtin in his prepolyphony phase, *before* he came to understand the word as dialogic. The spoken word is not yet conceived as something that contains potentially infinite, unresolvable dialogue within itself. Only with *Problems of Dostoevsky's Creative Art* does Bakhtin begin to insist that the word *must* be uttered to make its potential available; precisely as concrete utterance is the word rescued from having "nothing more."

In Bakhtin's ruminations on rhythm and pretendership, we see an important difference between his ideas in the 1920's and Voloshinov's later Marxification of them. For the author of *Marxism and the Philosophy of Language* and "Discourse in Life and Discourse in Poetry," communication between people is made possible by the rhythms and intonations they *share*, by their "common surroundings, common knowledge and understanding," and by their common evaluation.[7] Although Voloshinov discusses individuality and insists that a theory of culture must acknowledge its role, the thrust of his argument is to establish the value and determining significance of what is shared, of the "chorus." Bakhtin places the reverse emphasis, on how I can transcend the chorus, and on how, *beginning from* the given social and natural world, I can produce the new.

We may also detect an important difference between Bakhtin's early manuscripts and his later ideas in *Rabelais and His World*. In his carnival period, it is precisely the rhythms of the collective that promise salvation; outsideness is eliminated, and the individual is consummated through dissolution in the collective body. By contrast, in his early manuscripts, as in his fourth-period writings, Bakhtin stresses the need to resist a collapse into communality and rhythm, and the difficulty, loneliness, and risk taking that are part of "oughtness." I am alive only "in the sense of a constant possibility, a constant need to transform my life formally, to insert new meaning into my life (the ultimate word of consciousness)" (AiG, pp. 107).

In fact, Bakhtin writes, to value pretendership over potential is to experience a loss of self. A true self is "yet-to-be." What "constitutes my inner self-confidence, strengthens my back, lifts up my head, directs my gaze forward" is the knowledge that "the real center of gravity of my self-definition lies in the future" (AiG, p. 111) and will always lie in the future.

From the Nonpolyphonic to the Polyphonic Hero

In applying the concepts of his early manuscripts, Bakhtin arrived at his first descriptions of selfhood in art. Created characters are necessarily viewed from the outside, which means they are seen as "souls" rather than "spirits," and are inevitably rhythmicized. Like Gogol's Chichikov, authors deal in souls, and "a soul is always predetermined (in contrast to spirit)" (AiG, p. 114). Echoing his earlier comments on the "hopelessness of meaning" in selves that are fully rhythmicized, Bakhtin concludes: "The aesthetic embodiment of the inner human being anticipates from the very beginning the hero's hopelessness as far as meaning is concerned; artistic visualizing gives us the *whole* hero, enumerated and measured to the full extent; there must not be for us any meaning-related secrets to him, our faith and our hope must be silent" (AiG, p. 115). Such a hero is accompanied his whole life long by the "tones of a requiem" (ibid.). Art gives us dead souls.

"Author and Hero" is a meditation on authorship that emphasizes the enabling powers of literal physical embodiment. In that essay, Bakhtin consequently argues that aesthetic form requires a sort of outsideness that fully contains a hero in a pregiven structure. He therefore concludes that artistic visualization leaves us with little or no access to spirit, to unfinalizability, or—in his special sense of the word—to hope. He soon changed his mind. The theory of the polyphonic novel, developed in Bakhtin's second period, described how it *is* possible for a work of art to portray people as unfinalizable, responsible, and open.

Bakhtin's fascination with the physicality of bodies (which somewhat constricted his definition of aesthetic authorship and the whole of the hero) thus gave way to other individualizing forces. These new forces also serve to make personality concrete and responsible, but in ways more complex and flexible than those available to the body. First Bakhtin turned to polyphony and then, in the 1930's, to dialogized heteroglossia.

Because our next chapter is devoted to the concept of polyphony, we will not discuss it here. But it would be helpful to note at present that polyphonic works reduce plot to a mere "service function" (PTD, p. 100; TF1929, p. 277) incapable of fully defining the hero; "the real connections begin where the ordinary plot ends" (TF1929, p. 277). That conclusion was clearly called for by the problematic of the early manuscripts and its ideas about the weight and hopelessness of the story line.

The exposition of polyphony in the 1929 Dostoevsky book also continues the attack on false psychologies present in the early manuscripts. Bakhtin opens his discussion of the Dostoevskian self with the novelist's celebrated comment in his notebooks: "I am called a psychologist; that is not true, I am only a realist in the higher sense." Dostoevsky considered himself a realist, Bakhtin argues, because his perspective on his heroes' selves (unlike that of some Romantics, with whom he otherwise shares so much) is entirely *external*, that is, not cast in categories of the hero's own "I." Dostoevsky does not confuse this approach, however, with the wrong *sort* of outsideness, which is psychology. A psychological approach to a character would sanction the objectification of the other while not sharing with the other; it would create images by keeping something up one's sleeve, attacking from behind, or using a person's back to expose his face (TF1929, p. 278). Dostoevsky avoided finalizing a character with information that was in principle inaccessible to that character's consciousness. Despite his reputation, "Dostoevsky is no psychologist. But at the same time Dostoevsky is objective, and has every right to call himself a realist" (ibid.). He is objective because he describes consciousness in all the complexity and potential freedom really available to it.

In his second edition of the Dostoevsky book, Bakhtin expanded this critique of psychology and psychologists in a passage devoted to Dmitri Karamazov's trial. "In place of this living core [of personality] . . . they [psychologists] substitute a sort of *ready-made definitiveness . . . predetermined* in all its words and acts by 'psychological laws'" (PDP, p. 62). In his notes for the second edition, Bakhtin also develops his idea that the "depths" Dostoevsky explored—again despite Freud and conventional wisdom—had nothing to do with the unconscious, but rather with an extraordinarily complex and rich view of consciousness. Returning to his early categories of spirit and soul, Bakhtin observes:

Dostoevsky made spirit, that is, the ultimate semantic position of the personality, the object of aesthetic contemplation, he was able to *see* spirit in a way in which previously only the body and soul of man could be seen. He moved aesthetic visualization into the depths, into deep new strata, but not into the depths of the unconscious; rather, into the depths of the heights of consciousness. The depths of consciousness are simultaneously its peaks. . . . Consciousness is much more terrifying than any unconscious complexes. [TRDB, p. 288]

Evidently, Bakhtin never tired of enlisting Dostoevsky in his war against psychology.[8] He presents an impressive case for reading Dostoevsky in a way very difficult to do in an age that takes Freudian categories so much for granted.

In our view, Bakhtin was surely right to stress Dostoevsky's sense that consciousness is immensely complex. But Bakhtin probably overstated his case. Just as he interprets some of Dostoevsky's most pathological characters and situations as benevolent, open-ended, and thus "hopeful," so he strips Dostoevsky of much that is mystical and apocalyptic. Dostoevsky, who even advanced a theory of the collective unconscious in *The Diary of a Writer*, probably did believe in something resembling a Freudian unconscious as well as a Bakhtinian consciousness (or so we suppose).

Bakhtin assigns all the "depths and heights" of man—creativity, activity, rebellion, freedom—to the conscious sphere. Later, in his 1961 notes, Bakhtin refers critically to theories of "forces that lie outside consciousness, externally (mechanically) defining it: from environment and violence to miracle, mystery, and authority. Consciousness under the influence of these forces loses its authentic freedom, and personality is destroyed. There, among these forces, one must also consign the unconscious (the 'id')" (TRDB, p. 297). Here Bakhtin links political and psychological denials of human freedom.

The phrase "miracle, mystery, and authority" alludes, of course, to the entire problematic of Dostoevsky's Legend of the Grand Inquisitor, from which this famous triad is drawn. The entire legend, and that phrase in particular, is a classic allusion to political totalitarianism and to any system of thought based on an image of human beings without choice or responsibility. For Bakhtin, it appears, political totalitarianism—with which he had so much experience—and Freudianism were connected in this complex way. We hope we are not reading too much into his observations if we see in them a condensed form of the argument that Sir Isaiah Berlin developed in his essay "Political Ideas in the Twentieth Century." Berlin derived much of his thought from reflecting on the prosaic trend in Russian literature.

Berlin contends that twentieth-century radical political thought has often relied on a new argument (if it can be called that) largely absent from earlier such thought. Believing that people are not in fact motivated by conscious reasons, such radical thinkers dispensed with the necessity of proving the rationality of their case. "One of the elements of the new outlook," Berlin contends, "is the notion of unconscious and irrational influences which outweigh the forces of reason; another the notion that the answers to problems exist not in rational solutions, but in the removal of the problems themselves by means other than thought and argument" (Berlin, "Political Ideas," p. 7). One does not appeal to reason "because the springs of human actions lay in regions unthought of by the sober thinkers whose views enjoyed prestige among the serious public" (ibid., p. 14). Berlin cites Lenin as exemplary of this new outlook.

For a Russian of Bakhtin's time, such a view of Leninist thought in the Soviet Union would have been commonplace. One does not need to reason with class enemies, who are precluded from understanding the causes of their own views. For Berlin, some versions of Bergsonism and Freudianism taught similar lessons. However different he may have been from Lenin in other respects, "Henri Bergson had . . . been speaking of something not too unlike this when he had contrasted the flow of life with the forces of critical reason which cannot create or unite, but only divide, arrest, make dead, disintegrate" (ibid., pp. 20–21). Freudianism, if not Freud, often pointed in the same direction:

By giving currency to exaggerated versions of the view that the true reasons for men's beliefs were most often very different from what they themselves thought them to be, being frequently caused by events and processes of which they were neither aware nor in the least anxious to be aware, these eminent [Freudian] thinkers helped, however unwittingly, to discredit the rational foundations from which their own doctrines derived their force. For it was but a short step from this to the view that what made men most permanently contented was not . . . the discovery of solutions to the questions that perplexed them, but rather some process, natural or artificial, whereby the problems were made to vanish altogether . . . because their psychological 'sources' had been diverted or dried up. [Berlin, "Political Ideas," p. 21]

To any careful reader of the Grand Inquisitor legend (or *The Possessed*) the basic outlines of this argument would be immediately apparent, even if in the Soviet context it could not be expressed. Concerned throughout his life to affirm and define human responsibility, wary as he was of Freud and Bergson, opposed to all forms of dialectical thinking and to Marxism in its Soviet redaction, Bakhtin could well observe that "consciousness under the influence of these forces loses its authentic freedom, and personality is destroyed" (TRDB, p. 297).

The imperative to devise an alternative to the Freudian view was therefore great, and it was closely connected with Bakhtin's fundamental devotion to ethics, creativity, and freedom as he understood them. The idea of consciousness as inner speech served as such an alternative, because it located "Dostoevskian" complexities not in an unconscious, but in a more complicated view of consciousness. It is unclear whether Bakhtin or Voloshinov deserves the primary credit for an initial formulation of this model in terms set by the Bakhtin group, but it seems likely that each influenced the other and that both drew on ideas of dialogue and inner speech circulating at the time. We turn first to Voloshinov's exposition of the concept.

Voloshinov: Psychology and Ideology

Voloshinov opens the third chapter of *Marxism and the Philosophy of Language* with a difficult (some would say impossibly difficult) charge for Marxism. Among Marxism's most urgent tasks, he writes, "is to construct a genuinely objective psychology, which means a psychology based on *sociological*, not physiological or biological, principles" (V:MPL, p. 25). (Voloshinov, incidentally, clarifies why biological approaches are inadequate but not why they lack objectivity.) The nub of the problem is to find "an objective—but also subtle and flexible—approach to the conscious, subjective human psyche" (ibid.).

This search for an objective approach to the subjective psyche draws on terms and values that are already familiar to us from Bakhtin's early work. They might be said to characterize the shared "ideological horizon" of the Bakhtin group. Specifically, both Voloshinov and Bakhtin insist on the essential role of otherness in shaping and defining the self. For Bakhtin, as we have seen, otherness means "outsideness," the "surplus," and the activities that follow from each, such as aesthetic finalization and the radical singularity of worldviews. As a Marxist, Voloshinov reinterprets otherness in sociological terms: "The conscious psyche is a socio-ideological fact . . . [and] the processes that basically define the content of the psyche occur not inside but outside the individual organism, although they involve its participation" (V:MPL, p. 25).

Bakhtin added a sociological dimension to his psychology in the 1930's as an attempt, it would seem, to enrich his theory with Voloshinov's insights while avoiding the latter's Marxism.

We also recognize similarities between the two thinkers in their shared rejection of the Saussurean communication model. According to Voloshinov, an utterance is not sent from speaker to receiver, but is constituted from the outset as a "two-sided act. It is determined equally by whose word it is and for whom it is meant" (V:MPL, p. 86). Thus, when Voloshinov and Bakhtin write of thought as inner speech, they are asserting that other people—as the other side of each two-sided act—necessarily participate in our most intimate thoughts, which would not have to be the case if language were understood in a Saussurean spirit.

For Voloshinov, the fact that the psyche is socially constituted means that it is a mistake to seek purely separate and autonomous psychic laws. Of course, different people think differently, and psychologists must be attentive to that fact (which is to say, to individuality). But it is not necessary to resort to special psychological laws to explain those differences; indeed, doing so still leaves unanswered how general laws permit different people to think and experience the world differently.

For Voloshinov, neither the material of psychic life nor the fundamental principles by which it is organized are discontinuous from the more general materials and principles of social and ideological life. There are no special psychic laws per se, at least not in the sense that Freud and others have assumed. Instead, there are principles of psychic-ideological life, principles that allow for variation depending on the degree to which an experience is shared.

One reason that so many attempts to understand both ideology and psychology have proved inadequate, Voloshinov intimates, is that the two spheres are held to be radically distinct entities that only subsequently come to interact. The whole history of argument about the relation of the content of thought to the psychology of thought has reflected this mistake. According to Voloshinov, the key problem derives from a confusion between two meanings of the word *individual*—as biological specimen and as person. As biological specimen or natural object, the concept of individual is fundamentally different from the concept of the social, but the category of *person* (or personality) is in fact not essentially opposed to the social. "What most complicates our problem of delimiting psyche and ideology," Voloshinov explains, "is the concept of 'individuality.' The 'social' is usually thought of in binary opposition with the 'individual,' and hence we have the notion that the psyche is individual while ideology is social. Notions of that sort are fundamentally false" (V:MPL, p. 34).

On the one hand, the individual personality is "just as social as is ideology" (ibid.). On the other hand, ideological phenomena are as ineluctably individual as psychological phenomena. "Every ideological product bears the imprint of its creator or creators" (ibid.) and it can only continue to exist as an ideological phenomenon if it is variously implemented by particular people. Just as individuality is constituted socially, ideological phenomena require individual "impletion" to exist at all. "The ideological sign must immerse itself in the element of inner, subjective signs; it must ring with subjective tones in order to remain a living sign and not be relegated to the honorary status of an incomprehensible museum piece" (V:MPL, p. 39).

As a social product then, the psyche in an important sense is not located "within" a person at all. My brain is within me, but my psyche is not. "By its very existential nature the subjective psyche is to be localized somewhere between the organism and the outside world, on the *borderline* separating these two spheres of reality" (V:MPL, p. 26). On this borderline, a special encounter takes place between the organism and the outside world, "but the encounter is not a physical one" (ibid.); it is rather a semiotic encounter. "Psychic experience is the semiotic expression of the contact between the organism and the outside environment" (ibid.).

In Voloshinov's model—which Bakhtin was to develop productively, if in a prosaic rather than a semiotic spirit, in the 1930's—every individual engages in two kinds of communicative activity. He forms relationships with other individuals in specific utterances, and simultaneously forms relations between the outer world and his own psyche. These double activities, which are constant, constitute psychic life as a boundary phenomenon. Voloshinov uses a political metaphor: as people living abroad may claim the right to jurisdiction only by their home country, so the psyche enjoys similar "extraterritorial status in the organism. It is a social entity that penetrates inside the organism of the individual person" (V:MPL, p. 39). Any objective definition of "inner experience" must be included "within the unity of objective, outer experience" (V:MPL, p. 26) because the difference between them is not qualitative but a matter of degree.

Voloshinov: The Outer Word and Inner Speech

All of psychic life is semiotic, and almost all of it is linguistic. We think in inner speech, and inner speech is outer speech that we have learned to perform in our heads. "Language" is to be understood socioideologically and dialogically, beginning with the fact that every utterance, outer or inner, is a two-sided act. To understand psychic life is therefore to understand the content and shape of inner speech, generally and as it takes place in the minds of particular people. These are the fundamental tenets of Voloshinov's theory of psychology.

The theory leads to a number of specific questions, which for Voloshinov constitute the agenda for a viable discipline of psychology: "What is the nature of the word in its role as inner sign? In what form is inner speech implemented? How does it tie in with the social situation? What is its relation to the external utterance? What are the procedures for uncovering, for seizing hold, so to speak, of inner speech?" (V:MPL, p. 38). These questions require empirical work. In the meantime, Voloshinov offers a few tentative clarifications of the questions themselves.

Although it is not yet clear what forms inner speech assumes, it is clear "from the outset" that those forms cannot be reduced to purely linguistic categories (in the narrow sense of that term): "Without exception, all categories worked out by linguistics for the analysis of the forms of external language (the lexicological, the grammatical, the phonetic) are inapplicable to the analysis of inner speech or, if applicable, are applicable only in thoroughly and radically revised versions" (ibid.). Bakhtin would remind us that these linguistic categories pertain to sentences, but that inner speech, like outer speech, takes place in utterances; Voloshinov seems to have basically the same point in mind.

As Voloshinov explains, inner utterances resemble most of all "the *alternating lines of a dialogue*. There was good reason why thinkers in ancient times should have conceived of inner speech as *inner dialogue*" (ibid.). Utterances in dialogue are linked neither by grammatical nor by logical relations, but by specifically dialogical ones, that is, "by the laws of *evaluative* (emotive) *correspondence, dialogical deployment*, etc. . . . Only by ascertaining the forms of whole utterances, and, especially, the forms of dialogic speech, can light be shed on the forms of inner speech as well as on the peculiar logic of their concatenation in the stream of inner speech" (ibid.).

It should now be clear why Voloshinov chooses to devote the last third of his book to the problem of reported speech. Not only is that topic a good way to illustrate his theory of utterances as two-sided phenomena, but it also has a special bearing on the problems of psychology. For what happens in every act of reported outer speech is analogous to what goes on in every act of understanding as we think in inner speech. After all, Voloshinov asks, what is understanding if not the setting of another's utterance in the context of our own "apperceptive background" (V:MPL, p. 118), which is itself the totality of the dialogues within us? What is such a setting if not an analogue to reported speech in its various forms and functions? "After all, it is not a mute wordless creature that receives an utterance, but a human being full of inner words. All his experiences—his so-called apperceptive background—exist encoded in his inner speech, and only to that extent do they come into contact with speech received from the outside. Word comes into contact with word" (ibid.).

The forms of outer reported speech, it will be recalled, are all documents of active reception, in which complex interactions take place between the reported utterances and the reporting context (see Chapter Four). Presumably, the same or analogous kinds of interactions take place in inner speech. In inner speech, as in outer speech, active reception will perform "factual commentary" and "internal retort" (ibid.); and in understanding inner speech, too, we must keep in mind that these two functions "are organically fused in the unity of active reception, and . . . can be isolated only in abstract terms" (ibid.).

Inner speech, Voloshinov supposes, may be at varying distances from outward expression. When we prepare or memorize a speech for delivery, inner speech may approach outer speech in form. At other times, it often lacks such distinct outlines. Inner speech may then be closer to a "total impression" linked by dialogic principles to other inner total impressions, and so be rather distant from anything that could be shared or understood by some imagined eavesdropper on the psyche. We may even project a continuum of shareability, which also extends outside us, because outer utterances, too, are more or less shareable. Some utterances demand that the speaker and listener have the same field of vision, very similar attitudes, and essentially identical information.[9] By contrast, other utterances presume much less overlap of contingent circumstances and so are open, at least in principle, to a wider audience. The most shareable (even if not necessarily most widely shared) utterances are the fully worked out ideological systems of a culture.

Understanding the specific features of utterances along this and similar continua is necessary for understanding psychic life. Voloshinov sums up his model with a striking simile: "The process of speech, broadly understood as the process of inner and outer verbal life, goes on continuously. It knows neither beginning nor end. The outwardly actualized utterance is an island rising from the boundless sea of inner speech; the dimensions of this island are determined by the particular *situation* of the utterance and its *audience*" (V:MPL, p. 96).

Voloshinov Versus Vygotsky and Bakhtin

Even more than Bakhtin in his third period, Voloshinov is remarkably *logos*-centric in his model of the psyche. Although the range of expressive material and "motor reactions" available to the self is very wide, Voloshinov insists, nothing can match the "subtle and pliable semiotic material" provided by the word (V:MPL, p. 29). Only the word "can be shaped, refined, and differentiated in the extra-corporeal milieu in the process of outward expression. . . . It is the word that constitutes the foundation, the skeleton of inner life" (ibid.). Bakhtin, who is himself no stranger to *logos*-centrism, would agree with this line of reasoning; in "The Problem of the Text" he observed that "language and the word are almost everything in human life" (PT, p. 118). But he stops short of reducing consciousness entirely to language.

Voloshinov contends that "*independent of objectification, independent of embodiment in some particular material* (the material of gesture, inner word, outcry), *consciousness is a fiction*. . . . an improper ideological construct" (V:MPL, p. 90). Taken to this extreme, the argument would have to imply that either animals and neonates have something resembling language or else they are unconscious. Voloshinov's theory, remarkable in many ways, does not address the problem of the genesis of language, that is, how an individual first learns it.

We emphasize that this way of thinking about consciousness does not necessarily follow from the idea of inner speech. Lev Vygotsky, the influential Soviet developmental psychologist active in the 1920's and 1930's, explores precisely these developmental questions, as we discuss below. He inquires about the *relation* of thought to inner speech, the ways in which they become intertwined *when* children learn language, and the changes that take place when thought *becomes* inner speech.

Vygotsky's questions do not arise for Voloshinov, who believes in "the expressivity of all phenomena of consciousness" (V : MPL, p. 28, n. 4). In Voloshinov's view, if an experience is not expressible, it has not taken place. *"Experience exists even for the person undergoing it only in the material of signs.* Outside that material there is no experience as such. In this sense, *any experience is expressible,* i.e., is potential expression" (V : MPL, p. 28). The difference between Voloshinov's and Vygotsky's positions can perhaps be traced to the fact that Vygotsky intended his work for other empirical psychologists, whereas Voloshinov seems to have intended his for Marxist theorists. The doctrine of the expressivity of all phenomena allowed Voloshinov to describe his theory, unlike its rivals, as thoroughly monistic.

It also allowed him to intimate that what some have taken as private, speechless, isolated experience—the realm of the mystic, the visionary, not to mention the worlds of the deaf and blind—is essentially impossible *as experience.* Either the alleged experience does not exist or it is not in fact voiceless; it may, however, be erratic, bordering on the pathological. In any case, Voloshinov insists, experience that "lacks a socially grounded and stable [potential] audience" cannot "take firm root and will not receive differentiated and full-fledged expression" (V : MPL, p. 92).

By pulling the psyche up into the light, insisting upon its expressibility, and explaining its ideological content as a (largely verbal) dialogue with the outside world, Voloshinov echoes many of Bakhtin's concerns in the 1920's. In the course of his discussion, however, Voloshinov takes his account of the word-saturated, "borderline," sociological psyche in a direction that Bakhtin would not have followed at the time and did not follow later. In our reconstruction of events, Bakhtin, reacting to some of Voloshinov's formulations, arrived at theories of language, literature, and the psyche that were not only sociological without being Marxist, but also precise without being semiotic. What did Voloshinov add to Bakhtin's earlier work on the psyche, and what of Voloshinov did Bakhtin himself later accept and creatively incorporate?

As we have seen, Voloshinov adds the concept of the sign. To be sure, his use of the concept is a good deal more "subtle and pliable" than its use in various structuralisms and theories of semiotic modeling that were to come. But for Bakhtin, the sign was still too close to the whole framework of theoretism.

For Voloshinov, the continuity of inner and outer experience was guaranteed by the fact that "the inner psyche . . . can only be understood and interpreted as a sign" (V:MPL, p. 26). Much as he argues that grammatical and stylistic norms form a continuum, so he also contends that the continuum between inner and outer experience, which are both semiotic, enables objective analysis of them in the same terms.

Along with the sign comes a commitment to the act of decoding. Here Voloshinov differs markedly from Bakhtin, who rarely evinces any interest in signs (in this sense) and none at all in codes (except as negative examples of flattening, reduction, or "killed context"). Indeed, Bakhtin almost never uses the word *sign*. For Voloshinov, the sign guarantees the ultimate primacy of the social over the individual, and it permits him to link individual change with dialectical history. It also provides him with a fully adequate translation tool—and "complete translation" is again something that Bakhtin cautiously rejects throughout his life.

Voloshinov suggests, in short, that the psyche is a "system" in the strong sense (V:MPL, p. 35), whereas for Bakhtin, order, in the psyche as elsewhere, is at best a project. For Bakhtin, wholeness and integrity are lifelong and ever-unfinished tasks; for Voloshinov these concepts were more or less unproblematic. Voloshinov described individuation of the personality as the process of working over the "ideological themes" that penetrate consciousness and "there take on the semblance of individual accents."[10] Bakhtin described it as an ethical person's quest for identity and responsibility, and wondered about the meaning of those terms for a self that could never be completely ordered. With his messier and less "coincident" understanding of self and world, Bakhtin continually reexamined this quest, which led him to new experiments with new provisional solutions.

Bakhtin never ceased worrying about the possibility of self-expression. It was a topic of his work from the early consideration of I-for-myself and I-for-another to his late ideas about the super-addressee and elusive genres of "pure self-expression" (SG, p. 153). For Voloshinov, the "expressivity of all phenomena of consciousness" seemed to render this problem almost transparent, in effect no problem at all.

One more crucial difference between Bakhtin's and Voloshinov's approaches to the psyche is worth noting. Voloshinov disparages "causal" approaches to the psyche, but by this he means explanations in terms of "mechanical" or "biological" causality. He proposes to substitute for them the much more sophisticated determinations of the psyche by Marxist socioideology. By contrast, for Bakhtin it is causality per se that is troubling, because causality pertains only to the given and leaves no conceptual room for the created. Exhaustive causal explanations *of whatever sort* ultimately deny unfinalizability and responsibility. Dostoevsky denied being a "psychologist," a believer in potentially exhaustive laws of human behavior. In this sense of the word, Voloshinov was a psychologist (even if a remarkably sophisticated one); Bakhtin emphatically was not.

For different reasons, then, the idea of inner speech served both thinkers as an alternative to Freud's notion of the unconscious. Neither resorts to the unconscious realm, nor to deception of the inner censors, because both offer a sufficiently complex view of multileveled, diverse consciousness.

When Bakhtin himself took up these ideas in the 1930's, he kept the notion of inner speech but rejected that of the sign. In so doing, he disregarded coding and decoding, and reintroduced large amounts of untranslatability, singularity, uncoordinated centrifugal forces, and—mess. Inner speech became not a semiotic mechanism but something resembling a Tolstoyan battlefield. Before moving to that period, however, we should first briefly consider two texts that will serve to set off Bakhtin's later thought: Voloshinov's book on *Freudianism*, where the case against Freud is cruder and more explicit than in *Marxism and the Philosophy of Language*, and Vygotsky's *Thought and Language*, which is anything but crude.

Freudianism: Bourgeois "Insideness" as the Hopelessness of History

Much less profound than his theory of inner speech is Voloshinov's polemical *Freudianism: A Critical Sketch*. From the book's opening pages, Voloshinov makes it clear that Freudianism should be regarded primarily as a social symptom rather than a serious theory, still less a scientific theory. Voloshinov marks out rather conventionally what had become a Marxist line: psychoanalysis saves bourgeois man by taking him out of history and by explaining him not as a social being but as an abstract biological organism (V:F, pp. 9–11). As Voloshinov understands him, Freud always would have us seek answers within; those who follow him forget the social crisis and "take refuge in the organic warmth of the animal side of life" (V:F, p. 11). Freudianism's "ideological motif" is therefore an emphasis on two factors relatively unaffected (in Voloshinov's view) by social forces: sex and age. Sex and age become predominant motifs in an era of social decline; during such times, nature (including "human nature" understood in terms of biological drives) is seen as all-powerful and history as impotent. This oversimplified critique is, unfortunately, not uncommon in Voloshinov's work, and marks an important difference between his formulations and Bakhtin's.

Voloshinov is evidently rather selective in his reading of Freud. Nowhere does he engage Freud's most provocative works, the great sociopsychological essays of the war years and the 1920's. Rather, he is concerned to counter the challenge posed by Freud's early clinical work, the founding assumptions of psychoanalysis, and the basic concept of the Freudian unconscious.

At his worst, Voloshinov descends to something not very different from name-calling. But at his best, he presents an alternative to Freud's central ideas through his theory of the multiple voices in inner speech. He also advances his idea of the "unofficial conscious"—consciousness that is not yet sufficiently articulate—as an alternative to the unconscious. Earlier than most, he stresses the dialogic factors affecting the psychoanalytic interview and shaping the analyst's conclusions. According to Voloshinov, the forces of id and ego that emerge so colorfully in Freud's accounts of psychoanalytic sessions are not repressed inner realities in the process of discharge, but more likely the reflection of overt social dynamics, including those between doctor and patient (V:F, p. 79).

At various points in his exposition, Voloshinov contends that Freud's projection of autonomous drives and non-negotiable demands constitutes a mere "psychologization of the somatic" (V:F, p. 71). In Voloshinov's view, such scenarios can make no greater claim to scientific accuracy than, let us say, myth. Freud's "mythical unconscious" in turn leads to an evasion of history and to a denigration of the sort of social understanding that makes meaningful change possible. Eliminate time and society, and a structure cannot be modified: it can only be satisfied or repressed.

Voloshinov's *Freudianism* is a negative polemic, directed against a rival model of the psyche but not much concerned to elaborate positive alternatives. *Marxism and the Philosophy of Language*, along with Bakhtin's related works, do offer promising alternative models to the Freudian tradition. Supplementing them are Vygotsky's studies of the concept of the psyche as inner speech. In particular,

Vygotsky's final work *Thought and Language* (1934) seems to exploit the rich potential of this approach. A brief exposition will give some idea of that potential.[11]

Lev Vygotsky: Speaking, Thinking, and the Emerging of Self

We cannot close our survey without mentioning the perspectives that our investigation opens up . . . [on] the general problem of consciousness. We studied the inward aspects of speech, which were as unknown to science as the other side of the moon. . . . *Thought and speech turn out to be the key to the nature of human consciousness.*

. . . The word is a thing in our consciousness . . . that is absolutely impossible for one person, but that becomes a reality for two. The word is a direct expression of the historical nature of human consciousness.

Consciousness is reflected in a word as the sun in a drop of water. . . . A word is a microcosm of human consciousness.

—Vygotsky, *Thought and Language*, pp. 255–56

Voloshinov and Vygotsky both objected to the prevailing tendencies in psychological thought to think away history and development. Voloshinov argued that both "individual subjectivism" and "abstract objectivism" have made it impossible to understand language historically and to interpret consciousness as something constituted by social language. Vygotsky agreed: in such formulations, the loser is time. Vygotsky lamented the positing of "two poles—either the behaviorist concept of thought as speech minus sound or the idealist view, held by the Würzburg school and Bergson, that thought could be 'pure,' unrelated to language, and that it was distorted by words." He continues: "Whether inclining toward pure naturalism or extreme idealism, all these theories have one trait in common—their antihistorical bias. . . . Only a historical theory of inner speech can deal with this immense and complex problem" (Vygotsky, *Thought and Language*, pp. 254–55).

Vygotsky argued that time has long been misunderstood and misapplied in the psychological sciences. The development of the child was once described in terms of "botanical" models (maturation, "kindergarten") and then in terms of zoological models (the performance of animals under laboratory conditions), but it is precisely what can *not* be learned from plants and lower animals, namely, the uniquely human assimilation and production of language, that psychologists should examine. What truly marks the development of the human self, Vygotsky argued, is its mastery of tools and the signs that mediate them; and language is the human child's greatest tool. In order to study human development properly, psychologists should focus on the task-oriented utterance itself.

If language is always a means of problem-solving and of interaction with the world, then it is perilous to study it in isolated environments or in the traditional "controlled experiment." Vygotsky replaced these conventional locales of science with much looser "task situations" that confront the subject with real problems in a real social setting.

Vygotsky's distrust of the classic psychological experiment (what he called the "stimulus-response framework") recalls Voloshinov's and Bakhtin's distrust of the classic communication model, with its ideal speaker and ideal (or nonexistent) listener. Voloshinov and Vygotsky, as Marxists and semioticians, were more sympathetic than Bakhtin could have been to an integration of conceptual and communicative acts into some shared or collective system. Where Bakhtin in the early manuscripts everywhere stresses asystematicity, noncontiguity of worldviews, and unavoidable singularity as guarantors of true authoring and communication, Voloshinov emphasizes "choral support" and "the I [that] can realize itself verbally only on the basis of 'we'" (V:DiL, p. 100). Like Voloshinov (but again unlike Bakhtin), Vygotsky can entertain the idea of system as a prerequisite for consciousness. But all three were suspicious of idealized language models, like Saussure's, that posited a "sender" and a "receiver," a one-way message projected and received in what might as well be a void. Only the historical event could constitute human communication or lead to an act of learning.

Vygotsky believed that psychological events must be studied in history, concretely, and over time. He saw maturation and instruction as processes that were methodologically independent but still continually interacting, shaping at any given point what the self can do and the patterns of its further dynamic development. Vygotsky also posited the external social environment as the starting point for consciousness. These two premises are closely allied, for whatever we can acknowledge in the external world we can try to change over time.

In ingenious experiments, Vygotsky extended (and then modified or rejected) language-learning maps offered by Piaget, Stern, and Freud. His primary target was Piaget's interpretation of "egocentric speech," a stage between autistic play and directed (reality-oriented) thought. Vygotsky's actual attack was in fact much broader, for underlying Piaget's assumption that a child's thought is originally autistic and becomes realistic only under social pressure is a dichotomy akin to Freud's pleasure and reality principles. What all three Russian thinkers found objectionable in these Western views was the notion that individuality is given and is then socialized; according to the Russian theorists, individuality is always being made as a social process. Vygotsky was particularly unsympathetic to the assumptions that an individual is fundamentally reluctant to adjust to his environment and that reality, work, and social intercourse are somehow intrinsically not "pleasurable." In order to test the opposite assumption, Vygotsky devised his own set of experiments and then constructed an alternative model.

According to this model, thinking and speaking do not have common origins for children, and the two processes are not connected by a primary bond. For children, prelinguistic thought is biological (as it is for animals), and prerational speech is social and external. Here Vygotsky seems more convincing than Voloshinov, who does not allow for nonlinguistic thought and thus does not offer a hypothesis about how a child learns language in the first place. For Vygotsky, the child's first efforts at perception result in isolation of word meanings—but "meanings" only in the sense of verbal stimuli, which still function in context as signals rather than proper signs.

A truly critical moment in human maturation occurs when the child begins to ask for the names of things. At this point, Vygotsky postulates, thought becomes verbal as speech becomes rational. No longer is it possible to isolate the two processes because "*the nature of the development itself changes*, from biological to sociohistorical" (Vygotsky, *Thought and Language*, p. 94). One can no longer isolate and study the changes *within* each of the two functions, but must now study the relations between the functions, which become qualitatively different in consequence. These relations extend from the uppermost levels (where thought is closest to external speech) to the lowest, where it is so changed and abbreviated that interiorized speech resembles "thinking in pure meanings" (ibid., p. 249).

Believing that thinking is inner speech—which is to say outer speech that has undergone a process of "internalization" and an "ingrowth stage"—Vygotsky examined the phenomenon of "egocentric" speech, which could be examined in task situations. Uncomfortable with Piaget's conclusion that this speech was fantasy talk generated asocially, Vygotsky ran a series of experiments to complicate and socialize the child's environment at precisely the age when children "talk to themselves" (ibid., ch. 2). He demonstrated that a child talks twice as much when presented with obstacles, and that this externalized "conversation with oneself," this commenting on and predicting the results of an action, is in fact the natural dynamic of problem solving.[12] Furthermore, this talk proved to be extremely sensitive to social factors. Piaget, it should be noted, also observing that egocentric speech occurs in a social context, remarked that such speech is not truncated or whispered but uttered out loud, and therefore concluded that the child assumes he or she is being understood by other people. The two psychologists differed in the implications of these observations, and Vygotsky devised experiments to detach them from Piaget's conclusions.

When Vygotsky varied the social factors—by isolating the child, placing him with deaf-mutes, having him play in a room filled with deafening music—egocentric speech dropped off drastically (ibid., pp. 232–34). Vygotsky concluded that egocentric speech is not, as Piaget had thought, a compromise between primary autism and reluctant socialization, but rather the direct outgrowth (or better, ingrowth) of speech that from the start was socially and environmentally oriented.

In other words, Piaget was correct in his hypothesis that private speech and socialized speech intersected at this stage, but he was incorrect about the *direction* of the development. The child was not *ex*ternalizing internal thoughts, but learning to *in*ternalize external verbal interactions. Much as we learn first to count on our fingers and then in our heads, children learn to speak to others and then to internalize these dialogues in inner speech. Once this lesson is learned, consciousness becomes radically different and much richer. We become the voices that inhabit us, and we hold conversations with those voices. "The true direction of the development in thinking," Vygotsky concluded, "is not from the individual to the social, but from the social to the individual" (ibid., p. 36).

When internalization begins, egocentric speech drops off; the child becomes, as it were, his own best interlocutor. Crucial to this process, however, is the presence of a challenging verbal and physical environment. The descriptive "monologue" of which egocentric speech is composed can be internalized creatively only if questioned and challenged by outside voices. In this way alone is intelligence made possible, with "intelligence" defined not as the measurement of already mastered skills but as an address to the external world and as a dialogue with one's own future tasks.

It should come as no surprise that Vygotsky was unsympathetic to standard intelligence tests, which measure, in a competitive and isolating context, only *prior* achievement, and which punish children for seeking help—that is, for "cheating." A true test of intelligence, Vygotsky argues, is one that posits problems beyond the capacity of the child to solve and then makes help available. *How* a person seeks help, utilizes his or her environment, and asks questions of others: these are the proper test questions, for they address the child's "zone of proximal development" where all true learning occurs.[13] As Bakhtin would say, intelligence is a matter not of the given but of the created.

In sum: speech, behavior, and mental activity interact dynamically in a child's development. First speech accompanies action, then precedes it, finally displaces it; that is, speech assumes a planning function. In the final "ingrowth stage," inner speech and its distillate, verbal thought, crucially structure memory, hypothesis formation, and other mature mental processes.

Influx of Sense and the Work of Utterance

Bakhtin, Voloshinov, and Vygotsky all stress that inner speech differs in many ways from outer speech. "Inner speech is speech for oneself; external speech is speech for others," Vygotsky observes. "It would be surprising indeed if such a basic difference in function did not affect the structure of the two kinds of speech" (Vygotsky, *Thought and Language*, pp. 225–26). Briefly put, Vygotsky concludes that the most evident structural difference between inner speech and outer speech is syntactical. Because one takes for granted the subject and context of one's own inner speech, one characteristically omits the subject and specifies only the predicate of an inner utterance—much as a person asked whether he wants coffee or tea may answer simply, "Tea." Vygotsky suggests that this sort of abbreviation and condensation may be even more extensive in inner speech, where one would not need to specify shared knowledge and context. He points to a corresponding process, somewhat analogous to linguistic agglutination, whereby a word may come to surround itself with a whole field of meanings that it would not have for others.

Words are affected by a process Vygotsky calls the "influx of sense," which recalls Bakhtin's concepts of the already-spoken-about and of the capacity of words to "remember" their contexts.

In inner speech, Vygotsky observes, "the senses of different words flow into one another—literally 'influence' one another—so that earlier ones are contained in, and modify, the later ones" (ibid., pp. 246–47). The process is something like what happens to words recurring in a novel or poem and progressively absorbing the varieties of contextual sense. "In inner speech, the phenomenon reaches its peak. A single word is so saturated with sense that, like the title *Dead Souls*, it becomes a concentrate of sense. To unfold it into overt speech, one would need a multitude of words" (ibid., p. 247). And one would have to make a multitude of thoughtful choices.

When we externalize our thoughts, we *must* make them shareable, intelligible to others. We must, Vygotsky argues, choose among different sorts of connections, decide which sense of a word we wish to use, and negotiate a new definition of the situation with our listener—a definition possibly different from the ones we vaguely imagined in inner speech. For all these reasons, we can almost never make the speeches we often compose in our heads (as Vygotsky might have illustrated his point). Our rehearsals implicitly testify to the power of the dialogic situation, its capacity to surprise us or even to render us speechless, and to the difficulty of the choices we must make in "putting a thought into words," that is, in translating it from inner to outer speech in a real social context. The term *ex-pression*, implying as it does the mere externalization of something already there, is misleading, and can lead us to overlook the mix of impotence and real creativity at work in every prosaic utterance.

When we find these choices problematic, we may go through a succession of "drafts" in our heads or on paper, and then, switching roles, listen to or read our words from the point of view of the anticipated listener. None of this preparatory articulation, of course, guarantees successful communication in an actual dialogue with others, which is yet another task and considerably more risk laden. For all these reasons,

The relation of thought to word is not a thing but a process, a continual movement back and forth from thought to word and from word to thought. In that process, the relation of thought to word undergoes changes that themselves may be regarded as developmental in the functional sense. Thought is not merely expressed in words; it comes into existence through them. [Vygotsky, *Thought and Language*, p. 218]

Creation is genuine *making* and the most ordinary thing in the world.

Bakhtin in the Third Period:
The Novelistic Self

Consciousness finds itself inevitably facing the necessity of *having to choose a language.*   —DiN, p. 295

In our periodization of Bakhtin's thought, we divided the third period into two phases. The primary concerns of each phase led Bakhtin to a corresponding meditation on the nature of the self. In period IIIa, he described selfhood as essentially novelistic, that is, in terms of inner dialogues and the processes that shape them over time into a personality. Here Bakhtin drew on his own earlier study of psychology and language in the final chapter of the 1929 Dostoevsky book as well as on Voloshinov's theories of inner speech. (In this phase, Bakhtin also developed a theory of the "image of a person" and the self in terms of social time and space; we postpone discussion of that theory until Chapter Nine.) In period IIIb, he outlined a carnivalistic theory of the self to correspond to his theories of laughter, carnival, and the body in the *Rabelais* book. We turn first to the earlier construct, the novelistic self.

It would be helpful to begin by reviewing some concepts developed in Bakhtin's first period, in a chapter of "Author and Hero" entitled "The Whole of the Hero as a Whole of Meaning." Here Bakhtin approaches the self as an entity that performs "acts," in his special sense of that word (AiG, pp. 121–23). Bakhtin argues against the idea that people act out of a sense of a whole identity, out of what is *given* rather than what is being *created.* As a rule, Bakhtin claims, when I act, my whole identity or "determinateness" is not a factor for me: the acting consciousness needs not a sense of wholeness, but rather, goals and values. As it acts, consciousness is asking, "what for?," "to what end?," "is this right?"—and not "who am I?" or "what am I?" (AiG, p. 122). One acts, one does not need to make oneself into a hero of a projected work who acts. In this sense, selfhood is *not* a kind of text.

Action without full determinateness (or textualization) is what guarantees the ethical freedom of the act; for the one who acts, the pregiven self is not wholly determinate. Rather, the self is partially brought into being by the commitment of the act itself. Each act grows out of a self that is partially finalized, partially unfinalized.

Bakhtin then examines several genres—confession, autobiography, biography—from the point of view of the finalizability of the self. In confession, the self is unfinalizable; it does not even admit of another who could consummate it (AiG, p. 125). In this sense, confession does not allow for a separate author and hero, but rather fuses the two into one: spirit predominates over soul and thus cannot complete itself. There is no plotted story. By contrast, in autobiography the ratio of unfinalizability to finalizability, of I-for-myself to I-for-another, is more balanced. When we tell the story of our own lives autobiographically, what speaks in us most often is not direct experience or memory but a narrator with an imagined other's values and intonations. "I-for-myself," Bakhtin says, "is not capable of telling any stories," because projected goals are not whole enough to secure a narrative position (AiG, pp. 134–35). Autobiography from this perspective resembles biography more than it resembles confession. Presumably, Bakhtin would allow for intermediate stages between confession and autobiography, but the two are conceptually quite different.

In neither biography nor autobiography does I-for-myself determine the crucial moment of form (AiG, p. 131). They cannot do so, because both genres tell a story of the self from the outside. In autobiography, the story is told by a sort of double, projected and assembled by the I-for-myself; in biography, real others tell the story. If one imagines an ideal biography of oneself, it would be told not by oneself, but by "that potential other" who is "with us when we look at ourselves in the mirror, when we dream of glory, when we lay down the external plans for our life" (AiG, p. 133).

The special potential other can live alongside my I-for-myself and not be in conflict with it. He is always a loving other, the one who remembers my past, and he can have special authority for me, because I will agree with the story of my life that he tells. His voice, when I can hear it, is (to use terms Bakhtin coined later) both innerly persuasive and authoritative. As an "aesthetic finalizer," this ideal kind of biography offers "the valued other in me" (AiG, pp. 133–34). This idea of the potential friendly other reflects Bakhtin's naively appealing benevolence and seems to look forward to his later concept of the superaddressee.

Concerned to describe selfhood as both creative and responsible, Bakhtin characteristically chooses confession, autobiography, and biography when he needs examples of narrative genres. Bakhtin's Dostoevsky book and, still more, his discussions of the novel in the 1930's retain this interest in selfhood and in the shifting ratio of finalizability to unfinalizability, but largely abandon the model of I-for-myself and I-for-another. Instead, Bakhtin relocates the central opposition in language as it shapes the self in inner speech. He imagines the self as a conversation, often a struggle, of discrepant voices with each other, voices (and words) speaking from different positions and invested with different degrees and kinds of *authority*. Exemplary of this approach are the scattered discussions of self-hood in "Discourse in the Novel."

These passages stress a constant symmetry between the word in society and the self as an orchestration of social words. Observations like the following are characteristic: "The word lives, as it were, beyond itself, in a living impulse toward the object. . . . To study the word as such, ignoring the impulse that reaches out beyond it, is just as senseless as to study psychological experiences outside the context of that real life toward which it was directed and by which it was determined" (DiN, p. 292; second sentence italicized in original). The comparison is not simply an analogy. Both the self and the word must be understood dialogically, and it is impossible to understand the self without understanding dialogue.

Innerly Persuasive and Authoritative Discourse

The novelistic self is constituted by and as language, understood in Bakhtin's metalinguistic sense of the term. Accordingly, Bakhtin's discussion of selfhood occurs as part of his discussion of the "speaking person" in the novel. In Chapter Eight, we will discuss the novel's special use of language, but we may note here that for Bakhtin, the novel, like the self, is a highly complex combination and dialogue of various voices and ways of speaking, each incorporating a special sense of the world. Dialogue is essential to self-hood, and the novel is the most dialogical genre. Thus, for Bakhtin (as for many others), the novel is the best form for psychological investigation.

Bakhtin adopts the idea of psychic life as inner speech. But rather than concentrate on the earliest stages of language acquisition, as Vygotsky does, he focuses on the process at a later point, when the worlds inside and outside the individual are already thoroughly saturated with words. He considers an example from pedagogy, which suggests analogies with both psychology and the novel. "When verbal disciplines are taught in school, two basic modes are recognized for the appropriation and transmission—simultaneously—of another's words (a text, a rule, a model): 'reciting by heart' and 'retelling in one's own words.' The latter mode poses on a small scale the task implicit in all prose stylistics" (DiN, p. 341).

In the psyche, a similar distinction may be drawn to define poles of a continuum. Corresponding to words that must be "recited by heart" is "authoritative discourse"; corresponding to retelling in one's own words is "internally persuasive discourse." The psyche (or the social world) may know several examples of each kind of discourse, as well as countless kinds of voices that lie between, or are on their way toward, either extreme. The interaction and dialogue of these kinds of discourse shape the history of the psyche and the development of the self.

As Bakhtin was later to observe in his essay on speech genres, authoritative discourse plays a role in all social groups, down to "each small world of the family, friends, acquaintances and comrades in which a human being grows and lives" (SG, p. 88). Authoritative discourses set the tone for action in a given sphere of life; and they are assimilated into the psyche to set the tone for a particular sphere of thought. One can disobey authoritative discourse, but, so long as it remains fully authoritative, one cannot argue with it. By definition, it precludes dialogic relations. It is sensed as something that is inherited and unquestionable, as a voice from a zone infinitely distant. Rather, it "demands that we acknowledge it, that we make it our own; it binds us, quite independent of any power it might have to persuade us internally; we encounter it with its authority already fused to it" (DiN, p. 342). Demanding unconditional allegiance, authoritative discourse does not allow us to play with it, integrate it, or merge it with other voices that persuade us. We cannot select what we like from it or accept only a part of it; that would be heresy (in the root sense of *selection*).

So long as it remains such, authoritative discourse in the psyche is closed to growth and unfinalizability. If the psyche were composed only of it, then people would fully "coincide with themselves," be defined once and for all in a way potentially knowable by all. Bakhtin perhaps has in mind here the image of the "new Soviet man," the opposite of the novelistic self. In true novels (as opposed to socialist realist fiction), authoritative discourse can play no role, because the essence of the novel is to enter into dialogue with all discourses, to drag them from the "distanced plane" into "the zone of familiar contact." If the novel succeeds in dialogizing the authoritative word, it fundamentally changes the status of that word; if the novel fails in its dialogizing effort, authoritative discourse remains unintegrated into the work, a mere "dead quotation, something that falls out of the artistic context (for example, the evangelical texts in Tolstoy at the end of *Resurrection*)" (DiN,

p. 344). To the extent they rely on such dead quotations, novels fail.

Bakhtin's dismissal of the creative uses of authoritative discourse in novels weakens his readings of certain texts—not only *War and Peace* (in the few allusions to it), but also works by authors he admires most and understands best, such as *The Brothers Karamazov*. Clearly, the charge to make novels analogous to selves can work to crimp Bakhtin's own critical imagination and to narrow the types of novels he can accommodate. If one follows the logic of Bakhtin's argument, it becomes clear that just as novels fail in proportion to their reliance on authoritative discourse, so selves fail to grow in proportion to their reliance on it. The truly novelistic, mature, and responsible self knows a minimum of authoritative discourse.

To prevent misunderstanding, we must stress that Bakhtin does *not* mean to suggest that mere hostility to authority is a mark of maturity. Nor does he mean to condemn agreement with authority as a mark of immaturity or irresponsibility. On the contrary, agreement, as we recall, is a truly dialogic relation, and to agree with a discourse is already to have tested it, deprived it of unconditional allegiance, and integrated it into one's own framework. One has retold it in one's own words, and, whether those words seem acceptable or unacceptable, they are still partially one's own. Conversely, mere hostility to authoritative discourse may leave its status as absolutely authoritative unchallenged, much as some rebels remain the most passionately servile believers. To take on responsibility with respect to a discourse, or to any kind of authority, it is necessary not to dislike it, but to enter into dialogue with it—that is, to *test, assimilate,* and *reaccentuate* it.

"Assimilation" (*usvoenie*) is Bakhtin's general term for the processes by which the speech of others comes to play a role in our own inner speech. When utterances are assimilated they may retain the aura of something alien, or, to one degree or another, they may be reworked and endowed with "varying degrees of 'our-own-ness'" (SG, p. 89). Assimilation involves "reaccenting the word," giving it a new aura, developing potential meanings in it, placing it in dialogue with another voice that it may adumbrate as its antagonist, or, for that matter, entirely distorting it. Novels constantly assimilate and reaccentuate the discourses of daily life, and, as our psychic life grows more and more complex, we develop new ways to reaccentuate the discourse of others. In this respect, too, the self, as an assimilator of discourses, resembles a novel.

The process of assimilation and reaccentuation may affect the psyche's authoritative discourse and deprive it of its absolute authority. Previously authoritative words become overlaid with different registers and "accents." In understanding novels, it is crucial to distinguish between discourse that *is* still authoritative in the social milieu or work from discourse that *has once been* authoritative but has now been dialogized and reaccentuated; in reading novels from remote cultures or insufficiently accessible times, one may find it difficult to detect this crucial difference. The same distinction must be drawn with respect to the psyche, where an extremely important category is authoritative discourse that has only just begun to be assimilated. Such discourse is characteristically unstable in tone and effect, for its former authority may at any moment reassert itself, albeit somewhat defensively and polemically. Genuine authoritative discourse never sounds strident or defensive. It does not need to, for it does not know the test.

Just as authoritative words are compelling only because of their authority, so "innerly persuasive" words bind us precisely because they are persuasive. Innerly persuasive discourse, as other people's voices that we have learned, has become assimilated to the point where it is "half-ours and half-someone else's" (DiN, p. 345). It is not wholly our own, because nothing ever is; what *is* our own is our way of orchestrating the voices of others and the complex and highly specific character of inner speech within us. "Our own discourse [*svoe slovo*] is gradually and slowly wrought out of others' words that have been acknowledged and assimilated, and the boundaries between the two are at first scarcely perceptible" (DiN, p. 345, n. 31). We will see that for Bakhtin the true style of novels is in fact the combination of styles; by analogy, selfhood is not a particular voice within, but a particular way of combining many voices within. Consciousness takes shape, and never stops taking shape, as a process of interaction among authoritative and innerly persuasive discourses.

Innerly persuasive discourse thrives when it grows and changes in response to experience and to other innerly persuasive voices. Above all, it is never a dead thing, never something finished; rather, it is a kind of impulse toward the future. "Its creativity and productiveness consist precisely in the fact that such a word awakens new and independent words, that it organizes masses of our words from within, and does not remain in an isolated and static condition. It is not so much interpreted by us as it is further, that is, freely developed, applied to new material, new conditions" (DiN, pp. 345–46).

In this sense, it is unfinalized and unfinalizable, and is unlike any finished text, even a novel; it is perhaps closest to a voice in a polyphonic novel.

Because the mind is never whole and experience is always heterogeneous, innerly persuasive voices always differ from each other in unpredictable ways. "Our ideological development is just such an intense struggle within us for hegemony among various verbal and ideological points of view, approaches, directions and values" (DiN, p. 346).[14] Not only is this intense struggle an effect of the multiplicity of innerly persuasive voices, it is also the consequence of the very structure of each innerly persuasive word. "The semantic structure of an innerly persuasive discourse is *not finite*, it is *open*; in each of the new contexts that dialogize it, this discourse is able to reveal ever newer *ways to mean*" (ibid.).

Much as authoritative discourses may come to lose their authority, so innerly persuasive discourses can come to seem less persuasive, *more* than half "someone else's." When this happens, we typically begin to play with the discourse, make an objectified image of it, turn it into a "word of the second type," or attach it to a specific other person one holds at some distance. One investigates it from various perspectives in order to understand its limitations. One may begin to stylize or even parody the formerly persuasive voice.[15] Like assimilations of authoritative voices beginning to lose their authority, such parody of formerly persuasive voices is inherently unstable, because the earlier persuasiveness may at any moment reassert itself.

The process of distancing innerly persuasive voices is of great importance in psychic and ideological development. "One's own discourse and one's own voice, although born of another or dynamically stimulated by another, will sooner or later begin to liberate themselves from the authority of the other's discourse" (DiN, p. 348). One may suppose that it is often painful to encounter a reminder—an old letter, old notes, a diary entry, something that brings to mind an intense inner argument—of how one used to orchestrate inner dialogues, because we recognize how large a role was played by voices and perspectives that we have since rejected or outgrown in ourselves and criticized in others. Writers may reject old works that are in fact quite successful because the inner voices informing them now seem alien, threatening, or in danger of reasserting themselves.

Bakhtin suggests that if one truly understood the complex process of assimilation and reaccentuation of inner voices, one would understand a great deal about the development of a writer. The concept of influence, for instance, might be given a richer meaning; one would describe it in terms of a complicated reprocessing and dialogization of another voice, whether authoritative, persuasive, or anything in between. Novelistic language and images especially "are born in such a soil, seek to objectivize the struggle with all types of innerly persuasive alien discourse that had at one time held sway over the author" (DiN, p. 348). Here again we see Bakhtin's lifelong preoccupation with the creative process.

In the Dostoevsky book, and still more in "Discourse in the Novel," conceptualizing the world in language is described as the quintessentially human event, central to each self and to society. Bakhtin insists that "an independent, responsible, and active discourse is *the* fundamental indicator of an ethical, legal, and political human being" (DiN, pp. 349–50). Ethical responsibility and the project of selfhood require a constant readjustment of "one's own word," of "authoritative words," and of "innerly persuasive words." Far from representing a suspicion of language's conceptualizing and ethical powers, these readjustments bespeak a deep commitment to them.

The Novelistic Self on Trial: Carnival and the Uncloseable Loophole

The novel . . . is plasticity itself.   —EaN, p. 39

All existing clothes are too tight, and thus comical, on a man.
                                                          —EaN, p. 37

In period IIIb, under the aegis of Rabelais, Bakhtin shifts the balance of openness in the direction of pure unfinalizability. The shift has important consequences for Bakhtin's new description of the essential self.

In "Epic and Novel," Bakhtin adumbrates a new theory of the self by changing his understanding of the novel. Taking to an extreme some of his favorite earlier concepts—the positive role of laughter, of radical multilanguagedness, the loophole as pure potential—Bakhtin recharacterizes the novel and its sense of a human being. We immediately sense this change in the very personification of the genre of the novel itself. It now becomes not only a "living impulse" but a whole personality; now the novel "struggles," "gets on poorly with other genres" (EaN, p. 4), criticizes everything including itself, ridicules everything, and utterly forgets its past. The novel becomes the genre of permanent revolution and its favored image of the self becomes a *picaro* in time, pursuing novelty for its own sake.

Later in his career, Bakhtin would insist that without memory and a rich sense of the past, freedom and meaningful change are illusory. The revision of the 1929 Dostoevsky book and Bakhtin's final statement to the journal *Novyi mir* develop complex models of "genre memory" and culture memory to explain the intimate link between a sense of the past and an unfinalizable future. Memory establishes identity, enables responsibility, and creates meaningful potential. In period IIIb, however, Bakhtin displays a passion for *non*continuity and celebrates our ability to laugh events away and wholly to forget.

That difference is immediately apparent in his tendency toward extreme statement and inspirational hyperbole. He speaks in Heraclitian dicta, often cast as imperatives or exclamations: Time laughs and weeps! Dominion belongs to the child! In contrast to "Discourse in the Novel," which traced two long stylistic lines in the development of the genre, "Epic and Novel" asserts the novel's total freedom from any past, even its own. The novel is now not only different from other genres, but "a creature from an alien species" (EaN, p. 4).

In this formulation, the spirit of laughter becomes not only central to the novel, but essentially the whole of novelness. Laughter not only banishes "fear and pity before an object" (EaN, p. 23), it seems altogether loosed from bonds of responsibility and memory. In the pure comedy of novelness, Bakhtin writes, "the role of memory is minimal; in the comic world, there is nothing for memory and tradition to do. One ridicules in order to forget" (ibid.). The novel now takes on a distinct personality: it curses, brawls, parodies, probes crudely with its own hands, and lives in a perpetual present.

The past becomes incidental to novelness, inasmuch as the genre is oriented toward the *next* step and novels "speculate in what is unknown" (EaN, p. 32). The "unknown," understood as undefinability, also becomes fundamental to the novelistic heroes Bakhtin now celebrates. Out of the many more or less stable types of selves that can occur in novels, Bakhtin in this phase emphasizes comic heroes and popular masks. Immortal, cunning, and indifferent to biography, such heroes not only "cannot exhaust their possibilities

. . . always retaining a happy surplus of their own" (EaN, p. 36) but also never perish; they are figures of "free improvisation," and embody a "life process that is imperishable and forever renewing itself" (ibid.). Crucially, Bakhtin's emphasis here is on life process in the abstract and as a collective activity, not, as in the earlier manuscripts, on the individual life itself. There is no more I-for-myself, but, so to speak, only we-for-ourselves. For this reason, Bakhtin can describe fields of activity very different from the matrix of responsibility that was once his central concern.

In "Toward a Philosophy of the Act," we recall, Bakhtin everywhere stressed the self's radical singularity and irreplaceability in time and space, qualities that, in his view, make each person's life ethically responsible at every moment: "What can be accomplished by me cannot be accomplished by anyone else, ever" (KFP, p. 112). In "Discourse in the Novel," the self is portrayed as an interanimation of discourses that one shapes and reshapes, remembers and reaccentuates, throughout life: the "voice of conscience" becomes "the dialogue of conscience." By the time Bakhtin wrote "Epic and Novel," however, a reorientation toward a more extravagant self had taken place, a self that has no regrets because it has no past, a self that is not just open but pure loophole.

The Carnivalistic Self

Judged within the context of Bakhtin's career, then, the Rabelais book represents a rather atypical set of attitudes toward the self. One way to place *Rabelais and His World* in context might be to consider its characterizations of two fundamental markers of selfhood, the body and the voice.

In the early manuscripts, especially in "Author and Hero," one's form in space—one's body—becomes a main hero and an indispensable category for Bakhtin, as indeed is the case in the Rabelais book. As we have seen, whole chapters of "Author and Hero" are devoted to external appearance, to the outer boundaries of the body, and to the aesthetic role of the body in history. Nevertheless, these descriptions of the body could not be more different from those of the carnival body in *Rabelais*.

In "Author and Hero," what is important is the body's boundedness, its location in a given space and time, and its unique point of view on other bodies and on the world. From these situations, Bakhtin derives his special description of human responsibility, of mortality, of vulnerability to pain, and of the dangers inherent in "the event of being." When the word replaces the embodied act as the central metaphor in Bakhtin's descriptions of the world, self-other relations become more flexible and articulate. Processes of language, rather than the body, begin to trace the growth of the personality; novelistic language measures and ensures potential, loopholes, and futurity. These categories offer a possible exit from the boundedness of bodies. We confront the extreme of this process in *Rabelais and His World*, where the act of exiting becomes the primary, if not only, value-generating event.

In *Rabelais*, it is not the boundaries of the body that matter, but its orifices—which are important precisely because they *violate* the boundary between the individual self and the world. The carnival self of the Rabelais book is in many ways the antithesis of the responsible self of "Author and Hero," because it is not just shaped socially but is entirely collective: "This is not the body and its physiology in the modern sense of these words, because it is not individualized" (RAHW, p. 19). In carnival, an individual body is important only as a part of the body of the people: "The material bodily principle is contained not in the biological individual, not in the bourgeois ego, but in the people, a people who are continually growing and renewed" (ibid.).

For the carnivalistic self, death is like cell division. The old cell "dies in a sense but also reproduces" (RAHW, p. 52); in essence, there are no dead bodies. Thus the "utopian" sense of the self produced by a carnival vision is one in which all the consequences of mortality for selfhood disappear. The carnival self can laugh at itself dying because it has literally nothing to lose. No wonder that Bakhtin calls the work of Rabelais the most fearless book in world literature.

The carnivalistic self also inverts Bakhtin's description of the self in terms of voice and "the word." In contrast to "Discourse in the Novel," the Rabelais book generalizes the functions of the voice to a few collective activities: blasphemy, billingsgate, and choral support. It is not the guilty, agonized moral dialogues of a Dostoevskian hero but the loud oral forms of the public square that define the human voice. The word is not spoken, but shouted; it does not persuade, it hawks, profanes, curses. The speech forms that now interest Bakhtin are those that create "a free collectivity of familiar intercourse" (RAHW, p. 188), and they are interchangeable, unprintable, and strangely impersonal.

Bakhtin describes the appropriation of this discourse into literature as a diminution of its power and vitality. The Rabelais book thus rings with tones of nostalgia for an older and more popular orientation toward the future, a sense of time that is long past. Once the words of carnival joined the discourse of high satire and lost their full measure of blasphemy and degradation, the enfeeblement of carnival set in. Carnival became a matter of authors and audiences, its kings and queens mere characters in someone's telling, and its world a mere shadow of its former universally participatory "utopia." The best we can achieve now is the carnival grotesque "transposed into a subjective, idealistic philosophy" and the drama of a "chamber" carnival (RAHW, p. 37).

Because carnival is oriented to the collective, it does not speak in individual voices. Rather, it cultivates masks and disguises to separate voice from the individual and attach it to the collective. Celebrating liberation from any defining core of personality, carnival does *not* advance dialogue as the ideal of speech (RAHW, pp. 40–41). Whereas dialogue presupposes at least two responsible discrete selves, each outside the other, carnival strives everywhere toward *fusion*, which makes true dialogue impossible.

The distinction between fusion and dialogue is crucial. Before and after the Rabelais book, Bakhtin was to stress how fusion with the other—as in empathy—destroys the effectiveness, indeed the very possibility, of dialogue. But *Rabelais* describes an ideal in which all merge in "the people's second life," a life "organized on the basis of [common] laughter" (RAHW, p. 8). This laughter without outsideness "knows no inhibitions, no limitations" and consequently no fear (RAHW, p. 90).

Bakhtin counterposes the people's second life to its first, "official life" that celebrates "the triumph of a truth already established" (RAHW, p. 9) and a "seriousness" transmitted in tones of "violence, intimidation, threats, prohibitions" (RAHW, p. 94). For many readers, Bakhtin's opposition of the official and the unofficial has suggested his other binary pairs, monologic and dialogic, authoritative and innerly persuasive. But in fact the parallel is misleading. From the standpoint of Bakhtin's theories of dialogue, both the official and the unofficial (when it is organized, as in carnival) must be seen as opposite monologisms, confronting each other as unproductive antitheses.

The entire theory of novelistic selfhood is a theory of how innerly persuasive and authoritative words interact, are mediated, combined, and hybridized in the constant activity and project of forming a self. That self is unique, irreplaceable, noncoincident with itself and with every other self at every moment, as is the

Dostoevskian self of the polyphonic novel. But in contrast to these images of the self in which noncoincidence produces a *growth* in complexity, carnival liberates basically by simplifying and negating. In contrast to the novelistic self, which is oriented to ever new tasks, the carnivalistic self has no concrete task. Bakhtin's two heroes, Dostoevsky and Rabelais, are emblems of radically different moves in his thought.

One can see the difference between Bakhtin in this period and in his other periods if one considers his approach to "wholeness." As we have seen, Bakhtin sought numerous ways to describe selves, languages, or other cultural entities as meaningful wholes without describing them as fully integrated systems. In the early writings, the "whole" was described as a responsible individual signing (and coalescing around) an act; the wrong sort of wholeness was the various forms of system offered in the tradition of theoretism. In the second period, wholeness was the product of relationship and demanded a minimum of two consciousnesses in communication with each other. From this idea Bakhtin developed his concept of the open unity of a dialogue, as he had earlier described the open unity of the event. In both periods, proper wholes were not described as static, nor were they seen as developing in a predetermined way, but were understood as open-ended, productive, full of potential and "event-potential."

In his first two periods, Bakhtin cautioned that potential is bound to be empty, as the dictionary meanings of words are empty, unless a commitment is made in a specific context. Ambivalence and potential richness cannot remain real if they are uncommitted. One must act on them, or seek to realize potential in a way that produces something new and meaningful, and one must produce still more potential.

By contrast, in Bakhtin's carnival phase, pure—what he once called empty—potential itself becomes the prime, if not the sole, value. Inasmuch as the idea of the chronotope stresses the specific, historically bounded time and space that enables individual acts, carnival could be understood as an *anti*chronotope. The ethic of responsibility is replaced by the ethic of the loophole, and the wholeness of self by a totality of pure ambivalence. Such wholeness demands no risk and requires no self that exploits potential in a specific way. Indeed, from the perspective of Bakhtin's earlier and later writings, it allows for no self at all.

Carnival laughter is inspirational and restorative, to be sure, but only to the extent that it is impersonal and detached from individuality in spirit and in body. "The heart of the matter," as Bakhtin writes on Goethe's experience of Roman carnival, "is not in the subjective awareness but in the consciousness of [the people's] eternity" (RAHW, p. 250). In all Bakhtin's other writings on the self, what he here casually dismisses as "subjective awareness" is the fundamental value: the sense of one's own location at a specific time and place and one's unique responsibility for what "I alone can accomplish." Under carnival conditions, the self expands, rejoices, devours—and disappears.

The Later Writings:
A Return to the Beginnings

Bakhtin's final writings do not display the dogmatic antidogmatism and exuberant fascination with pure unfinalizability that we see in the book on Rabelais. The two other global concepts of his work, dialogue and prosaics, reassert themselves, and balance is restored. Self-building is again seen as a function of delimitation, individuation, and responsible socialization as well as of unfinalizability and the development of potential. Bakhtin again acknowledges that constraints, so long as they are not total, are in fact necessary to creativity and openness.

Thus, in his essay on speech genres, Bakhtin stresses that language enables the creation of the new through its "relatively stable thematic, compositional, and stylistic types of utterances" for everyday use (SG, p. 64). Generally speaking, Bakhtin returns to his earlier interest in genres, literary and nonliterary, as a way of understanding how a relatively stable heritage permits true creativity (see Chapter Seven of the present study). Patterns as well as loopholes allow for the integral position of a personality, and the key to personality again becomes dialogic relations (PT, p. 121).

Bakhtin once more sees the value of the given, which serves as a set of resources for what is created. The right sort of finalization makes unfinalizability possible; the "sclerotic deposits" of earlier activity become once again the starting point for new "living impulses" which will, in turn, leave more residues. Bakhtin expresses renewed interest in memory, which he conceives as an unsystematic accumulation of past experience that exists not only for the sake of preservation but also for creative transformation. Thus, the second edition of the Dostoevsky book develops his theory of "genre memory," and other late writings introduce the concept of "great time." Timelessness, the pure presentness celebrated in the work on carnival, is now seen as limiting because it derives from an obsession with "small time," a present without perspective, that separates us from the resources of real creativity in the future.

Bakhtin returns as well to his earlier ideas about the importance of an individual's separateness, his specific place in time, space, and culture. Not the collective body of the people but the separate body of a person interacting with and shaped by others reemerges as the precondition for all dialogue and creativity. He sees the positive side of boundaries and what they make possible, which is "creative understanding": "*Creative understanding* does not renounce itself, its own place in time, its own culture; and it forgets nothing. In order to understand, it is immensely important for the person who understands to be *located outside* the object of his or her creative understanding—in time, in space, in culture" (RQ, p. 7). In the context of his intellectual development, Bakhtin's insistence that creative understanding "forgets nothing" reads like a reply to his own carnival writings, which tend to link liberation with the banishment of memory. Creativity is reaffirmed as prosaic and dialogic. It requires both a gradual accumulation of real personal experience and the existence of genuine others as the ground for true learning. In a spirit almost stoic, Bakhtin acknowledges that individuals are never entirely at the mercy of events so long as they retain the power to reconceive them.

It is impossible to change the factual, thing-like side of the past, but the meaningful, expressive, speaking side can be changed, for it is unfinalized and does not coincide with itself (it is free). The role of memory in this eternal transformation of the past. Cognition/understanding of the past in its open-endedness (in its noncoincidence with itself). [Zam, pp. 516–17]

Bakhtin's description of freedom in his last years has little to do with carnival license and everything to do with noncoincidence. As long as difference can be charted between oneself and some other self, and between one's remembered past and a creative reassessment of it, one possesses the conditions for creativity and freedom. One needs the limitations of one's own past and of other selves. It is in this sense that we may understand Bakhtin's remark that "Quests for my own word are in fact quests for a word that is not my own, a word that is more than myself; this is a striving to depart from one's own words, with which nothing essential can be said. . . . These quests led Dostoevsky to the creation of the polyphonic novel" (N70–71, p. 149).

6

Polyphony: Authoring a Hero

> One could put it this way: the artistic will of polyphony is the will
> to combine many wills, a will to the event.   —PDP, p. 21

Polyphony is one of Bakhtin's most intriguing and original
concepts. Unfortunately, as Bakhtin wrote to his friend and col-
league Vadim Kozhinov, polyphony "has more than anything else
given rise to objections and misunderstanding."[1]

At times, careless reading of Bakhtin's Dostoevsky book has led
some critics to attribute to him arguments he has not made, and
has, in fact, explicitly denied making. The misreading began with
the very first reviews of the 1929 edition.[2] But not all misunderstanding is the fault of the critics. Bakhtin chose to explicate polyphony in a curious way, which has made misreading rather difficult to avoid.

To begin with, Bakhtin never explicitly defines polyphony. In
the first chapter of *Problems of Dostoevsky's Poetics* (and in the 1929
edition entitled *Problems of Dostoevsky's Creative Art* [or Creativ-
ity]), he selectively reviews the critical literature on Dostoevsky,
and, after each summary, specifies his reasons for agreeing or dis-
agreeing. This piecemeal exposition leads to repetition of some
points and ambiguity on others. By the end of the chapter, he has
provided a great deal of information about polyphony, but no explicit definition of it. If one expects this omission to be corrected in
subsequent chapters, one will be disappointed. The remainder of the
book discusses the implications of polyphony for representation of
the hero and of ideas, for the shape of plots and the use of double-
voiced language, but Bakhtin never specifies just what is and what
is not constitutive of polyphony per se.[3]

Bakhtin clearly states that Dostoevsky invented polyphony, but
that it is not limited to his works. Polyphony has been used subsequently—he does not tell us precisely where—and it could and
should be used in many more ways. The reader may therefore hope
that Bakhtin will distinguish between the defining features of po-

lyphony and the specific ways in which Dostoevsky implemented it. And Bakhtin does seem to imply some of these necessary distinctions. It is relatively clear, for instance, that carnivalization is a good but not necessary way to realize polyphony; by contrast, a "dialogic sense of truth" is absolutely constitutive of polyphony. But many other distinctions are never drawn. Bakhtin does not explicitly separate the contingent features of his prime example from the defining features of the concept.

Unwittingly creating still greater grounds for confusion, Bakhtin discusses polyphony in terms of dialogue, but he rarely tells us which sense of dialogue he has in mind.[4] Other key terms are also used inconsistently.

Even if Bakhtin's exposition were clearer, however, the possibility of confusion would still be great because the concept itself must be called deeply counterintuitive. Bakhtin was quite aware of its strangeness, and his method of presentation may have been an ill-considered strategy to preclude the misunderstanding that he correctly anticipated. In a manner perhaps resembling the verbal behavior of Dostoevsky's characters, Bakhtin's first chapter of the Dostoevsky book (especially in the 1963 edition) almost seems to "cringe" in the presence of potential misreaders and to take a "sideward glance" at future critics. In "Toward a Reworking of the Dostoevsky Book" (TRDB, 1961), Bakhtin seems to alternate between experiments with new expository strategies and expressions of hope that somehow future generations will come to appreciate what he has in mind.

Because misunderstandings have accumulated over the years, it will be helpful at the outset to enumerate some of the more common ones. According to Bakhtin, polyphony is *not* an attribute of all novels; Dostoevsky was the first polyphonic writer, and although there have presumably been others, the phenomenon is still relatively rare. Also, polyphony is not even roughly synonymous with heteroglossia. The latter term describes the diversity of speech styles in a language, the former has to do with the position of the author in a text. Many literary works are heteroglot, but very few are polyphonic. The two concepts pertain to fundamentally different kinds of phenomena, although the critical practice of conflating Bakhtin's categories has tended to blur the distinction for many readers.

Polyphony is often criticized as a theory that posits the absence of authorial point of view, but Bakhtin explicitly states that the polyphonic author neither lacks nor fails to express his ideas and values. Time and again, Bakhtin speaks of the commitment and "activity" of the polyphonic author. He also maintains that a work without "an authorial position . . . is in general impossible. . . . The issue here is not an absence of, but a *radical change in, the author's position*" (PDP, p. 67). In a polyphonic work, authorial viewpoint differs in kind and method of expression from its monologic counterparts. Neither does a polyphonic work lack unity, as critics of Bakhtin often understand him to be saying. By Bakhtin's criteria, a work without some kind of unity would simply be a flawed work. Rather, polyphony demands a different *kind* of unity, which Bakhtin calls "a unity of a higher order" (TRDB, p. 298).

Bakhtin attributes these and other misunderstandings to monologic habits of thought nurtured by centuries of what he earlier called theoretism. In the concluding sentence of the 1963 Dostoevsky book, he calls on critics to think in fundamentally new ways: "We must renounce our monologic habits so that we might come to feel at home in the new artistic sphere which Dostoevsky discovered, so that we might orient ourselves in that incomparably more complex *artistic model of the world* which he created" (PDP, p. 272). As we have seen, Bakhtin rejected the Hobson's choices of modern thought: either there is a system or there is nothing; either there are comprehensive closed structures or there is chaos; either there is in principle an all-encompassing explanatory system or there is total relativism (or perhaps: either God exists, or all is permitted). The assumption that these are the only alternatives has blinded critics to the possibility of radically different kinds of truth, unity, and perspective.

This assumption has also led to the mistaken identification of polyphony with relativism, in spite of Bakhtin's explicit warning against such a reading: "The polyphonic approach has nothing in common with relativism (or with dogmatism). But it should be noted that both relativism and dogmatism equally exclude all argumentation, all authentic dialogue, by making it either unnecessary (relativism) or impossible (dogmatism)" (PDP, p. 69).

On these grounds, Bakhtin would undoubtedly have dismissed the influential forms of relativism dominating current critical debate. If, as some have recently argued, all disputes ultimately reduce to questions of power or interest, then "authentic dialogue" about values and meanings is pointless. And if all divergent perspectives are fundamentally "incommensurable," then the possibility of genuine dialogue becomes illusory. As a form of thinking and of artistic visualization, polyphony presupposes the possibility and asserts the value of meaningful dialogue. Bakhtin not only describes polyphony, but endorses the view of the world it conveys.

Polyphony and the Dialogic Sense of Truth

As we interpret Bakhtin, two closely related criteria are constitutive of polyphony: a dialogic sense of truth and a special position of the author necessary for visualizing and conveying that sense of truth. In fact, these two criteria are aspects of the same phenomenon, the polyphonic work's "form-shaping ideology." They can be separated only for purposes of analysis.

Aware that his own discussion is cast in the monologic genre of literary criticism, Bakhtin repeatedly cautions us that it will necessarily be somewhat inadequate to its subject. Nevertheless, he suggests, if we proceed as far as monologic criticism can go, we may be better able to recognize and understand the essence of polyphony when we encounter it.

In the third chapter of the Dostoevsky book, Bakhtin discusses in some detail the difference between the monologic and dialogic conceptions of truth. These conceptions are not specific theories, but fundamental approaches to the very act of theorizing. They are, so to speak, theories "of the second order." For the past few hundred years, Bakhtin argues, modern thought has been dominated by a monologic conception of truth, reflected not only in philosophy but also in literature. It is to be found not only in Kant, Hegel, and other great thinkers, but also in the entire tradition of the monologic novel, which includes all novels before Dostoevsky. "These basic [monologic] principles go far beyond the boundaries of artistic creativity alone; they are the principles behind the entire ideological culture of recent times" (PDP, p. 80). It follows for Bakhtin that to explicate the nature of Dostoevsky's polyphonic works, one must first challenge the modern world's "entire intellectual culture," which represents its idea of truth as the only one possible.

Here we begin to see why the Dostoevsky book is really two books, something like a gestalt "duck-rabbit" drawing. On the one hand, it is a study of Dostoevsky, which happens to digress into metaphilosophical, metapsychological, and metalinguistic issues. On the other, it is itself a metaphilosophical work that challenges all of theoretism and semiotic totalitarianism by proposing a non-monologic, antisystemic conception of truth. To show that this different conception is possible, Bakhtin demonstrates that it actually exists in the novels of Dostoevsky. Read this way, his analysis of Dostoevsky's works is designed to bring out the dialogic conception of truth overlooked by Dostoevsky's critics and unsuspected by modern thought generally. These two frames of reference in Bakhtin's book compete for ascendancy, switch places, and—unfortunately—produce some ambiguity in the explication of polyphony.

Given the Soviet context in which the book was published, this strategy of exposition is understandable. How else could Bakhtin attack dialectics (Hegelian and Marxist), which he describes as deeply monologic? For Bakhtin, the opposition of Marxist and non-Marxist ideologies was itself a dispute *within* the tradition of monologic thought. Bakhtin was concerned to surmount that tradition altogether.

As Bakhtin describes it, the monologic conception of truth is built out of two distinct elements, the "separate thought" and the "system of thoughts" (PDP, p. 93). In "ideology" (by which Bakhtin here means monologic thought; PDP, p. 80), we encounter "separate thoughts, assertions, propositions that can by themselves be true or untrue, depending on their relationship to the subject and independent of the carrier to whom they belong" (PDP, p. 93). To the extent that these propositions describe the world accurately, they are regarded as true; to the extent they are inaccurate, they are untrue. No other scale of evaluation is relevant. In principle, it does not matter who enunciates these thoughts; or to be more precise, the content of these thoughts is not materially affected by their source.

To be sure, if the source of a proposition is authoritative, we may choose to believe it for that reason, or we may expend the effort to specify additional propositions implied by the source. A proposition in a scientific discipline, for instance, may carry with it unstated definitions of the subject matter, which could in principle be enunciated. But once this enunciation takes place, the truthfulness of the thought is entirely separable from the person who utters it. The proposition is "repeatable," as a scientific experiment is repeatable, by others. Someone may have discovered the particular idea in question, but it belongs to all and does not require the voice or particular context of the discoverer. In this sense, "separate thoughts" are what Bakhtin calls "'no-man's' thoughts" (PDP, p. 93).

Separate thoughts "gravitate" toward a system, the second aspect of monologic truth. "The system is put together out of separate thoughts, as out of elements" (ibid.). Bakhtin appears to have Hegel (or Marx) in mind as exemplary of monologic thought. To be sure, not all separate thoughts have been united into all-encompassing systems, but in principle they are formulated with systematicity as a goal. Thus, the great intellectual heroes of monologic thought are the great synthesizers, who shape apparently disparate insights and propositions into a coherent, all-encompassing system.

A system is also "no-man's." Or to put the point as Bakhtin also does, a system can be comprehended and fully contained by a *single* consciousness—in principle, by any consciousness with sufficient intellectual power. Even if a thought has been produced collectively, it is imagined as spoken by a single abstract entity: science, history, or the spirit of an age or people. Individuals can either accept or reject the truth, but as individuals they do not participate in its content. From the perspective of a believer in the system, there is "only one principle of cognitive individualization: *error.* True judgments are not attached to a personality, but correspond to some unified, systematically monologic context. Only error individualizes" (PDP, p. 81).

Bakhtin insists that this model of truth has been mistaken for the only one. In a key passage of the Dostoevsky book, he observes:

It is quite possible to imagine and postulate a unified truth that requires a plurality of consciousnesses, one that in principle cannot be fitted within the bounds of a single consciousness, one that is, so to speak, by its very nature *full of event potential* [*sobytiina*] and is born at a point of contact among various consciousnesses. The monologic way of perceiving cognition and truth is only one of the possible ways. It arises only where consciousness is placed above existence. [PDP, p. 81]

We may recall that in his early manuscripts, Bakhtin criticized theoretism for "transcribing away" the "eventness" of the event—everything about it that makes it particular, unfinalizable, and open to multiple unforeseen possibilities. In the passage just cited, the word translated as "full of event potential" (*sobytiina*) might also be rendered as "eventnessful"; what Bakhtin has in mind is a conception of truth that allows every moment of existence to be rich in potential. This alternate, prosaic conception of truth would not be "placed above existence," but would arise from the experience of the "open present" in each moment. Here Bakhtin's three global concepts—prosaics, unfinalizability, and dialogue—combine.

The dialogic sense of truth manifests unfinalizability by existing on the "threshold" (*porog*) of several interacting consciousnesses, a "plurality" of "unmerged voices." Crucial here is the modifier *un-*

merged. These voices cannot be contained within a single consciousness, as in monologism; rather, their separateness is essential to the
dialogue. Even when they agree, as they may, they do so from different perspectives and different senses of the world.

Bakhtin often refers to the participants in a dialogic conception
of truth as "voice-ideas." By this phrase he has in mind a unity of
idea and personality: the idea represents a person's integral point of
view on the world, which cannot be abstracted from the person
voicing it. Conversely, the person who holds the idea becomes a
full personality by virtue of that idea; the idea is not just something
he happens to believe, but is an essential shaping force throughout
his life. Such ideas are, as Dostoevsky observed, "felt." When two
such voice-ideas come to interact, they may produce a dialogue
changing both of them and giving rise to new insights and new dialogues. The "unity" of truth becomes the unified "feel" of a conversation, not the unity of a single proposition, however complex,
that may result from it. When monologic thinkers encounter such
conversations, they usually try to extract just such a finalizing proposition, but in doing so they are false to the dialogic process itself.

In such a conception of truth, the fundamental unit is no longer
the separate, "no-man's" thought, which does not play a major role
in an authentic dialogue. No, "the ultimate indivisible unit is not
the assertion, but rather the integral point of view, the integral position of a personality" (PDP, p. 93). According to Bakhtin, "Dostoevsky—to speak paradoxically—thought not in thoughts but in
points of view, consciousnesses, voices" (ibid.). The combination
of individual units of this sort does not "gravitate" toward systematicity. It yields "not a system" but "a concrete event made up of
organized human orientations and voices" (ibid.). The word *event*
here is to be understood not as a mere incident as we normally
understand it, but in Bakhtin's special sense of "eventness."

Polyphony and the New Position
of the Author

Then call thou, and I will answer; or let me speak, and answer
thou me.   —Job 13:22

In its structure Job's dialogue is internally endless, for the opposition of the soul to God—whether the opposition be hostile or
humble—is conceived in it as something irrevocable and eternal.
                                                    —TF1929, p. 280

Because the dialogic sense of truth requires a plurality of consciousnesses, a single author is bound to have immense difficulties in representing or conveying it. In fact, the "form-shaping ideology" of most literary genres, and of the novel before Dostoevsky, embodied one or another monologic truth. To understand Dostoevsky's achievement, it would be helpful to explore the effect of a monologic form-shaping ideology on a literary work.

In a monologic work, only the author, as the "ultimate semantic authority," retains the power to express a truth directly. The truth of the work is his or her truth, and all other truths are merely "represented," like "words of the second type." By this, Bakhtin means that in a monologic work each character's truth must be measured against the author's own ideology, because authorial ideology dominates the work and creates its unity. Monologic works may convey the author's position in various ways. Sometimes a given character may express it; at other times, the author's truth may be dispersed through a variety of characters. In some works, it may not receive direct or explicit expression; nevertheless, the author's truth informs the entire structure of the work, which cannot be comprehended without it.

In monologic works, other nonauthorial truths are either refuted or, more commonly in novels, they are represented as mere "characterological traits." By this and similar terms, Bakhtin means that the author represents these "other truths" as partial, as typical of and explained by a particular social perspective or psychological complex. The reader comprehends these truths by tracing them to a character's social group or personal history, but does not allow them to "mean directly." He locates their genesis and envisages their consequences, but does not engage in dialogue with them. Other truths do not have the right to demand an answer from the reader; that right is allotted only to the author's truth. The author's truth does not lie in the same plane as the truths of his characters. However complex, ambiguous, or fraught with contradictions and doubt the author's truth may be, it never treats the truths of other consciousnesses as equals. The author retains full control over the work and never surrenders the right to mediate between characters and readers. If that control is lost, the work becomes flawed.

By contrast, in a polyphonic work the form-shaping ideology itself *demands* that the author cease to exercise monologic control. This, then, is the second criterion of polyphony: a change in the author's position in the work. Polyphony demands a work in which several consciousnesses meet as equals and engage in a dialogue that is in principle unfinalizable. Characters must be *"not only objects of authorial discourse but also subjects of their own directly signifying discourse"* (PDP, p. 7). The direct power to mean, which in a monologic work belongs to the author alone, belongs to several voices in a polyphonic work. By surrendering his monologic powers, Dostoevsky created a way to embody a dialogic conception of truth.

According to Bakhtin, there is all the difference in the world between a contradictory or ambiguous truth and a truth that requires two or more voices. The same distinction must be drawn between merely expressing the monologic thought that "others have equal rights to the truth" and actually *embodying* a dialogic truth. The former expression is at best a monologic distillate of the latter, but does not take us out of the monologic world. Monologic works may point beyond themselves, but do not *go* beyond themselves. For that, it is necessary to grant another consciousness full semantic authority and the direct power to mean. A polyphonic work embodies dialogic truth by allowing the consciousness of a character to be truly *"someone else's* consciousness" (PDP, p. 7).

It may seem that this reorientation is impossible, because, after all, the author is still the sole creator and designer of the work. And, Bakhtin suggests, we might indeed conclude that polyphony was impossible if we did not have the example of Dostoevsky, who actually created it. He did so not by giving up his power of design but by changing the nature of the design. He made the encounter with other consciousnesses a part of his very project.

In order to create a truly polyphonic work, the author must be able to confront his characters as equals. His own ideology may receive expression in the work; indeed, in Dostoevsky's novels, at some level it always does. It may be defended passionately by one or another character or by the narrator. What is new in Dostoevsky's works is that others may and do contest the author's ideology *as equals.* And it is the author himself who sets the stage for these contests he is not foreordained to win and the outcome of which he does not foresee. The polyphonic author, in short, necessarily plays two roles in the work: he creates a world in which many disparate points of view enter into dialogue, and, in a quite distinct role, he himself participates in that dialogue. He is one of the interlocutors in the "great dialogue" that he himself has created.

Bakhtin explores this sense of the author through theological analogies. In the text of the Dostoevsky book, he compares the polyphonic author to Goethe's Prometheus, who "creates not voiceless slaves (as does Zeus) but *free* people, capable of standing *along-*

side their creator, capable of not agreeing with him and even of re-belling against him" (PDP, p. 6). In his notes "Toward a Reworking of the Dostoevsky Book," he appeals to the Judeo-Christian idea that God created morally free people (TRDB, p. 285). God may ar-gue with people, as he argues with Job, but Job retains the power to agree or disagree, if only silently. Similarly, Dostoevsky may an-swer his characters, but he does not manipulate them as passive ob-jects. "It is one thing to be active in relation to a dead thing, to voiceless material that can be molded and formed as one wishes, and another thing to be active in relation to *someone else's living, au-tonomous consciousness*" (ibid.).

To be sure, characters in a polyphonic work have been created by the author, but once they come into being, they partially escape his control and prevent him from knowing in advance how they will answer him. The polyphonic novel is therefore characterized by a *"plurality of independent and unmerged voices and consciousnesses, a genu-ine polyphony of fully valid voices"* (PDP, p. 6).

Using another favorite analogy, Bakhtin characterizes the mono-logic world as "Ptolemaic": the earth, representing the author's consciousness, is the center around which all other consciousnesses revolve. The polyphonic world is Copernican; as the earth is but one of many planets, the author's consciousness is but one of many consciousnesses. Elsewhere in the Dostoevsky book and in the notes for its revision, Bakhtin likens the polyphonic world to the universe of Einstein, in which one finds a "multiplicity of systems of measurement" (PDP, p. 272) that in principle cannot be reduced to a single system.

The Russian mathematician Nicholas Lobachevsky formulated his "non-Euclidian" model of space in order to answer Kantian contentions that even if space did not conform to Euclid's geome-try, we would never know it because any other kind of geometry is inconceivable to the human mind. Lobachevsky proved the con-ceivability of non-Euclidian space by conceiving of it. For Ivan Karamazov, non-Euclidian geometry suggests the possibility of non-Euclidian truth, which he urges Alyosha to reject. In alluding to Einstein's non-Euclidian universe, Bakhtin seems to be replaying Lobachevsky's and Ivan's strategy. He demonstrates that polyphonic works may exist by describing ones that already do exist. Even if his interpretation of Dostoevsky's works should prove mistaken, Bakhtin's polyphonic reading of them at least accomplishes his most important purpose: to prove the conceivability of polyphony. However counterintuitive polyphony may appear to critics nurtured by centuries of theoretism, Bakhtin suggests, it is a genuine possibility and perhaps an accomplished fact.

Polyphony and the Surplus

Drawing on concepts developed in his early manuscripts, Bakhtin explains polyphony's new authorial position in terms of the "surplus." It will be recalled that each of us enjoys a "surplus of vision" with respect to others we encounter. One person can see the back of another's head, and can appreciate the "blue sky" constituting the background to the other's suffering. One can know what the other looks like when he is unself-conscious of his appearance, knowledge forever inaccessible to the other. Others have the same surplus of knowledge with respect to us. In monologic works, authors enjoy an immense surplus of vision with respect to their characters, but the characters do not have the same surplus—indeed, often no surplus at all—with respect to the author.

In fact, the surplus enjoyed by monologic authors is much greater than the surplus we normally encounter in daily life. After all, the author has created the character, knows his psychology better than the character ever could, and knows the character's fate. This sort of "essential" surplus (knowledge of essential facts unavailable to the character) makes it impossible for the author and character to "exist on a single plane" and hence to enter into dialogue as equals. An author's surplus *finalizes* a character and definitively establishes his identity.

Real dialogue, however, demands partners who encounter each other on the same plane. Each must be unfinalizable with respect to the other. It would therefore seem impossible for there to be a genuinely polyphonic novel as Bakhtin describes it. And indeed, the obstacles to polyphony are immense, as Bakhtin concedes— which is why so much literary and social history was required before they were overcome. Dostoevsky's great discovery was to find a way to encounter his characters as unfinalizable others and engage them in a genuine open-ended dialogue.

To do so, it was necessary to renounce the author's "essential surplus of *meaning*" (PDP, p. 73). Only such a renunciation can enable characters to be relatively free and independent. This freedom and independence of characters is "relative" because in order to create the work at all the author must retain a second kind of surplus, which Bakhtin calls "that indispensable minimum of pragmatic, purely *information-bearing* 'surplus' necessary to carry forward the story" (ibid.). The author creates the world in which the unfinalizable character lives, and may put chance encounters or provocative incidents in his way. What he may not do is retain for himself a superior position beyond these purely pragmatic necessities. It is as if the author could pick the hour and room for a dialogic encounter with a character, but once he himself had entered that room, he would have to address the character as an equal.

In addressing the character, the author may also make use of one other kind of surplus; indeed, if the polyphonic novel is to be successful, the author ought to exploit this third type of surplus and must do so with great tact. Bakhtin does not give this third surplus a name, but it might be called the *addressive* surplus. Characters themselves use it in dealing with each other, so it is not a privilege confined to authorship. Indeed, we may use it in everyday life, and, Bakhtin intimates, would be wise to do so more often.

The addressive surplus is the surplus of the good listener, one capable of "live entering" (*vzhivanie*). It requires "an active (not a duplicating) understanding, a willingness to listen" (TRDB, p. 299). Without trying to finalize the other or define him once and for all, one uses one's "outsideness" and experience to ask the right sort of questions. Recognizing the other's capacity for change, one provokes or invites him to reveal and outgrow himself. As Bakhtin observes, "final significance is limited significance" (ibid.). Among Dostoevsky's characters, Tikhon in *The Possessed*, Myshkin in *The Idiot*, and Zosima in *The Brothers Karamazov* all make especially effective use of addressive surplus. "This surplus is never used as an ambush, as a chance to sneak up and attack from behind. This is an honest and open surplus, dialogically revealed to the other person, a surplus expressed by the addressed and not the secondhand word. Everything essential is dissolved in dialogue, positioned face to face" (ibid.).

As a participant in dialogue with the character, the author has at his disposal almost the whole range of dialogic interactions. He may tease and provoke the character, cajole and caress him, irritate and insult him. Indeed, the polyphonic author must avoid only two specific kinds of relation with the character. As we have seen, he must shun those that retain the essential surplus and so finalize the character, because then real dialogue would be impossible. The polyphonic author must also avoid merging entirely with the character. In that case, the author gives up his surplus, the two voices collapse into one, and real dialogue again becomes impossible.

Bakhtin's argument here parallels his distinction in chapter five of the Dostoevsky book between "imitation" (in the narrow sense) and "stylization"; it also recalls the distinction drawn in his early manuscripts between "empathy" and "live entering." Empathy (or imitation) precludes real dialogue by replacing "active understanding" with "duplicating understanding" and fusing two voices into one (TRDB, p. 299). A work in which author and character merge is not polyphonic, and perhaps not even a literary work at all, but rather a confession in varying degrees of disguise.

Polyphony as a Theory of the Creative Process

Concepts such as "renunciation of the essential surplus," "relative freedom" of the characters, and change in the "position" and "activity" of the author all suggest that polyphony is in fact a theory of the creative process. A polyphonic work must be created in a special way, Bakhtin argues, or it will inevitably become monologic. If the wrong creative methods are used, the work will not be a genuine dialogue but rather an "objectivized and finalized *image of a dialogue*, of the sort usual for every monologic novel" (PDP, p. 63).

According to Bakhtin, "Dostoevsky's creative process, as reflected in rough drafts, differs sharply from that of other writers" (PDP, p. 39). Drawing on what he perceives as Dostoevsky's method, Bakhtin apparently wants to construct an alternative to received models of the creative process, both "Romantic" (or "inspirational") and "classical" (or "formalist"). The inspirational model, which has its origin in Plato and includes most Freudian revisions, represents the creative process as a sudden burst of inspiration, whether from a muse, the unconscious, or an unidentified source. Crucially, it denies the importance of methodical work and of the moment-to-moment process of making decisions. In this respect, it is at odds with Bakhtin's prosaics.

Shelley's "Defense of Poetry" contains an exemplary statement of this view: "Poetry is not like reasoning, a power to be exerted according to the determination of the will. A man cannot say, 'I will compose poetry.' . . . for the mind in creation is as a fading coal, which some invisible influence, like an inconstant wind, awakens to transitory brightness" (Shelley, "Defense," p. 511). In this view, creation is strictly speaking not a process at all, inasmuch as the work comes essentially full blown to the author; the act of recording the inspiration is for Shelley not truly creative at all. "When composition begins, inspiration is already on the decline. . . . for

Milton conceived the *Paradise Lost* as a whole before he executed it in portions" (ibid.). This sort of creation—if it actually exists—would clearly not be suitable for a polyphonic work because it is not temporally extensive. There is no place in the model for un-finalizable encounters altering the shape of what is to come. Instan-taneously received and essentially complete from the outset, Ro-mantic inspiration does not allow for genuine, ongoing dialogic activity on the part of either the author or the characters.

The usual alternative to this model, the classical or formalist one, is no more suitable for polyphonic works. According to this ac-count, the author proceeds by following a plan given at the outset and fills in details with the rigor and care of a mathematician solv-ing a problem. Poe's essay "The Philosophy of Composition," a fa-vorite text of the Russian Formalists, offers a classic version of this position. Selecting the creative history of "The Raven" as typical, Poe writes: "It is my design to render it manifest that no one point in its composition is referrible either to accident or intuition—that the work proceeded, step by step, to its completion with the preci-sion and rigid consequence of a mathematical problem" (Poe, "Phi-losophy," p. 530). "Rigid consequence" is hardly what a poly-phonic author is after. Solving a mathematical problem is really a form of discovery rather than of creation, because the solution in some sense already exists. By contrast, a polyphonic author en-gages in dialogues that can always potentially create something genuinely new. Poe's creator makes maximal use of the "essential surplus," which the polyphonic author must renounce.[5]

Like genuine dialogue, polyphonic creation is an open process that seeks "surprisingness" at almost every step of the way. In the second edition of the Dostoevsky book, Bakhtin discusses a num-ber of reactions to the first edition, and cites with approval Victor Shklovsky's observation that "Dostoevsky's plans contain by their very nature an open-endedness which in effect refutes them as plans" (Shklovsky, *Za i protiv*, as cited in PDP, p. 39). Paraphrasing Bakh-tin, Shklovsky observes that Dostoevsky's nervous, hurried method of creation repeatedly testifies to his openness to new insights and directions. Indeed, Shklovsky contends, Dostoevsky continually went back to already written dialogues, opened them anew, tried to provoke new responses, and so changed their outcomes—which in turn necessitated rewriting dialogues to follow and altered the pre-liminary shape of those only dimly imagined. "As long as a work remained multi-leveled and multi-voiced, as long as the people in it were still arguing, then despair over the absence of a solution would not set in" (ibid.). As a result, concluding his works was especially painful to Dostoevsky: "The end of a novel signified for Dostoevsky the fall of a new Tower of Babel" (ibid.).

Bakhtin imagines Dostoevsky's creative process as profoundly active. In his account, Dostoevsky did not first work out a structure, plan, or overall plot of the work. Rather, he first imagined specific "voices," that is, integral personalities with their own ideas and sense of the world. "Dostoevsky begins . . . with idea-heroes of a dialogue. He seeks the integral voice, and fate and event (the fates and events of the plot) become means for expressing voices" (TRDB, p. 296). Dostoevsky sometimes begins with specific real people, whose voices and worldviews he already knows well, and in his first rough drafts, the names of these people—Herzen, Chaadaev, Granovsky—sometimes appear.

Dostoevsky then makes use of his "pragmatic" surplus to contrive situations that could provoke these people into dialogue with each other and with his own views. Characters join in dialogue, Dostoevsky himself may in some form participate, and the characters (perhaps also the author) outgrow themselves in the process. Sometimes Dostoevsky continues the dialogue in new scenes; at other times, he leaves preliminary dialogues in his notebooks and starts anew with characters recently made more complex.

Dostoevsky's creative methods may explain why so many readers have found his notebooks to be doubly dramatic: not only are their scenes in themselves riveting, but the very process by which the work emerges so frenetically has a drama of its own. Although Bakhtin does not say so, Dostoevsky's published *Diary of a Writer*, which included drafts of stories along with their finished text, was presumably an attempt to capitalize on the excitement of his own process of work. Throughout this process, "Dostoevsky seeks words and plot situations that provoke, tease, extort, dialogize. In this lies the profound originality of Dostoevsky's creative process. The study of his manuscript materials from this angle is an interesting and important task" (PDP, p. 39).

Bakhtin also cites with approval a response to the first edition of the Dostoevsky book by Anatoly Lunacharsky, a leading Bolshevik intellectual and People's Commissar of Education from 1917 to 1929. Paraphrasing Bakhtin's thought, Lunacharsky observed:

Dostoevsky—if not in the final execution of the novel, then certainly *during its original planning stage and gradual evolution*—was not in the habit of working from a preconceived structural plan. . . . we have here instead a true polyphonism of the type that links together and interweaves *absolutely free personalities*. Dostoevsky himself was perhaps interested, extremely and intensely interested, to discover the ultimate outcome of this ideological and ethical conflict among the imaginary persons he had created (or, more precisely, who had created themselves in him). [Lunacharsky, "O 'mnogo-golosnosti,'" as cited in PDP, p. 46, n. 51]

This technique works only if the author has such a vivid sense of the characters that he can truly address them.[6] They seem to answer him, which is to say, he can imagine their answers but cannot predict them before he actually addresses them. In this sense, although Dostoevsky remains their creator, they are truly unfinalizable.

Bakhtin's crucial point is that the dialogues that compose the novel—that make the entire novel one "great dialogue"—are not shaped beforehand, not "planned" in the usual sense. Rather, they take place "right now, that is, in the *real present* of the creative process" (PDP, p. 63). What we read is not a mere "stenographer's report of a *finished* dialogue, from which the author has already withdrawn and *over* which he is now located as if in some higher decision-making position" (ibid.). In that case—a common one in monologic works—we have the mere "image of a dialogue," something finalized and not truly dialogic. In the polyphonic work, we sense the dialogue as it actually unfolded; we sense the author addressing characters like people "*actually present . . .* and *capable of answering him*" (ibid.).

Dostoevsky was able to compose dialogues of this sort because he could intuit not only the explicit and implicit content of an idea, but also some of its "potentialities" (PDP, p. 91). By provoking and teasing the carrier of the idea, he could induce that character to produce something new. Thus, readers see how particular ideologies with which they are familiar might (but would not have to) lead to new concepts never before expressed. They learn not only what Herzen or Granovsky actually said, but what they might have wound up saying in spite of themselves in different circumstances. Some of the idea's potentials emerge before the readers' very eyes, as Dostoevsky depicts how it might "develop and function under certain changed conditions, what unexpected directions it would take in its further development and transformation" (ibid.). Dostoevsky would, in effect, draw "dotted lines" (*punktir*) between positions that had still not encountered each other in real life; he "placed the idea on the borderline of dialogically intersecting consciousnesses. . . . and forced them to quarrel" (ibid.). He starts with the "given" and turns it into the "created"—and creating.

Toward Prosaics: Plot and Structure Versus Polyphony and Eventness

What, then, is the status of the plot in a polyphonic work? Clearly, it must differ from its monologic counterparts. Because the polyphonic author does not know the outcome of dialogues "in the real present of the creative process," he cannot decide in advance what will happen to the characters. He may, of course, sketch out various possibilities, which one can find in the notebooks. But these potential outcomes serve not so much to direct action as to create a better sense of characters at a given time and to arrive at a conceptualized "whole" of their personalities. The author understands characters in each present moment by imagining futures that are, at that moment, conceivable for them. Anticipation is not a plan for the future, but a "dotted line" drawn and redrawn as the creative process proceeds. Since characters may always surprise their author as their potential dialogues and acts become concrete, and since the dialogues in which they engage may change them in unexpected ways, possible outcomes are continually outdated. Like the characters, the work remains unfinalizable throughout its creation. Plot is no longer the sequence characters are ordained to follow, but the result of what they happen to say or do.

Thus, Dostoevsky handles plot in a special way. He avoids using a character's predetermined destiny as a way of "ambushing" and "finalizing" him. Instead, plot becomes a way of setting optimally favorable situations for intense dialogues with unforeseen outcomes. "Its goal is to place a person in various situations that expose and provoke him, to bring people together and make them collide in conflict—in such a way, however, that they do not remain within this area of plot-related contact but exceed its bounds" (TF1929, pp. 276–77). It follows that the "clamps" holding the work together are indeed enabled by the plot but not contained in it: "The real connections begin where ordinary plot ends, having fulfilled its service function" (TF1929, p. 277). However intriguing (or banal) Dostoevsky's plots may be, they are the wrong place to look for the central moments of his works. Plot exists so that it may be transcended by characters achieving "extra-plot connections" (PDP, p. 105).

Bakhtin provides no sustained readings of whole novels, and so one must guess at how he would analyze the role of extra-plot connections in a specific work. His analysis suggests that the truly central moments of *The Brothers Karamazov* are its great dialogic encounters, which although enabled by the plot seem to arise out of it. They seem to be somehow "excessive" in terms of the novel's action. Most likely, Bakhtin would focus on the Grand Inquisitor legend, which seems to have a life of its own; on Ivan's conversation with the devil; and on Dmitri's "Confession of a Passionate Heart—in Verse," in which he describes "the beauty of Sodom" to Alyosha.

The earliest "excessive" dialogue occurs in book two when the Karamazovs gather in Father Zosima's cell supposedly to work out their family differences. As the narrator observes, however, not only is this reason a pretext, it is not even a true pretext ("The pretext for this gathering was a false one" [Dostoevsky, *Karamazov*, bk. 1, ch. 5, p. 32]). In this atmosphere of multiple feigning, characters discuss ultimate questions, and the discussion achieves a momentum that makes even Ivan take it seriously for a few moments in spite of himself. The scene's central chapter, "Why Is Such a Man Alive?," takes its title from Dmitri's Job-like question about his father as the self-proclaimed incarnation of evil; this title provides the text for future dialogues of the novel. Almost immediately, Dmitri's question provokes Zosima's silent bow, which concentrates in a single gesture immense dialogic potential. Like the Inquisitor's kiss, it is an unexpected, wordless microdialogue. It is not fundamentally a prediction of future action, as the more naive characters assume, but is itself a high point of a key dialogue in a novel of plot-transcending dialogues.

Bakhtin apparently sees the dialogues in Dostoevsky's works as interrupted but never ended. Dramatic incidents occur in order to place characters in "critical moments" that force them to speak out their deepest thoughts and feelings, which may change suddenly in the process. To read these speeches and conversations in terms of the plot is to turn the novel on its head. Dmitri's dream of "The Babe" is not to be read primarily as indicative of his mental state when he is arrested; rather, it is the arrest that is to be understood in terms of the dream. The dream itself is, characteristically, an imagined dialogue about an ultimate question. It leads to Dmitri's later dialogues with Rakitin, and to his dialogue with Alyosha about his dialogue with Rakitin, in which Dmitri rejects the chemical theory of consciousness as a threat to freedom, responsibility, and the meaningfulness of questioning itself. When Dmitri accepts God, he does so dialogically, as someone to call upon from imprisonment beneath the earth.

What, then, defines the structure of the work in a Bakhtinian reading? It is clearly not the plot, because such a reading would lead to explaining the dialogues in terms of past and future action. Such an explanation, perfectly appropriate for monologic works, would decisively change the nature of these dialogues. Their participants would lose the power to "signify directly," and their utterances would become simply signs of their character or indications of their destiny, rather than "directly signifying ideas" inviting the reader to respond dialogically with his or her own answers.

Dostoevsky's novels are designed to turn readers not into ana- lyzers of character, action, and circumstance, but into dialogic part- ners of the characters and author. Their "interaction provides no support for the viewer who would objectify an entire event accord- ing to some monologic category (thematically, lyrically, or cog- nitively)—and this makes the viewer also a participant. . . . every- thing in the novel is structured so as to make dialogic opposition inescapable. Not a single element of the work is structured from the point of view of a non-participating 'third person'" (PDP, p. 18). For the reader, as well as for the characters, it is impossible to be just an "eyewitness" (Ivan Karamazov's journalistic pseudonym); the novel "destroys footlights" (PDP, p. 237).

Characters who are mostly interested in events and causes turn out to be fools, like the spectators or attorneys at Dmitri's trial. Ivan eventually learns that it really does not matter whether he him- self plotted the death of his father; his responsibility lies on an en- tirely different plane. Similarly, readers who understand ideas in terms of their origins and consequences find they are left hanging on too many crucial issues. One must read not for the plot, but for the dialogues, and to read for the dialogues is to participate in them. The compelling quality of Dostoevsky's novels derives in part from this intense reaction produced—or rather provoked—in the reader.

The classic analysis of Dostoevskian structure, Robert Belknap's *The Structure of "The Brothers Karamazov,"* offers just the sort of so- phisticated analysis that Bakhtin would probably characterize as the best possible monologic reading of the work. We may suppose that Bakhtin would react to Belknap's study as he reacted to the best Formalist work and would respectfully treat it as exemplary (in both senses) of a mistaken view. To understand Bakhtin's under- standing of polyphonic plot and structure, it would be useful to imagine his likely objections. Belknap sees the novel as a complex "structure of inherent relationships" (Belknap, *Structure*, p. 89), consisting of scenes and incidents resonating with each other in a complex network of symbolic cross-references, echoes, and fore- shadowings. For Bakhtin, this approach, like all readings grounded in essentially structuralist categories, makes a closed *structure* out of an ongoing *event*.

To detect a structure is to read a work essentially synchronically: the plot, symbols, and resonances are already in place and may properly be contemplated at a single moment. These elements are regarded as elements of a structure that unfolds in time but is not essentially *constituted* by time in all its unfinalizability. Novels read this way become essentially similar to lyric poems as, let us say, Roman Jakobson reads them. The richness of the novel, like the richness of a poem, lies in the density of a network with ever finer interconnections. The plan of the whole overdetermines all incidents, symbols, and words as they interweave with other incidents, symbols, and words. The more complex the weave, the better the plan; and the better the plan, the better the work.

Bakhtin accepts the power of this model for certain kinds of works, such as lyric poems and monologic narratives, but denies its appropriateness for polyphonic works. Born of poetics and well suited to poetry, it necessarily misses the defining feature of polyphonic prose. Here Bakhtin takes his first steps toward prosaics as a special theory of prose. In the Dostoevsky book, he contrasts polyphonic works, which demand his new approach, with monologic ones, which may be approached in terms of traditional poetics. Later, he will expand the domain of prosaics, adjusting its categories in the process, to all novels and to all prose "gravitating" toward the novel. The fourth ("menippean satire") chapter of *Problems of Dostoevsky's Poetics*, most of which was added in 1963 after he had worked out his general theories of the novel, already reflects this broader prosaics, which is probably why the chapter is not fully integrated into the rest of the book.

For Bakhtin, Dostoevsky's novels are not structures because there is no plan in the usual sense. Their great dialogues are not constructed with an eye to their integration in a yet-to-be-completed whole, for such construction would turn a dialogue into a mere "objectivized and finalized image of a dialogue" (PDP, p. 63). Rather, the dialogues take place "in the *real present* of the creative process" (ibid.) with their outcomes unknown, and their implications for the whole unspecified in advance. Consequently, parallels with later events and similarities that look like structural correspondences to monologic readers are in reality nothing of the sort. Apparent echoes and foreshadowings are not the product of the author's plan, but of the characters' obsessions. Possessed by ideas, the characters return to them over and over again, and so naturally certain repetitions develop. It is important to recognize that even in life, habits and obsessions may produce repetitions that could appear as parallels plotted in advance if we did not know better. *Karamazov* reflects not an integral plan but what might be called the "return of the obsessed."

As Bakhtin also puts the point, the plot that happens to have developed is conceived as only one of many possible plots that could have developed. We are invited to draw "dotted lines" to other possible plots that could have developed out of the same initial dialogic material. Plot by itself is merely a "Procrustean bed" that characters escape in quintessential moments of dialogic exchange beyond all plot—and beyond all structure of any kind. Structure would require the kind of "essential surplus" that the polyphonic novel abjures. Like the dialogic sense of truth, the polyphonic novel is not made up of elements united in a system but of voices full of event potential. Instead of a finalized plot, Dostoevsky gives us "a *live event*, played out at the point of dialogic meeting between two or several consciousnesses" (PDP, p. 88). Rather than structure, we have "eventness" (*sobytiinost'*).

Of course, Bakhtin may be wrong in his analysis of Dostoevsky's novels. Certainly, the concept of polyphony applies better to some works than to others. In our view, Belknap's reading is convincing—or will be until a truly polyphonic reading of *Karamazov*, worked out in detail and over the course of the novel, becomes available. But even if Belknap should prove to be correct, we would still be left with Bakhtin's remarkable concept of polyphony, which may have (and was meant to have) much broader applications. Bakhtin aimed at nothing less than the replacement of a monologic approach to culture with a truly polyphonic approach, one requiring a plurality of irreducible consciousnesses.

Closure and Unity

> The unity of the whole in Dostoevsky is not a matter of plot nor of monologic idea, that is, not mono-ideational. It is a unity above plot and above idea.   —TRDB, p. 298

By now it should be clear why the common objection to Bakhtin's theory of polyphony—that it describes the author as somehow passive—is based on misunderstanding. According to Bakhtin, the polyphonic author is supremely active in conceptualizing whole personalities, setting up open-ended dialogues, and provoking characters to speak. If anything, Dostoevsky is more active than most monologic authors, and the nervous, frenetic quality of his works reflects Dostoevsky's constant and energetic participation.

It is also inaccurate to charge Bakhtin with attributing no point of view to the author. On the contrary, the author passionately expresses a point of view in two distinct ways. He may participate in the novel's dialogue, principally by creating characters who express various aspects of his ideology (Shatov in *The Possessed*, Zosima in *Karamazov*, Sonia in *Crime and Punishment*, and Myshkin in *The Idiot*). In addition, Dostoevsky's perspective is embodied in the form-shaping ideology of the work, with its dialogic conception of truth.

According to Bakhtin, this double expression has occasioned considerable confusion, because the two kinds of authorial views are radically different. The diatribes of Shatov and Myshkin express monologic truths; the works as wholes express a dialogic conception of truth. What then is the relationship between the two authorial expressions, and how should we approach the ideas of Dostoevsky the journalist when they appear in his novels? Bakhtin's answer is categorical and clear: we should approach "Dostoevskian ideas" in his novels

in exactly the same way we regard the ideas of Napoleon III in *Crime and Punishment* (ideas with which Dostoevsky the thinker was in total disagreement), or the ideas of Chaadaev and Herzen in *The Adolescent* (ideas with which Dostoevsky the thinker was in partial agreement). . . .

In fact, the ideas of Dostoevsky the thinker, upon entering his polyphonic novel . . . are combined in an indissoluble unity with images of people (Sonya, Myshkin, Zosima), they are liberated from their monologic isolation and finalization, they become thoroughly dialogized and enter the great dialogue of the novel on *completely equal terms* with other idea-images (the ideas of Raskolnikov, Ivan Karamazov, and others). It is absolutely impermissible to ascribe to these ideas the finalizing function of authorial ideas in a monologic novel. Here they fulfill no such function, for they are all equally privileged participants in the great dialogue. [PDP, p. 92]

Not only does Dostoevsky actively express his views, but he does so in a way that in effect sets him in dialogue with his own form-shaping ideology as well as with his characters. What Dostoevsky does not do is take unfair advantage of his position as author to arrange in advance for the triumph of his own most cherished convictions.

This account, however, suggests another set of objections to Bakhtin's thesis, which he is at some pains to answer adequately. How can a work that is in principle unfinalizable achieve closure or function as a whole? And what specific solutions did Dostoevsky devise for this problem?

Bakhtin answers the second of these questions with a concession: Dostoevsky usually failed to work out a way to end his novels without violating their polyphonic essence, which is why his endings are so often out of keeping with the tone of the works they conclude. The exemplary case of such an ending that is unsuccessful by Bakhtin's criteria is the epilogue to *Crime and Punishment*, which has, in fact, struck many readers as a "falling off." Faced with "a unique conflict between the internal open-endedness of the characters and dialogue, and the *external* (in most cases compositional and thematic) *completedness* of every individual novel," Dostoevsky often resorted to "a *conventionally literary, conventionally monologic* ending" (PDP, p. 39). The notable exception to such failures, according to Bakhtin, is the ending to *The Brothers Karamazov*, which ends polyphonically and openly and which invites us to draw dotted lines to a future, unresolved continuation that the narrator "promises."

Bakhtin here presumes, as many critics have not, that *Karamazov* is complete as it stands, and that it would have been complete even if Dostoevsky had lived long enough to continue it (should he have chosen to do so). Interestingly enough, Belknap also argues that Dostoevsky used the device of the deliberate fragment in *Karamazov*, as he did in some other works (most notably, *Notes from Underground*). But Bakhtin's polyphonic interpretation of this ending nevertheless differs markedly from Belknap's structuralist reading.

For Belknap, Dostoevsky's deliberate fragment is essentially similar to the deliberate fragments of numerous other works, including "unfinished" Romantic poems and Gogol's "unfinished" stories (such as "Ivan Fyodorovich Shponka and His Aunt"). For a structuralist, the anticlosure of such endings is really a highly wrought and appropriate form of closure, which does in fact complete the structure of the whole. The wit and ingenuity of the device lies in its successfully doing just what it denies doing at the very moment it denies doing it. A work about the failure of inspiration breaks off as it meditates on the unaccountability of the muse; a story about the devices of suspense leaves us hanging just as it reaches a turning point.

Bakhtin would probably concede that in monologic works, the structuralist analysis is correct. But he maintains that in polyphonic works the same device performs a radically different function. Specifically, it allows the work to achieve not closure by anticlosure but

genuine *lack* of closure. Instead of metaliterary wit, we sense dialogic unfinalizability; instead of witnessing a virtuoso assertion of
control just when it seemed to be lost, we realize that completion in
the usual sense is not needed because structure in the usual sense is
not present. As a polyphonic work has a plot without a structure,
so it also has a conclusion in which—genuinely, not just ostensibly—nothing is concluded.

What sort of unity is possible under such circumstances? What
sort of unity can be open and polyphonic? Bakhtin's answers are not
entirely satisfying, but they do indicate where more adequate formulations might be sought. In part, Bakhtin answers by analogy:
the Einsteinian world has many separate systems of measurement
that cannot be combined into a single Newtonian system of reference, but the Einsteinian universe is nevertheless a unity. Bakhtin
evidently saw his idea as part of a broader trend in modern thought,
in which, ironically, the sciences were ahead of the humanities in
formulating concepts that the humanities urgently require. But argument by analogy can be unsatisfying if the correspondence remains unclear. What precisely does an Einsteinian unity mean when
applied to novels or culture?

In a polyphonic work, we recall, each major hero retains the
capacity to "mean directly." That is, the role played solely by the
author in a monologic work is multiplied, so that several characters
may play it. Each character has his own word, and neither the
author nor any other character can turn that word into a mere object or character trait. The polyphonic work has several distinct
and irreducible centers. It follows that the work's unity cannot be
monologic, because monologism achieves unity by incorporating
all elements of the work into a single design governed by a single
ultimate semantic authority. The presence of many heroes, each
of whom speaks in an autonomous and "relatively independent"
voice, "breaks down the monologic unity of the work (without, of
course, violating artistic unity of a new and nonmonologic type)"
(PDP, p. 51).

A nonmonologic unity joins but does not merge several "semantic authorities," each of which would be capable of endowing a
monologic work with a monologic unity. Polyphony, in other
words, achieves a unity of several potential unities. For this reason,
Bakhtin repeatedly calls polyphonic unity a unity of the second
order or a unity of a higher order (see PDP, pp. 15, 51; TRDB,
p. 298). Higher unity is roughly analogous not to a set, but to a set
of sets, with the important exception that a set of sets may be closed

whereas a polyphonic unity is necessarily open. Bakhtin provisionally compares polyphonic unity to "the church as a communion of unmerged souls, where sinners and righteous men come together" and to "Dante's world, where multi-leveledness is extended into eternity" (PDP, pp. 26–27). But then he immediately rejects these comparisons, because they seem too static, too closed and structured, and too easy to conflate into an ideological and monologic unity.

Monologic readings of Dostoevsky's novels typically attribute to them a unity of the first, or lower, order—a Newtonian rather than an Einsteinian unity. Some critics assume that the novel is meant to illustrate the viewpoints Dostoevsky advocates in his journalism and therefore read that ideology into the novels. Other critics argue that in spite of his intentions, the controlling voice of his works belongs to characters he ostensibly refutes but brilliantly develops, such as Ivan Karamazov. Still others try to construct a dialectical system in which all the characters participate as preliminary thesis or antithesis; Bakhtin deems this approach furthest of all from a true polyphonic understanding.

According to Bakhtin, the most sophisticated monologic critics dimly sense the work's dialogic sense of truth, but monologize it into a single theme or moral imperative: "Be a personality!" (Askoldov), or "affirm someone else's 'I'" (Vyacheslav Ivanov). A theme of this sort, however, "is altogether possible in a novel of the purely monologic type, and is in fact often found in that sort of novel. . . . the affirmation of someone else's consciousness does not in itself create a new form or a new type of novelistic construction" (PDP, pp. 10–11). In short, Ivanov, "having arrived at a profound and correct definition of Dostoevsky's fundamental principle—the affirmation of someone else's 'I' not as an object but as another subject—proceeded to monologize this principle, that is, he incorporated it into a monologically formulated authorial worldview and perceived it as merely one of the interesting themes in a world represented from the point of view of a monologic authorial consciousness" (PDP, p. 11).

Each of these attempts is what we might expect from critics steeped in the "monologic habits" of traditional poetics. The history of Dostoevsky criticism seems to exhaust the resources of monologic poetics in its encounter with a polyphonic work. Lacking an alternative tradition, critics "reduce a new artistic form to an already familiar artistic intention" (ibid.). Curiously, Bakhtin finds the most adequate traditional response to be one that at first glance would seem the most naive: the attempt of some critics to argue directly with the characters, as if they were not part of a literary work and somehow lived and spoke on their own. Critics who would not think of arguing directly with Flaubert's characters find themselves polemicizing with Ivan Karamazov, Raskolnikov, the Grand Inquisitor, and Kirillov; these polemics inadvertently testify to the unprecedented power of these characters to "mean directly." However naive this approach may be, it at least preserves the characters' status as "*subjects of their own directly signifying discourse*" (PDP, p. 7). In describing polyphonic unity, we must take into account this special power and status of characters.

Polyphonic unity is "unity not as an innate one-and-only, but as a dialogic *concordance* of unmerged twos or multiples" (TRDB, p. 289). What precisely is the nature of this concordance? Bakhtin answers rather vaguely that it is "unity of the event" (PDP, p. 21). He seems to have two kinds of event in mind. To begin with, there is the event of the dialogue itself. In conversations with independent participants arguing intensely about matters of great concern to them, the whole may have a unifying spirit, regardless of the divergence among positions. We lack a vocabulary for this kind of unity, which is one reason it is so hard to convey. We give the name *structure* to static unities, and we discriminate among kinds of structure, but we lack a comparable term for the unity of event, and for the different kinds of "eventness" we have experienced. Rather than provide such terminology, Bakhtin seems to project it as a topic for future inquiry.

The Unity of Creative Eventness

In speaking of the "unity of the event," Bakhtin also seems to have in mind the event of the creative process. It will be recalled that polyphony is in essence a theory of creativity: it describes a special method of creation necessary for the production of polyphonic works. As readers, we sense the "throb" of this process as the "clamps" holding the work together. Bakhtin's point is that authors do not just "invent" or fabricate whatever comes into their mind. Rather, they subject themselves to certain procedures, which they cannot violate without ruining the integrity of the work. Even children do as much when they play games, Bakhtin observes. What distinguishes polyphonic works from monologic ones is that (1) the procedures are different in kind, and (2) our sense of unity derives primarily from our sense of the integrity of the process itself. Bakhtin does not himself make this last point explicitly, but we think it follows from his argument.

We must here extend Bakhtin's logic. It seems to us that Bakhtin may not have been fully aware when he published the 1929 edition of his book that polyphony was essentially a theory of creativity; many of the citations we have used to illustrate this point first appear in the 1963 edition. Creativity is present as a topic in both editions, but it is more central to the second. It seems still more central to his "Toward a Reworking of the Dostoevsky Book" and to some other of his late essays. But Bakhtin never developed the potential of this idea as rigorously or fruitfully as he might have.

That potential argument seems to run as follows: A polyphonic author begins with a specific type of material different from that of a monologic author. Every good author, whether monologic or polyphonic, creates characters whose characteristics must not be arbitrarily violated if the work is to ring true. Monologic authors may at times sense resistance to what they want to do, because what they want to do may contradict a given character's image. As the work progresses, the fleshed-out character may make the preplanned plot seem contrived. In this way, even characters in monologic works may surprise their authors. But that surprise is not part of the author's design, and so the monologic author will usually revise the work in order to make his or her surprise invisible. It is left in the notebooks and becomes mere "scaffolding" that is designed not to be seen. Alternatively, the monologic author may recast the work as metaliterary, so that the unexpectedness appears to the readers as scripted and planned from the outset; only the reader, but not the author, may be truly surprised.

The polyphonic author goes one step further and makes surprise part of his design so that it *is* supposed to be seen. He is genuinely caught unaware by his heroes' responses, and the finished work retains that sense of unexpectedness. Indeed, the polyphonic work's design can be realized *only if* there is genuine surprise, which is one reason why polyphonic design is incompatible with structure or plan in the usual sense. Polyphonic design can succeed only if characters are imagined as unfinalizable from the outset and as on the threshold of essential and unpredictable change. Clearly, a special sort of imagination is necessary for the creation of "living others" in this way.

Once the polyphonic author has imagined genuinely unfinalizable heroes, he deploys an arsenal of techniques to provoke unexpected reactions from them and to induce them to argue with each other and with the author's own views. These techniques may vary from author to author and work to work, but in Dostoevsky's case they usually include special methods of plotting. Typically, Dostoevsky sets up scandalous scenes and critical moments, the need to confess a terrible crime, the impulse to cross various "thresholds" of behavior or faith, and the explosive mixture of intense insult with self-assertive pride. As Bakhtin discusses these scandalous confrontations in Dostoevsky: "Catastrophe is not finalization. It is the culmination, in collision and struggle, of points of view . . . catastrophe is the opposite of triumph and apotheosis. By its very essence it is denied even elements of catharsis" (TRDB, p. 298). Rather than catharsis, Dostoevsky focuses on internal dialogues, in which characters pass their favorite ideas through the voices of important others, and so, in a sense, repeat the logic of the novels in which they appear. The use of active double-voiced words by both characters and narrator is obviously well suited to this technique.

Dostoevsky also embeds in his novels heterogeneous literary genres (legends, folk tales, saints' lives, detective stories, dialogues with ghosts and the devil, family chronicles, and journalistic exposés) in order to test characters' ideas in radically different frameworks. Voice-ideas resonate in new ways as they find themselves accumulating new "accents" and meanings in new environments, and so sound differently in future dialogues. As the work proceeds, its own development also suggests new kinds of authorial provocations to dialogue.

In short, the dynamic parameters have been set at the outset, but the *event* that is the making of the work constantly surprises author and readers. This dramatic event constitutes the true unity of the work, a unity of dynamic process and not of finished product. Again, it is necessary to emphasize that we are not speaking of the scripted process and merely ostensible spontaneity visible in *Tristram Shandy*, "The Overcoat," and other metaliterary classics. Those works give us the objectivized "image of an event," not "eventness" itself. Their unity is still the unity of a plan. Only polyphonic works give us the "unity of the event." In polyphonic works, unity derives from our sense of a specific kind of creative process at work, a process that may itself evolve in unexpected ways as the event of creation proceeds.

Bakhtin writes as if polyphonic creation were the only one that is "eventful" in this sense, but to us it appears as one of a class of eventful creative methods and literary works. Other authors seem to have cultivated methods, quite different from the one Bakhtin attributes to Dostoevsky, that nevertheless depend essentially on "surprisingness" and achieve a true unity of process. Bakhtin himself briefly mentions Pushkin's novel in verse *Eugene Onegin* only to dismiss it as not quite what he has in mind. He observes that although Pushkin may have been surprised, and may even have written so as to be surprised, his characters nevertheless do not retain the direct power to mean. In our view, that difference would seem to indicate that polyphonic creation is a member of a larger class, one that might be called "creation by potential." A discussion of this class would take us beyond the bounds of the present study.[7]

Bakhtin's own essays, it might be noted, sometimes read as if they were created more or less by potential, polyphonically. He seems to begin with a set of ideas, which he then passes through several diverse contexts (rather than voices), thus generating new insights to guide his future discussion. This method is especially visible in Bakhtin's unfinished essays, but it also seems to be present in completed—or are they?—works, such as "Discourse in the Novel," *Rabelais and His World*, and the two editions of the Dostoevsky book. An advantage of the method was that it showed how a given theme could generate quite distinct sets of insights when approached from different angles. In short, it was a good way to dramatize an idea's rich potential. But the method also led to the repetitiveness that is a hallmark of Bakhtin's style and which many readers (and translators) find so trying.

Time and Character in Dostoevsky

"At that moment I seemed to understand the extraordinary saying that *there shall be no more time*. Probably," he added, smiling, "this is the very second which was not long enough for the water to be spilt out of Mahomet's pitcher, though the epileptic prophet had time to gaze at all the habitations of Allah."
—Dostoevsky, *The Idiot*, pt. 2, ch. 4, pp. 214–15

Oh, if I had done nothing simply out of laziness! . . . I would have respected myself because at least I would have been capable of being lazy; there would have been in me one positive quality, as it were, in which I could have believed myself. Question: Who is he? Answer: a sluggard. . . . It would mean that I was positively defined, it would mean that there was something to be said about me. "Sluggard"—why, after all, it is a calling and an appointment, it is a career, gentlemen.

—Dostoevsky, *Notes from Underground*, pt. 1, ch. 6, p. 17

So far, we have identified two constitutive features of polyphony: a specific form-shaping ideology that incorporates a dialogic sense of truth (dialogue in the third sense) and a changed position of the author needed to embody that kind of dialogue. We have also described some corollaries to these criteria: a special kind of creative process, which in turn entails a new approach to plot, structure, and unity. By contrast, some features of Dostoevsky's works, such as the use of active double-voiced discourse, seem to be well suited to but not necessary for polyphony. We now turn to some other features of Dostoevsky's novels that appear to fall into this last category. As Bakhtin describes them, these features clearly derive from and contribute to Dostoevsky's polyphony, but in principle could be omitted or replaced by alternative techniques in the polyphonic writing of other authors.

According to Bakhtin, Dostoevsky was able to make his dialogues especially intense and dramatically open because of his special sense of time. Here we may detect Bakhtin's interest in the complex of ideas that began with the discussion of architectonics in his early writings and eventually matured into his essay on the chronotope. He identifies Dostoevsky's chronotope—but still without using that word—as one of *simultaneity*. "The fundamental category in Dostoevsky's mode of artistic visualizing was not evolution, but *coexistence* and *interaction*. He saw and conceived his world primarily in terms of space, not time" (PDP, p. 28). This kind of visualizing explains the "whirlwind motion" and the "catastrophic swiftness of action" in his works, "for speed is the single means of overcoming time in time" (PDP, p. 29).

Dostoevsky understood social phenomena by imagining a dialogue among them. He embodied trends in voices, and then forced those voices to encounter or quarrel with each other. To do so, he represented them as simultaneous, even if they were not. Bakhtin contrasts this form of visualization with Goethe's. Where Dostoevsky would "*juxtapose* and *counterpose*" ideas at the same time, Goethe "gravitates organically to an evolving sequence. He strives to perceive all existing contradictions as various stages of some unified development" (PDP, p. 28). For Goethe, everything came with marks of pastness and intimations of futurity; for Dostoevsky, temporal difference could always be overcome and a dialogue of simultaneous ideologies thereby created.

Each kind of visualization has its advantages and disadvantages, Bakhtin suggests. Goethe was able to understand real development and historicity better than Dostoevsky, but he ran the risk of making development more "unified" than it really was. Dostoevsky's method was ideally suited to representing the openness and irreducible disorder of the world, but it blinded him to real change over extensive time, a central concern of Bakhtin's and the main theme of his chronotope essay. Bakhtin in fact describes "Dostoevsky's extraordinary artistic capacity for seeing everything in coexistence and interaction" as "his greatest strength, but his greatest weakness as well. It made him deaf and dumb to a great many essential things; many aspects of reality could not enter his artistic field of vision" (PDP, p. 30). Bakhtin intimates that a superior version of polyphony would be able to represent open-endedness in development over long periods of time.

Dostoevsky's weakness was also a strength because "this capacity sharpened, and to an extreme degree, his perception of the cross-section of a given moment" (ibid.). Dostoevsky saw variety, conflict, and dialogue where others sensed uniformity:

Where others saw a single thought, he was able to find and feel out two thoughts, a bifurcation; where others saw a single quality, he discovered in it the presence of a second and contradictory quality. Everything that seemed simple became, in his world, complex and multi-structured. In every voice he could hear two contending voices, in every expression a crack, and the readiness to go over immediately to another contradictory expression; in every gesture he detected confidence and lack of confidence simultaneously; he perceived the profound ambiguity, even multiple ambiguity, of every phenomenon. [PDP, p. 30]

Characteristically, Bakhtin immediately cautions us not to interpret these contradictions and bifurcations dialectically. No synthesis is possible between them, and they can hardly be contained within a single voice or consciousness. Rather, they exist "as an eternal harmony of unmerged voices or as their unceasing and irreconcilable quarrel" (ibid.). In contrast to Voloshinov, Bakhtin rarely misses an opportunity to contrast dialogue to dialectics.

This sense of time has important implications for Dostoevsky's portrayal of his characters. It became a criterion for distinguishing "the essential" from "the nonessential" in them. For Dostoevsky as Bakhtin describes him, the essential is what troubles characters in the present moment. "That which has meaning only as 'earlier' or 'later,' which is sufficient only unto its own moment, which is valid only as past, or as future" is for him "nonessential and is not incorporated into his world" (PDP, p. 29). As a result, Dostoevsky's characters, unlike those of Tolstoy, Turgenev, and George Eliot, "have no biography in the sense of something past and fully experienced" (ibid.). We learn only those facts about Raskolnikov's past that he himself considers in the novel's present; they must be experienced here and now, must trouble the hero as a present problem, or readers do not learn of them at all. The extraordinary intensity of Dostoevsky's novels in part derives from this attitude toward causality and biography, which also shapes the sense of crisis so important to his novel's great dialogues.

Dostoevsky chose this method of representation because it allowed him to represent characters as maximally free, in fact, as wholly free. In this respect, too, Dostoevsky goes beyond the demands of polyphony, which requires only that characters be partially unfinalizable and free. Polyphony requires that characters be able to respond unexpectedly and to change something important about themselves, but it does not require that they be wholly free and able to change everything. Perhaps Dostoevsky's extremism in this respect was what prompted him to invent the polyphonic novel, but it is not binding on future polyphonic writers. And it may also have led him to misrepresent certain aspects of human nature as Bakhtin understands it. For Bakhtin, "humanness" is temporally extensive, biographically dispersed, historically evolving, and responsible over time.

In Bakhtin's view, Dostoevsky's characters are never subject to "genetic or causal categories." In his journalism, Dostoevsky argued against "environmentalist" explanations of behavior when they aspired to be all-encompassing. Such a view necessarily made moral responsibility impossible and crime nothing but the sign of social inequity. But Dostoevsky's journalism does concede that *some* crime is the result of social, and even biological, causes; he even argued for the acquittal of a pregnant woman whose crime could be explained through the psychological stress of her pregnancy. In his novels, however, Dostoevsky's form-shaping ideology—his way of visualizing the world—led him to portray people as *completely* beyond genetic approaches and as ultimately capable of remaking everything about themselves (or so Bakhtin contends).

When in the 1930's Bakhtin turned to novels as a genre, he did not attribute to them the radical extreme of a Dostoevskian form-shaping ideology. Rather, he described the genre's great discovery as a proper understanding of the relation of historical or genetic categories to the unfinalizable essence of each person. The novel as he describes it requires an interaction of these two factors. People are shaped in essential ways by their social and historical environment, but their "surplus of humanness" still transcends that environment and makes them the unique and unfinalizable beings that they (and we) are. From the perspective of this later work, Dostoevsky's representation of people seems one-sided and somewhat naive.

Personality and Noncoincidence

In his notes "Toward a Reworking of the Dostoevsky Book," Bakhtin draws a distinction central to his analysis of Dostoevsky's heroes. Monologic writers represent their heroes as "characters"; Dostoevsky represented them as true "personalities." As Bakhtin uses these terms, a character is a bundle of psychological and social traits. A character's psychology may be immensely complex, but it is in essence something "objectivized" and finalized. By contrast, a "personality" is a genuine other person, capable, as real people are, of changing his or her essential identity. To represent a hero as a personality is to portray him as truly unfinalizable. "Personality is not subordinate to (that is, it resists) objectified cognition and reveals itself only freely and dialogically (as *thou* for *I*)" (TRDB, p. 298). However complexly drawn, a character is all "given"; a personality is always being "created."

Bakhtin explores the ways in which Dostoevsky learned to represent his heroes as personalities in this sense. He begins with a traditional topic, Dostoevsky's debt to Gogol in his early stories. The Russian Formalists approached this problem in a remarkably interesting way. Focusing on such passages as Makar Devushkin's reading of Gogol's story "The Overcoat" (in Dostoevsky's *Poor Folk*), they stressed Dostoevsky's use of parody and metaliterary techniques as a method of artistic innovation and the renewal of "the device." Without rejecting this insight, Bakhtin contends that something much more important was going on when Dostoevsky reworked Gogol's themes and plots: a "small-scale Copernican revolution" (PDP, p. 49) in the representation of people, a revolution that turned "character" into "personality."

Beginning with Belinsky, most Russian critics have seen Devushkin and Golyadkin (in *The Double*) as Gogolian poor clerks with a new trait added: self-consciousness. Thus, it was appropriate that Devushkin should agonize over his reflection in the mirror or resent the demeaning picture of poor clerks in Gogol's story. Bakhtin argues that the real drama here is a "revolt of the hero" (PDP, p. 58) against all "secondhand" and "causal" definitions of him.

According to Bakhtin, the self-consciousness of Dostoevsky's heroes was not just another trait, it was a fundamentally new principle of representation. Dostoevsky could have made Devushkin simply a self-conscious Akaky Akakievich, but he did something much more radical: he not only changed the hero, but also changed the way in which the hero is visualized. In this way, he made the Gogolian character into the Dostoevskian personality.

Dostoevsky's heroes are never described, they describe themselves. (Bakhtin exaggerates this point.) They are never represented "at second hand," and no authorial "surplus" finalizes them. Strictly speaking, we do not see them at all; we see, instead, their self-conscious image of themselves. Whatever might require an external perspective to depict, whatever the hero could not himself be conscious of, we do not learn about. "The author retains for himself, that is, for his exclusive field of vision, not a single essential definition, not a single trait, not the smallest feature of the hero: he enters it all into the field of vision of the hero himself, he casts it all into the crucible of the hero's self-consciousness" (PDP, p. 48). Consequently, "we do not see how he [Devushkin or Golyadkin] is, but *how* he is conscious of himself" (PDP, p. 49). The world external to the hero is seen only as a function of his self-awareness, and so the novel gives us reality at one remove, "reality of the second order" (ibid.).

Whereas the external world serves to define and explain Gogol's heroes, Dostoevsky's heroes, as we have seen, remain untouched by "causal or genetic factors" (ibid.). Outside of the hero's consciousness in these works there can be no independent objective reality, but only "another consciousness; alongside its field of vision [there can be only] another field of vision; alongside its point of view on the world, another point of view on the world" (ibid.). In other words, we see "I" encounter "thou," but we never see "I" as shaped by "it."

In principle, this method of representation could be used with any sort of hero, but it is best suited to maximally self-aware and self-conscious ones. The "poor clerk" was poor material; he was not self-conscious enough for the method to illuminate a broad compass of experience. Dostoevsky therefore turned to a different kind of hero, "who would be occupied primarily with the task of becoming conscious, the sort of hero whose life would be concentrated on the pure function of gaining consciousness of himself and the world" (PDP, p. 50).

In short, Dostoevsky created types that were to figure repeatedly in his later works: the dreamer and the underground man. The hero of *Notes from Underground* thinks constantly about what he is thinking about; he worries most of all about what others might think of him, about what others may think of the very fact that he is thinking about what they are thinking about him, and about what he thinks of all that, ad infinitum. Dostoevsky's hero is "infinite function" (PDP, p. 51), and so the object of representation is maximally suited to the method of representation. Self-consciousness is represented by a method that filters everything through self-consciousness.

Indeed, the underground man is also an ideologist of self-consciousness. He constantly complains about how self-consciousness paralyzes action, and he repeatedly refutes determinism as well as all other "causal or genetic explanations" of the self. Like so many of Dostoevsky's heroes, he not only is unfinalizable, but also explicitly insists on his unfinalizability. In paraphrasing the underground man's defense of "surprisingness," Bakhtin expresses one of his own most cherished convictions:

As long as a person is alive he lives by the fact that he is not finalized, that he has not yet uttered his ultimate word. . . . man is free and can therefore violate any regulating framework that might be thrust upon him. . . .
A man never coincides with himself. One cannot apply to him the formula of identity $A \equiv A$. In Dostoevsky's artistic thinking, the genuine life of the personality takes place at the point of noncoincidence between a man and himself, at his point of departure beyond the limits of all that he is as a material being, a being that can be spied on, defined, predicted apart from his own will, "at second hand." [PDP, p. 59]

Unlike sentences, utterances as Bakhtin describes them are unrepeatable and can never be made to coincide "like geometrical figures." In much the same way, personalities are defined—or, rather, remain partially undefined—by their eternal "noncoincidence" with themselves.

Ethics and "Secondhand" Definitions

We have seen that the Dostoevsky book is really two books: on the one hand, it is an analysis of that author, and on the other, it is a broader consideration of polyphony and the dialogic sense of truth. By now, it may be apparent that it is also possible to see the book in yet a third way, as a meditation on ethics.

For Dostoevsky as Bakhtin understands him, and for Bakhtin himself, "secondhand" definitions of others are fundamentally unethical. One must approach another as a "personality," that is, as someone "who has not yet uttered his ultimate word" (PDP, p. 59). Although Bakhtin does not attack specific opponents, it would

seem that he has in mind such finalizing approaches to the self as
Freudianism and Marxism; indeed, he is thinking of the entire tradition of Western "Newtonian" thought that seeks to explain life in
purely causal terms.

Bakhtin mentions several heroes of Dostoevsky's works who object on ethical grounds to secondhand definitions of living people.
Bakhtin unambiguously sympathizes with these heroes. They argue that even when secondhand definitions say something essentially correct about a person, the very fact that they are secondhand
renders them, in a deeper sense, both false and morally wrong.
"The truth about a man in the mouths of others, not directed at him
dialogically and therefore a *secondhand truth*, becomes a lie degrad-
ing and deadening him, if it touches upon his 'holy of holies,' that
is, 'the man in man'" (PDP, p. 59). In *The Idiot*, Aglaya objects to
Myshkin's analysis of Ippolit's attempted suicide: "I find all this
very mean on your part, for it's very *brutal to look on* and *judge a
man's soul*, as you judge Ippolit. You have no tenderness, *nothing but
truth, and so you judge unjustly*" (Dostoevsky, *The Idiot*, pt. 3, ch. 8,
as cited in PDP, p. 60; italics Bakhtin's). Bakhtin comments: "Truth
is unjust when it concerns the depths of *someone else's* personality"
(PDP, p. 60).

When Alyosha Karamazov analyzes Captain Snegiryov's state of
mind and predicts that the captain will *without fail* take charity next
time it is offered, Lise replies: "Aren't we showing *contempt* for him,
for that poor man—*in analyzing his soul like this*, as it were, *from
above*, eh? In deciding so *certainly* that he will take the money?"
(Dostoevsky, *Karamazov*, bk. 5, ch. 1, p. 257). Passages like these
seem to echo Bakhtin's own ethical position.

It is in this context that Bakhtin discusses Dostoevsky's remarkable statement that he was *not* a psychologist. Critical reaction to
Dostoevsky has tended to assume that he was, and Freud in particular valued Dostoevsky's novels for their psychological depth. But
Dostoevsky himself wrote: "They call me a *psychologist; this is not
true*. I am merely a realist *in the higher sense*, that is, I portray all the
depths of the human soul."[8]

For Bakhtin, this passage is crucial and is connected with Dostoevsky's satire on the psychologists at Dmitri Karamazov's trial as
well as with Lise's and Aglaya's reactions to "secondhand definitions." The "psychology" that Dostoevsky rejected was precisely
"secondhand psychology," which reduced a person's consciousness
to a play of unconscious, biological, or chemical forces beyond his
control. Psychologists as different as Freud and Pavlov have tradi-

tionally taken pride in such reduction, which Bakhtin abhorred. As we saw in Chapter Five, this "scientific" approach to personality partially explains Bakhtin's dislike of Freud and his attempt to describe the psyche in terms of unconscious drives: "Dostoevsky . . . moved aesthetic visualization into the depths, into deep new strata, but not into the depths of the unconscious; rather into the depths of the heights of consciousness. . . . Consciousness is much more terrifying than any unconscious complexes" (TRDB, p. 288).

The proper way to understand others is not "psychologically" but dialogically. The heroes who really understand other people in Dostoevsky are those who possess "dialogic intuition" (PDP, p. 61), that is, the ability to sense the inner dialogues of others *in all their unfinalizability* and then participate in that dialogue while respecting its openness. They renounce the desire for "essential" surplus and seek instead addressive surplus. According to Bakhtin, this approach is not only more accurate with respect to human nature, but is also the only truly ethical one.

It seems likely that the ethical agenda of the Dostoevsky book is related to a theological one: we may imagine that God created the world in an "Einsteinian" way, polyphonically. He created unfinalizable beings, who are truly free and capable of surprising Him, as Dostoevsky's characters surprised their creator. To participate directly in the "world symposium," God allowed Himself to be incarnated and tested, as Dostoevsky tested his own ideas by incarnating them in Shatov, Zosima, and Tikhon. Christ "lived into" the world and proved himself to be the perfect dialogic partner, addressing people with a "dialogic intuition" that never finalized them.

Finally, the Dostoevsky book also seems to have an implicit political agenda, which is anti-Marxist. Obviously, in the Soviet context such a view could not be expressed directly. But Bakhtin comes remarkably close to doing so in his lengthy attacks on "dialectics" (in the Soviet Union, as every schoolchild knows, Marxism-Leninism is officially identified with dialectical materialism). The length and vigor of Bakhtin's "anti-dialectics" go considerably beyond their ostensible purpose in explicating Dostoevsky's polyphony; and when Bakhtin had the chance to expand the Dostoevsky book in 1963, he took the occasion to lengthen the critiques of dialectics. Bakhtin also explicitly criticizes Hegelianism and utopianism, which are indeed permissible targets in the Soviet Union; but together with his critiques of dialectics, these passages triangulate the unnamed opponent, Marxism, to which we may draw "dotted lines."

Bakhtin's characterization of utopian thought—all of it—is re-

markably similar to his passages on dialectics. Both kinds of thinking are quintessentially monologic, both reflect the worst in modern European thought, and both are fundamentally at odds with
respect for distinct, unfinalizable personalities: "All of European
utopianism was likewise built on this monologic principle. Here
too belongs utopian socialism, with its faith in the omnipotence
of the conviction. Semantic unity is everywhere represented by a
single consciousness and a single point of view" (PDP, p. 82). It
was, of course, Soviet Marxism that claimed infallibility and "omnipotence," and which above all maintained "the omnipotence of
the conviction . . . and a single point of view." Greater explicitness
would hardly have been possible, either in 1929 or in 1963.

For Bakhtin, utopianism in all its forms was monologic because
it claimed to "have the last word" about people and the world in
which they live. But "the final word of the world and about the
world has not yet been spoken . . . everything is still in the future
and will always be in the future" (PDP, p. 166). And if utopianism
should ever prove true, our daily lives would become mere instantiations of a pattern, not only describable but already described by a
"secondhand" theory. As Dostoevsky's underground man observes, people would become "piano keys" or "organ stops," and
life would turn into uncreative behavior that could be determined in
advance by something analogous to "a table of logarithms." Instead
of real being, we would have only its alibi.

PART III

Theories of the Novel

7

Theory of Genres

To a considerable extent Bakhtin's reputation in the West rests on his theories of genre and of the novel. Among literary critics, he is identified with the essays from the 1930's translated as *The Dialogic Imagination*, all of which are devoted to the history of narrative genres; scholars in other fields often think first of his book on Rabelais, parodic social forms, and the novel as a "carnivalized" genre.

It is therefore something of a shock to recognize that the categories of genre and novel did not become central to Bakhtin until his third period. Only in the 1930's did he seem to realize their rich potential for solving his favorite problems. Much as a new interest in language propelled Bakhtin into his second period, so the turn to "novelness" and more general questions of genre marks his transition to a third period.

Those who know only the revised edition of the Dostoevsky book may find this statement surprising, inasmuch as that book's fourth chapter and conclusion deal extensively with genre theory. Those passages, however, are not present in the 1929 edition, and are in fact the product of Bakhtin's thought in his third and fourth periods. At best, the original Dostoevsky book, when viewed retrospectively, contains the germ of concepts later to be enriched by Bakhtin's theories of the novel (specifically, his interest in "the prosaic word" and of a dialogic conception of truth).

Perhaps still more surprising, the Bakhtin group's first serious discussion of genre belongs not to Bakhtin himself, but to Medvedev. *The Formal Method in Literary Scholarship* devotes a chapter to demonstrating that any good sociological approach to literature must be grounded in genres, which, Medvedev argued, carry and shape social experience for individual people. Although it is presently impossible to determine priority of discovery, Bakhtin seems to have been impressed and influenced by Medvedev's argument, enough so to have refined, extended, and recast it. Over the next few decades and with varying degrees of success, Bakhtin was to pass all his favorite concepts and concerns through the prism of genre and the novel.

Reading from the Bottom Up

Medvedev's preliminary discussion may serve as a useful introduction to Bakhtin's ideas. Contrasting his approach to that of the
Formalists, Medvedev attacks the very way in which Shklovsky,
Boris Tomashevsky, and others asked and answered questions. As
Medvedev describes them, the Formalists approached genre from
"part to whole" and from the "bottom up"; but what is needed is
an approach from the top down and from the whole work to its
constituent parts. For the Formalists, the first topic of literary theory was the elements of language, which meant that a complex of
those elements, such as genre, necessarily came later. For Medvedev, the first topic was the work as a social fact oriented toward
an audience, which for him meant that the forms of whole utterances—their genre—must be the starting point. After all, we respond to utterances, not to phonemes; fairy tales and novels, not
syntactical or grammatical elements, are what most affect us. "Poetics should really begin with genre, not end with it. For genre is
the typical form of the whole work, the whole utterance" (M:FM,
p. 129).

To Medvedev, a "whole work" is a specific conceptualization of
the world and a genre is an overall way of conceiving it, a starting
point for a particular conceptualization. The selection of specific
elements, devices, or themes is a consequence of the work's "vision." The Formalists' defense of the opposite position made them a
convenient target. In criticizing them, Medvedev clearly, if briefly,
outlined the fundamental tenets of an alternative theory.

Specifically, Medvedev objected to the following premises culled
from his reading of the Formalists:

1. A work's theme (or overall meaning) is the sum of the themes
of its constituent parts. Medvedev cites Tomashevsky: "The various sentences of the artistic expression combine according to meaning and result in a definite construction unified by a common idea
or theme. Theme (what is talked about) is the unity of meanings of
the separate elements of the work. One may speak of the theme of
the whole work and of the themes of its separate parts" (Tomashevsky, *Teoriia literatury*, as cited in M:FM, p. 131).

2. The parts of a work are linguistic in nature; that is, the work
can ultimately be divided into sentences, clauses, and words.

3. These parts are combined by means of "devices." Certain aspects of works that often interest unsophisticated readers, such as
character or philosophy, are in fact merely the by-product of a
given combination of devices, the artist's only real concern.

4. Genre is a specific way of deploying a hierarchy of devices; the hierarchy is constrained by its apex, the dominant.

5. In the course of literary history, various hierarchies "wear out" and are replaced by other hierarchies. Old hierarchies recede into popular culture or to the margins of high culture until their successors also wear out, at which point the two may switch places.

Medvedev objects at length to each of these premises before presenting his own alternative view of genre. He argues, to begin with, that literary works cannot be divided into linguistic elements. Here his argument closely resembles Bakhtin's later distinction between utterances and sentences. Only utterances mean; works are utterances; and sentences are units of a different order. Although linguistic elements are necessary for utterances, they are anything but sufficient. As Medvedev insists, "the thematic unity of the work is not the combination of the meanings of its words and individual sentences. . . . The theme is not composed of these meanings; it is formed with their help, but they only help to the same extent as all the other semantic elements of language. Language helps us to master the theme, but we should not make theme an element of language" (M:FM, p. 132).

Like Bakhtin, Medvedev consistently opposed all forms of linguistic reductionism, whether foundationalist or relativist, essentialist or what we would now call deconstructive. In his attack on Formalist atomism, Medvedev pointed out that "theme always transcends language. . . . It is the whole utterance and its forms, which cannot be reduced to any linguistic forms, which control the theme. The theme of the work is the theme of the whole utterance as a definite sociohistorical act. Consequently, it is inseparable from the total situation of the utterance to the same extent that it is inseparable from linguistic elements" (ibid.). The second Formalist premise above, which reduces works to linguistic (not metalinguistic) elements, is consequently mistaken. "It is not the sentence, the period, or their aggregate that implement the theme, but the novella, the novel, the lyric, the fairy tale. . . . The fairy tale as such does not consist of sentences and periods" (ibid.).

Formalist linguistic atomism is wrong for yet another reason. Because sentences have only potential meaning, and only utterances have real meaning, one cannot speak of the meaning of particular parts. As we recall, Bakhtin argued that linguists often attribute real meaning to sentences because they covertly and unwittingly imagine situations in which those sentences function as utterances; and so the sentence becomes a sort of quasi-utterance into which meaning is "smuggled." Medvedev argues that the Formalists are engaged in a similar kind of smuggling when they speak of the meaning of works' separate parts. Strictly speaking, Medvedev contends, parts can be imagined as having meaning only "by imagining these parts to be separate and finished [whole] utterances independently oriented in reality" (ibid.). But *as* parts, they do not mean in that way, but rather contribute to the whole utterance's meaning. Thus, the first Formalist premise described above is also mistaken, because it makes the meaning of the whole the sum of the meaning of the parts, which in fact do not have such meaning.

The third Formalist premise—that works are organized through devices—was often expressed in terms suggesting that people interested in questions of morality or character were somehow philistine. Taken together, the third, fourth, and fifth Formalist premises implied that only naive readers regard great authors as moral teachers, social researchers, philosophers, or psychological analysts, whereas the proper sort of theory teaches us that authors are really skillful artificers: they exploit effective ways of combining ready-made elements into an artistic whole. To illustrate these Formalist premises, Medvedev cites Victor Shklovsky's discussion of the origin of the novel and the "making" of *Don Quixote*.

According to Shklovsky, novels arose from collections of short stories. First, authors wrote stories separately, then they found ways of combining them in "a common frame" (e.g., *The Decameron*) (Shklovsky, "Kak sdelan *Don-Kikhot*"; as cited in M:FM, p. 136). The next step was to find a better way to link stories. Authors discovered the "stringing together" (*nanizyvanie*) of stories: instead of framing them as separate narratives about separate people, they transformed them into episodes of a single character's life. In this way, the modern novel was born.

At first, Shklovsky argued, this technique was bound to produce main characters who behaved inconsistently. The complex and paradoxical figure of Don Quixote arose not to illustrate some philosophical or psychological insight, but as the purely accidental result of stringing inconsistent adventures together. Shklovsky concluded: "The type of Don Quixote, so glorified by Heine and beslobbered by Turgenev, was not the primary aim of the author. The type was the result of the process of constructing the novel, just as the mechanism of performance often creates new forms of poetry" (ibid.).[1]

In Medvedev's view, the special value of Shklovsky is that he never flinches from the extreme conclusions that logically follow from Formalist premises. Better than his more sensible and less consistent allies, Shklovsky foregrounds the ultimate folly of those premises. The notion that "aesthetic philistines" like Turgenev misread and "beslobbered" Cervantes' masterpiece by finding subtle characterization and timeless wisdom in it is, for Medvedev, Formalist "bottom up" reasoning reduced to the absurd.

The Eyes of Genre

If genre is neither a collection of devices nor a particular way of combining linguistic elements, then what is it? Medvedev answers this question quite clearly: it is a specific way of visualizing a given part of reality.

In this respect, genres are not unique to literature, but govern our daily speech, both "outer" and "inner." Inner speech (or thought) is not "a string of words and sentences" (M:FM, p. 134). Rather, "we think and conceptualize in utterances," and utterances are ultimately formulated according not to "syntactic" but to "generic" principles (ibid.). Those principles establish ways of seeing; the variety of experiences and social purposes necessitates a multiplicity of genres. "One might [therefore] say that human consciousness possesses a series of inner genres for seeing and conceptualizing reality. A given consciousness is richer or poorer in genres, depending on its ideological environment" (ibid.).

Bakhtin was later to make a similar point when he argued that people may know a language well (in terms of grammar, syntax, vocabulary, pronunciation, and other "linguistic" categories) but still "feel quite helpless in certain spheres of communication precisely because they do not have a practical command of the generic forms in the given spheres. . . . Here it is not a matter of an impoverished vocabulary or of style, taken abstractly; this is entirely a matter of the inability to command a repertoire of genres of social conversation" (SG, p. 80). Something similar occurs in the process of learning a foreign language: although comprehension and vocabulary might be strong, learners continue to use the genres of their native language. In both one's own and a second language, the ability to command a wider set of genres enriches one's capacity to conceptualize and participate in varying aspects of social life.

According to Medvedev, it is hopelessly naive to assume, as Formalists and many others do, that a speaker (or writer) first understands reality and then finds the forms and genre with which to express his understanding. It is untrue, for example, that a painter "sees everything first and then shapes what he saw and puts it into the surface of his painting according to a certain technique" (M:FM, p. 134). Rather, seeing is shaped by genres of expression; "seeing and representation merge" (ibid.). As one learns new genres, one learns to see differently and one expands one's repertoire of vision. "New means of representation force us to see new aspects of visible reality. . . . The artist does not squeeze pre-made reality onto the surface of his work. The surface helps him to see, understand, and select his material" (ibid.).

To create successfully, Medvedev explained, "the artist must learn to see reality with the eyes of the genre" (ibid.). The artist must come to see those aspects of reality to which the given genre is adapted, to visualize them in the genre's way, and to exploit the potential of that vision to express something genuinely new and valuable.

In the same spirit, Bakhtin later described a particular type of failure that results from a writer's misunderstanding of his chosen genre and his attempt to use it for purposes alien to its ethos. Bakhtin's example is Gogol's ill-fated effort to turn the satiric novel *Dead Souls* into the first volme of an epic *Divine Comedy*, an effort which led to the hopeless failure of volume two. Bakhtin was to contend: "Gogol could not manage the move from Hell to Purgatory and then to Paradise with the same people and in the same work; no continuous transition [from satiric novel to epic] was possible" (EaN, p. 28) because the two genres view the world in fundamentally incompatible ways. "[Epic] pathos broke into the world of Menippean satire like a foreign body," became "abstract and simply fell out of the work" (ibid.).

In short, Gogol's failure was due neither to a lack of talent nor to a lapse in imagination, but to his project of taking a genre where it could not go. Such projects lead to a special kind of creative tragedy: "The tragedy of Gogol is to a very real extent the tragedy of a genre (taking genre not in its formalistic sense, but as a zone and a field of valorized perception, as a mode for representing the world). Gogol lost Russia, that is, he lost his blueprint for perceiving and representing her; he got muddled somewhere between [epic] memory and [novelistic] familiar contact—to put it bluntly, he could not find the proper focus on his binoculars" (ibid.).

As this discussion suggests, Medvedev—and later Bakhtin—regarded genres as combinations of specific blindnesses and insights. Each is adapted to conceptualizing some aspects of reality better than others. That, indeed, is why people and cultures need continually to learn new genres as the compass of their experience expands. "Each genre is only able to control certain definite aspects of reality. Each genre possesses definite principles of selection . . . and a definite scope and depth of penetration" (M:FM, p. 131).

Medvedev therefore responds to Shklovsky's description of the origin of the novel with yet another objection. According to Med-vedev, it is a fundamental mistake to view the sole difference be-tween short stories, anecdotes, or novellas on the one hand and novels on the other as nothing more than quantity of words. On the contrary, difference in length of narrative genres is itself usually a consequence of a difference in vision. *War and Peace* is not just a very long anecdote, nor is *Middlemarch* a collection of short stories artfully "strung together." One could expand a short story to a few hundred pages and still not produce a "novel."

In Medvedev's view, short stories tend to see life in essentially anecdotal terms; the genre is well adapted to capture what Medvedev calls the "anecdotal aspect of life" (M:FM, p. 134). By contrast, novels are well adapted to describing the fundamental character of an epoch or other large social phenomenon. Each genre will prove ill suited to the other's topic or purposes. As Medvedev observed, "in order to create a novel it is necessary to learn to see life in terms of the novelistic story, necessary to learn to see the wider and deeper relationships of life on a large scale. There is an abyss of dif-ference between the ability to grasp the isolated unity of a chance situation and the ability to understand the unity and inner logic of a whole epoch" (M:FM, pp. 134–35).

It follows that the creation of new genres cannot be the result of purely mechanical processes or the revival of neglected devices. "If no unity of life incapable of being fit within the framework of the novella enters the artist's horizons, he will confine himself to the novella or collection of novellas. And no external combination of no-vellas can replace the inner unity of reality adequate to the novel" (M:FM, pp. 136–37). New genres reflect changes in real social life. Those changes lead to new views of experience and to different genres of speech, social behavior, and literature. Conversely, liter-ary genres, once they arise, may teach people to see aspects of real-ity in a new way, and so these genres may become common in spheres remote from their origin. As a rule, "genre appraises reality and reality clarifies genre" (M:FM, p. 136).

Literary History

Medvedev's argument that genres respond to social experience shades into his polemic with Formalist views of literary history. Literary forms change not because devices wear out, but because real people create new ways to understand their changing lives. Medvedev was especially disturbed by Formalist attempts to offer mechanical explanations for human efforts, as if it were necessarily a blow against superstition every time one found a new way to explain away creativity or deny historicity. For somewhat different reasons, Bakhtin appeared to find Medvedev's arguments congenial to his own war against theoretism, and he came to apply them not only to Formalism, but also to structuralism, semiotics, and Marxism.

In particular, Medvedev objected to

the formalists' basic tendency to see creativity as the recombination of ready-made [*gotovye*] elements. . . . [According to the Formalists,] a new genre is made from genres at hand; within every genre a regrouping of already prepared elements [*uzhe gotovyi material*] takes place. Everything is given [*dan*] to the artist—all that remains is to combine the ready-made material in a new way. The story is given; all that is necessary is to combine it into a plot. The devices of the plot are also given and only need to be rearranged. The hero is given, and it is only necessary to string the ready-made motifs on him. [M:FM, pp. 140–41]

For Medvedev, a real theory of literary history would discuss the interaction of historically shaped human experiences with ways of conceptualizing reality in genres. Genres would be described as taking shape over centuries; and one could also fix more rapid changes leading to subgenres, trends, or even short-lived schools.

Bakhtin came to share this view, and to speak with some disdain of those who overlook long-term changes and see in literary history "merely the struggle of literary tendencies and schools. Such struggles of course exist, but they are peripheral phenomena and historically insignificant. Behind them one must be sensitive to the deeper and more truly historical struggle of genres, the establishment and growth of a generic skeleton of literature" (EaN, p. 5). In his final published essay, Bakhtin repeated this criticism of literary history understood as a "superficial struggle of literary schools" (RQ, p. 3) rather than the profound story of genres.

In short, Medvedev's critique of Formalist models of literary history is the first of several attempts in the Bakhtin group to treat genres as "the drive belts from the history of society to the history of language" and literature (SG, p. 65).[2]

As Medvedev points out, Formalism, especially in its earliest stages, tended to ignore or deny that real experience, leading to new views of life, also leads to new genres and new kinds of works. The Formalists never entirely abandoned the idea that new forms result from boredom with old ones rather than from new views of the world needing expression. Medvedev focuses on Tynyanov's four-stage model of literary change: first, an already automatized "constructive principle" for making literary works is replaced by an opposite constructive principle; next, that new principle "seeks its easiest application"; third, the principle becomes dominant and widespread; fourth, it, too, "becomes automatized and elicits opposing constructive principles," and so the process repeats itself (Tynyanov, "O literaturnom fakte"; as cited in M:FM, p. 166).

Medvedev raises numerous objections to this model, a few of which are of special importance for an understanding of Bakhtin. To begin with, no real sense of history informs the Formalist model. Uncanonized lines replace canonized lines ad infinitum, but it makes no difference *when* the replacement occurs. No mention is made of social experience. "In terms of the scheme itself, the location of the Derzhavin tradition in the eighteenth century and the Pushkin tradition in the early nineteenth century is absolutely accidental" (M:FM, p. 163). Moreover, since mere opposition is all that is necessary for one constructive principle to replace another, old constructive principles may return; in fact, the Formalists argued that such repetitions are quite common in literary history. In theory, two constructive principles could alternate forever. To argue in this way, Medvedev contends, is to make literary history entirely "reversible." Thus, a constituent element of any true concept of historicity—namely, anachronism—is entirely absent from Formalist theory.

Perhaps most troubling of all to Medvedev, the identification of "automatization of perception" and "the wearing out of devices" as the engine driving literary history requires that changes be accomplished in a brief period of time. Specifically, they cannot take longer than a single generation because what is worn out for one generation need not be for its successor. For the Formalists, history is always a "permanent present" and a "permanent contemporaneity" (M:FM, p. 171). Medvedev then asks a question that was also to prove important for Bakhtin: how are we to account for changes that "can only really be accomplished over a long series of generations and a succession of epochs? For such tasks are the real, historical tasks" (ibid.).

If one adopts the Formalist view, Medvedev reminds us, then any generation continuing the work of its predecessors would be a generation of unoriginal epigones; real originality in literature, science, or anywhere else would always be a matter of revolutions. "From the Formalist point of view, every scientist is an epigone, except for sensationalists" (ibid.).

As we have seen, Bakhtin was most comfortable with models in which change is usually prosaic and continuous, rather than revolutionary; only such a vision would allow both daily creativity and ordinary responsibility to be meaningful. This prosaic view in turn implied for Bakhtin that fundamental changes require long stretches of "great time." Such developments, which have adapted to differing worlds and contingent events, fit no simple pattern; they constitute no neat structure; and they lead to unforeseeable results.

A view of literary history with developments over great time demands some "organ of memory," some way in which experiences can carry over from one generation to subsequent ones. The past must contain the potential to shape, though not wholly to determine, new visions of the world. Bakhtin came to identify genre as a key organ of memory and an important vehicle of historicity.

Forms of Artistic Thinking

The literary theories of Bakhtin's third period vary considerably, but they all proceed from the twin hypotheses that genres are really forms of thinking, and that the novel is the most accurate conceptualization of human experience ever developed. In his fourth period, when he revised the Dostoevsky book, Bakhtin in effect claimed that polyphonic novels are as superior to monologic novels as monologic novels are to other literary forms.

In creating what was essentially a new genre, Bakhtin insists, Dostoevsky "created, in our opinion, a completely new type of artistic thinking [*khudozhestvennoe myshlenie*], which we have provisionally called *polyphonic*. . . . It could even be said that Dostoevsky created something like a new artistic model of the world" (PDP, p. 3).

Bakhtin develops this claim in his book's new conclusion, which is largely devoted to problems of genre. According to Bakhtin, Dostoevsky created a revolution in prose genres; and because genres are forms of thought, it follows that Dostoevsky also created a revolution in ways of thinking about the world. "We consider the creation of the polyphonic novel a huge step forward not only in the development of novelistic prose, that is, of all genres developing within the orbit of the novel, but also in the development of the *artistic thinking* of humankind. It seems to us that one could speak directly of a special *polyphonic artistic thinking* extending beyond the bounds of the novel as a genre" (PDP, p. 270). Bakhtin's favorite comparison is with Einstein, who, like Dostoevsky, enriched humanity with a whole new conceptualization of the world.

What is most important about Dostoevsky's new kind of thinking is that it makes available aspects of human experience never before accessible. Prior to Dostoevsky, novelists could write about moral responsibility and human choice, but their "essential surplus" and advance knowledge of the plot prevented them from visualizing freedom in all its unfinalizable "eventness." Neither could philosophers, employing their characteristic discourse of abstract transcription, write about more than a pale shadow of eventness and "oughtness." But Dostoevsky's special new kind of novel for the first time "makes available those sides of a human being, and above all the *thinking human consciousness and the dialogic sphere of its existence*" that could not be assimilated "from *monologic* positions" (PDP, p. 270).

Thus, Dostoevsky's creation of polyphony constitutes a Copernican revolution bound to extend far beyond the cultural sphere in which it first appeared. Indeed, all new genres, if they are based on profound enough forms of artistic thinking, have this potential for wide application, as do great philosophical or scientific theories. A new genre enriches our repertoire of visions of the world and may prove useful at distant times for unforeseeable applications, much as the non-Euclidian geometry of Lobachevsky and others found an unexpected application in relativistic models of the universe.

According to Bakhtin, intellectual historians often overlook the greatest discoveries in the history of thought because they do not recognize genres and artistic forms *as* forms of thought. They limit themselves to explicit statements in texts or tracts, or, if they consider literary works at all, examine only those passages whose *content* is philosophical. But some of the greatest discoveries in world thought have taken place first—or exclusively—in the concrete visualization of artistic *form*. Philosophical transcription, if it has taken place in any adequate way at all, has often followed the creation of a genre or subgenre.

Bakhtin's central example of this error on the part of intellectual historians occurs in his discussion of the novel of education (the Bildungsroman). It is a commonplace in discussions of eighteenth-century thought to argue that a real historical sense was absent from the era. According to Bakhtin, this judgment is the product of the usual parameters of research, which unwittingly exclude precisely those texts that would disconfirm it. "In general, the whole notion of the notorious lack of historicity during the Enlightenment should be radically revised" (BSHR, p. 26) by changing the research parameters to include previously unappreciated kinds of evidence. Bakhtin maintains that the eighteenth century developed a series of new ways to conceptualize time and history; but those experiments, routinely misunderstood by historians of thought, took the form not of philosophical tracts but of new kinds of narrative. "This process of preparing for the disclosure of historical time took place more rapidly, completely, and profoundly in *literary creativity* than in the abstract philosophical and strictly historical, ideological views of Enlightenment thinkers" (ibid.).

Just as philosophical treatises are better adapted than novels for discussing some kinds of problems, so novels lend themselves better to understanding others. Specifically, novels are best adapted to those forms of experience not easily "transcribable" into rules and abstractions, either because the principles of transcription are unknown or because transcription itself would decisively change the essence of the phenomenon described. As we have seen, ethical problems necessarily change their character in fundamental ways when transcribed. The same may be true of different senses of time and history.

It is unclear whether Bakhtin means to say that specific senses of time are *still* untranscribable or whether he means that they are *in principle* untranscribable. It is clear, however, that Bakhtin maintains (1) that it is difficult to imagine something so concrete and so complex as a specific sense of time being explored profoundly in any non-narrative form, and (2) that to date there is no form offering as rich a sense of the varieties of temporal experience as the novel. The essay "The *Bildungsroman* and Its Significance in the History of Realism" and the book-length study "Forms of Time and of the Chronotope in the Novel" are devoted to translating, so far as that is possible, some novelistic insights into time.

Genres convey a vision of the world not by explicating a set of propositions but by developing concrete examples. Instead of specifying the characteristics of a worldview, as philosophical theories might, they allow the reader to view the world in a specific way. A particular sense of experience, never formalized, guides the author's efforts in creating his or her work. Each author who contributes to the genre learns to experience the world in the genre's way, and, if the work is significant and original, to enrich the genre's capacity for future visualization. In short, a genre, understood as a way of seeing, is best described neither as a "form" (in the usual sense) nor as an "ideology" (which could be paraphrased as a set of tenets) but as "form-shaping ideology"—a specific kind of creative activity embodying a specific sense of experience. One might say that Bakhtin's objection to Formalism is that it undervalues the significance of form.

In Chapter Six, we saw that the form-shaping ideology of the polyphonic novel involves a dialogic sense of truth realized by a change in authorial position. We saw as well that Bakhtin cautions us against mistaking such critical paraphrases for the real thing. The best way to convey a given form-shaping ideology may be to discuss its sense of truth and the form in which that sense is realized, but this very division necessarily oversimplifies the genre. In offering it, one should realize that it necessarily lacks the "life" of the genre. The form-shaping ideology of any reasonably complex genre is never reducible to a set of rules, nor is it wholly transcribable in any other way. Here as elsewhere, the proper use of transcriptions, as analytic tools, is either to point in the direction where real vision lies or to recoup for abstract analysis as much of the genre's wisdom as can be captured. So long as one does not confuse transcribed propositions for the essence of the genre, they can be helpful. In this sense they are like sets of linguistic rules, which may be quite useful even if language is not ultimately a matter of rules.

Genres are neither lifeless collections of formal features nor abstract combinations of philosophical premises, although critical descriptions may involve both. Indeed, when authors write in a given genre, they sometimes hold views at odds with the genre's form-shaping ideology. We saw, for instance, that Dostoevsky held some monologic views incompatible with the dialogic sense of truth serving as his artistic "principle of seeing." In part, this conflict and its working out constitute the dynamics of Dostoevsky's creative process. Indeed, one reason that authors often express truths they did not know they knew, and learn new ideas in the process of composing, is to be found in the conflict of personal convictions with form-shaping ideology. The author must adapt one to the other or the work will fail. Creation produces the new in part because, in choosing a genre, an author adopts a partially alien vision and imposes on himself a difficult set of constraints. Dostoevsky is especially great, Bakhtin intimates, because he not only *used* but himself *created* the partially alien form-shaping ideology of polyphony.

For Bakhtin, Dostoevsky's real contribution lay not in his rather conventional social theories but precisely in his new form-shaping ideology. The contribution of Dostoevsky's novels "to questions of *form* is more profound, more condensed, more general than is the concretely ideological, changeable content that fills them. . . . The content of autonomous consciousnesses changes, ideas change, the content of the dialogues changes, but the new forms Dostoevsky discovered for the artistic cognition of the human world remain the same" (TRDB, p. 285). Once discovered, the polyphonic form-shaping ideology could be used for dialogues of many philosophical positions Dostoevsky never imagined, just as the novelistic conception of social space could be used to explore societies that the earliest novelists never considered. One could subtract all the specific philosophical content of Dostoevsky's works and something of great value—the form-shaping ideology with its dialogic *sense* of truth—would be left. Such a statement could not be made about most authors. "If, for example, in Turgenev, one were to cast out the content of the disputes between Bazarov and Pavel Petrovich Kirsanov, no new structural forms would remain" (ibid.).

Bakhtin's most cherished artists are those who enrich humanity's ways of visualizing the world by creating new form-shaping ideologies. The greatness of Goethe lies in his contribution to the sense of time conveyed by narrative genres; Rabelais played a decisive role in the novel's ability to sense conventions and assess popular social forms. Bakhtin also believed that the most valuable contribution of Western thought in the humanities was its diversity of genres. In this context, we can understand his impatience with literary histories stressing either the conflict of local schools, or the psychology of individual authors, or the "reflection" of social conflicts. By finding better ways to explore the wisdom of genres, criticism has much more important contributions to make.

Meanings and Potentials

> Semantic phenomena can exist in concealed form, potentially, and be revealed only in semantic cultural contexts of subsequent epochs that are favorable for such disclosure.
>
> —RQ, p. 5

Bakhtin's understanding of genre allowed him to offer an interesting solution to "the question of meaning" that has vexed modern theory. Bakhtin rejected the solutions offered by both "semiotic totalizers" and by absolute "relativists." On the one hand, he argued that no procedure could be found to determine the fixed meaning of great literary texts, because those texts do not have a fixed meaning. For Bakhtin, meaning is neither located entirely *in* the text nor is it identical with the author's original intentions (in the usual sense). Works genuinely *grow* in meaning over time, which would be impossible if meaning were fixed. On the other hand, Bakhtin also rejected the contrary view, that meaning is entirely the product of interpreters. If we could get out of texts only what we bring to them, then literature could never teach us anything of value.

For Bakhtin, these two alternatives are equally the product of a naive scientism that assumes knowledge must either be a system or else is nonexistent. Bakhtin saw in both opposing positions the sort of errors he found either in the Jakobson communication model, which leads to an enormously oversimplified understanding of "context," or in all relativist models of meaning, which appeal to historical change but lack a sense of genuine historicity. Both semiotic totalizers and relativists usually fail to appreciate another key concept in Bakhtin's thought: potential.

According to Bakhtin, no author of a great literary work could fully command all its important implications, because great literary works exploit resources that have developed over centuries and contain potentials for development over centuries to come. The most important source of these resources is genres. Having accumulated centuries of conceptualizations, and carrying wisdom irreducible to any set of propositions, genres carry potentials that great writers may sense but which are ever beyond the capacity of any writer to ascertain specifically.

Contrary to the telegraphic communication model, or everyday notions of "expression," Bakhtin does not assume that authors formulate their thought and then "encode" it by using the resources of language and genre. In that case, an author's failure to understand his work's potential meanings could result only from his own lack of skill or from the random vagaries of literary history, which, for example, might change a work's meaning by altering interpretive conventions. Turning to one of his favorite problems, Bakhtin offers a different model of the creative process, a model that allows for a third, alternative explanation of great works' growth in meaning.

Bakhtin suggests that when great authors are in the process of creation, they judge their work not only by its "expression" of what they mean, but by the richness of its possible meanings. The author senses the complexity of his work's use of the language, of tradition, and, especially, of the many resources of genre. Having responded to the rich potential of other works he has read, the author cultivates the ability to sense whether his own text has rich potential for meaning in unforeseen circumstances and whether such changes are likely to make his text richer or poorer in potentials. This sense guides his work as much as his desire to express specific

meanings he has clearly in mind. A great author knows the difference between a work that simply expresses what he "means to say"
but can do nothing more and a work that exploits the resources of
the past to produce rich "semantic treasures" (RQ, p. 5).

Stated simply, a work's potential is its capacity to grow in unforeseeable circumstances. In a universe of uncertainty, capacity to
perform a present, specific function is not the sole value; no less important is the flexibility to adapt to the unexpected. Major genres
contain that kind of flexibility, and major works exploit it.

Thus, in Bakhtin's view, there are three broad ways in which
works can be interpreted. First of all, one can identify the meanings
the author specifically had in mind or that his contemporaries may
have discovered. Bakhtin refers to this sort of interpretation as one
that "encloses" the work "within the epoch" (RQ, p. 4), and he
finds it both limited and limiting. "Enclosure within the epoch . . .
makes it impossible to understand the work's future life in subsequent centuries; this life appears as a kind of paradox" (ibid.). Second, one can "modernize and distort" the work by reading it entirely in terms of current interests. As the first interpretive method
reduces the reader's creative activity to zero, the second method does
the same to the author's activity; it simply makes a work mean whatever the interpreter wants or is trained to make it mean. In Bakhtin's
view, modernization and distortion are even more limiting than enclosure within the epoch because at least enclosure within the epoch
allows us to learn *something* we did not know before. By enclosing
the work within its epoch, we at least learn about the epoch; but by
making it a version of ourselves, we learn nothing.

For Bakhtin the real problem with intentional criticism is that it
is not intentional *enough*. Typically, intentionalists understand only
one of two kinds of intention; what they overlook is the author's
"other intention"—to make his work rich in potentials. Enclosing
the work within its epoch, practitioners of the first interpretive
method can never reveal the author's intentions adequately because
they rule the richest of them out of consideration in advance. To put
the point paradoxically but precisely, authors *intend* their works to
mean more than their *intended* meanings. They deliberately endow
their works not only with specified meanings they could paraphrase, but also with "intentional potentials" for future meanings
in unforeseen circumstances (DiN, p. 421). The most important
thing wrong both with the usual intentional criticism and with the
most common criticisms of it is an extraordinarily impoverished
understanding of intention itself.

It follows for Bakhtin that works accumulate meanings for *two* distinct reasons. Later generations of readers may either (1) modernize or distort the work, which tends to impoverish both the work and the readers; or, quite the opposite, (2) readers can interpret the work so as to develop and exploit the potentials actually present in it. This second process, while requiring discipline and care, may enrich both readers and work. (Of course, it may be difficult for readers of a given time to decide whether an interpretation is a distortion or an exploitation of potentials, just as it is always difficult to recognize the ways in which one is shaped by one's own times; but this difficulty does not compromise the distinction itself.)

Bakhtin insists on the centrality of this distinction, which depends entirely on the idea that a work can truly *contain* something that is necessarily only *potential*. This idea is important to Bakhtin's approach to all the humanities, and grows out of his global concept of unfinalizability. Thus, what Bakhtin maintains about great works he also maintains about individuals and entire cultures. Both contain potentials they could not specify. Or as Bakhtin sometimes puts the point, potentials are why great works, individuals, and cultures are "noncoincident" with themselves, why they always have a loophole, and why, no matter how *fully* they are described, they have not been *exhaustively* described. Just as individuals always have a "surplus of humanness" (EaN, p. 37), great works and cultures have a "surplus" of unexploited potentials. Potentials, noncoincidence, and the surplus make all three unfinalizable and able to render untrue any definition of them.

By their very nature, the implications of potentials cannot be fully specified. Thus, Shakespeare's works have grown in meaning over the centuries in "great time" (RQ, p. 4). Like other great works, they have lived a "posthumous life" even richer, "more intense and fuller than are their lives within their own time" (ibid.). Indeed, all truly great works "outgrow what they were in the epoch of their creation. We can say that neither Shakespeare himself nor his contemporaries knew that 'great Shakespeare' whom we know now. There is no possibility of squeezing our Shakespeare into the Elizabethan epoch" (ibid.). Bakhtin cryptically predicts a similar destiny for Shakespeare's modern rival in potentiality: "When Shakespeare became *Shakespeare*. Dostoevsky has not yet become Dostoevsky, he is still becoming him" (TRDB, p. 291).

Bakhtin insists that Shakespeare's rich "posthumous life" is *not* the product of modernization and distortion. His works have grown in meaning not only because of the efforts of later readers, but also because of what is really *in* them. They have grown because of the potential present from the outset, the capacity for growth put there and presumably sensed by the author precisely *as* potential. "Modernization and distortion, of course, have existed and will continue to exist. But that is not the reason why Shakespeare has grown. He has grown because of that which actually has been and continues to be found in his works, but which neither he himself nor his contemporaries could consciously perceive and evaluate in the context of the culture of their epoch" (RQ, p. 4).

Shakespeare and other great writers are able to exploit more than they understand because they intuitively have a sense of cultural wealth accumulated over history. "The semantic treasures Shakespeare embedded in his works were created and collected through the centuries and even millennia: they lay hidden in the language, and not only in the literary language, but also in . . . the diverse genres and forms of speech communication," in the forms of popular culture, "in plots whose roots go back to prehistoric antiquity, and, finally, in forms of thinking" (RQ, p. 5). In other words, Shakespeare did not "encode messages," as semiotic models tend to imply; rather, he constructed works with "semantic depths" that "exist in concealed form, potentially" (ibid.). He was able to do so—to include the potential to mean in remote times—because he "constructed his works not out of inanimate elements . . . but out of forms that were already heavily laden with meaning, filled with it" (ibid.).

In short, artists create potentials for the future by exploiting the resources of the past. In literature, the most important carrier of past resources—the central organ of memory—is genre. "Genres are of special significance. Genres (of literature and speech) throughout the centuries of their life accumulate forms of seeing and interpreting particular aspects of the world" (ibid.). Artists who are less than great use a genre as "an external template" (ibid.) for creating a work; truly great artists exploit "generic potentials" (DiN, p. 390). "Shakespeare took advantage of and included in his works immense treasures of potential meaning that could not be fully revealed or recognized in his [own] epoch" (RQ, p. 5).

It follows for Bakhtin that a special role of critics is to disclose potential. "The author himself and his contemporaries see, recognize, and evaluate primarily that which is close to their own day. The author is a captive of his epoch, of his own present. Subsequent times liberate him from this captivity, and literary scholarship is called upon to assist in this liberation" (ibid.). The technique of liberation is called "creative understanding."

In creative understanding, as we have suggested earlier, the interpreter creates a special sort of dialogue. "A meaning only reveals its depths once it has encountered and come into contact with another, foreign meaning; they engage in a kind of dialogue, which surmounts the closedness and one-sidedness of these particular meanings, these cultures" (RQ, p. 7). The result of these dialogues is to enrich both the text and its interpreter. The exchange creates new and valuable meanings possessed by neither at the outset. The text contains the potentials for the new meanings, but the specific meanings revealed also require the special contribution of the interpreter and his or her unrepeatable experience. Both sides of the dialogue are active. "Without *one's own* questions one cannot creatively understand anything other or foreign. . . . Such a dialogic encounter of two cultures does not result in merging or mixing. Each retains its own unity and *open* totality, but they are mutually enriched" (ibid.). In his insistence on one's own questions, Bakhtin is returning to the tenet of his early manuscripts: No one can ever do what I can do now from my position.

Unlike alternative forms of interpretation, then, creative understanding demands a double and dialogic activity. In contrast to relativism and modernization, it presumes that the text is truly *other* and contains semantic depths otherwise unavailable; in contrast to enclosure within the epoch, it demands what Bakhtin calls the interpreter's own "outsideness," which includes the resources of his or her own culture's experience. The interpreter is not satisfied with recreating the text's original context, he also takes advantage of his own. "*Creative understanding* does not renounce itself, its own place in time, its own culture; and it forgets nothing. In order to understand, it is immensely important for the person who understands to be *located outside* the object of his or her creative understanding—in time, in space, in culture" (RQ, p. 7).

By invoking the concept of outsideness, Bakhtin builds on the work of his first period. He observes that "one cannot even really see one's own exterior and comprehend it as a whole, and no mirrors or photographs can help; our real exterior can be seen and understood only by other people, because they are located outside us in space and because they are *others*" (ibid.). By analogy, the great texts of any culture require the perspective of other cultures to develop their potential. In fact, they are great in large measure *be-*

cause of potentialities and semantic depths that can be revealed only by another culture.

As the reference to other cultures may suggest, Bakhtin maintains that ethnographic and historical interpretation involves essentially the same issues as the interpretation of great works. What is true of Shakespeare is true of distant times and remote places; other cultures both contain potentials that they themselves do not suspect and promise semantic rewards attainable in no other way. Cultural history and anthropology, no less than literary criticism, will contribute most if they exploit their own outsideness and engage in creative understanding.

For Bakhtin, cultures are never semiotic "systems" with a closed totality. "In each culture of the past lie immense semantic possibilities that have remained undisclosed, unrecognized, and unutilized throughout the entire historical life of a given culture" (RQ, p. 6) but which can still be utilized at other times and places. Thus,

antiquity itself did not know the antiquity that we know now. There used to be a school joke: the ancient Greeks did not know the main thing about themselves, that they were *ancient* Greeks. . . . But in fact the temporal distance that transformed the Greeks into *ancient* Greeks . . . was filled with increasing discoveries of new *semantic* values in antiquity, values of which the Greeks were in fact unaware, although they themselves created them. [RQ, p. 6]

Speech Genres

Context and code. A context is potentially unfinalized; a code must be finalized. A code is only a technical means of transmitting information; it does not have cognitive, creative significance. A code is a deliberately established, killed context.

—N70–71, p. 147

Many people who have an excellent command of a language often feel quite helpless in certain spheres of communication precisely because they do not have a practical command of the generic forms used in the given spheres.   —SG, p. 80

Genres are the residue of past behavior, an accretion that shapes, guides, and constrains future behavior. Bakhtin uses a series of metaphors to describe the origin and nature of genres; he compares them to "crystallizations" of earlier interactions and refers to them as "congealed events." Their form is not mere form, but is really "stereotyped, congealed, old (familiar) content . . . [that] serves as a necessary bridge to new, still unknown content" because it is "a familiar and generally understood congealed old world view" (MHS, p. 165).

Genres provide a specific field for future activity, and such activity is never just an "application," "instantiation," or repetition of a pattern. Genres carry the generalizable resources of particular events; but specific actions or utterances must use those resources to accomplish new purposes in each unrepeatable milieu. Each utterance, each use of a genre, demands real work; beginning with the given, something different must be created.

As this paraphrase indicates, genres for Bakhtin are not a strictly literary phenomenon. Rather, literary genres are themselves just a specific type of "speech genre"; Voloshinov went still further and argued that speech genres are themselves part of another complex he called "life genres" (*zhiznennye zhanry*; the phrase is translated in *Marxism and the Philosophy of Language* as "behavioral genres"). The fact is, that whenever we speak we necessarily do so in one or another speech genre. We use speech genres skillfully in practice even though they have remained largely undescribed by scholarship.[3]

If one remembers that for Bakhtin, speech always takes the form not of repeatable sentences but of unrepeatable utterances, one can immediately see that much more than grammar and syntax are needed for speech. One must situate one's utterance in a given context. One needs to suggest the social relations between the speakers and their relation to outsiders; to indicate a set of values; to offer a set of perceptions and ways of perceiving; to outline a field of possible, likely, or desirable actions; to convey a vague or specific sense of time and space; to suggest an appropriate tone; to rule in or rule out various styles and languages of heteroglossia; and to negotiate a set of purposes.[4] Since it is impossible to do all this work before each utterance—and in any case, even such preliminary work would require its own set of initial premises—we rely on speech genres, the "relatively stable types" of utterance (SG, p. 60), as a starting point for particular exchanges.

Indeed, we necessarily begin to learn speech genres from the very first time we speak; we "are given these speech genres in almost the same way that we are given our native language, which we master fluently long before we begin to study grammar" (SG, p. 78). To know a language is to command a repertoire of its speech genres, which means to understand more than "language" in the narrow sense. Each genre implies a set of values, a way of thinking about kinds of experience, and an intuition about the appropriateness of applying the genres in any given context. An enormous amount of unformalized cognitive content is acquired each time we learn a new kind of social activity with its attendant genres, content whose very nature has remained largely unexamined.

Because each culture engages in a vast array of activities practiced by many different social groups in a variety of circumstances, each culture possesses a vast number of speech genres. As the culture's "congealed events" and "crystallized" activity, these genres constitute an important part of its memory and carry a great deal of its wisdom. This is the prosaic, unformalized, and highly concrete wisdom of daily life, the appreciation of which is central to what Bakhtin calls prosaic consciousness, "prosaic intelligence," "prosaic wisdom," and "prosaic vision" (DiN, p. 404), and to what the present study calls "prosaics."

Speech genres "differentiate and grow as the particular sphere [of social activity] develops and becomes more complex" (SG, p. 60). As individuals or cultures acquire a larger set of activities or a wider compass of experience, their repertoire of genres grows. Taken as a whole, then, a culture's speech genres tend toward heterogeneity and form anything but a system.

Each individual genre records the minutest shifts in daily practices and values. Indeed, "there is not a single new phenomenon (phonetic, lexical, or grammatical) that can enter the system of language without having traversed the long and complicated path of generic-stylistic testing and modification" (SG, p. 65). Speech genres are therefore a key link between social and linguistic history. If one is to understand the history of a language, "one must develop a special history of speech genres . . . that reflects more directly, clearly, and flexibly all the changes taking place in social life" (ibid.).

Genres accumulate experience. Just as the topics of our discourse are always "already spoken about" in diverse ways, so genres carry with them the layered record of their changing use. Genres form not by legislation but by accretion. The genuine results of a historical process, they resemble a patchwork rather than a preconceived design. One cannot understand them unless one recognizes that they are compromises, never designed from the outset for the purpose they currently serve, but adapted for that purpose from forms previously serving other purposes. Like most products of evolution, they are imperfectly suited to their present use—and for that very reason are relatively adaptable to future uses, to which they will also be acceptably but not optimally suited. Made from ingredients at hand, they become part of a culture's mixed plate—its prosaic *satura*—of hastily confected offerings.

As we have seen, Bakhtin at times prefers an organic metaphor to describe the formation of genres: genres *grow together*, *inosculate*, or *knit together* (as bones are said to knit together). Never shaped by design or integrated as a structure, genres cannot be adequately described as or by a system of rules.

Because genres are so often adapted from previous genres, they may carry the potential to resume their past usage and so to redefine a present experience in an additional way. Some genres easily lend themselves to this kind of "double-voicing"; they recover old contexts or intimate the possibility of new ones. The unsuspected potential of a genre may also be used to "reaccentuate" a voice. This process is a common part both of individual psychic life, in which we arrive at our own inner discourse through reaccenting the discourses of others, and of collective social life, in which it serves as a method for adapting the lessons of one kind of experience to another.

Genres shaped in one area of life may be imported into another. For example, in many historical eras specific kinds of extraliterary speech genres have set the tone for the development of literary language. Diverse kinds of written discourse or oral conversation—the discourse of the salon, or of a certain type of philosophical discussion, for instance—may penetrate literature and set the tone for various literary genres. A complex interaction of genres necessarily takes place, as each reaccents the other. When oral genres penetrate written ones, the interactions may be especially complex. One observes "the more or less distinct dialogization of secondary genres, the weakening of their monological composition, the new sense of the listener as a partner-interlocutor, new forms of finalization of the whole, and so forth. Where there is style, there is genre. The transfer of style from one genre to another not only alters the way a style sounds, under conditions of a genre unnatural to it, but also violates or renews the given genre" (SG, p. 66). Specific genres may carry the record of numerous "transfers" from one social realm to another; one may sense within them many such violations and renewals.

As conversational genres may invade literature, so the reverse process may and frequently does happen. Norms of speech or behavior are borrowed from literature, set the tone for certain kinds of everyday behavior in given social groups—and may, after suitable reaccentuation, penetrate literature once again.

Because confusion about Bakhtin's concept of speech genres is fairly common, it is worth stressing that in speaking both of "literary" genres and of "secondary" genres Bakhtin is *not* using synonymous designations. As Bakhtin defines his terms, secondary genres are not necessarily literary. They are distinguished not from nonliterary but from "primary" genres, which are, in a sense, the atoms (or amoebic forms) of genre; several of them may be combined to form a more complex secondary genre. "During the process of their formation, they [secondary genres] absorb and digest various primary (simple) genres" (SG, p. 62). Secondary genres take shape in every social sphere; they include philosophical commentaries, scientific treatises, forms of practical communication that typically combine simpler types of report, command, or request, and countless other kinds of exchanges. Literary genres are but one kind of secondary genre.

The formation of all secondary genres necessarily involves reaccentuation of the primary genres that are absorbed. Once they become part of secondary genres, primary ones "lose their immediate relation to actual reality and to the real utterances of others. For example, rejoinders of everyday dialogues or letters found in a novel . . . enter into actual reality only via the novel as a whole, that is, as a literary-artistic event and not as everyday life" (ibid.). When incorporated into secondary genres, primary genres may retain much of their characteristic tone or definition of experience, in which case a complex kind of double-voicing and generic dialogization will be visible. In other cases, the act of assimilation involves a consistent muting of the incorporated genre's tone. The problem of "inserted genres"—both primary and secondary—is discussed at length in "Discourse in the Novel."

As genres "remember" the contexts in which they have been established and adapted, so may the words that typically appear in those genres. Indeed, much of what we loosely refer to as a word's "connotations" may in fact be the "stylistic aura" resulting from the word's usual generic context (SG, pp. 87–88). Typical contexts "seem to adhere to words" (SG, p. 87). After all, we do not select the words we use from the dictionary; rather, we "usually take them from *other utterances*, and mainly from utterances that are kindred to ours in genre" (ibid.). Although a word's aura may seem to belong "to the word of language as such"—to its dictionary meaning—the aura actually belongs "to that genre in which the given word usually functions. It is an echo of the generic whole that resounds in the word" (SG, p. 88).

Genre Memory

The idea of "genre memory," though perhaps implicit through-out Bakhtin's third period, was first explicitly developed in the 1963 edition of the Dostoevsky book. As we have noted, genre only be-came central to Bakhtin's thought after the original edition ap-peared (1929). When he turned to his revisions, Bakhtin altered the text considerably to include theories of genre he had been develop-ing over the previous three decades.

Bakhtin addresses general questions of genre ostensibly in order to justify his lengthy digression about carnivalistic forms in Western literature. Dostoevsky, Bakhtin contends, saw the rich "potential" of these forms better than any earlier writer and discovered a way to develop that potential to the fullest: by combining the genre's tradi-tional techniques with his own radical innovation, polyphony. Dostoevsky's novels are therefore the greatest menippean satires ever written—the "peak" of a tradition extending back to antiquity (PDP, p. 121).

Having made this claim, Bakhtin raises a possible objection to it: Dostoevsky may have known very little about menippean satire. He certainly knew considerably fewer examples of it than Bakhtin did. Moreover, Dostoevsky was probably unaware of the source of these forms in carnival; as with "the majority of other eighteenth- and nineteenth-century writers . . . carnival proper was perhaps not even perceived by him [Dostoevsky] in any clearly precise way" (PDP, p. 157). How then can it be claimed that Dostoevsky best realized the potential of a genre he barely knew and found the most effective realization of a "carnival spirit" whose existence he perhaps did not consciously suspect?

This sort of question is evidently important with respect not only to Dostoevsky, but also to many other writers, and is, indeed, fundamental to "historical poetics" generally. One frequently en-counters writers who apparently develop the potentials of tradi-tions they barely know; in such cases, critics search in vain for "in-fluences." If critics truly understood the nature and development of genres, Bakhtin contends, they would look not for influences, but for "generic contacts" (PDP, p. 157). This distinction is central to Bakhtin's argument in the Dostoevsky book's chapter devoted to "Characteristics of Genre."

To study influence is to study a relationship that is essentially binary, Bakhtin explains. One traces the source of one writer's work to another's; for example, one discovers in Balzac the source of well-known ideas in Dostoevsky. For studies of this sort, generic tradition is not especially important, whereas it is important to Bakhtin's own discussion of Dostoevsky's relation to menippean satire. Bakhtin stresses: "We are not interested in the influence of separate individual authors, individual works, individual themes, ideas, images—what interests us is precisely the influence of the *generic tradition itself* which was transmitted through the particular authors" (PDP, p. 159). The important word here is *through*.

In reading Balzac, Dostoevsky may have looked for Balzac's specific contributions; he was influenced by what he found *in* Balzac. But in reading the handful of menippean satires he knew (Voltaire's "Micromegas," Diderot's *Rameau's Nephew*), Dostoevsky also looked "through" the works and sensed the generic tradition to which those works belonged. In this sense, the works in question were not "sources of influence" but "contacts" with the genre. "It is certainly possible [and justified] to study individual influences . . . that is, the influence of one individual writer on another . . . but this is already a special task and one which we do not set for ourselves here. We are interested only in the tradition itself" (PDP, p. 159).

Dostoevsky did not need to know many menippean satires in order to discover the genre's special kind of "artistic thinking." Generally speaking, to understand a genre's way of perceiving and representing the world, "a writer need not know all the links and all the branchings of that tradition. A genre possesses its own organic logic, which can to a certain extent be understood and creatively assimilated on the basis of a few generic models, even fragments" (PDP, p. 157). After understanding the genre's logic, a great writer can guess the uses to which it must have been put by someone or other at some time or other; and the writer can also imagine how the resources of his own age or experience might better realize the genre's potential. Having understood the spirit of menippean satire, Dostoevsky recognized how his own polyphonic method could combine with it so that both would be enriched.

In short, Dostoevsky did not have to remember very much of the past, because the genre remembered for him. "Dostoevsky linked up with the chain of a given generic tradition at that point where it passed through his own time. . . . Speaking somewhat paradoxically, one could say that it was not Dostoevsky's subjective memory, but the objective memory of the very genre in which he worked, that preserved the peculiar features of the ancient menippea" (PDP, p. 121).

Great writers—Shakespeare, Dostoevsky—have a special relation to tradition. More fully than others, they intuit the rich resources of the past carried by genres; they imagine the potential
uses, both past and possible, to which those resources could be put;
and they plant more potentials for unexpected development in the
future. Such special use and renewal of the heritage of "great time"
constitutes the "life of the genre. . . . A genre lives in the present,
but always *remembers* its past, its beginning. Genre is a representative of creative memory in the process of literary development"
(PDP, p. 106).

Genres and Sociological Reductionism

One can appreciate at this point why Bakhtin objected so strenu-
ously to naive Marxist (or other sociological) "explanations" of
great works in terms of their own epoch. Regardless of the time or
social milieu in which they are composed, great works draw upon
the resources of centuries past and develop potentials for ages to
come. Never exhausted by the circumstances of their origin, they
are unfinalizable and noncoincident with themselves.

In Bakhtin's view, an understanding of a work's epoch is necessary but far from sufficient for an adequate understanding of the
work. To be sure, it is not accidental when great works appear;
most likely, Dostoevsky's works could only have been produced at
their time and place. Nevertheless, they cannot be reduced to that
time and place. As Sartre observed, "Valéry was a petit bourgeois
intellectual, no doubt about it. But not every petit bourgeois intellectual is Valéry" (Sartre, *Search*, p. 56). And Bakhtin might have
added: *Crime and Punishment* is a product of the Russian capitalist
era; but not every product of that era is *Crime and Punishment*.

As Bakhtin formulates the issue, an age provides favorable or
unfavorable conditions for a work's appearance, and may shape the
work in important ways, but a great work's richest potentials have
nevertheless developed over many ages. No matter how exhaustively we study Shakespeare's or Dostoevsky's time, and no matter
how thoroughly we probe their personal psychological complexes,
we will not plumb all the semantic depths present in their works. It
is perhaps for this very reason that biographies of writers, however
well researched, often seem unsatisfying at the most important moment—when they move from the experiences of a writer's life to
the rich meanings of his works. We may recall Medvedev's insistence that great works or creative projects often take many genera-

tions to complete. Great works are impoverished by "enclosure within the epoch," as is the "open totality" of the epoch itself.

In the second edition of the Dostoevsky book, Bakhtin took advantage of the opportunity to clarify his views on "sociologism." Responding to Lunacharsky's generally positive 1929 review of the first edition, Bakhtin objected strongly to Lunacharsky's rather naive identification of Dostoevsky's polyphony with the capitalist conditions in which it appeared. In Bakhtin's view, this sociologism was what led Lunacharsky, as it has led so many others, to a misunderstanding of literature's significance. Specifically, it led Lunacharsky to view Dostoevsky's novels as nothing but a symptom of an era soon to pass, at which point polyphony would be of merely historical interest. In Lunacharsky's view (as it is expressed in the passage Bakhtin cites), "Dostoevsky has not yet died, neither here nor in the West, because capitalism has not yet died, and even less the vestiges of capitalism" (Lunacharsky, "O 'mnogogolosnosti,'" as cited in PDP, p. 35).

Bakhtin replies that "poetics cannot, of course, be divorced from social and historical analyses, but neither can it be dissolved in them," (PDP, p. 36) as Lunacharsky dissolved it. Polyphony was developed over many ages, not just "under capitalism." "New forms of artistic visualization prepare themselves slowly, over centuries; a given epoch can do no more than create optimal conditions for the final ripening . . . of a new form" (ibid.). Bakhtin adds that what has taken shape over centuries may also have the potential to enter into new and significant dialogues with later centuries and cultures. Regardless of when polyphony was discovered, its future development is bound to be rich. Both Dostoevsky's epoch and his personality "have long since faded into the past, but the new structural principle of polyphony, *discovered* under these conditions, retains and will continue to retain its artistic significance under the completely different conditions of subsequent epochs. Great discoveries of human genius are made possible by the specific conditions of specific epochs, but they never die or lose their value along with the epochs that gave them birth" (PDP, p. 35).

We have stressed that an important objective of Bakhtin's work was to show that creativity is real, ongoing, and immanent in the process of daily living. Thus, he sought to describe creativity without resorting to inspiration from the muse, intimations of the transcendental, or eruptions from the unconscious. Those models are usually used to explain the fact, noted at least since Plato, that poets seem to know more than they "know"—to place more meaning in their works than they themselves could ever adduce. Without resorting to the irrational or mystical, Bakhtin's theory of genre memory and of an individual writer's relation to potential meanings accounts for this "surplus" knowledge. Bakhtin is careful neither to explain away that surplus knowledge nor to call it inexplicable. Rather, it is the understandable consequence of prosaic creativity at work across cultures and through ages of great time.

Novels and Other Genres

> The utter inadequacy of literary theory is revealed when it is forced to deal with the novel. . . . Aristotle's poetics, although occasionally so deeply embedded as to be almost invisible, remains the stable foundation for the theory of genres. Everything works so long as there is no mention of the novel. But the existence of novelized genres already leads theory into a blind alley. Faced with the problem of the novel, genre theory must submit to a radical restructuring.   —EaN, p. 8

Much as various languages of heteroglossia seem to grow out of specific social experiences, so genres offer a repertoire of visualizations. Historical experience enriches both.

The comparison of genres with languages of heteroglossia suggests another set of questions central to Bakhtin's thought. Languages of heteroglossia can become "relativized" and "dialogized"; that is, they may lose their status as the unquestioned way of speaking about a given aspect of life. Forced to compete with other languages, they enter a "Galilean" universe (there are many linguistic worlds, none of which is at the center). A similar phenomenon happens with genres: at times, they may be forced to compete with rival genres as the best way to visualize a given aspect of life. No longer sensed as indisputably correct within its sphere, a genre may instead be perceived as one participant in an ongoing dialogue about its characteristic topic.

In other words, literary theory and literary history must consider the *interaction* of genres (much as metalinguistics must consider the interaction of languages). To be sure, this problem is far from new; it has been a central topic of poetics since the ancients. But inasmuch as genres have been misunderstood, so has their interaction. In Bakhtin's view, traditional poetics has repeatedly made fundamental errors that only a radically new approach guided by "prosaic consciousness" can correct. To understand the interaction of genres properly, one needs not only poetics, but also prosaics.

According to Bakhtin, poetics tends to suppress the competition, dialogization, and conflictual interaction of genres. Itself a "centripetal" cultural force, poetics has never given adequate attention to the "centrifugal" forces shaping the history of genres. "The great organic poetics of the past—those of Aristotle, Horace, Boileau—are permeated with a deep sense of the wholeness of literature and the harmonious interaction of all genres contained within this whole. It is as if they literally hear this harmony of the genres" (EaN, p. 5). From this concern with harmony, poetics derives its "fullness and exhaustiveness" (ibid.). The price it pays is an almost total deafness to *dis*harmony. Poetics fails to appreciate all those genres deliberately concerned with upsetting order, the genres that belong to "the 'dialogic line' in the development of European artistic prose" (PDP, p. 270). The greatest of these disharmonious genres is the novel.

If the novel and related genres did not exist, there would be less need to go beyond poetics. A structuralist approach to literary history would be more or less adequate; genres could be described either as static elements in a sort of periodic table or at least as dynamic entities changing in a regular and lawful manner. The harmony of genres would produce the quadrille of literary history. Once the novel and related genres are seriously considered, however, this entire approach becomes untenable.

Bakhtin's third period may be viewed as a series of attempts to describe "novelness" in ways antithetical to the spirit of traditional poetics (including Formalist and structuralist). In so doing, Bakhtin depicts literary history as a continuous conflict of the novel with other genres.

Novels and Novelization

Bakhtin developed three major theories of the novel and its relation to other genres. These three theories (and a few minor ones) are discussed in Chapters Eight, Nine, and Ten of the present study. Perhaps the most successful and original of the three (developed in "Discourse in the Novel" and "From the Prehistory of Novelistic Discourse") describes the novel in terms of its special use of language. Almost equally impressive is Bakhtin's classification of genres as distinct conceptualizations of historical time, social "space," individual character, and moral action. (Bakhtin outlines this approach in "Forms of Time and of the Chronotope" and "The *Bildungsroman* and Its Significance in the History of Realism.") Bakhtin's third major theory of the novel, which is based on his ideas regarding carnival, was the first to become widely known in the West. In our view, it is, for all its occasional brilliance, often hyperbolic and ultimately not as durable as the other two.

It will be recalled that we distinguish two lines of thought in Bakhtin's third period (IIIa and IIIb). Generally speaking, the theories belonging to IIIa are more convincing to us than the theories of IIIb. The latter tend to a radical "novelistic imperialism," to ecstatic but somewhat imprecise thinking, and to overdramatized accounts of literary history. When writing in this mode, Bakhtin treats the novel not just as a favorite topic but also as a "hero," and he consequently novelizes the novel's history. We follow the picaresque adventures of this rogue genre, learn of its wise foolishness, and admire its Rabelaisian jokes at the expense of "high heroizing" forms. By contrast, in period IIIa, Bakhtin's prosaics achieves a formulation that is more adequate because less extreme. He still expresses his preference for the novel's view of the world, but less categorically; he avoids absolute endorsements of the novel's rejection of absolutes. Other genres are treated with greater appreciation and respect. Skeptical rather than antinomian, Bakhtin acknowledges many "visions of truth," and endorses prose and "prosaic intelligence" in a measured, prosaic spirit.

In his fourth period, Bakhtin preferred the less extreme formulations of IIIa. In his new conclusion to the Dostoevsky book, he asks whether polyphony makes monologism "obsolete," a question he immediately broadens to ask whether new genres, such as the novel, superannuate older ones. In period IIIb, Bakhtin looked for ways to answer in the affirmative; in the revised Dostoevsky book, he answers unreservedly: "Of course not. A newly born genre never supplants or replaces any already existing genres. Each new genre merely supplements the old ones, merely widens the circle of already existing genres. For every genre has its own predominant sphere of existence" (PDP, p. 271).

Thus, polyphony does not make monologism obsolete (and presumably the novel does not end the life of rival genres) because life is too changeable, too messy and diverse, for any single way of conceptualizing the world to claim unchallenged superiority. "There will always continue to exist and expand those spheres of existence, of man and nature, which require precisely objectified and finalizing, that is, monologic forms of artistic cognition" (ibid.). Even the novel must operate in a Galilean conceptual universe, where it is but one of many worlds. "Thus no new artistic genre ever nullifies or replaces old ones" (ibid.).

Bakhtin never explicitly clarified the relation of his three theories of the novel to each other. They differ in a number of obvious respects. As a consequence of describing the novel according to differing criteria, they arrive at overlapping rather than identical genre membership. One theory's "early novels" are another's "pre-novels"; texts within the bounds of novelness from one point of view lie just outside it from another. How are we to reconcile these differences?

In our opinion, Bakhtin probably saw his theories as complementary rather than contradictory. Because each specific way of understanding the world is extremely complex, it can be treated from different vantage points, each of which is bound to yield somewhat different results. When viewed as a way of thinking about action and character, novels most prominently exhibit one set of characteristics and seem best represented by a corresponding group of texts; when considered as a specific approach to language, the genre looks somewhat different and suggests other exemplars. Because genres are shaped historically by the accretion and interaction of numerous contingent factors over long periods, it would be surprising if they *did* look the same from every perspective. Properly interpreted, then, variability of description may indicate not inconsistency but asymmetry. It also implies that critics need to specify questions and purposes of inquiry carefully before choosing among generic characterizations.

Readers of Bakhtin also need to clarify which concept of novelness he has in mind at any given point in his argument. They would be ill advised to assume that the term *novel* has the same meaning in all essays, even those within the same period. Used most broadly in his texts, the term indicates the entire "dialogic line" of European prose. Extending from ancient seriocomic works to the present, this line includes low genres as well as high and seems to incorporate such nonliterary institutions as carnival, parodic rituals, and "genres of billingsgate."

Taken in its narrowest sense, however, Bakhtin sometimes appears to use *novel* to indicate a highly restricted class; membership demands that all of Bakhtin's major criteria be satisfied. The novel in this sense would seem to begin around 1800 and to include only a portion of the texts often called novels. As far as we can tell, the works of Goethe (or Jane Austen?) would seem to be the first novels in the narrowest sense. Although this restricted class would include *Crime and Punishment, Great Expectations, Middlemarch, Anna Karenina, Eugenie Grandet, The Charterhouse of Parma, Madame*

Bovary, Eugene Onegin, Barchester Towers, and many other works usually called novels, it would *not* include *Dead Souls* (better classified as a menippean satire), *Moby Dick* (as a kind of allegory), *Looking Backward* (as a utopia), *Wuthering Heights* (as a romance), *Life on the Mississippi, Erewhon,* and *The Sot-Weed Factor* (as modern menippean satires). By one set of criteria, Richardson is an important "pre-novelist," by another, a novelist and, in fact, a central representative of the first of two lines in the genre's history.

Bakhtin's various descriptions of the novel do have a number of important features in common. Whatever the principle governing his generic classification, Bakhtin always treats the novel as the form best satisfying his favorite values and expressing his global concepts. The novel is sure to be the genre that is most dialogic. More than any competitor, it treats character, society, and knowledge as unfinalizable; it is closest to prosaic values, an appreciation of centrifugal forces, and a sense of the world's essential messiness. In any given classificatory scheme, genres antithetical to the novel are given to claims of certainty, expressions of absolute truth, and assertions of timeless wisdom; by contrast, the novel is ever skeptical, experimental, and open to the unpredictable experience of every present moment. Rivals are set at a reverential distance from their readers; the novel partakes of everyday life. Other genres claim to know, the novel asks how we know; novels are most aware of the multiplicity of languages, conceptual schemes, and social experiences; where others might prophesy, the novel merely conjectures.

Another way in which Bakhtin likes to express such points is to refer to the relative "naivete" (*naivnost'*) of other genres and to describe the novel as a force for overcoming such naivete. Thus, a genre based on the unquestioned assumption that there is only one way of speaking, one set of values, or one conceptual scheme adequate to a given topic is wholly naive. It is like a "word of the first type." When that assumption comes to be questioned, naivete begins to erode. We see something analogous to a "word of the third type."

After losing its naivete, a genre may still reassert its initial values, continue to employ its perceptual scheme, and speak again in its favored language, but even if it does so it will nevertheless have changed. For as we noted earlier, there is all the difference in the world between accepting something without question and accepting it after it has been questioned. A genre that has encountered the novel has been *tested*, and for ever after its values become a choice among alternatives. Its style turns into stylization; authors and audience no longer just assume the genre's values but *agree* with them; and agreement, as we have noted, is a truly *dialogic* relation. (One difference between periods IIIa and IIIb is that in the latter, Bakhtin is more likely to write as if disagreement were necessarily less naive than agreement; in IIIa, he does not.)

In principle, all genres can force rival genres to become more self-conscious, "to better perceive their own possibilities and boundaries, that is, to overcome their *naivete*" (PDP, p. 271). But the novel and related genres perform this function best because their very spirit is Galilean. Overcoming naivete is part of the novel's generic "task." Novels invade a tranquil realm to dispute territory, violate generic decorum, and upset poetic harmony. Faced with such behavior, other genres must adapt. If they do not, they come to sound hopelessly anachronistic and unsophisticated, or even like unintended self-parodies. Perhaps contradicting his earlier statements that genres are never supplanted, Bakhtin at one point even pictures a Darwinian struggle in which genres that do not adapt may "die a 'natural death'" (PDP, p. 272).

Usually other genres do adapt by changing. In ages when novels predominate, they "novelize" or "prosify" other genres. Moreover, the social forces that lead to the novel's preeminence—say, a skeptical sense of the world—also act directly on other genres; at such times, novelization happens both directly and indirectly. "All literature is then caught up in the process of 'becoming,' and in a special kind of 'genre criticism.' This occurred several times in the Hellenistic period, again during the late Middle Ages and the Renaissance, but with special force and clarity beginning in the second half of the eighteenth century" (EaN, p. 5).

In Bakhtin's view, novelization is a key process in literary history. Depending on the novelistic characterization he has in mind at a given moment, Bakhtin uses the term *novelization* in varying ways. Common to all uses is the "reaccentuation" of a naive genre, that is, a change in the way it "sounds" owing to a revision in its sense of the world. Where language was once unself-conscious and categorical, after being novelized it becomes polemical and double-voiced; it takes a sideward glance at other ways of speaking. Laughter and self-parody complicate tones of previously unquestioned seriousness; revered values find themselves in the daily marketplace of ideas and heroes from the "absolute past" are reborn in the "familiar zone" of the "open-ended present."

Bakhtin offers a number of examples of "novelized" works and genres: Byron novelized the epic when he wrote *Don Juan* and

Childe Harold, Ibsen novelized the drama, and Heine prosified the lyric poem. Ultimately, Bakhtin suggests, some degree of novelization is unavoidable in a novelistic epoch.

Bakhtin concedes that some earlier scholars have described features of novelization, but they have nevertheless not understood its significance. Literary historians

usually reduce this struggle between the novel and other already completed genres, all these aspects of novelization, to the actual real-life struggle among "schools" and "trends." A novelized poem, for example, they call a "romantic poem" (which of course it is) and believe that in so doing they have exhausted the subject. They do not see beneath the superficial hustle and bustle of literary process the major and crucial fates of literature and language, whose great heroes turn out to be first and foremost genres. [EaN, pp. 7–8]

8

Prosaics and the Language of the Novel

> The dialogic orientation of a word among other words (of all kinds and degrees of otherness) creates new and significant artistic potential in discourse, creates the potential for a distinctive art of prose, which has found its fullest and deepest expression in the novel. —DiN, p. 275

> What is realized in the novel is the process of coming to know one's own language as it is perceived in someone else's language, coming to know one's own conceptual horizon in someone else's horizon. —DiN, p. 365

> Two myths perish simultaneously: the myth of a language that presumes to be the only language and the myth of a language that presumes to be completely unified. —PND, p. 68

For Bakhtin, as we have seen, a genre is neither a hierarchy of devices nor a complex of themes and forms nor a set of interpretive conventions. Rather, it is a specific form of thinking, a way of visualizing the world with "the eyes of the genre." When a genre is significant, its way of thinking is no mere expression of principles already formulated in philosophy; it offers insights that often precede or entirely elude philosophical transcription. Like great works and remote cultures, major genres have enormous unrealized potential for future insights and for still more complex modeling of the world.

Great writers—Shakespeare, Dostoevsky—sense, exploit, and contribute to this "generic potential," the artistic possibilities of the genre (DiN, p. 390). Thus, a genre must be understood not only in terms of the works it contains—not just as a classification of works written or to be written—but as an ongoing creative energy, which, as it encounters unforeseen kinds of experience, responds and grows. The great works belonging to a genre do not constitute it, but rather are the results of its "living impulse," and are among the shapers of that impulse. Genres are truly historical not only because they carry with them the memory of the past, but also because they are more or less capable of responding to the sort of contingency constitutive of historicity itself.

"Form-shaping ideology" (or "form-shaping force") is Bakhtin's name for all that makes a genre what it is: its way of seeing the world, the forms that carry the traces of earlier creative thinking, its record of interactions with other genres, its potential for future development, and—above all—its distinctive kind of generic energy. A genre's form-shaping ideology is not "transcribable with no residue" into a set of propositions or complex of forms; such a transcription would necessarily oversimplify the genre's way of visualizing and would think away its generic potential. Still, such transcriptions may be quite valuable as a stepping-stone to an understanding of the genre, a way of pointing one in the right direction. So long as one does not mistake the transcription for a full explication, and so long as one is aware of the kind of thing necessarily left out, transcriptions can be a key critical tool for literary studies.

In the Dostoevsky book, Bakhtin offered a sample of such a transcription of his concept of polyphony. Repeatedly cautioning us about what "monological" paraphrases necessarily omit, he offers to approach polyphony's form-shaping ideology in terms of a set of beliefs and the "forms" realizing it. To be sure, polyphony is not a content plus accompanying forms, but a way of seeing the world that generates both. Nevertheless, Bakhtin tells us, we can get a rough appreciation of that way of seeing by this somewhat artificial analytic practice. Bakhtin then discusses polyphony's ideological predisposition to a "dialogic conception of truth" and Dostoevsky's discovery of a form to realize that conception.

All these considerations also inform Bakhtin's theories of the novel in the 1930's and 1940's, especially the works belonging to period IIIa. Once Bakhtin had presented polyphony as a way of seeing and had found an analytic technique for discussing that way of seeing, he saw the potential of this approach for genres in general. Because genres were for Bakhtin central to the dynamics of literary history, he could now boldly turn to questions spanning thousands of years of Western "artistic thought." As the discovery of language as a key problem shaped his work of the second period, his turn to history, genres, and the novel creates the special excitement present in his works of the third period.

For Bakhtin, the novel was not just a complex form of thinking, but was also the supreme achievement of Western thought, greater than all other genres as well as all schools of philosophy. It should be stressed at the outset that although Bakhtin's reasons for *distinguishing* the novel from other genres grow directly out of his theories of literature and language, his reasons for *preferring* the novel to all other genres do not. It would be entirely possible to accept Bakhtin's descriptions of the novel while still rejecting his evaluation of it.

Bakhtin's very high evaluation of the novel reflects some of his essentially extraliterary concerns. Specifically, it derives from his ethical agenda, his war on theoretism, and his global concerns of dialogue, unfinalizability, and, especially, prosaics. Bakhtin speaks repeatedly of the novel as the form that best embodies "prosaic intelligence," "prosaic vision," and "prosaic wisdom" (DiN, p. 404), terms he does not define, but which are probably meant to allude to what we have called the "prosaic sense of the world." For Bakhtin, this sense was so central to his whole intellectual enterprise that the genre embodying it became his hero.

Bakhtin seems to have regarded prosaic wisdom as a kind of overarching form-shaping ideology of the novel. But that ideology was so complex that he apparently decided not to proceed directly to discussing the genre in terms of it, but rather to isolate two distinct aspects of prosaic wisdom and take each of them as subordinate form-shaping ideologies. An overall sense of the novel would come from the combination of these two (and perhaps others only hinted at). One subordinate form-shaping ideology concerns the novel's special sense of language, the other its sense of social space, historical time, character, and human action. In period IIIa, Bakhtin devoted his book-length essay on time and the chronotope and his study of the Bildungsroman (apparently also at one time much longer than the present surviving fragment) to the second aspect of novels. He devoted "Discourse in the Novel" and the briefer "From the Prehistory of Novelistic Discourse" to the novel's special approach to language, which is our concern in the present chapter.

Throughout his discussion of discourse in the novel, Bakhtin uses the words *prosaic* and *novelistic* as roughly synonymous. Of course, Bakhtin was well aware that not only prose is found in novels, and, still more important, that most prose does not occur in novels. If one were to develop a theory of prose focusing on expository prose, for example, one would arrive at a prosaics quite different from the one Bakhtin offers, and, in fact, Bakhtin devotes a good deal of attention, in this period and after, to expository prose of various kinds.[1] His point is not that all prose is novelistic,

but that the special energy embodying a prosaic wisdom is best realized in novels. That is, the novel best realizes the "potential" of
prose.

Here as elsewhere, Bakhtin's approach is guided by a sense of the
organic connection between his prosaic view of the world and his
belief in a special theory of literature that privileges prose—between
what we have called the two senses of prosaics. Only great prose
can convey the prosaic sense of life. Some prose conveys it better
than others; and so Bakhtin proposes to consider the novel, which
conveys it best, and "all prose gravitating toward the novel," that
is, other forms that exploit the potential of prose to a lesser degree.
Of course, other approaches to prose are not in principle excluded.

The Galilean Linguistic Consciousness

The novel as a form-shaping ideology embodies and develops
a special view of language, specifically language understood as
Bakhtin describes it and as we have paraphrased his description in
Chapter Four. The novel keenly senses two aspects of language in
their interaction and combinations: dialogicality (especially "dialogue in the second sense") and heteroglossia. The novel takes as its
special concern the ways in which various languages of heteroglossia may enter into dialogue with each other and the kinds of
complex interactions that such dialogues produce.

In a number of respects, languages of heteroglossia already resemble genres. As we have seen, languages, like genres, are ways of
conceptualizing the world in words. One may speak of the eyes of a
language as one may speak of the eyes of a genre. A "language" (of
heteroglossia) is a complex of beliefs. Each language of heteroglossia has arisen from a vast array of social and psychological experience. Its sense of the world has been shaped by the accretion
and reaccentuation of contingent evaluations and perceptions of the
world over time, and so the language carries with it the wisdom of
its speakers' historical experience.

Also like genres, languages of heteroglossia are best understood
not as a specifiable set of propositions, but as a "living impulse"
that responds to experience and changes, and thus grows in potential. This potential is realized—as it is in the case of genres, great
works, or whole cultures—by interaction with other languages and
other belief complexes. We have seen that the potential of great
works is realized by an act of creative understanding from an alien
perspective reflecting experiences the author never knew; and so

Shakespeare grows in meaning by virtue of what his works contain but could only be realized by active understanding from a new perspective. We have also seen that cultures contain a wealth of wisdom that can only be actualized when viewed from the perspective of another culture, in which case a dialogue enriching to both cultures may take place. The same logic applies to languages of heteroglossia. Each has more to say than it has said; but what it has to say can be provoked when it is addressed dialogically from the alien perspective of another language of heteroglossia. To realize and develop the potential of a language, "outsideness"—the outsideness of another language—is required. That outsideness may lead to an exchange in which each language reveals to the other what it did not know about itself, and in which new insights are produced that neither wholly contained before.

The dialogue of social languages is not always so enriching, of course, but if rich enough it will be in principle endless, "unfinalizable," and "interminable." It will not just exploit (and risk exhausting) potential, but will produce still greater potential.

When languages enter into dialogue, complex changes take place. Some of these changes are particular to each dialogue, but others may be described in more general terms. To begin with, a language that has entered into dialogue with another language, especially if that dialogue concerns the topic or experience to which the language is specially adapted, loses its "naivete." It becomes self-conscious, because it has seen itself from an alien perspective and has come to understand how its own values and beliefs appear to the other language. When it is used subsequently, such a language can no longer directly and unself-consciously talk about its topic as if there were no other plausible way of doing so. The language begins not just to speak, but to hear how it sounds; it not only represents the world, but imagines itself as the object of representation; its words, therefore, more or less turn into "words of the third type." Some elements of stylization or double-voicing may appear, as the language takes a sidelong glance at listeners who may be comparing it to another language's possible words on the same topic. The language is, so to speak, more or less self-conscious of its "face" because it has encountered an "image" of itself.

This loss of unself-consciousness may have profound results on the language's sense of itself. Specifically, speakers begin to compare belief complexes, examine how the same topic may be approached in terms of different conceptualizations, and come to consider social facts in the light of different languages. They begin to examine religious questions in the language of the kitchen, and to look at their daily lives from the perspective of another class or profession. Each language the speaker knows changes its tone; no longer indisputable in its own domain, the language becomes simply one of many possible languages. It has been *tested*, and even if it has passed the test, it can never be the same. It can never again naively assume itself to be indisputable, because it has been disputed, may be disputed again, and is always guarding itself against possible disputes. It is now, as Bakhtin writes, "contested, contestable, and contesting" (DiN, p. 332). Even if the language should, so to speak, polemically assert that it is *not* disputable, the very act of doing so betrays its own sense of possible disputes. There is all the difference in the world between naive unself-consciousness and the polemical assertion of one's rights.

The whole universe in which the language lives has changed. To use Bakhtin's metaphor, that universe is no longer Ptolemaic, but Galilean. Like the earth, the language has ceased to be at the center, and has become one of many planets. It "knows" that different languages understand the world differently, and that each must compete with the others.

Of course, in actual life, no language is entirely Ptolemaic; naivete and Galilean linguistic self-consciousness are poles of a continuum. But the difference between various points on the continuum may be immense in its effects on one's sense of the world.

Galileo the Novelist

We may now describe the novel's form-shaping ideology when that genre is approached in terms of language. As Bakhtin describes it, the novel is based on a maximally intense Galilean linguistic consciousness:

The novel is the expression of a Galilean perception of language, one that denies the absolutism of a single and unitary language—that is, it refuses to acknowledge its own language as the sole verbal and semantic center of the ideological world. It is a perception that has been made conscious of the vast plenitude of national and, more to the point, social languages—all of which are equally capable of being "languages of truth," but, since such is the case, all of which are equally relative, reified and limited, as they are merely the languages of social groups, professions, and other cross-sections of everyday life. The novel begins by presuming a verbal and semantic decentering of the ideological world, a certain linguistic homelessness of literary consciousness, which no longer possesses a sacrosanct and unitary linguistic medium for containing ideological thought; it is a consciousness manifesting itself in the midst of social languages. [DiN, pp. 366–67]

It is worth stressing here that by saying all languages are "relative" Bakhtin does not mean to endorse an absolute philosophical relativism, which would make competition among languages pointless. He means that in the "eyes of the novel," no language enjoys an absolute privilege, inasmuch as each must be and is continually tested and retested with respect to (relative to) others, any one of which may turn out to be capable of becoming as good or better a language of truth—if only tentatively, on a specific set of occasions, or with respect to particular questions.

Shaped by a Galilean linguistic consciousness, novels stage dialogues between and among languages. Each language of heteroglossia is allowed to view other languages, each is viewed by others, and each glimpses its own image in the eyes of others. From diverse perspectives and standpoints, the novel offers a "vast plenitude" of maximally rich *images of languages*. The genre is based on the assumption that to create such an image, "outsideness" is required. "An image of a language may be structured only from the point of view of another language, which is [temporarily] taken as a norm" (DiN, p. 359).

The basic impulse of the novel as a genre, then, is to dialogize heteroglossia as intensely as possible. The creation of images of languages is a form of sociological probing, an exploring of values and beliefs, and not a mere play of forms. "The image of a language" in a novel "is the image assumed by a set of social beliefs, the image of a social ideologeme that has been fused with its own discourse, with its own language. Therefore such an image is very far from being formalistic, and artistic play with such languages far from being formalistic play" (DiN, p. 357). These images are tools for understanding the social belief complexes that make up a society and for exploring the unsuspected riches of its existing languages.

Still more important, novelistic images also activate and develop some of the *potential* of these languages, the wisdom they could impart in the right dialogic situation. The novel is not just a description, but also an act of creative understanding for each language and by each language. The novel presumes of any language that "we have not yet learned from it all it might tell us; we can take it into new contexts, attach it to new material, put it into a new situation in order to wrest new answers from it, new insights into its meaning, and even wrest from it new words of its own" (DiN, p. 346).

The novel "conducts experiments and gets solutions in the language of another's discourse" (DiN, p. 347).

One experimental method is to draw "dotted lines" between languages that in everyday life have not yet entered into a profound dialogue. The novelist, concerned with hearing the diversity of languages, creates new dialogues among them, examines the results, and then takes those results—languages reaccented in the light of other languages—and stages dialogues among them as well.

The novelist may also exaggerate features of a given language in order to imagine how it might develop in special circumstances or interact in milieus distant from its usual one. In the novel,

social language . . . becomes the object of a re-processing, reformulation and artistic transformation that is free and oriented toward art: typical aspects of language are selected as characteristic of or symbolically crucial to the language. Departures from empirical reality of the represented language under these circumstances may be highly significant, not only in the sense of their being biased choices or exaggerations of certain aspects peculiar to the given language, but even in the sense that they are a free creation of new elements—which, while true to the spirit of the given language, are utterly foreign to the actual language's empirical evidence. [DiN, pp. 336–37]

Even when the novelist remains close to the empirical language, his concern is not mere representation but a maximal use of "outsideness"—the outsideness of other languages—to produce a dialogue. If the dialogue is truly successful, truly novelistic, "the image [of the language so produced] reveals not only the reality of a given language but also, as it were, its potential" (DiN, p. 356), including the new languages that could develop out of its fissures. Every language of heteroglossia teems with future languages, threatens to revive old languages, and harbors "countless pretenders to the status of language" (DiN, p. 357).

Because the novel works by dialogizing languages—by creating images of one language from the standpoint of others—it will be appreciated that the one kind of discourse the novel cannot work with is that kind of absolute, authoritative language that does not condescend to dialogue. Bakhtin has in mind the absolutely "authoritative word," which, to those who accept it as such, is insulated from dialogic interaction, either by taboos, or by a special script, or by an attitude of reverence. He speaks of languages set at an absolute "distance," languages with which we do not even have the right to agree, since agreement, too, is dialogue and already concedes the possibility of disagreement. To those who accept it as such, absolute language is unconditional, and dialogue, including agreement, always attaches conditions.

When such absolutely authoritative language is included in a novel, one of two things happens. On the one hand, it may (like authoritative discourse in inner speech) be dialogized and so lose its absolute authoritativeness. In that case, it becomes but one of many languages aspiring to authority, or it becomes a language polemically (and therefore insecurely) asserting its authority, or perhaps it turns into a language sensed as one that at one time was authoritative but is now "decentered." On the other hand, if the absolute language is not dialogized, then it remains an inert mass within the work, alien to the work as a whole. To the degree that this inert mass is central to the work, the work becomes a failure. Bakhtin's example of this second possibility is the Gospel quotations at the end of Tolstoy's *Resurrection*, but he presumably has other didactic novels in mind, including the beginnings of socialist realism.[2]

In a successful novel, no language can remain naive or undialogized. Even the language of the author, "literary language," becomes a carrier of social values, specifically, the values of high literary culture. The author may accept those values, as Turgenev does; and he may invite us to accept them. But he nevertheless treats that language as "contested, contestable, and contesting," as one of the languages in a Galilean linguistic universe. He cannot use it naively. If he does, we either have a failed novel, or something that resembles a novel but is really something else.

Bakhtin stresses that *both* heteroglossia and intense dialogization are necessary for language to be truly novelistic. Some readers of Bakhtin have been content to point to a diversity of speech styles in a work as evidence that they meet his criteria for novels, but Bakhtin is clear that heteroglossia alone is not enough. The true novelist is not concerned "to achieve a linguistically (dialectologically) exact and complete reproduction of the empirical data of those alien languages he incorporates into his text" (DiN, p. 366). What is vital is that the languages be viewed from each other's perspectives, that they be "hybridized" so that an "interminable" dialogue is created among them. Such hybridization "demands enormous effort; it is stylized through and through, thoroughly premeditated. . . . This is what distinguishes it from the frivolous, mindless and unsystematic mixing of languages . . . characteristic of mediocre prose writers" (ibid.). Such writers give us "a random mix of the elements out of which languages are made" (ibid.), but they do not dialogize, orchestrate, and hybridize language. "The [true] novel demands a broadening and deepening of the language horizon, a sharpening in our perspective of socio-linguistic differentiations" (ibid.), and a deepening of our sense of the potentials of languages.

As heteroglossia by itself does not produce a novel, neither does mere dialogization or double-voicing. After all, "double-voiced internally dialogized discourse is also possible . . . in a language system that is hermetic, pure, and unitary, a system alien to the [Galilean] linguistic relativism of prosaic consciousness" (DiN, p. 325). In fact, such nonheteroglot double-voicing is common in poetic or rhetorical genres, which are alien to the fundamental Galilean spirit of novelness. Double-voicing by itself may contribute to the depth and interest of a work, but cannot do what novels do: explore the richness, ambivalence, and depth of social languages by creating images of them and forming hybridizations from them. In poetic and rhetorical double-voicing, "there is no soil to nourish the development of such discourse" (ibid.). So long as it remains "within the boundaries of a single language system, [double-voicing] is not fertilized by a deep-rooted connection with the forces of historical becoming that serve to stratify a language, and therefore, rhetorical genres are at best merely a distanced echo of this becoming, narrowed down to an individual polemic" (ibid.).

As Bakhtin further explains, dialogue without heteroglossia is essentially individual—"[an] argument and conversation between two persons" (ibid.)—but not fundamentally social. It does not exploit the conceptual horizons of languages, and so this double-voicing, "without any fundamental socio-linguistic orchestration, may be only a stylistically secondary accompaniment. . . . The internal bifurcation (double-voicing) of discourse, sufficient to a single and unitary language and to a consistently monologic style, . . . is merely a game, a tempest in a teapot" (ibid.).

By contrast, the double-voicedness of true novels "draws its energy, its dialogized ambiguity, not from *individual* dissonances, misunderstandings or contradictions" (DiN, p. 325), however tragic, profound, or "firmly grounded in individual destinies" (ibid.) those dissonances may be. Rather, novelistic double-voicedness "sinks its roots deep into a fundamental, socio-linguistic speech diversity and multi-languagedness" (DiN, pp. 325–26). To be sure, even in novels social languages are personified, and dialogue takes place among individuals, but these individual "wills and minds are submerged in *social* heteroglossia, they are reconceptualized through it" (DiN, p. 326). Individual consciousnesses are "saturated" with the conflict of social values, which interact when they do.

For this reason, novelistic dialogism is essentially inexhaustible and so reflects the infinite potential of social languages in dialogue with each other. True double-voiced prose discourse "can never be developed into the motivation or subject for a manifest dialogue, such as might fully embody, with no residue, the internally dialogic potential embedded in linguistic heteroglossia" (ibid.). Heteroglossia, in sum, is used to make the discourse unfinalizable. "Authentic prose discourse . . . cannot fundamentally be dramatized or dramatically resolved (brought to an authentic end)," and can never be made to fit "into the frame of a mere conversation between persons" (ibid.). For this and other reasons, real novelistic discourse is fundamentally different from the "manifest dialogue" of plays.

Of course, some writers of fiction do not keenly hear social heteroglossia, and, in failing to draw on a "relativizing linguistic consciousness" (ibid.), produce works that are really plays with stage directions, dramas in fictional form. A sort of complement to chamber drama (to works in the form of plays but best realized by reading), these play-like fictions are what Bakhtin calls "un-novelistic novels" (DiN, p. 327, n. 25). He accuses the Russian Formalists, and other critics who approach novels in terms of primarily formal criteria, of not understanding how such quasi-novels differ from true novels. Indeed, formalists of various types and traditions characteristically take such works as model novels.

Authors of "unnovelistic novels" lack a sense of the true novel's fundamental spirit and energy. They see some portion of the residue of that energy and imitate that residue while ignoring the energy itself. Critics who fail to understand the novel as a genre take the imitation for the real thing. But what makes a novel a novel, what makes any genre what it is, is its form-shaping ideology, which for the novel means a Galilean linguistic consciousness. "If the novelist loses touch with this linguistic ground of prose style, if he is unable to attain the heights of a relativized Galilean linguistic consciousness, if he is deaf to organic double-voicedness and to the internal dialogization of living and evolving discourse, then he will never comprehend or even realize the actual possibilities and tasks of the novel as a genre" (DiN, p. 327). Instead, the writer will "create an artistic work that compositionally and thematically will be similar to a novel, will be 'made' exactly as a novel is made; but he will not thereby have created a novel. The style will always give him away" (ibid.).

The use of the word *made* here alludes to the Russian Formalist concept of literary works as artifacts put together by assembling "devices," and to the titles of such well-known essays on the theory of prose as Eichenbaum's "How Gogol's 'Overcoat' Is Made" and Shklovsky's "How *Don Quixote* Is Made." Bakhtin's point is that however skillful the "making" and however interesting the product, such a work does not partake of novelness. Critics fail to notice the absence of novelness because they approach literature from the wrong perspective, the perspective of poetics.

Poetics Versus Prosaics

For Bakhtin, the Russian Formalist conception of "making," like their approach to novels generally, is far from an isolated error. It is, instead, profoundly characteristic of the entire tradition of poetics. In approaching novels, poetics (understandably enough) errs by applying techniques developed in the study of epic, drama, and, especially, lyric poetry. Those genres derive their artistic power and significance from form-shaping ideologies profoundly different from that of the novel. In effect, the critics who presume that poetics is universally applicable interpret with a Ptolemaic standard, whereas a Galilean one is required. In order to understand the genre of the novel, it is necessary to acknowledge fundamental differences between poetry and prose and to approach prose with a theory adapted to its constitutive features. In addition to poetics, we need, but do not yet have, prosaics.

Prosaics, as Bakhtin developed the concept, regards novelistic discourse not as a style but as a style of styles, or, more accurately, as the dialogization of styles. Novels are dedicated to the hybridization and mutual "interillumination of languages" (DiN, p. 362). By contrast, the tradition of poetics regards style as a particular instantiation of the resources of language as a system or as a specific use of "poetic language" in general. Poetics focuses on tropes, poetic structures, and a host of rhetorical devices present in diverse genres, but does not recognize in any essential way the constitutive features of novelistic discourse. Whether it presumes a single literary language or a single-voiced speaker, poetics is bound to miss the sort of discourse that derives from a Galilean linguistic consciousness. To be sure, given critics have responded to the particularities of specific novels, but they have not done so on the "principled basis" of a fully articulated prosaic theory, and so their observations, however locally significant, are necessarily ad hoc.

In Chapter One, we surveyed some of the characteristic limitations of poetics when applied consistently to novels. Confronting works that are not especially rich in tropes or other typically poetic techniques, poetics may pronounce novels nonartistic or semiartistic. For if literature is defined in terms of poetic language—as the Formalists for a while insisted—then, except for some atypical "lyrical" novels, novels as a genre become one of the "contemporary forms of moral propaganda" (Shpet, *Vnutrenniaia forma slova,* as cited in DiN, p. 268). Alternatively, poetics may locate the literariness of novels in features other than language, such as plot, structure, or narrative devices—and then apply poetic techniques to the analysis of these features. This approach was also used by the Formalists and, beyond them, by the entire tradition of "narratology," which tends to flatten out the differences between novels and other narrative genres. Novels in effect become epics in prose, narrated dramas, or long short stories, rather than something fundamentally different, as Bakhtin regards them. Poetics may also approach novels in terms of tropes, see them as allegories or parables, or treat them as a special sort of metaliterary artifact. Each of these viewpoints can contribute and has contributed a good deal to our understanding of novels, much as, for example, it is possible to learn a good deal about a foreign culture by treating it as one that has some features, but not others, of one's own culture. But there is clearly also something lost by this technique, and the losses are multiplied if one is unaware of them. One fails to recognize in novels the "distinctive features of novelistic discourse, the stylistic *specificum* of the novel as a genre" (PND, p. 42).

When poetics and traditional stylistic analysis are applied to novelistic language, misleading results are obtained. For, strictly speaking, novels do not *have* a style in the sense stylistics understands the term; their style of styles constitutes a style "of another order" (DiN, p. 298). Thus, traditional stylistics substitutes one of a number of other linguistic features for the genre's true stylistic *specificum.* Among these substitutes analyzed by critics, Bakhtin includes the "style" of the "author's portions alone . . . that is, only the direct words of the author more or less correctly isolated—an analysis constructed in terms of the usual, direct poetic methods of representation and expression (metaphors, comparisons, lexical register, etc.)" (PND, p. 42). Alternatively, the critic may discover "in a given novelist's language elements characteristic of his particular literary tendency . . . be it Romanticism, Naturalism, Impressionism, etc." (ibid.). Or language may be taken as an "expression of the specific individual personality" of the novelist (ibid.); or the genre can be viewed as rhetorical, and its devices treated in terms of rhetorical categories. Each of these approaches may also be applied to specific characters in the novel, to its inserted or defining genres (as in the epistolary novel), or, in principle, to any one of the "subordinate stylistic unities" that have entered the work.

Taken as a whole, these approaches "serve to conceal from us the genre itself with the specific demands it makes upon language and the specific possibilities it opens up for it" (PND, p. 43). The result is that critical attention is focused on the relatively "minor stylistic variations" of particular authors or schools at the expense of an understanding of the genre itself. Critics fail to see the forest of the genre for the trees of specific authors or movements. "And all the while discourse in the novel has been living a life that is distinctively its own, a life that is impossible to understand from the point of view of stylistic categories formed on the basis of poetic genres in the narrow sense of that term" (ibid.).

Prose Versus Poetry

Bakhtin insists: "The differences between the novel (and certain forms close to it) and all other genres—*poetic* genres in the narrow sense—are so fundamental, so categorical, that all attempts to impose on the novel the concepts and norms of *poetic* imagery are doomed to fail" (PND, p. 43). What are these differences between prose (especially the novel) and poetry (especially the lyric)? In "Discourse in the Novel," Bakhtin devotes some remarkable and often misunderstood passages to this essential contrast.

Bakhtin cautions us in advance and repeatedly that in characterizing novels and poems he does not mean to offer empirical generalizations about those texts often called novels and poems. His concern is not with the use of terms, nor is it with the problems of classification per se. Rather, he is interested in two distinct views of language and the world, two form-shaping ideologies that have found expression in a large number of novels and a large number of lyric poems. "It goes without saying that we continually advance as typical the extreme to which poetic genres [as such] aspire; in concrete examples of poetic works it is possible to find features fundamental to prose, and numerous hybrids of various generic types exist" (DiN, p. 287). His concern, in other words, is with novel*ness* and lyric*ness*. In order to make his rejection of poetics clear, he brackets for a moment historical problems and returns to them only later in the essay.

The "stylistic limit" to which poetry aspires is one in which the poet speaks in a language free from heteroglossia and dialogization. "The poet is a poet insofar as he accepts the idea of a unitary and singular language and a unitary monologically sealed-off utterance. These ideas are immanent in the poetic genres with which he works" (DiN, pp. 296–97). Galilean linguistic consciousness is entirely alien to poetry; the effort of the poet is to find a language over which he has full control, and when he has found that language, he recognizes no need for some other, actually existing language to express his meaning. That is, he tries to speak "directly and without mediation; there must be no distance between the poet and his word" (DiN, p. 297). One does not sense, as one does in novels, that the author's language takes a "sideward glance" at other languages, which could compete for adequacy with his own poetic language. His language is not offered and not used as just one of the languages of heteroglossia, because he speaks, as it were, "from language as a single intentional whole" (ibid.)—that is, from out of *the* language, from out of language itself, but not from *a* language.

For Bakhtin it follows that "any sense of the boundedness, the historicity, the social determination of one's own language is alien to poetic style, and therefore a critical qualified relationship to one's own language as but one of many languages in a heteroglot world is foreign to poetic style" (DiN, p. 285). Of course, both poet and reader realize that they live in a heteroglot world, but that realization is suspended "by convention" (ibid.) because it is not part of the "task" of the poem, as it is of the novel.

The poet can speak alone, and does not require interaction with other consciousnesses and with other languages in order to say what he wants to say. He selects his own society—he *is* his own society—and then he "shuts the door," except, perhaps, to other poets and other poems. Whereas the novelist tries to represent, even exaggerate, heteroglossia, the poet escapes it in order to write in a language that is timeless—timeless in the sense that it does not call attention to its specific historical shaping as the point of view of one, merely partial, kind of experience. The language of the poet, as Shelley observed, is "the echo of the eternal music" (Shelley, "Defense," p. 502). By contrast, the language of the novelist is still "warm" from its social use in everyday contexts (DiN, p. 331); the novelist speaks the language of specific passing days, whereas "poetry depersonalizes days" (DiN, p. 291). Only the earlier history of poetry itself enters into the poet's project. Here, however, a rich intertextuality is possible, for as the poet speaks out of language itself, he speaks as it were out of poetic tradition itself, taken as a whole.

Bakhtin sometimes puts it this way: the novelist speaks "with quotation marks." Aware that his language is one of many possible languages, the novelist, to one degree or another, uses it with qualifications, withholds full commitment to it, which is what Bakhtin means when he speaks of the "distance" of the novelist from his language. The distance may vary from minimal to great, but, to some extent, one senses that the novelist is saying: "I myself am not speaking directly; perhaps I would speak quite differently."

What one senses in a novel, and what is essential to its task, is a *play* of distances from languages. The novelist in the course of writing is exploring the potentialities and limitations of languages. He sees different potentials, depending on purpose or perspective.

The language of the prose writer deploys itself according to greater or lesser proximity to the author and to his ultimate semantic instantiation: certain aspects of language directly and immediately express (as in poetry) the semantic and expressive intentions of the author, others refract these intentions; the author does not meld completely with any of these words, but rather accents each of them in a particular way—humorously, ironically, parodically, and so forth. [DiN, p. 299]

Some words in the novel are denied any authority at all, although, perhaps, on other occasions the author may return to them from a new perspective, intone them respectfully, or find a different kind of "quotation marks" for them. Quotation marks of some kind are essential to novelistic style, but not to poetic style.

The novelist's impulse is to measure "his own world by alien linguistic standards" (DiN, p. 287), which is one reason he includes alien languages in the novel. He tries to get a reading on his own words from alien perspectives, and so may use a nonliterary narrator; or he may include a character who speaks the author's favorite language in a way that tests its adequacy, as Turgenev does. By contrast, poets typically do not use alien languages in this way. To be sure, some "low" poetic genres introduce heteroglot languages through the speech of characters, but not in a way that permits a real dialogue with poetic language. As Bakhtin puts it, this low language "does not lie on the *same* plane with the real language of the work; it is the depicted gesture of one of the characters and does not appear as an aspect of the word doing the depicting" (ibid.). These are mere "words of the second type."

In this sense, we may say that the novelist's language is one of doubt, not because he uses language to express doubts, but because he doubts his own language. By contrast, poetic language is not doubted, even when it expresses doubt. "In poetry, even discourse about doubts must be cast in a discourse that cannot be doubted" (DiN, p. 286). Poetic language that expresses doubt is sensed— undoubtedly—as the maximally best way to express that doubt in all its complexity and nuanced ambiguity. Certainly, no mere everyday social language of a particular profession or group is imagined as possibly expressing that doubt more adequately.

Much of the work of creating poetry, therefore, lies in stripping away the marks of presentness, of current and transitory daily life, from language. Rhythm itself flattens out the diversities of hetero-glot speech. "Rhythm, by creating an unmediated involvement be-tween every aspect of the accentual system of the whole . . . de-stroys in embryo those social worlds of speech and of persons that are potentially embedded in the word" (DiN, p. 298). Or if it does not destroy them, rhythm at least does not permit their rich devel-opment. "Rhythm serves to strengthen and concentrate even fur-ther the unity and hermetic quality of the surface of poetic style, and of the unitary language that this style posits" (ibid.).

Similarly, the creation of poetic diction, the poet's effort at per-fect expression, is a striving for purification from the taint of pos-sible recollections of everyday social languages. "Behind the words of a poetic work one should not sense . . . professions, tenden-cies, . . . nor typical and individual images of speaking persons, their speech mannerisms or typical intonations" (DiN, p. 297). To achieve the special richness that only poetry possesses, the poet must first *forget*: "Everything that enters the work must immerse itself in Lethe and forget its previous life in any other contexts: lan-guage may remember only its life in poetic contexts (in such con-texts, however, even concrete reminiscences are possible)" (ibid.; entire sentence in italics in original).

Heteroglossia has always been present in reality, of course, and poetry has been written in the face of it. But exploiting the richness of heteroglossia is not part of the poem's tasks, and heteroglossia is left "in the slag of the creative process, which is then cleared away (as scaffolding is cleared away once construction is finished), so that the finished work may rise as unitary speech, one co-extensive with its object, as if it were speech about an 'Edenic' world" (DiN,

p. 331). A poem's success in speaking timelessly, free from merely particular concerns and outside the passing speech of a passing world, creates its special poetic value.

Bakhtin's reference to the Edenic world of poetry suggests a fundamental philosophical difference he finds between the form-shaping ideologies of poetry and novels. In presuming the adequacy of a single language of truth—a "purely poetic extrahistorical language far removed from the petty rounds of everyday life" (ibid.)—poetry is ultimately utopian. The contingencies of history and the messiness of daily life are thought away. In their place, the poet speaks his language that sees into the essence of things and so removes the obscuring garb of contemporaneity or any specific historicity. Again Shelley: "A poet considers the vices of his contemporaries as a temporary dress in which his creations must be arrayed . . . to temper this planetary music for mortal ears. . . . Poetry lifts the veil from the hidden beauty of the world" (Shelley, "Defense," pp. 502–3).

It is telling that when poets do come to doubt their language, they do not turn to another social language, a merely historical way of speaking. When poetic language fails, poets tend to doubt *language itself*, and they "will sooner resort to the artificial creation of a new language specifically for poetry" (DiN, p. 287) than to existing dialects, with all their socially localized and historically dated particulars. Thus arose the dream among Russian symbolists and Futurists of creating "a special 'language of poetry,'" a "language of the gods" (ibid.). Novelists do not share that dream.

Far from a mere aberration, such efforts of poetry foreground the essentially utopian presuppositions of poetry per se. "The idea of a special unitary and singular language of poetry is a typical utopian philosopheme of poetic discourse; it is grounded in the actual conditions and demands of poetic style, which is always a style . . . from whose point of view other languages (conversational, business and prose languages, among others) are perceived as objects that are in no way its equal" (ibid.). In this sense, novels are radically anti-utopian, because they presuppose the impossibility of a single language of truth and imagine social discourse as an unfinalizable discovery of new and unforeseeable truths.

We saw in Chapter One that for Bakhtin prosaics was not a mere supplement to poetics, to be placed alongside it as the tool for analyzing a different genre. Rather, Bakhtin argued, prosaics changes poetics as well. "Novelistic discourse," he argued, "is the acid test" for poetics and the theory of poetic language in general; and theory must either "acknowledge the novel . . . an unartistic or quasi-artistic genre, or [else it must] . . . radically reconsider that conception of poetic discourse in which traditional stylistics is grounded and which determines all its categories" (DiN, p. 267). In effect, *prosaics does to poetics what one language of heteroglossia may do to another and apparently authoritative language*: it decenters it, confronts it with a fundamentally different universe.

Like the universe of poetic language, the universe of poetics is Ptolemaic; to place it in the same universe with—to force it to confront dialogically—an alternative is to change the universe itself. Poetics in a Galilean universe is no longer the same poetics, much as poetry in a period when the novel predominates can never sound quite the same.

In his remarkable essay on Bakhtin, Paul de Man recognizes the challenge that prosaics—de Man calls it dialogics—poses to all received poetics, including (or perhaps especially) deconstructive poetics. To confront this challenge, de Man focuses on yet another contrast Bakhtin drew between poetic and novelistic language, the contrast between "the trope" and "the double-voiced word." That contrast is worth examining in detail.

Bakhtin's argument here is a difficult one, and it must be stressed in advance that he is *not* arguing that poetic language is any less rich or complex than prosaic language. Rather, he contends that each develops a different kind of complexity. The poet develops the richness of the trope, and has at his disposal the entire "treasure-house of language" to help him. Tropes or symbols in poetry create a polysemous, complex, and powerfully ambiguous discourse no less profound than the discourse of novels. Nevertheless, there is a fundamental difference "between ambiguity [or polysemy] in poetry and double-voicedness in prose" (DiN, p. 328). "If the central problem in poetic theory is the problem of the poetic symbol, then the central problem in prose theory is the problem of the double-voiced, internally dialogized word" (DiN, p. 330).

However one understands the "interrelationship of meanings in a poetic symbol (a trope)," Bakhtin observes, "this interrelationship is never of a dialogic sort" (DiN, p. 327). Whether that interrelationship is understood logically, ontologically, emotively, evaluatively, or in any other way, one is still speaking of the relation of words to their objects. One can discuss its complexity through the theoretical discourse of "signified" and "signifier." However complex the trope, it requires only a single voice to utter it; "one voice, a single accent system, is fully sufficient to express poetic ambiguity," however rich (DiN, p. 378). A double-voiced word by definition requires two voices, two distinct speakers, and suggests an unfinalizable dialogue. By contrast, a poetic symbol "cannot presuppose any fundamental relationship to another's word, to another's voice. The polysemy of the poetic symbol presupposes the unity of a voice with which it is identical, and it presupposes that such a voice is completely alone with its own discourse" (ibid.). If the poet introduces a second voice, "the poetic plane is destroyed and the symbol is translated onto the plane of prose" (ibid.).

De Man replies that Bakhtin's project is in effect a bold but doomed attempt to go beyond formal analysis by way of form itself. In attempting to bridge the social and poetic worlds, he argues, Bakhtin turns to dialogue, but in so doing he has made dialogue itself into a trope, which means that he has not in fact escaped the poetic world. To this Bakhtin would probably have answered that de Man's objection is itself a typical sort of monologic relativism, which presupposes the Ptolemaic universe of poetics as the only possible one. He might have added that in his very reply, de Man has had recourse, if not to heteroglossia and prosaics, then at least to dialogue. As Mathew Roberts has shrewdly observed, the confrontation between these two thinkers—and between deconstruction and dialogics—is unresolvable in terms set by either (Roberts, "Poetics Hermeneutics Dialogics"). In our view, the dialogue between them is ultimately between two fundamental views of the world: poetics and prosaics.

Hybridization: The Real Life of Novels

Bakhtin suggests that one way to appreciate the difference between poetic ambiguity and novelistic double-voicing is to double-voice a piece of direct unmediated discourse. Such double-voicing will not necessarily make novelistic use of heteroglossia, but it will at least insert distance between the author and his words and enclose those words in some sort of intonational quotation marks.

In fact, this sort of "reaccentuation" is quite common in daily life. We are continually citing and alluding to others' words, or using a discourse with some degree of reserve. Distancing has infinite shadings, can be from countless positions, and is used for an indefinitely large number of reasons, only a few of which receive an explicit marker or statement, but all of which may be keenly felt. Only in extreme instances is our distance great enough to warrant using (or saying we are using) actual quotation marks. In essence, "quotation marks" are a matter of degree.

Novels as a genre exploit the resources of daily life and constantly reprocess direct unmediated discourse—poetic, authoritative, aphoristic, or otherwise "naive"—by distancing and double-voicing. We do to naive language what Aleksey Aleksandrovich Karenin routinely does, as in this example Bakhtin offers: "'Yes, as you see, your tender spouse, as devoted as in the first year after marriage, is burning with impatience to see you,' he said in his deliberate, high-pitched voice, and in that tone which he almost always took with her, a tone of derision for anyone who would really talk like that" (Tolstoy, *Anna*, pt. 1, ch. 30, pp. 110–11; as cited in DiN, p. 328, n. 26). As Tolstoy makes clear, and as Anna still understands, Karenin double-voices his professions of love although he really feels them. He does not directly say what he means because the discourse of love is alien to him, and its language and tones are unnatural for him, even when he really feels devotion and love. Characters in novels—and people in life—often resort to a stylized or otherwise distanced version of a language for similar reasons. Sometimes we use a discourse from a field of life we sense as questionable, outmoded, or otherwise under suspicion because there is no better discourse available. Novels, given as they are to exploring the belief complexes of discourse and the various ways they are used, foreground and exaggerate such practices.

The real action of novels as Bakhtin describes them is of this kind: a complex play of values and tones, as discourses and their speakers orient themselves to each other. The most important place where this complexity is developed is in the voice of the author. Wayne Booth had good reason to conclude that Bakhtin's theories of the novel were an especially rich endorsement of "telling" as opposed to "showing" (Booth, "Introduction to *PDP*").[3] Authorial telling enacts the hybridizations of discourse and the encounter of conceptual horizons that are the real life of the novel.

Bakhtin's point here is often misunderstood, so it is worth stressing: the dialogues that constitute novelness are to be found *not* primarily in the "compositionally expressed dialogues" among the characters, but in the hybridized, double-voiced, dialogized heteroglossia of the author's own voice. "Inside this area a dialogue is played out between the author and his characters—not a dramatic dialogue broken up into statement-and-response, but that special type of novelistic dialogue that realizes itself within the boundaries of constructions that externally resemble monologues" (DiN, p. 320). This sort of dialogue is the novel's special preserve, for which drama has no equivalent and which the form-shaping ideologies of other genres have not led them to exploit so fully. "The potential for such dialogue is one of the fundamental privileges of novelistic prose, a privilege available neither to dramatic nor purely poetic genres" (ibid.).

Bakhtin's most extensive case study of novelistic play with distance is Pushkin's *Eugene Onegin*, which we might consider as exemplary. The choice is curious because that work, of course, is (and is subtitled) "a novel in verse." Pushkin's astonishing achievement lies in his full development of a "prosaic linguistic consciousness" in a tightly wrought verse form, which distances itself in dizzyingly complex ways from all poetic discourse, not to mention every other socially available discourse. His distance from poetic discourse seems maximal in some of his paraphrases of Lensky's naively and extremely romantic poems:

> He sang love, he was obedient to love,
> And his song was as clear
> As the thoughts of a simple maid,
> As an infant's dream, as the moon. . .
> [a development of the comparison follows].
> [Pushkin, *Onegin*, canto 2, stanza 10, lines 1–4; as cited in PND, p. 43][4]

In these lines, as Bakhtin analyzes them, we hear Lensky's voice and style, but only as it is interwoven with and permeated by "the parodic and ironic accents of the author; that is the reason why it need not be distinguished from authorial speech by compositional or grammatical means" (PND, p. 44). We have here a rather simple case of hybridization, as Lensky's Germanized Russian romantic verse encounters the author's Byronic values. The result is an *image* of Lensky's language (and, implicitly, of the author's Byronic language as well), in which Lensky's discourse appears in a special kind of intonational quotation marks.

The Formalists notwithstanding, Pushkin's voice is not always or even primarily parodic in this way. Distance and the kind of "language images" vary considerably. At times, the author seems much closer to Lensky and appears to wonder whether the contrast between his discourse and Lensky's is always to his own advantage. He surreptitiously forms an image of his own language from the imagined perspective of a Lensky—or rather, a hypothetical, somewhat less naive Lensky capable of forming such an image. Bakhtin also considers the author's use of language typical of Onegin and close to the author's own characteristic irony:

> He who has lived and thought can never
> Look on mankind without disdain;
> He who has felt is haunted ever
> By days that will not come again;
> No more for him enchantment's semblance,
> On him the serpent of remembrance
> Feeds, and remorse corrodes his heart.

[Bakhtin continues:] One might think that we had before us a direct poetic maxim of the author himself. But these ensuing lines:

> All this is likely to impart
> An added charm to conversation

(spoken by the posited author to Onegin) already give an objective coloration to this maxim. [Pushkin, *Onegin*, canto 1, stanza 46, lines 1–9; as cited in PND, pp. 44–45]

We have here an example of the author's speech, but constructed within the discursive realm of his "pal" Onegin, with its attendant tones and values. Lensky's poem was *represented* discourse, but here the image of Onegin's language is simultaneously represent*ed* and represent*ing*. For the author's discourse is fairly close to Onegin's and he agrees with Onegin to a considerable extent, though he has his reservations as well. Functioning both inside and outside this language, the author is "located in a zone of potential conversation" with his hero, "in a zone of *dialogical contact*" (PND, p. 45). Well aware of the limitations and shallowness of Onegin's values and language, and keenly sensing their artifice and absurdity, the author nevertheless knows that he "can express some of his most basic ideas and observations only with the help of this 'language,' despite the fact that as a system it is a historical dead end" (ibid.).

Passages like these bespeak the author's and the work's Galilean linguistic consciousness, the sense that no language is sufficient by itself. And this linguistic consciousness in turn implies a sense of the unfinalizability of truth that requires multiple voices and languages in potentially endless acts of exploration. "Just as all there is to know about a man is not exhausted by his situation in life, so all there is to know about the world is not exhausted by a particular discourse" (ibid.).

Where novelistic discourse is handled well, an immense array of distances and standpoints treat the "vast plenitude" of languages. Characters in novels, as we have seen in the case of Karenin, are themselves always reprocessing the languages they encounter, and, still more important, their particular assembly of languages infects the author's speech. Not only does the author enclose characters' speech in intonational quotation marks, but his own discourse seems continually invaded and qualified by challenging discourses of the characters. Bakhtin here is developing both his own concept of double-voicing and Voloshinov's idea that report*ed* speech may resolve the report*ing* context—a key insight underlying "Discourse in the Novel" and therefore apparently an important influence of Voloshinov on Bakhtin.[5]

Character Zones

Because so much of the discourse and inner speech of characters is presented as the author reaccents them in hybridized forms of "quasi-direct discourse," "prepared-for discourse," and other kinds of double-voicing, characters who infect the author's speech may come to infect our sense of other characters' speech as well. Through the medium of the author's voice, characters in novels enter into a kind of dialogue—a peculiarly novelistic dialogue—with characters who are not present to them, whom they have not met and may never meet.

A given character's values and language are first

diffused throughout authorial speech that surrounds the characters, creating highly particularized and sensitized *character zones*. These zones are formed from the fragments of character speech, from various forms for hidden transmission of someone else's word, from scattered words, sayings, and verbal tics belonging to someone else's speech, from those invasions into authorial speech of others' expressive indicators (ellipsis, questions, exclamations). Such a character zone is the field of action for a character's voice, encroaching in one way or another upon the author's voice. [DiN, p. 316]

Once such a character zone is created, it may then be, and typically is, used at a distance from the character; we hear the potential dialogue of two characters, of each with the author, and of all three together. Each character's "sphere of influence . . . extends—and often quite far—beyond the boundaries of the direct discourse allotted to him. The area occupied by an important character's voice must in any event be broader than his direct and 'actual' words" (DiN, p. 320). In a character zone, and in overlapping character zones, the "most varied hybrid constructions hold sway" (ibid.). One can encounter particularly intense and complex examples of that special kind of novelistic dialogue "that realizes itself within the boundaries of constructions that externally resemble monologues" (ibid.).

One may now see why Bakhtin's examples of "hybrid discourse" in the novel are relatively simple. The most complicated examples of hybridized discourse develop and accumulate over the course of a novel, and unless the critic discusses the particular character zones *as* they are being established, their presence in later passages is likely to be invisible. What Bakhtin really needed to do in order to illustrate his concept was to study a whole novel—*Eugene Onegin? Anna Karenina? Middlemarch?*—from his special perspective, but he never undertook such a study. Instead, he chose to discuss passages where the languages dialogized would be immediately comprehensible out of context, either because the interaction is relatively simple or because the passages include explicit commentary about the languages in interaction. Turgenev, with his precise "ethnographic" interest in dating changes in the ways various groups speak, often resorts to such explicit statements, and so he serves as a convenient example. Of course, as Bakhtin notes, the very ethnographic discourse that comments on characters' speech itself takes place from within the framework of a particular language and its attendant beliefs. Therefore, it is completely dialogized.

The English Comic Novel and "Common Language"

It is worth pausing briefly on some of Bakhtin's examples because they introduce several interesting concepts of broader applicability. He chooses his first set from a subgenre of the novel that he calls the "English comic novel," and digresses briefly to discuss novelistic subgenres. Basically, a genre's various subgenres all realize its form-shaping ideology, but they do so in different ways and, indeed, with different degrees of success. Or to put the point in another way, some subgenres realize "genre potential" more fully than others. Other comparisons between subgenres reveal different emphases and means rather than different degrees of depth.

The English comic novel, as Bakhtin describes it, includes some non-English examples, but its central exemplars are Fielding, Smollett, Sterne, and, later, Dickens. Elements of the English comic novel appear in other types of novels as well. Characteristic of this subgenre is its "specific treatment of 'common language'"

(DiN, p. 301). Common language, the language of a given social group defining "public opinion"—that is, the opinion of the group investigated by the novel—carries "the *going point of view* and the going *value*" (DiN, pp. 301–302). It defines, so to speak, *The Way We Live Now* and the "way we talk now." At times, the author's distance from this common language is at a maximum:

> The conference was held at four or five o'clock in the afternoon, when all the region of Harley Street, Cavendish Square, was resonant of carriage-wheels and double-knocks. It had reached this point when Mr. Merdle came home *from his daily occupation of causing the British name to be more and more respected in all parts of the civilized globe capable of appreciation of world-wide commercial enterprise and gigantic combinations of skill and capital.* For, though nobody knew with the least precision what Mr. Merdle's business was, except that it was to coin money, these were the terms in which everybody defined it on all ceremonious occasions, and which it was the last new polite reading of the parable of the camel and the needle's eye to accept without inquiry. [Dickens, *Little Dorrit*, bk. 1, ch. 33; as cited in DiN, p. 303; emphasis Bakhtin's]

The example here is rather elementary, because in the final section of the passage the author explicitly comments on the language in the portion in italics. Though not set off in quotation marks, the portion in italics is evidently a "parodic stylization of the language of ceremonial speeches (in parliaments and at banquets)" (ibid.), an image of the values carried by such speech, and (as in other examples Bakhtin cites), an "unmasking" of "the chorus's hypocrisy" (DiN, p. 304). As we examine the passage more closely, we see that the section preceding the portion in italics is already rather ceremonious as it prepares for the unmasking; the words of banquet speeches have been present there "in concealed form" all along (DiN, p. 303). Retrospectively, we identify a more pronounced set of intonational quotation marks and, throughout the passage, an intensifying of irony. This example is, again, rather primitive. But it serves to illustrate that a sensitivity to the uses, intensity, and implicit vantage points of intonational quotation marks is central to an understanding of novels: for that is where the real action of novels is to be found.

The unmasking of expressions in common language can infect the words unmasked with alien intentions, so that the later use of those words carries a reminder of the kind of irony to which they have been subjected. "So, bolstered by this mark of Government homage, the *wonderful* Bank and all the other *wonderful* undertakings went on and went up; and gapers came to Harley Street, Cavendish Square, only to look at the house where the golden wonder lived" (Dickens, *Little Dorrit*, bk. 2, ch. 12; as cited in DiN, p. 303; italics Bakhtin's). Such an "influx of sense" (to use Vygotsky's phrase in a somewhat different context) can then carry over into later scenes, infecting the author's or another character's inner speech unawares. In describing characters to whom he is unsympathetic, Dickens will use such "objectionable" words to set up a dialogue of values.

Pseudo-Objectivity

Focus on common language also leads to rather extensive use of a technique that Bakhtin calls "pseudo-objective motivation": "But Mr. Tite Barnacle was a buttoned-up man, and *consequently* a weighty one" (Dickens, *Little Dorrit*, bk. 2, ch. 12; as cited in DiN, p. 305; emphasis Bakhtin's). If one were to analyze this sentence as single-voiced or by its formal markers, its logic would belong to the author, but in fact the logic belongs to common opinion or the beliefs of characters who share it. The "consequently" is justified only from such a standpoint. Pseudo-objective motivation, which is characteristic of novels in general, may be much more complex than this example; the whole logic of particular passages may be of this type and presented so plausibly that the reader may accept it as the author's or even as the reader's own logic. Jane Austen (whom Bakhtin evidently did not know) comes to mind. And we might also add that much of the difficulty in interpreting *Anna Karenina* derives from different estimations of such passages. When we read the author's descriptions of Karenin in Anna's language, do we take them as pseudo-objective or not?

To understand novelistic discourse of great complexity, it would perhaps be most helpful to indicate the sort of problems that arise. For this purpose, we will use examples from a single work, *Anna Karenina*. Consider, for instance, Tolstoy's paraphrase of Anna's speech and thoughts before she has left Karenin and her son Seryozha to live with Vronsky:

"Seryozha? What about Seryozha?" Anna asked, with sudden eagerness, recollecting her son's existence for the first time that morning. . . .

The recollection of her son suddenly roused Anna from the helpless condition in which she found herself. She recalled the partly sincere, though greatly exaggerated, role of the mother living for the child, which she had taken up of late years, and she felt with joy that in the plight in which she found herself she had a support, quite apart from her relation to her husband or to Vronsky. This support was her son. In whatever position she might be placed, she could not lose her son. Her husband might put her to shame and turn her out, Vronsky might grow cold to her and go on living his own life apart (she thought of him again with bitterness and reproach); she could not leave her son. She had an aim in life. And she must act so as to secure this relation to her son, so that he might not be taken from her. Quickly, indeed, as quickly as possible, she must take action before he was taken from her. She must take her son and go away. Here was the one thing she had to do now. She needed consolation. She must be calm, and get out of this insufferable position. The thought of immediate action binding her to her son, of going away somewhere with him, gave her this consolation. [Tolstoy, *Anna*, pt. 3, ch. 15, p. 306]

We watch here the process of Anna's thoughts, expressed in quasi-direct discourse. A play of several voices is apparent, and still more diversity is felt if one recalls the rest of the novel. We hear how she intones to herself her response to Vronsky's characteristic words as she has heard them; Tolstoy alludes to the tone of reproach at his assertion of his "masculine independence," a phrase not actually present in this passage but probably hinted at. We hear a similar play of her inner thoughts with respect to her husband, and an anticipation of the dialogue with her son soon to follow, in which she provokes him to the first of several hysterical outbursts of eternal devotion to her. In the phrase "the aim in life," which is uncharacteristic of Anna, we may detect Levin's character zone, and beyond that, his conversations with Anna's brother Stiva about the aim of life. The subtlety of these hints differs greatly from the blatant irony of the passages from *Little Dorrit*: if one does not know the novel well, their presence may be missed, and if one does, the *kind* of intonational quotation marks around key words may be a subject of dispute. Disputes of this kind are disputes about the central action of the novel, and of novels generally. Bakhtin suggests that they are the proper arena of criticism.

Permeating all the hinted dialogues with other characters we hear some degree (but how much?) of authorial irony at Anna's unfairness. That unfairness leads her to blame Vronsky, as we recall she repeatedly does, for things he might do but which (as she sometimes admits candidly to herself) she knows he has not done and would not do. That irony appears deeper with respect to Anna's vaguely narcissistic dialogues with her son, in which the child exists to comfort the parent, and in which the relationship is considered only from the vantage point of the parent's problems. That dialogue continues a page later: "'And can he ever join his father in punishing me? Is it possible he will not feel for me?' Tears were already flowing down her face, and to hide them she got up abruptly and almost ran out of the room" (Tolstoy, *Anna*, pt. 3, ch. 15, p. 307). The entire exchange with her son is prepared by the author's comment that this is her first recollection "of her son's existence" that day, and by her own recollection (soon forgotten) of the "partly sincere, though partly exaggerated role of the mother living for the child"—the last phrase apparently cited from social discourse, a discourse Anna adopts with a complex mix of irony and attempted devotion. The varying traces of irony set her somewhat hysterical inner discourse in shifting intonational quotation marks.

These observations only minimally establish the *kind* of complexities in this (and many similar) passages. What is the degree and what is the direction of irony of the author's voice? How are we to evaluate the standpoint of the paraphrase and how much variation in irony takes place in the course of the passage? How do the barely audible voice zones of Karenin, Vronsky, and Seryozha sound? How are we to detect the voices of others who might put Anna to shame (Betsy Tverskaya? Countess Lydia Ivanovna? common opinion?) or, for that matter, justify her? Is her brother audible in the very pattern and logic of self-justification here, in the entire discourse of denying blame associated with him from the novel's beginning and passed through the languages and beliefs of several characters? To what extent do we hear not just Anna but the tonality of the Oblonsky family? What resonances does this passage have later in the book, for example, in establishing a character zone that affects descriptions of Seryozha? We do not propose to answer these questions here, but rather to indicate that this type of question, the complex tracing of intonational quotation marks and interacting character zones, is part of the special activity necessary to understanding novels.

This activity is generally very complex, because the novelist, creating within character zones, accomplishes a delicate task. Properly visualized by the author, zones make it possible to show from within how a character thinks and feels from moment to moment. Even if the author ultimately condemns the character, the reader may be infected with a special sort of novelistic sympathy that comes from having lived with and dialogically shared the character's perspective. Questions about the author's ultimate view of a character are therefore likely to be particularly intricate in such cases.

Hybridization: Some Refinements and Extensions

Different kinds of Bakhtinian complexities apply in the following passage:

Vronsky's life was particularly happy in that he had a code of principles, which defined with unfailing certitude what he should and what he should not do. This code of principles covered only a very small circle of contingencies, but then the principles were never doubtful, and Vronsky, because he never went outside that circle, had never had a moment's hesitation about doing what he ought to do. These principles laid down as invariable: that one must pay a card shark, but need not pay a tailor; that one must never tell a lie to a man, but one may to a woman; that one must never cheat anyone, but one may cheat a husband; that one must never pardon an insult, but one may give one; and so on. These principles were possibly not reasonable and not good, but they were of unfailing certainty, and as long as he adhered to them, Vronsky felt that his heart was at peace and he could hold his head high up. Only quite lately, in regard to his relations with Anna, Vronsky had begun to feel that his code of principles did not fully cover all possible contingencies, and to foresee in the future, difficulties and perplexities for which he could find no guiding clue. [Tolstoy, *Anna*, pt. 3, ch. 20, pp. 322–23]

This passage not only illustrates some of Bakhtin's concepts, but also suggests ways in which they might be extended. Like the citations from Dickens, this paragraph from Tolstoy displays a considerable distance between the values and language paraphrased and the values and language from which the paraphrase is made. As in the English comic novel, we have the hybridized elucidation of a particular type of common opinion, in this case the opinion of officers and gallant young bachelors. But Tolstoy's paraphrase is, though similar in effect, quite different from Dickens's in method. In Dickens's "pseudo-objective motivation," the logic ostensibly belongs to the author and so to an objective standpoint, but in fact belongs to the characters who would speak that way; thus, the paraphrase is "pseudo-objective," which is to say, truly subjective. By contrast, Vronsky would never say, "one must never tell a lie to a man, but one may to a woman." He might indeed believe as much, might assent to each part of the proposition in distinct circumstances, but the very drawing of the contrast in that way is alien to him, because it suggests a kind of hypocrisy we know he would abjure. The author discovers that hypocrisy for him. Although the passage might seem to be paraphrasing Vronsky's beliefs from within, it is in fact reconstructing them from without. We might therefore extend Bakhtin's terminology and call this an example of "pseudo*subjective* motivation." One may suppose that this technique appears in Dickens as well, and that our two examples define not a difference between the two authors, but different exploitations of possibilities given by novelistic discourse.

In this passage, we may note as well the workings of another technique quite common in Tolstoy and other novelists, the repetition of the same (or semantically very similar) words frequently in a short piece of prose: *code of principles, principles,* and *rules; circle of contingencies, circle,* and *contingencies; unfailing certitude* and *invariable rules.* As readers of Tolstoy are aware, this sort of repetition is central to his writing, and as critics know, Tolstoy quite consciously avoided elegant variation of the sort used so masterfully by Turgenev and other "fine writers." Bakhtin's approach offers a starting point for exploring the function of Tolstoy's technique.

We may observe generally that each time a phrase is repeated, its "already-spoken" quality is foregrounded. As it is incorporated into different contexts, passed through different voices, and made to figure in different projected acts of self-justification, we detect an "influx of sense" from each hybrid to the next. One of the reasons why it is hard to read aloud the richness of novelistic passages of this sort is that they involve too many layers of hybridization for the voice to register with precision.[6] Such repetitions may themselves reappear in later passages, and so recall earlier ones. Variations of the phrases "It was all my fault, though I am not to blame" (Stiva's self-justification before an imagined audience of his peers in "the going value") are reaccented in the different value horizons of Anna, Karenin, even Kitty and Levin, in various ways and in terms of discrete experiences.

In using such repetitions, Tolstoy may well have been borrowing from Anthony Trollope, whom he admired and in whose prose constant repetition of this sort is a hallmark. Readers of *Anna Karenina* will recall that Anna reads an English novel on the train, a novel that Tolstoy paraphrases in complex novelistic hybrids carrying the imprint of (at the very least) the novel itself, Anna's reactions, the voice of Vronsky sounding in her ears, and the author's complex play of irony in his paraphrase. The novel Anna reads, as it happens, is almost certainly one of Trollope's Palliser novels. Though not explicitly identified, it involves speeches in Parliament and fox-hunting, both of which were Trollope's signatures and characteristic of him to the point of being the most obvious targets of parody. In cases like this, we may ask an important question in analyzing such allusions in novels generally: Is Tolstoy's use of Trollopean stylistic devices meant to be detected as such, or not? Is it part of the "scaffolding" that has entered into the creative process but is designed not to be noticed, or, on the contrary, are we meant to hear an example of novelistic double-voicing and dialogue with a text outside the one we are reading? Both alternatives are in principle possible for novelists.

It is clear, for example, that Pushkin does want us to hear a number of such voices in constructions he self-consciously borrows from Byron, Sterne, Karamzin, and, indeed, from his own earlier works. In Tolstoy's case, the answer to this question is not so obvious, and may turn out to be a matter not of presence or absence of double-voicing, but of degree and kind of double-voicing. Moreover, the information we might need to resolve the question could easily involve a sense of what the reader could be expected to hear, that is, a sense of the work's "dialogizing background" at a given time. As that dialogizing background changes, and different voices are intensified or muted within it, the kinds of hybridizations operative in the text may change. The text, as Bakhtin observes, is "reaccented" and in that sense becomes a somewhat different one. Exploitative as they are of the dialogizing background of social heteroglossia, novels undergo a great deal of reaccentuation in the course of a long historical life. That kind of change may add, as well as subtract, hybridizations the text holds in potential.

As we have seen, characters in novels may establish character zones that work in the characters' absence, infecting the speech of the author and the hybridized paraphrases of other characters' thoughts. We might now add that in addition to character zones, works establish "other-author zones," in which the values and beliefs of those authors become part of the dialogue of the novel. We easily notice such zones when the other author is the object of a direct parody (Richardson in *Shamela* and in *Joseph Andrews*), but more often the allusion is subtler. Those zones may appear in countless shadings, nuances, and registers, used in ways much less hostile or obvious than in clear-cut parodies.

If we recall Bakhtin's distinction between "influence" and "generic contact" (Chapter Seven of the present study), we may extend this insight as well. At times the voice of another author may be used to suggest not the author's own idiosyncratic values and language, but the values and language of his genre or subgenre. We may be meant to detect, for example, not Trollope, but the tradition of the "English novel" (as opposed, let us say, to the French novel); we may have what might be called a "genre zone" or a "tradition zone." Readers who interpret *Anna Karenina* in this way may then listen for the work's many echoes of "Englishness"—in the names Dolly, Kitty, and Stiva, in the characters' use of English phrases, English jockeys, or English agricultural techniques, and in Anna's worked-up interest in an English child instead of in her daughter. If they understand the spirit of Bakhtin's analysis, they will expect not one authorial tone with respect to the English novel and Englishness, but a shifting diversity of tones and accumulating layers of "already-bespokenness." Again, our interest here is not so much in Tolstoy, as in the novelistic possibilities the examples from *Anna* make visible.

The passage about Vronsky suggests another about Stiva, in which novelistic dialogization serves to interweave the psychological, moral, and broadly social issues of the work:

Stepan Arkadyevich Oblonsky's affairs were in a very bad way.

Two thirds of the money for the forest had been spent already, and he had borrowed from the merchant in advance, at ten per cent discount, almost all the remaining third. The merchant would not give more, especially as Darya Aleksandrovna, for the first time that winter insisting on her right to her own property, had refused to sign the receipt for the payment of the last third of the forest. All his salary went on household expenses and in payment of petty debts that could not be put off. There was positively no money.

This was unpleasant and awkward, and in Stepan Arkadyevich's opinion could not go on like this. . . . And he began keeping his eyes and ears open, and toward the end of the winter he had discovered a very good berth and had formed a plan of attack upon it, at first from Moscow through aunts, uncles, and friends, and then, when the matter was well advanced, in the spring, he went himself to Petersburg. It was one of those snug, lucrative berths of which there are so many more nowadays than there used to be, with incomes ranging from one thousand to fifty thousand rubles. It was the post of secretary of the committee of the amalgamated agency of Southern Railways and certain banking companies. This position, like all such appointments, called for such immense energy and such varied qualifications that it was difficult for them to be found united in any one man. And since a man combining all the qualifications was not to be found, it was at least better that the post be filled by an honest than a dishonest man. And Stepan Arkadyevich was not merely an honest man in the ordinary sense of the word, he was an honest man—emphatically in that special sense the word has in Moscow, when they talk of an "honest" politician, an "honest" writer, an "honest" newspaper, an "honest" in-

stitution, an "honest" tendency, meaning not simply that the man or institution is not dishonest, but that they are capable on occasion of taking a
line of their own in opposition to the authorities.

Stepan Arkadyevich moved in those circles in Moscow in which that
expression had come into use, was regarded there as an honest man, and so
had more right to this position than others. [Tolstoy, *Anna*, pt. 7, ch. 17,
pp. 748–49]

In this passage, we hear intonational quotation marks that distance the author about as far from Stiva as the earlier passage distances him from Vronsky. As the passage progresses, a complex interweaving of vantage points and languages develops Stiva's inner
voice as he justifies himself against his wife's almost audible re-
proaches, rehearses the language of the circle in which he hopes to
be employed, and fuses with a political language of manifest benefit
to him.

Stiva's role in the book as chameleon, who easily takes on the
appearance (or rather the sound) of any group, becomes central to
the novel's exploration of social heteroglossia. The opening statement—"Stepan Arkadyevich Oblonsky's affairs were in a very bad
way"—sets the tone of the passage from within his own inner
speech, as it might be spoken with imagined others of his own
circle in mind. We hear the tone in which he has appealed for
Levin's sympathy in part one, a sympathy that Levin does not in
fact feel and which the author evidently does not share. Forced by
his wife's unexpected and (as he would see it) unfair recalcitrance at
surrendering her property to her philandering husband (as she
would see it), Stiva regrets that his whole salary goes to pay "petty
debts." The discourse of debt has been central to the book up to this
point, and we recognize that by "petty debts" Stiva means the
butcher, the tailor, and other "household expenses" used to support his wife and children. This sentence, and the conclusion that
"there was positively no money"—for the amusements money is
really *for*—are spoken with his voice, in which we hear the echoes
of Dolly's and Levin's objections as well as the assenting voices of
his fellow debtors. Perhaps—it is hard to tell without examining
the dialogizing background—this and similar passages about debt
in the same section of the book come from an other-author zone,
specifically from the chapters on "How to Live on Nothing a Year"
in *Vanity Fair* and from the discourse on the impoverishment of the
nobility in the Russian press at the time.

We hear different tones in the two phrases for the position Stiva
seeks: "one of those snug, lucrative berths of which there are so

many more nowadays than there used to be" and "secretary of the committee of the amalgamated agency of Southern Railways and certain banking companies." The first phrase is spoken as Stiva and everyone else in his circle would describe it to themselves (the all-important salary range follows), the second phrase as Stiva rehearses it to himself so he may pronounce it without a slip in the presence of the "two ministers, one lady, and two Jews" who have the power to hire him (Tolstoy, *Anna*, p. 749). Evidently his rehearsal is not complete, because he still has not learned which banking companies are involved; but Tolstoy will later tell us that the process of memorization here underway was soon completed. In the extraordinarily wide range of the salary—from one to fifty thousand rubles—we may detect the voice of Karenin, who elsewhere interprets such a wide range of salary as evidence of an objectionable system of remuneration in proportion to social connections rather than utility, a way of thinking and speaking that Stiva knows and regards as naive.

The discussion of the word *honest* foregrounds the process, constantly at work in these passages, by which words acquire meaning through the genres, contexts, and groups for which those words figure. This "honesty," of course, has nothing to do with honesty, but with a fashionable pose of liberalism constantly parodied in the book. We know that if Stiva takes up a position in opposition to the authorities, it is only by associating himself with the "liberal group" from which he gets his employment and which is less likely to condemn what old-fashioned people would consider his evident dishonesty, namely, his infidelity to his wife and his appropriation of her money in the process. We may detect an echo of that irony with which the author has first introduced Stiva as an honest, "truthful man with himself. He was incapable of persuading himself that he repented of his conduct. . . . All he was sorry about was that he had not succeeded better in hiding it from his wife" (Tolstoy, *Anna*, pt. 1, ch. 2, p. 5). Throughout the book, the discourse of "truthfulness" and "honesty" is interwoven through characters and social groups, and the complex play of voices we hear in it each time draws on earlier hybridizations. Again, this is one reason why illustrative examples are rather difficult to provide without consideration of earlier passages through which the work's "influx of sense" has been developed. Because the words of such passages also echo usage in the social context of the time, this extension of Bakhtin's concepts points to the importance of understanding the highly particular and socially variable discourse of the period. Each novel, as Bakhtin describes it, contains the germ of Flaubert's dictionary of received expressions.

The Mutual Interillumination of Languages: Organic and Intentional Hybrids

Bakhtin distinguishes between two types of hybridization: hybridization proper and the "mutual interillumination of languages." In hybridization proper, only one discourse is explicitly present; the dialogizing other discourse is felt in its effect on the first. It is sensed as the other language from which the image of the first language is made, but it is not itself directly visible. In what Bakhtin calls the mutual interillumination of languages, both languages are explicitly present. As should be apparent, these two possibilities are poles of a continuum, and at times it may be difficult to say whether a given discourse is present in part or only strongly implicit. Understanding such difficulties, and the complex kinds of double-voicing that produce them, is central to the work of understanding novels.

Karenin's meditation on the complex and varied discourses at Stiva's dinner party illustrates this and closely related problems:

Unconsciously going over in his memory the conversations that had taken place during and after dinner, Aleksey Aleksandrovich returned to his solitary room. Darya Aleksandrovna's words about forgiveness had aroused in him nothing but annoyance. The applicability or nonapplicability of the Christian precept to his own case was too difficult a question to be discussed lightly, and this question had long ago been answered by Aleksey Aleksandrovich in the negative. Of all that had been said, what stuck most in his memory was the phrase of that silly, good-natured Turovtsyn— "*Acted like a man, he did! Challenged him and shot him!*" Everyone had apparently shared this feeling, though from politeness they had not expressed it. [Tolstoy, *Anna*, pt. 4, ch. 17, p. 430]

Karenin finds it easy to answer Dolly's Christian appeal to forgive, and we hear him reprocess her words in the bureaucratese and legalese characteristic of him. Forgiving those who have wronged us becomes a precept, the particular situation becomes a case, and the logic of examination becomes a question of "applicability" or "nonapplicability," which Aleksey Aleksandrovich had long since "answered in the negative." One character's discourse is "unconsciously" reaccented in the language of another, and the author's discourse illuminates (and is perhaps illuminated by) both.

What Karenin finds difficult to reprocess is the language of "common opinion," which he usually is rather poor at hearing. Here he senses a palpable expression impossible not to detect. The contrast of Turovtsyn's direct way of speaking and the values it implies with Karenin's bureaucratese will echo in Karenin's inner speech, give it an increasingly irritated edge, and add overtones of aggressive self-justification and resentment, which in turn produce complex sidelong glances of his word at the words of others. Conversely, Karenin's language will also illuminate Turovtsyn's values, as we see the destructive effect of its rather "silly," and Vronsky-like, overtones.

Karenin's bureaucratic rendition of Christianity is presented as an exaggerated form of a discourse actually present in society. To understand its use, we may invoke another of Bakhtin's distinctions, between "organic" and "intentional" hybrids. Both are common in everyday life. In unintentional (or organic) hybridization, speakers and groups come to mix existing discourses they know and encounter with each other in order to come to terms with changing daily experience. In the crucible of the utterance, discourses are fused by use to yield new discourses; a particular kind of Christian language joins with official legalisms to create a strange though easily recognizable amalgam. Since all people participate in many different groups and master diverse social languages, and since all institutions draw diverse members who interact with multiple outsiders, this kind of amalgamation is always taking place. And as it does, speech genres, words, and syntactic structures come to be differently intoned and to change. Consequently, "unintentional, unconscious hybridization is one of the most important modes in the historical life and evolution of all languages. We may say that language and languages change historically primarily by means of [such] hybridization, by means of various co-existing 'languages'" (DiN, pp. 358–59). Novelists detect and explore the implications and potentials of old and new hybrid languages.

Bakhtin supposes it likely that all languages of heteroglossia were formed by a process of hybridization no longer detectable by its speakers. They use these organic hybrids directly, as single-voiced discourse. But speakers also produce intentional hybrids by double-voicing available discourses, and thus produce their own *images* of languages. Novelists illuminate both organic and intentional hybrids with their own intentional hybrids. The amalgam of Christian bureaucratese meets the common language of duels and challenges in the crucible of Karenin's inner speech. The work of novels is to choose, create, and intensify such hybrids:

The artistic image of a language must by its very nature be a linguistic hybrid (an intentional hybrid): it is obligatory for two linguistic consciousnesses to be present, the one being represented and the other doing the representing, with each belonging to a different system of language. Indeed, if there is not a second representing consciousness, if there is no second representing language intention, then what results is not an image [obraz] of a language but merely a *sample* [obrazets] of some other person's language. [DiN, p. 359]

Novelistic Language and Inner Life

Bakhtin believed that novelistic discourse of the type we have described is especially well adapted to portraying the dynamics of psychological life. As we saw in Chapter Five, Bakhtin understood psychology in terms of inner speech, and he described inner speech as a complex orientation among voices and dialogues that we have internalized and brought into interaction. We form a self from "innerly persuasive words," which are a kind of hybrid, "half-ours, half-someone else's" (DiN, p. 345). Such innerly persuasive words may become less persuasive and may come to be overlaid with ironic quotation marks; or, at times, they may reassert their persuasiveness through all layers. Selfhood, in short, is a process remarkably similar to novelization, and novels are consequently the best form for conveying psychological life, at least as Bakhtin understood it.

In "Discourse in the Novel," Bakhtin discusses the dialogic nature of psychological life and the special potential of novels as a psychological genre, but provides no examples. However, examples are available in the Dostoevsky book. When Raskolnikov receives a letter from his mother describing how his sister Dunya has become engaged to Luzhin, Raskolnikov immediately recognizes from his mother's very overstatements about the marriage's desirability that his mother and sister are sacrificing themselves for his benefit. As Dostoevsky traces Raskolnikov's inner speech about this letter, we hear how voices of mother and sister, the imagined voices of other people mentioned in the letter, and the social voices who might comment on the situation, all enter into an intensified dialogue. The fact that Raskolnikov is verging on delirium and murder makes the sort of psychological processes present in all of us particularly intense and open to inspection. And of course there is special irony in the fact that this intense inner dialogue takes place in someone barely capable of speaking with real individual others.

Conveyed in quasi-direct discourse and complex forms of direct discourse, Raskolnikov's inner speech is "filled with other people's words that he has just recently heard or read. . . . He inundates his own inner speech with these words of others, complicating them with his own accents or directly reaccenting them, entering into a passionate polemic with them. Consequently his inner speech is constructed like a succession of living and impassioned replies to all the words of others he has heard or been touched by" (PDP, p. 238). We witness a dizzying sequence of reaccentuations and a series of imagined dialogues among people who address each other for the first time in his consciousness, which is, in turn, addressed by the author's.

Here again we see the special potential of novelistic dialogue: "All the voices that Raskolnikov introduces into his inner speech come into a peculiar sort of contact, one that would be impossible among voices in an actual dialogue. Because they all sound within a single consciousness, they become, as it were, reciprocally permeable. They are brought close to one another, made to overlap; they partially intersect one another, creating the corresponding interruptions in areas of intersection" (PDP, p. 239). "Reciprocal permeability"—through dialogized heteroglossia and the infinitely varied kinds of double-voicing—conveys the moment-to-moment processes of selfhood as no other tool can.

Bakhtin apparently believed that the immense potentials of the novel as it was shaped in the nineteenth century are far from exhausted. From a current perspective, it also becomes evident that his approach to novels represents an unusual combination of sophisticated close reading with sociological analysis. His way of reading focuses on the complex play of discourse that is socially heterogeneous, variously and multiply intoned, and still "warm" from its daily use.

The Novel's Two Stylistic Lines

Bakhtin devotes the sixty-page final chapter of "Discourse in the Novel" to historical problems. How has the novel's distinctive use of language developed over time? What forms and subgenres have been shaped by a Galilean linguistic consciousness? How successful have these subgenres been in exploiting the potential of the novel's form-shaping force? And how have the various types of novels interacted?

To answer these questions, Bakhtin sketches the broad outlines of a history of the genre from the perspective of dialogue and heteroglossia. Bakhtin evidently intended this sketch as a series of initial suggestions for a more detailed treatment. In the course of his exposition, he also offers a number of intriguing new concepts about language and its use in literature.

Bakhtin identifies two broad lines in the stylistic history of the novel, two rival traditions identified by the ways in which they exploit the resources of heteroglossia to create dialogized "images of languages." He favors the "second stylistic line" because it more fully and more richly exploits the genre's "potential." This way of viewing the novel's history explains a form of argument that might otherwise seem puzzling: although Bakhtin divides novels into two groups, he nevertheless often contends that characteristics present only in the second stylistic line are nevertheless definitive of the entire genre. In offering such formulations, Bakhtin evidently has in mind what he identifies as the novel's essence—"novelness" per se. Novelness is much more fully developed in the second line, and so to understand the second line is to understand the genre. Though important historically, the first line, as Bakhtin treats it, merely approximates true novelness.

According to Bakhtin, the great novels of the nineteenth century, from which we have drawn our examples in the present chapter, derived from a fusion of the two stylistic lines. In that fusion the second line clearly predominates over the first. "It could even be said that in the nineteenth century the distinctive features of the Second Line become the basic constitutive features for the novelistic genre as a whole. It was in the Second Line that novelistic discourse developed all its specific stylistic potential, unique to it alone. The Second Line opened up once and for all the possibilities embedded in the novel as a genre; in it the novel became what it in fact is" (DiN, p. 414). The kinds of novelistic language that we have so far described as the real life of novels are all developments of the second line's basic features.

Prior to the latter part of the eighteenth century, the two stylistic lines developed largely independently, although there are some isolated examples of mixtures before then. The first line reached fruition earlier. In the ancient world, the first line found "a sufficiently full and finished expression" (DiN, p. 375) in the "Sophistic novel" (and elsewhere), whereas the second line achieved only a few preparatory elements. Nevertheless, the second line was to develop both the most significant subgenres of the novel and the greatest individual works.

From the late middle ages or Renaissance on, it is relatively easy to identify unambiguous representatives of each line. Bakhtin offers paired contrasts representing the two: he writes of "the opposition between *Amadis* on the one hand [first line] and *Gargantua and Pantagruel* and *Don Quixote* on the other [second line]; between the high Baroque novel and *Simplicissimus*, the novels of Sorel, Scarron; between the chivalric romance on the one hand and the parodic epic, the satire novella, the picaresque novel on the other; between, finally, Rousseau and Richardson [belonging to the first line], and Fielding, Sterne, and Jean Paul [belonging to the second]" (DiN, p. 414).

The two lines exploit the resources of Galilean linguistic consciousness in fundamentally different ways. Basically, the first line strives for a finished, elegant style, which is studiously polished and never interrupted by heteroglot expressions from real life. Or if heteroglossia does interrupt the style, the intrusions are isolated and never lie on the same plane as the elevated language that establishes the tone of the whole. The contrast between elegance and heteroglossia, if it is present at all, only serves to set off the elegance of the dominant language more palpably. By definition, then, works of the first line know "only a single language and a single style (which is more or less rigorously consistent); heteroglossia remains *outside* the novel, although it does nevertheless have its effect on the novel as a dialogizing background in which the language and world of the novel is polemically and forensically implicated" (DiN, p. 375). Conversely, the second line "incorporates heteroglossia *into* a novel's composition, exploiting it to orchestrate its own meaning and frequently resisting altogether any unmediated and pure authorial discourse" (ibid.).

One might wish to ask at this point why the first line is novelistic at all. For if the dialogization of heteroglossia and the Galilean decentering of languages is definitive of the genre, how can one call works dominated by a single style and tone novels? Are not such works in fact closer to lyric poetry as Bakhtin understands it? After all, lyric poems (in their essence) also work with a single language ignorant of heteroglossia.

Bakhtin anticipates this objection and clarifies his point. Unlike poetry, the first line is highly conscious of heteroglossia. It does not "forget" speech diversity, as poetry by convention does, nor does the polished style of these novels suggest that there is in essence no other way of speaking about its topics. On the contrary, the style of the first line seems beleaguered by heteroglossia at the gates, heteroglossia waiting to overwhelm it. Far from ignorant of speech diversity, it is polemically directed at it; the style of the first line is offered as something tested, contested, and retested.

This polemic with heteroglossia is part of the generic "task" of novels belonging to the first stylistic line, whereas the task of lyric poetry, which is quite different, could not be fulfilled at all in an atmosphere of such polemics. Of course, the lyric poet and his readers live in a heteroglot world, but, "bathed in Lethe," they suspend their awareness of it. Novelists of the first line, however, do not forget for a minute the motley enemies surrounding them. One can sense the style of the first line answering the rival languages outside it; that style is really diatribe, in the basic sense of an argument with an absent or silent interlocutor. That is what Bakhtin means when he says that the very tasks of the first line *presume* heteroglossia as a "dialogizing background." As Bakhtin observes, "such stylization involves a sideways glance at others' languages, at other points of view and other conceptual horizons. . . . This is one of the most fundamental distinctions between novelistic stylization and poetic stylization" (DiN, pp. 375–76).

Bakhtin also offers a spatial analogy: "Poetry behaves as if it lived in the heartland of its own language territory, and does not approach too closely the borders of this language, where it would inevitably be brought into dialogic contact with heteroglossia; poetry chooses not to look beyond the boundaries of its own language" (DiN, p. 399). By contrast, the prose of the first stylistic line of the novel "stands on the very borderline of its own language and is dialogically implicated in the surrounding heteroglossia, resonates with its most essential features, and consequently participates in an ongoing dialogue of languages" (ibid.).

Both stylistic lines of the novel rely on and exploit heteroglossia in a dialogizing fashion. The second line does so by incorporating heteroglossia into the text, the first relies on heteroglossia's presence and activity in the "dialogizing background." It is apparent, therefore, why the first line does belong to the genre, but also why the second line has been more successful in exploiting the genre's potential.

Special risks attend the reliance on a dialogizing background as the main technique of dialogization. Most obviously, the first stylistic line necessarily presumes readers who possess an intimate sense of that background and the ability to detect its specific kinds of interaction with given passages and with the work as a whole. Such works have great difficulty conveying their dialogicality to remote cultures and generations, who do not know the original background. In some cases, it may be possible for readers to supply equivalents from their own time, if they think to do so; but a great deal of the dialogicality and parodic quality of such works is bound to be lost.

Except in those cases where it is grossly apparent, the presence of parody is in general very difficult to identify (that is, difficult to identify precisely in literary prose, where it rarely is gross), without knowing the background of alien discourse against which it is projected, that is, without knowing its second context. In world literature there probably are many works whose parodic nature has not even been suspected. . . . And yet we look at world literature from a tiny island limited in time and space. [DiN, p. 374]

We can now see the origin and mistaken assumptions behind traditional stylistics of the novel. Based on beliefs ultimately derived from poetics, Bakhtin argues, such studies typically (1) take the first line as definitive of the genre, and (2) misunderstand the first line by not taking into account the essential role of the dialogizing background (DiN, p. 399). When dealing with representatives of the second line, traditional stylistics adds a third unjustifiable step: by isolating a few "polished" passages, it in effect transforms the works into novels of the first line, and then proceeds to apply its misplaced poetic analytic techniques. Such a process only compounds the errors of poetics.

"Extrageneric Literariness"

The discourse of the first stylistic line raises intriguing problems for Bakhtin. He remarks that this "style" does not, strictly speaking, conform to the definition of style with which he has so far been working, even though that definition is broad enough to encompass the diverse languages of everyday speech genres, the epic and lyric genres, and the modern novel. In other words, the language of the first stylistic line turns out to be something quite special. As Bakhtin analyzes it, it also turns out to have great importance in understanding broader tendencies and norms in social life.

Bakhtin reminds us that style, as he has defined it, involves a specific complex of relations between speaker, listeners, generic forms, an estimation of social circumstances, the anticipated discourses of others, sets of values, presumed or rejected purposes, and projected topics of conversation. Or as Bakhtin sometimes explains more briefly, "style strives organically to assimilate material into language and language into material" (DiN, p. 378). Whether it "permeates the topic directly, as in poetry, or refracts its own intentions, as in literary prose" (ibid.), style depends on a specific fit between value-charged forms of discourse and the material to be discussed. This sort of *specific* relationship is precisely what is lacking in the discourse of the first stylistic line.

Shifting briefly to historical problems, Bakhtin observes that the rise of early novelistic prose in Europe—he takes Germany, rather than France, as the typical case—involved a process of constant "translation, reworking, re-conceptualizing, re-accenting" (DiN, p. 377) of numerous alien discourses and genres, including ancient literature, early Christian legend, Breton-Celtic oral tales, and many other forms from various cultures. "It could even be said that European novel prose is born and shaped in the process of a free (that is, reformulating) translation of others' works" (DiN, p. 378). Add to this a number of other crucial social factors shaping the development of European prose: the self-conscious "cultural internationalism of its creators" and audience (DiN, p. 379); the fact that the prose "lacked a firm unitary social basis, possessed no calm and assured self-confidence as would derive from association with a fixed social stratum" (ibid.); and, finally, the new effects of printing, which allowed the novel to begin "a period of wandering among social classes" (ibid.). The result of these various factors was to create a kind of "homelessness" and "rootlessness" of prose, to divorce "the word . . . from its material" and to separate it from "the unity of a [specific] social ideology" (ibid.). Prose was cleansed of the marks of experience reflecting a specific kind of life and world-view. "Wandering among social classes, lacking any roots, this word was forced to assume a character compounded of specific conventions; this was not however the healthy conventionality of poetic discourse but rather one resulting from the impossibility, under these conditions, of making full artistic use of discourse, or of formulating it in a wide variety of aspects" (ibid.). In other words, it was necessary to develop something to substitute for a genuine style (strictly defined).

The substitute for style that emerged was what Bakhtin calls "sheer exposition," a phrase that only defines the substitute for style negatively. Stated positively, what emerged was a "special conventionality" that took the form of "mere decorativeness" and general "literariness" (DiN, p. 380).[7] This conventionality offered a new way to deal with the wealth and possibilities of language that, in the absence of genuine style, still had to be dealt with. In some forms of decorativeness, the goal was "an empty ease of manner, a smooth finish" for syntax and "empty euphony" for sound (ibid.). In other forms, discourse seeks "an equally empty rhetorical complexity, something florid and overblown, an ornamented exterior" (ibid.). This ornamental discourse may make use of poetic tropes, which, in such a context, will necessarily function quite differently from the way they do in poetry. These and other forms of decorativeness serve to "legalize and (as it were) canonize the absolute rupture between language and material" (ibid.).

What is special about this substitute for style is that, because it does not grow out of specific speech genres adapted to specific situations and materials, it is, by design and by convention, universally applicable to any material, at least in principle. "Language used in this way is a neutral element that appeals precisely because it is dressed up, permitting its surface charms to be emphasized" (ibid.). It is in this sense that the language is "extrageneric," that is, not tied to any particular speech genre.

Of course, such discourse could also be understood as a style of a special sort, adapted, however broadly, to particular occasions of use. Freedom from mere style could be regarded as just another style. Indeed, the second stylistic line of the novel will understand the style of the first line in just this way, and in the process of representing it, will deflate its pretensions. Nevertheless, the discourse of the first line can only be comprehended if one realizes that its fundamental task is not to allow itself to be regarded as just another language; but to be seen as an alternative to all mere jargons. Its very success indicates that the claims of this discourse were widely accepted, even if, at a later point, those claims were unmasked with great effectiveness by the more thoroughgoing prosaics of the second line.

The Roots of Homelessness

It is worth pausing here to consider the *way* in which Bakhtin arrives at his concept of the substitute for style, the "general literariness" of the first line. The sort of move he makes is in fact an important new element in his style of thinking during his third period. Stated most generally, what Bakhtin learned to do was to offer a definition of some important aspect of culture—style, institution, or genre—and then imagine a particular ostensible style, institution, or genre that defined itself as violating the definition. That is, he would discover an apparent member of the category, but one whose central "task" was to challenge or ostentatiously ignore the features that make the category what it is. In this sense, the style becomes antistyle, the institution an anti-institution, the genre an antigenre.[8]

These "substitutes" challenging a category, it must be stressed, are anything but "naive." That is, they may be compared to double-voiced, rather than single-voiced, discourse, because they are deeply aware of the norms that they are violating. They are, in a profound sense, dependent on those norms, which may in consequence be altered, at which point the substitute may rejoin the revised system. Should that happen, the substitute style, genre, or institution will of course cease to be antistyle, antigenre, or anti-institution. Its special potency will be "reduced." To understand these intriguing substitutes, one must recognize that the possibility of rejoining the category is ever present. From the perspective of the category defied, it is also always an open question whether the existence of the challenger truly threatens the category or whether, on the contrary, it strengthens it—by serving as a "safety valve" or as an exception that proves the rule.

In Bakhtin's third period, he discovered three major examples of such substitutes. His evaluation of them varies. As should be evident by now, he seemed to regard "extrageneric literariness" rather negatively, as a kind of pretender style that derived from a contempt for heteroglossia. By contrast, he clearly celebrated his example of an anti-institution—carnival—although he remained unsure whether it ultimately weakened or strengthened "official" institutions. It offers an alternative to institutions per se. In "Epic and Novel," he described the novel as an antigenre and interpreted this special status as a cause of the novel's superiority over all other genres. How are such differences in evaluation to be explained?

We offer an admittedly speculative, and genetic, explanation. If one looks for an equivalent for "substitutes" in Bakhtin's earlier writings, one may single out a chain of reasoning in "Toward a Philosophy of the Act." It will be recalled that in this essay Bakhtin insists that moral responsibility pertains to every moment of life and that there is no legitimate escape from it. But there are illegitimate escapes; one may live as if there were "an alibi for being"; one may live as a "pretender." In a world that is moral to the core, people have self-consciously constructed moments in which their obligations are ostensibly suspended. Bakhtin's point here is that the very act of constructing these suspensions itself has (negative) moral value.

In period IIIa, it will also be recalled, Bakhtin retains a concern with responsibility, and his theories of the novel are in part designed to describe how that genre may deepen our sense of prosaic obligations. A central purpose of "Discourse in the Novel" and "Forms of Time and of the Chronotope" is to represent the novel as a special form of thinking that allows us to comprehend the reality and nature of daily responsibility. Novels, as these essays describe them, presuppose the fundamental rootedness of life in specific social practices and in inescapable fields of evaluation.

By contrast, in period IIIb Bakhtin experimented with his global concepts by taking one of them, unfinalizability, to an extreme, and by suspending the others. Living by pure unfinalizability makes life a single "loophole," a view of life he had previously regarded as irresponsible and futile. In period IIIb, pure unfinalizability is treated positively. Thinking this way, Bakhtin came to describe suspension of rootedness not as an illegitimate alibi but as a form of liberation. Because novels always embodied his positive values, we conjecture, they are described as an antigenre only in period IIIb—that is, in "Epic and Novel"—but not in period IIIa (in "Discourse" and in "Chronotope"). Whereas "Discourse" represents the claims of extrageneric literariness as a deliberate and futile attempt to avoid the heteroglossia, chaos, and "vulgarity" of daily life, *Rabelais and His World* describes carnival as a liberating escape from official institutions.

The terms Bakhtin uses for these forms of anticulture suggest one avenue that led to their positive reevaluation in period IIIb. He repeatedly describes them as "homeless," "rootless," and "wandering." As it happens, those are also the terms he uses to describe some key figures in the development of the modern novel, namely, the clown, the fool, and the rogue. These three figures are "life's maskers" (FTC, p. 159), by which Bakhtin means that they expose the conventional masks of life; they are, in fact, life's *un*maskers. "Essential to these three figures is a distinctive feature that is as well a privilege—the right to be 'other' in this world, the right not to make common cause with any single one of the existing categories that life makes available; none of these categories quite suits them, they see the underside and falseness of every situation" (DiN, p. 159). Like the forms of anticulture, these figures do not belong to social categories, but exist in homeless, defiant opposition to them.

The rogue continually dons and discards masks so as to expose the falsity of those who presume their roles and institutions are natural. Bakhtin goes on to state that the stance of the rogue is precisely the stance of the novelist. Thus, although roguish "masks" occupy a place in Bakhtin's new theory analogous to that of "alibi" or "pretender" in his early texts, they are represented as agents of truthfulness and authenticity rather than as futile tools for an escape. Irresponsibility, now recast as mockery of the "official," has assumed a positive value.

In his fourth period, Bakhtin modified or abandoned his celebrations of pure unfinalizability, but he seems to have retained the habit of imagining, for each institution, genre, or practice, a kind of antipractice that self-consciously defines itself as defiant of the category as a whole. He again stresses that such defiance is futile, much like the underground man's effort to *show* his friends that he is *ignoring* them. But however futile, these efforts may have the value of teasing thought, of allowing us to imagine what an impossible state would be like if it were not impossible—of hinting, by untenable metaphors, at what we must otherwise pass over in silence.

It is in this sense, we imagine, that Bakhtin intends a number of otherwise puzzling passages in his last writings, where he often speculates about the nature of things he has deemed impossible. In his often cryptic "Notes of 1970–71," for instance, he toys with an unimaginable "supra-existence" (N70–71, p. 137), with the speech of pure silence (N70–71, p. 133), and with direct access to the "primary author" of an utterance. As a character in Dostoevsky asks, is it possible to imagine as an image that which has no image? If language is necessarily dialogic, can one still somehow conceive of an impossible speech beyond dialogue? There are vague overtones of mysticism, or of "negative theology," in such passages. Bakhtin alludes to Christ's silent kiss of the Grand Inquisitor and asks what it would be like—if it were not admittedly impossible—to have "genres of pure *self*-expression (without the traditional authorial form)? Do there exist genres without an addressee?" (N70–71, p. 153).

"Ennobled" Language

Let us now return to the discourse of the first stylistic line. That discourse conceives of itself as (1) not tied to specific contexts or genres (it is extrageneric), and (2) opposed to the vulgar heteroglossia of daily life, against which it is tacitly but polemically directed. It is informed by a sense of general "respectability" and propriety. Deeply aware of the heteroglossia of daily life, it offers itself as an alternative, "ennobled" discourse; it is analogous to, and often makes use of, euphemism. Such discourse implies that any merely professional or daily jargon necessarily "reeks of specific contexts" (DiN, p. 384). Those contexts are sensed as contaminating all languages of heteroglossia with merely utilitarian purposes, and so one detects in them "a narrowly practical direction, overrun with petty philistine associations" (ibid.).

By contrast, the "rootlessness" of "extrageneric literariness" enables it to claim a kind of universality and noncontextual purity. Wherever it is used, whatever it may describe, it remains unstained and its topic becomes ennobled. Exquisitely aware of all low and impolite things and actions, it refuses to acknowledge their presence. "The way of perceiving objects and expressions peculiar to this novelistic discourse is not the ever-changing world view of a living and mobile human being . . . it is rather the restricted world view of a man trying to preserve one and the same immobile pose, someone whose movements are made not in order better to see, but quite the opposite—he moves so that he may turn *away* from, *not* notice, be distracted" (DiN, p. 385).

Existence is experienced at a protective distance. "This world view, filled not with real-life things, but with verbal references to literary things and images, is polemically set against the crude heteroglossia of the real world and painstakingly (although in a deliberately polemical, and therefore tangible, way) cleansed of all possible associations with crude real life" (ibid.).

Discourse of this sort exercised great influence in extraliterary social life. Lying somewhere between language and style, it could (and did) affect extraliterary discourse by moving to either extreme. On the one hand, "ennobled" language could offer itself as the essence of the national language—as if to say, "This is true French." When this happens, ennobled discourse "achieves a maximal degree of generality but is deprived of almost all ideological coloration and specificity" (DiN, p. 382) because it is now offered not as the language of an elite but as the proper national language in principle spoken by or taught to everyone. Used in this way, "extrageneric literariness" became a force for the codification and "centripetal" normatization of national languages.

On the other hand, extrageneric literariness may tend in the opposite direction and "seek its *stylistic* (as opposed to linguistic) limit" (ibid.). In this case, it becomes even more ideologically concrete and definite. Its sense of itself could be expressed as: "This is the way respectable people speak and write." It becomes a force for redefining elevated norms of behavior in daily life: for specifying how to conduct conversations, how to write letters or diaries, and how to suffuse diverse activities with refinement, sensitivity, and nobility. Under its influence, previously nonliterary genres become "semiliterary" (DiN, p. 383). Its force and area of operation may vary from time to time and culture to culture, but its tendency is always to subjugate all those areas, encountered in the lives of ennobled speakers, that are low and vulgar. It is likely to have greatest success where social shifts have produced new kinds of exchanges not yet subject to firm generic norms and where existing norms are felt to be weak or already questionable. One can sense its effect especially strongly when it affects the shape of whole spheres of behavior or, indeed, the shape of whole lives: it leads, in such cases, to the creation of "literary deeds" and "literary people." Life becomes "novelized" (according to the first stylistic line of the novel).

Despite its pose of immobility, ennobled discourse undergoes constant change, in both literature and extraliterary life. Given the fact that the pose of immobility is just that—a pose, polemically ignoring vulgar life—such change is implicit in the very nature of the discourse. It carries the traces of whatever it is at the moment straining not to see. As new kinds of vulgarity and heteroglossia accumulate, new kinds of literariness arise to "ignore" them. Thus, Bakhtin sketches a brief history of literariness in the novel. (He also indicates the need for such a history in social life, a history that would go beyond the topic of his essay.) In passages like these, we see Bakhtin engaging sociological problems while avoiding a Marxist framework: his apparent answer to Voloshinov and Medvedev.

The Discourse of Pathos

The first stylistic line of the novel developed what Bakhtin calls "the discourse of pathos" (or "the pathetic word"). It is important to note at the outset that the Russian words *pafos* and *pateticheskoe*, although routinely translated into their English equivalents from the same Greek roots, differ in meaning from English *pathos* and *pathetic*. Whereas the English terms carry overtones of sadness and suggest a quality that arouses pity, sorrow, or compassion, common translations of Russian *pafos* include "enthusiasm," "inspiration," "animation," "passionate ardor or fervor." Soviet dictionaries offer as sample phrases "revolutionary pathos," "to speak with pathos," and "the pathos of creative labor."

Characteristically for this essay, Bakhtin distinguishes "prosaic pathos" or "novelistic pathos" (terms he uses interchangeably) from "poetic" or "authentic" pathos. Poetic pathos is expressed directly and without distance between the speaker and his discourse. It is "fully sufficient to itself and its object. Indeed, the speaker completely immerses himself in such a discourse, there is no distance, there are no reservations" (DiN, p. 394). By contrast, prosaic pathos always appears with "quotation marks"; it must be double-voiced.

The novelist, Bakhtin notes, uses prosaic pathos as a discourse distant from himself, one which he might like to be able to speak directly, but which he cannot. It belongs to another time, another genre. "In the novel a discourse of pathos is almost always a surrogate for some other genre that is no longer available to a given time or a given social force—such pathos is the discourse of a preacher who has lost his pulpit, a dreaded judge who no longer has any judicial or punitive powers, the prophet without a mission, the politician without political power, the believer without a church" (DiN, p. 395). To clarify Bakhtin's point: he is speaking *not* about the language of a character, but of the author. It is his discourse that resembles the judge who has lost his powers. Although the author knows that he cannot use the pathetic discourse directly and in the conditions that nourished it, he also knows that there is no adequate substitute for it. He therefore uses it conditionally: "He must, against his will, mount the pulpit, assume the role of preacher or judge" (ibid.). This act of assuming a role in order to speak confers on the discourse a sense of its limitation that conflicts with its professed enthusiastic tone: "In this lies the 'curse' of novelistic pathos" (ibid.).

The discourse of pathos dominates the baroque novel, where it is linked to the basic plot of testing a hero's "irreproachability." Its overtones are exalted, grand, and public; this is "high heroizing pathos," the "pathos of heroism and terror" (DiN, pp. 397, 398). But in the Sentimental novel, a quite different discourse of pathos arose. No longer a matter of the grand, the political, or historical, the sentimental discourse of pathos self-consciously concerns itself with the "moral choices of everyday life and satisfies itself with the narrowly personal and family spheres of life" (DiN, p. 396). It becomes "chamber pathos," spoken within the privacy of one's own room, and associated with a new conception of small space—or, to use the term of Bakhtin's other essay of this period, with a new chronotope.

As a result, this sentimental discourse presupposes two kinds of language to which it is opposed. Neither are directly present in the text of sentimental novels, but both figure in the presumed dialogizing background. Like "high heroizing pathos," sentimental pathos is tacitly opposed to the vulgar heteroglossia that would describe its favored topics quite differently. But it is also tacitly opposed to its predecessor, high heroizing pathos itself, which is now understood as "quasi-elevated and false" (DiN, p. 397). As Bakhtin sums up his point:

The finely detailed descriptions, the very deliberateness with which petty secondary everyday details are foregrounded . . . and finally a pathos occasioned by helplessness and weakness rather than heroic strength, the deliberate narrowing down of the conceptual horizon and the area of a man's experience to his most immediate little micro-world (to his very own room)—all this is accounted for by the polemical opposition to a literary style in the process of being rejected. [DiN, pp. 397–98]

By comparison with baroque style, sentimental style and topics have clearly moved closer to great nineteenth-century novels. The concern with the everyday is a step in that direction. Nevertheless, the gulf between *Middlemarch* and sentimental narratives remains large. Sentimental style is still very much a product of the first stylistic line. "In place of one conventionality . . . Sentimentalism creates another—and one similarly abstract. . . . A discourse made respectable by Sentimental pathos, one that attempts to replace the crude discourse of life, inevitably ends up in the same hopeless dialogic conflict with the actual heteroglossia of life" (DiN, p. 398). Generally speaking, the first stylistic line of the novel fails to go beyond a peculiar "one-sided dialogism" (ibid.).

Incomprehension and Gay Deception

When it appears in the second stylistic line, the language of the first line loses its privilege. It becomes just another language of heteroglossia to be set into dialogue with others. The discourse of chivalric romances, of baroque novels, and of sentimental narratives no longer represents the world, but is represented as part of it. It loses the privilege of turning away from the languages of heteroglossia, and is forced to encounter them and to defend itself; it becomes *actively* double-voiced. Exemplary in this regard is the parodic treatment of *Amadis* in *Don Quixote*. "For the Second Stylistic Line, the respectable language of the chivalric romance . . . becomes only one of the participants in a dialogue of languages, it becomes the prosaic image of a language—most profoundly and fully instanced in Cervantes—capable of internal dialogic resistance to new authorial intentions; it is an image that is agitatedly double-

voiced" (DiN, p. 386). To the extent that first line discourse claims
not to be "just another language," it is especially vulnerable to parody by the second line. To the extent that it refuses to be parodied
with impunity and offers active resistance, first line discourse appearing in second line novels enriches the dialogue of heteroglossia.

In novels of the second line, general "literariness" of language—
the language of respectable or highly literate people—of course
plays an important role. Indeed, it would be hard to imagine most
of the greatest works of the second line without it. Such discourse
may even be offered as the author's own favored way of speaking
and writing, as it is in Turgenev. Nevertheless, "literary" discourse
in the second line functions quite differently from the way ennobled
discourse functions in the first line. However much the author of a
second-line novel may favor it and the values it carries, he knows
that it is still just another professional or class jargon that enjoys no
special privilege. It contributes to the novel's dialogue on the same
plane as other languages, is tested by them, and is not guaranteed to
pass the test.

The second stylistic line also changes the function of a device
common to both lines, namely, the use of inserted genres. As part
of its project of refining extraliterary life, novels of the first line
often included samples of well-written letters, proper conversation,
and other types of "good style." Written in the decorous language
of the whole, these parts were made to be easily detachable, and
were, indeed, often detached so as to be used as models. "Special
books such as *Treasures of Amadis* and *The Book of Compliments* were
compiled that brought together models of conversations, letters,
speeches and so forth extracted from the novel. . . . The chivalric
romance provided a discourse proper to all possible situations and
events in life" (DiN, p. 384). In considering such detachable parts,
it is necessary to reconsider critics' usual blanket condemnation of
excerpting or taking a passage out of context; for it is characteristic
of some works to allow or encourage readers to take certain parts
both in context and out of context.[9] Here again we see Bakhtin's
lifelong interest in the complexities of "wholeness."

Novels of the second line, as we have seen, use inserted genres in
a quite different way. Extraliterary genres (or other literary genres)
are included so as to be mined for their multiple discourses, which
are set into dialogue with the other discourses of the work. Thus, in
the first line, inserted genres are designed to *ex*port literariness
from the novel; in the second line, they *im*port heteroglossia into
the novel.

Bakhtin next turns to two devices of the second stylistic line that reflect especially clearly its entire sense of the world and of language: "gay deception" and "incomprehension." He digresses to explain initially that all sorts of "minor epic genres (*fabliaux*, *Schwänke*, minor parodic genres)" (DiN, p. 400) lying outside the mainstream of the dominant chivalric romances continued work begun in satiric genres of antiquity, the work of finding ways to sense and represent the "image" of social languages. In these genres, styles of double-voicing, parodic discourse, *skaz* "in all degrees and nuances" (ibid.) coupled particular ways of speaking with specific kinds of speakers. Rather than making speech an instantiation of a "depersonalized language," these genres sensed the social typicality and evaluative habits of given ways of speaking. They moved toward a "form-shaping impulse" according to which "every discourse has its own selfish and biased proprietor; there are no words with meanings shared by all, no words 'belonging to no one'" (DiN, p. 401).

Like Ambrose Bierce's *Devil's Dictionary* (which defines *impunity* as wealth and *egotist* as a person who cares more about himself than he does about me), these satiric forms were suspicious of "the false front of the word. What matters is rather the actual and always self-interested *use* to which this meaning is put and the way it is expressed by the speaker—a use determined by the speaker's position (profession, social class, etc.) and by the concrete situation. *Who* speaks and under what conditions he speaks: this is what determines the word's actual meaning" (DiN, p. 401). The "philosophy of discourse" inherent in such forms therefore tends toward a radical skepticism. When it appears in Rabelais, that skepticism becomes still more extreme and borders "on rejection of the very possibility of having a straightforward discourse at all that would not be false" (ibid.).

In its subsequent development, this "philosophy" led to the creation of an important category of novelistic speech, which Bakhtin calls "gay deception." This kind of speech presumes that all "pathos" is a "lie," and that no language of any class, group, or profession contains a "straightforward truth." It is, we might say, a sort of deconstruction before the name.

Gay deception is the language of the merry rogue, who answers the lie of pathos—who answers everything—with his own "intelligent deception, a *lie* justified because it is directed precisely to *liars*" (DiN, p. 401). The rogue parodies and reprocesses discourses of falsity so as to reveal what is false about them and to rob them of their harmful power. In this way, "what was a lie [turns] into gay deception. Falsehood is illuminated by ironic consciousness and in the mouth of the happy rogue parodies itself" (DiN, p. 402). Although Bakhtin's praise of answering lies with deception may be understandable in the Soviet context, it may also seem like a sentimental response to falsehood.

Gay deception is closely connected to another device of the second stylistic line that is even more central to its form-shaping impulse and its historical development. Indeed, this device, which Bakhtin calls "incomprehension," is *so* important that the second line would almost disappear if it were eliminated. As gay deception belongs to the rogue, incomprehension belongs to one or another type of fool.[10]

The fool *fails to understand* pathos-charged discourses that have become habitual. When heard by someone who does not understand them and who asks naive but probing questions about them, these discourses betray their conventionality and pretensions. In other words, the stupidity of novelistic foolishness is dialogic: "At its heart always lies a polemical failure to understand someone else's discourse, someone's pathos-charged lie that has appropriated the world" (DiN, p. 403). Thus, the fool is often coupled with another character—with a poet, a scholar, a moralist, or a priest (Cervantes, Diderot)—who presumes, and then tries to explain, a discourse of pathos. In some works, such as *Candide* or *The Charterhouse of Parma*, incomprehension becomes the most basic style-shaping force; in others, such as Pushkin's Belkin tales, it pertains only to specific languages, narrators, or kinds of experience. Sometimes the work describes a particular character who fails to understand (in *The Persian Letters*); at other times, it creates a fool of a narrator (Gulliver); at still others, incomprehension characterizes the fundamental position of the author (common in Tolstoy). We shall see that in his chronotope essay Bakhtin argues that the fool exercised such a determining influence on the relation of an author to his story that in many works a "foolish" stance of incomprehension may be detected even where no specific fool is represented.

Bakhtin stresses that the author need not demonstrate solidarity with the foolish perspective. At times, indeed, mockery of the fool may even be paramount. But even in such cases, the author needs the fool: "For by his very uncomprehending presence he *makes strange* the world of social conventionality. By representing stupidity, the novel teaches *prosaic intelligence, prosaic wisdom*. Regarding fools or regarding the world through the eyes of the fool, the novelist's eye is taught a sort of *prosaic vision*" (DiN, p. 404; italics ours). One might say that every novel and every novelistic trend "will feature one or another aspect of stupidity or incomprehension" (ibid.).

As Bakhtin observes, incomprehension "bestranges" (makes strange, defamiliarizes) the world: the term *bestrangement* belongs, of course, to the Formalists. Many of the examples Bakhtin mentions—Pierre on the battlefield in *War and Peace*, Levin at the elections in *Anna Karenina*, numerous stories about foreigners, supernatural beings, or animals trying to describe European civilization—were, in fact, standard Formalist illustrations of their central concept. Nevertheless, Bakhtin's interpretation of "bestrangement," though indebted to the Formalists, diverges markedly from theirs. For the Formalists, bestrangement was the defining feature of literature itself; it is what makes *all* of literature literary. Thus, for Shklovsky, there is fundamentally no difference between the various forms of this device: poetic language makes strange everyday language, literary narrative defamiliarizes everyday stories to produce artistically "deformed" plots (*fabula, siuzhet*), and poets or novelists choose metaphors that are sufficiently unfamiliar to impede perception and thus focus attention.

For Bakhtin, this approach overlooks the all-important category of genre as a specific way of seeing the world. As we saw in the previous chapter, for the Bakhtin group the absence of such a concept of genre constituted a crucial shortcoming of Formalist poetics. Without genre, one loses the sense that distinct forms are characterized not just by the use of different devices, but also by fundamentally different "eyes" perceiving life and "ears" attuned to the play of values. To identify poetic rhythm with Pierre on the battlefield is to miss the specifically novelistic features of Tolstoy's scene. Before one moves to "literariness" (in the Formalist sense), one needs to inquire about "novelness"—and lyricness, and epicness. Unlike Shklovsky, for whom bestrangement in Tolstoy is an instance of a universal literary principle, Bakhtin stresses the ways in which incomprehension expresses the form-shaping ideology of the novel's second stylistic line. In this way, bestrangement becomes a vehicle for "prosaic intelligence, prosaic wisdom."

Canonization and Reaccentuation

Bakhtin's theory of novelistic languages provides new kinds of close reading and demands a reinvigorated attention to novelistic texts. But it also points to crucial limitations inherent in any exclusive focus on the text itself. These limitations are immediately apparent in the case of novels belonging to the first stylistic line, because the most basic features of these works would be lost if one treated them—as so many have—in isolation from their social world. Without an awareness of the dialogizing background to which it is opposed, the style of first-line novels cannot be adequately understood. As we have observed, these novels presume, and depend upon, an awareness of social heteroglossia—indeed, on specific features of contemporaneous heteroglossia—not explicitly represented in the text. To see only the text is not to see the whole work. It is to misunderstand the genre's fundamental conventions and "philosophy of discourse." Just as one cannot understand the style of a double-voiced utterance if one perceives only a single voice within it, so one cannot understand novels of the first line unless one detects the palpable traces of presumed social languages.

As we have seen, novels of the second stylistic line make explicit, rather than implicit, use of social heteroglossia. For this reason, their dependence on their dialogizing background differs in significant ways from the dependence of first-line novels on their background. In second-line novels, much more information about social heteroglossia is provided in the text itself. To be sure, not all novelists of the second line are as explicit as Turgenev—who often comments in detail on the social implications of particular words, expressions, and kinds of pronunciation, and who often traces the changing evaluative aura of speech forms as they move from group to group, generation to generation, and year to year. But all second-line novels (by definition) offer enough examples of dialogized heteroglossia for readers aware of the issue to detect the complex uses to which heteroglossia may be put. Indeed, that is presumably one reason why such novels may serve as excellent documents of their times.

It might therefore seem that second-line novels are simply *less* dependent on their background than are first-line novels. That is true, in the sense that without an awareness of specific features of heteroglossia, the basic Galilean consciousness of second-line works is still readily visible. Nevertheless, novels of the second line do interact with their dialogizing background in crucial ways, some of which are different in *kind* from first-line interactions. Unless one understands the various relations of second-line novels to their background, a good deal of their meaning and potential will be lost.

Bakhtin describes two broad types of interaction. He calls the less important type "canonization" (not to be confused with what is now called canon formation). As we have seen, novelists of the second line orchestrate the language of particular professions or groups by combining them with the literary language or with the language of other professions and groups. But the linkage of a given expression with a particular group is not fixed: in the course of even a decade, a form that carries the aura of a provincialism or a jargon may become part of the general literary language; it may be "canonized." In that case, the author will no longer sense it as a previous author would have sensed it. Jargon for Jane Austen may be canonized for George Eliot.[11] But a reader from another time and culture, who has not lived through the change and whose sense of historical experience is "flattened," may find it difficult to detect the difference. A reader who does not have an intimate knowledge of the shifting dialogizing background may find it hard to tell what was canonized at a given time and, therefore, the kind of orchestration present in a given part of the work. Anyone who has tried to teach students to avoid colloquialisms or expressions marked as "merely current," but which the students take as unmarked expressions of the English language, will appreciate the sort of phenomenon Bakhtin has in mind. "The more distant the work to be analyzed is from contemporary consciousness, the more serious this difficulty becomes" (DiN, p. 418). Great care in interpretation must be taken because "it would be a gross mistake to ascribe to such [canonized] aspects [of language] an orchestrating function" (ibid.).

In some eras, the process of canonization takes place relatively slowly and in ways that can be easily traced. But the novel tends to flourish in times when canonization, decanonization, and shifts among jargons entirely outside the literary language take place rapidly and without leaving sufficient documentation for adequate reconstruction of the process. Nevertheless, Bakhtin adds, in spite of such difficulties, novels of the second line usually do not depend in *fundamental* ways on an intimate knowledge of such extratextual particulars. "For anyone who grasps the basic orchestrating languages and the basic lines of movement and play of intentions, canonization is no [major] obstacle" (DiN, p. 418).[12]

Bakhtin regards as much more important the second type of interaction between novels of the second stylistic line and their dialogizing background. Indeed, it raises problems central to the dynamics of literary history and to the nature of literary value generally. Bakhtin calls this type of interaction "reaccentuation." It occurs with all literary genres, but is especially important with novels inasmuch as the fundamental energy and tasks of novels are already a type of reaccentuation.

Reaccentuation changes the value, nature, and interrelation of voices visible in a genuinely "prosaic image" of a language or languages. Against a different background, double-voiced images can turn into single-voiced ones, or the reverse; comic or ironic intonations can alter in kind or degree; the dialogic angle at which voices interact may shift. A voice that was once a relatively inert parodied target may become active and offer powerful resistance to the parodying voice; its original meaning may "under changed conditions . . . emit bright new rays, burning away the reifying crust that had grown up around it and thus removing any real ground for a parodic accentuation, dimming or completely extinguishing such re-accentuation" (DiN, p. 419). Significant change is always a possibility for every true "prosaic image" (ibid.). Much as the number of possible relations among voices and languages of heteroglossia is indefinitely large, so are the number of possible reaccentuations.

The process of reaccentuation may at times impoverish a text. In Chapter Seven, we observed that current understanding of a text may serve to "modernize and distort" it; in the case of novels, distortion may result from silencing a complex play of voices or suppressing the "otherness" of other cultures and worldviews. But understanding may also be "creative" without being distorting. Great works contain great potentials that are really *in* them, and which the author has deliberately created, even though he is not aware of the specific meanings to which they may lead. For those new meanings to arise, the potentials of the text must enter into dialogic relations with other perspectives the author cannot predict or concretely imagine. This sort of understanding is not distorting because it serves to unlock potentials really there, and it enriches the text. Reaccentuation is an important vehicle for such creative understanding, and a principal one for novels.[13]

Not only do readers reaccentuate great works, so do other authors; for authors, after all, are also readers. One of the ways in which novelists create new images of language is by reaccentuating old ones. A figure (and his language) who once appeared only in comic images, in minor genres, or as a secondary character, may be "transferred" to a "higher plane"—by, let us say, being represented as suffering and unfortunate. For example, "the traditionally comic image of the miser helps to establish hegemony for the new image of the capitalist, which is then raised to the tragic image of Dombey" (DiN, p. 421).

In such ways, authors and readers activate the "intentional potentials" of a text or genre—the potentials that are intentionally "embedded" in it (ibid.). Thanks to these potentials, great works "have proved capable of uncovering in each new era and against ever new dialogizing backgrounds ever new aspects of meaning; their semantic content literally continues to grow, to further create out of itself" (ibid.).

Radical relativism and a sense of history are often perceived as closely allied, if not absolutely identical. Positing timeless, inherent, and inert value or meaning as the only existing position, theorists sometimes offer the polar opposite as the only conceivable alternative and then claim for that opposite the honorific title "historical." In Bakhtin's view, such an equation of radical relativism with a sense of historicity is extraordinarily naive, no less so than its equally untenable opposite. It is equivalent to equating "modernization and distortion" with "creative understanding" and it renders impossible a comprehension of the complex ways history works. A rich sense of history cannot proceed without a recognition of potentials that have developed over "great time" and that make possible genuinely new developments; potentials make the process of historical life one of genuine becoming. For a radical relativist, history seems to teach only one Heraclitian lesson, that everything changes. But since that lesson is universal, and applies a priori to every change in every period, it makes a knowledge of particular cultural and historical facts superfluous. Under the aegis of "history," views that are at base antihistorical gain ascendancy.

The evaluation and meaning of works change for countless reasons, but one of them is the activation through dialogue of potentials present in the works themselves. To say that value is entirely "relative" is to overlook the difference between works that do and do not have great potential. True, to detect such potentials is supremely difficult and is ultimately possible only over great time; but to say as much is not to say that the potentials are not truly there. It is, rather, to approach a sense of historicity not reducible to system and not dissolvable in abstractions, whether absolutist or relativist. Value is not just "economic" but also profoundly "historical." As Bakhtin observes in the final sentence of "Discourse in the Novel": "For, we repeat, great novelistic images continue to grow and develop even after the moment of their creation; they are capable of being creatively transformed in different eras, far distant from the day and hour of their original birth" (DiN, p. 422).

9

The Chronotope

Bakhtin viewed literary genres as specific modes of thought. Intellectual historians typically focus on products of "abstract cognition" but, in so doing, they overlook the fact that intellectual activity may take a quite different form, namely, "artistic thinking."

Literary genres do not simply "transcribe" into artistic form discoveries made elsewhere; they themselves make discoveries. Some of these discoveries have anticipated insights of later philosophers, some have not yet been made by abstract cognition, and some may not be "transcribable" at all into abstract terms without significant loss. For example, if ethics is (as Bakhtin contends) a matter of particular, concrete cases, and not of rules to be instantiated, then novels may be the richest form of ethical thought—and, perhaps, the only one to retain to a significant degree the "eventness" of events and the "oughtness" of obligation. Various literary genres may be best at understanding different realms of experience.

"Forms of Time and of the Chronotope" argues that the richest discoveries about the relation of people and events to time and space have been made by narrative genres of literature. The great advantage of narrative genres is to be found in their "density and concreteness" (FTC, p. 250). If we are to grasp the variety of ways in which the relation of people to their world may be understood, we need to examine the many concrete and highly detailed possibilities that literary genres have worked out. Bakhtin calls these concrete possibilities, each of which may be taken as defining the "living impulse" and "form-shaping ideology" of a genre, a *chronotope*. Not surprisingly for Bakhtin, novels turn out to have the richest chronotope and therefore to be arguably the greatest contribution of Western thought.

The Chronotope and Time-Space: Kant and Einstein

What precisely is a chronotope? Characteristically for Bakhtin, he never offers a concise definition. Rather, he first offers some initial comments, and then repeatedly alternates concrete examples with further generalizations. In the course of this exposition, the term turns out to have several related meanings.

In its primary sense, a chronotope is a way of understanding experience; it is a specific form-shaping ideology for understanding the nature of events and actions. In this sense, the chronotope essay may be understood as a further development of Bakhtin's early concern with the "act" (in "Toward a Philosophy of the Act"). Actions are necessarily performed in a specific context; chronotopes differ by the ways in which they understand context and the relation of actions and events to it.

All contexts are shaped fundamentally by the kind of time and space that operate within them. Kant, of course, argued long ago that time and space are indispensable forms of cognition, and Bakhtin explicitly endorses this view. But he differs from Kant by stressing that in chronotopic analysis, time and space are regarded "not as 'transcendental' but as forms of the most immediate reality" (FTC, p. 85, n. 2). Bakhtin's crucial point is that time and space vary in *qualities*; different social activities and representations of those activities presume different kinds of time and space. Time and space are therefore not just neutral "mathematical" abstractions. Or, to be more precise, the concept of time and space as mathematical abstractions itself defines a specific chronotope that differs from other chronotopes.

Bakhtin mentions Einstein in order to elucidate a key defining feature of chronotopes, a feature he has tried to capture in the neologism itself. "We will give the name *chronotope* (literally, 'time space') to the intrinsic connectedness of temporal and spatial relationships that are artistically expressed in literature. This term is used in mathematics and was introduced as part of the theory of relativity (Einstein)" (FTC, p. 84; trans. emended). Bakhtin explains that he is not concerned with the specific meaning the term time-space (or space-time) has in physics; "we are borrowing it for literary criticism almost as a metaphor (almost, but not entirely)" (ibid.). By this cryptic comment Bakhtin appears to mean that the relation of "chronotope" to Einsteinian "time-space" is something weaker than identity, but stronger than mere metaphor or analogy.[1]

It would be a mistake to assume that everything pertaining to the theory of relativity applies to the chronotope. But the comparison is important for at least five reasons, present both explicitly and implicitly, in Bakhtin's subsequent argument:

1. In the chronotope, as in Einsteinian physics, time and space are not separate but are rather "intrinsically interconnected"; each

chronotope specifies a "*fused*" sense of time and space. Time and space constitute a whole, and can be separated out only in an act of abstract analysis, which runs the risk of distorting the nature of the chronotope under discussion. What precisely this "fusion" means in concrete instances, we shall examine presently.

2. The very formulation of Einstein's theory, as Bakhtin understands it, demonstrates that there are a *variety* of senses of time and space available. In light of Einstein's theory, Newtonian time-space is revealed not as absolute but as one of many possible time-spaces; so, indeed, is Einsteinian time-space. Other time-spaces may govern particular spheres, such as the interaction of subatomic particles. The discovery of a second time-space must change our whole orientation; we can no longer look at time-space "naively," but must entertain the possibility, or consider the necessity, of choosing among available ones or discovering new ones. This line of thought in effect recapitulates Lobachevsky's reasons for formulating a non-Euclidian geometry. (In opposition to Kantians—who thought that even though Euclid's geometry could not be proven correct, we cannot conceive of space in any other way—Lobachevsky offered an alternative geometry to prove that various conceptualizations of space are indeed possible. Which geometry is to be chosen on a particular occasion cannot be naively presumed in advance.) For Bakhtin, what is true of geometries of space is also true of chronotopes. We live, so to speak, in a universe of "heterochrony" (*raznovremennost'*). Or to adapt another of Bakhtin's phrases, the Einsteinian model invites us to develop a "Galilean chronotope consciousness."

3. Different aspects or orders of the universe cannot be supposed to operate with the same chronotope. To begin with, biological organisms may have their own special rhythms that are not identical with astronomical ones or with each other. Bakhtin notes that "in the summer of 1925, the author of these lines attended a lecture by A. A. Ukhtomsky on the chronotope in biology" (FTC, p. 84, n. 1).[2] Bodies must organize their own external activities and internal processes in time and space. Organisms operate by means of, and must coordinate, a variety of rhythms differing from each other and from those of other organisms. Furthermore, different social activities are also defined by various kinds of fused time and space: the rhythms and spacial organization of the assembly line, agricultural labor, sexual intercourse, and parlor conversation differ markedly. Although Bakhtin focuses on the chronotope in literature, he means us to understand that the concept has much broader applicability and does not define a strictly literary phenom-

enon. To use his own terms, we may say that he reveals the concealed "potential" of the Einsteinian concept of space-time.

4. It follows from the variety and multiplicity of chronotopes that they may change over time in response to current needs; they are in fact, and in potential, *historical*. This is apparently part of what Bakhtin means by subtitling his study "Notes Toward a Historical Poetics." Moreover, in society and in individual life, chronotopes also compete with each other. As senses of the world, they may implicitly dispute (or agree with) each other. That is, the relation of chronotopes to each other may be *dialogic*.

5. Chronotopes are not so much visibly *present* in activity as they are the *ground* for activity. To use one of Bakhtin's favorite distinctions, they are not represented in the world, they are "the ground essential for the . . . representability of events" (FTC, p. 250). They are not contained in plots, but they make typical plots possible. It is in this sense that "the chronotope is the place where the knots of narrative are tied and untied. It can be said without qualification that to them [chronotopes] belongs the meaning that shapes narrative" (ibid.). Because for Bakhtin all meaning entails evaluation, chronotopes also define parameters of value.

Chronotopic Questions and Possibilities

In culture and in literature, the concept of the chronotope immediately raises a number of problems to which every specific well-developed chrontope offers answers: What is the relation of human action to its context? Is the context mere background, or does it actively shape events? Are actions dependent to a significant degree on where or when they occur? Is a particular space "replaceable"? Are the same kinds of actions plausible or possible in different historical and social contexts (the problem of anachronism and "anatopism")? Would it in principle be possible for the order of incidents to be different, for events to be "reversible" or "repeatable" (as Bakhtin puts it)? What kind of initiative do people have: are they beings to whom events simply happen, or do they exercise choice and control, and if so, how much and of what kind? Is time open, with multiple possibilities, or is it scripted in advance? Depending on the degree and kind of initiative people have, what kind of ethical responsibility obliges them? What kind of creativity is possible? Does social context itself change, and if so, in what ways? Are time and space shaped by the events that take place in them? Do personal identity and character change in response to events or are they fixed?

If they change, how, when, and to what degree? What role, if any, do particular sets of social and historical factors play in shaping personal identity?

For that matter, is there a concept of the "personal" or private as opposed to the public? Are people understood as entirely "exterior" or is there real interiority, and if so what kind? If that interiority is socially and historically shaped, does that shaping happen differently from the shaping of public selves and roles? Is there any everyday realm distinct from the historical or from everyday realms of other people or groups? If such distinct realms exist, how do they interact with each other? How does the past impinge on the present, and what is the relation of the present to possible futures? Is the greatest value placed on the past, the present, the immediate future, or the distant future?

Each of these questions may be asked about specific chronotopes; the solutions are to be found not in explicit answers enunciated in given works, but in the ways in which the genres and works represent events. Not the embedded essays in *War and Peace* but the very sense of time shaping its narrative determines its chronotope, and determines it more profoundly than the essays ever could. That sense of time and space—that chronotope—is itself the answer to the questions we have mentioned. As critics, we must probe not just representations but also the very ground for representing.

Bakhtin also raises a series of questions concerning the relation of the chronotopes representing the world described in the work to the chronotopes of the author and reader, or, more accurately, of authoring and reading.

It should be evident from the kinds of questions Bakhtin wants to ask about particular chronotopes that each genre offers a different "image of a person" (*obraz cheloveka*, sometimes translated as "the image of man"). Each genre also suggests a different concept of history, society, and other categories essential to an understanding of culture. We may appreciate why the study of chronotopes has such broad implications.

In short, Bakhtin understands narrative as shaped by a specific way of conceptualizing the possibilities of action. It is as if each genre possesses a specific *field* that determines the *parameters* of events even though the field does not uniquely specify particular events. To study the field is to study the chronotope; and no study of the particular plot of a given work exploits the work's richness unless it illuminates the chronotope as well as the particular sequence of events.

So important are chronotopes that we all intuitively recognize what Bakhtin has in mind. We know, for instance, that actions that would be highly implausible, if not impossible, in a nineteenth-century realist novel may be fully expected in a chivalric romance or other adventure tale; and we tend to shape our expectations to given works based on a sense of what is plausible in a work of that kind. We know as well some of the parameters of value and meaning in works of a given type; indeed, that is one reason why people tend to prefer some genres (not just some works) to others.

To sense a genre's field of possibilities is part of what reading is all about (and part of what criticism should be about). In each chronotope, "time, as it were, thickens, takes on flesh, becomes artistically visible; likewise, space becomes charged and responsive to the movement of time, plot and history" (FTC, p. 84). In literature and culture generally, time is always in one way or another *historical* and *biographical*, and space is always *social*; thus, the chronotope in culture could be defined as a "field of historical, biographical, and social relations." Because our lives unfold in a variety of such fields, an understanding of their characteristics is important to our lives as individuals and social beings.

At any given time, literature offers a multiplicity of chronotopes. Taken as a whole, literature is a heterochronous. A great number of literary genres are available for conceptualizing the "image of a person," the processes of history, and the dynamics of society. Familiarity with a variety of genres therefore offers a rich store of choices for understanding particular aspects of experience. In any given instance, some chronotopes may be more adequate than others.

Genres (and their attendant chronotopes) constitute a part of a particular society's contribution to understanding actions and events. When they are new or vital, specific genres may be highly "productive" in shaping thought or experience. But genres also continue "to exist stubbornly" even after they have exhausted their capacity to generate new insights, "up to and beyond the point where they had lost any meaning that was productive in actuality or adequate to later historical situations" (FTC, p. 85). Adventure time now seems a rather primitive way to understand human action, but it continues to thrive in dime-store novels, comic strips, in movies like *Rambo* or *Raiders of the Lost Ark*, and in countless television programs. It is of course an important sociological or psychological question why this ancient chronotope still has such great appeal, but whatever the reason, the chronotope does not seem to be especially productive of new insights about the nature of actions and events. Any culture will presumably have numerous survivals of this sort. "This explains the simultaneous existence in literature of phenomena taken from widely separate periods of time, which greatly complicates the historico-literary process" (ibid.).

Chronotopic Thinking and the Novel

None of what has been said so far indicates that some chronotopes are intrinsically superior to others. But although Bakhtin's description of chronotopes does not necessarily entail a qualitative ranking, he still wants to claim that some genres do a better job than others of "assimilating real historical time and space" and "actual historical persons in such a time and space" (FTC, p. 84). As Bakhtin views the matter, the understanding of actions and "the image of a person" in Greek romances is not only different from, but also less profound than, the understanding of actions and people in novels like *Middlemarch*. It would be entirely possible to accept the utility of the concept of chronotope without accepting his argument that some genres come closer to an accurate understanding of the "actual historical chronotope" than others. But for Bakhtin, the evaluation of chronotopes was important to his project of understanding what historicity really is, and for his goal of defining the world in such a way that responsibility and creativity could be real. Those concerns may in fact have been the main reasons he developed the concept of the chronotope in the first place, much as he may have chosen to celebrate the novel because it allowed him to experiment with his three global concepts.

Indeed, the chronotope essay and related writings were part of Bakhtin's great project of his third period to elucidate and exalt the genre of the novel. In "Discourse and the Novel" and "The Prehistory of Novelistic Discourse," Bakhtin described the novel as having the most complex sense of language, an argument suggesting that novels also have the richest sense of the world. What is true of languages of heteroglossia is also true of chronotopes. Having the most complex sense of chronotopicity, the novel offers our most profound image of people, actions, events, history, and society.

In effect, the discourse and chronotope theories of the novel are two aspects of the same theory. The form-shaping ideology of the novel includes both a view of languages of heteroglossia and a way of understanding time and space. To be sure, the choice of examples and the shape of the genre's history are not identical in "Discourse" and in the chronotope essay. But these differences, which never reach the point of contradiction, are what one might expect from the examination of the same class according to different criteria. So close are these two essays in spirit and basic conceptualization that in several places they overlap to a considerable degree—for example, in the discussions of the "testing" plot in some novels, of the role of the clown, fool, and rogue in the genre's development, and of competition among languages or chronotopes. Novels that "test" the image of a person also test his language; fools defamiliarize our sense of social context as they defamiliarize the falsities of official languages; Rabelais plays a decisive role in developing the modern novelistic chronotope as he does in developing the novelistic sense of language.

As we discuss in the next chapter, however, Rabelais is described quite differently in the chronotope essay from the way he is in *Rabelais and His World*. This dissimilarity reflects many others between Bakhtin's period IIIa and IIIb, especially Bakhtin's different theories of the novel. Whereas the discourse and chronotope theories are almost fully complementary, the carnival theory is only occasionally complementary with, and more often contradictory to, the other two.

A curious aspect of the chronotope essay is worth stressing at the outset: although Bakhtin's main impulse is evidently to celebrate the novel since the eighteenth century, he focuses almost entirely on much earlier works. We learn what the novel is by examining works that contrast with it or are deficient in comparison with it. Bakhtin traces the development of the literary chronotope from the Greek romance to Rabelais, but never reaches the genre that best assimilates "real historical time." To be sure, the essay often digresses to discuss some features of nineteenth-century novels clearly related to the chronotopes he discusses in detail, but basically those works are present in his essay's "dialogizing background." One can therefore construct Bakhtin's view of the novel by a cautious process of inverting the features of other genres that Bakhtin regards as most naive.

At times, the chronotope essay reads as if it were written intermittently, its author occasionally running out of steam or leaping over topics and periods less interesting to him. And, as we have noted, the essay's history of the assimilation of history ends, for no discernible reason, with Rabelais. As if to fill in some of the gaps, Bakhtin in two other essays offered further observations clearly derived from the same complex of ideas: "The *Bildungsroman* and Its Significance in the History of Realism (Toward a Historical Typology of the Novel)," apparently a surviving fragment of a complete book on the novel of education,[3] and portions of "Epic and Novel."

Chronotopic Motifs

In the course of his chronotope essay, and especially in its "Concluding Remarks" appended in 1973, Bakhtin distinguishes between the chronotopes of whole genres and what he calls "chronotopic motifs." The latter term may perhaps best be understood by analogy with Bakhtin's theory of language. When a word figures frequently in utterances belonging to a specific genre, the values and meanings of that genre will somehow be sensed when the word is spoken. The word acquires a "stylistic aura," and that aura is likely to remain even when the word is used in a different genre; the word in effect "remembers" its past. Strictly speaking, the stylistic aura belongs *not* "to the word of language as such but to that genre in which the given word usually functions. It is an echo of the generic whole that resounds in the word" (SG, pp. 87–88). Something similar happens with typical scenes or events in literary genres.

A particular sort of event, or a particular sort of place that usually serves as the locale for such an event, acquires a certain chronotopic aura, which is in fact the "echo of the generic whole" in which the given event typically appears. Chases and rescues in the nick of time, for example, are highly characteristic of adventure narratives, and the very possibility of a chase or last-minute rescue may suggest adventure time. Idyllic rural settings may adumbrate the sort of events typical of pastoral. Salons may intimate the tone of dialogues or social climbing typical for them in certain kinds of narrative. When these events or locales are used in other genres, they may "remember" their past and carry the aura of the earlier genre into the new one; indeed, they may be incorporated for this very reason. A chronotopic motif is, to use one of Bakhtin's terms, a sort of "congealed event," and a chronotopic place is a sort of condensed reminder of the kind of time and space that typically functions there. Because chronotopes also govern nonliterary life, chronotopic motifs may be drawn from extraliterary sources as well.

Bakhtin offers a few intriguing examples of chronotopic motifs and the aura they carry with them. As it came to be used in literature, for example in Gothic fiction, the castle became not just a kind of building, but an image, "saturated through and through" with a specific sort of time and a special sense of history (FTC, pp. 245–46). Everything about the castle carries "the traces of centuries and generations" (FTC, p. 246), visible, for instance, in its architecture, portrait gallery, weapons, furnishings, and archives, all of which suggest "particular human relationships involving dynastic succession and the transfer of hereditary rights" (ibid.). Legends and traditions seem to "animate" each corner of the castle and its environs, and to suggest the kind of narratives developed in Gothic fiction. (Jane Austen's parody of Gothic fiction, *Northanger Abbey*, of course, focuses on the aura of different parts of the castle.) Bakhtin also stresses the sort of time suggested by "the chronotope of the threshold" and related areas (stairways, front halls, corridors), exploited so brilliantly by Dostoevsky. The threshold's aura, evidently acquired in life as well as in literature, is one of "*crisis* and *break* in life" (DiN, p. 248); this is where decisions are made or indecisiveness becomes crucial, where boldness or the fear of "stepping over the threshold" take on profound meanings. The threshold seems to have crisis time attached to it. By contrast with time in idyllic motifs, for example, "in this chronotope, time is essentially instantaneous; it is as if it has no duration" (FTC, p. 248). Bakhtin is thinking, for instance, of Razumikhin's realization in the corridor that Raskolnikov is a murderer. He may also have in mind Prince Myshkin's epileptic fit on a staircase; Myshkin meditates on how his fits speed up time to the point where he can understand the promise of the Apocalypse that "there shall be time no longer" (Dostoevsky, *Idiot*, pt. 2, ch. 4, p. 214).

Some chronotopic motifs have remained remarkably constant in literary history, and have retained the power to evoke a particular kind of event. Others have changed greatly over time, such as "the chronotope of the road" (FTC, pp. 243–45). In reading Bakhtin, it is useful to keep in mind that the word *chronotope* is in such cases used in a different sense than it is in phrases such as "the chronotope of the Greek romance." A generic chronotope is not a congealed event, but a whole complex of concepts, an integral way of understanding experience, and a ground for visualizing and representing human life.[4]

Time and Space in the Greek Romance

> The adventure chronotope is thus characterized by a *technical, abstract connection between space and time,* by the *reversibility* of moments in a temporal sequence, and by their *interchangeability* in space.   —FTC, p. 100

The chronotope essay proceeds chronologically but does not treat in detail the rise of specific chronotopes or the causal factors shaping their sequential development. The essay is therefore best conceived not as a history but as a series of illustrations in chronological order. The central examples are drawn from the history of prose fiction, but numerous digressions (occasionally quite lengthy) offer contrasts with chronotopes from other genres, such as epic, tragedy, mythology, and forms of folklore.

Bakhtin contends that the ancient novel developed three major chronotopes. As points of contrast, he also mentions some minor types, such as the "ancient novel of travel." For each of his major examples, he briefly indicates some forms in later European literature that drew upon the ancient chronotopes.

His first, best-known, and probably clearest example is the Greek romance or, as he also calls it, "the ancient novel of ordeal" (FTC, p. 86). He has in mind "the so-called 'Greek' or 'Sophist' novels written between the second and sixth centuries A.D." (ibid.), including such works as the *Aethiopica* of Heliodorus, and Longus's *Daphnis and Chloë*. His central illustration is Achilles Tatius's *Leucippe and Clitophon*.

These works display remarkably similar plots, so similar that it is easy to construct a composite plot schema: A boy and girl of marriageable age, exceptional beauty, and perfect chastity meet unexpectedly and are overcome by a sudden and instantaneous passion, but cannot marry. The lovers are parted, and for the major part of the novel, they seek one another across vast expanses of space, overcome obstacles, lose and find each other, suffer shipwrecks, captivity, slavery, and prison, almost lose their lives, barely but successfully preserve their chastity, are presumed dead but turn up miraculously alive, are accused and tried falsely. Unexpected meetings, prophecy, and dreams play an important role. At last they are reunited and married in a happy ending.

Bakhtin observes that all the elements of this plot were old, but that the whole chronotope was nevertheless more than the sum of its inherited motifs. Old elements were fused into a new conceptualization of time and space; "they entered into a new and unique artistic unity, one, moreover, that was far from being a mere mechanical mélange of various ancient genres" (FTC, p. 104). Bakhtin describes this new chronotope as "an alien world in adventure-time" (FTC, p. 89). Because for Bakhtin time is generally more important than space in characterizing a chronotope, he begins by elucidating the nature of adventure time.

The crucial point to note about the adventures in a Greek romance is that they "leave no trace" (FTC, p. 94). They affect nothing, and, for all the difference they make, might just as well not have happened. If there had been no obstacles, if the hero and heroine had married as soon as they fell in love, nothing would have been any different for them in the end, although, of course, we would not have a novel. Hero and heroine do not change, mature, grow, or even age biologically as a result of their adventures. (This unreal conception of the effect of experience and time in traditional romance is precisely what is parodied in Voltaire's *Candide* and Pushkin's *Ruslan and Lyudmila*. When Candide and Cunegonde are reunited at the end of their adventures, she *has* aged and turned into a shrew; in Pushkin's poem, a "hero" is similarly shocked at the change in the object of his love. He asks in amazement, Has it been long since I left you? "Exactly forty years/ Was the maiden's fateful answer" [*Rovno sorok let/ Byl devy rokovoi otvet*; Pushkin, *Ruslan*, p. 19]).[5]

The entire action of the Greek romance, in other words, takes place in "an extratemporal hiatus between the two moments in biographical time" (FTC, p. 90). It is a time of "pure digression" rather than of "real duration," that is, the time is opposite to what we find in the nineteenth-century novel, where experience changes people. Because events in the Greek romance do not change the hero and heroine, their reunion is certain to be happy no matter when they are reunited. In other words, there is no reason in the internal logic of the genre why the string of adventures could not be longer or shorter than they are in a given work. In the seventeenth century, works written in this chronotope stretched over many volumes; they were ten to fifteen times longer than Greek romances, and in principle "there are no internal limits to this increase" (FTC, p. 94).

Moreover, there is no reason why the adventures in a given work could not have happened in a different order, inasmuch as none of them change anything in the protagonists and their world. As Bakhtin puts the point, time in the Greek romance is "reversible." In this respect, too, the ancient novel of ordeal differs markedly from the modern novel of "becoming," in which experience does change the protagonists. Anna Karenina and Kitty Shcherbatskaya are not the same people on page 500 as they are on page 50, and would not behave similarly in similar circumstances; they learn from their experiences, and this learning is, in fact, central to the main theme of the novel.

Within each adventure of a Greek romance, however, time is of great importance. Measured "technically" within each series of incidents, adventure time is "highly intensified but undifferentiated" (FTC, p. 90). By "intensified," Bakhtin means that a moment earlier or later tends to make a decisive difference; rescues occur at the last possible moment, a passing procession saves the hero from torture, a fortuitous circumstance unexpectedly saves the heroine's chastity just when it seems certain to be lost. Things happen in the nick of time, and we may say that adventure time is furrowed with nicks.

Thus, key concepts and phrases are *suddenly* and *at that moment.* This is a world in which simultaneity, random contingency, miraculous coincidence, and sheer chance play a key role. Wars happen unexpectedly and without apparent cause at crucial moments; storms come from nowhere to cause fatal shipwrecks. The time of the Greek romance is therefore one of "adventuristic 'chance time,'" (FTC, p. 94), a time in which irrational forces erupt into human life to change its course. In older novels, such forces may take the form of gods, demons, or sorcerers; in later works, villains who "lie in wait" or "bide their time" may play a similar role. These forces create "a veritable downpour of 'suddenlys' and 'at just that moments'" (FTC, p. 95).

Actual historical context and historical time are entirely irrelevant to these adventures, which is what Bakhtin means when he says that adventure time is "undifferentiated." If a war should break out, it does not matter which war or why; and nothing that happens to the hero and heroine in any way shapes or reflects the historical process, which remains entirely abstract, just another source of random disruptive forces. That is one reason why adventuristic plots are so easy to adapt by authors of different countries and eras and so difficult to date accurately. By contrast, it would be exceedingly difficult to transform *Middlemarch* into a Russian novel or to transpose it into the eighteenth century. In the great nineteenth-century novels, character and personality are shaped in important ways by the specifics of the social and historical world in which people live; and the sort of actions that are possible or the opportunities that are available (for example, to women) are dependent to great degrees on the values, laws, and customs of a specific and changing locale. Such dependency is absent from adventure time.

As time is reversible in the Greek romance, space is "interchangeable." For a shipwreck, one needs a sea, but which sea makes no difference. For chance meetings and miraculous occurrences, one needs an alien country, but any alien country will do. In the realist novel, London is not simply English for Paris, or Petersburg for Moscow; but in the Greek romance, what happens in Ethiopia could just as easily have happened in Persia.

What is required in the Greek romance is an *"abstract expanse of space."* No particular space is required, but a great deal of it is necessary—for pursuit, separation, and various obstacles. The adventures may take place across a vast geographical expanse. The only place they may not take place is in the hero or heroine's home, which is another reason why captivity, shipwreck, and abduction are so important. Indeed, the hero and heroine usually come from different places or countries (one does not fall in love with the boy or girl next door). It is necessary to break the links to any particular place so that the world may be sufficiently alien.

Why is an alien world necessary? Because if adventures took place at home, a network of specific habits, customs, and relations would limit the power of pure chance. "Every concretization, of even the most simple and everyday variety, would introduce its own *rule-generating force*, . . . its own *inevitable ties* to human life and to the time specific to that life" (FTC, p. 100). If one were to depict one's native world, some such concretization would be almost unavoidable. "A depiction of one's own world—no matter where or what it is—could never achieve that degree of abstractness necessary for Greek adventure-time" (FTC, p. 101).

Thus, the adventures take place in countries that the hero and heroine experience for the first time. Those countries are therefore not simply foreign, but also unknown and "indefinite" (ibid.). Crucially, though, they are not *exotic*, for exoticism implies a constant measurement against a native standard, which is therefore an active and evaluating force. To describe something as exotic, something else must be ordinary and familiar, at least by implication; but Greek adventure time functions in a world where everything human is alien. Exoticism, such as appears in the ancient novel of travel, would also hamper the free play of chance. For the Greek romance, "everything is foreign, including the heroes' homeland" (ibid.). To be sure, there must be some standard of normality or else exceptional occurrences could not be marked as such, but the degree of specificity of the normal is "so minuscule that scholarship has been almost entirely unable to devise a method for analyzing in these romances the presumed 'real world' and 'real era' of their authors" (ibid.). That, too, could hardly be said of George Eliot's *Romola* or Dmitri Merezhkovsky's novel about Leonardo da Vinci, which strongly bear the stamp of their English and Russian origins.

Greek romances do contain descriptions of the foreign countries in which adventures take place, but these descriptions do not really serve to concretize or specify those countries. They describe neither the texture of daily life nor the country as a whole; rather, they focus on wonders and unique occurrences, detached from everything. Instead of a matrix of human relationships, we are given natural wonders, strange animals, "some strange isolated quirk, connected to nothing" (FTC, p. 102). Such rarities are really made of the same material as the adventures; they are, as Bakhtin observes, "congealed 'suddenlys'" (ibid.).

The Greek Romance: The Image of a Person and the Idea of Testing

By now it should be clear that the image of a person in a Greek romance is necessarily different from the image of a person in a nineteenth-century novel (or other genres). For one thing, the role of fate and chance in Greek romances ensures that people lack initiative; good and bad things happen *to* them, for it is fate, the gods, or some other nonhuman force that is in control. The protagonists may *happen* to be abducted, or to win a kingdom. Individuals are "completely *passive*" (FTC, p. 105), and their actions "are reduced to *enforced movement through space* (escape, persecution, quests); that is, to a change in spatial location" (ibid.).

Because characters cannot shape events, what they basically do is *endure*. In such a world, calculation and planning can do nothing to thwart the blind power of fate and chance; and so instead of forethought, the novel depicts oracular predictions, omens, and prophetic dreams. "Fate and the gods hold all the initiative in their hands, and they merely inform people of their will" (FTC, p. 95). They do so not in order to warn people of some disaster that might be avoided, but, as Clitophon observes in Achilles Tatius's romance, simply so that the hero and heroine may endure their sufferings more easily.

In the subsequent development of the European novel, Greek adventure time often reappears, and when it does, initiative "is handed over to chance . . . either as an impersonal, anonymous force in the novel or as fate, as divine foresight, as romantic 'villains' or romantic 'secret benefactors.' Examples of the latter one can still find in Walter Scott's historical novels" (ibid.). Even if a novel is constructed only partially in Greek adventure time, the "accompanying effects" of that time may play an important role.

The basic idea governing such plots is *testing*. The hero and heroine have a fixed identity, which nothing can change. As we have seen, real growth and "becoming" are absent from the Greek romance. "This distinctive sameness with oneself is the organizing center of the image of a person in the Greek romance" (FTC, p. 105).[6] Sufferings and dangers are conceived as trials of the hero's and heroine's identity, especially of their fidelity and chastity to each other; and they pass the test. (Some modern readers may object that a test one always passes is no test at all.) The novel as a whole, and each adventure in it, *affirms* who the hero and heroine are. The plot is a sort of judicial proceeding verifying innocence; and indeed judicially shaped rhetoric of the time is used in Greek romances and was clearly important in developing their ethos. The more severe the test, the greater the proof of the protagonists' integrity. Hero and heroine are and remain whole. "The hammer of events shatters nothing and forges nothing—it merely tests the durability of an already finished product" (FTC, p. 107).

The idea of testing had immense influence on the subsequent development of European narrative. In both "Discourse in the Novel" and "Forms of Time and of the Chronotope," Bakhtin digresses to enumerate a few of the important developments of this organizing idea. He indicates, first of all, that pure suspense can never be the basis for an artistic genre "for the very good reason that to be suspenseful there must be matters of substance to engage" (ibid.). Something human must be at stake, and suspense is always tied, at least to some degree, to a sense of identity and to qualities that are tested. To be sure, there are adventure novels that reduce "the potential of the novel as a genre to a minimum, but nevertheless a naked plot, naked adventure cannot in itself ever be the organizing force in a novel" (DiN, p. 390). We can always discover at least "the traces of some idea that had organized it earlier, some idea that had structured the body of the given plot and had animated it, as if it were its soul, but that in pure adventure novels has lost its ideological force, so that the idea continues to flicker but only feebly" (ibid.).

Differences in kind, as well as in the degree of forcefulness, of the quality undergoing a test may also be detected in the history of the novel. The vast variety of tests in the European novel is hardly surprising, inasmuch as "the idea of testing the hero . . . may very well be the most fundamental organizing idea of the novel" (DiN, p. 388). Highly "malleable" (FTC, p. 107), this "compositional idea" (ibid.) is present, for example, in Christian hagiography and the literature of martyrdom; in the chivalric romance in verse (which unites the test of lovers' fidelity with the test of Christian devotion); in the baroque novel, which tests the hero's "irreproachability" (ibid.), and in many other forms.

After the baroque, "the organizational importance of the trial diminishes sharply" (ibid.), but in no sense does it die out completely. Combined with other organizing ideas, or subservient to them, it "is retained as one of the organizing ideas of the novel in all subsequent eras" (ibid.). At times it leads to "negative results" (ibid.) as the hero fails the test. Among the later variants of this idea, Bakhtin mentions trials of the hero's "chosenness" or genius, for example, tests of the Napoleonic parvenu in French novels (FTC, pp. 107–8); tests of immoralists, moral reformers, Nietzscheans, and emancipated women; in Russia, tests of the intellectual's fitness for life (novels about the "superfluous man"); and tests of the hero's "biological worth" (in Zola). Extremely complex adaptations of the idea of testing structure Dostoevsky's novels, which "are all sharply etched novels of trial" (DiN, p. 391). Nevertheless, in the great nineteenth-century novels, a new element has been introduced, which changes the very concept of the test, that is, adapts its traditional forms and motifs to a new image of a person.

That new element is the idea of *becoming*. Novels of pure testing presuppose either a stable identity (as in the Greek romance) or, in other variants, an identity that undergoes a single crisis of rebirth. What these novels do not contain is the concept of true development, by which Bakhtin means "becoming, a person's *gradual* formation" (DiN, p. 392). In traditional novels of testing, the hero displays unchanging "inert nobility" (ibid.), whereas in the nineteenth century, major novels show a hero *continually* growing with experience, changing in response to external events and his or her own decisions. Choices not only *reveal* the hero and heroine, but *make* them.

Novels of becoming often use the resources provided by novels of testing for new purposes. Essentially, what happens is that events *test* the hero, and in response, the hero learns, acquires experience, and *becomes*. The two ideas are already present in equal proportion in Fielding and Sterne; in "the continental type of *Bildungsroman* . . . the testing of an idealist or an eccentric does not result in naked exposure of them as such in the novel, but rather facilitates their becoming more like real thinking people; in these novels, life is not a touchstone, but a school" (DiN, p. 393).

To return to the image of a person in Greek romance: the genre contrasts with all other genres of ancient literature in that it represents people entirely as individuals and as "private persons" (FTC, p. 108). This image of a person "corresponds to the *abstract-alien world* of the Greek romance: in such a world, a person can *only* function as an isolated and private individual, deprived of any organic connection" (ibid.) with his native land, his social network, or even his family. "He is a solitary person, lost in an alien world" (ibid.). He has no mission; he lives in "privacy and isolation" (ibid.).

But profound ways of describing interiority do not accompany this focus on privacy. In general, Bakhtin observes, "the ancient world did not succeed in generating forms and unities that were adequate to the private individual and his life" (FTC, p. 110), except, to some extent, "in the minor, lyrico-epic genres and in the small everyday genres, the comedy and novella of common life" (ibid.). In the major genres of antiquity, the focus was on the public; private life, if it figured at all, "was only externally and inadequately arrayed, and, therefore, in forms that were inorganic and formalistic, either public and bureaucratic or public and rhetorical" (ibid.). We might say: it is as if *Anna Karenina* had to be told entirely by Karenin or *Middlemarch* by Casaubon.

Thus, a curious contradiction shapes the image of a person in the Greek romance. On the one hand, people are private, isolated individuals; all public events have meaning "only insofar as they relate to private fates" (FTC, p. 109), for example, "at the level of the heroes' love activities" (ibid.). Public life is interpreted in terms of private life, and not the reverse. On the other hand, the depiction of private life takes place in highly rhetorical and juridical forms of public accounting (as opposed, let us say, to intimate confession). That, indeed, is one reason why legal procedures often play so important a role in these novels. Bakhtin observes that a curious weakness of Greek romance is that the unity of private individuals can only be a "public and rhetorical unity" (FTC, p. 110).

He therefore concludes that the chronotope of the Greek romance is "the most abstract of all novelistic chronotopes" and also "the most static. . . . As a result of the action described in the novel, nothing in its world is destroyed, remade, changed or created anew. What we get is a mere affirmation of the identity between what had been at the beginning and what is at the end. Adventure-time leaves no trace" (ibid.). Of course, in the great realist novels, people do have genuine potential, and experience does leave its trace. Throughout his discussion, Bakhtin seems to be not

only describing the chronotope of the Greek romance but to be eu-
logizing its implicit opposite, the nineteenth-century novel.

Time in the Adventure Novel
of Everyday Life

> Metamorphosis serves as the basis for a method of portraying the
> whole of an individual's life in its more important moments of
> *crisis*: for showing *how an individual becomes other than what he was.*
> We are offered various sharply differing images of one and the
> same individual, images that are united in him as various epochs
> and stages in the course of his life. There is no evolution in the
> strict sense of the word; what we get, rather, is crisis and rebirth.
> —FTC, p. 115

The second type of ancient novel Bakhtin discusses is a curious
one, because it has very few surviving examples from antiquity.
The characteristic features of the "adventure novel of everyday life"
appear in some other genres, such as satires and Hellenistic diatribes, but in a strict sense only two extant works of antiquity are
based primarily on this chronotope: *The Golden Ass* of Apuleius
and the *Satyricon* of Petronius. Even the *Satyricon* emerges as less
than a perfect example in the course of Bakhtin's discussion, which
focuses primarily on *The Golden Ass*. The importance of this chronotope lies, first of all, in its effect on later literature, including
Christian narratives of temptation and rebirth, and second, in the
relative complexity of its spatio-temporal sense.

As the phrase *adventure novel of everyday life* indicates, this chronotope fuses two different senses of time, a version of adventure
time and a version of everyday time. The fusion is far from "a
merely mechanical mix" (FTC, p. 111), but for purposes of analysis
it is helpful to discuss the two elements separately.

The adventure time of *The Golden Ass* differs in significant ways
from the adventure time in the Greek romance. To be sure, it is a
time of chance events, exceptional occurrences, and relatively discrete adventures. Over and over again, the plot is propelled by accidental events that prevent Lucius's transformation back into a human being. But this adventure time is enclosed within another kind
of time and so its "logic of chance is subordinated to another and
higher logic" (FTC, p. 116). The string of adventures is but a moment of the whole story, the overall logic of which is a kind of
metamorphosis. The adventures of Lucius the Ass take place as one

phase of a three-part story of crisis and rebirth, and the sense of the adventures is thereby changed by their role in the larger story.

Bakhtin first examines the logic of metamorphosis as a way to understand change in individual lives and in history. Of course, Apuleius did not invent, but adapted, that logic, which had a long and varied history in the ancient world. Metamorphosis figures prominently in Greek philosophy, in cultic mysteries (including "the original forms of the early Christian cult"; FTC, p. 112), in various "crude magical forms that were exceedingly widespread in the first and second century A.D." (ibid.), and in folklore, as well as in literature proper. And in literature, too, this kind of thinking had a long and complex history.

Conceiving change in terms of metamorphosis involves the following fundamental assumptions: (1) Change is real; identity is not static as it is in the Greek romance. (2) The time and changes of metamorphosis are irreversible, by contrast to the sequence of changes within a Greek romance or some other forms that may be reordered or expanded indefinitely. (3) Most important, the course of change is understood in a very specific way. It "unfolds not so much in a straight line as spasmodically, a line with 'knots' in it. . . . The makeup of this idea is extraordinarily complex, which is why the types of temporal sequences that develop out of it are extremely varied" (FTC, p. 113).

In Hesiod, for example, there are numerous kinds of sequences of changes governed by one or another form of this logic, including "the myth of the five ages: Golden, Silver, Bronze, 'Trojan' or Heroic and Iron" (ibid.). Because the official "historical materialism" of Soviet Marxism has also insisted on five stages of history separated by "leaps" (revolutions), this passage may have been intended as an oblique commentary on the relatively primitive logic of the Marxist scheme—one of the "extremely varied" types of this model?—which has not progressed beyond an understanding of change in terms of the ancient logic of metamorphosis.

According to Bakhtin, Hesiod does not use the term *metamorphosis* with magical overtones, but in later periods, for example in Ovid, "the general idea of metamorphosis has already become the private metamorphosis of individual, isolated beings and is already acquiring the characteristics of an external, miraculous transformation" (FTC, p. 114). In Apuleius, metamorphosis is understood still more strongly as miraculous and as individual. It becomes "a vehicle for conceptualizing and portraying personal, individual fate, a fate cut off from both the cosmic and the historical whole" (ibid.). Its importance for the novel lies in the fact that it comprehends "the *entire life-long destiny of a person*, at all its critical *turning points*" (ibid.).

The concept of critical moments, of turning points, is essential to this logic, because development is not understood as constant, gradual, and prosaic, as it is for example in Jane Austen's novels, but as taking place in a limited set of specific moments. It is a logic of "punctuated equilibrium."[7] Precisely for this reason, it served as an ideal vehicle for Christian "crisis hagiographies" (FTC, p. 115). In *The Golden Ass*, we get three periods of the hero's life, separated by two crises (becoming an ass and returning to human form). In Christian crisis hagiographies, there are usually only two periods— before and after the redemption—but the essential logic of the story remains the same.

In contrast to the Greek romance, then, the events depicted in this type of story cannot be described as "an extratemporal hiatus" from life. On the contrary, this plot is a way to define an entire life. Of course, the entire life is not given to us; we are given only a few images and an explanation of the moments of transformation. Strictly speaking, the events do not unfold in full "biographical time" (FTC, p. 116), most of which takes place outside the frame of the novel. We see Lucius at three moments and Psyche (in the novel's embedded story of Cupid and Psyche) at two. But the moments described nevertheless "*shape the definitive image of the person, his essence as well as the nature of his entire subsequent life*" (ibid.). The events emphatically do leave a trace. Having passed through his initiations, Lucius becomes for the rest of his life a rhetorician and priest, and the redemption that makes a Christian holy man is conceived of as permanent.

Thus, in *The Golden Ass* we have some characteristics of adventure time—in particular time as "exceptional and unusual events . . . dominated by chance" (ibid.)—but not others. We have a series of adventures, in each one of which time is measured "technically" in terms of speed and fortuitous conjunctions, but which, *as a series*, has a purpose and a direction.

Corresponding to this new logic is a different image of a person. Specifically, the hero, though buffeted by fortune, is not merely the object of forces over which he has no control and for which he has no responsibility. A measure of agency, initiative, and accountability enters the world of this kind of novel. Lucius becomes an ass in the first place because of his own weaknesses, because of his voluptuousness and curiosity; as in later Christian versions of the plot, he is truly guilty. That guilt is, indeed, why he is delivered over to the realm of blind chance for a limited period of time; the adventures become retribution leading eventually to redemption. Lucius's transformation back into a man is also not the result of chance, but of the intervention of the goddess. Thus, the rule of chance is strictly limited, serves a purpose, and is itself the result of the hero's actions. In the Greek romance, its time was also limited, but, as we have seen, it served no purpose and the hero bore no responsibility for it.

Although initiative does play a role in the adventure novel of everyday life, Bakhtin contends, that role is understood in a relatively primitive way. To begin with, it affects the hero of *The Golden Ass* only twice, before he becomes an ass and, still more briefly, when he follows the goddess's instructions to effect the reverse transformation. Initiative is intermittent, not constant. Or to use Bakhtin's earlier terminology, for most of the hero's life he does have an air-tight "alibi." Second, initiative is understood as purely negative and so is fully describable as error or moral weakness: "This initiative is *not positive in a creative sense*" (FTC, pp. 116–17). We do not have profound differentiations in kinds of initiative and responsibility, as we do in the nineteenth-century novel.

The nature of this initiative is felt in the use Apuleius makes of dreams. Whereas in Greek romances dreams served simply to allow the hero and heroine to bear their sufferings more easily but could not affect the course of events, in *The Golden Ass* a dream provides Lucius with instructions from the goddess; if he follows them, he can be saved. Thus, dreams allow for initiative, even if only one choice between two clear alternatives is possible.

Given his values, Bakhtin describes this conceptualization of time as "progressive" with respect to the Greek romance, but immediately adds that "some crucial limitations remain" (FTC, p. 119). In addition to those already described, these limitations include the genre's understanding of the relation of the individual to his social world. Like the Greek romance, the adventure novel of everyday life understands the individual's biography as separate from the rest of society. His life is his own business, is unaffected by specific social forces or historical changes, and leaves no mark on society, from the perspective of which the hero's changes are entirely irrelevant. "Therefore, the connection between an individual's fate and his world is *external*. . . . metamorphosis has a merely personal and unproductive character" (ibid.).

For Bakhtin, as we have seen, real individuals are truly *individual*, but that individuality is nevertheless essentially and decisively shaped by particular social and historical forces; indeed, it is the variety and unrepeatability of social contexts that ensures the uniqueness of each person. Moreover, social forces are themselves generated by the dynamics of particular people and groups in everyday life. Thus, by implicit contrast with the adventure novel of everyday life, the nineteenth-century novel links the individual's story to society in complex ways. If one thinks of a novel such as Turgenev's *Fathers and Children* (1862), one recognizes that the hero's story is itself shaped by historical forces and would have been quite different or utterly impossible had it taken place even five years earlier or later. And it is also apparent that this story, and others like it, have had a profound effect on Russian society. That, indeed, is one reason why novelists often imagine their works as forms of sociological exploration, and criticism of those works often becomes a way to analyze and change society.

The nineteenth-century novel as a genre understands anachronism; but the plot of the adventure novel of everyday life is "not localized in historical time (that is, it does not participate in the irreversible historical sequence of time, because the novel does not yet know such a sequence)" (FTC, p. 120).

Spying on Everyday Life

The chronotope of *The Golden Ass* is much more concrete than that of the Greek romance. "Space becomes . . . saturated with a time that is more substantial: space is filled with real, living meaning, and forms a crucial relationship with the hero and his fate" (FTC, p. 120). As a result, the genre does what the Greek romance did not: it portrays everyday life. To be sure, the hero is not essentially shaped by that life, and the facts of that life do not alter his own biographical life. The daily world "is, so to speak, spread out along the edge of the road itself, and along the sideroads. The main protagonist and the major turning points of his life are to be found *outside everyday life*" (FTC, pp. 120–21). Nevertheless, daily life is portrayed at length and substantially. This feature of the genre and its specific means for representing the quotidian world were to exercise great influence on the development of the novel.

In the chapter of the chronotope essay from which we have been quoting and in the chapter that follows it, Bakhtin stresses that the very concept of a *private* daily realm was itself a relatively late discovery in ancient literature and its conception of a person. The modern perspective, in which distinct (if related) public and private spheres exist, is not a universal; and many debates about ancient literature, in Bakhtin's view, have been miscast because of the unexamined and anachronistic assumption that a later discovery was always available.

The everyday life that Lucius observes while an ass "is an *exclusively personal and private life*. By its very nature there can be nothing *public* about it" (FTC, p. 122). Lucius sees and hears things that could not occur publicly, let us say, in the marketplace or in front of a chorus. These events "take place between four walls and for only two pairs of eyes" (ibid.). And what this essential privacy meant is that new technical problems had to be solved for portraying it. Authors required a new *perspective* from which events could be portrayed. Something had to be devised better than the "external, inadequate public and rhetorical forms" (FTC, p. 123) used for the portrayal of personal life (what there was of it) in Greek romance.

The technical problem is simultaneously a conceptual one. When life is thought of as entirely public, or when only public life is to be represented, the very phenomena to be described already presume an audience. "Public life and public man are by their very essence *open, visible*, and *audible*" (ibid.). Thus, no special problems arise for portraying this life or explaining how it came to be known. By contrast, "when the private individual and private life entered literature (in the Hellenistic era) these problems inevitably were bound to arise" (ibid.). How does one know—from what perspective does one describe—what goes on in intimate spheres? What perspective would not implicitly violate and change the very nature of the life to be described? "By its very nature this private life does not create a place for . . . that 'third person' who might be in a position to meditate on this life, to judge and evaluate it" (FTC, p. 122)—as public life inevitably does. In short: "*A contradiction developed between the public nature of the literary form and the private nature of its content*" (FTC, p. 123).

The first significant steps toward resolving this contradiction take place in the adventure novel of everyday life: "The process of working out *private genres* began. But this process remained incomplete in ancient times" (ibid.). Part of the interest of *The Golden Ass* derives from its earliest solution to this problem. In the course of literary history a large number of such solutions were devised.

One possible solution, available to antiquity, was the criminal trial, in which eyewitness accounts, documents, confessions, and analogous devices could subsequently make public acts that had been committed under the presumption of concealment or privacy. What is revealed could and usually does go beyond the criminal activities themselves. This method, of course, has had a long history in fiction.

In *The Golden Ass*, Lucius's transformation affords him the special perspective needed to observe intimate actions, because human privacy is not compromised by the presence of an ass. Lucius also remarks on the great advantage he enjoyed by having large and keen donkey ears, which made distinct what would normally be inaudible. In short, the position of an ass is extremely well adapted to spying and eavesdropping.

Generally speaking, Bakhtin observes, "the literature of private life is essentially a literature of snooping about, of overhearing 'how others live'" (FTC, p. 123). In a sense, much of the history of the novel is a history of eavesdropping, and, although Bakhtin does not explicitly make this point, it would seem to follow that the position of the reader in such cases becomes that of a voyeur. When Svidrigailov, by chance lodging next to Sonya's quarters, moves his chair to the wall in order to overhear Raskolnikov's private confession in the adjoining room, he does what Dostoevsky's readers are always invited to do. In the novel, the walls have ears. "A fly flew by and saw it" (to use another Dostoevskian formulation [*Crime and Punishment*, pt. 3, ch. 6, p. 268]).

Lucius's special position has analogues in later literature for ways to place a "third person" in a private scene. For example, rogues and adventurers are witnesses who do not "participate internally in everyday life . . . [and] do not occupy in it any definite fixed place, yet who at the same time pass through that life and are forced to study its workings" (FTC, p. 124). The same holds true for the servant, a figure who might be described as "the eternal 'third man' in the private life of his lords" (FTC, pp. 124–25). Because lords may be as little embarrassed before a servant as they would be before an ass, the servant came to play an exceptionally important role in the novel. Prostitutes, courtesans, and parvenus serve an analogous function. To build his career, the parvenu studies private life, eavesdrops on its secrets, and investigates its hidden workings. He "begins his journey 'to the depths' (where he rubs shoulders with servants, prostitutes, pimps, and from them learns about life 'as it really is')" (FTC, p. 126); his whole passage through various spheres of life allows for an encyclopedic portrayal of society.

Bakhtin especially admires Diderot's inventive use of these devices in *Rameau's Nephew*, whose eponymous hero "embodies and distills in himself, in a wonderfully complete and profound way, all the specific attributes of an ass, a rogue, a tramp, a servant, an adventurer, a parvenu, an actor" (ibid.). In his very being, as well as in the speeches he delivers, he offers us a whole "*philosophy of the third person in private life*" (ibid.): "This is the philosophy of a person who knows only private life and craves it alone, but who does not participate in it, who has no place in it—therefore sees it in sharp focus, as a whole, in all its nakedness, playing out all its roles but not fusing his identity with any of them" (ibid.).

These passages about spying and eavesdropping could (but do not have to) be taken as allusions to Stalinist conditions and culture: to a world where the walls have ears (the constant fear of the "third person") and in which a sustained assault was being made on the idea of a private realm beyond the reach of public scrutiny. One might observe, for instance, that the doctrine of the "new Soviet man" in Socialist Realism was a new image of a person as entirely public, as striving for pure "exteriority"—in short, a person with no concept of having "something to hide." Whether or not Bakhtin intended this application, a great deal of Soviet literature, from Zamyatin's *We* to Bulgakov's *The Master and Margarita*, could be understood in terms derived from this chapter of the chronotope essay.

As we have seen, in Apuleius and Petronius, everyday time is understood not as a part of life but somehow as lying outside it. Lucius experiences it as a punishment, temporarily; it is a descent, the equivalent of a journey to the dead. "Everyday life is the nether world, the grave, where the sun does not shine, where there is no starry firmament" (FTC, p. 128). Consequently, it is characterized as essentially obscene, priapic, cut off from the cycles of nature, scattered and segmented, and fundamentally different from the overall plot of redemption that structures the work as a whole. To use Bakhtin's simile, the everyday world lies along a different axis from the work's basic story, and everyday time "is not parallel to this basic axis and not interwoven with it, but separate segments of this time—those parts into which everyday time breaks down—are perpendicular to this basic axis and intersect it at right angles" (ibid.). The implicit contrast is again with the nineteenth-century novel, in which everyday time is not temporary and forms the basic chronotope of the work as a whole (e.g., in *Anna Karenina*).

In Apuleius, the diverse and fragmentary aspects of everyday life reveal social heterogeneity, but in a static way: there is no social becoming, no real sense of historical change in *The Golden Ass*. But in Petronius, "the earliest traces of historical time" (FTC, p. 129) are evident, because Petronius not only represents various social spheres but also suggests that they may interact so as to change society itself—so that "the world would start to move, it would be shoved into the future, time would receive a fullness and historicity" (ibid.). Nevertheless, even in Petronius, "this process [of understanding historicity] is . . . far from completed" (ibid.). Again, the implicit contrast is with the nineteenth-century novel, with Balzac and Dostoevsky.

Ancient Biography and Autobiography

Bakhtin next turns to his third type of ancient novel, which he calls "biography and autobiography." He immediately qualifies this designation with the reservation that "antiquity did not produce the kind of novel that we (in our terminology) would call a 'novel,' that is, a large fiction influenced by biographical models" (FTC, p. 130). What it did produce was "a series of biographical and autobiographical forms" (ibid.) at the heart of which lay "a new type of *biographical time* and a human image constructed to new specifications, that of an individual who passes through the course of a whole life" (ibid.). These works differ substantially both from Greek romances, which portray only an "extratemporal hiatus" in life, and from the adventure novel of everyday life, which, focusing on one or two metamorphoses and the period in between, suggests that the period after the final conversion needs no further elucidation.

In the course of his analysis, Bakhtin continually qualifies his characterizations and subdivides his categories to the point where it is not entirely clear whether he is speaking of a single phenomenon or even of a relatively unified class of texts. In general, it might be said that for Bakhtin elaborate classifications were a mental habit— one may think of the classification of "prosaic words" in the final chapter of the Dostoevsky book—that proved more or less successful in varying circumstances. To us, this section of the chronotope essay reads as if Bakhtin had an inkling of a unity in ancient biography and autobiography, but did not succeed in specifying it, either because his broad knowledge of ancient literature continually suggested qualifications as he went along or because he had not really thought through his analysis as well as he had in the case of the Greek romance. Distinctions between different conceptualizations, forms, and periods abound; so do cultural and historical typologies covering broad periods and the varieties of Greek, Hellenistic, and Roman thought. We offer only a few highlights of his discussion.

Bakhtin contends that a real sense of interiority and of a private realm distinct from the public developed relatively late in antiquity. Antiquity's sense of the self was decisively shaped by the idea of public man and "the public self-consciousness of a man" (FTC, p. 140). Bakhtin cautions us that this very description of ancient autobiography is necessarily somewhat anachronistic, because it examines antiquity in terms of categories that did not emerge until later.

In discussing one special type of ancient biography that he calls "rhetorical," Bakhtin observes that "at the base of this type lies the 'encomium'—the civic funeral and memorial speech that had replaced the ancient 'lament'" (FTC, p. 131). Encomia are public orations extolling selves presumed to be public. To understand encomia, and the forms of biography based on them, we need to keep in mind not so much their "internal chronotope" as their "exterior real-life chronotope" (ibid.), that is, the circumstances in which encomia are delivered. Those circumstances are resolutely public, and everything about the form is shaped by this publicity. "In ancient times the autobiographical and biographical self-consciousness of an individual and his life was first laid bare and shaped in the public square" (ibid.).

In this real-life chronotope of the square, a person is conceived as "open on all sides, he is all surface; there is in him . . . nothing that could not be subject to public or state control and evaluation" (FTC, p. 132). This statement may have been intended to have a muffled, ominous ring in the context of the Soviet 1930's. What is essential to public-square images of a person is the impossibility of anything that is in principle "private, secret or personal, anything relating solely to the individual himself" (ibid.). Everything could be seen or heard: "A mute internal life, a mute grief, a mute thought, were completely foreign to the Greek [of this period of early antiquity]" (FTC, p. 134). One consequence of this kind of publicity and "utter exteriority" (FTC, p. 133) was that there was no difference in principle between the autobiographical and biographical points of view (FTC, p. 132). Everything important that I could say about myself could be said by another. From the perspective of the nineteenth-century novel, what is most remarkable about such an image of a person is that "there is no mute or invisible core to the individual himself" (FTC, p. 134).

But in the Hellenistic and Roman periods, crucial changes occur.

Bakhtin singles out as symptomatic debates among rhetoricians—Plutarch, Tacitus, and others—about the permissibility of praising and appraising one's own self. To Bakhtin, what is important about these debates is that they should have occurred at all. For what stirs beneath this problem is "a more general question, namely, the legitimacy of taking the same approach to one's own life as to another life, to one's own self as to another self" (FTC, p. 133). Evidently, by this point there was a difference in principle between biographical and autobiographical points of view; "the classical *public wholeness* of an individual had broken down" (ibid.).

This change made possible "the beginnings of a translation of whole spheres of existence . . . onto a *mute register*, and into something that is in principle invisible" (FTC, p. 134). To be sure, this change was far from fully exploited in antiquity, but what matters is that people could now be understood as having a private realm for which public approaches, discourse, and categories were inadequate. A person, or the image of a person, could now participate in "mute and invisible spheres of existence. He was literally drenched in muteness and invisibility. And with them entered loneliness" (FTC, p. 135). We are on the way to Raskolnikov. Whereas previously the image of a person had neither core nor shell, it now had both. In contrast to earlier forms in which even an individual's self-consciousness relied completely on public categories and was entirely "turned outward" (FTC, p. 137), now it could be composed to some degree of "aspects that might be intimately personal, unrepeatably individual, charged with self" (ibid.).

Antiquity did not develop new forms based on this changed view of self; instead, it modified already existing forms. In part because antiquity barely exploited this insight, the project of describing interiority was only begun in the ancient world. Bakhtin lists three kinds of "modifications." In the first, "personal and private topics, unable to find a positive form for their expression, are clothed in *irony* and *humor*" (FTC, p. 143). Bakhtin cites the ironic self-characterizations present in verse by Horace, Ovid, and Propertius as examples.

A more interesting modification is represented by Cicero's letters to Atticus. Though still highly conventionalized, and still saturated with exteriority, the familiar letter nevertheless provided a vehicle for exploring "the private sense of self" in "an intimate and familiar atmosphere" (ibid.). This shift is reflected in a reinterpretation of various aspects of a life, which now are somewhat detached from their public character. For example, nature can now be understood as "landscape," that is, "as horizon (what a particular person sees) and as the environment . . . for a completely private, singular individual who does not interact with it" but rather contemplates it while out on a walk or glancing randomly about (ibid.). In one's field of vision one discovers "picturesque remnants" that "are woven together in the unstable unity of a cultured Roman's private life" (FTC, p. 144). Similarly, the private drawing room becomes important, as do petty details of daily life, and selfhood begins to take its sense from these prosaic facts. Being "at home" and in private spaces takes on a biographical and psychological value.

Bakhtin calls the third modification of public forms toward privacy and interiority "stoic." Among other works, he has in mind various "consolations" (discussions with Philosophy the Consoler), Seneca's letters, Marcus Aurelius's "To Myself," and St. Augustine's *Confessions*. What these works offer is a "new relationship to one's own self, one's own particular 'I'—with no witnesses, without any concessions to the voice of a 'third person,' whoever it might be" (FTC, p. 145). Indeed, in Marcus Aurelius, the point of view of another has a purely negative character and becomes the source of vanity. This third modification increases the importance of events that could mean something only privately and have little or no public significance—for example, the death of a daughter in Cicero's *Consolations* (ibid.). Events that do have a public significance may now be described primarily in terms of their private implications; and the sense of individual mortality comes to the fore.

All these modifications are important, but they are still, in Bakhtin's view, rather primitive in comparison with what was to come. "There is, as yet, nothing of that authentically solitary individual who makes his appearance only in the Middle Ages and henceforth plays such an enormous role in the European novel" (ibid.). Selfhood, though it encompasses the private sphere, is still basically rooted in the public; symptomatically, Augustine's *Confessions* seem to require a loud public declamation. "Solitude here is still a very relative and naive thing" (ibid.).

Throughout this discussion, Bakhtin's prosaic set of values is clearly at work. We see him drawing on another of his global concepts, unfinalizability, when he turns to the next characteristic of ancient biography and autobiography: the lack of genuine "becoming," growth, or emergence in selves. Bakhtin stresses the importance for "the mature biographical forms of the Roman-Hellenistic epoch" (FTC, p. 140) of Aristotle's concept of entelechy, which does not allow for genuine becoming as Bakhtin understands it. For if "the ultimate purpose of development is at the same time its first cause" (ibid.), then any genuine creation of a self is ruled out. In effect, there is a sort of "inversion in a character's development" (ibid.); the end is always there, shaping what happens, and the course of a life simply reveals ready-made qualities. In such an image of a person, time forges nothing new. Obstacles or opportunities may impede or encourage the expression of qualities, but they do not truly form them. Identity is given, as in the genetic code of a seed. In this respect, the nineteenth-century novel is a direct contrast to these ancient autobiographical forms inasmuch as the novel describes a process of genuine becoming in which experience qualitatively shapes an ever-changing identity.

Bakhtin singles out two types of "mature" Roman-Hellenistic biography. In the "analytic" type, exemplified by Suetonius, biography is presented by "rubrics." The whole of a character is given at the outset as a set of qualities, and incidents from widely separate periods are used to illustrate each of them. Genuine change is discounted in advance. In using the term *analytic*, Bakhtin may have had in mind more recent examples of this technique, for example, Formalist or structuralist approaches to a writer's career as a series of variations on an initially given theme.

Opposed to analytic biography is "energetic" biography, exemplified by Plutarch. Here Aristotle's concept of *energia* is crucial: "The essence of a man is realized not by his condition, but by his activity" (FTC, p. 140). Actions do not simply illustrate essential qualities, which constitute the real man; they themselves "constitute the character's being, which outside its energy simply does not exist" (FTC, p. 141). Thus, one cannot approach a person by enumerating static qualities, but must describe his or her deeds.

Nevertheless, even in the energetic biography there is no genuine becoming. Actual experience and historical events serve "merely as a means for disclosure" of a person's characteristic energy (ibid.). "Historical reality is deprived of any determining influence on character as such" (ibid.). Entelechy still reigns supreme, and so the energetic ancient biography, no less than biography by rubrics, is opposed to the modern novel. In all works governed by entelechy, there is no reason in principle why the same person could not have appeared and developed the same way in a different culture or period. Thus, although it is important in energetic biography actually to narrate a life (not just enumerate and illustrate qualities), time is still "reversible" (ibid.) in the sense that it really does not matter which feature of character is manifested first. In different circumstances, one or another quality may appear before or after others, but the totality of qualities and their relation to each other remain unchanged. "Character itself does not grow, does not change, it is merely *filled in*" (ibid.).

Historical Inversion and Eschatology

When prosaics and unfinalizability combine, as they do in the chronotope essay, the result is a resolute anti-utopianism. All forms of utopian thought are understood as denying openness and the importance of daily creative efforts. Utopia and the realist novel are traditional enemies, of course, and they have frequently parodied each other. It is hardly surprising, then, that Bakhtin's novel-centered chronotope essay should include a section critical of utopian thought, which is described as rendering impossible a sense of real historical time and a genuine sense of becoming.

For there to be a real sense of becoming, according to Bakhtin, the future, and especially the immediate or near future in which we concretely act, must be seen as significant, valuable, and open to change. As in "Toward a Philosophy of the Act," Bakhtin wants to represent the world as one in which the actions that each of us undertakes actually count. Indeed, ethical responsibility, no less than creativity, is thoroughly impoverished unless the future is viewed in this way. Bakhtin discusses two kinds of utopian chronotopes, each of which "empties out the future, dissects and as it were bleeds it white" (FTC, p. 148).

One kind, characteristic of certain types of "mythological and artistic thinking" (FTC, p. 147), empties out the future by an act of "historical inversion." Myths of paradise, a state of nature, a heroic age, or a Golden Age locate purpose, justice, and perfection in the past rather than in the future. In this kind of "trans-positioning" or "historical inversion," we witness "a special concept of time, and in particular of future time" (ibid.). Specifically, the future is felt as something unreal, as something that does not exist and never did exist; it is not "homogeneous" with the present and past. Composed, so to speak, of a different substance, the future "is denied a basic concreteness, it is somehow empty and fragmented—since everything affirmative, ideal, obligatory, desired has been shifted, via the inversion, into the past (or partly into the present)" (ibid.). The present and past are "enriched" (ibid.) at the expense of the future, and so ideals are located either in a distant and inaccessible past, or, if in the present, in a remote place (utopia). Such a utopia is located in another world felt as somehow extratemporal even if it is simultaneous with the present. Justice so conceived is not a *project*, something with respect to which each of us has obligations in the immediate future of our lives.

In another type of utopian thought, eschatology, the immediate future is emptied out in a different way—not by the past, but by an absolute end. Whether that end is near or remote, whether it is a coming of perfection, of catastrophe, or of catastrophe leading to subsequent perfection, the effect of such thinking is to devalue the concrete immediate future into which we live moment to moment. "Eschatology always sees the segment of the future that separates the present from the end as lacking value; this separating segment of time loses its significance and interest, it is merely an unnecessary continuation of an indefinitely prolonged present" (FTC, p. 148).

Because Soviet Marxist-Leninist ideology is itself a form of utopian thought, which officially acknowledged the entire tradition of utopian thinking as its predecessor, Bakhtin's comments would appear to constitute a critique of some aspects of Soviet ideology. The precise implications of this critique remain unclear, however, and it seems more prudent to stress the general anti-utopianism of the chronotope essay than to recommend a specific political reading.

The Chivalric Romance and the Vision

As Bakhtin analyzes it, the chivalric romance uses a form of adventure time, in most cases resembling that of the Greek romance, but in some instances (such as Wolfram von Eschenbach's *Parzival*) resembling the everyday adventure time of *The Golden Ass*. Time is segmented into a series of discrete adventures "within which it is ordered abstractly and technically; the connection of time to space is also merely technical" (FTC, p. 151). As in the Greek romance, we see in the chivalric romance the typical adventure plot of testing the hero; the same chronotopic motifs of simultaneities, disjunctions, recognition and nonrecognition, and presumed deaths; and we see the same sense of time shaped by "suddenlys." Nevertheless, the chivalric romance adds a new element, which makes its chronotope quite different from that of the Greek romance.

In the chivalric romance, the whole world is given over to suddenlys and becomes thoroughly miraculous. Instead of erupting into normal life and propelling the hero and heroine into a string of adventures destined to end with a return to normal life, chance events take over completely and define a thoroughly "*miraculous world in adventure time*" (FTC, p. 154). "The 'suddenly' is normalized . . . it becomes something generally applicable without ceasing at the same time to be miraculous" (FTC, p. 152). "Unexpectedness" becomes the rule, and so "the unexpected, and only the unexpected is what is expected" (ibid.). Numerous other differences between the Greek and chivalric romances follow from this one.

Whereas the hero of Greek romance wishes to restore normal life, the hero of the chivalric romance seeks adventures; they are his native element, in fact, and so the world is no longer alien to him, as the adventure world is alien to the hero and heroine of the Greek romance. The chivalric hero is an adventurer per se, and "by his very nature he can live only in this world of miraculous chance, for it alone preserves his identity" (ibid.). It follows that the chivalric hero, who looks for and finds adventures, possesses a measure of initiative, whereas the hero of the Greek romance, as we have seen, does not.

In the Greek romance, chance and adventure motifs are "unadorned" (ibid.), but in the chivalric romance, chance is seductive. It is personified by good and evil fairies and operates in enchanted groves and magical castles, which are tantalizingly attractive. The heroes of a chivalric romance "*glorify themselves*" (FTC, p. 153); the Greek romance did not know the heroic deed in this sense. From this perspective, Bakhtin remarks, the chivalric romance is closer to epic: "In fact the early chivalric romance in verse lies on the boundary between epic and novel" (FTC, p. 154).

Moreover, the heroes of chivalric romances are to some extent both individualized and symbolic, whereas the heroes of Greek romances are neither. Resembling each other, the Greek heroes belong to a specific novel and author; other novels center around other heroes. But in the chivalric romance, heroes differ from each other: "Lancelot in no way resembles Parzival, Parzival does not resemble Tristan" (FTC, p. 153). The temptation arises, therefore, to continue the adventures of a specific person, for not just anyone will do. Thus, we get not only heroes of individual romances, but also heroes of cycles. These heroes, like those of epic, "belong to a common storehouse of images, although this is an international storehouse and not, as in the epic, one that is merely national" (ibid.).

Finally, the chronotope of the chivalric romance allows for a subjective playing with space and time in a way quite foreign to the Greek romance. In the Greek romance, time within each adventure is technically correct in the sense that a day is always a day and an hour an hour. But in the thoroughly miraculous world of the chivalric romance, time and space themselves become miraculous. Whole events may disappear as if they had never happened and, as in the fairy tale, hours may be extended and days compressed; time itself may be bewitched. Spatial categories are played with in the same way. Time can become like the time of dreams, and so dreams themselves take on new functions and influence events. In later prose forms of the chivalric romance, the wholeness of this miraculous world begins to disintegrate, and elements more like those of the Greek romance become more prominent; but "separate aspects of this distinctive chronotope—in particular the subjective playing with spatial and temporal perspectives—now and then re-emerge in the subsequent history of the novel (of course, with somewhat changed functions)" (FTC, p. 155). Bakhtin has in mind some works of the Romantics, symbolists, expressionists, and surrealists.

The genre of the encyclopedic dream-vision exhibits a still more interesting conceptualization of time and space. The most important works Bakhtin has in mind are the *Roman de la Rose*, *Piers Plowman*, and, especially, *The Divine Comedy*. Characteristic of these works is a feeling for the social contradictions at the end of a given epoch, a sense that impels the form toward a historical sense; and yet, at the same time, these works display an even more powerful impulse to overcome time entirely.

Thus, on the one hand, one sees in Langland and in Dante a "contradictory multiplicity" (FTC, p. 156) of diverse social classes and kinds of people, an image that is "profoundly historical" (FTC, p. 157). On the other hand, the genre creates a vertical world "perpendicular" to this horizontal historical axis. That is, the genre's form-shaping impulse creates a temporal logic designed to rein in and to overcome time—to "synchronize diachrony" (FTC, p. 157). In Dante's various circles of Hell, Purgatory, and Paradise, we see that impulse producing a time of "sheer simultaneity" (ibid.), a time in which everything coalesces into "pure simultaneous existence" (ibid.). The concepts of "earlier" and "later" lose their substance. The sense of the genre is that only "under conditions of pure simultaneity—or what amounts to the same thing, in an environment outside of time altogether—can there be revealed the true meaning of 'that which was, and which is, and which shall be'" (ibid.). But the people of Dante's world nevertheless "bear the marks of time" (ibid.). Populating an eternal world with people who are "saturated" by historical time, the work reads as if its characters seek to escape from their vertical world into a horizontal, historical existence. "Each image is full of historical potential, and therefore strains with the whole of its being toward participation in historical events—toward participation in a temporal-historical chronotope. But the artist's powerful will condemns it to an eternal and immobile place on the extratemporal vertical axis" (ibid.). In short, the special power of the work derives in large part from the tension between the form-shaping principle of the whole and the temporality of its separate parts, "between living historical time and the extratemporal otherworldly ideal" (FTC, p. 158). According to Bakhtin, a great deal of the parodic energy of Rabelais was directed against the otherworldliness of this static sort of chronotope.

We can see a much later attempt to exploit this Dantesque chronotope in Dostoevsky. Bakhtin has in mind Dostoevsky's fascination with "the cross-section of a single moment," which we discussed in Chapter Six, and which adapts a logic similar to Dante's "cross-section of pure simultaneity" (FTC, p. 158).

Prosaic Allegorization and the Intervalic Chronotope

Chapter six of the chronotope essay, entitled "The Functions of the Rogue, the Clown, and the Fool," contains perhaps the most opaque writing of Bakhtin's third period. Obscure coinages are introduced not only without explicit definition, but also without sufficient illustration to make clear their meaning or their connection with the whole. This opacity is all the more frustrating because Bakhtin clearly attributes special importance to the topics of this section.

Bakhtin's key point seems to be closely related to his discussion of "everyday life" in *The Golden Ass*, to which he alludes. It will be recalled that the position of the author, of a "third person," presented special problems in the portrayal of the private because the very presence of a witness to intimacy seemed to be self-contradictory. A public language and form would somehow change the private world represented. The figure of the ass, and analogous figures in later literature, constituted a special solution to this problem, but better solutions were needed. More than technical considerations are involved here.

The deeper issue involved in the problem of the "third person" is, of course, how we are to understand the complex world of the "*internal man*" (FTC, p. 164), that is, the world of individual and subjective experience. An author describing a character's subjective experience is necessarily an author describing an *other's* subjective experience.[8] The author's position becomes problematic not just because his vantage point would seem to be impossible, but also because the very nature of inner experience was unclear and had to be thought through by the artistic imagination. What exactly is "the 'internal man' and his 'free and self-sufficient subjectivity'" (ibid.)? Real *artistic thinking* had to be done, not just formal solutions devised, to solve this problem. And it is evident that the nineteenth-century novel Bakhtin values so highly depended on this type of thinking.

Some traditional figures helped writers think the problem through. The clown, the fool, and the rogue are, of course, ancient figures in social life and folklore, as well as in literature. "If one were to drop a historical sounding-lead into these artistic images, it would not touch bottom in any of them—they are that deep" (FTC, pp. 158–59). That depth gave this triad great potential, and the novel, with its need to solve the problem of the internal man, exploited some of that potential.

To begin with, the novel seized upon these figures to solve the problem of the author's position. Instead of the elaborate and unwieldy device of an ass, or of a devil lifting the roofs off houses, or of a supposedly deaf man who turns out to have been able to hear all along, the *novelist himself* assumed the position of the fool, clown, or rogue. The point is not that one of these three figures must be introduced into the novel to narrate it (although that often happens), but that even without such a narrator explicitly present, the authorial position itself becomes "foolish."

In order to understand inner life, Bakhtin observes, it is necessary, first of all, to strip away all those conventional layers that conceal it. Becoming a fool grants the author the right "not to understand," the right of "incomprehension." Not just Pierre at Borodino, but Tolstoy himself, narrates from the position of a fool who does not grasp the simplest social conventions that readers and most characters take for granted. "At last a form was found to portray the mode of existence of . . . life's perpetual spy and reflector" (FTC, p. 161).

No less important, the image of a fool, when presented as a character *in* the work, provided a way to explore the nature of people's inner life. What is important here is, first of all, that in the absence of any direct access to the inner man a sort of "metaphorical" approach was needed; Bakhtin here uses the word *metaphorical* to mean "indirect." Second, the figure of the fool could be used to stand for all humanity, as an extreme that allows us to see the norm. In this special sense, metaphorization also becomes "allegorization." In using the fool in this way, the novel is drawing on the tradition of fool figures who underwent various metamorphoses (as both tsar and god) in order to suggest the entire human experience, the image of man per se and of all human life. Bakhtin cites as an example "Christ's passion [with its] . . . metamorphosis of god or ruler into slave, criminal or fool. Under such conditions man is in a state of allegory. The *allegorical state* has enormous form-generating significance for the novel" (FTC, pp. 161–62).

Finally, this allegorization is used for specifically *prosaic* purposes. Metaphor and allegory (in the sense Bakhtin uses these terms in this passage) become "prosaic metaphor" and "prosaic allegorization" (FTC, p. 166). They are used specifically to explore the life of people in their most intimate and prosaic activities and thoughts.

A version of the fool as character suggested a way that this exploration could be undertaken. Transformed into the *chudak* (oddball, crank), the fool "becomes an important means for exposing the 'internal man.'" (FTC, p. 164). Bakhtin's defining example is Tristram Shandy, a fool whose consciousness can be explored because of his very oddities, a person whose eccentricities make the nature of all our inner lives more visible. This kind of eccentricity is central to what Bakhtin means by prosaic allegorization.

At this point in his argument, Bakhtin pauses to discuss terminological problems. As it happens, there is no adequate term for this phenomenon, and so novelists themselves have sometimes coined terms based on their central characters—*Pantagruelism, Shandyism*. Other terms, such as *irony, parody, joke, humor, whimsy,* and the *grotesque*, do not catch the specific function of eccentricity that lies at the base of this phenomenon. And to speak of clownishness, holy foolishness, or even eccentricity is also to miss the point that this figure is *allegorical*, as is Christ—its use provides an indirect approach to the inner life of all people. Bakhtin thus proposes the term *prosaic allegorization* to cover the phenomenon—but he seems aware that it, too, has its limitations.

Unfortunately, the terms *prosaic allegorization* and *prosaic metaphor* may suggest a direct contrast with poetic allegorization and metaphorization. Bakhtin does not appear to be drawing such a contrast. A prosaic metaphor is not opposed to a poetic metaphor, it quite literally "has nothing in common with the poetic metaphor" (FTC, p. 166). One needs to understand Bakhtin's coinages in three steps: metaphor as indirection; allegory as metaphoric indirection plus suggestion of the entire human condition; and prosaic allegorization as the use of allegorization to solve the novel's problems of conceptualizing and representing ordinary, intimate, and ongoing life.

Once established, prosaic allegorization could be and was itself exploited to produce a new phenomenon (more accurately, a new use of an older phenomenon): the "intervalic chronotope." The eccentricity of Shandyism could be extended in a special scene that interrupts—is an interval in—the predominant chronotope of the work. Bakhtin's prime example is *Vanity Fair*, the title of the work referring to the intervalic chronotope that interrupts and casts light upon the chronotope of the main narrative. Most often, the intervalic chronotope tends to be one of theatricality, of a kind of play separated from but related to the life in which it is an interval. To make matters still more complex, this chronotope may not be developed explicitly as it is in *Vanity Fair*; it may be a "hidden chronotope," sensed only at particular moments. "At the heart of *Tristram Shandy* lies the intervalic chronotope of the puppet theatre, in disguised form. Sterneanism is the style of a wooden puppet directed and commented upon by the author himself" (FTC, p. 166). A similar hidden chronotope also informs Gogol's "The Nose."

The intervalic chronotope serves another function, present long before Sterne. By foregrounding the possibility of viewing action from two different chronotopic perspectives, it highlights the fact that each chronotope is one of many possible chronotopes. To adapt some other Bakhtinian terms, the intervalic chronotope allows no chronotope to be "naive" and "Ptolemaic"; it creates a "Galilean chronotope consciousness." Bakhtin's term for this phenomenon is *hybridization*, which suggests he means to draw on the logic of novelistic hybridization (of various languages of heteroglossia) to project a hybridization of time-spaces. We witness such a hybridization in *Don Quixote*, which creates a complex dialogue of "the 'alien, miraculous world' chronotope of chivalric romances, with the 'high road winding through one's native land' chronotope that is typical of the picaresque novel" (FTC, p. 165). As in any real dialogue, the interaction is not just a combination but "radically changes" the character of each chronotope; "both of them take on metaphoric significance and enter into completely new relations with the real world" (ibid.). The intervalic chronotope is also well suited to exploiting this potential of dialogically interacting chronotopes.

The Essay on Goethe and
the Bildungsroman: The Prehistory
of Becoming

Bakhtin's chronotope essay was apparently written during 1937 and 1938 and his study of Goethe and the Bildungsroman between 1936 and 1938. Because only a small fragment of the Goethe essay has survived, and part of that appears to be in the form of a prospectus or outline, it is difficult to ascertain the precise relation of the two studies, but it is clear that they were closely connected. Indeed, they read as if they were different parts of the same study—as if the Goethe essay demanded clarification of its key concepts, or the chronotope essay, which ends with Rabelais, demanded a continuation. As it has come down to us, the essay on Goethe frequently uses the term *chronotope* but never explains it, an omission that in retrospect makes it wise to read this work as another chapter of the chronotope essay.

The basic topic of the Bildungsroman essay is the emergence in Goethe's time, and especially in Goethe's work, of a genuine sense of "becoming." For Bakhtin, such a sense involves at least the following three elements: (1) Individuals must genuinely grow: their identity must develop and they must be capable of developing it. Identity so conceived does not simply unfold or reveal what was somehow present all along. (2) The same is true of history: present, past, and future must be linked by a process of genuine growth, which means that change does not take place in an arbitrary fashion (not just anything can happen). Genuine growth also means that processes can be exhaustively explained neither by the operation of automatic impersonal forces, nor by mechanical causal laws, nor by any other wholly deterministic sequence. In short, genuine historical becoming involves both continuity and creativity (each within limits). We may sense in this argument essentially the same logic Bakhtin used to describe the relation of "genre memory" to a text's "potentials" for the future.[9] (3) The two processes—individual and historical becoming—are neither versions of each other nor wholly independent. Individual growth is decisively but not wholly shaped by history and social forces, which are not just mere background. An understanding of personality and its growth requires the concept of historical anachronism. At the same time, individuals are in no sense wholly reducible to "products of their era"; they retain the capacity to surprise, and that sort of surprise is, indeed, what ultimately produces historical change. The inner man, the private and intimate spheres, have a relative integrity of their own. The logic resembles that in Bakhtin's descriptions of linguistic history.

Without these three elements—each of which allows for complex variations—there can be no genuine sense of historicity and no sense of "the fullness of time"; neither can individuals be understood as they truly are. Bakhtin writes:

> The main theme of our essay is the time-space and the image of a person in the novel. Our criterion is the assimilation of real historical time and the assimilation of the historical person that takes place in that time. This problem is mainly theoretical and literary in nature, but no theoretical problem can be resolved without concrete historical material. . . . Hence our more specific and special theme—the image of *a person in the process of becoming* in the novel. [BSHR, p. 19]

Bakhtin begins by classifying fiction before the rise of a genuine sense of becoming as "novels without emergence" (see the chart on pp. 412–13). This classification is in effect a set of supercategories, each of which incorporates several related genres. He identifies three broad classes of novels without emergence; when we read this classification in the context of the chronotope essay, it becomes evident that each class includes one of the three ancient chronotopes as well as some later genres related to these three.

Bakhtin's first broad class is the "travel novel," which includes *The Golden Ass* (the wanderings of Lucius), the *Satyricon* (the wanderings of Encolpius), picaresque novels (*Lazarillo de Tormes, Francion, Gil Blas*), the "adventure-picaresque novels of Defoe (*Captain Singleton* and *Moll Flanders*)" (BSHR, p. 10), and Smollett's *Roderick Random, Peregrine Pickle,* and *Humphrey Clinker,* as well as a number of other works. In this type of narrative, the hero "is a moving point in space" and "has no essential distinguishing characteristics, and he himself is not at the center of the novelist's artistic attention" (ibid.). Instead, the author uses the adventures to describe the social diversity of the world.

That diversity is understood ahistorically; what we are given is "a purely spatial and static conception of the world's diversity. The world is a spatial contiguity of differences and contrasts" (BSHR, p. 11). Thus, "temporal categories are extremely poorly developed" (ibid.) and there is no real sense of history or individual development. The hero's growth and age are either completely missing or only mentioned for the sake of form, without any essential shaping effect. These works rely primarily on adventure time, and their temporal determinations are those that measure time technically within the limits of an adventure. Displaying social contrasts, this type of novel often focuses on the "exotic." Describing static people in a static world, it "does not recognize human emergence and development" (ibid.). Even if the hero changes status, from beggar to rich man for instance, "he himself remains unchanged" (ibid.).

Bakhtin's second broad class, "the novel of ordeal," is described as the one including the largest number of works, in fact, the "considerable majority of all the [European] novels [ever] produced" (ibid.). It includes the Greek and chivalric romances, early Christian hagiography (especially of martyrs), and two types of baroque novel, the "adventure-heroic novel" of Radcliffe, Lewis, Walpole and others, and the "pathos-filled psychological, sentimental novel (Rousseau, Richardson)" (BSHR, p. 14). At the heart of this category is the idea of *testing* the hero. As we have already seen, this sort of story understands identity as complete, unchanging, and given in advance; qualities are affirmed and verified, but do not emerge or develop. In Bakhtin's view, the potentials of this category were best realized in the baroque novel, which was "able to draw from the idea of testing all the plot possibilities it held for the construction of large-scale novels" (BSHR, p. 13).

The most important contribution of the novel of ordeal, especially in its baroque versions, was a richer sense of "psychological time." Such time comes to possess a "subjective palpability and duration" (BSHR, p. 15), for example, in the depiction of reactions to danger, agonizing suspense, and passion. Nevertheless, this kind of psychological time is not linked organically with anything else, not even with the rest of the hero's life.

In this type of novel, everyday life tends to be less important than in the travel novel. The social world here, in contrast to the nineteenth-century novel, is mere background. The hero neither affects nor is affected by the world in a profound way, nor does he seek to change it; in general, it might be said that "the problem of the interaction between subject and object, man and the world, was not raised in the novel of ordeal. This explains why the nature of heroism is so unproductive and uncreative in this type of novel (even when historical heroes are depicted)" (BSHR, p. 16).

Nevertheless, the idea of testing succeeded in organizing a novel around the hero and, when combined with concepts of emergence developed in the Bildungsroman, was able to make important contributions to the shape of the great nineteenth-century novels.

Bakhtin's third broad category of novels without emergence, the "biographical novel," "has never actually existed in pure form" (BSHR, p. 17). It is thus, like ancient biography and autobiography in the chronotope essay, a strange class indeed. It includes ancient biographical works, early Christian confessions, hagiographies, and, most important, the "family-biographical" novel of the eighteenth century. The only example Bakhtin mentions is *Tom Jones*. This type of novel concerns the whole of a hero's life, not some adventuristic departures from it; in other words, it displays a sense of "biographical time" (ibid.). Events in a life are consequently "unrepeatable and irreversible" (BSHR, pp. 17–18). Moreover, the biographical conception of a person introduces the idea of generations in a profound way. Because that idea involves "the contiguity of lives taking place at various times" (BSHR, p. 18), these works take an important step toward an understanding of real historical time, even though they never actually reach that understanding. Exoticism now disappears, as the social world begins to be more than mere background. Whereas in picaresque novels, social positions were mere masks, here they "acquire a life-determining essence" (ibid.).

A hero now has real, concrete features, both positive and negative; and "he is not [just passively] tested, but strives for actual results" (BSHR, p. 19). Nevertheless, these features are "readymade" and given in advance. The hero remains essentially unchanged throughout the work. Events may shape his destiny, but do not touch his identity.

Novels of Emergence

The family-biographical novel in its eighteenth-century variant was an important step toward a full and genuine sense of becoming. The next step was taken by the novel of education. According to Bakhtin, Goethe was the key figure who thought through a fuller sense of time and development essential to the development of the nineteenth-century novel, the narrative form possessing the richest sense of time and becoming in European history. If the whole of Bakhtin's study were extant, it would probably be clear that in his thought the great triumvirate of literary figures are Dostoevsky, Rabelais, and Goethe.

After surveying the novels of travel, ordeal, and biographical time, Bakhtin turns to the "incomparably rarer type" (BSHR, p. 21) that is his main concern: "*the novel of a person's emergence*" (or "becoming": *roman stanovleniia cheloveka*) (ibid.). In the several variants of this kind of novel, the hero and the image of the hero change, become, develop; moreover, these changes in the hero himself (as opposed to changes that merely alter the hero's status) "acquire *plot significance*, and thus the entire plot of the novel is reinterpreted and reconstructed" (ibid.). Such novels are *about* how people develop their identity, rather than just reveal it. Entelechy no longer prescribes identity. Instead, "time is introduced into a person, enters into his very image, changing in a fundamental way the significance of all aspects of his destiny and life" (ibid.).

The idea that people genuinely emerge in this way is a profound one, but here, too, one may discern degrees of profundity (as well as alternative formulations) in the conception of *how* emergence happens. Bakhtin chooses to focus on one important variable, which he uses as the basis for identifying five types of novels of emergence. That variable is "the degree of assimilation of real historical time" (ibid.), by which Bakhtin means the extent to which a given kind of novel understands the relation of an individual's becoming to social and historical changes. The most profound novels of emergence, as we have suggested, represent not only individual becoming but also social becoming; and they represent these two processes as irreducible to each other but nevertheless closely linked.

Bakhtin's first type of novel of emergence uses an "idyllic-cyclical" chronotope. Here emergence is viewed as a consequence of advancing years and the progress from childhood to youth, maturity, and old age. It is cyclical because it repeats itself in each life, regardless of where and when that life takes place. Consequently, it lacks any real sense of historical, as opposed to individual, becoming. As it happens, this chronotope does not exist in pure form, but is combined with others—for example, in "the work of eighteenth-century idyllists and the work of novelists of regionalism" (BSHR, p. 22), as well as in Sterne and Tolstoy, whose works are mainly guided by other chronotopes.

A different type of cyclical time identifies the chronotope of the second type of novels of emergence, the Bildungsroman "in the narrow sense" (ibid.). Here Bakhtin suggests that for his purposes, it is worth adopting this narrow understanding of the Bildungsroman, inasmuch as a broader classification—including everything from the *Cyropedia* to *Vanity Fair*—would obscure the distinctive chronotopic features of the subclass he has in mind. In the Bildungsroman—"the classical novel of education in the second half of the eighteenth century" (ibid.)—it is not the cycle youth-to-age that shapes identity, but the path from idealism to skepticism and resignation. Life is seen as experience and as a school "through which every person must pass and derive one and the same result: one becomes more sober" (ibid.). Bakhtin's examples are Wieland and Wetzel, and he identifies elements of this chronotope in Hippel, Jean Paul, and Goethe. Here, too, genuine historical becoming is not evident.

Type three dispenses with cyclicality; emergence is seen in terms of individual and unrepeatable changes. "Emergence here is the result of the entire totality of changing life circumstances and events, activity and work. Man's destiny is created [rather than ready-made] and he himself, his character, is created along with it" (ibid.). *David Copperfield* and *Tom Jones* are said to exemplify this type. (Bakhtin does not explain how *Tom Jones* could simultaneously be a novel *without* emergence—the family-biographical novel—and a novel *of* emergence.)

The "didactic-pedagogical novel," traceable to the *Cyropedia* and including *Emile*, constitutes a fourth type. Elements of this chronotope can be found in Rabelais and Goethe. Bakhtin does not really describe this type, perhaps because the logic of his classification would seem to dictate that many of these works be assigned to one of the categories of novels without emergence. In general, one could fault Bakhtin's classification for some inconsistency. Once again, we may detect Bakhtin's habit, evident since "Author and Hero," of thinking through an idea by elaborating a set of categories that then take on a momentum of their own and produce inconsistencies that may or may not be noticed and resolved.[10]

Bakhtin's main concern is the fifth type, the novel of "historical emergence," which exhibits the most profound chronotopicity. What distinguishes this type, and marks it off from every other class and subclass of novel ever written, is its assimilation of "real historical time" (BSHR, p. 23). In the first four types of novels of emergence, man truly developed, but his development was "his private affair, as it were, and the results of this emergence were also private and [purely] biographical in nature" (ibid.). Each person changed and developed, but the world in which he or she lived was represented as stable; the hero, for example, would learn to adapt himself to the unchanging laws of life. The experience provided by the world shaped the hero in the Bildungsroman, but the world itself remained unaffected, "fundamentally immobile and ready-made, given" (ibid.). A full sense of real time could only be achieved when the form-shaping impulse of a specific chronotope conceived of the world not as given (*dan*) or ready-made (*gotov*)[11] but as created (*sozdan*) by human effort in the lives of real, specific people.

This step is taken by the fifth type of novel of emergence, which most fully exploits the potential of the genre. "Aspects of this [chronotope of] historical emergence can be found in almost all important realist novels" (BSHR, p. 24). Novels of this sort represent the furthest point that the understanding of real historical time has reached.

In novels of historical emergence, a person "emerges *along with the world* and he reflects the historical emergence of the world itself" (BSHR, p. 23). For example, he may be "at the transition point" between two historical epochs, in which case the transition itself "is accomplished in him and through him" (ibid.). Historical time saturates his identity, but he himself nevertheless retains initiative and is not just a product of historical time. In such a chronotope, for the first time "the organizing force held by the future is therefore extremely great" (ibid.).

By "the future," Bakhtin means, first, a future that is not understood purely in private biographical terms, and second, a future that is not utopian or eschatological, but rather immediate and concrete. This type of novel understands the future—the realm in which real, individual decisions are made—as the "zone of proximal development." This future is of supreme importance, and novels of this type value it more highly than any other literary form has ever valued it before.

As people live into this future, new kinds of character and identity emerge along with the world and shape the world's emergence. This type of novel understands anachronism and its relation to personality; that is, it understands why personal types are not repeatable from age to age and culture to culture.

Finally, and perhaps most important, in this type of novel "problems of reality and human potential, problems of freedom and necessity, and the problem of creative initiative rise to their full height" (BSHR, p. 24). It will be recalled that one of Bakhtin's lifelong concerns was to conceive a model of the world in which creativity and potential could be real. To be real, creativity had to be more than "extracting square roots," and the new not just a mechanical or inevitable result of the past. People must make the new by their own efforts, and not just be the passive vehicle through which innovation takes place. The chronotope of the novel of historical emergence, with its rich understanding of "freedom," "initiative," and "human potential," became for Bakhtin just such a model of people at creative work.

Classification of Novels in the Bildungsroman Essay

I. Novels Without Emergence (the image of a hero lacks development).
  A. Travel novel.
      1. Includes "the adventure novel of everyday life" in the chronotope essay (*The Golden Ass*, the *Satyricon*).
      2. Other examples: picaresque novels (*Gil Blas*); the adventure-picaresque novels of Defoe; Smollett's novels.
      3. Uses adventure time.
      4. The hero is a moving point in space.
      5. Focuses on the world's diversity and on the exotic.
      6. Temporal categories are weak.
  B. Novel of ordeal.
      1. Includes the Greek romance and the chivalric novel described in the chronotope essay.
      2. Other examples: early Christian hagiography (especially of martyrs); two types of baroque novels, the "adventure-heroic novel" of Radcliffe, Lewis, Walpole and the "pathos-filled psychological, sentimental novel" of Rousseau and Richardson.
      3. Includes the great majority of all novels ever produced.
      4. Basic plot is *testing*. Hero's identity is affirmed but does not emerge or develop.
      5. In variants that best exploit genre's potential, main contribution is a sense of "psychological time."
      6. Social world is mere background.
  C. Biographical novel.
      1. Has never existed in pure form.
      2. Includes ancient biographical novels as described in the chronotope essay.
      3. Other examples: early Christian confessions, hagiography, and the "family-biographical novel" of the eighteenth century (*Tom Jones*).
      4. Entelechy structures a life.
      5. Works in biographical time and sense of a whole life, perhaps of generations.
II. Novels of Emergence (the image of a person develops). Much rarer than novels without emergence.
  A. Type one: The idyllic-cyclical chronotope.
      1. A chronotope that does not exist in pure form but only in combination with others.
      2. May be found in eighteenth-century idyllists and novels of regionalism; in Sterne; in Tolstoy.
      3. Cyclical time: emergence as a result of the life cycle from childhood to old age.

B. Type two: The Bildungsroman in the narrow sense.
   1. Includes the classic eighteenth-century novel of education (Wieland, Wetzel).
   2. Cyclical time: the path from idealism to sobriety shapes a life.
C. Type three [unnamed].
   1. Includes *David Copperfield* and *Tom Jones*.
   2. Dispenses with cyclical time.
   3. Experience shapes changes; destiny and the image of a person created by a character's own activity.
D. Type four: Didactic-pedagogical novels.
   1. Traceable to the *Cyropedia* and including *Emile*.
   2. Not described.
E. Type five: Novels of historical emergence.
   1. Bakhtin's main concern.
   2. Aspects of this chronotope can be found in almost all important realist novels.
   3. The only chronotope that assimilates real historical time.
   4. The hero emerges along with the world; includes both individual and social change shaping each other.

"Creative Necessity" and "The Fullness of Time"

Goethe . . . saw everything not *sub specie aeternitatis* . . . as his teacher, Spinoza, did, but in time and in the *power of time*. But the power of this time is a productive and creative power. Everything—from an abstract idea to a piece of rock on the bank of a stream—bears the stamp of time, is saturated with time, and assumes its form and meaning in time. . . . [Moreover,] in Goethe's world there are no events, no plots or temporal motifs that are not related in an essential way to the particular space of their occurrence, that could occur anywhere or nowhere ("eternal" plots and motifs). Everything in this world is a *time-space*, a true *chronotope*.   —BSHR, p. 42

Goethe's immense importance for Bakhtin derives from two closely related factors. First, Goethe made the crucial chronotopic discoveries that led to the development of the nineteenth-century novel; second, those discoveries offered a solution to some of Bakhtin's lifelong concerns, specifically the nature of action and the meaning of creativity.

Goethe understood "the fullness of time" (BSHR, p. 42), by which Bakhtin means the inner connectedness of past, present, and future. Actions and events at any moment respond to specific circumstances in which they take place, and create new circumstances, which provide constraints and opportunities for future action. In his fourth period, Bakhtin used the term *great time* to refer to the sense that past events, as they become congealed in institutions, languages of heteroglossia, and genres, pose specific problems and offer specific resources for each present moment that follows. One cannot understand a work or an action by "enclosing" it entirely in its own moment. It will be recalled that Medvedev had objected to Formalist models of literary history for making it impossible to comprehend developments that extend over many generations.

A feeling for the fullness of time allowed Goethe to understand the nature of creativity. Creativity is always real, is always going on, and so cannot be understood as sudden, mysterious eruptions from nowhere. On the contrary, creativity is always a response to problems that are posed in particular circumstances at a particular time. Bakhtin is here opposing romantic notions of creativity to creativity conceived in terms of prosaics. It grows out of the fabric of daily life, responds and contributes to local opportunities and needs, and, in the process, plants potentials for future creativity.

Bakhtin tries to capture this view of the creative process with a pair of paradoxical phrases: "creative necessity" (BSHR, p. 51) and "the necessity of creativity" (BSHR, p. 39). These phrases, which seem to border on contradiction, require a gloss in terms of Bakhtin's use of them in context. By "necessity," Bakhtin cautions, he does *not* mean that particular novelties are the merely automatic result of past processes; on the contrary, "this Goethean necessity was very far from both the necessity of fate and from mechanical natural necessity" (ibid.). If the world were governed by necessity in a fatalistic, mechanical, or strictly deterministic sense, then creativity in a real sense would not exist at all. Rather, this is "a materially creative, historical necessity" (ibid.). The term *necessity* is used in opposition to an inspirational or utopian understanding of creativity. The point of necessity is that not just anything is produced by creative work; a true sense of creativity excludes "any arbitrariness, fabrication or abstract fantasy" (ibid.). Creativity is rooted in the real actions of real people, who use the resources provided by the past, which is to say, of earlier creativity: "Such a creatively effective past . . . to a certain degree predetermines the future" (BSHR, p. 34).

"To a certain degree": as so often in his work, Bakhtin is trying to avoid abstract and reified oppositions that think away the phenomenon he is examining. If the past exhaustively determines the future, then creative work is meaningless because real agency does not belong to people but to impersonal laws; and if the past has no effect on the future, then human work is evidently also meaningless because it surrenders initiative to the irrational transcendental impulse that produces the creative product. Bakhtin finds that Goethe properly understood that a real sense of creativity would have to involve human work—"man the builder" (BSHR, p. 35; *chelovek-stroitel'*). It must involve work growing out of concrete needs but producing something that is also genuinely new and not exhaustively specified by the past. The essay on Goethe exemplifies Bakhtin's conceptualization of responsive unfinalizability as inseparable from prosaics.

It is useful to recall Bakhtin's approach to genres in his fourth period. Genres, he argued, "remember" the past and make their resources and potentials available to the present; authors exploit those potentials and in the process create new potentials for the future; as a result, works always contain more potential meanings (but not every conceivable meaning) than the author and his contemporaries know. Such potentials are activated in unexpected ways by later generations or different cultures in a process of creative understanding, in which a dialogue is produced between the work's potentials and the interpreter's unforeseeable and unique perspective. This model of genres grows out of Bakhtin's own sense of the "fullness of time" and of "creative necessity." It adds Bakhtin's third global concept of dialogue to the matrix of unfinalizability and prosaics in the Goethe essay.

Seeing Time

> The ability to *see time*, to *read time*, in the spatial whole of the world and, on the other hand, to perceive the filling of space not as an immobile background, a given that is completed once and for all, but as an emerging whole, an event—this is the ability to read in everything signs *that show time in its course*, beginning with nature and ending with human customs and ideas (all the way to abstract concepts). . . . The work of the seeing eye joins here with the most complex thought processes.   —BSHR, p. 25

This passage, which begins the third and final extant section of the essay on Goethe, points to important connections between Bakhtin's work on the chronotope and his early essays. We note first of all that for Bakhtin what is important is to perceive the world as an *emerging event*—or, in the phraseology of "Toward a

Philosophy of the Act"—to understand *eventness*. Eventness cannot be reduced to a ready-made or underlying abstract system, extends over time and across all cultural spheres, and continually produces the new. According to Bakhtin, Goethe understood the world in this way; he saw the world not as a totality of things, nor as a background to events, but as itself an ongoing event. That is why he was able to *see time*.

Bakhtin dwells on the great importance of vision and visibility for Goethe. Goethe understood time not just as an abstraction, but as a visible process, and so for him it was necessary to *see* time in concrete objects that bear the marks of pastness. Bakhtin's fascination with this aspect of Goethe's artistic imagination perhaps reflects the concerns of Bakhtin's own early work, in which the "field of vision" of each person in a particular space and time was central. He evidently detected in Goethe the historical and social dimension missing from the scenarios of vision in "Author and Hero" and from his description of the particular details shaping each person's "outlook."

To see time involves seeing "heterochrony" (*raznovremennost'*).[12] When Goethe "read" a landscape, he saw in it evidence of many different kinds of time: natural cycles, cycles marked by human labor, "the growth of trees and livestock, the age of people" (BSHR, p. 25), and "historical time in the strict sense of the word . . . visible vestiges of man's creativity, traces of his hand and mind, cities, streets, buildings, artworks, technology, social organizations, and so on" (ibid.). Each of these is itself heterochronous: nature has many different kinds of rhythms, and different spheres of human activity operate by different kinds of time. "Behind each multiformity he [Goethe] saw heterochrony" (BSHR, p. 28). To read time is to see the interactions of a world rich in temporalities.

Such temporal literacy, as we might call it, involves seeing in apparently static objects or institutions the "congealed" activity of the past and everything that still "pulsates" in the present (BSHR, p. 29). Just as the low chronotopicity of adventure time produced spatial objects that are "congealed suddenlys," so the high chronotopicity that Goethe valued turned the whole world into a congealed sequence. In an apparently static world, active forces are always shaping action. For this reason, Goethe was passionate about understanding historical events in their specific geographical and local setting; he wanted "to read Tacitus in Rome."

For a truly chronotopic imagination, then, time must be understood in its interconnection with specific space, and space must be understood as saturated with historical time. "The creative past must be revealed as necessary and productive under the conditions of a given locality, . . . which transforms a portion of terrestrial space into a place of historical life for people, into a little corner of the historical world" (BSHR, p. 34). For this reason, Goethe disliked fabricated tales for tourists, fake historical buildings, manufactured ruins, or museum-like artifacts that merely mixed up past and present without suggesting inner linkages between time and space or between past and present. "Goethe's chronotopic artistic imagination" (BSHR, p. 46) keenly sensed spacial falsity and temporal hypocrisy.

Finally, Goethe would always sense "the fresh wind of the future" in a given scene (BSHR, p. 36). That is, he sensed the opportunities, problems, and constraints shaping action in the concrete (not utopian or eschatological) future. He registered with great precision what work there was for man the builder to do. In short:

The main features of this [chronotopic] visualization are the merging of time (past with present), the fullness and clarity of the visibility of the time in space, the inseparability of the time of an event from the specific place of its occurrence (*Localität und Geschichte*), the visible *essential* connection of time (present and past), the creative and active nature of time (of the past in the present and of the present itself), the necessity that penetrates time and links time with space and different times with each other, and, finally, on the basis of the necessity that pervades localized time, the inclusion of the future, crowning the fullness of time in Goethe's images. [BSHR, pp. 41–42]

The realist novel of the nineteenth century was to incorporate this rich sense of time and further develop its potentials.

The extant fragment of the Goethe essay concludes by contrasting Goethe's rich sense of time with the relatively poor sense in Rousseau and Walter Scott. Focusing primarily on Rousseau's *Confessions*, Bakhtin observes that "Rousseau's artistic imagination was also chronotopic" (BSHR, p. 50) but less so than Goethe's. To be sure, Rousseau was able to see time in nature; nevertheless, in his artistic imagination "the only time that was separated from the background of natural time was idyllic time (also still cyclical) and biographical time, which had already surmounted its cyclical nature, but had not yet completely merged with real historical time. Therefore, creative historical necessity was almost completely foreign to Rousseau" (ibid.).

When Rousseau contemplates a landscape, for example, he succeeds in humanizing it, in transforming it from a piece of merely terrestrial space to a locus of human life. Nevertheless, that life is merely idyllic and biological. What one does not get in Rousseau, as one does in Goethe, is an image of people as creators and builders; the emphasis is not on the immediate concrete future in which people solve specific problems but on an image of a utopian Golden Age, "that is, the utopian past that is transferred into the utopian future" (BSHR, p. 51). Bakhtin cites Rousseau as a prime example of "historical inversion" that "bleeds" the real future. In such inversion, nature "bypasses" history, and we go straight from nature to utopia, without any intervening historical process. Thus, in Rousseau "the desired and the ideal are torn away from real time and necessity"; actions are not located as shaped by a particular time; we miss a rich sense of anachronism. Rousseau's time "lacks real duration and irreversibility" (ibid.). Idyllic days just repeat each other, and arbitrary fantasies shape Rousseau's meditations in a way that Goethe, with his truly historical sense of time, found distasteful.

What strikes Bakhtin about Walter Scott's poems is the author's ability to "see time in space" (BSHR, p. 53). In a way reminiscent of much folklore and of Pindar, Scott populates particular places with legends and history: "Local folklore interprets and saturates space with time, and draws it into history" (BSHR, p. 52). Nevertheless, in Scott "time still had the nature of a *closed past*" (BSHR, p. 53), by which Bakhtin means that the past events and picturesque ruins Scott describes are *merely* past, and have no creative effectiveness in the present. Scott, too, lacks Goethe's profound appreciation of "the *fullness of time*" (ibid.).

In Bakhtin's thought, Goethe and Dostoevsky represent two different impulses taken to their extremes. It will be recalled that Dostoevsky (as Bakhtin describes him) thought away development in order to present a world of pure simultaneity—"the cross section of a single moment." He also tended to confine his heroes to small spaces (thresholds, corridors, and other locales for scandal). This way of visualizing the world allowed Dostoevsky to create the most intense dialogues among people from different ideological camps, professions, backgrounds, even different eras. Developing the resources of menippean satire, with its dialogues among heroes in the underworld, Dostoevsky was the master of the threshold dialogue outside of time. For Goethe, by contrast, time was all. With his impulse to see time and read space, Bakhtin's Goethe exemplifies a vision maximally suited to a prosaic understanding of development over lifetimes, over great time.

For Bakhtin, Dostoevsky was the extreme dialogist, even though

his works lacked a sense of everyday life and historical development; Goethe, on the other hand, was the model for prosaics, even
at the expense of some dialogic complexity. Each exhibited an
understanding of unfinalizability, but their versions of it differed.
For Dostoevsky, unfinalizability resulted from the unpredictabil-
ity of dialogue, and became part of a world in which anything
might "suddenly" happen. For Goethe, unfinalizability was prosaic; bounded by constraints as well as endowed with potentials,
people change through the slow processes of accumulated small
decisions.

The spokesman for "creative necessity," Goethe understood the
inseparability of freedom and constraints. If Bakhtin had summed
up the import of Goethe's vision in the same terms as he paraphrased Dostoevsky's, he might have written: "For nothing absolutely conclusive has yet taken place in the world, a penultimate
word of the world and about the world is always being prepared
and always slowly changing, the world is more or less open and free
within limits, everything comes from the past and is reworked in
the present as we live into an open future."

Epic Versus Novel, "Absolute Past" Versus the "Zone of Familiar Contact"

The field available for representing the world changes from genre
to genre and from era to era as literature develops. It is recognized
in different ways and limited in space and time by different
means. But this field is always specific.   —EaN, p. 27

The novel, from the very beginning, developed as a genre that
had at its core a new way of conceptualizing time.

—EaN, p. 38

As we have seen, the overall tone of Bakhtin's essay "Epic and
Novel" is set by the concerns of period IIIb. But several sections of
the essay develop the arguments of period IIIa, especially his thinking about the chronotope of various genres. These sections in effect
extend the trajectory of the chronotope and Goethe essays to the
great novels of the nineteenth century.

In "Epic and Novel," Bakhtin describes the novelistic chronotope (he uses the concept but not the term) in two ways: first, by
focusing on the non-novelistic features of the epic as a point of con-

trast; and second, by dwelling on new elements that make the novel what it is.

He begins, characteristically, by developing Goethe's and Schiller's concept of "the absolute past." Bakhtin uses this term to characterize the particular sense of time *immanent* in epic as a formally constitutive feature, as the ground or field through which it represents the world. The epic conceives of time in a way radically different from, in fact opposite to, time in the novel.

In the novel, the author and readers are assumed to exist in the same *kind* of time as the world the novel describes. As Bakhtin puts the point, the novelist and his readers exist in a "zone of familiar contact" with the heroes. Thus, Pushkin can be personally close to his hero Eugene Onegin, whereas an epic poet could never be so with Achilles, Aeneas, or Adam. Readers of novels can identify with the heroes and heroines they read about in ways that the audience of epic poems could not. At times, this special novelistic identification may be naive, as in the "local cults" of novelistic places (journeys to the pond where "Poor Liza" drowned herself) or in various forms of "Bovaryism" (EaN, p. 32). Indeed, there may arise a special type of novelistic risk, a "specific danger inherent in the novelistic zone of contact: we ourselves may actually enter the novel. . . . It follows that we might substitute for our own life an obsessive reading of novels, or dreams based on novelistic models" (ibid.). We may become like Madame Bovary or like the hero of Dostoevsky's *White Nights*. This very phenomenon attests to the fact that the readers and the heroes of novels live in the same kind of time, and so their two worlds are more readily interchanged.

No such zone of familiar contact is possible in epic. Epic time is sealed off from the present (the time of the singer and audience) by a qualitative distance. One cannot go back by a series of "gradual, purely temporal progressions" (EaN, p. 15) until one reaches the time of the epic world, because epic time is understood not just as a long time ago, but as fundamentally different and totally remote. It is in this sense that absolute past is *absolute*, not just a "*merely transitory past*" (EaN, p. 19). By contrast, the novel understands the past as simply another present, as a time in which different events happened that do not happen now, but which can be reached by a series of backward steps and which at the time described felt open-ended, inconclusive, and problematic, just as our own time feels to us. Thus, it is in the novel, and the novel alone, that "we have the possibility of an authentically objective portrayal of the past" (EaN, p. 29) because only the novel understands contemporaneity and presentness well enough to represent the feel of presentness experienced by people of another era.

The absolute boundary that separates the epic poet and audience from the world of epic heroes makes it necessary to speak not of merely temporal categories (past, present, future) but of "*valorized-temporal categories*" (EaN, p. 15). In the novel, greatest value is placed on the immediate future, in which real problems must be solved and in which real becoming takes place. In the epic, all real value belongs to the absolute past; it is the world in which values originated and were fixed forever, beyond our power to modify them. "In the past, everything is good; [indeed,] all the really good things (i.e., the 'first' things) occur *only* in this past" (ibid.).

As a result, tradition in epic has a special meaning beyond being its "factual source" (EaN, p. 16). "What matters rather is that a reliance on tradition is immanent in the very form of the epic" (ibid.). Novels, too, can reflect upon and make use of tradition, of course, but they do so in a different way. In novels, tradition is made accessible to personal experience, and individual evaluations of tradition are possible. One can enter into dialogue with tradition, and one has the right to agree or disagree with it, both of which are dialogic relations. But in epic no such stance with respect to tradition is possible: "One cannot glimpse it, grope for it, touch it; one cannot look at it from just any point of view; it is impossible to experience it, analyze it, take it apart, penetrate its core. It is given solely as tradition, sacred and sacrosanct, evaluated in the same way by all and demanding a pious attitude toward itself" (ibid.). Epic tradition is apparently analogous to an "authoritative," not an "innerly persuasive," word. Bakhtin here is speaking not of all epics, but of "epicness," much as in characterizing poetry in "Discourse in the Novel" he speaks of the "ideal limit" to which the form-shaping ideology of lyric poetry strives.

In epic, everything really important is sensed as already over. "There is no place in the epic world for openendedness, indecision, indeterminacy. There are no loopholes in it through which we glimpse the future; it suffices unto itself, neither supposing any continuation nor requiring it" (ibid.), as the novel by its very nature does.

Certain temporal categories present in Greek romance are also well developed in epic—for example, "nuances of 'earlier,' 'later,' sequences of moments, speeds, durations, etc." (EaN, p. 19). But because these events are "not localized in an actual historical sequence" (ibid.) potentially leading up to the present, they appear as a completed and closed "circle" on which "all points are equidistant from the real, dynamic time of the present" (ibid.). It is as if the entire "fullness of time" (ibid.) were contained in the epic world in which we cannot participate.

This sense of time explains why "epic is indifferent to formal beginnings and can remain incomplete" (EaN, p. 31) with no loss of a sense of wholeness. Formal closure in a novelistic sense is not needed "because the structure of the whole is repeated in each part, and each part is complete and circular like the whole. One may begin the story at almost any moment, and finish at almost any moment" (ibid.). The *world* is whole, complete, and sensed as complete in advance. "The *Iliad* is a random excerpt from the Trojan cycle. Its ending (the burial of Hector) could not possibly be the ending from a novelistic point of view" (EaN, p. 32)—although, of course, it is always possible to "novelize" the epic by reading it with the presuppositions of novels and seek a novelistic reason for this ending.

Read in terms of the epic form-shaping ideology, epics do not require an answer to novelistic questions—"How does the war end? Who wins? What will happen to Achilles? and so forth" (ibid.). These answers are already known, and the locus of interest does not lie with them. The fullness and completedness of the epic world, in other words, excludes the sort of "impulse to continue" and "impulse to end" (ibid.) that we find in novels, because such impulses are possible only in a world with an open future and a world in which everything important is not already over.

"It is impossible to achieve greatness in one's own time" (EaN, p. 18)—a saying Bakhtin interprets *not* to mean that contemporaries cannot achieve greatness but that epic greatness is not possible in time felt as an open-ended present, as something located in the "zone of familiar contact." The important point is not when events happen but the *kind* of time in which they happen. Contemporaries can achieve greatness in their own time if they are represented and sensed as existing in a special sort of world beyond familiar contact. Bakhtin might well have had in mind the epic treatment of heroes in Socialist Realist fiction, in the Soviet press (Stakhanovites), and in official representations of Stalin.[13] One also senses an allusion to Soviet conditions in Bakhtin's cryptic observation that an epic attitude toward present figures has been used "up to the nineteenth century, and even further" (EaN, p. 20).

The opposite phenomenon is also possible: one can represent heroes traditionally accorded epic treatment in the zone of familiar

contact, in contemporary time, and thereby change them in fundamental ways. In the ancient world, for example, some works represented the heroes of the Trojan cycle as if they lived in just another
present, and so we witness "epic . . . being transformed into novel"
(EaN, p. 15). In menippean satire, for example in Lucian or Julian
the Apostate, epic heroes may be brought together in the underworld, where they jostle each other, brawl, and argue with living
contemporaries. A "radical shift of the temporally valorized center
of artistic orientation" (EaN, p. 26) has brought the heroes into a
zone of familiar contact, in fact, of "crude contact, where we can
grab at everything with our own hands" (ibid.). By dragging epic
heroes out of the absolute past, ancient menippean satire helped
shape the chronotope of the modern novel.

In short: "The epic past is a special form for perceiving people
and events in art. . . . Artistic representation here is representation
sub specie aeternitatis" (EaN, p. 18). The "eyes" of the epic genre see
differently from the eyes of the novel.

Presentness and the "Surplus of Humanness"

> Reality as we have it in the novel is only one of many possible
> realities; it is not inevitable, not arbitrary, it bears within itself
> other possibilities.   —EaN, p. 37

More than any other genre, the novel understands "presentness": the sense of time as it is lived, the relation of that time to the
past, and the value of the imminent future to which it is always oriented. "The present, in its so-called 'wholeness' (although it is, of
course, never whole) is in essence and in principle inconclusive; by
its very nature it demands continuation, it moves into the future,
and the more actively and consciously it moves into the future the
more tangible and indispensable its inconclusiveness becomes"
(EaN, p. 30). So conceived, presentness is never a complete structure in which everything has its place; it is "never whole," always
messy, and that messiness is essential to its identity.

Presentness is also by its nature open in the sense that it can lead
to many different futures; one cannot properly narrate the present
backwards, from the point toward which it ultimately happened to
lead, because it did not *have* to lead there. In fully realized novels,
the plot is understood as only one of many possible plots. In other
words, when the novel realizes its potential, events, people, and the
world can realize theirs.

Thus, the world of the novel "becomes a world where there is no first word (no ideal word), and the final word has not yet been spoken" (EaN, p. 30). Here Bakhtin is echoing a phrase from his book on Dostoevsky (or vice versa), and the logic of his observations about presentness would appear to establish Dostoevsky as the writer who best developed this aspect of novelistic generic potential.

The consequences of the novelistic sense of present and imminent future, whether Goethe's or Dostoevsky's, are immense for Bakhtin, because "for the first time in artistic-ideological consciousness, time and the world become historical: they unfold, albeit at first still unclearly and confusedly, as becoming, as an uninterrupted movement into a real future" (EaN, p. 30). Perhaps Tolstoy best developed novelistic potential in this sense: he understood change as gradual becoming and so "did not value the [separate] moment, he did not strive to fill it with something fundamental and decisive. . . . Tolstoy loves duration, the stretching out of time" (FTC, p. 249). What Goethe, Dostoevsky, and Tolstoy understood—what the form-shaping ideology of the genre in which they worked allowed them to understand—was that there can be no real sense of historicity unless the future is open and the present contains multiple potentials to be developed, or left undeveloped, by the efforts of real people.

Multiple possible futures—another aspect of heterochrony—are conceivable only in a world where prophecy, at home in epic and other genres, has no place. Not prophecy but uncertain prediction is characteristic of the novel, which speculates in categories of ignorance. In the novel, knowledge is always a genuine problem, and so the novel becomes a profoundly epistemological genre.

In the world according to the novel, the image of a person necessarily changes over time. Main characters in novels can and do become different, and they never exhaust the possibilities they can become and could have become. At every moment, old potentials die, seem as if they had never been, and new ones, only some of which can be realized, come into existence, at which point other potentials are lost and still newer ones are produced. Man is ever "noncoincident" with himself (EaN, p. 36). By contrast, an epic hero *is* his destiny, and there is nothing else he can be. Outside that destiny, the epic or tragic hero "is nothing; he is, therefore, a function of the plot fate assigns him; he cannot become the hero of another destiny or another plot" (ibid.). But novels ask us to imagine the "what if," and novelists sometimes make new novels out of the "what if."

It could be said that one of the most fundamental themes of novels is "precisely the theme of the hero's inadequacy to his fate or situation. The individual is either greater than his fate, or less than his condition. He cannot become once and for all a clerk, a landowner, a merchant, a fiancé, a jealous lover, a father and so forth" (EaN, p. 37). A main character has an interior, a subjectivity, in tension with his exterior; he cannot be described the same way from outside as he senses himself. (Here Bakhtin develops the dilemma of "consciousness perceiving itself" discussed in "Author and Hero.") Deep within the character there are potentials, and these potentials could be made visible by novels only because of their new sense of time and "the zone of contact with an inconclusive present (and consequently with the future)" (ibid.). Always essentially what he is not but could perhaps become, the novelistic hero, conceived with all his "unrealized potential and unrealized demands" (ibid.) is a creature made in part of the future: "The future exists, and this future ineluctably touches upon the individual, has its roots in him" (ibid.).

Bakhtin thus opposes the novelistic image of a person with the image common in vulgar (and some sophisticated) Marxism and in the more common kinds of sociological thought. However much people are shaped by history and society, "an individual cannot be completely incarnated in the flesh of existing sociohistorical categories" (ibid.). That is so first because "real historical time" itself contains not just "categories" and qualities but also potentials; and second, because individuals contain potentials to be found nowhere else. "There is no mere form that would be able to incarnate once and forever all of his human possibilities and needs, no form in which he could exhaust himself down to the last word . . . no form that he could fill to the brim and yet at the same time not splash over the brim. . . . All existing clothes are always too tight, and thus comical, on a man" (ibid.). What makes a person what he truly is, and what novels correctly understand a person to be, is what Bakhtin calls his "surplus of humanness": "there always remains a need for the future, and a place for this future must be found" (ibid).

Chronotope and Dialogue

In 1973, Bakhtin added a final chapter to his chronotope essay. "Concluding Remarks" first clarifies and summarizes the main points already made in previous chapters and then extends chronotopic analysis to new subjects, which are only briefly sketched out. Made in a terse, even aphoristic style, the arguments of this section require special attention.

So far, Bakhtin observes, he has described only the "major chronotopes" that define genres and constitute the principal field for events in particular works. But works often contain more than one chronotope. Some may be drawn from life, others from literary works of various genres; still others may be present as congealed events in specific chronotopic motifs. In life, too, particular institutions or activities combine and are constituted by diverse chronotopes. "Chronotopes are mutually inclusive, they co-exist, they may be interwoven with, replace or oppose one another, contradict one another or find themselves in ever more complex interrelationships" (FTC, p. 252).

What is the nature of the interactions among chronotopes? It is clear that such interactions cannot themselves be exhaustively, or even primarily, described in chronotopic terms. Chronotopes provide the ground for particular kinds of activity and carry with them a particular sense of experience; but the relation of several chronotopes to each other is not a depicted action in any one of them. We are dealing with relations of a different order. These relations are, for example, relations of agreement or disagreement, of parody or polemic, in all their various nuances: in other words, the interactions among chronotopes in a work are *dialogic* in nature.

Here and elsewhere in "Concluding Remarks," Bakhtin recognizes the value of exploring the links between his two great concepts of dialogue and chronotope. Chronotopes may interact dialogically; indeed, this idea is already implicit in his concept of "heterochrony" (in the Bildungsroman essay), a term evidently coined by analogy to heteroglossia (*raznorechie* and *raznovremennost'*; literally, varied-speechedness and varied-timeness).

Much as diverse languages of heteroglossia may confront each other dialogically, so may diverse chronotopes. In that case, the sense of experience in each language or chronotope is seen in the light of the other language's or chronotope's sense of experience. We may be asked to imagine the same event placed in different fields, or the same topic discussed in different languages of heteroglossia, and so come to appreciate the limitations and potentials of each chronotope or language with respect to rivals. In the process, we may come to lose linguistic or chronotopic "naivete."

Not only do chronotopes behave like languages, Bakhtin suggests, but they are also intrinsic to certain metalinguistic categories, such as speech genres. In specifying the norms, assumptions, and values for a particular kind of exchange, a given speech genre also sets expectations for the kind of time and space on which the exchange will rely. (Here we are drawing "dotted lines" from Bakhtin's brief comments, so examples are necessarily our own.) One may observe, for example, that the exchange of information at a railroad information desk takes place in a different chronotope from the one governing a public lecture, but a very specific sense of time and space is an intrinsic part of each. Bakhtin apparently has in mind the sort of insights that Edward Hall later developed (in *The Hidden Dimension*) as "proxemics," which from a Bakhtinian perspective might better have been conceived as something like "chronoproxemics."[14]

Thus, all dialogues take place in a given chronotope, and chronotopes enter into dialogic relations. Each concept is needed for a full understanding of the other, but the two are nevertheless distinct.

In order to understand the dialogue among chronotopes in a work, we must recognize that "the relationships themselves that exist *among* chronotopes cannot enter into any of the relationships contained *within* chronotopes" (FTC, p. 252). Interchronotopic relations thus are not part of the world represented in the work—which is always represented within a given chronotope—but they *are* definitely part of the work itself "as a whole" (ibid.). Works that create chronotopic dialogues of this sort, in other words, seem to envelop the world they represent with a special dialogic field that "enters the world of the author, of the performer, and of the world of the listeners and readers" (ibid.).[15]

To take the argument one step further, the worlds of author, reader, performer, and listener are necessarily chronotopic as well: these activities take place in a specific kind of time and space. We may therefore ask: "How are the chronotopes of the author and the listener or reader presented to us?" (ibid.). To answer this question, we need to recognize that the text, insofar as it figures in culture, is not just a dead thing (although it is always partially that)—that is, it is not just writing on parchment or paper, but also an utterance. "We not only see and perceive it but in it we can always hear voices (even while reading silently to ourselves). . . . we always arrive, in the final analysis, at the human voice, which is to say we come up against the human being" (FTC, pp. 252–53). The readers, too, are real people engaged in an activity that is performed in a specific time and place. Both author and reader, in other words, are "located in a real unitary and as yet incomplete historical world" (FTC, p. 253), which is to say, a world that is unfinalizable and in which the activity of writing and reading is shaped by presentness.

That world is "set off by a sharp and categorical boundary from the *represented* world in the text" (ibid.). Failure to understand the nature of this boundary can lead to two broad types of errors. On the one hand, if the boundary is not taken seriously enough, the result is likely to be either naive realism, or naive biographism, or naive reader reception (which confuses readers of different periods with readers of one's own time).[16] Although the first two kinds of naivete are well known, the third, conceived as parallel to the other two, would seem to be Bakhtin's response to much reader reception theory.

On the other hand, if the boundary between the world of reading or writing and the represented world is mistakenly understood as impermeable, the result is likely to be "an oversimplified, dogmatic hairsplitting" (FTC, p. 254), visible, for instance, in Formalist and more recent narratology. By speaking of a *categorical* boundary, then, Bakhtin means that there is always a distinction to be drawn, but *not* that interaction is ever impossible. On the contrary, interaction is always taking place, and if it did not, the work could not be meaningful, could not survive. Between the represented world and the world of the readers and authors—the creating world—"uninterrupted exchange goes on . . . similar to the uninterrupted exchange of matter between living organisms and the environment that surrounds them. As long as the organism lives, it resists a fusion with the environment, but if it is torn out of its environment, it dies" (ibid.). This comparison, like that of chronotope with Einsteinian time-space, appears to lie in that realm that is more than mere metaphor but less than total identity.

Bakhtin's thinking about the relation of the creating to the represented worlds, and about the dangers of naive reader reception, seems to be grounded in Bakhtin's fourth-period work on genres, interpretation, and great time. Thus, an important set of points concerns the differences that often obtain between the unfinalized world of the author and the unfinalized world of the reader, because the two worlds may be ages or cultures apart. And of course, if the work survives, readerships will also differ from each other. The themes of the chronotope essay therefore lead us to the line of thinking present in Bakhtin's "Response to a Question from the *Novyi mir* Editorial Staff," "Toward a Reworking of the Dostoevsky Book," and in the conclusion to "Discourse in the Novel."[17]

How do works rich in potential grow in meaning by acts of creative understanding taking place over great time? Just as the processes of "canonization" and "reaccentuation" may affect or enrich the meaning of works, so may analogous changes in the chronotopes of the reader's world. We may presumably speak of a changing chronotopic background as well as a changing dialogic background. These factors, and many more, establish the differences of culture—the *outsideness*—that makes real dialogue among cultures and periods possible.

Basically, changing chronotopes offer the same interpretive alternatives as do changing languages. Readers may "enclose the work within its epoch" by trying to see only the chronotope of original and ostensibly passive readers; that is, they may try to engage in pure empathy and to give up their outsideness as much as possible. Or, still less fruitfully, readers can "modernize and distort" the work by suppressing chronotopic differences in the opposite way, by seeing only their own chronotope. Finally, they can take maximal advantage of the differences and of their outsideness by an act of creative understanding that is truly dialogic in the best sense. Readers may make the differences an occasion for exploring the potentials of the work in a way not available to its original author and readers, and so become enriched by something truly in the work but needing their own special experience to provoke.

Bakhtin elsewhere describes creative understanding in terms of his metalinguistic framework, that is, in terms of dialogue; here he postulates a special *chronotope* in which such dialogues may take place:

The work and the world represented in it enter the real world and enrich it, and the real world enters the work and its world as part of the process of its creation, as well as part of its subsequent life, in a continual renewing of the work through the creative perception of listeners and readers. Of course this process of exchange is itself chronotopic: it occurs first and foremost in the historically developing social world, but without ever losing contact with changing historical space. We might even speak of a special *creative* chronotope inside which this exchange between work and life occurs, and which constitutes the distinctive life of the work. [FTC, p. 254]

The "Image of the Author"

Bakhtin suggests that to understand literary works it would be necessary to explore more fully the chronotopes of reading and creating. With regard to the listener or reader, "his chronotopic situation, and his role in renewing the work" (FTC, p. 257), Bakhtin observes briefly and cryptically that "every literary work *faces outward away from itself*, toward the listener-reader, and to a certain extent anticipates possible reactions to itself" (ibid.). He appears to want to develop the sort of insights implicit in his concept of a work's "exterior" chronotope and in his combination of dialogic and chronotopic analysis. With regard to the chronotope of authorship, he offers somewhat more substantial comments. These comments, which rework and reaccentuate ideas from his first period, may seem opaque if one does not approach them from the perspective of Bakhtin's other writings, especially those not yet available in English.

Bakhtin distinguishes between the author as a particular person living at a given time (the biographical author) and the author as creator of the work (the so-called image of the author), but his main concerns lie with other issues. Much as in other writings he suggests that authorial intention is far more complex than either intentionalists or their opponents have imagined, in the chronotope essay he suggests that the very concept of "the image of the author," for all its wide circulation, has not been clearly thought through.

The basic problem with this concept is that, properly speaking, the author as creator of the work has no image. For authorship is an activity, a process of moment-to-moment work, not a fixed image; the author senses himself not as a person executing a preformed plan but as a person at work over an incomplete task in an open world. To the extent that we sense the author as creator, we sense him in that way, which means, without an "image." In these observations, we see how Bakhtin's recurrent interest in the creative process and his global concepts of unfinalizability and prosaics shape, and occasionally undo, the very terms he tries to explicate.

To put Bakhtin's point differently, the author-as-creator, strictly speaking, has no image because the author-as-creator is a creat*ing*, not a creat*ed*, thing; he represents, but is not himself represented. Or to use the terminology of "Author and Hero," he exists primarily in the realm of "I-for-myself," which means that he is not part of the world (or work); rather, he is himself an unfinalizable component *entering into* the work. To say as much does not mean to say that we cannot know the author-as-creator, but it does mean that we know him by sensing his activity. Bakhtin also does not mean to say that we cannot *construct* an image of the author; on the contrary, he says that we usually do construct such an image, because in some important respects the construction aids the work of interpretation. For example, a constructed image of an author may allow us to relate the work to the specific social and historical context in which it was created, and thus to make use of biographical data. Such an image "can help the listener or reader more correctly and profoundly to understand the work of the given author" (FTC, p. 257). But the image we create is still not the author-as-creator. It is our version of "the-other-for-me" and not the actual "I-for-myself" who creates.

Bakhtin does not specify the errors that the confusion of a constructed image with the author-as-creator might produce, but he may have in mind two types of false leads. First, there are mistakes involving the kind of work the reader is doing in the act of interpretation, which lead to fruitless debates about objectivity or relativism. Second, there can be oversimplifications regarding the nature of creativity as a genuine process. In that case, what typically follows is a misunderstanding of intention, of the relation of work to life, and, in general, of everything connected with creativity as a process of real and open work.

The I-for-myself, the author-as-creator, is always outside the work, or tangential to it, Bakhtin contends. For example, if I tell a tale, "then I as the *teller* (or writer) of this event am already outside the time and space in which the event occurred" (FTC, p. 256). That narrated event is completed, but the act of telling itself is not.

From this perspective, Bakhtin recasts some well-known distinctions, drawn by the Formalists and inherited by narratology. In Bakhtin's view, the real difference between *fabula* and *siuzhet* is not primarily that one is raw material for artistic reshaping into the other. The important distinction is that between the "different worlds" in which the represented events unfold, on the one hand, and in which, on the other, the author is in the process of describing those events. These worlds combine to produce the "fullness of the work in all its wholeness and indivisibility" (FTC, p. 255).

The apprehension of a work involves the recognition of these two different kinds of worlds. From the perspective of the author-as-creator, the represented world may be finalized whereas his own cannot be. (The argument of the Dostoevsky book would suggest that only in the polyphonic work can there be openness in the represented world, just as there is in the world of the author at work.) The author's *activity* can always be sensed in one way or another, for example, in the act of segmenting the work, or in the very choosing of a starting point. Such a choice must be made from outside the world represented, but it figures in our apprehension of the work.

The author can convey (and we can perceive) the traces of authorial activity, but what we cannot perceive, and what the author cannot convey, is either the creating activity itself or the creating self that acts. That is what Bakhtin appears to mean when he writes: "It is just as impossible to forge an identity between myself, my own 'I,' and that 'I' that is the subject of my stories as it is to lift myself up by my own hair. . . . That is why the term 'image of the author' seems to me so inadequate: everything that becomes an image in the literary work, and consequently enters its chronotopes, is a created thing and not a force that itself creates" (FTC, p. 256).

The Gates of the Chronotope

Bakhtin concludes with some observations about "the boundaries of chronotopic analysis" (FTC, p. 257). Many meanings are chronotopic, that is, intrinsically shaped by a specific time-space, but not all of them are. We have already seen, for example, that dialogic relations are not reducible to chronotopic ones. Moreover, numerous meaningful elements in science, art, and literature "are not subject to temporal and spatial determinations" (ibid.). Thus, mathematical concepts may be used for measuring time and space, but they are not in themselves chronotopic. There are numerous similar concepts in "abstract cognition"; indeed, nonchronotopic meaningful elements figure even in "artistic thinking."

Nevertheless, our concrete *apprehension* of these nonchronotopic elements is necessarily chronotopic. For in order to become part of our experience, these elements must be understood in a given context; that context is necessarily chronotopic and partially shapes the act of understanding. In short, although some kinds of meanings are not in principle chronotopic, understanding itself cannot escape chronotopicity. Or as Bakhtin puts the point, "without such temporal-spatial expression, even abstract thought is impossible. Consequently, every entry into the sphere of meaning is accomplished only through the gates of the chronotope" (FTC, p. 258).

This final sentence is often misunderstood to mean that all meaning is by nature chronotopic, but if our interpretation of this passage is accurate, that interpretation is incorrect. Meanings can dwell outside the gates of the chronotope, but we must live within them. For us to understand those meanings, they must reach us; they must pass through the gates of the chronotope.

10

Laughter and the Carnivalesque

We have so far discussed two ways in which Bakhtin sought to specify the nature of "novelness." The first, "dialogized heteroglossia," involves a special multivoiced use of language; the second, novelistic "chronotopicity," denotes an increasingly historical, concrete, and differentiated use of time and space. The present chapter is devoted to the third model that Bakhtin offered for understanding novels, what might loosely be called "the carnivalesque." Novels are described as inspired by a laughing truth, indebted to parodic genres and to the spirit of carnival. As Dostoevsky is exemplary for the first set of criteria and Goethe for the second, so Rabelais is the hero of the third.

The first two markers for the novel, heteroglossia and a high degree of chronotopicity, are quite compatible. In both, high value is placed on particularity and heterogeneity, either in voice or in "timespace." Each represents an aspect of the same form-shaping ideology, for each commits diverse individuals and voices to specific situations. But the third category is quite different: in the writings of period IIIb, values become ritualistic, collective, and generalizable. Both voice and body begin to function in ways inconsistent with Bakhtin's earlier and later formulations. Thus, we can speak of the "carnival writings" as a distinct group or period within Bakhtin's work, with their own motivation and internal consistency.

In this chapter, we will proceed chronologically for several reasons. First, Bakhtin's numerous "carnival terms" occur in various contexts, with significantly different emphases, evaluations, and theoretical implications. Second, a chronological approach will allow us to explore Bakhtin's grounds for turning to this complex of ideas. To do so, it will be necessary to discuss carnival "from within" Bakhtin's thought. What problems was the concept formulated to solve, and why did Bakhtin experiment with this solution?

Parody and Parodic Doubles

Bakhtin makes his first extensive statement about the liberating potential of laughter in his essay of the late 1930's, "From the Prehistory of Novelistic Discourse." Almost nostalgically, he asserts that the so-called literary parody we study today is an impoverished and reduced thing. "In modern times," Bakhtin notes, "the functions of parody are narrow and unproductive. Parody has grown sickly, its place in modern literature is insignificant" (PND, p. 71). Today we laugh one-way, *at* people and things. Ridicule of the serious word is everywhere, but much of parody's ancient complexity and strength has been lost.

According to Bakhtin, the true and healthy parody of earlier times was "free of any nihilistic denial" (PND, p. 55). All parties to the exchange laughed in all directions. In contrast to its impoverished modern variant, such parody does not undermine a hero or his exploits; it parodies only their tragic heroization. "The genre itself . . . [is] put in cheerfully irreverent quotation marks" (ibid.). This sort of parody can generate true heroes, who are heroic precisely because they contain more possibilities for growth and change than can be encompassed by any single given genre. The serious word is not discredited; it is complemented and supplemented.

Throughout "Prehistory," Bakhtin presumes this fundamental distinction between two types of parody or laughter. When he observes that every serious word in antiquity had its parodic double (PND, p. 53), he does not mean to imply that the double discredited the serious word itself, but only a one-sided interpretation of it. Parody emerges here as a subcategory of creative potential. It is the "corrective of reality," always richer and more contradictory than any single genre or word can express (PND, p. 55). This corrective is the real value of the laughing word, which "proved to be just as profoundly productive and deathless a creation of Rome as Roman law" (PND, p. 58).

Thus, the parodies of epic texts, prayers, grammars, and liturgies that Bakhtin enumerates here and in other essays were not necessarily perceived by their contemporaries as disrespectful. Such parodies were understood as "intentional dialogized hybrids" (either linguistic or stylistic). The author distanced himself from an authoritative style so that a new point of view could be brought to the topic, which enriched it, stressed its multiple potential, and thereby foregrounded a special role for the creative artist. "Linguistic consciousness . . . constituted itself *outside* [the] direct word . . . the creating artist began to look at language from the outside, with another's eyes, from the point of view of a potentially different language and style" (PND, p. 60). In this emphasis on the importance of *potential* and *outsideness* to true parody, we see a close continuity with concerns central to Bakhtin ever since the early 1920's. Laughter becomes the sound outsideness makes.

Bakhtin reminds us that in antiquity and the Middle Ages an enormous variety of parodic genres existed in literature, in folklore, and in behavior (even if their surviving traces are few). In "Prehistory," Bakhtin emphasizes the legality and thus the conservative nature of "parodic-travestying" forms and festivals. There is little suggestion of the radical or revolutionary aspects of parodic laughter that were to play so large a part in his later, Rabelaisian, carnival view of the world.

"Prehistory" thus maps out a generous and positive agenda. Parody undermines not authority in principle but only authority with pretensions to be timeless and absolute. Parodic forms enable us to distance ourselves from words, to be *outside* any given utterance and to assume our own unique attitude toward it. Thus, the parodic words we use are important not because they can change reality (they need not), but because they increase our freedom of interpretive choice by providing new perspectives. As Bakhtin was later to develop this more or less stoic idea, true human freedom and responsibility lie not in the ability to change concrete facts, but in the contemplative power of the "witness and the judge" (N70–71, pp. 137–38).

Compared with his treatment of carnival laughter and the grotesque body in the Rabelais book, Bakhtin's concerns in "Prehistory" center more on the individual speaker and on the tone and content of the speaker's utterance. In retrospect, the "utopianism" of period IIIb is inconsistent with the modest and more restrained understanding of parody we find in "Prehistory."

Laughter Chronotopes: Embodiment Versus Potential

"Forms of Time and of the Chronotope" devotes several chapters to laughter and "folkloric structures." In these chapters, Bakhtin forges a connection between the novel and the carnivalesque. In the context of the chronotope essay, the trajectory toward carnival is often at odds with the main argument, and Bakhtin seems to be in transition between his two theories.

Bakhtin focuses in these chapters on two concepts that figured in his early writings: *embodiment* and *potential*. Both are celebrated, but they differ from and sometimes seem to conflict with each other. Embodiment as a value is expressed by "folkloric identity," in which a hero equals his physicality. In this chronotope, ideas are spatially and temporally embodied in such a way that good ideas take up more space than bad ones and everything good grows bigger. When a person grows, the world grows; we witness a direct proportionality of size to value. In this special sense, the "folklore chronotope" is not symbolic but mimetic.

But alongside this principle of direct material embodiment (and as if on the same plane), Bakhtin introduces the idea of *potential*, that which is by its very nature unrepresented and perhaps unrepresentable in any direct way. Rather than illustrate this concept through mythic figures, Bakhtin turns to three marginalized characters: the rogue, the clown, and the fool. Symbols of *noncoincidence* wherever they appear, this triad represents the right to be more than any given role: "the right to be *other* in this world, the right not to make common cause with any single one of the existing categories that life makes available" (FTC, p. 159). Thus, they can exploit any position—but only as a mask.

The clown and the fool, Bakhtin claims, are the world's primordial laughers, and they laugh not just at others but at themselves. Laughter serves to externalize them, to liberate them from the constraints that might be dictated both by some internal essence and by outside conditions of class, status, profession, or environment. Rogues and fools, therefore, enjoy a peculiar "chronotope of the entr'acte" (FTC, p. 163) related to, but not to be identified with, the "intervalic chronotope" (discussed in Chapter Nine). In the chronotope of the entr'acte, rogues and fools exercise the right to rip off masks and to survive any particular delimiting plot. The body we see in any given time and space is *not* wholly representative of a personality or its possible future development. Embodiment makes a body and its size all, whereas potential makes it *not* all, and not what it appears to be.

The oxymoron that Bakhtin invokes to join these two opposing concepts is the "realistic fantastic" (FTC, p. 150). In his view, this chronotope, adapted from folklore, is folklore's most substantial contribution to the novel. In chapter seven of the essay, Bakhtin then provides his first sustained application of these folkloric chronotopes to literature—as it happens, to the work of Rabelais.

Bakhtin's rarely discussed analysis of Rabelais in the chronotope essay offers a fascinating glimpse into what we might call "responsible carnival," carnival still tied down to concrete personalities in a recognizably real space and time. It is quite different in tone and spirit from *Rabelais and His World*. Carnival in this redaction is directed toward affirmative, positive, and humanist action to be undertaken within the historical process. In the chronotope essay, Bakhtin emphasizes the continuity between the earthbound folkloric chronotope and the Rabelaisian chronotope, and identifies the common foe of both as the "medieval worldview" that has "bled" history as well as the body of any concrete significance. Under these historical circumstances, Rabelais's task was "the re-creation of a spatially and temporally adequate world able to provide a new chronotope for a new, whole and harmonious man, and for new forms of human communication" (FTC, p. 168). In other words, Rabelais's carnival laughter was integral to Renaissance humanism.

Although the ultimate goal of Rabelaisian thought is described as wholeness and harmony, Bakhtin argues that to confront a foe as powerful as the medieval worldview it was necessary to resort to grotesquerie. Rabelais's manifest passion for extreme (and extremely "uncultured") acts of the body and the word was an exuberant rejection of all "ideologically negative things" produced by the "transcendental ascetic world view" of the Middle Ages, which could only be countered by an exaggeration in the opposite direction (FTC, p. 185). This oppositional strategy was designed to destroy all habitual linguistic and ideological "matrices." To do so, unexpected connections of words and images were created in order to upset languages and conceptions "shot through with centuries and millennia of error" (FTC, p. 169). The result of this strategy was another paradox, "realistic folklore fantasy" (FTC, p. 175).

At this point in Bakhtin's thinking, the grotesque in Rabelais is seen as serving a clearly defined purpose. It was a temporary means to a new world, whose matrices would not themselves turn out to be grotesque. Rather, that newborn world would be "permeated with an internal and authentic necessity. . . . The destruction of the old picture of the world and the positive construction of a new picture are indissolubly interwoven with each other" (FTC, p. 169). In the Rabelais of "Chronotope," the grotesque and laughter are strategies for getting creativity back into time and the body (FTC, p. 170).

In contrast to *Rabelais and His World*, the chronotope essay does not glorify orifices and protuberances for their own sake, and does not revel in the "lower bodily stratum" and its activities. Instead, Rabelais's novel is presented as the first attempt to structure a picture of the world around the human being as a positive and value-generating *body*. To this end, the body is literally opened up "in order to demonstrate its complexity and depth . . . to uncover a new place for human corporeality" (FTC, p. 170). The medieval world is said to have viewed the body as licentious, crude, self-destructive, and to have divorced it from any meaningful relationship to human speech. A general campaign had to be waged, therefore, against "finishedness," against roundedness in space and cyclicity in time, and against the linear, transcendent medieval view of history "where real time is devalued and dissolved in extratemporal categories" (FTC, p. 206). In Bakhtin's view, medieval temporality was purely destructive; it could create nothing new. Rabelais fought a Rabelaisian war against medieval time.

Reading these chapters on the Rabelaisian and carnival chronotopes, one is constantly aware of the extent to which they are, as the subtitle proclaims, an essay in *historical* poetics. In the spirit of his hymns to heteroglossia in period IIIa, Bakhtin describes Rabelaisian language as both rich and enriching, as aimed polemically against a dessicated medieval usage. Rabelais constructed new "associative matrices" for words and thus, to use a Formalist phrase, "de-automatized" them. His manipulation and crossing of "drinking series," "food series," "sex series," and "death series" turned common verbal clusters into monsters. Death somehow merges with defecation and sex with overeating. Indecency and comic juxtaposition forced a rethinking of all fixed categories.

A grotesque-word matrix drags the messy body into territory previously occupied by disembodied, hierarchical word systems. It spreads obscenities throughout learned talk, and degrades language in order to transform abstract thought into something more material, concrete, and widely shareable. These indecencies are thus understood as *part of a dialogue*, which is not the way such language works in *Rabelais and His World*.

In "Chronotope," grotesque-word matrices serve quite literally to embody the world, to measure everything on the scale of the human body—in other words, to give the world a chronotope that grows, much as bodies grow. The body in the Middle Ages, Bakhtin notes, was represented as repellent in its hawking, farting, spitting, drinking; the humanist body would be elegant, cultured, and harmoniously developing (FTC, pp. 177–78). To make the transition, an intermediate step was needed; the body had to be experienced in all its corporeality. Bakhtin evaluates these changes positively.

Bakhtin's encomium here to the affirmative humanist body is in marked contrast to his better-known celebration in the Rabelais book of the hawking, guffawing, grotesque body for its own sake. In the chronotope essay, Bakhtin goes so far as to argue that Rabelais was in fact an advocate of *moderation*. "The theme of culture and moderation in food is discussed in connection with spiritual productivity," Bakhtin reminds us (FTC, p. 186). "Rabelais by no means advocates crude gluttony and drunkenness. But he does affirm the lofty importance of eating and drinking in human life, and strives to justify them ideologically . . . to erect a culture for them" (FTC, p. 185). The key emblem here, of course, is the Abbey of Thélème, which Bakhtin praises for its attention to the culture of the body. He promises to "return to this harmonious, affirmative pole of Rabelais's world view, to this harmonious world with its harmonious human being" (FTC, p. 178).

Nevertheless, one can also discover some loopholes in "Chronotope" that appear to face in the direction of *Rabelais*. Traces of carnivalesque utopia are present, if understated. Although the word is still primarily a carrier of individual personality, there are hints of the later view, according to which carnival diminishes the word's narrative power so as to reassert the carnivalesque body. The new body of a Renaissance human being is described not only as progressive but also as joyously "retrogressive," as drawing its strength from the ancient chronotope of folklore. This new image concerns "not the individual body, trapped in an irreversible life sequence . . . [but rather] the impersonal body, the body of the human race as a whole, being born, living, dying the most varied deaths, being born again" (FTC, p. 173). An important question looms for Bakhtin: can language and meaning be returned to the body if at the same time the body is abstracted from individual experience, as it is in carnival?

In this question we see the first full confrontation between embodiment and potential—between, as it were, the "folkloric" and the "novelistic" chronotopes. As a provisional (but unstable) resolution, Bakhtin puts forward the "elegant cultured body of the humanist" (FTC, p. 178) as an ideal image both embodied and rich in cultural potential. It is a body that engages in dialogue. In the chronotope essay, as we have seen, Renaissance humanism and the "harmonious, affirmative pole" (ibid.) of Rabelais's work *is* an important subtext. In the dissertation (and later book) on Rabelais, however, the "humanist body" hardly appears. Instead, Bakhtin idealizes the brawling, spitting, medieval body—which is granted no special historical task, nor any "historical momentum" toward a more harmonious and articulate form. If the carnival image of the body in the chronotope essay is specifically transitional, then its later redaction in *Rabelais* is retrofitted to the old folkloric chronotope, with its timeless one-on-one equation of goodness to brute size and crude vitality.

Even in "Chronotope," Bakhtin takes a few steps away from the ideal of the humanist body toward the exuberant and ambivalent body reveling in excess that he praises in *Rabelais*. For example, laughter is introduced into the chronotope essay precisely as "laughing death." In this broadest possible parody on the medieval worldview, death is not an absolute end for anyone or any thing; therefore it must occur only in passing, without any special pathos, on a grotesque and clownish plane. Death begins and ends nothing decisive "in the collective and historical world of human life" (FTC, p. 204). The wholeness of a triumphant life—one of the goals of Renaissance humanism—may no longer be possible for an individual body while remaining possible for the *abstract* folkloric body. That is, the inner logic by which Bakhtin defended Renaissance humanism would, if extended, point beyond humanism. Taken to an extreme, the original defense of humanism might become an attack on everything cultural and historical, humanism included. And that is the revised view that *Rabelais and His World* attributes to carnival and Rabelais.

In sum, Bakhtin's two studies of Rabelais present two images of carnival. Each relates to a distinct set of ideas Bakhtin developed in the 1920's. The chronotope essay, which describes Rabelais and carnival as destructive only in order to affirm, holds that "humanism" and "moderation" are Rabelais's real goals. In this image of carnival, laughter is not only grotesque but also serious and historically active. It counters the medieval worldview that so overvalued death and the afterlife with an image of "laughing death." This humanist and restorative strand of thinking about carnival should recall Bakhtin's concerns in his early manuscripts and in the Dostoevsky book. Human mortality and rhythm are underplayed, to be sure, but Bakhtin's analytic framework is still recognizably "architectonic." That is, carnival strives to redistribute the available world around the value system of a human being. The very concept of chronotope can be understood as an interpretation of architectonics in terms of genre, and so a carnival *chronotope* is necessarily oriented toward historical human values and specific human experience.

Bakhtin's second set of ideas about carnival, investigated at length mainly in *Rabelais and His World*, is essentially "antichronotopic." In Rabelais and the folklore he imbibed, value is divorced from any specific time frame, real history is not registered, and space becomes thoroughly fantastic. Laughter under these conditions *merely* decrowns, and any finished image is portrayed as repressive. Language is limited to cheerful obscenity and epithets. This strand of thinking appears to derive from a second development in Bakhtin's thought, the idea of unfinalizability, interpreted as pure loophole.

When dialogue is connected with specific utterances and speaking persons (as it is in the Dostoevsky book and in the essay "Discourse in the Novel"), Bakhtin tends to stress the particularity and concreteness of the human image. But if the "loophole aspect" of the dialogic word is stressed—and especially if this "word with a loophole" is combined with laughter—the unit that emerges can communicate in a different way. The laughing word becomes a general attitude toward the world instead of a specific utterance engendering a specific response. Laughter tends not to combine with the word, but to replace it. When this happens, the word's openness typically becomes dehistoricizing and depersonalizing.

Thus, these two images of carnival, the "humanistic" (or chronotopic) and the "antihumanistic" (or antichronotopic), co-exist in Bakhtin's thinking as he moves from period IIIa to IIIb. Before looking at the antichronotopic alternative as fully realized in *Rabelais and His World*, we should examine the fate of the novel treated as a carnivalized genre. The programmatic statement of this theory of the novel is to be found in Bakhtin's essay of 1940, "Epic and Novel."

Carnival Comes to Bakhtin's Favorite Genre

What happens to the ideas of body, laughter, and folkloric time when they are applied not only to the created characters within a novel but also to the genre itself? The novel becomes a sort of carnival body. The opposition between the immortal collective folkloric body and the mortal, individualized, compartmentalized body is then redrawn as that between the immortally embodied genre of the novel and all other genres. The novel has a body; other genres do not. The novel can be touched, groped, entered; it not only contains real people but is itself a sort of person, one who "comes to self-consciousness" and laughs (EaN, p. 11).

The sort of laughter that is available to the novel as a genre significantly changes Bakhtin's ideas on creativity and freedom. The "laughing novel"—as contrasted with, say, a laughing person *in* the novel—has no special task; it is not a specific response and therefore need not be responsible. It is most of all an *anti*force, and thus begins to display antinomian traits. Bakhtin authorizes the novel to play the same role in literature that carnival is alleged to play in the real life of cultures.

Bakhtin describes this radically personified novel as "dialogized." But the term is no longer associated primarily with specific dialogues, voice zones, and markers of heteroglossia within a work. Now dialogization works hand in hand with another force, "novelization," which may be understood as an imperialist strategy aimed at other, more monologic genres and subverting them through "laughter, irony, humor, and elements of self-parody" (EaN, p. 7). The interpenetration of chronotopes and complex gradations among genres that Bakhtin celebrates in his earlier essays on the novel now give way to absolute boundaries. The epic is "walled off from all subsequent times by an impenetrable boundary"; "as closed as a circle," there are "no loopholes in it" (EaN, pp. 16–17). The novel, by contrast, is *all* loophole.

To be sealed off is to be serious, but laughter is the eternal loophole. When novels are seen in terms of loophole, then, laughter becomes absolutely essential to novelistic sensibility. In Bakhtin's new hierarchy of times, the *past* and genres of the past are always somber, serious, and monovalent; the *present* is always comic, cheerful, and ambivalent. Epic material can thus be transformed into novelistic material merely by passing it through the realms of familiarization and laughter. Indeed, in "Epic and Novel" this dragging of an event into the comic "contact zone" is the single technical requirement that Bakhtin specifies for "novelizing a genre."

Laughter makes us free. It "demolishes fear and piety before an object," and is thus "a vital factor in laying down that prerequisite for fearlessness *without which it would be impossible to approach the world realistically*" (EaN, p. 23; italics ours). Realism in the novel is ultimately the gift of laughter, which delivers objects into "the fearless hands of investigative experiment—both scientific and artistic" (ibid.). It would seem to follow that the most fundamental and responsible relation to the objects of this world is a comic one, and that the primary way to be "realistic" about the world, both as a scientist and as an artist, is to laugh at it. From this perspective, "Epic and Novel" discusses both the paradoxical ambivalence of the Socratic dialogue and the "more powerful, sharper and coarser" laughter of menippean satire (EaN, p. 26).

Not only is this laughter provocative and unafraid; it is also without memory. In the comic world, there is "nothing for memory and tradition to do. One ridicules in order to forget" (EaN,

p. 23). Prosaics and dialogue—two of Bakhtin's global concepts richly dependent on the consciousness of the past—are beginning to be overwhelmed by laughter, the most effective instrument of unfinalizability. Genres, as organs of memory, are no longer seen as creating potential but as limiting it. As soon as memory becomes dispensable to the authentic spirit of the novel, laughter can enter as abuse, as a specifically *crude* familiarity. The "comical operation of dismemberment" that Bakhtin begins to celebrate here (EaN, p. 24) can be seen as the beginning of the carnivalistic body that does not hurt, or remember, or die.

To be sure, Bakhtin is more cautious in "Epic and Novel" than in *Rabelais and His World*. He concedes that novels need not travesty the past, and he praises abusive laughter not for its own sake but as a *formal* constituent necessary to destroy epic distance. Only familiarization makes possible access to inner reality, potential, and a multiplicity of truths. Thus, in "Epic and Novel" laughter and parody do not always involve the grotesque. They need only celebrate familiarization and noncoincidence. The argument Bakhtin makes in *Rabelais* for the ambivalent grotesque was to be yet another stage in his typology of laughter.

Rabelais and the Rest of Bakhtin's World

The "carnival sense of the world," as a process and a technical term, covers many interconnected ideas in Bakhtin. First, it is a view of the world in which all important value resides in openness and incompletion. It usually involves mockery of all serious, "closed" attitudes about the world, and it also celebrates "discrowning," that is, inverting top and bottom in any given structure. Discrowning points symbolically to the unstable and temporary nature of any hierarchy. Bakhtin generalizes these two actions into one ambivalent gesture: "debasement" or "casting-down."

Under noncarnival conditions, such debasement might signify humiliation and loss of power. In the carnival symbolic, however, a casting-down is always a positive gesture as well, a bringing-down-to-earth and thus a renewal and refertilization. "To degrade [carnivalistically]," Bakhtin writes, "is to bury, to sow, and to kill simultaneously, in order to bring forth something more and better" (RAHW, p. 21). Or, in a more concrete image, carnival insults are like the slinging of excrement, which fertilizes and fosters growth. "The slinging of dung and the drenching in urine" represent "the gay funeral of this old world; they are (in the dimension of laughter) like handfuls of sod gently dropped into the open grave, like seeds sown in the earth's bosom" (RAHW, p. 176). The primary reflex of the carnival body, when it is not defecating or ingesting, is to laugh. Carnival laughter is neither negative nor unidirectional and does not pass authoritative judgments: valuing the unfinished in everything, it is always ambivalent.

Debasement and mockery are idealized in a special carnivalistic image, the grotesque body. In this image, the body's protuberances and apertures are primary: they help the body outgrow itself because they are the passageways that ingest and communicate with the world. "Thus the artistic logic of the grotesque image ignores the closed, smooth, and inpenetrable surface of the body and retains only its excrescences (sprouts, buds) and orifices, only that which leads beyond the body's limited space or into the body's depths" (RAHW, pp. 317–18). This body eats, drinks, laughs, and curses—but does not necessarily contemplate the world or hold dialogues with it.

Bakhtin associates this inverted hierarchy of bodily activities with carnivalistic images, in which "the confines between bodies and between the body and the world are overcome" (RAHW, p. 317). Carnival banishes fear of individual pain and death, for "the grotesque body is cosmic and universal" (RAHW, p. 318). Death is fused with new birth and ends with new beginnings. This body always acts as part of a collective and with collective implications; it has no private spaces and almost no private memory. There is an element of "utopian" radicalism here as well, for unlike the fate of real-life bodies, potential in the grotesque body is always realized: the old always dies and the new always flourishes and grows bigger.

The grotesque body cannot be a spectator to events, it can only be a participant. As Bakhtin puts it, a carnival sense of the world "does not know footlights." "Footlights would destroy a carnival, as the absence of footlights would destroy a theatrical performance. Carnival is not a spectacle seen by the people; they live in it. . . . While carnival lasts, there is no other life outside it" (RAHW, p. 7). Thus carnival—and its eventual seepage into literary forms, "carnivalization"—accomplishes two mergings: one between realism and a utopian ideal, the other between literature and real, generative life.

Up to now, Bakhtin writes, "[Rabelais] has been merely modernized: he has been read through the eyes of the new age, and mostly through the eyes of the nineteenth century" (RAHW, p. 58). Such "modernization" can result in a "reduced" idea of what laughter can do. Bakhtin himself, for all his neglect and apparent disdain of modern*ism* as an aesthetic program, was nevertheless writing from a "reduced" period in the twentieth century. Perhaps he feared that his own conceptual structures for understanding the self, dialogue, and authorial position in a text were themselves reduced—thus distorting his view of Rabelais. If so, Bakhtin could be in dialogue here with his own earlier writings.[1] If indeed his belatedness has misled him, he seems to ask, would not the conflict between his new work on Rabelais and his "chronotopic" treatment of the same material indicate that he had moved beyond "modernizations"? Would not the divergence between radical unfinalizability (so characteristic of carnivalized forms) and his other prosaic and dialogic global concepts indicate the correctness of his readings, his successful reconstitution of them in their own time?

These questions are not easy to answer, and suggest a prior one: does Bakhtin employ his global concepts primarily to serve his readings, or his readings to probe his global concepts? The Rabelais and Dostoevsky books, with their great insights alongside their great eccentricities, can hardly resolve the issue. The monograph on Rabelais has been much praised, as well as severely criticized, by Renaissance scholars; we will not engage that criticism here. *Rabelais and His World* serves us in the present chapter as an illustration of the fate of a global concept and as the medium for a new stage in Bakhtin's use of carnival laughter. How do the ideas at this new stage supplement and reshape ideas from earlier periods? At what point does unfinalizability (in the form of unreduced laughter) decisively part company with dialogue and prosaics? And what might be gained as well as lost by such a reorientation in Bakhtin's ideology?

Polarization and the "Public-Square Word"

The tone of *Rabelais* differs markedly from that of Bakhtin's earlier and later works. Investigative modesty and hypothesis disappear; Bakhtin barely acknowledges the historicity of his own historical account. Some of this self-confidence might be due to the original framing of the work as a dissertation, and some, perhaps, to the heightened background noise of authoritative rhetoric and hyperbole during the Stalin years.

But even more striking than the exaggeration that marks the tone of the book is its greatly increased binariness of thought. In the Rabelais sections of the chronotope essay, the emphasis falls not on contradiction or opposition but on *mess*. Bodily matrices overlap, interlock, and create grotesque scenarios, but in no sense are they neatly polarized. In "Epic and Novel," Bakhtin moves toward binary formulations: the "absolute past" of epic is contrasted with the immediate present of novels. In *Rabelais*, the logic of either-or is even stronger.

Consider, first, the discussion of language in the Rabelais book. In Bakhtin's other writings, beginning with his earliest comments on the word in "Author and Hero" and extending through the Dostoevsky book to "Discourse in the Novel," Bakhtin rigorously avoids dualistic formulations (social versus individual, langue versus parole). Instead, he stresses the irreducible multiplicity of speakers, situations, discourses, and purposes. Language serves one consciousness as it orients itself toward another consciousness in a specific setting. When he arrived at the concepts of heteroglossia and dialogue, he could see in every utterance the crossing of numerous intentions, worldviews, and evaluations at intricate dialogic angles. The avoidance of binaries was essential to Bakhtin's account. It marked an important difference between his thought and both Formalism (with its taste for categorical oppositions) and Marxism (with its dialectical model). Bakhtinian dialogue cannot be reduced to "contradiction"; neither can the novelist's coordination of various individual truths.

In the writings on carnival, individualized language fades away. Instead, Bakhtin focuses on two extreme alternatives: the authoritative language of state or church power, and the shouted, unprintable word. Bakhtin devotes the entire second chapter of *Rabelais* to the antiauthoritative kind of language, "the language of the marketplace" (more precisely *ploshchadnoe slovo*, the "public-square word"). What does this word do?

Unlike other types of discourse in Bakhtin's lexicon, public-square words are both collective and interchangeable. As his model, Bakhtin takes a prologue from *Pantagruel*, which is replete with the verbal genres of the quack and the hawker: "The words are actually a cry, that is, a loud interjection in the midst of a crowd, coming out of the crowd and addressed to it. . . . [The speaker] is one with the crowd; he does not present himself as its opponent, nor does he teach, accuse, or intimidate it. He *laughs* with it. . . . This is an absolutely gay and fearless talk, free and frank" (RAHW, p. 167).

Bakhtin presents this "public-square atmosphere" as a positive value—although, from previously established Bakhtinian perspectives, his reasons for doing so might seem obscure. Hawking is, after all, rather indifferent to specific meaning. It reduces the distinction between speaker and audience, and is "fearless and free" only to the extent that no individual person risks anything by uttering it.[2] The word as a carrier of one's own truth (which is the task of language in the Dostoevsky book and in the other writings on the novel) has completely disappeared. In fact, the carnival word does not really communicate. Rather, it *mediates*, much as excrement is said to mediate (between body and earth); and it is far from the case that words are the more potent fructifier. In this odd semantic system, defecation and scatology emerge as the real guarantors of kinship.

Double-Voiced Criticism?

From an ethical perspective as well, the role of the "public-square word" is somewhat inconsistent with Bakhtin's other formulations. For the success of popular self-advertising—the word of the hawker and the quack—derives largely from cunning and deceit. As Bakhtin writes: "At the fair, even cupidity and cheating have an ironical, almost candid character" (RAHW, p. 160). This separation of the word from any grounding in the ethical speaking person is said to be one of the privileges of the people's laughter.

In several passages, Bakhtin reads real history through a carnival lens, in a grotesque (and presumably exculpatory) presentation of famous episodes from the Russian past. Ivan the Terrible's killing campaigns against his own subjects "could not escape the influence of popular forms of mockery and derision" (RAHW, p. 270); Bakhtin comes close to representing these campaigns as a war on seriousness, a struggle "against Russian feudal sanctimonious traditions" (ibid.). (Given Stalin's idealization of Ivan, is this passage double-voiced? Is Bakhtin's statement that "the *oprichnina* was suppressed and disavowed, and an attack was made on its very spirit" [ibid.] a plea for a similar fate for the NKVD?) To support these historical readings, Bakhtin cites the famous nineteenth-century radical critic Nikolai Dobrolyubov, who argued that radical change and renewal required a firm belief "in the need and possibility of a complete exit from the present order of this life" (RAHW, p. 274). Rather implausibly, Bakhtin takes this line as a justification of carnival license. At this point it becomes difficult to tell whether Bakhtin is parodying Stalin's identification with (and idealization of) Ivan the Terrible, or if he is providing us with a counteridealization of his own. It is also possible to detect irony in his citation of an officially praised critic to justify antiofficial rituals.

We may also see an intriguing parallel between Bakhtin's verbal aesthetics of the carnival period—the period of high and repressive Stalinism—and the Futurist aesthetic of the early 1920's, an era of sanctioned radicalism and free experimentation. For it was a cardinal tenet of Futurism to celebrate the "word as such," its inexpressible potential and its license to be "transrational" and absurd. The word so conceived could promise a "complete exit from the present order." In the 1920's, Bakhtin polemicized against precisely this exiling of content and tradition from the word; in fact, he constructed his own aesthetics of verbal art largely around a rejection of the Futurist and related Formalist positions. In the 1940's, however, under protection of the Middle Ages, Bakhtin adopted a version of the discredited (and by that time dangerous) "Futurist defense." As the embodiment of unfinalizability, carnivalized speech was "released from the shackles of sense" (RAHW, p. 423) and also, we might add, from the shackles of history. In a stance that was somehow both resistant to and compliant with Socialist Realism, Bakhtin celebrated the "verbal absurdities" of a "completely liberated speech that ignores all norms, even those of elementary logic" (RAHW, p. 422). The extent and kind of double-voicing operative in such passages is exceedingly difficult to determine.

The Polarized Body, the Abbey of Thélème, and the Reevaluation of Renaissance Humanism

Given his lifelong concern with responsiveness and responsibility, Bakhtin would not have dispensed lightly with the dialogic and ethical component of language. We must ask, then, what function this new public-square word fulfills in Bakhtin's intellectual projects. Whatever irony may be present in Bakhtin's formulations, it would seem unwise to dismiss them as a mere political allegory. Here we should turn to a second binary opposition that emerges in *Rabelais and His World*: in addition to polarized language, we are presented with the "polarized body."

Two types of bodies are discussed in *Rabelais*, and they exhibit diametrically opposed behavior. The first is associated with a discredited "bourgeois ego"; the second is the "collective ancestral body" of popular folklore. The former is said to be entirely possessive and selfish, living a closed private life of "egotistic lust and possession" (RAHW, p. 23); the latter is entirely generous and selfless, "triumphant and festive" (RAHW, p. 19). The ailing, one-legged Bakhtin is clearly much taken by the spiritual potential of a robust "collective body," and, again in contrast with his earlier and later writings, he expresses sympathy for its liberating aspects. The mortal body—whose very mortality now makes it "fleeting and meaningless"—is directly opposed to the timeless elements in popular-festive images of the body and the world (RAHW, p. 211).

These two polarizations, within language and within images of the body, can be seen as attempts by Bakhtin to explore the implications of unfinalizability. That global concept is the necessary link between the public-square word (with its laughter and ambivalent abuse) and the ancestral body (with its facelessness, anaesthesia, and immortality). Taken together and made concrete, they produce the grotesque image: open, "interfaced," forever active and reevaluating.

In Bakhtin's other work, the endlessness of dialogue must always elude the closure of death. The Dostoevsky book, for example, argues that the polyphonic portrayal of consciousness from within in effect banishes death from Dostoevsky's world. Developing ideas from his earliest writings, Bakhtin insists that there can be no death experienced from within; death can only be a fact for others. Thus, Bakhtin evinces dialogic distaste for Tolstoy as a poet of death. The immortality of the collective body, which sprouts new limbs even as it loses them and relishes the incompleteness of any bodily part, may have appealed to the amputee scholar as a guarantor of life's endlessly open processes.

Unfinalizability is not the only value celebrated in this image of the body. The grotesque also unites two qualities or orientations in the world that Bakhtin deeply respected: the interdependence of bodies and the messiness of life. The grotesque body is "composed of fertile depths and procreative convexities"; it is "never clearly differentiated from the world but is transferred, merged, and fused with it" (RAHW, p. 339). If Socialist Realist art (and what today might be called fascist art) emphasizes the clean, closed-off, and narcissistic body, the art of the grotesque stresses exchange, mediation, and the ability to surprise. The grotesque restores "the ever uncompleted whole of being" (RAHW, p. 379, n. 3).

Such values were important to Bakhtin throughout his life. But in its carnival dress, the Rabelaisian version of "embodied potential" departs significantly from earlier formulations. Bakhtin's discussion of embodiment in his early writings focuses to such an extent on unrepeatable points of view and perceptual horizons that one can almost speak of an "ethics of vision." The grotesque body, however, does not emphasize the eyes. The organs that matter most to it are the nose and the mouth, which protrude into the world or ingest from the world. This new status that Bakhtin grants to the public-square word and to its embodiment, the grotesque image, leads to a thorough reevaluation and displacement of Renaissance humanism.

Bakhtin's discussion of the Abbey of Thélème may serve as a convenient touchstone for this reevalution. In the context of the chronotope essay, we recall, the Abbey and its cultivation of the "harmonious, affirmative body" were described as representing—for Rabelais and for Bakhtin himself—the humanist ideal, the goal that inspired postmedieval man. In *Rabelais and His World*, the Abbey of Thélème is presented in a very different light. Criticizing a prominent nineteenth-century Russian scholar who saw Thélème as "a key to Rabelais' philosophy," Bakhtin counters: "In reality, Thélème is characteristic neither of Rabelais' philosophy nor of his system of images, nor of his style. Though this entire episode does present a popular utopian element, it is fundamentally linked with the aristocratic movements of the Renaissance. This is not a popular-festive mood but a court and humanist utopia" (RAHW, p. 138). In a subsequent footnote, the Abbey's absence of a clearly demarcated kitchen (and of banquet imagery generally) is taken to undermine its legitimacy (RAHW, p. 280). Bakhtin now attributes the peculiar tameness of the Abbey, and Rabelais's manifest affection for it, entirely to the mechanisms of Rabelaisian negation: whatever was once forbidden is now allowed, in accord with the logic of "constructing the positive image by means of the negation of certain aspects" (RAHW, p. 412). The positive image becomes merely a parody of its opposite, not an ideal in its own right.

Humanism itself comes to be recharacterized. Whatever is healthy in it is brought closer to folklore: "All the images of the new humanist culture. . . . are steeped in the atmosphere of the market [literally, "public-square atmosphere"]" (RAHW, p. 170). The rest, especially more restrained or intellectual pursuits, become the province of the "chamber humanists," a term of near-abuse that Bakhtin links with the Church and the government as suppressors of popular speech and profanity (RAHW, p. 189).

In place of humanism, Bakhtin appears to invoke an idealized female principle—one of several indications that Bakhtin was not quite so blind to gender issues in Rabelais as has sometimes been supposed.[3] According to Bakhtin, the popular tradition that inspired Rabelais was not at all hostile or negative toward woman. She was perceived as the source of all flow and change, the bodily grave of the medieval Gallic man. Only when the image was trivialized did it become sensual and base (RAHW, p. 240); it was "the new, narrow conception" of gender and sexuality, described within the "moralizing and scholastic humanist philosophy" of the sixteenth century, that reduced women to a negative image (RAHW, p. 241).

One final and more general comment might be made about this overall discrediting of the harmonious, humanist ideal. Along with the changed function of the word and the newly idealized grotesque, Bakhtin reassesses the value of particularity as well. As we have seen, his earlier philosophy of the deed and the word tied the individual person to specific events and located in each utterance as many specific voices and hybrids as possible. Attempts to collapse the many into one, to project golden ages into the future ("historical inversion"), or to abstract the specificity of events all came under unremitting criticism from Bakhtin—first as "theoretism," then as "monologism," then as "abstract cognition." In the Rabelais book, by contrast, Bakhtin shifts his emphasis from the particular and irreplaceable to a new, universalist category: the "ideal-real" or "utopian-realistic." When they experienced the world in this carnivalistic way, "people were, so to speak, reborn for new, purely human relations" (RAHW, p. 10).

From the perspective of "Toward a Philosophy of the Act" and "Author and Hero," one inevitably asks: can there be "purely human relations"? Such relations would obtain only between persons reborn *out* of their lives and biographies, persons with no marked surfaces, no points at which the specific voice and body can be adjoined to other individual people. Otherwise, relations are necessarily *im*purely human. In most of Bakhtin's writings, "purity" is a pejorative term; in the context of "Toward a Philosophy of the Act," purely human (not particular) people would possess no more than "mere empty potential" and would be said to live life as "pretenders" with a spurious "alibi."

In those early essays, Bakhtin insisted on a constantly renegotiated balance between givenness and positedness. According to the new carnival worldview, however, people are all either permanently fixed or else in random flux, pure possibility. Again we ex-

perience the appeal and the daring of the carnivalesque, its pushing
to extremes the two contradictory ideals of embodiment and of potential. We also see the consequences of Bakhtin's new and short-
lived taste for binary oppositions.

The Consolations of Carnival

Up to this point, we have assessed the grotesque body and the
public-square word from the perspective of Bakhtin's earlier writings. From the perspective of the Rabelais book itself, this assessment might in turn appear "reduced." We would now like to take
Bakhtin at his Rabelaisian word, and attempt to enter the spirit of
those popular folkloric sources as he understands them. For even as
the spirit of carnival laughter in many parts of *Rabelais and His
World* can be targetless and indiscriminate, utopian and Bakuninesque, it can also function in fundamentally positive and value-
generating ways. By detaching Bakhtin's concepts from his specific
application of them, we might better appreciate the appeal of the
carnival view of the world—much as Bakhtin invites us to understand polyphony not only as a theory about Dostoevsky but also as
a concept with other possible applications. The radical unfinalizability of the carnivalesque both complements and undermines
Bakhtin's other global concepts. Where carnival differs from those
two concepts, we will suggest why it might have seemed a useful
corrective to them.

What is "form-shaping" or "genre-shaping" about the laughing
folkloric genres is *not* the external shape of their plots, nor the verbal form in which a given work is cast (myth, lyric, epic), but,
rather, some prior "vision" of the world. To see the world as authentic laughter sees it is not just to find something ridiculous.
Rather, laughter is more generally therapeutic. According to Bakhtin, Renaissance thought assumed laughter to be an essential part of
humanity's identity and birthright. It functioned much as philosophy did for earlier and later centuries, as something that "comforts
and advises" us in our lives. Rabelais, at least, believed that unreduced laughter was one possible point of view on the world, one of
the forms of truth concerning the world. It seems to repeat, over and
over: That which you thought was finished is not yet finished; that
which you thought was dead is not necessarily dead. If we bear in
mind Bakhtin's idea that each specific genre is especially well suited
to understanding some aspects of life and uniquely poorly adapted
to others, we can appreciate his assertion that "certain essential as-

pects of the world are accessible only to laughter" (RAHW, p. 66).

"Laughing truth" is valuable, Bakhtin argues, not because it conveys a concrete set of ideas but because it never worships, commands, or begs. For this reason, it can banish fear, mystic terror and guilt (RAHW, p. 90)—three reactions to the world, we might add, that Bakhtin neither respected nor understood especially well. In any given historical situation, Bakhtin concedes, the truth of laughter is ephemeral, for everyday anxieties and terrors always return. Nevertheless, carnival images offer an "unofficial truth," "the defeat of fear presented in a droll and monstrous form, the symbols of power and violence turned inside out" (ibid). The central lesson of Menippus, according to Bakhtin, was just such an independence of spirit: laughter may be persecuted on earth, but it is always at home in the eternal Kingdom of the Dead—where unofficial truth rules supreme (RAHW, p. 69).

To be sure, laughter rarely alters actual material conditions. Renaissance laughter in particular was legalized, enjoyed privileges, and kept evil at bay only by altering people's attitudes toward it. "Laughter is essentially not an external but an internal form of truth" (RAHW, p. 94), Bakhtin explains. It frees people "to a certain extent from censorship, oppression, and the stake" not by eliminating those realities but by liberating people from "the great interior censor . . . from the fear that developed in man during thousands of years: fear of the sacred, of prohibitions, of the past, of power" (RAHW, pp. 93–94).

Again, the argument Bakhtin makes here on behalf of laughter closely resembles the case he was to make at the end of his life for the freedom of "the witness and the judge." This freedom "cannot change existence, so to speak, materially (nor can it want to)—it can change only the *sense* of existence" (N70–71, p. 137). The truth of laughter is also, in this sense, a stoic truth. Bakhtin's final notes, in which he rethinks and reintegrates some of his most important concepts, link the freedom to "change the sense of existence" exclusively with the *word*. In the Rabelais book, which represents an experiment with unfinalizability at the expense of dialogue, it is laughter and the grotesque body that play this reevaluating and rehabilitating role.

We should note, however, that *Rabelais and His World* does not take an unequivocal stand against the serious word. According to Bakhtin, folk humor was not directed against all types of seriousness (RAHW, pp. 121–23). There can be complex, productive forms of the serious, among which Bakhtin mentions tragic seriousness with its understanding of "creative destruction" (RAHW, p. 121) and certain genres (epic, lyric, drama) that possess a "deep and pure, but open seriousness" (RAHW, p. 122). What all these forms share is fearlessness: "True open seriousness fears neither parody nor irony . . . for it is aware of its attachment to an uncompleted whole [*prichastnost' nezavershimomu tselomu*]" (ibid.; trans. emended). The right sort of serious affirmation, then, is always, like laughter, *prichastnyi*, "attached to or in communion with" a nonconsummatable whole. With their resonances of dialogue and responsible unfinalizability, these passages bear the marks of Bakhtin before and after *Rabelais*.

The Historical Fate of Folklore Laughter

According to Bakhtin, Rabelais's contemporaries understood the philosophical import of laughter in his works. Only later generations found his images problematical—or simply obscene, vulgar, and shallow, even if entertaining. Indeed, Bakhtin remarks, the folk humor complex, dependent as it is upon participation rather than performance, is rather fragile and resistant to chamber reading and transcription. Once moved into literature, it quickly disintegrates and tends to become either trivial (in which case it is presumed that nothing important or essential can be comical) or a one-way gesture from laugher to target. When read in this second way (that is, as satire), carnival laughter takes on the burden of a didactic or political agenda. In absolute opposition to folk humor's central mission, laughter is used to "inspire disgust or fear" for the "negative purpose of satiric mockery and moral condemnation" (RAHW, p. 63).

Bakhtin's brief account of the disintegration of folk humor (RAHW, pp. 102–36) counts among the most interesting sections of *Rabelais and His World*. Amid chapters that otherwise engage in lengthy exposition of an ahistorical, routinely ecstatic "carnival symbolic," Bakhtin offers an essay in literary history. He narrates laughter's fate through history as a nostalgic story of laughter's diminishing power and shrinking gifts.

According to Bakhtin, the ancient world witnessed a similar decline. Folkloric laughter first gave way to menippean satire. This genre's laughing images, though still ambivalent and robust, were already somewhat compromised by "moral meaning" (RAHW, pp. 62–63). In the early Christian era, laughter was domesticated or exiled altogether. But in the early Middle Ages, folk humor proved too powerful a force to ignore. Church and state authorities tolerated and integrated it, set aside special days when exiled laughter could be celebrated, and thus "licensed" carnival even as they regulated its scope.

The richest and most differentiated period for laughter occurred in the Renaissance, when folk humor broke into official literature. But a successful transposition into literary genres led to further distortion, enfeeblement, and disintegration. Carnival moved from the marketplace to the court masquerade; Rabelaisian laughter yielded to ballets based on Rabelaisian scenes. In the seventeenth century, Rabelais's works were subjected to a new distortion: they began to be read as abstract allegory by commentators who offered an "entire system of interpretation" and a key to the code (RAHW, p. 113). Even when this scholarship was technically accurate in deciphering allusions, Bakhtin argues, it narrowed the meaning of the texts. For a great work's image is "always deeper and wider, it is linked with tradition, it has its own aesthetic logic independent of the allusion" (RAHW, p. 114).

The reception of Rabelais in the modern period provided Bakhtin with a good lens through which to view the fate of folk humor. Rabelais began to be read not as allegory but as prurient comic realism. A new bodily canon worked to finish off and polish up the body: bulges and sprouts from which new bodies might come were smoothed over, and all attributes of an incomplete world were removed along with all signs of the body's vigorous, messy internal life (RAHW, pp. 320–22). The body lost its power to mediate, and death ceased to laugh. As bodies and biographies were increasingly individualized and "privatized" in literature, direct discussion of the body in the public square came to be replaced by a realism of eavesdropping and Peeping Tomism.

With the ascendancy of eighteenth-century scientific empiricism, the resistance to a sympathetic reading of Rabelais (and of carnival images in general) shifted ground. The Enlightenment developed an epistemology that specifically aspired to avoid ambivalence. It is not surprising, Bakhtin remarks, that this century marked a low point for appreciating Rabelais, for whom ambivalent images, such as pregnant death and exalting degradation, were essential. Voltaire saw in Rabelais's laughing images only "erudition, dirt, boredom," and negating satire (RAHW, pp. 116–17).

In the nineteenth century, Rabelais again came into vogue, although for somewhat trivial reasons. Either "the fantastic degenerated into mysticism" (RAHW, p. 125) or Rabelais was interpreted univocally in ethical and philosophical terms. Russian studies of Rabelais hardly existed. One great thinker of the period who did understand the larger meaning of carnival, however, was Goethe, and in *Rabelais* Bakhtin digresses to describe one of his favorite literary texts, Goethe's experience of Roman carnival. "Goethe understood that seriousness and fear reflect a *part* that is aware of its separation from the whole. As to the whole itself in its 'eternally unfinished' condition, it has a 'humorous' character" (RAHW, p. 254). In Goethe's reading, the individual who takes himself seriously as a complete whole is opposed to the larger whole of the people, a whole that Rabelais understood. As Bakhtin discusses Goethe's interpretation of carnival, we recognize a revalued and revised version of the case Bakhtin made against "monologic wholes" in chapter three of the book on Dostoevsky.

Carnival and the Two Editions of the Dostoevsky Book

As rewritten in the early 1960's, Bakhtin's book on Dostoevsky registers traces of his thought from disparate periods. The 1929 text focuses on polyphony and differs markedly from the work now usually read. The principal difference between the two editions is to be found in the new fourth chapter, which reflects (and revises) Bakhtin's thoughts in the 1930's and 1940's on carnival. How organic is this new section to the whole work?

The fourth chapter of the 1929 edition, "Functions of the Adventure Plot in Dostoevsky's Work," is barely nine pages long. Most of it remains in the second edition (PDP, pp. 101–5), but is so overshadowed by the new seventy-five-page discussion of menippean satire and carnivalization that one can easily overlook it. The original chapter, which deals solely with the adventure plot and its function in Dostoevsky, appears to be a sort of early draft for what in the 1930's would become Bakhtin's account of the "adventure chronotope" in the Greek romance.

The "adventure hero" suits Dostoevsky, Bakhtin states, because Dostoevsky's works are not unified by plot. He therefore required protagonists who do not depend upon plot for their self-definition.[4] "Anything can happen to the adventure hero, and he can become anything" (PTD, p. 94). But to be free of plot is to be free of destiny and a purpose. The 1929 chapter, in all likelihood produced alongside and under the influence of Bakhtin's early writings on moral responsibility and the architectonics of authorship, highlights the degree to which Dostoevsky's characters *resist* their plot-less state and strive to be responsibly "embodied." "[Whereas in the biographical novel] the hero and the objective world surrounding him must be made of one piece, Dostoevsky's hero is not embodied in that sense, nor can he be embodied. He cannot have a normal biographical plot. And the heroes themselves fervently dream of being embodied, they long to attach themselves to a life-plot" (PTD, p. 95). Dostoevsky denies them this solace, because he does not want the human being's freedom fettered by any fixed social, family, or biographical ties.

Thus, in Bakhtin's reconstruction of Dostoevsky's intent we see traces of his earliest author-hero scenario. Author and hero are at odds (as they also are in Dante as Bakhtin reads him; FTC, p. 158). Dostoevsky creates free beings, but they, like humanity as described by the Grand Inquisitor, seek the security of a normal biographical plot. Dostoevsky insists on polyphonic freedom because a biographical plot can become not only a hero's "clothing," but also his body and soul (PTD, p. 98), which would mean the end of polyphony.

The adventure plot is never body and soul, but always *mere* clothing. Like a suit, it can always be exchanged, so the hero is not dependent on any "readily available or stable positions" (PTD, p. 99). Such a plot is singularly favorable to Dostoevsky's polyphonic design and connected to it in a negative way: neither allows for a hero who is "fully embodied" in social roles, as the heroes of Tolstoy, Turgenev, and Goncharov are said to be. Positively, however, the adventure hero and the polyphonic hero differ substantially. The adventure plot is suitable not because of what it contains but because of what it lacks. Carnival, of course, lacks even more, and the features it does exhibit are experienced not as alternative institutions but as parodies of institutions per se. Carnival, in essence, is pure adventure, pure lack: the embodied void. Thus, when Bakhtin returned to the Dostoevsky book, the fourth chapter provided an opportunity for approaching Dostoevsky in terms of carnival.

In the original chapter, then, Bakhtin is critical of traditional plotting and insists that Dostoevsky did not invest such plots with real value. In a passage Bakhtin himself might later have called a defense of the "antichronotope" (and which he removed from the revised edition), he asserts: "Plot in Dostoevsky is deprived of any finalizing functions whatsoever. . . . In essence all of Dostoevsky's heroes come together outside of time and space, like two creatures in infinity. . . . At the points where their fields of vision intersect lie the culminating points of the novel. . . . They are external to the plot" (TF1929, pp. 276–77). This passage makes clear why the line of Bakhtin's thought that led to *Rabelais* was notably at odds with the line that led from "architectonics" to "chronotope." Chronotopes offer constraints that provide opportunities for new kinds of self and creativity; antichronotopes liberate by abolishing constraints in an atmosphere of "joyful relativity."

Bakhtin opens his notes toward reworking the Dostoevsky book (1961) with the words: "Rework the chapter on plot in Dostoevsky. Adventurism of a special sort. The problem of Menippean satire . . . the public square in Dostoevsky. Sparks of carnival fire" (TRDB, pp. 283–84). And, indeed, "adventurism of a special sort" is exactly what Bakhtin develops as he applies carnival to his favorite novelist.

The opening lines in these notes from 1961 can be understood in a number of ways. Most likely, Bakhtin really saw Rabelaisian carnival and various forms of "reduced laughter" in Dostoevsky's works. But pragmatic considerations might also have played a role. A revised edition of the Dostoevsky book was the first work Bakhtin agreed to prepare for publication after his "rediscovery," and its fate was far from certain. Bakhtin was not yet "rehabilitated." His essays on the history of the novel written during the exile years, his dissertation on Rabelais, and various lectures he had delivered on literary history were known to Soviet scholars, but there was no way of predicting when, if ever, they would appear in print. Perhaps Bakhtin wished, or was advised, to include some of his ideas on the history of laughter and folk culture under pretext of a "revised edition." Combining manuscripts, in any case, was a common practice for Bakhtin, who had a rather weakly developed sense of the conventional scholarly essay. He seems to acknowledge such ulterior motives when he writes that his "historical digression" on menippean satire is, in fact, a question with "broader significance for the theory and history of literary genres" (PDP, p. 106).

In reading the new chapter four, therefore, we must ask ourselves how organic its discussion of carnival and menippean satire is to the structure and logic of the book as a whole. The carnival excursus is flanked by chapter three, "The Idea in Dostoevsky," and chapter five, "Discourse in Dostoevsky," whose content is essentially unchanged from 1929. Are "carnival time" and "loophole logic" natural extensions of the concepts developed elsewhere in the study? Or does chapter four drag the specific gravity of the whole too much toward unfinalizability, to the detriment of the other two global concepts that are otherwise in reasonably good balance in this book? These questions matter, for it has often been noted with regard to the second edition that its best and most comprehensive readings are of Dostoevsky's early fiction and of his late "carnivalized" stories ("Bobok" and "The Dream of a Ridiculous Man"). The greater the novels, it seems, the more restricted and nonloadbearing do the carnival structures within them become, and the more unsatisfactory does Bakhtin seem as a reader.

As Bakhtin integrated the tradition of menippean satire into his reading of Dostoevsky, his polemic against "plot" as such apparently became less intense. Such a shift in position might have resulted from his work on literary history over the previous three decades: clearly there were "menippean plots" and plot traditions, much as dialogues may have prototypes. One of the ways menippean satire works is to "provoke the word by setting up plot situations" (PDP, p. 111). In contrast to his attempt in the Rabelais book to free that author from literary tradition, in the 1963 Dostoevsky book Bakhtin introduces carnival as a moment in literary history. Thus, he begins the new fourth chapter by promising "to shift the question onto the plane of *historical poetics*" (PDP, p. 105). As a result, his tone loses the hyperbole of the Rabelais book when he turns to a scholarly consideration of Dostoevsky's debt to parodic genres.

In the Dostoevsky book, Bakhtin treats carnival as a quasiliterary genre. What distinguishes carnival from literary genres per se is its lack of a readership or audience; everyone participates in it. If there are viewers who do not participate, there can be no true carnival; instead, we have a performance. Carnival is not a form of theater. As Bakhtin stresses in both *Rabelais* and in *Problems of Dostoevsky's Poetics*, carnival allows for no "footlights." But in other important respects, carnival as described in the Dostoevsky book does resemble literary genres as Bakhtin usually understood them. Like all genres, it is a way of understanding the world and figures a sense of experience. The "carnival sense of truth" is for carnival what "the dialogic sense of truth" is for the polyphonic novel and what the "Galilean language consciousness" is for the novel. That is, the carnival sense of truth is an essential part of a form-shaping ideology and as such has "genre-shaping significance" (PDP, p. 131).

As with all genres, it is the form-shaping impulse that really counts. The specific forms that carnival takes vary over time and from culture to culture, and some forms exploit the generic potential of carnival more fully than others. But whatever forms it may take, carnival is a mode not of "abstract thinking" but of "artistic thinking." It is not a set of propositions about the world but a way of viewing the world; it is not so much a set of views as a ground for vision. After describing a number of carnival's typical forms, Bakhtin cautions us:

These carnivalistic categories are not *abstract thoughts* about equality and freedom, the interrelatedness of all things or the unity of opposites. No, these are concretely sensuous ritual-pageant "thoughts" experienced and played out in the form of life itself, "thoughts" that had coalesced and survived for thousands of years among the broadest masses of European mankind. This is why they were able to exercise such an immense, *formal, genre-shaping* influence on literature. [PDP, p. 123]

The Carnivalization of Literature and the Seriocomic Genres

Bakhtin's argument about carnival's form-shaping ideology contributes to the broader historical argument of the Dostoevsky book's new fourth chapter. Bakhtin contends that from antiquity to the present, literary history has been shaped by both "serious" genres, such as tragedy and epic, and by a set of genres quite different from serious genres in tone and spirit. This second "line of development," shaped by a "carnival sense of the world," cannot be translated "into a language of abstract concepts, but it is amenable to a certain transposition into a language of artistic images that has something in common with its sensuous nature; that is, it can be translated into the language of literature" (PDP, p. 122). To effect this transposition, it was necessary to turn the quasi-genre into a fully realized literary genre, that is, to find a way to restore the footlights while still maintaining something of the carnival spirit. Strictly speaking, Bakhtin's term *the carnivalization of literature* refers to this transposition, which is to say, it might also be thought of as the "literization of carnival" (although Bakhtin does not use that phrase).

The ancients explicitly recognized a group of genres distinct from the high serious forms, a group they called "seriocomic." All these genres took the "living present" as their starting point, set their action in a "zone of familiar contact," and represented people as acting or speaking in "the open-ended present." A radical change "takes place in that time-and-value zone where the artistic image is constructed" (PDP, p. 108). These genres were also characterized by a spirit of "free invention" (ibid.), which often led them to treat myths and legends in a tone of "cynical exposé. . . . This is a complete revolution in the history of the literary image" (PDP, p. 108). Finally, the seriocomic genres tended to use language not only to represent the world but also as an object of representation, which means that they developed a multistyled form and techniques of double-voicing. "What appears here, as a result, is a radically new relationship to the word as the material of literature" (ibid.).

These features of ancient seriocomic literature, of course, were to become central to the novel as Bakhtin celebrates it. He therefore argues that it is impossible to understand the modern novel without understanding the seriocomic genres of antiquity. "Speaking somewhat too simplistically and schematically, one could say that the novelistic genre has three fundamental roots: the *epic*, the *rhetorical*, and the *carnivalistic* (with, of course, many transitional forms in between)" (PDP, p. 109). Bakhtin apparently means to include the Greek romance as belonging to the class of "rhetorical" works shaping the novel; *The Golden Ass* and the *Satyricon*, which are described in the chronotope essay as partially growing out of the Greek romance, are here classed with the "carnivalistic" works of antiquity.

Ancient seriocomic works initiate the "carnivalistic line" in Western literature. Of special importance was the Socratic dialogue, which Bakhtin describes as having only limited success in capturing a carnivalistic sense of truth. Its disintegration led to a variety of other forms, the most important of which was menippean satire.[5] Bakhtin stresses that it would be a mistake to regard "Menippean satire [as] a pure product of the decomposition of the Socratic dialogue (as is sometimes done), since its roots reach *directly* back into carnivalized folklore, whose decisive influence is here even more significant than it is in the Socratic dialogue" (PDP, p. 112). Indeed, from antiquity to the Renaissance, whenever carnival forms arise, they have a double genealogy. They reflect both the direct influence of carnival and its indirect influence through prior carnivalized forms, whose specific ways of making literature out of the carnival spirit are then adapted.

The importance of menippean satire tends to be underestimated, Bakhtin argues, in part because the *term* largely fell out of use, even though the form-shaping impulse of the genre has continued to produce important works up to the present. "The application of such [classical] terms as 'epic,' 'tragedy,' 'idyll' to modern literature has become generally accepted and customary, and we are not in the least confused when *War and Peace* is called an epic, *Boris Godunov* a tragedy, [Gogol's] 'Old-World Landowners' an idyll. But the generic term 'menippea' [menippean satire] is not customary (especially in our literary scholarship), and therefore its application to works of modern literature . . . may seem somewhat strange and strained" (PDP, p. 178, n. 10). Nevertheless, authors who do not know the term have developed the spirit of the genre—or, as Bakhtin often calls it, its "generic essence" (PDP, p. 161). Classified or named in many different ways by critics who have not always recognized these works' consanguinity, menippean satires have flourished throughout the postclassical world, right up to the modern period. "In fact, it continues to develop even now (both with and without a clear-cut awareness of itself as a genre). . . . Menippean satire became one of the main carriers and channels for the carnival sense of the world in literature" (PDP, p. 113).

The only menippean satirist since the Renaissance whom Bakhtin mentions is Dostoevsky, but he presumably also has in mind the Sterne of *Tristram Shandy* and the Gogol of *Dead Souls*. His detailed description of the genre suggests that Mark Twain's "Letters from the Earth," Bulgakov's *The Master and Margarita*, Grass's *The Tin Drum*, and Barth's *The Sot-Weed Factor* might also be considered almost perfect examples of menippean satire. Some of these authors may have had a "clear-cut awareness" of the genre; others had a less defined, de facto awareness through the "memory of the genre." (It is in this context that Bakhtin introduces the concept of genre memory.)

Other carnivalized forms in addition to menippean satire arose in Europe throughout the Middle Ages. But it was in the Renaissance that carnivalization burst powerfully into all canonized literary forms, according to Bakhtin. A carnival sense of the world "took possession of all genres of high literature and transformed them fundamentally" (PDP, p. 130). Carnival laughter, symbols, and ambivalence "penetrated deeply" into Renaissance literature and thought; indeed, "even antiquity, as assimilated by the humanists of the epoch, was to a certain extent refracted through the prism of the carnival sense of the world" (ibid.).

Thus, when eighteenth- and nineteenth-century writers imbibed this "carnival sense" from earlier literature, they had numerous different texts that could serve as "generic contacts."[6] In addition to menippean satire and other carnivalized forms of antiquity and the Middle Ages, they could turn to the major writers of the Renaissance—Boccaccio, Shakespeare, Cervantes, and, of course, Rabelais. They could also turn to "the early picaresque novel (directly carnivalized)" (PDP, p. 157).

After the Renaissance, the echoes of carnival laughter grew weaker for an obvious reason: carnival itself diminished drastically in importance in people's lives. After the second half of the seventeenth century, the source of carnivalization in literature was pretty much limited to earlier carnivalized literature. Before that time, "people were *direct participants* in carnivalistic acts and in a carnival sense of the world. . . . Therefore carnivalization was experienced as something unmediated (several genres in fact directly served carnival). *The source of carnivalization was carnival itself*" (PDP, p. 131). But in the masquerade, in the satires of Swift and Voltaire, we can hear the echoes of carnival laughter that has been "reduced." For to sound fully in literature, a sense of having been *only just* transformed into literature must be preserved. Unlike Swift's works, Rabelais's seem to lie on the boundary between art and life, as if life itself had somehow come to enjoy "extraterritorial" rights in the kingdom of literature.

Reduced Laughter

Laughter is a specific aesthetic relationship to reality, but not one that can be translated into a logical language; that is, it is a specific means for artistically visualizing and comprehending reality and, consequently, a specific means for structuring an artistic image, plot, or genre. Enormous creative, and therefore genre-shaping, power was possessed by ambivalent carnival laughter.

—PDP, p. 164

It is in this context that Bakhtin at last explains what he means by "reduced laughter." In contrast to his observations in the Rabelais book, Bakhtin here treats the phenomenon as a significant and interesting fact in its own right, not just as enfeebled carnival. "The phenomenon of reduced laughter is of considerable importance in world literature," he observes. "Reduced laughter is denied any direct expression, which is to say 'it does not ring out,' but traces of it remain in the structure of an image or a discourse and can be detected in it. Paraphrasing Gogol, we can speak of 'laughter invisible to the world'" (PDP, p. 178, n. 4). Such laughter can acquire, as well as lose, profound meaning as a result of its reduction or "invisibility." In Dostoevsky, for instance, reduced laughter figures prominently and contributes an essential element to the great dialogues of his novels.

But what exactly is reduced laughter? To explain this concept, Bakhtin adapts his ideas on genre. For analytic purposes, one can say that laughter is a form-shaping ideology or "genre-shaping power," which means that it can be described—again, analytically—in terms of two aspects: its sense of the world ("the carnival sense of truth") and its particular formal realizations. The former is the more important. When laughter shapes an image, a scene, or a work, its genre-shaping power (or form-shaping ideology) imparts a carnival sense of the world and of change. Laughter can "grasp and comprehend a phenomenon in the process of change and transition . . . [and] fix in a phenomenon both poles of its evolution in their uninterrupted and creative changeability: in death, birth is foreseen and in birth, death, in victory, defeat and in defeat, victory. . . . Carnival laughter does not permit a single one of these aspects to be absolutized or to congeal in one-sided seriousness" (PDP, p. 164).

In reduced laughter, the form-shaping ideology still permeates the image or scene, but explicit humor provoking outright laughter is either absent or muffled. This change reflects the transformation of the quasi-literary form of carnival into a specific literary genre and work; laughter is adapted to the needs and vision of its literary use. For any genre to which it is adapted must have its own prior form-shaping ideology—which shapes everything in the work, including laughter. Thus, the kinds, not just the degrees, of laughter in literature are very diverse. At times, the adaptation of carnival laughter to literature eliminates explicit humor, but laughter's inner logic "continues to determine the structure of the image. . . . we see, as it were, the track left by laughter in the structure of represented reality, but the laughter itself we do not hear" (PDP, p. 164). For example, in Plato's early Socratic dialogues, "laughter is reduced (but not entirely), but it remains in the structure of the image of the major hero (Socrates), in the methods for carrying on the dialogue, and—most importantly—in authentic (not rhetorical) dialogicality itself" (ibid.).

In Renaissance literature, Bakhtin contends, laughter tends not to be very much reduced, although even here there are degrees of "volume." It rings out fully in Rabelais, somewhat less so in *Don Quixote*, still less in *The Praise of Folly*. By the eighteenth and nineteenth century, laughter is usually reduced considerably, "to the level of irony" and related reduced forms. We must emphasize that in the Dostoevsky book, this observation is not meant to suggest that the works in question are any less profound in their use of laughter. This appreciation of reduced laughter marks an important difference between *Problems of Dostoevsky's Poetics* and *Rabelais*, and between Bakhtin's fourth period and his third.

Polyphony and Menippean Satire

However distant or muffled the echoes of carnival may have been in the works that Dostoevsky read (Gogol, Diderot, Voltaire), he nevertheless succeeded, according to Bakhtin, in exploiting the "genre potential" of the carnivalized genres better than any other writer.[7] "In his creative utilization of this generic potential, Dostoevsky departed widely from the authors of the ancient menippea. In its posing of philosophical and social problems, in its artistic qualities, the ancient menippea seems in comparison with Dostoevsky primitive and pale" (PDP, p. 121). Dostoevsky formulated his own questions and drew on the resources of his own time; that is, he read menippean works with "creative understanding." As it happened, polyphony was ideally suited to developing the rich potential of the genre, and the polyphonic novel found in menippean satire a sense of experience and a set of forms well adapted to conveying its dialogic sense of truth.

In short, "the menippean satire, like the Socratic dialogue, could only prepare certain genre conditions necessary for polyphony's emergence" (PDP, p. 122). A weak sense of the dialogic nature of truth had been present in the form-shaping ideology of the Socratic dialogue and was the heritage of menippean satire and later carnivalized forms; it was only when Dostoevsky invented polyphony, however, that a rich way was found to convey and develop that sense of truth. Dostoevsky learned from earlier works but went beyond them.

Dostoevsky also breathed new life into menippean satire by adapting other traditional features of the genre to polyphony. The extraordinary situations and extreme frankness of speech so characteristic of menippean satire were well suited to Dostoevskian clashes of "voice-ideas," and Dostoevsky also borrowed the ancient technique of provoking the word by the word (anacrisis). Polyphony also suggested ways to extend traditional menippean techniques for exploring ultimate questions and ultimate positions about the world: journeys to the underworld or heaven (present in the dreams and fantasies of Dostoevsky's characters); dialogues in the other world and in extreme or liminal situations ("threshold dialogues," as in Ivan Karamazov's conversation with the devil); and circumstances temporarily free from quotidian consequences and social positions in which people can discover and articulate their most fundamental beliefs and the sense of their lives. In such a "carnival space and time," a character experiences a "life outside of life" that permits a special type of conversation to take place, one based on each character's "pure humanness" (PDP, p. 173). Reaccenting it for his own purposes, Bakhtin cites Shatov's appeal to Stavrogin in *The Possessed*: "We are two *beings*, and have come together *in infinity* . . . for the *last time in the world*. Drop your tone, and speak like a *human being!*" (Dostoevsky, *Possessed*, pt. 2, ch. 1, as cited in PDP, p. 177; italics and ellipses Bakhtin's). We sense here the same "utopian-realistic" intonations that accompanied Bakhtin's celebration in *Rabelais and His World* of people's rebirth into "new, purely human relations" under conditions of carnival (RAHW, p. 10). But in a Dostoevskian context, these "purely human" interactions are not merged into a collective body nor estranged from genuine dialogue. Here, this special carnival chronotope for dialogue "makes it possible to extend the narrow scene of a personal life in one specific limited epoch to a maximally universal *mystery play scene*, applicable to all humanity" (PDP, p. 177).[8]

Genre Conditions

In his analysis of polyphony's relation to carnival and menippean satire, Bakhtin combines three key concepts of his "historical poetics": potential, genre memory, and "genre conditions." We have already seen (in Chapter Seven) that the first two concepts have wide application in Bakhtin's thought. The third, "genre conditions," also seems to invite extension. Crucially, it offers a way of describing how the resources of the past may allow for change without wholly determining it. New conditions enable innovations in a genre and the creation of new potentials within it, but the innovations are in no sense automatic, predetermined, or "ready-made." They are not just discovered, but truly created by the real work of a writer. That writer's particular vision, which is shaped but not exhaustively determined by current conditions, allows him or her to enter into a productive dialogue with available genre resources. Always concerned to demonstrate the genuineness of creativity, Bakhtin concludes his chapter by stressing Dostoevsky's true originality:

Having linked Dostoevsky with a specific tradition, it goes without saying that we have not in the slightest degree limited the profound originality and individual uniqueness of his work. Dostoevsky is the creator of *authentic polyphony*, which, of course, did not and could not have existed in the

Socratic dialogue, the ancient menippean satire, the medieval mystery play, in Shakespeare and Cervantes, Voltaire and Diderot, Balzac and Hugo. But polyphony was [nevertheless] prepared for in a *fundamental* way by this line of development in European literature. This entire tradition, beginning with the Socratic dialogue and the menippea, was reborn and renewed in Dostoevsky in the uniquely original and innovative form of the polyphonic novel. [PDP, p. 178]

Problems with the Carnival Approach to Dostoevsky

In his discussion of Dostoevsky's works under the star of carnival, Bakhtin seems to exaggerate the menippean element. After describing (persuasively enough) Dostoevsky's odd late trifle "Bobok" as a "perfect menippea," he deems it "almost a microcosm of [Dostoevsky's] entire creative output" (PDP, p. 144). In general, Bakhtin attempts to sustain a role for the menippean worldview that may give it too substantial a weight in the Dostoevsky canon. Perhaps this explains the episodic nature of Bakhtin's treatment of the later works—where, by his own admission, carnivalization is severely "reduced" (PDP, p. 164). Doubtless, the logic of this sort of satire permeates certain scenes in the longer novels, but it hardly determines their larger structure or ideology. And one cannot help feeling at times that, however illuminating the concept of "reduced laughter" may be, it also lends itself to fast and loose application. In much the same way as some Freudians take the absence of evidence as proof of repression and therefore as the strongest kind of evidence, Bakhtin often seems to take the absence of laughter as a sign of its utter "reduction" and silent, pervasive presence.

In Bakhtin's discussion of *The Idiot*, readers of that novel may feel that an important and genuinely tragic dimension has disappeared (PDP, pp. 173–74). Bakhtin places Prince Myshkin in a "carnival heaven" because Myshkin strives so mightily to finalize others benevolently, to release them from their most desperate selves, and even to deny the existence of those negative selves. Surely, however, this reading ignores a crucial paradox in the novel. When the Prince exclaims to Rogozhin, who is posed over him with a knife, "Parfyon, I don't believe it!," or when he assures the scandalous heroine Nastasya Filippovna that, contrary to all evidence, she is not really "that sort of woman," he reveals a weakness that Bakhtin also at times exhibits—a failure to appreciate evil that cannot be laughed away. Myshkin, in fact, causes harm precisely by crediting only the most benevolent qualities of people, a "monologizing"

evaluation that those people resent and resist. Bakhtin, too, seems
to turn a blind eye to the tragedy and murder that follow everywhere in Myshkin's wake. In his ethical writings, Bakhtin—inspired as he always is by creative potential—stressed the opportunities for good rather than the need to resist evil. It is a stance notably
at odds with the problematics of his favorite writer.

Still, Bakhtin's "carnivalization" of Dostoevsky is not entirely
gratuitous. Not every Dostoevsky work resembles "Bobok," but
"Bobok" may be seen as an extreme example of features indeed
present in Dostoevsky's great novels. Those features have received
scant attention apart from Bakhtin. Humor, and not all of it reduced, really does play an important role in Dostoevsky's works
and contributes fundamentally to the special experience of reading
him. The trajectory from Bakhtin's analyses could be traced through
the problematic of buffoonery in Dostoevsky to that of laughter
turned inward, ressentiment, as a potent social force: the grim humor, dark ethos, and political challenge of a bitter Saturnalia. It is a
trajectory that takes us farther than Bakhtin, with all his benevolent
optimism or accommodating stoicism, ever went.[9]

Bakhtin seems especially thoughtful when he discusses the contribution carnivalization made to closure in Dostoevsky's works
(and potentially elsewhere). Like polyphony and true dialogue, "the
carnival sense of the world also knows no period, and is, in fact,
hostile to any sort of *conclusive conclusion*: all endings are merely
new beginnings; carnival images are reborn again and again" (PDP,
p. 165). It follows for Bakhtin that critics have been hasty in applying Aristotle's concept of catharsis (or purification) to Dostoevsky's
works. To be sure, all works of art, as conceptualized wholes, must
have some sort of catharsis (if the term is taken broadly enough),
but "tragic catharsis (in the Aristotelian sense) is not applicable to
Dostoevsky" (PDP, p. 166). Such catharsis is incompatible with the
unfinalizability of laughter, carnival, menippean satire, and to Dostoevsky as a writer who developed the potentials of all three. It is
in this context that Bakhtin observes: "The catharsis that finalizes
Dostoevsky's novels might be—of course inadequately and somewhat rationalistically—expressed in this way: '*nothing conclusive has
yet taken place in the world . . . the world is open and free, everything is
still in the future and will always be in the future.*' . . . But this is, after
all, also the *purifying sense* of ambivalent laughter" (PDP, p. 166).

To be sure, Bakhtin's analysis is a partial reading of Dostoevsky,
one that ignores (among much else) Dostoevsky's apocalyptic and
mystical side. But in the context of Bakhtin's other writings on car-

nival, the new chapter four does more to rehabilitate than to discredit "literary laughter"—which is seen not as a pale reflection of carnival but as highly productive in its own right. Above all, literary laughter and menippean satire "made possible the creation of the *open* structure of the great dialogue and permitted social interaction between people to be carried over into the higher sphere of the spirit and intellect, which earlier had been primarily the sphere of a single and unified monologic consciousness, a unified and indivisible spirit unfolding within itself" (PDP, p. 177).[10] Dostoevsky's debt to menippean satire and the carnival sense of the world helped him to "overcome gnoseological as well as ethical solipsism. A single person, remaining alone with himself, cannot make ends meet even in the deepest and most intimate spheres of his own life; he cannot manage without *another* consciousness. One person can never find complete fullness in himself alone" (ibid.). In this passage, we see quite clearly that, unlike *Rabelais and His World*, the revised Dostoevsky book amends the concept of carnival so that it can be combined with that of dialogue.

The return to carnival in the Dostoevsky book thus accomplishes an important task in Bakhtin's recapitulation of his major ideas during the last two decades of his life. As carnival is subordinated to dialogue, Bakhtin avoids Bakuninesque or maximalist rhetoric. He returns to quiet registers and more prosaic dialogues. "Laughter," he writes, "can be combined with profoundly intimate emotionality" (N70–71, p. 135). What interests Bakhtin now in his analysis of laughter is not its invulnerability and cosmic impersonal force, not breasts and buttocks at a carnival feast, but the "analysis of a serious face (fear or threat). The analysis of a laughing face" (N70–71, p. 134).

The Carnivalesque Among Bakhtin's Global Concepts

What can be offered by way of a balance sheet? In periods IIIa and IV, Bakhtin subordinates "unfinalizable" carnival elements to his other two global concepts, prosaics and dialogue. In period IIIb, the potential of carnival is *itself* let free, as a sort of disembodied embodiment, and both the prosaic and the dialogic lose ground. It is as if Bakhtin recognized shortcomings in those two global concepts and used the third as a way of reexamining them in a questioning spirit.

The most vulnerable side of dialogue, Bakhtin may have sensed, is its benevolence. For even a cursory reading of Bakhtin reveals that the implied potential other in his dialogues lives on friendly boundaries and continuums. Bakhtin's other is as a rule benignly active, always at work to define us in ways we can live with and profit from. The worst that this other can do is fail to answer. The self, awaiting a response, is presumed resilient or vigorous enough to incorporate, or counter, any definition the other might thrust upon it. Bakhtin presumes no absolute conflict between an organism and its surroundings, just as he presumes no conflict in principle between self and society.

Except for the occasional reference to hell as the "absolute lack of being heard" (PT, p. 126), Bakhtin does not investigate life's terrors. Carnival, however, does address them, if only to banish them in a new way. Carnival laughter provides a mode of inner adjustment that does not depend upon the benign dialogic scenario of "talking it out." Prosaics as a worldview may also tend to excessive emphasis on the small or almost invisible adjustments at the expense of crises and abrupt changes. Carnival, with its Gargantuan images and radical inversions, may have appealed to Bakhtin as a corrective.

Still, it must be added that carnival itself addresses catastrophe and terror in a highly benevolent and unrealistic way. Bakhtin ignores the dangers of carnivalistic violence and antinomian energy. In short, it is not carnival but the "carnival symbolic" that inspires him, not real individual bodies in interaction but the potential for extending, transcending, and rendering immortal the collective body. Unless we assume that the carnival construct is itself parodically double-voiced (as some have done), it would seem that Bakhtin did not seriously consider the philosophical—and much less the political—implications of carnival at its least "reduced." In contrast to the author of *The Possessed*, the author of *Rabelais and His World* did not sufficiently appreciate that it is but a step from Bakunin to Shigalyov. "I am perplexed by my own data and my conclusion is a direct contradiction of the original idea with which I start," Dostoevsky's character observes. "Starting from unlimited freedom, I arrive at unlimited despotism" (Dostoevsky, *Possessed*, pt. 2, ch. 7, sec. 2, p. 409). Bakhtin's three global concepts do not completely cohere, to be sure, but in the larger perspective of his life they appear to have subjected each other to unexpected critiques and form-shaping insights.

Reference Matter

Notes

Introduction

1. For more on models for biography, see Tomashevsky, "Literature and Biography." See also Morson, "Dostoevsky's Anti-Semitism."

2. As the rest of the present study indicates, there is another problem with Todorov's formulation. In his last years, Bakhtin returned to the problematics of his earliest work, which he had long set aside. Thus, although one can find points from his earliest writing repeated fifty years later, one is less likely to find them repeated ten or twenty years later.

3. But Todorov is right that some of Bakhtin's ideas on the novel do not cohere with other crucial ideas he held on language, culture, and the novel itself. See Chapters Two and Seven through Ten of the present study.

4. Obviously, Freudian biographies typically use this approach, which the Bakhtin group distrusted in part because it denied true development throughout a lifetime.

5. The first installment, an excerpt from this long essay, appeared in the Soviet periodical *Sotsiologicheskie issledovaniia*, no. 2 (1986), pp. 157–69. It was published under the title "Arkhitektonika postupka" [The architectonics of the act]. The full text was published soon after as "K filosofii postupka" [Toward a philosophy of the act] in a yearbook of the Soviet Academy of Sciences (see Abbreviations). The titles appear to be the work of editor Sergei Bocharov; on page 156 of the periodical excerpt, Bocharov notes: "We have supplied a title to the fragments of the manuscript proffered below, since the author's title is unknown to us."

6. For an example of a recent and powerful use of this model, see Gustafson, *Leo Tolstoy*. Gustafson is rigorous, consistent, and thorough in applying this approach, which he formulates explicitly and concisely: "Just as in any human utterance a sound takes its meaning only from within the total statement, so any Tolstoy text takes its meaning only from within the complete oeuvre. To understand any part of his life's text, a story or novel, an essay or tract, a diary entry or a letter, we must see the particular set of words in their relationship to all his words. The pattern of this relationship is shaped by the process of articulation. *The primary rule in reading Tolstoy, therefore, is that the later clarifies the earlier.* This does not mean that an earlier work of art is better than a later one or vice versa. It does mean, however, that an earlier work may be an experimental version of a later one and that the later works may reveal the hidden patterns and meanings of earlier ones" (Gustafson, *Leo Tolstoy*, pp. 6–7; italics ours).

7. One set of questions we have not sought to address is Bakhtin's various debts to earlier thinkers, an immense and important topic. We have mentioned these debts only where it was necessary in order to grasp Bakhtin's own points, our central concern. That is, we focused on Bakhtin's "tasks" rather than on his debts. The most common occasions on which we mention earlier thinkers occur when Bakhtin explicates his ideas by explicitly differentiating himself from them.

Chapter 1

1. So far as we can tell, the term *prosaics* first appeared in print in Morson, *Hidden in Plain View*, pp. 126–28, 218–23. Later in the same year, the term also appeared in Kittay and Godzich, *The Emergence of Prose: An Essay in Prosaics* (1987). Apparently, the term was coined independently and essentially simultaneously.

Our use of the term differs from Kittay and Godzich's. As explained below, in our usage, prosaics refers to both an approach to prose and a view of the cultural world; Kittay and Godzich's use overlaps the first of these two meanings. Their illuminating study concerns the origins (emergence) of prose; our usage focuses primarily on its development in the nineteenth-century novel.

Morson developed the idea in two lectures subsequently published as "Prosaics: An Approach to the Humanities" and "Prosaics and *Anna Karenina*."

2. In effect, Bakhtin's early writings approach lyric poetry from a prosaic standpoint. Consider his discussion of Pushkin's lyric "Razluka" [Parting] in KFP, pp. 131–38, 141–45.

Kittay and Godzich arrive at a position that in many respects recalls Bakhtin's: "In all the theories of literature at our disposal, from Aristotle's *Poetics* onward, we have been taught that verse is a form of discourse more elaborate than prose, which suggests two things: first, that verse is the result of work on a discourse that is taken to be prose, and, second, that prose is anterior to verse. The various poetics, including medieval ones, take prose for granted, treating it as if it were natural, artless, just a given, and turn their attention to verse. . . . It is for this reason that we have so many studies of versification and none of prosification" (Kittay and Godzich, *Emergence of Prose*, p. 11).

3. Greene's comments are cited in Morson, *Literature and History*, p. 270.

4. Characteristically, Chekhov gives this line to an unappealing character who, even when she is right, cannot avoid the temptations of apocalyptic language.

5. Although they do not mention him, Bakhtin and Tolstoy here develop Aristotle's (anti-Platonist) idea that "all law is universal but about some things it is not possible to make a universal statement which shall be correct" (Aristotle, *Nichomachean Ethics*, p. 1020). Universal justice must be corrected by "the equitable, a correction of law where it is defective

owing to its universality" (ibid.). Equity is a matter of a kind of "judgment, which is the right discrimination of the equitable," and judgment in turn depends on "experience" (ibid., pp. 1032–33). For a recent revival of these ideas, see Stephen Toulmin, "Tyranny of Principles," especially his sensitive reading of Tolstoy, pp. 34–35; and Jonsen and Toulmin, *Abuse of Casuistry*.

6. There are, of course, still more stringent definitions.

7. See our article, "Penultimate Words"; see also Morson, *Hidden in Plain View*, pp. 84–86; and Morson, "Prosaics: An Approach to the Humanities."

8. "If it had not rained on the night of the 17th and 18th, the future of Europe would have changed; a few drops of rain more or less made Napoleon oscillate" (Hugo, *Miserables*, vol. 2, bk. 1, ch. 3, p. 10).

9. Our thanks to Gerald Graff for asking probing questions that helped to clarify these possibilities.

10. Chapter one of Gleick's *Chaos* is devoted to "the butterfly effect." See also Freeman Dyson, *Infinite in All Directions*.

11. Bakhtin also draws a distinction between "great time" and "small time." Small time is locked in the superficial great events of its epoch, which appear important because they are so noticeable. An understanding of great time requires the perspective of ages and includes "the experience of the life of worlds and of atoms"—atoms not noticed from the perspective of "small time" (MHS, p. 167; see also Zam, p. 519).

12. We discuss Bakhtin's concept of "eventness" in our summary of "Toward a Philosophy of the Act" in the introduction to *Rethinking Bakhtin*.

13. As we explain in the next chapter, Bakhtin, but not Voloshinov and Medvedev, also criticized Marxism for this sort of error; Voloshinov and Medvedev limited their critique to Freudianism, Formalism, and structuralism, but preferred to exempt Marxism.

14. See Jackson, "Aristotelian Movement."

15. See, for instance, Part one of Gould, *Panda's Thumb*, pp. 19–44.

16. On Bakhtin's interest in the sciences, see Holquist, "Answering as Authoring." At the beginning of the chronotope essay, Bakhtin expresses a debt to Einstein; and there are references to quantum mechanics. We discuss the Einstein connection in Chapter Nine.

17. Both Prigogine and Bakhtin try to overcome the radical opposition of the humanities and the hard sciences. See, for instance, Bakhtin's "From Notes Made in 1970–71": "The distinction between the human and natural sciences. The rejection of the idea of an insurmountable barrier between them. The notion that they are opposed to one another (Dilthey, Rickert) was refuted by subsequent developments in the human sciences. The infusion of mathematical and other methods—an irreversible process, but at the same time specific methods, a general trend toward specifics (for example, the axiological approach)—is and should be developing" (N70–71, p. 145).

18. Gould stresses that we are wrong to think only of physics and astronomy when we consider scientific attitudes to time: some sciences, such as evolutionary biology and geology, are inconceivable without a strong sense of historicity. Whereas physicists tend to think of "overarching, simplified and unifying law," evolutionary biologists focus on "the messy diversity of a world so largely regulated by the chancy interventions of history" (from Gould's fascinating essay, "Pleasant Dreams," p. 204). See also the contrast of "Athens" and "Manchester" in Dyson, *Infinite in All Directions.*

19. As translated in PDP, p. 301, n. 7.

20. Bakhtin's suggestions have in fact been influential in the evolution of Soviet "culturological" writing over the last several decades, especially in the work of Yuri Lotman and Boris Uspensky of the Tartu school.

For an initial statement, see the so-called Tartu Theses that launched the semiotic study of culture in the Soviet Union: Lotman et al., *Theses on the Semiotic Study of Culture*, and for a more recent update of that position, Lotman, "O semiosfere."

21. We correct a printer's error in the first printing of the English text, which reads: "but it also has cognitive, creative significance." The second printing corrects the error.

22. On the relation of Bakhtin's theories of language to speech act theory and sociolinguistics, see Stewart, "Shouts in the Street." But it would be possible to understand speech act theory or pragmatics as a set of maxims rather than a system of rules.

23. Bakhtin offers an interesting qualification of this description of Plato's monologic tendencies: "The idealism of Plato is not purely monologic. It becomes purely monologic only in a neo-Kantian interpretation. Nor is Platonic dialogue of the pedagogical type, although there is a strong element of monologism in it" (PDP, p. 100, n. 1). We can see how far Bakhtin has come in a short time from his early neo-Kantian influences.

24. For a discussion of Bakhtin's concept of the "form-shaping idea" in a genre, see Chapters Six and Seven of the present study.

25. As we understand it, this is the sense of Bakhtin's comments in "Toward a Methodology of the Human Sciences": "Meaning cannot (and does not wish to) change physical, material, and other phenomena; it cannot act as a material force. But it does not need to do this: it is itself stronger than any force, it changes the total contextual meaning of an event and reality without changing its actual (existential) composition one iota; everything remains as it was but it acquires a completely different contextual meaning (the semantic transformation of existence)" (MHS, p. 165).

Chapter 2

1. Our periodization roughly corresponds with Michael Holquist's in his biographical entry on Bakhtin in the *Handbook of Russian Literature*, (Terras, *Handbook*, pp. 34–36).

2. The second installment, published in 1986 under the title "Toward a Philosophy of the Act," probably predates the 1979 segment that appeared in *Estetika* as "Author and Hero in Aesthetic Activity." It is still untranslated. A summary of its contents and major lines of argument can be found in our introduction to *Rethinking Bakhtin*.

3. See Perlina, "Funny Things," and see also Vadim Liapunov's annotation to his translation of Bakhtin's early writings, forthcoming from University of Texas Press, which contains detailed information on sources and influences.

4. Two versions of Bakhtin's analysis of Pushkin's lyric have been published, one at the end of "Toward a Philosophy of the Act" and the other assigned by Bakhtin's editors to "Author and Hero." David Powelstock (in his "Remarks Regarding Baxtin's View on Poetry") has contrasted these two readings. He notes that in the first (earlier) version the hero is equated with the "objectified author"; their joint viewpoint is juxtaposed to the heroine's, and thus the dialogue takes place within the parameters of a dualistic "I-other." In the later version, the author-artist is explicitly separated from the hero-narrator, and the resulting three-way tension becomes much more formally complex. We see here in miniature Bakhtin's movement from the universe of I-other acts toward more flexible triangulated aesthetic structures (I, thou, and the hero) characteristic of his later work.

5. In Bakhtin's late essay "The Problem of the Text" (1959–61), we find an extreme instance of this shift of emphasis: "For the word (and, consequently, for a human being) there is nothing more terrible than a *lack of response*. Even a word that is known to be false is not absolutely false, and always presumes an instance that will understand and justify it, even if in the form: 'anyone in my position would have lied too'" (PT, p. 127).

6. *Marxism and the Philosophy of Language* begins its exposition of a properly Marxist linguistics with two poles, "abstract objectivism" and "individualistic subjectivism," and finds both wanting; similarly, in the book on Freud, Voloshinov marks out two trends in modern psychology, "objective" (grounded in observed behavior) and "subjective" (dependent upon personal experience transmitted through language)—and criticizes both.

7. It may seem odd to call Formalism "materialism" (because it reduces content to mere raw material organized by devices). Is the formulation perhaps designed to imply a broader critique of all materialist aesthetics?

8. Smirnov distinguishes three discrete disciplines of the word: the study of *slovesnost'* (the linguistic word as such); *literatura* (all analysis of the fragmentable kind: literary history, biography, and also the activity of Formalist devices upon material); and, finally, *poeziia* (the study of "indivisible content"). Along Bakhtin's lines, Smirnov divides poetic value into its aesthetic, cognitive, and ethical aspects. He also rehabilitates Potebnia's definition of art as "thinking in images": Potebnia did not necessarily intend a *finalized* poetic image, Smirnov correctly points out, but a *potential* one (Smirnov, "Puti," p. 96).

9. Further information on the differences between the two editions of the Dostoevsky book appears in Chapter Ten.

10. As early as 1922, a work by Bakhtin on Dostoevsky was advertised as "being prepared for publication," but that manuscript has not survived. See *Zhizn' iskusstva* (Petrograd: November 1922) as cited in *Pamiat'*, no. 4 (Paris: YMCA, 1979–81), p. 279, n. 37.

11. For more on this point, see our discussion of Ann Shukman's essay on Bakhtin and Tolstoy in part three of the introduction to *Rethinking Bakhtin*.

12. Mathew Roberts ("Bakhtin and Jakobson") suggests that Bakhtin's primary antagonist in the 1920's was not Shklovsky at all (a relatively simple target, taken on by Bakhtin's associate Medvedev), but the much more powerful Roman Jakobson. The idea of device and its defamiliarization was nowhere near as serious a threat as a "linguistic poetics" supported by a theory of language.

13. For this reason, it serves as the focal point for Paul de Man's critique of Bakhtin. See de Man, "Dialogue and Dialogism," and Mathew Roberts, "Poetics Hermeneutics Dialogics."

14. For a reading of the Rabelais book in these terms, see Clark and Holquist, *Bakhtin*, ch. 14.

15. The title of the first essay was supplied by Bakhtin's editors, but it appears apt. The second essay was based on an abandoned draft originally entitled by Bakhtin "Toward the Philosophical Bases of the Human Sciences."

16. Bakhtin refers to "the positive significance of Formalism" and "high evaluations of structuralism"; "what is new always assumes one-sided and extreme forms in the early, more creative stages of its development" (MHS, p. 169).

Chapter 3

1. See Clark and Holquist, *Bakhtin*, especially the chapter entitled "The Disputed Texts," pp. 146–70.

2. We note here that we do not bring to this reconsideration any new archival material or oral evidence. Our conclusions were reached through a rereading of Bakhtin's texts and those of other members of his circle; and through an assessment of the major arguments and the evidence about the authorship question currently in print. We note that reservations about conflation were registered in the United States at least as early as 1981; see Kochis and Regier: "The controversial question of Bakhtin's relationship to works formerly ascribed to V. N. Vološinov and P. N. Medvedev is summarily dismissed by the editor in a short paragraph. Until facts can be substantiated by more than hearsay, and until distinct stylistic features are isolated, the most reasonable solution would be Titunik's" (Review of *The Dialogic Imagination*, p. 535, n. 8).

3. In his essay "The Baxtin Industry," Morson characterized Clark and

Holquist's case as unconvincing but did not himself take a stand on the authorship question. In their reply, "A Continuing Dialogue" (considered below), Clark and Holquist concentrated on Titunik's objections.

4. See Perlina, "Bakhtin-Medvedev-Voloshinov," pp. 35–47, and Brown, "Soviet Structuralism," pp. 118–20.

See also part 3 of Carroll, "The Alterity of Discourse." Carroll questions the inner logic of Holquist's idea of "ventriloquization," as well as the twin assumptions that Bakhtin's early manuscripts contain in embryo all his later ideas and that those ideas were primarily theological.

5. Caution is needed in reading Seyffert's excellent study to allow for his expressed preference for the semioticians, but he wisely includes numerous direct and lengthy quotations from influential articles so that readers can draw their own conclusions.

6. Recently, there has been a call within the Soviet academic establishment for a thoroughly annotated Academy Edition of Bakhtin School writings, with the disputed texts provisionally attributed to Bakhtin. See Averintsev, Review. In a footnote to a review of Eichenbaum's *O literature*, Nemzer calls for a reprinting of Medvedev's critique of Formalism "so that the serious reader will be able to see the strength and weakness of this book and understand what in it is from Bakhtin, and what from the style of polemics at the end of the twenties" (Nemzer, Review, p. 262). The rehabilitation of Voloshinov and Medvedev, should it come, will be welcome for Bakhtin studies and for the history of Marxist thought.

In a review of a 1989 Bakhtin commemorative conference in the Siberian city of Kemerevo, Vladimir Turbin makes reference to "Bakhtin's remarkable book *The Formal Method*, for some reason ascribed not to him but to Pavel Medvedev, who was (as far as I know) in no way even a close friend" (Turbin, "Bakhtin," p. 8). The cult of Bakhtin extends into deeper and deeper realms of mythmaking.

7. The first American edition of *The Formal Method* (Johns Hopkins Univ. Press, 1978, translated by Albert Wehrle) originally published under Medvedev's name gives its author as "P. N. Medvedev/M. M. Bakhtin"; the Harvard University Press paperback reprint (1985) reverses the order and attributes the work to "M. M. Bakhtin/P. N. Medvedev." A Russian-language edition printed in New York (published by Serebrianyi vek in 1982) attributes the book solely to "Mikhail Bakhtin." The introduction to this edition takes a high moral tone, as it claims to be restoring the book to its true author. It offers as proof that the Wehrle translation mentions a document Bakhtin signed for the Soviet copyright agency, in which Bakhtin allegedly claimed authorship (Bakhtin [sic], *Formal'nyi*, pp. 5–6). (See M:FM in Abbreviations for bibliographic information on the various editions.) In fact, Wehrle's statement is not so categorical. He claims only that Vadim Kozhinov informed him of the existence of such a document. As we mention below, Clark and Holquist indicate that Bakhtin *refused* to sign such a document.

On the other hand, Harvard University Press reprinted Voloshinov's *Marxism and the Philosophy of Language* and his *Freudianism: A Critical Sketch* without any attribution to Bakhtin, perhaps because I. R. Titunik, co-translator of *Marxism* and sole translator of *Freudianism*, has been the most consistent and long-standing opponent of "Bakhtin imperialism."

Clark and Holquist also mention translations of the disputed texts into other languages, with authorship attributed to Bakhtin. According to their biography, the Soviet copyright agency VAAP insists that credit be given to Bakhtin. See Clark and Holquist, *Bakhtin*, p. 147.

8. Brown comments on Ivanov's methodological assumptions in "Soviet Structuralism," pp. 118–20.

9. Elsewhere in the same chapter, Clark and Holquist write: "The earliest 'Voloshinov' text that seems a candidate for Bakhtin's authorship is 'Beyond the Social,' which was published in *The Star* early in 1925. Many sections in this article are similar to sections in 'Voloshinov's' later *Freudianism*, published in the summer of 1927, which is also by Bakhtin" (Clark and Holquist, *Bakhtin*, p. 162). They continue: "The next 'Voloshinov' publication, 'The Latest Trends in Linguistic Thought in the West,' was published in 1928. It was presented as a synopsis of three chapters of 'Voloshinov's' forthcoming book *Marxism and the Philosophy of Language*. Inasmuch as the book is Bakhtin's, the article is presumably his likewise, though Bakhtin could have assigned to Voloshinov the onerous task of preparing a synopsis. The authorship of *Marxism and the Philosophy of Language*, published in 1929, is clearly Bakhtin's" (Clark and Holquist, *Bakhtin*, p. 166). Although toward the end of their chapter Clark and Holquist concede that the problem is "one about proportion and ratio rather than identity as such" (ibid., p. 170), this chapter and their book as a whole clearly limit Voloshinov and Medvedev to purely mechanical roles: preparing a synopsis or making a few minor insertions. All the creative energy and everything from main specific points to overall argument are said to belong to Bakhtin.

10. The error here, which is a fundamental one, has recently been discussed in Furbank and Owens, *The Canonisation of Daniel Defoe*:

> The first rule to observe in regard to author-attribution is the one that Baron Gilbert, in his classic *Law of Evidence* lays down . . . that it is not necessary to prove a negative: "And here it is first to be considered, that in all Courts of Justice the Affirmative ought to be proved, for it is sufficient barely to deny what is affirmed until the contrary is proved. . . . The Civil Law says 'The Proof lies on him who makes the Allegation, for it is against the Nature of Things to prove a negative.'" When an anonymous work is ascribed to an author, the onus of proof lies entirely with the person making the ascription, and in theory at least, there is no corresponding obligation to disprove it; it may be assumed to be untrue until proved true. It is this that makes the attribution of a work such a momentous business. [Furbank and Owens, *Canonisation*, p. 29]

11. A translation of these prefaces appears in *Rethinking Bakhtin*. They are also discussed in that volume in Shukman, "Bakhtin's Tolstoy Prefaces," and Emerson, "Tolstoy Connection."

12. In his article "The Politics of Representation," Holquist argues that Bakhtin deliberately published his books under the names of his friends to illustrate his theories: this is "the example provided by the relation he himself bears to certain texts that he authored [the disputed texts]" (Holquist, "Politics," p. 167; similar passages appear throughout the article).

13. These arguments are presented in Holquist, "The Politics of Representation," and criticized by Titunik in "The Baxtin Problem." Holquist writes: "At this point [in the latter half of the 1920's], the theoretical epicenter of his work—how to reconcile modern linguistics with the biblical assurance that the Word became flesh—overlapped with his own pressing practical needs: How was he to find an appropriate ideological flesh for the spirit of his own works so that he could sell his work before wasting away completely? . . . If the Christian word were to take on Soviet flesh it had to clothe itself in ideological disguise" (Holquist, "Politics," pp. 172–73). This theological comparison is not meant as a mere analogy: Holquist discusses Russian Orthodox theology to demonstrate the theological terms of Bakhtin's thought and action with regard to the authorship question.

14. See Titunik, "Baxtin & / or Vološinov & / or Medvedev," p. 8, n. 8.

15. Titunik observes: "Baxtin's interest in carnival (and associated topics such as Menippean satire) seems to have originated with his work on Rabelais. Yet, the authors identify Baxtin as 'carnival man' from the start, asserting that the very ambience of his life from the earliest period of his career was 'carnivalesque'" (Titunik, "Baxtin Problem," p. 93). In their reply, Clark and Holquist note that Bakhtin had long been familiar with menippean satire. But that does not mean, of course, that he had thought of analyzing menippean satire in terms of carnival and carnivalization.

16. Titunik asks, "Perhaps it is just a matter of one's sense of humor?" (Titunik, "Baxtin Problem," p. 93). Clark and Holquist reply that Voloshinov did not finish his dissertation and no notes survived, so "a definitive answer simply does not exist" (Clark and Holquist, "Continuing," p. 98).

17. On this point, see Godzich's foreword to the paperback reprint of *The Formal Method* (1985).

18. Our own reading of Bakhtin on this point appears later in the present volume (see Chapter Seven). See Shukman, "Bakhtin's Tolstoy Prefaces."

19. For example, see Bakhtin's response to Engelhardt's theory of Dostoevsky's "dialectical development of the spirit" (PDP, pp. 22–26). This critique occupied a proportionately even more prominent place in the first edition of the Dostoevsky book.

20. Clark and Holquist write: "For Kanaev is, as we state very clearly, *still alive* (or, at least, was alive when we wrote our book), and is thus able to deny or validate claims that it was Baxtin who actually wrote the text [on vitalism] in question" (Clark and Holquist, "Continuing," p. 97). To

whom did Kanaev confirm Bakhtin's authorship? "As we make clear in the book, we did not personally interview him (not, as we hasten to add, for want of trying)" (ibid.).

21. Titunik writes: "The result of their efforts is not, in my opinion, a study, but something like an *apologia*, or even more than that: Clark and Holquist have produced what can be described . . . as *hagiography*, that is, an account both of a 'saint' of ideas (like Einstein, to whom the authors compare Baxtin) and of a Christian, even—in the authors' view—a specifically Russian Orthodox saint. . . . I do not mean to say that Clark and Holquist have not attempted to prove Baxtin's intellectual and Christian sanctity, but—and this is my major objection—hagiography is not at all what is needed now" (Titunik, "Baxtin Problem," p. 91). According to Titunik, one must judge by the overall tenor of the work and by the reliability, precision, and care of the assertions that can be verified. And, Titunik adds, these aspects of their work are not wholly reassuring. Titunik enumerates errors in fact and documentation in the Clark-Holquist biography; see "Baxtin Problem," p. 95.

With regard to "hagiography": Occasionally, reminiscences in the current Soviet press suggest the origins of the Bakhtin cult in the 1960's. In the Conversations About Literature and Life section of the popular journal *Don*, Vadim Kozhinov relates the first trip that he and his fellow graduate students Sergei Bocharov and Gennadi Gachev made to Bakhtin in Saransk—during which one of their number, Gachev, fell down on his knees and implored, "Mikhail Mikhailovich, tell us how to live so we can become like you" (Kozhinov, "Tak eto bylo," p. 159).

To this spiritually orphaned generation, Bakhtin seemed like a miraculous survivor from some more creative and far-distant time.

22. Titunik notes that for all the categorical assertions that "Bakhtin was a religious man" (Clark and Holquist, *Bakhtin*, first sentence of ch. 5), there is very little to put one's finger on. Clark and Holquist, he points out, repeatedly describe religious circles at the time, only to conclude that there is no evidence Bakhtin belonged to them; nevertheless, Titunik continues, they do not qualify their categorical claims of his religiosity. Their readers may not be aware of how much their account depends on evidence and how much depends on "supposition, speculation, and surmise" (Titunik, "Baxtin Problem," p. 92).

23. In "The Politics of Representation," Holquist's projected title is still *The Architectonics of Responsibility* (Holquist, "Politics," p. 171).

24. Perlina, "Funny Things," especially pp. 15–17 (on Lossky's philosophical writings and their importance for Bakhtin) and pp. 17–21 (on the problematic "Kanaev" article).

25. Once one accepts that the relations were dialogic, another question, which we do not address here, comes into view: what are the differences between Voloshinov's and Medvedev's "monologizations" of Bakhtin and between their respective versions of Marxist poetics?

Chapter 4

1. And in quoting or in indirect discourse, we can never quite "get it right"; we always add another voice that distorts. A voice can never be reproduced, only quoted; for tone, like utterances, is unrepeatable.

2. For an account of these fascinating models, see Galan, *Historic Structures*, especially ch. 2, "Language Diachrony and Literary Evolution," pp. 6–44.

3. For a shorthand guide to individual terms and concepts in Bakhtin's writings, including many not considered in the present volume, see our companion volume, *Heteroglossary*.

4. For a more extended Bakhtinian approach to parody, see the section Theory of Parody in *Rethinking Bakhtin*, pp. 63–103.

5. A more literal rendition of the terms Voloshinov uses for reporting and reported speech are "author's speech" (*avtorskaia rech'*) and "someone else's speech" (*chuzhaia rech'*).

6. For a contemporary Marxist account of language that uses Voloshinov and is written in his spirit, see Williams, *Marxism and Literature*, pp. 35–44. Williams assumes (in our view, correctly) that Bakhtin did not write *Marxism and the Philosophy of Language* and that the book represents a sophisticated attempt to develop an adequate Marxist approach to language.

7. See Vygotsky, *Thought and Language*, pp. 210–56. Vygotsky's title, *Myshlenie i rech'*, would be more accurately rendered as *Thinking and Speaking* to reflect the Russian original's emphasis on process and orality.

8. In the original edition of the Dostoevsky book, Bakhtin does not mention *metalingvistika* but rather concurs with Voloshinov in recommending a "sociological" approach. We may compare the parallel passages in the two versions of the Dostoevsky book: "The problem of the orientation of speech toward another person's word is of paramount sociological significance. The word is by its very nature social" (1929; PTD, p. 131); "Stylistics must be based not only, and even not as much, on linguistics as on metalinguistics, which studies the word not in a system of language and not in a 'text' excised from dialogic interaction" (1963; PDP, p. 202).

Chapter 5

1. On Soviet psychology and its nineteenth-century predecessors, see Graham, *Science, Philosophy and Human Behavior*, ch. 5 ("Physiology and Psychology"); Joravsky, *Russian Psychology*; and Kozulin, *Psychology in Utopia*.

2. On the shortcomings of Bakhtin's overly benign approach to Dostoevsky, see Emerson, "Bakhtin, Dostoevsky," and Emerson, "Problems."

3. See Holdheim, "Idola Fori Academici," especially p. 11.

4. On theoretism, see pages 27–32 of the present study. See also our overview of "Toward a Philosophy of the Act" in the introduction to *Rethinking Bakhtin*; and the entry in Morson and Emerson, *Heteroglossary*.

5. See V:F, and Vygotsky, *The Psychology of Art* (1925), especially pt. 2, ch. 4 ("Art and Psychoanalysis").

6. On this story and the larger problems it raises, see Jackson, *Dostoevsky's Quest*, pp. 158–62.

7. See V:DiL, especially pp. 98–100. For a thorough discussion of this divergence between Bakhtin's and Voloshinov's ideas in the light of Bakhtin's early manuscripts and V:DiL, see Roberts, "Neither a Formalist nor a Marxist Be." Roberts correctly points out that Voloshinov's "Marxist monism," however sophisticated it might be, departs from Bakhtin's project by collapsing the aesthetic, cognitive, and ethical realms into mere varieties of the social. In other words, Roberts argues, Voloshinov's "sociology of art" is based on "shared evaluative contexts" rather than differentiated ones (as for Bakhtin).

8. For more detail, see Pirog, "Bakhtin Circle's Freud," especially p. 605. Pirog distinguishes between Voloshinov's explicit (and Bakhtin's implicit) critique of psychoanalysis, and draws some parallels with Habermas's revisioning of Freud.

9. This is a key point of Voloshinov's discussion of the utterance "Well!" in V:DiL, pp. 98–102 (section 3).

10. In his early programmatic essay, "Discourse in Life and Discourse in Poetry," Voloshinov argues that a poet's style "is engendered from the style of his inner speech, which does not lend itself to control, and his inner speech is itself the product of his entire social life" (V:DiL, p. 114). The same case is made in *Marxism*: "People do not 'accept' their native language; it is in their native language that they first reach awareness" (V:MPL, p. 81). The very act of introspection is modeled on external social discourse; it is self-observation, communion with the self, "the understanding of one's own inner sign" (V:MPL, p. 36).

11. There is no evidence that Vygotsky ever met any member of the Bakhtin circle, and Vygotsky makes no reference in his work to any of them. More likely, his interest in dialogue derived from the writings of Lev Yakubinsky, which may mean that Vygotsky began by reinventing the wheel—perhaps a wheel designed somewhat differently. The Vygotsky scholar James Wertsch correctly and perceptively observes that "Bakhtin" (so he identifies the author of *Marxism and the Philosophy of Language*) "emphasized the dialogic nature of inner speech more than Vygotsky did." By conflating Bakhtin and Voloshinov, Wertsch is led to discuss Bakhtin's work on the novel in his third period in "semioticized" terms, that is, to read Bakhtin through Voloshinov. See Wertsch, *Vygotsky*, pp. 223–31, 237.

Vygotsky's title recalls Alexander Potebnia's 1862 work *Mysl' i iazyk* (Thought and language), which he doubtless knew; he may have been contrasting his process-oriented title to Potebnia's theory of art (or language) as image.

12. See also the discussion in Vygotsky, "Tool and Symbol."

13. See *Thought and Language*, pp. 186–96, and Vygotsky, "Interac-

tion," pp. 84–86. The concept of a "zone of proximal development" has been developed productively by some American psychologists. Compare Vygotsky's views with those of the American philosopher of education John Holt: "The true test of intelligence is not how much we know how to do, but how we behave when we don't know what to do" (Holt, *How Children Fail*, p. 205).

14. Passages like these suggest that Bakhtin may have had in mind a theory of schizophrenia. Described in terms of inner voices, schizophrenia would presumably have been seen as an exaggeration of tendencies already present in normal daily life.

15. One internally persuasive voice may lose its tolerance for another and begin to manipulate, undermine, and parody it. Bakhtin's analysis of Dostoevsky's early novella *The Double* is in fact a brilliant reading of the self at war with itself through various alliances between authoritative and innerly persuasive words (PTD, pp. 146–62; and PDP, pp. 211–21).

Chapter 6

1. Letter of Bakhtin to Kozhinov, July 30, 1961, as cited in the editors' note to "K pererabotke knigi o Dostoevskom" [TRDB] in the 1979 Russian collection, p. 404.

2. See Berkovskii's largely negative review of *Problems of Dostoevsky's Creative Art* that appeared in "Zvezda," 1929. The critic appreciates only the "philosophical-linguistic part" of Bakhtin's study (i.e., its pt. 2, "Slovo u Dostoevskogo"), arguably because he does not understand what Bakhtin means by polyphony. After complimenting Bakhtin for his understanding of Dostoevskian heroes and their "words with a sideways glance," Berkovskii concludes (pp. 120–21): "The most damaging thing of all for Bakhtin's book is its absolutely unfounded, radically mistaken basic assertions concerning the alleged 'polyphonism' of the Dostoevskian novel. In Bakhtin's opinion, there is no authorial 'directing' in Dostoevsky's novels; what we are given are personal consciousnesses in equally valid measure ('voices'), not reduced to the unified consciousness of the author; every voice lives on its own, and as a result the novel turns out to be a multi-voiced thing, 'polyphony,' in no way encompassed by a unified authorial voice. [But] in fact, Dostoevsky's novel is extremely unified, and precisely by an authorial thought, by an authorial meaning. . . . The unsuccessful idea of 'polyphonism' destroys all of Bakhtin's constructs."

3. The musical metaphor of polyphony has also led to some misunderstandings, for only some aspects of musical polyphony pertain to Bakhtin's concept, as he himself cautions (PDP, p. 22). Bakhtin keeps the idea of an interweaving of independent "melodies" (or voices); he keeps multiplicity, dissonance or "unmergedness," and dynamic movement. He omits the necessity for *simultaneous* sounding and (as if following atonal or modern musical sensibilities) does not insist that polyphonic development move from dissonance to consonance.

4. It will be recalled that in Chapters One and Four we distinguish three main ways in which Bakhtin uses the term *dialogue*: as a description of language that makes all utterances by definition dialogic; as a term for a specific type of utterance, opposed to other, monologic utterances; and as a view of the world and truth (his global concept).

5. For a more detailed account of these accounts of creativity and for a discussion of Bakhtin's place among possible alternatives to them both, see the sections on "Creation by Potential" in Morson, *Hidden in Plain View*, pp. 173–89.

6. This "vivid sense" of a character results, perhaps paradoxically, from the author's success in conceptualizing a "whole personality." In the early manuscripts, Bakhtin draws a distinction between real-life and aesthetic "authoring" (AiG, pp. 7–8). In life, he writes, we author fragments; "we are not [usually] interested in the whole of a person but only in his separate acts." In art, however, an author must assume "a unified reaction to the whole of the hero." Getting the whole of a hero right is an arduous task, Bakhtin contends; and he remarks on "how many grimaces, random masks, false gestures" (AiG, p. 8) can result from the whims or caprices of the author. But the task is necessary, for only as a conceptualized whole can a hero be released to develop freely within the logic of his own reality. These observations seem to look forward to the problematic of the Dostoevsky book.

7. See Morson, *Hidden in Plain View*, pp. 173–89. Tolstoy in particular seems to have cultivated another kind of creation by potential. Bakhtin's deep antipathy to Tolstoy's monologism may have blinded him to Tolstoy's ideas. See Emerson, "Tolstoy Connection." It would be especially interesting to investigate the ways in which serial publication, in which the author may commit himself to a partial text before having a plan for the whole, may have been used to "create by potential." For other studies of creativity relevant to this argument, see *Hidden in Plain View*, p. 295, n. 16.

8. Cited in PDP, p. 60, from *Biografiia, pis'ma i zametki iz zapisnoi knigi F. M. Dostoevskogo* (St. Petersburg, 1883), p. 373.

Chapter 7

1. Shklovsky continues (and Medvedev cites): "In the middle of his novel, Cervantes was already aware that in loading his wisdom on Don Quixote he had made him a duality. Subsequently, he used or began to use this fact for his own artistic ends."

2. Voloshinov's arguments in this vein may be found in V:MPL, pt. 2, ch. 3 ("Verbal Interaction"). See especially the discussion of "speech genres" and their relation to "life genres" (translated in V:MPL as "behavioral genres"), pp. 91–92, 96–97.

3. "Like Moliere's Monsieur Jourdain who, when speaking in prose, had no idea that was what he was doing, we speak in diverse genres with-

out suspecting that they exist" (SG, p. 78). For more on the debate on speech genres, see Perlina, "Dialogue."

4. Thus, a standard comic or absurdist figure is a person who grasps the "language," but not the genres of speech (e.g., Gracie Allen).

Chapter 8

1. On a prosaics of expository prose, see Kittay and Godzich, *Emergence of Prose*.

2. In his preface to *Resurrection* (TP2), Bakhtin, with some degree of irony, explicitly recommends that novel as a model for the new Soviet "socioideological novel." See *Rethinking Bakhtin*, p. 257.

3. See Booth, *The Rhetoric of Fiction*. In his introduction to the Emerson translation of *Problems of Dostoevsky's Poetics*, Booth observes that Bakhtin found a still better way to analyze the novelistic features with which *The Rhetoric of Fiction* was concerned.

4. The lines from *Onegin* are modified from the Walter Arndt translation. The statement "a development of the final comparison follows" is Bakhtin's.

5. On this kind of resolution of reporting context by reported speech, see Chapter Four.

6. Bakhtin observes: "It is difficult to speak it [such discourse] aloud, for loud and living intonation excessively monologizes discourse and cannot do justice to the other person's voice present in it" (PDP, p. 198).

7. Readers familiar with Russian Formalism should be aware that Bakhtin is not using the term *literariness* in the Formalist sense of that which makes literature literary. But he may be alluding to the Formalists critically; he may mean to imply that they mistake for the essence of literature what is in fact a rather specific phenomenon that is not definitive of the whole.

8. This form of argument may be contrasted, for instance, with Voloshinov's habit of defining opposites and seeking a dialectical resolution.

9. This point is only implicit in DiN; we extend Bakhtin's reasoning in the direction we suspect he was going.

10. In both DiN and FTC, Bakhtin considers the debt of satiric genres and the novel to folkloric images of fools and rogues. The folkloric images proved fundamental to the novel, but the novel reprocessed and altered them to a great extent. The fool and his genre are soon parted.

11. An awareness of such changes may be consciously exploited by the authors of historical novels. *War and Peace*, for instance, allows its readers to sense the jargonish expressions used by characters even when those expressions have been canonized by the time Tolstoy is writing. We sense the difference between our own language and the language of "our grandfathers." The presence of French in the text, which would have been routinely understood by readers of 1805, required translation in footnotes in

1865, and so these footnotes mark the difference in linguistic sensibility. As if to stress the point, the Russian Tolstoy uses to translate the French is itself often dated; he often renders the French in the Russian of 1805. Problems of class are also involved in the chronological divergence that provides the text with so much of its linguistic energy.

12. Presumably, this is one reason why the "basic" dialogism of novels may be captured even in a translation, and why Bakhtin can use translations of English novels to illustrate his points. Presumably, it is also why readers of "Discourse in the Novel" and *Problems of Dostoevsky's Poetics* in English versions can grasp Bakhtin's fundamental points.

13. In the case of the *Quixote*, for instance, a vast history of reaccentuations has enriched the text. To be sure, some reaccentuations simply modernized and distorted it, but others were "an organic further development of the image, a continuation of the unresolved argument embedded in it" (DiN, p. 410). In this way, Bakhtin observes, works truly grow: "Thus are created the immortal novelistic images that live different lives in different epochs" (ibid.).

Bakhtin also notes that the activation of some potentials may silence meanings developed at an earlier time from interaction with other potentials. Gains and losses may both be present.

Chapter 9

1. We lack a commonly accepted term for the relation Bakhtin has in mind here, but a comparison from general systems theory might be helpful. General systems theorists often focus on specific functions that different systems must perform—for example, the allocation of resources. Different systems—whether cultural, economic, psychological, or hydraulic—have developed different mechanisms to perform these functions; indeed, they must have, because there are always some important resources in limited supply. In comparing systems, one can learn a great deal about their ways of working by comparing their mechanisms for performing this function and understanding why different ways of performing it have developed. For example, where economic systems may use "price" to allocate resources (in a market economy), cultural systems may use "value," and hydraulic systems "pressure." The relation among these three terms is not identity—pressure does not work the same way as value in many crucial respects and it would be wrong to assume it does—and yet the relationship is something stronger than metaphoric because it is based on the performance of similar functions in different systems. Our thanks to Aron Katsenelinboigen for helping us with this point.

2. On Bakhtin and Ukhtomsky, see Michael Holquist, "Answering as Authoring," especially pp. 67–70.

3. It appears that the publishing house where this book was in press was bombed shortly after the German invasion, and the manuscript was lost. As for Bakhtin's own copy, the going story (or legend?) is that, due to

the paper shortage, he made the better part of it into cigarettes—a story that would seem to be an interesting counterpoint to the famous line in Bulgakov's novel *The Master and Margarita*: "Manuscripts don't burn." It is unclear whether the portion published in Russian in 1979 and in English in 1986 is taken from page proofs, a finished manuscript, or drafts; nor is it clear what other documents in the Bakhtin archives might shed light on the problem.

4. Our thanks to Donald Fanger for pointing out the importance of distinguishing chronotopes as genres from chronotopic motifs.

5. The example from *Candide* is Bakhtin's, from Pushkin our own.

6. In DiN, the sentence is rendered: "*This distinctive correspondence of an identity with a particular self* is the *organizing center* of the human image in the Greek romance." We have preferred "sameness with one's own self" as a rendition of *tozhdestvo s samim soboi*. Here "sameness with oneself" seems synonymous with "coincident with oneself" in *Problems of Dostoevsky's Poetics*, and the opposite of *nesovpadenie* (noncoincidence) in the nineteenth-century realist novel as Bakhtin understands it.

7. Stephen Jay Gould and Niles Eldridge's use of this logic as an alternative to gradualist Darwinism may serve as a reminder that a store of diverse chronotopes may prove useful.

8. To support Bakhtin's point here, we might note that even in the nineteenth century, Konstantin Leontiev could object that in describing the last moments of a silent, dying character, Tolstoy put himself in an impossible position. "How does Count Tolstoy *know this?*" asked Leontiev. "He did not rise from the dead and visit us after his resurrection" (Leontiev, "Novels of Count L. N. Tolstoy," p. 245). Similar debate accompanied Victor Hugo's and Dostoevsky's specialized devices for describing a condemned man's last moments (e.g., the supposition of an impossible diary kept right up to the last instant). Dostoevsky discusses the question in his preface to the story "The Meek One" in the November 1876 issue of *The Diary of a Writer*.

9. See Chapter Seven of the present study.

10. Here again, the problem might be resolvable if the editors of the Soviet anthology had described just how they produced the published text (on which the English version is based). In general, Bakhtin scholarship would greatly profit by a comprehensive description of the Bakhtin archives, to which access is limited.

11. The Russian text combines these two essentially synonymous terms in the phrase *gotovaia dannost'* (ready-made givenness).

12. The term is translated in the Bildungsroman essay as "multitemporality." We prefer "heterochrony" because of the evident parallel with "heteroglossia" (*raznorechie*); and because *razno* indicates "variety" not "plurality." But if "vari-speechedness" or "vari-vocality" were accepted in place of "heteroglossia," then "vari-temporality" would be a good rendition for *raznovremennost'*.

13. On this aspect of Socialist Realism and Soviet culture, see Clark, *Soviet Novel*, and Clark, "Political History."

14. "Proxemics is the term I have coined for the interrelated observations and theories of man's use of space as a specialized elaboration of culture" (Hall, *Hidden Dimension*, p. 1). Bakhtin, of course, would insist on at least "equal time" for time and on the fusion of temporal and spatial categories.

15. Bakhtin's logic here seems less than fully consistent with his framework. For it would seem possible that there could be "double-voiced" chronotopes, chronotopes whose sense of the world and way of representing the world involves an allusion to a different chronotope. In that case, chronotopic dialogues would seem possible *within* a specific chronotope. To take one of Bakhtin's examples elsewhere in the chronotope essay, *Candide* works essentially by parodying the chronotope of adventure time, which would mean that the dialogue among chronotopes is already present in this "double-voiced" parodic chronotope. If so, then we may expect a broader panoply of double-voiced chronotopes to exist as well.

16. In this passage, Bakhtin gives no term for this third error; the term *naive reader reception* is our own.

17. Could this conclusion, like "Concluding Remarks" in the chronotope essay, belong to Bakhtin's last years?

Chapter 10

1. "Chronotope" (apart from the section "Concluding Remarks") was completed before *Rabelais*, but Bakhtin may nevertheless have been working on both simultaneously. At least until the archives are opened, dating must remain speculative.

2. In a sense, hawking—with its dependence upon the "I" recognizing itself on the basis of "we" and "choral support"—more resembles Voloshinov's "shared social purview" than any scenario in Bakhtin's own early writings. See "Discourse in Life and Discourse in Art" in V:F, especially pp. 102–3.

3. The best-known critique of Bakhtin from this perspective is by Booth, "Freedom of Interpretation."

4. For a discussion of the special role of plot in polyphony, see Chapter Six of the present study.

5. Bakhtin provides fourteen typical characteristics of menippea (PDP, pp. 114–18). Among them, he stresses an intensified comic element, a new freedom from the constraints of memoir literature and established legend, a bolder use of fantastic situations to test and interrogate truths, the setting of ideas in inappropriate locales (a sort of "slum naturalism"). Menippean heroes have no status to defend and fear only not having access to life's variety. All purely "academic" questions fall away: under these circumstances, even ultimate ethical questions are practical. Many menippean satires are constructed with three planes, "Earth/Olympus/Netherworld," because the experimental fantasticality of the genre requires observation

from some unusual point of view. Abnormal states such as peculiar dreams and insanity become ways of exploring the complexities of multileveled personality, "man not coinciding with himself." Likewise, the appearance of doubles serves to weaken or destroy the "epic and tragic wholeness of man" and to create the possibility of dialogue with oneself. Other traits of the genre are all related to this attack on "epic wholeness." Scandal scenes and inappropriate behavior abound; sharp contrasts, oxymorons, and abrupt changes of state are common. Inserted genres and an admixture of (usually parodied) poetry help to create a "multi-toned" whole. And lastly—recalling Bakhtin's focus on the tension between embodiment and potential so characteristic of carnivalized forms—there is a tendency to mix a passion for current and topical issues with vibrant scenarios of social utopia.

How are these carefully detailed traits of menippean satire, a form of "reduced folkloric laughter," different from the Rabelaisian carnivalesque? Similarities between the treatment of words, character, and plot in the two studies are obvious. But one great difference lies in Bakhtin's new—or rather, renewed—emphasis on the ordinary human body and individual personality as a vehicle for this impulse. Much less attention is paid to the "collective body of the whole people"; in fact, there is only a single, under-played reference to such an entity in the entire chapter (PDP, p. 128).

Moreover, the moral-psychological experimentation of dreams, insanity, and scandal, all designed to destroy the epic and tragic wholeness of the human being and his fate, serves here to *enrich* dialogue—not to simplify it, close it down, or absorb it into a large cacophonous whole. One need only note how Bakhtin deals with the ancient genres of the diatribe, soliloquy, and symposium, in a spirit quite foreign to their body-oriented Rabelaisian counterparts (PDP, pp. 120–22). Here, symposia are not only banquet tables for the sake of bellies and mouths; likewise, diatribes and soliloquies are vehicles for "internal dialogicality" and a dialogic relationship to one's own self and thought.

6. We discuss Bakhtin's concept of "generic contacts," as distinct from "influence," in Chapter Seven of the present study.

7. Bakhtin suggests that Dostoevsky definitely or probably knew numerous works of menippean satire, including those of Lucian (whose works were widely known in Russia and provoked imitations), *Pumpkinification* (Seneca), the *Satyricon*, *The Golden Ass*, and works of Hoffmann, Poe, and others, as well as Gogol, Diderot, and Voltaire.

8. Bakhtin himself does not use the term *chronotope* in this essay, but the concept is evident in his discussion of carnival space and time and their transposition into Dostoevskian "thresholds."

9. For such an extension of Bakhtin's ideas, see Bernstein, "When the Carnival Turns Bitter"; Bernstein, "Poetics of *Ressentiment*"; and Fogel, "Coerced Speech."

10. The contrast of dialogue with a monologic, "unified and indivisible spirit unfolding within itself" may also have been intended as another of Bakhtin's contrasts between dialogue and dialectics.

Works Cited

For works by Bakhtin, Medvedev, and Voloshinov cited throughout the text, see the list of abbreviations, pp. xvii–xx.

Aristotle. *Nichomachean Ethics.* The Basic Works of Aristotle. Ed. Richard McKeon. New York: Random House, 1941.

Averintsev, Sergei. Review of *M. M. Bakhtin. Literaturno-kriticheskie stat'i* (1986). *Druzhba narodov* 3 (1988), pp. 256–59.

Bateson, Gregory. "Why Do Things Get in a Muddle?" In *Steps to an Ecology of Mind.* New York: Ballantine, 1972, pp. 3–8.

Belknap, Robert. *The Structure of "The Brothers Karamazov."* The Hague: Mouton, 1967. Reprint. Evanston, Ill.: Northwestern Univ. Press., 1989.

Berkovskii, Naum. Review of "Problemy tvorchestva Dostoevskogo," in *Zvezda*, no. 7 (1929). Reprinted in N. Berkovskii, *Mir, sozdavaemyi literaturoi*. Moscow: Sovetskii pisatel', 1989, pp. 119–21.

Berlin, Isaiah. "Political Ideas in the Twentieth Century." In *Four Essays on Liberty*. London: Oxford Univ. Press, 1969, pp. 1–40.

Bernstein, Michael André. "The Poetics of *Ressentiment*." In *Rethinking Bakhtin: Extensions and Challenges*. Ed. Gary Saul Morson and Caryl Emerson. Evanston, Ill.: Northwestern Univ. Press, 1989, pp. 197–223.

———. "When the Carnival Turns Bitter: Preliminary Reflections upon the Abject Hero." In *Bakhtin: Essays and Dialogues on His Work.* Ed. Gary Saul Morson. Chicago: Univ. of Chicago Press, 1986, pp. 99–121.

Booth, Wayne C. "Freedom of Interpretation: Bakhtin and the Challenge of Feminist Criticism." In *Mikhail Bakhtin: Essays and Dialogues on His Work.* Ed. Gary Saul Morson. Chicago: Univ. of Chicago Press, 1986, pp. 145–76. Originally published in *Critical Inquiry* 9 (September 1982).

———. Introduction to M. M. Bakhtin, *Problems of Dostoevsky's Poetics.* Ed. and tr. Caryl Emerson. Minneapolis: Univ. of Minnesota Press, 1984, pp. xiii–xxvii.

———. *The Rhetoric of Fiction.* Chicago: Univ. of Chicago Press, 1961.

Borges, Jorge Luis. "Tlön, Uqbar, Orbis Tertius." In *Labyrinths: Selected Stories and Other Writings.* Ed. Donald A. Yates and James E. Irby. New York: New Directions, 1964.

Brandt, G. A. (Sverdlovsk). "Eticheskaia dominanta kul'tury v filosofii M. Bakhtina." *Estetika M. M. Bakhtina i sovremennost'*. Saransk: Mordovskii gosudarstvennyi universitet, 1989, pp. 22–24.

Braudel, Fernand. "History and the Social Sciences: The *Long Durée*." In *On History*. Tr. Sarah Matthews. Chicago: Univ. of Chicago Press, 1980, pp. 25–54.

———. "The Situation of History in 1950." In *On History*. Tr. Sarah Matthews. Chicago: Univ. of Chicago Press, 1980, pp. 6–22.

———. *The Structures of Everyday Life: The Limits of the Possible* (vol. 1 of *Civilization and Capitalism, 15th–18th Century*). Tr. Sîan Reynolds. New York: Harper & Row, 1981. Originally published as *Les Structures du Quotidien: Le Possible et L'Impossible*. Paris: Librairie Armand Colin, 1979.

Brown, Edward J. "Soviet Structuralism, A Semiotic Approach." In *Russian Formalism: A Retrospective Glance, a Festschrift in Honor of Victor Erlich*. Ed. Robert Louis Jackson and Stephen Rudy. New Haven, Conn.: Yale Center for International and Area Studies, 1985, pp. 118–20.

Bulgakov, Mikhail. *The Master and Margarita*. Tr. Michael Glenny. New York: Harvill, 1967.

Carroll, David. "The Alterity of Discourse: Form, History, and the Question of the Political in M. M. Bakhtin." *Diacritics* 13, no. 2 (Summer 1983), pp. 65–83.

Chekhov, Anton. *Uncle Vanya*. In *Chekhov: The Major Plays*. Tr. Ann Dunnigan. New York: Signet, 1964, pp. 171–231.

Clark, Katerina. "Political History and Literary Chronotope: Some Soviet Case Studies." In *Literature and History: Theoretical Problems and Russian Case Studies*. Ed. Gary Saul Morson. Stanford, Calif.: Stanford Univ. Press, 1986, pp. 230–46.

———. *The Soviet Novel: History as Ritual*. Chicago: Univ. of Chicago Press, 1981.

Clark, Katerina, and Michael Holquist. "A Continuing Dialogue." *Slavic and East European Journal* 30, no. 1 (Spring 1986), pp. 96–102.

———. *Mikhail Bakhtin*. Cambridge, Mass.: Harvard Univ. Press, 1984.

De Man, Paul. "Dialogue and Dialogism." In *Rethinking Bakhtin: Extensions and Challenges*. Ed. Gary Saul Morson and Caryl Emerson. Evanston, Ill.: Northwestern Univ. Press, 1989, pp. 105–14. Originally published in *Poetics Today* 4, no. 1 (1983).

Dostoevsky, Fyodor. *The Brothers Karamazov*. Tr. Constance Garnett. New York: Random House, 1950.

———. *The Idiot*. Tr. Constance Garnett. New York: Random House, 1935.

———. *Notes from Underground*. In *"Notes from Underground" and "The Grand Inquisitor."* The Garnett translation revised by Ralph Matlaw. New York: Dutton, 1960.

———. *The Possessed*. Tr. Constance Garnett. New York: Random House, 1963.

Dyson, Freeman. *Infinite in All Directions*. New York: Harper & Row, 1988.

Eliot, George. *Middlemarch*. New York: Random House, 1984.

Emerson, Caryl. "Bakhtin, Dostoevsky, and the Rise of Novel Imperialism." Unpublished ms.

———. "Problems with Baxtin's Poetics." *Slavic and East European Journal* 32, no. 4 (Winter 1988), pp. 503–25.

———. "The Tolstoy Connection in Bakhtin." In *Rethinking Bakhtin: Extensions and Challenges*. Ed. Gary Saul Morson and Caryl Emerson. Evanston, Ill.: Northwestern Univ. Press, 1989, pp. 149–70.

Emerson, Caryl, and Gary Saul Morson. "Penultimate Words." In *The Current in Criticism*. Ed. Clayton Koelb and Virgil Lokke. West Lafayette, Ind.: Purdue Univ. Press, 1987, pp. 43–64.

Fogel, Aaron. "Coerced Speech and the Oedipus Dialogue Complex." In *Rethinking Bakhtin: Extensions and Challenges*. Ed. Gary Saul Morson and Caryl Emerson. Evanston, Ill.: Northwestern Univ. Press, 1989, pp. 183–96. Excerpted from Fogel, *Coercion to Speech: Conrad's Poetics of Dialogue*. Cambridge, Mass.: Harvard Univ. Press, 1985.

Freud, Sigmund. *Civilization and Its Discontents*. Ed. and tr. James Strachey. New York: Norton, 1961.

———. "Creative Writers and Daydreaming." In *Critical Theory Since Plato*. Ed. Hazard Adams. New York: Harcourt Brace, 1971, pp. 749–53.

———. *The Psychopathology of Everyday Life*. Ed. James Strachey. Tr. Alan Tyson. New York: Norton, 1965.

Furbank, P. N., and W. R. Owens. *The Canonisation of Daniel Defoe*. New Haven, Conn.: Yale Univ. Press, 1988.

Galan, F. W. *Historic Structures: The Prague School Project, 1928–1945*. Austin: Univ. of Texas Press, 1985.

Gleick, James. *Chaos: Making a New Science*. New York: Viking, 1987.

Godzich, Wlad. Foreword to M. M. Bakhtin/P. N. Medvedev, *The Formal Method in Literary Scholarship: An Introduction to Sociological Poetics*. Tr. Albert J. Wehrle. Cambridge, Mass.: Harvard Univ. Press, 1985, pp. vii–xiv.

Gogol, Nikolai. "The Overcoat." In *The Collected Tales and Plays of Nikolai Gogol*. Ed. Leonard Kent. The Garnett translation revised by the editor. New York: Modern Library, 1969, pp. 562–92.

Gould, Stephen J. *The Panda's Thumb: More Reflections in Natural History*. New York: Norton, 1982.

———. "Pleasant Dreams." In *An Urchin in the Storm: Essays about Books and Ideas*. New York: Norton, 1987, pp. 199–207.

Graham, Loren R. *Science, Philosophy and Human Behavior in the Soviet Union*. New York: Columbia Univ. Press, 1987.

Gustafson, Richard. *Leo Tolstoy, Resident and Stranger: A Study in Fiction and Theology*. Princeton, N.J.: Princeton Univ. Press, 1986.

Hall, Edward T. *The Hidden Dimension*. Garden City, N.Y.: Anchor, 1969.

Holdheim, W. Wolfgang. "Idola Fori Academici." *Stanford Literature Review* 4 (1987), pp. 7–21.

Holquist, Michael. "Answering as Authoring: Mikhail Bakhtin's Trans-

Linguistics." In *Bakhtin: Essays and Dialogues on His Work*. Ed. Gary Saul Morson. Chicago: Univ. of Chicago Press, 1986, pp. 59–71.

———. "The Politics of Representation." In *Allegory and Representation*. Ed. Stephen J. Greenblatt. Baltimore, Md.: Johns Hopkins Univ. Press, 1982, pp. 163–83.

Holt, John. *How Children Fail*. New York: Pitman, 1964.

Hugo, Victor. *Les Misérables*. Tr. Lascelles Wraxal. New York: Heritage, 1938.

Ivanov, Viach. Vs. "The Significance of M. M. Bakhtin's Ideas on Sign, Utterance and Dialogue for Modern Semiotics." In *Semiotics and Structuralism: Readings from the Soviet Union*. Ed. Henryk Baran. White Plains, N.Y.: International Arts and Sciences Press, 1976, pp. 310–67. For the Russian text, see Viach. Vs. Ivanov, "Znachenie idei M. M. Bakhtina o znake, vyskazyvanii i dialoge dlia sovremennoi semiotiki," in *Trudy po znakovym sistemam* (vol. 6). Tartu, 1973, pp. 6–44.

Jackson, Robert Louis. "Aristotelian Movement and Design in Part Two of *Notes from the Underground*." *The Art of Dostoevsky: Deliriums and Nocturnes*. Princeton, N.J.: Princeton Univ. Press, 1981, pp. 171–88.

———. *Dostoevsky's Quest for Form: A Study of His Philosophy of Art*. New Haven, Conn.: Yale Univ. Press, 1966; second edition, Bloomington, Ind.: Physsardt, 1978.

Jonsen, Albert R., and Stephen Toulmin. *The Abuse of Casuistry: A History of Moral Reasoning*. Berkeley: Univ. of California Press, 1988.

Joravsky, David. *Russian Psychology: A Critical History*. Oxford: Basil Blackwell, 1989.

Kittay, Jeffrey, and Wlad Godzich. *The Emergence of Prose: An Essay in Prosaics*. Minneapolis: Univ. of Minnesota Press, 1987.

Kochis, Bruce, and W. G. Regier. Review of *The Dialogic Imagination*. In *Genre* 14, no. 4 (Winter 1981), pp. 530–35.

Kozhinov, Vadim. "Tak eto bylo . . ." *Don*, no. 10 (1988), pp. 156–59.

Kozulin, Alex. *Psychology in Utopia*. Cambridge, Mass.: MIT Press, 1984.

Kramer, Nic. J. T. A., and Jacob de Smit. *Systems Thinking: Concepts and Notions*. Leiden, the Netherlands: Martinus Nijhoff, 1977.

Kristeva, Julia. "Word, Dialogue and Novel" in *Desire in Language: A Semiotic Approach to Literature and Art*. Ed. Leon S. Roudiez. New York: Columbia Univ. Press, 1980, pp. 64–91. Originally published 1967.

———. "The Ruin of a Poetics." In *Russian Formalism: A Collection of Articles and Texts in Translation*. Ed. Stephen Bann and John E. Bowlt. Edinburgh: Scottish Univ. Press, 1973. Published in the United States by Harper & Row, 1973, pp. 102–19. Originally published 1970.

Leontiev, Konstantin. "The Novels of Count L. N. Tolstoy: Analysis, Style, and Atmosphere." In *Essays in Russian Literature: The Conservative View*. Ed. and tr. Spencer E. Roberts. Athens: Ohio University Press, 1968.

Losskii, N. O. *Intuitivnaia filosofiia Bergsona*. 3rd ed. Petersburg: Uchitel', 1922.

Lotman, Ju. M. "O semiosfere." In *Trudy po znakovym sistemam* (vol. 17). Tartu, 1984, pp. 5–23.

Lotman, Ju. M., V. A. Uspenskij, V. V. Ivanov, V. N. Toporov, and A. M. Pjatigorskij. *Theses on the Semiotic Study of Culture* [As Applied to Slavic Texts]. Lisse, the Netherlands: The Peter de Ridder Press, 1975. For a more recent update of that position see Lotman, "O semiosfere."

Morson, Gary Saul, ed. *Bakhtin: Essays and Dialogues on His Work.* Chicago: Univ. of Chicago Press, 1986.

———. "The Baxtin Industry." *Slavic and East European Journal* 30, no. 1 (Spring 1986), pp. 81–90.

———. "Dostoevsky's Anti-Semitism and the Critics." *Slavic and East European Journal* 27, no. 3 (Fall 1983), pp. 302–17.

———. *Hidden in Plain View: Narrative and Creative Potentials in "War and Peace."* Stanford, Calif.: Stanford Univ. Press, 1987.

———., ed. *Literature and History: Theoretical Problems and Russian Case Studies.* Stanford, Calif.: Stanford Univ. Press, 1986.

———. "Prosaics: An Approach to the Humanities." *The American Scholar* (Autumn 1988), pp. 515–28.

———. "Prosaics and *Anna Karenina*." *Tolstoy Studies* 1 (1988), pp. 1–12.

Morson, Gary Saul, with Caryl Emerson. *Heteroglossary: Terms and Concepts of the Bakhtin Group.* Forthcoming.

———., eds. *Rethinking Bakhtin: Extensions and Challenges.* Evanston, Ill.: Northwestern Univ. Press, 1989.

Nemzer, A. Review of Boris Eikhenbaum, *O literature. Raboty raznykh let* (1987). *Novyi mir*, no. 4 (1988), pp. 260–64.

Perlina, Nina. "Bakhtin-Medvedev-Voloshinov: An Apple of Discourse." *University of Ottawa Quarterly* 53 (1983), pp. 35–47.

———. "A Dialogue on the Dialogue: The Baxtin-Vinogradov Exchange (1924–65)." *Slavic and East European Journal* 32, no. 4 (Winter 1988), pp. 526–41.

———. "Funny Things Are Happening on the Way to the Baxtin Forum." Kennan Institute Occasional Paper no. 231. Washington, D.C., 1989.

Pirog, Gerald. "The Bakhtin Circle's Freud: From Positivism to Hermeneutics." *Poetics Today* 8, nos. 3–4 (1987), pp. 591–610.

Poe, Edgar Allen. "The Philosophy of Composition." In *Great Short Works of Edgar Allen Poe.* Ed. G. R. Thompson. New York: Harper & Row, 1970.

Powelstock, David. "Remarks Regarding Baxtin's View on Poetry." Unpublished ms., 1988.

Prigogine, Ilya. *From Being to Becoming: Time and Complexity in the Physical Sciences.* San Francisco: Freeman, 1980.

Pushkin, A. S. *Eugene Onegin: A Novel in Verse.* Tr. Walter Arndt. New York: Dutton, 1963.

———. *Ruslan and Lyudmila.* In *Polnoe sobranie sochinenii v desiati tomakh*, vol. 4. Leningrad: Nauka, 1977.

Roberts, Mathew. "Bakhtin and Jakobson." *Slavic and East European Journal*. Forthcoming.

———. "Neither a Formalist nor a Marxist Be." Unpublished ms.

———. "Poetics Hermeneutics Dialogics: Bakhtin and Paul de Man." In *Rethinking Bakhtin: Extensions and Challenges*. Ed. Gary Saul Morson and Caryl Emerson. Evanston, Ill.: Northwestern Univ. Press, 1989, pp. 115–34.

Sartre, Jean-Paul. *Search for a Method*. Tr. Hazel E. Barnes. New York: Random House, 1963; reissued in paperback in 1968.

Seyffert, Peter. *Soviet Literary Structuralism: Background, Debate, Issues*. Columbus, Ohio: Slavica, 1983.

Shelley, Percy Bysshe. "A Defense of Poetry." In *Critical Theory Since Plato*. Ed. Hazard Adams. New York: Harcourt Brace, 1971, pp. 499–513.

Shukman, Ann. "Bakhtin's Tolstoy Prefaces." In *Rethinking Bakhtin: Extensions and Challenges*. Ed. Gary Saul Morson and Caryl Emerson. Evanston, Ill.: Northwestern Univ. Press, 1989, pp. 137–48.

Slavic and East European Journal 30, no. 1 (Spring 1986), pp. 81–102: "Forum on Baxtin." Includes Gary Saul Morson, "The Baxtin Industry," pp. 81–90; I. R. Titunik, "The Baxtin Problem: Concerning Katerina Clark and Michael Holquist's *Mikhail Bakhtin*," pp. 91–95; and Katerina Clark and Michael Holquist, "A Continuing Dialogue," pp. 96–102.

Smirnov, A. A. "Puti i zadachi nauki o literature." *Literaturnaia mysl'* 2 (1923), pp. 91–109.

Stewart, Susan. "Shouts in the Street: Bakhtin's Anti-Linguistics." In *Bakhtin: Essays and Dialogues on His Work*. Ed. Gary Saul Morson. Chicago: Univ. of Chicago Press, 1986, pp. 41–57.

Terras, Victor, ed. *Handbook of Russian Literature*. New Haven, Conn.: Yale Univ. Press, 1985.

Titunik, I. R. "Baxtin &/or Vološinov &/or Medvedev: Dialogue &/or Doubletalk." In *Language and Literary Theory*. Ed. Benjamin A. Stolz, I. R. Titunik, and Lubomir Dolezel. Papers in Slavic Philology, no. 5. Ann Arbor: Department of Slavic Languages and Literatures, Univ. of Michigan, 1984, pp. 535–64.

———. "The Baxtin Problem: Concerning Katerina Clark and Michael Holquist's *Mikhail Bakhtin*." *Slavic and East European Journal* 30, no. 1 (Spring 1986), pp. 91–95.

Todorov, Tzvetan. *Mikhail Bakhtin: The Dialogical Principle*. Tr. Wlad Godzich. Minneapolis: Univ. of Minnesota Press, 1984. Originally published as *Mikhaïl Bakhtine: le principe dialogique suivi de Écrits du Cercle de Bakhtine*. Paris: Seuil, 1981.

———. *The Poetics of Prose*. Tr. Richard Howard. Ithaca, N.Y.: Cornell Univ. Press, 1977. Originally published as *La Poétique de la prose*. Paris: Seuil, 1971.

Tolstoy, Leo. *Anna Karenina*. Ed. Leonard J. Kent and Nina Berberova. Tr.

Constance Garnett. New York: Random House, 1965. For the Russian text, see the 90-volume "Jubilee" edition.

———. *War and Peace.* Tr. Ann Dunnigan. New York: Signet, 1968. For the Russian text, see the 90-volume "Jubilee" edition.

———. "Why Do Men Stupefy Themselves?" In *Leo Tolstoy: Selected Essays.* Tr. Aylmer Maude. New York: Random House, 1964, pp. 185–203.

Tomashevsky, Boris. "Literature and Biography." In *Readings in Russian Poetics: Formalist and Structuralist Views.* Ed. Ladislav Matejka and Krystyna Pomorska. Cambridge, Mass.: MIT Press, 1971, pp. 47–55.

Toulmin, Stephen. "The Tyranny of Principles." *The Hastings Center Report* 11, no. 6 (December 1981), pp. 31–38.

Turbin, Vladimir. "M. M. Bakhtin: Buenos Aires–Kemerovo." *Literaturnaia Rossiia,* no. 18 (May 5, 1989), p. 8.

Tynyanov, Yuri, and Roman Jakobson. "Problems in the Study of Literature and Language." In *Readings in Russian Poetics: Formalist and Structuralist Views.* Ed. Ladislav Matejka and Krystyna Pomorska. Cambridge, Mass.: MIT Press, 1971, pp. 79–81.

Vygotsky, Lev Semenovich. "Interaction Between Learning and Development." In *Mind and Society: The Development of Higher Psychological Processes.* Ed. Michael Cole, Vera John-Steiner, Sylvia Scribner, and Ellen Souberman. Cambridge, Mass.: Harvard Univ. Press, 1978, pp. 84–86.

———. *The Psychology of Art.* Tr. Scripta Technica. Cambridge, Mass.: MIT Press, 1971.

———. *Thought and Language.* Ed. and tr. Alex Kozulin. Cambridge, Mass.: MIT Press, 1986.

———. "Tool and Symbol in Child Development." In *Mind and Society: The Development of Higher Psychological Processes.* Ed. Michael Cole, Vera John-Steiner, Sylvia Scribner, and Ellen Souberman. Cambridge, Mass.: Harvard Univ. Press, 1978, pp. 19–30.

Wehrle, Albert J. "Introduction: M. M. Bakhtin / P. N. Medvedev." In M. M. Bakhtin / P. N. Medvedev, *The Formal Method in Literary Scholarship: A Critical Introduction to Sociological Poetics.* Tr. Albert J. Wehrle. Cambridge, Mass.: Harvard Univ. Press, 1985, pp. xv–xxix.

Wertsch, James. *Vygotsky and the Social Formation of Mind.* Cambridge, Mass.: Harvard Univ. Press, 1985.

Williams, Raymond. *Marxism and Literature.* Oxford: Oxford Univ. Press, 1977.

Wimsatt, William K., Jr. *The Prose Style of Samuel Johnson.* New Haven, Conn.: Yale Univ. Press, 1941; second printing, 1963.

Wittgenstein, Ludwig. *Philosophical Investigations.* 3rd ed. Tr. G. E. M. Anscombe. New York: Macmillan, 1958.

———. *Tractatus Logico-Philosophicus.* Tr. D. F. Spears and B. F. McGuinness. London: Routledge and Kegan Paul, 1961.

Index

In this index, an "f" after a number indicates a separate reference on the next page, and an "ff" indicates separate references on the next two pages. A continuous discussion over two or more pages is indicated by a span of page numbers, e.g., "57–58." *Passim* is used for a cluster of references in close but not consecutive sequence.

This index uses the abbreviations on pp. xvii–xx and the following additional abbreviations: B = Bakhtin; D = Dostoevsky; G = Goethe; M = Medvedev; R = Rabelais; T = Tolstoy; V = Voloshinov.

and politics, 198–200; and Vygotsky, 212; and secondhand definitions, 266–67
—works: *Civilization and Its Discontents*, 28–29, 174; "Creative Writers," 187; *Psychopathology of Everyday Life, The*, 28, 32
From Being to Becoming (Prigogine), 47–48
Fullness of time, 406, 413–15, 422
Function, 82, 424; pure or infinite, 264–65
Furbank, P. N., 480
Fused time and space, 368
Fusion and nonfusion, 53–54, 99, 102, 183ff, 227, 243
Future and futurity, 37, 177, 182, 193, 247, 260, 286, 370, 436; and creativity (by-products or imperfect design), 46, 230, 292–93; and self, 196, 221–30 *passim*, 397–98; and D, 261, 268; and relation to past, 288, 291, 296–97, 298; immediate vs. distant, 370, 397–98, 411, 418, 421, 423–25; and historical inversion, 397–98; vs. utopia, 397–98, 411, 418; and fullness of time or becoming, 405, 413–19 *passim*; and novel, 421–25
Futurism, 22–23, 65, 323, 448

Gachev, Gennadi, 482
Galan, F. W., 483
Galilean: universe of genres, 299, 301; linguistic consciousness, 309–17, 320, 325, 328, 344, 362, 459; chronotope consciousness, 368, 404
Games, 189, 256
Gargantua and Pantagruel (R), 92–96, 346, 445–47, 454–56; Abbey of Thélème, 92, 439, 450; FTC vs. RAHW on, 436–41, 445–46
Gates of the chronotope, 432
Gay deception, 359–60
Gender, 451
General systems theory, 27–28, 45, 488
Generations, 408, 412
Generic contact, 467; vs. influence, 295–96, 337
Generic energy, 307, 309, 316
Generic essence, 462
Generic potential, 276, 285, 288, 293, 295–97, 306–10 *passim*, 344–45, 347, 459, 465–66, 468; of Socratic dialogue, 60; of novel, 88–89, 381, 424; of novel of ordeal, 407, 412; and genre conditions, 466

Generic risks, 347–48
Generic skeleton, 278
Generic surrogate, 356
Generic task, 304, 347
Generic terms, 461–62
Genette, Gerard, 19
Genre and genres, 6, 19, 129, 229, 271–309, 355, 362, 428, 458; and prosaics, 16–20; and time and historicity, 47, 278–80, 307, 414f, 419; in B's development, 66, 87–89; and architectonics, 84, 440; Formalists on, 88–89, 272–80, 361; M on, 88, 271–77; and carnival, 93, 459, 463, 465–67; and canon of, 93–94; of billingsgate, 96, 302; origin of new, 273, 276–84, 293–94, 298; as modes of thought or ways of seeing, 275–77, 281–84, 299, 306–9 *passim*, 361, 367, 371–72, 452, 459–60; need for repertoire of, 275, 291f, 371–72, 452–53; inner and private, 275, 389; and literary history, 277–80, 307, 458–60; vs. schools, 278, 284, 305; formed over long time, 278–80, 290–97, 302, 305; as creators of new truths, 280–84, 298–99, 366; and form-shaping ideology, 282–84, 307–8, 461–62; transcription of, 282f, 307, 366; wisdom of, 284, 292; and history of language, 292–93; imperfect design of, 292–93; primary and secondary, 293–94; interaction among, 293–94, 299–305, 307, 309, 363; and sociological reductionism, 297–99; and heteroglossia, 299, 309; obsolescence of, 301, 304; naiveté of, 303–4; summary of B's approach to, 306–8; of pure self-expression, 353; surrogate for, 356; parodic, 359, 433, 434–35; and intellectual history, 366; and chronotopes, 370, 374–75, 440; as field of possibilities, 371; private, 389; and parodic doubles, 434–35; folklore, 452, 454–55; quasi-, 459; seriocomic, 460–63. *See also* Chronotope and chronotopic; Generic potential; Genre memory; Novels; Speech genres
Genre conditions, 465, 466–67
Genre criticism, 304
Genre memory, 89, 224, 295–97, 307, 405, 415, 462, 466; in B's development, 66, 229; and genres as organs of memory, 280, 288, 290–91, 292, 443

Theory and sense of theory, 62
"Theory of the Formal Method"
(Eichenbaum), 21
Thermodynamics, 47
Third person: as superaddressee, 135–
36; as hero (topic) of utterance, 136–
37; as audience of reported speech,
164; as nonparticipating reader of
work, 249; as witness of others' private lives, 389–91, 395, 401–4
Thought and Language (Vygotsky), 208,
210–15, 483, 484–85
Threshold: dialogues, 60–61, 62, 418;
chronotope of the, 375, 491
Time, 36–38, 43–52, 366–432; and biography, 3, 8–9; that forges nothing
new, 7, 38, 396; as open, 36–38, 369;
and freedom, 45–46; irreversibility
or reversibility of, 45–48, 369, 375,
377f, 385, 396–97; and historicity,
46–49; as operator, 47–48; and heterochrony and multiplicity of, 48–49,
52, 56, 368, 371, 416, 424, 426, 489;
and nature of chronotopes, 49, 366,
367–72; and untranscribability, 50,
281–82; and growth in meaning, 55,
284–90; of hero in early manuscripts,
75, 78; and self, 189–93 *passim*, 216,
224f, 229–30; and animals, 210; and
creativity, 246f, 250, 397, 413–19
passim; and literary history, 278–80;
and tradition, 290–97; -space, 368;
and anachronism, 369; key questions
about, 369–72; that thickens, 371;
and apocalypse, 375, 398, 411; that
leaves no trace, 376, 383; measured
technically, 377–78, 380, 406–7;
nicks in, 378; with knots, 385; with
critical moments or turning points,
386; and anti-utopianism, 397–98,
411; and becoming, 405–6, 408–13;
fullness of, 406, 413–15, 422; as
visible, 413, 415–19; and work,
417–18; and proxemics, 427, 490;
and nontemporal concepts, 432; and
parody of timelessness, 435; and
body, 436–38; -and-value zone, 460
—various writers or thinkers on: Aristotle, 395–96; Bergson, 177–79;
Braudel, 48–49; Cervantes, 404;
Dante, 400–401; D, 48, 259–63, 375,
382, 392, 401, 418–19, 424, 457; Einstein, 367–69; G, 260–61, 405, 410,
413–19, 420, 424; Gould, 45–46,
376, 489; Hesiod, 385; Kant, 367;

Ovid, 385; Petronius, 384, 391f; Prigogine, 47; Rousseau, 417–18; Scott,
380, 417f; Thackeray, 404; T, 19, 391,
409, 412, 424, 487–88; Voltaire, 377
—kinds and genres of: abstract, 379,
383; adventure, 371, 376–79, 380,
383, 398–400, 416; adventure, in adventure novel of everyday life, 384,
386; adventure, in chivalric romance,
398–400; adventure, in travel novel,
406–7, 412; adventure, parodied,
490; of adventure novel of everyday
life, 384–88, 391–92; of ancient biography and autobiography, 395–97;
of Bildungsroman, 281–82, 407–13
passim; biographical, 386, 408; of
biographical novel, 408, 412; carnival, 227, 229–30, 440, 449, 458,
466, 491; of chivalric romance, 398–
400; cyclical, 409–10, 412–13, 438;
of dream-vision, 400–401; epic,
419–23; everyday, 384, 391; extratemporal hiatus, 377; in fairy tale,
400; in family-biographical novel,
408, 412; great and small, 35, 66, 99,
229–30, 280, 287–88, 297, 299, 365,
414, 418, 428–29, 475; in Greek romance, 375–78, 380, 383, 398–400,
421; historical inversion, 397–98;
idyllic-cyclical, 409, 412, 417–18;
mathematical, 367; medieval, 438; in
novel (or novel of emergence), 19,
65, 224, 408–13, 419–25; in novel
before becoming, 406–8, 412; in
novel of ordeal, 407, 412; psychological, 407, 412; of pure digression, 377;
real historical, 43–45, 281–82, 372f,
378, 409, 410–11, 416f, 425; simultaneity, 260, 400–401; of suddenlys,
378, 380, 398–99; in travel novel,
379, 406–7, 412; undifferentiated,
378. *See also* Future and futurity; Past
and pastness; Present and presentness
Tin Drum, The (Grass), 462
Tiny alterations, 24, 33
Titunik, I. R., 102, 110, 112–15,
479–89
"Tlön" (Borges), 116
Todorov, Tzvetan, 5–6, 7, 19, 473
Tolstoy, Leo, 27, 30, 208, 448, 457,
473f, 486; and prosaics, 15, 36; and
Formalists, 16f; and ethics, 25–27;
and law of progress, 28; and systems,
28, 30, 35; and incomprehension,
360; and idyllic-cyclical time, 409, 412

Library of Congress Cataloging-in-Publication Data

Morson, Gary Saul, 1948–
  Mikhail Bakhtin : creation of a prosaics / Gary Saul
Morson & Caryl Emerson.
    p. cm.
  Includes bibliographical references.
  ISBN 0-8047-1821-0 (alk. paper)
  ISBN 0-8047-1822-9 (alk. paper : pbk.)
    1. Bakhtin, M. M. (Mikhail Mikhailovich), 1895–
1975. 2. Prose literature—History and criticism—
Theory, etc. 3. Criticism—History—20th century.
I. Emerson, Caryl. II. Title.
PG2947.B3M67 1990
801'.95'092—dc20   90-39855
                                                    CIP